Handbook of Indian Sociology

The Oxford India Handbooks are an important new initiative in academic publishing. Each volume offers a comprehensive survey of research in a critical subject area and provides facts, figures, and analyses for a well-grounded perspective. The series intends to provide scholars, students, and policy planners with a well-rounded understanding of a wide range of issues in the social sciences.

Handbook of Indian Sociology

Edited by
VEENA DAS

OXFORD
UNIVERSITY PRESS

OXFORD

UNIVERSITY PRESS

YMCA Library Building, Jai Singh Road, New Delhi 110 001

Oxford University Press is a department of the University of Oxford. It furthers the
University's objective of excellence in research, scholarship, and education
by publishing worldwide in

Oxford   New York

Auckland   Cape Town   Dar es Salaam   Hong Kong   Karachi   Kuala Lumpur
Madrid   Melbourne   Mexico City   Nairobi   New Delhi   Shanghai   Taipei   Toronto

With offices in

Argentina   Austria   Brazil   Chile   Czech Republic   France   Greece   Guatemala
Hungary   Italy   Japan   Poland   Portugal   Singapore   South Korea   Switzerland
Thailand   Turkey   Ukraine   Vietnam

Oxford is a registered trademark of Oxford University Press
in the UK and in certain other countries

Published in India
by Oxford University Press, New Delhi

© Oxford University Press 2004

The moral rights of the author have been asserted
Database right Oxford University Press (maker)

First published 2004
Oxford India Paperbacks 2006
Second impression 2007

ISBN-13: 978-0-19-568510-7
ISBN-10: 0-19-568510-5

Typeset in Sabon MT
by Eleven arts, Keshav Puram, Delhi 110 035
Printed by Pauls Press, Delhi 110 020
Published by Oxford University Press
YMCA Library Building, Jai Singh Road, New Delhi 110 001

Contributors

ARJUN APPADURAI, John Dewey Professor in the Social Sciences, The New School, New York, USA

LAWRENCE A. BABB, Professor, Department of Anthropology-Sociology and Asian Languages and Civilizations, Amherst College, Amherst, USA

ANDRÉ BÉTEILLE, FBA, Professor Emeritus of Sociology, University of Delhi, India

RITA BRARA, Reader in Sociology, University of Delhi, India

JAN BREMAN, Emeritus Professor of Comparative Sociology, Amsterdam University, The Netherlands

HEIDRUN BRÜCKNER, Professor of Indology, University of Tubingen, Germany

VEENA DAS, Krieger-Eisenhower Professor, Department of Anthropology, Johns Hopkins University, Baltimore, USA

SATISH DESHPANDE, Professor of Sociology, Institute of Economic Growth, Delhi, India

JÉAN DRÉZE, Visiting Professor, Delhi School of Economics, University of Delhi, India

DIPANKAR GUPTA, Professor, Centre for the Study of Social Systems, Jawaharlal Nehru University, New Delhi, India

NARAYANI GUPTA, Former Professor of History, Jamia Millia Islamia, New Delhi, India

SURINDER JODHKA, Associate Professor, Centre for the Study of Social Systems, Jawaharlal Nehru University, New Delhi, India

MALAVIKA KARLEKAR, Senior Fellow, Centre for Women's Development Studies (CWDS), New Delhi, India

SUDIPTA KAVIRAJ, Reader, Department of Politics, School of Oriental and African Studies (SOAS), University of London, UK

T.N. MADAN, Emeritus Professor (Sociology), Institute of Economic Growth, Delhi, India

OLGA NIEUWENHUYS, Researcher, Amsterdam Research School on Global Issues and Development Studies, University of Amsterdam, The Netherlands

THOMAS PANTHAM, Former Professor, Department of Political Science, Maharaja Sayajirao University, Baroda, India

ELIZABETH SCHÖMBUCHER, Lecturer, Department of Anthropology, South Asia Institute, University of Heidelberg, Germany

JONATHAN SPENCER, Professor of Anthropology, University of Edinburgh, UK

PATRICIA UBEROI, Professor of Sociology, Institute of Economic Growth, Delhi, India

DENIS VIDAL, IRD/Centre for the Study of India and South Asia, Paris, France

LEELA VISARIA, Professor, Gujarat Institute of Development Research, Gujarat, India

Late PRAVIN VISARIA (1937–2001) was Former Director, Institute of Economic Growth, Delhi, India

Late MYRON WEINER (1931–1999) was Former Professor of Political Science, Massachusetts Institute of Technology, Cambridge, USA

Contents

PART IV: FAMILY, CHILDHOOD, AND EDUCATION

PART V: ECONOMIC AND POLITICAL LIFE

Introduction

This book presents a selection of essays taken from the *Oxford India Companion to Sociology and Social Anthropology* that addresses broad trends in Indian society and culture. The companion is a critical review of the state of social science knowledge on India drawing upon scholars across disciplines and countries. The emergence of social sciences in Europe, as we know, is closely linked to the emergence of modernity. The combined forces of Industrial Revolution, new technologies of governance, and ideas about democracy and individual agency propagated in the French Revolution produced the idea of society both as an object of study and reform. However, many scholars forget that the nation-state, even as it provided a powerful impetus to the development of social sciences in Europe, arose more from the *constraints* of realizing the Enlightenment ideals rather than as a celebration of these. It is not surprising, then, that social sciences in non-western countries were linked initially with the needs of colonial governmentality, or evangelical missions—though it is equally important to remember that none of these projects were implemented in an empty or inert space. Given this history, the practice of constructing 'national traditions' in sociology or social anthropology is curious since it takes the political boundaries of the nations to be already given and settled.

The editorial advisors to the *Companion* and I did not conceptualize it as a project that could represent a national tradition but rather as a work that could delineate the tensions and contradictions between different stakes that scholars, administrators, and others had in the study of Indian society. It is the conversation and even the clash in these perspectives that shaped the understanding of social phenomena in India and contributed to the development of theory in these disciplines. In planning the *Companion*, I specifically rejected any gatekeeping concepts that would recognize only certain kinds of questions or concepts as 'authentic'. I believe that forms of power certainly shaped knowledge in the social sciences in India but public debate, translation between different kinds of concerns, and innovations resulting from conversations between Indian scholars and their counterparts in other countries, also played a major role in shaping the sociology and social anthropology of India. It is vital to recognize that the sites on which knowledge is produced today are undergoing rapid changes—universities do not hold the pivotal position they once did which is both a danger and an opportunity. It is in this context that one hopes that investigations in disciplinary histories that look at the relation between ideas and institutions in terms of their different temporalities, ruptures, and juxtapositions will continue to provide new terrains for rethinking social theory.

The aim of the *Handbook of Indian Sociology* is more modest. By presenting a smaller selection of essays from the original *Companion*, the editors of Oxford University Press and I hope that we will be able to meet the needs of readers who are looking for an understanding of broad trends in economy, polity, religion, culture and forms of family and kinship. Keeping this in mind, we have arranged a selection of the original essays in six sections. The first section includes two essays on the general idea of social sciences in India and the broad institutional framework within which sociology and social anthropology developed here. The second section on selected aspects of society and culture gives a broad overview of the demographic features, the ecological and environmental framing of social life, processes relating to stratification and mobility, urban social formations, and migration. The third section on religious and cultural landscape gives an account of the major religions in India including diversities within each religion. It also includes essays that explore the relation between religious and theatrical performances as well as the emergence of new forms of public culture. The fourth section is on family, child, and education. While the specific question of joint versus nuclear family has dominated the thinking on family in India, this section puts forward many other dimensions, such as the alliance between family and state, social reproduction and transformation through education, and failure of entitlements within the family. It also examines questions of gender, domestic violence, the impact of literacy and the specificity of local issues regarding the child against the global ideologies of childhood. The fifth section on economic arrangements provides connections between rural and urban concerns. It has essays on agrarian relations, markets as social institutions and the labour processes in the informal sector. The final section on politics considers democracy and the state and concludes with an analysis of collective violence.

◆

A persual of the general intellectual and social climate in which sociology and social anthropology developed in India makes it clear that one cannot see the developments in these subjects as a simple application of methods and concepts developed elsewhere. The conceptual innovations did not happen independently of the social processes and especially the struggles of different kinds of groups to find recognition in remaking the social. Thus, the sociological concepts we work with are not pure concepts shorn of all political plenitude. They carry the traces of social processes especially those arising from new forms of governmentality which were premised on the notion that society had to be made legible for the state; or from emergent forms of institutions such as caste formations forged as part of the electoral politics of post-independence India. This is a point elaborated in various chapters that follow (e.g. in the chapter on democracy) but the first two chapters by Veena Das and André Béteille pay special attention to these processes. A telling example that Das gives of this is the constitution of area studies in the United States after the Second World War and its impact on the development of the social/cultural anthropology of South Asia. Although the discovery of Sanskrit (through the route of Persian) had created a strong interest in Sanskritic studies in the constitution of Orientalism as a subject in nineteenth century, the idea that the *diplomatic* interests of the United States required an investment in Sanskritic studies was a curious assemblage. It consolidated a certain 'commonsense' propagated by some nationalists that Sanskrit provided a key to Indian civilization and hence was crucial to the understanding of contemporary India. The colonial construction of India had already bestowed it with the narrative of unchanging social forms. Curiously, the new sciences of statistics and ethnology also contributed to the picture of India as an unchanging society in which social formations such as caste had endured for thousands of years. This conclusion was, in fact, an artifact of the templates that were used for collection of data. While many Indian scholars (e.g. G.S.Ghurye) contested the way that race and caste were configured in colonial administrative practices, these constructions acquired great resilience because they carried the stamp of official approval and because the official archive, in turn, provided the texts through which much of India's past was researched. The influence of geopolitical interests in the post war era invites us to look at networks of knowledge shaped by strategic interests and power but these interests themselves shift, and in any case, should not be invested with some kind of omnipotence that acts upon an inert reality. This is where the role of public debate, translatability of ideas, and development of various sites of knowledge can play a crucial role in shaping these disciplines.

Geopolitical interests were important because flow of funds, materials, and ideas from research foundations, global institutions, and various western governments had an impact on research and pedagogy. The state in India also played a decisive role in expansion of universities and research institutions. A discipline comes to be stabilized through the material and institutional frame within which it is pursued. Béteille gives a panoramic view of the work of universities, their pedagogic modes, emergence of research institutes, professional journals, and role of professional bodies, showing how sociology and social anthropology acquired its character in a particular place and particular time. As anthropologists, we acknowledge the role of tacit knowledge even in the most formal of settings and we know that abstract thought often moves along concrete relations. Major innovations in science studies have demonstrated these observations. How is this relevant for sociology in India?

Consider Béteille's argument that an important feature of the debates in India has been the concern to integrate, or at least to respond to, classical studies in both sociology and social anthropology. The interesting point is that while classical studies, he thinks, were much more about the concerns of elite sections of society-anthropologists concentrated on the lives of the humble, the illiterate and the poor, providing a counterpoint to what M.N. Srinivas used to call the book view of Indian society. I am struck, though, that the imperative of responding to classical studies did not arise from vernacular concerns alone. It bore some relation to the colonial and post war constructions of India as a *Sanskritic* civilization. If vernacular cosmopolitan writings did not find much reflection in this scholarship, this was surely not unrelated to the undue reliance on official archives to construct India's past. Béteille's paper shows that the history of a discipline cannot be constructed as a linear succession of ideas—questions such as the curricula of these subjects in universities or the recruiting patterns of teachers, or anxieties around public opinion, which were coming from collateral concerns, had important implications for the development of these disciplines.

◆

In instituting new forms of governance, the British laid a great deal of emphasis on reliable data about subject populations. The institutional mechanisms for data collection were inherited and further augmented in post-independence India. The opening paper of the second section of the book by Praveen Visaria and Leela Visaria gives a detailed account of the institutional framework for the collection of data on population and the demographic trends. The decennial census began in 1867–72—India has now completed the sixth round of census after independence.

As Visaria and Visaria describe it, the legal and administrative framework for collection of reliable data as well as the conditions of relative political stability has enabled the government to collect consistently good data. The collection of vital statistics in the inter-census years, though, is not so impressive because the administrative framework for regular registration of births and deaths is not in place. Another way to put this is to say that collection of data that requires regular surveillance, such as birth statistics or mortality statistics, is inadequate. It is obvious that this is closely related to the way in which the functionaries of the state are embedded in social practices and further that numbers are not simply neutral statements but are politically volatile. Two examples that the authors give of this are telling. The first is the question of so-called 'religious demography'—the fact that the rate of increase of Muslim population is faster than the Hindus, is often used to incite communal hatred by politicians (but not only by them) while concealing the fact that this is related to the concentration of Muslims among relatively poor populations whose fertility rates among *all religions* tend to be higher than the rest. The second is the question of the declining sex ratio in some regions of India posing the question of gender discrimination and the role of new technologies in attaching themselves to existing social formations. As Visaria and Visaria point out, though, we can tackle the political questions best by providing sustained work on the specificity of the issues rather than by speculation.

Questions about ecology and environment are becoming increasingly important. These are often posed with regard to the population problem in India, but are much more complex. While the growth of technology in the service of human desire to modify nature has ameliorated many of the hazards relating to say, health and mortality, or helped in overcoming limitations of the human body—the long term consequences of many of these technological changes (including increase in population or unbridled consumption) have contributed to the vulnerability of the planet. The issue is not only that of global changes but also how local environments can change and become especially injurious to vulnerable sections of the population. Rita Brara gives us an informed account of how religious beliefs and practices might affect environment through the mediation of modes of livelihood or forms of consumption. She also describes how environmental concerns have led to a serious appraisal of religious and moral beliefs, not as texts but as practices that change and grow in relation to material needs. She shows how environmental movements have built upon the idea that local forms of knowledge can be evolved to address local needs and desires. One important factor that emerges from Brara's paper, as from many others, is that we cannot divide sociology into neat parcels of religion, economics, politics, and family, for these are not separate and divisible spheres of society. Instead, we need to see how social practices cut through these domains and thus generate new ways of understanding the problems of contemporary society. Thus, questions relating to environment are not about a stable and eternal nature but about social inequalities, both global and national, that impact on use of resources. Similarly, we might ask whether the religious values of any of the world religions or values of animism (a word now proudly and rightly claimed by indigenous groups), could provide intellectual resources for a new environmental ethics of responsibility to future generations. The point is not that of finding a grand ethics but of giving an account of resource use that is embedded in everyday life. From this point of view it is particularly illuminating to read the account of combinatory modes of livelihoods in rural and urban settings, for these show how environment and survival strategies are closely related at the level of the local.

It is interesting that certain aspects of social institutions of caste or religion can appear in a positive light when viewed from the perspective of environment but may be experienced as extremely unjust from other perspectives. For instance, some environmental historians feel that caste specialization in utilization of resources at the local level might have been conducive to environmental conservation. Alternatively, vegetarianism might be seen by many to preserve natural resources better than meat-eating practices do. However, it is the same ideology of caste specialization that restricts access to resources by lower castes in the former case, while in the latter case the ideology of purity with which vegetarianism is associated, was elaborated to hierarchicize other practices of lower castes . This aspect of the caste system becomes evident in Dipankar Gupta's essay on social stratification which emphasizes hierarchy and difference in the caste system. In later essays by T.N. Madan and Lawrence Babb this interplay is highlighted in the context of religion. For a broader understanding of caste, Gupta makes a contrast between closed systems of stratification (e.g. caste) and open systems of stratification (e.g. class). The point is not that the former was completely rigid and latter completely flexible but that the form that social mobility took in each was structured by different kinds of institutional constraints. For example, mobility took the form of group mobility in closed systems and individual mobility in the latter.

One interesting question with regard to close and open systems of stratification is the significance attached to natural differences in different kinds of societies. Thus, Gupta says that colour may become the basis of social identity or even legal regulation as in the case of race based discrimination—but other differences such as those in height may not carry the same weight. It is well to remember, though, that the molecular revolution in biology has led to a sea change in the place of biology in social life. Taking examples from Europe and North America, some anthropologists have argued that social action may be based upon biological conditions, as when populations with particular disabilities organize to influence social policy and resource allocation by the state. An example of this in India is the lobbying done by the disabled to have that category included in the 2001 census, since political mobilization of the disabled would depend on incidence and prevalence of different kinds of disabilities in the population. The emergence of critical disability studies points to new disciplinary configurations that will have profound influences on the relation between social sciences and biological sciences, for the way that technology attaches itself to social forms is decisively shaped by the politics of citizenship, forms of inequality, and geopolitical concerns. Thus what may appear as a natural difference with little or no significance could change as disability becomes an object of mobilization and intervention.

Sociology in India was, till recently, dominated by the study of villages. This, as Béteille notes in his paper, was salutary for correcting an undue reliance of classical texts. However, as Narayani Gupta points out in her essay on the Indian city, urban forms are not new in India. There is a rich vocabulary in Sanskrit and Persian for different kinds of urban spaces. Moreover, she finds that out of the 216 towns with a population over 1 lakh recorded in the 1981 census, 186 towns are over 200 years old. Unfortunately, the experience of Indian towns did not enter mainstream urban sociology or anthropology—there was often a tendency to assume that urbanization will follow the trajectories it followed in Europe. Gupta gives a succinct account of the different trajectories of changes in the urban landscape in India—for instance, the changes following the introduction of railways and later, the increasing use of automobiles. Urban spaces also offer rich terrains for understanding the experimentation on urban planning arising initially out of colonial concerns with zoning, public health or public order and then becoming routinized as statecraft. In the post-independence period the study of urban forms presents important opportunities for understanding how new imaginaries about space and place, the nature of emergent publics, and new kinds of survival strategies may be analysed and the relation between these survival strategies and the environment. Urban areas provide important sites for seeing how new forms of publics arise—a theme taken up later in Arjun Appadurai's paper.

Myron Weiner's essay on migration nicely complements the essay on cities. Weiner argues that as compared to many other low-income or middle-income (he uses the term 'developing') countries, migration accounts only for small flows of population from rural areas to urban areas in India. These flows, however, have an important impact upon both receiving and sending communities. He gives a rich account of the major phases of population flows into and out of India. Migration is always indicative of larger processes such as environmental changes, changes in forms of governmentality, and development of labour markets. Historically, the largest transfer of population in South Asian history happened at the Partition of India with tremendous implications for the politics of the region. There have been other forced movements of populations due to violence, insurgency movements and displacement of populations consequent upon various 'development' projects. There has also been a creation of internal refugees due to ongoing violence as in Kashmir with respect to Kashmiri Pandits or the insecurity created by the recent Gujarat riots (or pogroms) against Muslims with clear complicity of the state. These have important implications for human rights, citizenship, and access over resources. Studies of migration, urban processes, and the spatial contours of the city are not only about the city—they carry important implications for our understanding of collective violence— issues that Jonathan Spencer analyses in the concluding section.

It is important to remember that rural to rural migration is an important part of social life in India and that even with urban migration, the ties between town and village are not terminated once and for all. The linked social forms such as linked households or property arrangements are important to keep in mind so that we do not simply assume that the urban dweller is the atomized individual cut off from all social ties of kinship or from traditional forms of cultural performances. In fact, the unconscious equation made between country and city to tradition and modernity in public discourse is suspect in view of the nature of rural urban networks in India. The concluding essay of this section by Satish Deshpande on modernization is extremely interesting from this point of view because it provides a different genealogy of this concept than what one would find in modernization theory in North America. As I mentioned earlier, if we are justified in regarding social science, for some purposes, as the ideology of modernity, then it had a stake in presenting tradition as static and backward. However, in Srinivas's famous concepts of Sanskritization and Westernization, these are *both* processes of change though they derive their legitimacy from different sources. The interesting point about the research on modernity was that tradition and modernity were seen to be located in the same structural entities or even persons. Given that modernity privileges the time of the present and conceptualizes tradition, as that which is left behind—it was not surprising that forms of popular culture such as film or popular fiction mimicked this attitude. What is interesting is that such formulations also acquired a self-evidential character in social sciences research as in some famous sociological writings on Indian intellectuals and scientists that framed their practices as paradoxical or even schizophrenic. It was, as if, there was something inherently incongruous about the fact that one could work in the laboratory in the day and perform *puja* in the evening. There was little realization that this sense of incongruity was an artifact of the research designs itself. The research on modernity has become more sophisticated in the last decade as modernity's self-representation as essentially western has come to be questioned so that the dualism of tradition and modernity has been laid to rest. There is increasing recognition of the role of Indian diasporic intellectuals such as Arjun Appadurai, Homi Bhabha, Ranajit Guha, Gayatri Spivak (to name a few), in making decisive interventions in social theory, foregrounding the experience of India. Similar recognition of the impact of the work of South Asian scholars living and working in the region, on social theory has been slow to come. How space and location impact upon social theory and which kind of experience is fore-grounded are important areas of research which, if nothing else, have broken the monopoly of gate keeping concepts that always constructed India in terms of an exceptionalism—a point made with telling effect by Appadurai in his essay in this volume.

◆

The essays in the next section on religious and cultural landscape are not intended to offer examples of how 'expressive' values are realized as against 'instrumental' values. It was a widely held view in the sixties that religion and culture were domains for the understanding of 'meaning'—the term itself allowed a slippage between *meaning* constructed on the analogy of linguistic meaning and *significance* (as in the frequently asked question about the meaning of life). The dualistic conception of social action was premised on the idea that economic and political actors were primarily motivated by a rational pursuit of interests while religion, family or art were the domains of affective action. Although some scholars continue to make valiant attempts to explain such phenomenon as sectarian riots by rational choice theory, others have begun to think of rationality itself in more sophisticated ways than purely in terms of pursuit of interests. In any case, the events of the last decade in various parts of the world have invited deliberation on religion and culture in new ways and the essays in this section reflect the deep concern with this set of issues.

T.N. Madan's essay on the religious traditions in India takes up the theme of religious pluralism. Madan's theoretical quest is to see the way in which difference and pluralism was not only conceptualized but also lived. The point is not that we can simply replace 'modern' ways of conceptualizing difference with some imagined 'traditional' way but that we need to experiment with the points of entry and exit between these different formulations to arrive at answers that are adequate to contemporary quandaries of sectarian or communal conflict. While modern ideologies of secularism provide one way of thinking about religious difference, Madan argues that there were other ways embedded within different traditions that could accommodate and (sometimes celebrate) difference within their designs of life. For instance, some Hindu texts and practices, accorded a place of respect to the sacred texts or prophets of other faiths while simultaneously placing them within a hierarchical order. Madan gives some important examples of the experiments with difference, such as Dara Shikoh's attempts to think of Upanishadic or Buddhist texts in the context of Islamic revelation for which he was declared a heretic. Similarly, he points to the 19th century experiments with various religions as expressive of same human values in the Brahmo Samaj or in the twentieth century, Gandhi's attempt to find a language of difference from within Hinduism. There are scholars who would contest Madan's reading of the history of secularism in the West and others who would argue that secularism is primarily a legal concept dealing with citizenship in the modern state. Yet others, such as the anthropologist Talal Asad, argue that we need anthropological explorations into the very question of what accounts for the practices through which modern subjects are produced and that secularism in this sense is not only about law but also about deep transformations in subjectivity. The growth of identity politics in the 1980s is analysed in some detail in the essays by Thomas Pantham and Sudipta Kaviraj, who ask how forms of religiosity have been transformed by the electoral and other imperatives of democratic mobilization. The theme of secularism thus, brings questions of transformations of subjectivity under regimes of modernity, political citizenship, and religion within the same framework of analysis.

One important aspect of identity politics is that it underplays the internal divisions within groups that it mobilizes on grounds of some kind of primordial sentiment. Yet internal pluralism within a particular tradition has a grammar that frames the trajectories within which difference tends to move even if it does not determine these. For instance, division wihin Christian sects often results from disputes over dogma whereas , it is the specific figure of the world renouncer who has played a major role in the development of sects within Hinduism. Lawrence Babb analyses the figure of the renouncer as providing the standard against which caste practices (especially the Brahmanical ideology) was measured and in many cases emulated. Though it was Buddhism that first instituted monastic living within an organized collectivity or sangha, it is not correct to think of sectarian values in the Buddhist/Hindu/Jain complex as exclusively an expression of otherworldly values. Babb gives a subtle analysis of the power of the renouncer ideal on the one hand, and the engagement of sects with this-worldly affairs on the other. For instance, many ascetic orders were deeply engaged in trade and professional soldiery in the eighteenth century. Similarly militant asceticism was not seen as an anomaly. The role of ascetics and renouncers of various kinds in modern politics (as in the Ramjanmabhumi–Babri Masjid dispute) draws on this tradition while evolving new forms of political action. It is not sufficient to take this simply as evidence that the claim of the renouncer's disengagment with this worldly activities is invalid but rather to see how the force of the renouncer's voice in the public arena constituted a form of politics precisely because it claimed to speak from an otherworldly position. Babb's essay draws our attention to the highly mobile trajectories of identity within Hinduism and is a good corrective to those who think that Hinduism was always a religion of peace and toleration. Like any other religion it had possibilities for both, peace and conflict. How either of these two possibilities was realized is more a matter of looking at lived practices closely rather than at textbook formulation of values.

The last two essays in this section turn our attention to cultural forms through which different kinds of publics are defined. Heidrün Bruckner and Elizabeth Schömbucher deploy the concept of performance to bring religious and theatrical performances within the same framework of analysis. While many ritual performances such as the Vedic sacrifice was limited to upper castes, other forms such as possession rituals were open to all castes. When possession rituals were part of a well-ordered performance with theatrical props, costumes, masks, etc., they participated in dramatic conventions and took on the quality of a spectacle. The publics created around these were fully aware of the structure and sequence of these performances— in many ways these gave a material representation to aesthetic forms and values that were well-understood. However, the possibility of improvisation to make ironic commentaries on local events or to admonish the powerful local personages who had transgressed against moral norms, have also been documented in the literature. In contrast, when individuals experienced possession by malignant spirits and enacted personal conflicts or expressed fears and dangers, these too could be understood as performances. The authors make a plea for attention to agency and context in these performances without rushing to deploy categories of psychopathology. In fact one can detect a certain impatience in anthropological discourse against the usual public health depiction of such performances as forms of psychiatric pathology but the problem does not resolve that easily, for, sometimes the concerned person or the family may itself experience such possession as a sign of pathology. The popularity of the many exorcism cults from regional to local levels attests to this. As in many other cases, here too the joining of the social and the individual requires close attention to context and experience so that sometimes what anthropologists describe as possession may be better understood as dispossession, while at other times the haste to read signs of possession as symptoms of pathology might be evidence of the clash between folk and biomedical categories, or even of the power of psychiatry to strip cultural categories of their meaning.

It would be obvious that the disciplines of sociology or social anthropology now occupy the same space of interpretation and intervention as public health, or political science, or economics. Thus, many concepts that were used primarily by anthropologists have travelled to other sites. Anthropologists are also no longer satisfied with overarching or totalizing concepts, such as culture or society. In this context an important and productive concept that has emerged is that of 'public culture'. Appadurai offers this concept in his paper, in order to bring those interstitial practices, spaces, and institutions into mainstream sociology that have fallen outside the disciplinary gaze. By using the concept of public culture (as distinct from popular culture), Appadurai means those activities through which notions of publics come into being—activities that cannot be mechanically tied to social reproduction or to pre-determined social spaces. These can refer to new visual economies as displayed in film hoardings, hybrid forms of performances, strategies of survival in which urban common property becomes a resource, and many other such examples. Focusing on these gives a different direction to the meaning of culture, for it shifts the emphasis from shared values, or worldviews to contestation that relates as much to economic or political survival as to aesthetic practice. Together the essays in this section help us to conceptualize the domain of the public not simply as a space for rational discursive forms of argumentation, but rather as imaginaries in which corporal experience, visual economies, and discursive forms together make up the experience of the 'public'.

◆

The question of the public brings me to the public/private dichotomy. Despite criticism from the feminists, it is still sometimes assumed that themes of family, childhood, and reproduction belong to the realm of the private. Instead, I suggest that the essays in the next section might be read as deploying the notion of the person as the link that stitches the private and the public together. Family and the child are matters of intense public debate and while some of these debates are specifically Indian, one has to locate them within the general concern with social reproduction and the role of the state in ensuring this. The field of kinship studies within anthropology was an invention of legal scholarship in Europe and North America precisely because of the interest of early theorists such as Henry Maine and Louis Henry Morgan in rendering the field of kinship relations knowable in juridical terms. This development is related to the emergence of the biopolitical state with its interest in managing life—we can see the particular articulation between power and knowledge in the colonial government's attempt to determine the nature of family and kinship by commissioning translations of classical texts of Sanskrit, Arabic, and Persian to determine what rules of marriage, inheritance, and succession would be applicable to their subjects. Thus Patricia Uberoi shows how the dominance of the joint family versus nuclear family debate in India and the anxiety about 'disappearance' of joint family was generated by the mismatch between the ideals of joint family propagated in Sanskrit *vyavahara* texts and the preponderance of nuclear families that emerged in census reports. This is not to say that at the normative level the ideal of joint family is not addressed in family formations but rather that the conditions for formation of joint households are more complex as they are tied to demographic factors, political stability, and economic changes in local societies. The notion of household composition as an index of a phase in the domestic cycle of domestic groups assumes stable political and economic conditions and many anthropologists are now realizing that populations most affected by economic instability or political violence are unable to form families in the manner in which heterosexual normativity demands. The preponderance of women headed households during wars or epidemics with differential sex mortality is one example of this. The devastation by the HIV/AIDS epidemic in Africa that has led to large number of orphans who are either in foster care or who join clandestine armies as child soldiers, or live in the streets—are other examples of this process.

Just as many people simply do not have the resources to form the ideal family, so one cannot assume that once formed, the family is a haven against the violence or uncertainty of the larger world. Recent academic and advocacy work done primarily by various women's organizations and NGOs, has boldly exposed the high level of violence in the family in India. It is true that violence is unevenly distributed along social classes and along different phases of the life cycle. Nevertheless, violence against women is not a new issue—it was a major theme in the colonial construction of India and thus reform of practices such as *sati* or ban on widow remarriage animated many reform movements in nineteenth century Hinduism. Malvika Karlekar makes a strong plea for taking up this issue as a central concern of research and policy. Contesting the view that it is only young wives who are exposed to violence or that all violence against women in India is dowry related, Karlekar argues that infants, children, and adolescents can be subjected to direct violence, abuse or severe neglect that is gender related. In fact one can map out the special kinds of vulnerabilities in different phases of the life cycle—sex specific abortion, nutritional deprivation, sexual abuse, wife battering, and neglect or abuse of older women especially if they are widowed—all relate to the way in which entitlements are structured within the family. Some anthropologists have questioned whether global categories of gender justice are appropriate to analyse the culturally specific experiences of women who may value social relatedness above individual autonomy or may hold very different pictures of the social good. Yet, most anthropologists have long discarded the frame of putting universal values against cultural relativity—instead, they ask how one can take account of the fact that the power of global institutions may displace local agendas of reform or that utopian ideals may be pitted against desperate realities about which framers of global policies may have little understanding. The question is relevant, not only for womens' rights but also for the rights of children. The paper on child labour provides a superb discussion of these issues.

Olga Nieuwenhuys argues in her paper that global ideologies of childhood that cast it as a period of innocence often assume that the family and the school are the only two appropriate places for bringing up children and for educating them. These conceptions and their implementation in policy making have the intended or unintended effect of keeping children out of remunerative employment. Many studies on time allocation among children done under the label of the new sociology of childhood have produced convincing data that shows that even in industrial countries children perform labour ranging from care labour in the home to jobs in the informal economy. However, just as ideologies of gender were used to put low value on women's labour, argues Nieuwenhuys, so the ideologies of childhood are being used to keep children out of remunerative employment in the then labour market. It is not anybody's argument that children should not be protected against exploitative labour practices, but many sociologists and anthropologists have argued that we need to alter the practices of pedagogy in schools and think of learning as a life-long process, so that children whose survival depends upon their earning capacity are enabled to develop skills and can command fair price for their labour.

The point of this discussion is that children are often treated as if they were not agents in their own rights because it is assumed that adults have all the decision-making powers in the space of child-adult interactions. Yet childhood has undergone important transformations in the world and we need to think of many children as actively engaged in shaping their own survival. Some of the contexts within which children have to work are lethal as when children are employed in hazardous industry or are compelled to join armies as child soldiers. Other contexts in which children come to have greater decision-making power may be simply those involving decisions to attend or to drop out of school and these should concern us as much as the dramatic instances quoted above.

Jean Drèze's essay bears a direct relation to the issues regarding childhood. He argues that though India has made substantial improvements in literacy rates, the achievement is both uneven in regional terms and unimpressive when compared to other countries like China. He points out that neglect of primary education in policy making has meant that there is an addition of non-literate population in every new cohort. Despite the usual claim that parents neglect to send children to school because of the demand for their labour, this essay argues that the decision to drop school is often the child's decision because she finds school to be boring or because she cannot cope with school work. It is only when children have already taken the decision to drop school that they are put to work in the informal labour markets or at home. In any case, as Nieuwenhuys's essay shows, children sometimes use their earning to pay for their needs such as for books or uniforms even when primary education is free. Thus to simply blame parents while paying scant attention to the nature of school education and other supply side failures, is not likely to help solve the problem of high drop out rates in schools. It is also imperative to recognize that demand for literacy can stem from different kinds of concerns. For instance, the demand for female literacy in India was initially driven by the demand for educated brides, so that female literacy was a byproduct of male literacy. This also means that if we think of learning as a life long process rather than something that ends with childhood and early youth, then designing of institutions which allow different forms of inclusion at various points, as life circumstances change, would respond more effectively to the new needs for education that are generated. In other words we need to think of the plural conditions of childhood just as we need to consider educational institutions as changing entities that can meet life long demands for learning.

◆

The next section contains essays on different aspects of rural and urban economy. Surinder Jodhka reviews the major debates on peasantry and agrarian relations in India. Since the colonial government had a major interest in revenue collection and in securing peaceful conditions in the countryside, it generated substantial data on landholding patterns, cropping patterns, rural indebtedness, and so called rural unrest. As in many other cases, here too there was considerable experimentation by the colonial government so that as they learnt from failures in one region, they introduced new forms of property relations in others, leading to variations in revenue patterns in British India. The specific debates in social sciences (including sociology and economics) in the post-independent period were similarly tied to questions of development, imperatives of politics, and new notions of citizenship. For instance the debates about productivity of large farms and small farms, the impact of green revolution, or the research on land reforms had tremendous implications for policy. Similarly the entanglement of political and economic issues is evident in the various peasant movements or the emergence of middle peasants as a political force in various parts of the country. The issue of agrarian productivity and secure livelihoods is also related to the question of food security at the level of household and country. While India has been successful in preventing famines because of technological changes in agriculture, on the one hand and the functioning of democratic institutions, on the other its record in preventing hunger and malnutrition is still dismal. This is because increase in productivity in agriculture has not been accompanied with increase in purchasing power of poor households and increase in the reach of the public distribution system. Clearly we cannot understand the economic institutions independently of the political institutions. The emergence of the rich and middle peasantry as powerful political forces increased the range of interests represented in the political arena but it still excludes the rural and urban poor who find it difficult to have their demands met. Sudipta Kaviraj also makes this point in his paper on democracy in the next section.

As we saw in the chapter on migration, the volume of rural/urban migration is not large in percentage terms but its impact on receiving and sending communities is enormous. In addition, migration creates networks that connect rural and urban institutions in India because the migrants continue to maintain contact with home communities. The social formations that cut across rural and urban ties also influence urban markets. The next two essays on economics describe markets in commodities, the incorporation of money within forms of the social that were non-monetized as well as the labour processes in the urban sector. Dennis Vidal points out in his essay that markets and trade have played a very important role in Indian society—yet detailed studies of markets by sociologists and anthropologists are relatively few. He traces this to the suspicion in anthropology of money transactions as alien institutions. The centrality of the opposition between gifts and commodities, following Marcel Mauss and Karl Polanyi, led to the treatment of gift exchange as more integrated into social life than money transactions. However, many anthropologists in India have pointed to the danger that is seen to inhere in gift transactions precisely because these involve the self and other in totalizing relationships or because the exchange of gifts is seen to be fraught with danger because these can become mediums for the transfer of other properties such as inauspiciousness. However, exchanges in markets are also not simply anonymous transactions—in fact, the study of markets of various kinds reveals complex relations of trust, brokerage, and intricate networks of exchange. The interface between market and state also holds important implications for both academic and policy studies since failure of regulation and corruption are features of both economics and politics. The question of services, such as health and education that are particularly susceptible to market failures invites serious collaboration between social science and policy research.

The importance of the 'informal' sector in the Indian economy is directly tied to some of the processes described in earlier papers such as the importance of rural-urban networks, the nature of migration, and the use of casual labour in both industry and service sector. As Jan Breman points out, however, it is not as if the informal sector is completely separate from the formal sector. We all know of processes by which industrial organizations or even government offices devise hiring and firing practices so that employees can be kept in temporary positions in order to block the creation of institutional entitlements for them. This means that practices of organized labour are an essential component of any analysis of the informal economy for it is only the interrelationship between these that would illuminate the impact of one or the other. I would also suggest that the term informal labour might be a misnomer (hence my distancing quotes in referring to it) if we mean that the absence of regulation in this sector implies the absence of the state. Indeed, one of the implications of Jan Breman's analysis is precisely that it invites us to reconsider our theories of the state that privilege its order making functions—instead, we might find that it is in precisely these sectors that the state invents itself. One feature of this reinvention is that while formal regulation might be absent, there are regulatory practices such as the *haftas* (weekly payments) paid regularly to policemen as bribe by the self-employed poor as guarantee that they can practice their trade. Similarly, instead of thinking of vote banks as simply passive pools of people, it may be useful to conceptualize these in terms of active strategies pursued by the poor to use the gaps in the electoral system to make economic survival possible. I am not suggesting that the poor are not subjected to enormous risks and dangers because of the absence of welfare measures or due to the malfunctioning of welfare delivery mechanisms where these exist. However, to treat the poor as passive populations who are simply managed by the state, as some have suggested, is to ignore the tactics and strategies through which the poor claim economic and political citizenship.

✦

One theme that runs throughout the book is the question of how concepts, institutions, or disciplines that may have originated in the West (at least on a narrow definition of these) are translated or made one's own. When is it that such attempts at translation fail? As I indicated in the introductory remarks, the easy division between what is an authentic national tradition and what is alien often depend upon extremely simplistic notions of the authentic. The essays by Thomas Pantham and Sudipta Kaviraj on politics in the last section raise similar concerns. They both start with the important observation that the institutions and practices of nation-state and democracy are not simply western imports. While many take it for granted today that the nation is the most 'natural' expression of collective political life, it is important to guard against a historical teleology that assumes the inevitable arrival of the nation-state as the most enlightened expression of human rationality. In fact, forms of sociality prevalent in India have shaped the way that ideal and practices of the nation-state are realized. Furthermore, while the power that the state exercises makes it necessary for other forms of collective and social life to come to terms with its form of rationality (and irrationality), we should not reduce all politics to the politics of the nation-state.

In his paper on the state, Thomas Pantham argues that the modernity of the nation-state in India was located not in a complete break from tradition but in a reconfiguration of it. The leaders of the nationalist movement, despite the heavy use of Hindu symbols for mobilization, saw the post-colonial state as realizable only within a pluralistic, civic-communitarian nationalism, rather than a Hindu nationalism. Some scholars have contended that nationalism serves as a glue to attach the individual to the state, but in the case of India, belongingness seems to function in more complicated ways. Thus, for instance, the emergence of caste associations through which individuals are attached to the state give a different dimension to notions of choice and consent than the classical liberal theories of the state would suggest. Further, the idea of the state as an embodiment of universal rationality has been questioned in western social science itself. To take one example, Giorgio Agamben has resuscitated an obscure figure of Roman law, the figure of *homo sacer* to suggest that sovereignty is to be understood as the ability to resort to an endless state of exception so that the sovereign is both within the law and outside it. As the figure of the person who can be killed but not sacrificed, *homo sacer* comes to be placed outside both human and divine law. For Agamben this figure is necessary to understand the paradox as to how the biopolitical state that is committed to preserving life can sanction mass deaths as in the Nazi camps. So Agamben would construct the genealogy of the biopolitical state in a different manner from that of Michel Foucault, the other major theoretician of the biopolitical state. I gesture towards these questions because I think there is an urgent need to think whether and how notions of sovereignty have been inflected with other notions from Indian experience, whether this is in ideas of kingship in the *Shanti Parva* of the *Mahabharata* or in the notion of patrimonial bureaucracy in Mughal administration. However, it is not only from textual and historical sources but also from the experience of the state in everyday life in contemporary India that we can work towards these genealogical questions.

In his paper, Kaviraj argues that while Indian political thought was receptive to western ideas of equality and justice, it combined this with critiques of the ideology of individualism and tried to seek for other ways of grounding notions of consent. Thus democratic ideals, he submits, came to be infused with a sense of community and rights of communities were addressed in democratic and constitutional discourse. He is very perceptive in pointing out that an intellectual critique of western notions in itself would have been insufficient for mounting a movement against authoritarian colonial rule. It was Gandhi's genius of combining intellectual critique with mass mobilization that gave the nationalist movement its impetus and paved the way towards a democratic constitutional post-colonial polity. Like Pantham, Kaviraj also emphasizes the idea of the cultural unity of India as made up of a pluralistic, layered form of nationalism. The legacy of the Congress Party, in the first two decades of independence was not only an allegiance to a constitutional form of democracy but also the political style that put value on compromises between antagonistic conceptions and interests. While in the first two decades after independence, these antagonistic interests were accommodated within the Congress Party itself, after 1967, other political parties and powerful lobbies came to play an increasingly competitive role in national politics. This expanded the range of interests that found institutional expression in the political arena. Paradoxically there was an abrogation of internal democracy in political parties in the same period. Kaviraj regards the National Emergency declared by Indira Gandhi's government as a watershed—it not only demonstrated that democratic processes and procedural rules could be abandoned but also aggravated a politics of confrontation that was to find lethal expressions in various parts of the country. Kaviraj sees these trends in the politics of insurgency movements, the rise of militancy, and the growth of the security state in India, that could violate human and citizen rights on the grounds of threats to national security.

Pantham and Kaviraj, both regard the 1980s as a period of the growth of identity politics. Its most dangerous expression today is to be found in the demand for a Hindu nationalism that would form the basis of emotional unity and claims over citizenship. It is not that such ideas were completely absent earlier but what was at the periphery of state practices has acquired greater strength, so that the principle of a layered nationalism is severely threatened. Kaviraj does not suggest any simple opposition between a politics of recognition and a politics of redistribution. He points out that the politically blunt instrument of electoral mandate does not provide the means for the marginal and deprived sections of the polity to have their demands taken seriously by the state. To that extent the studies of electoral politics have limited use, for they fail to address questions of how those who are excluded from the wealth that is created due to economic inequalities, are to have their demands for regular employment, housing, medical care or education recognized. It seems that all demands for justice are now limited to asking for more reservations within the organized sector rather than attending to the urgent needs that arise from everyday hazards that the poor face.

The book ends with an essay on collective violence by Jonathan Spencer, not because that is an appropriate resting point for these issues but because to think through questions raised by the increasing violence in India requires conceptual boldness and a great sensitivity to the tremendous human costs of this violence. The communal riot was seen in colonial historiography as a particular pathology of Indian society and was assimilated in the administrative practices of the colonial state on the analogy of a natural eruption or an epidemic. Thus it neither had a history nor a possibility of being addressed as a form of politics. Spencer argues that social theory often mimicked this approach by replicating the so-called distinction between legitimate force and illegitimate violence. Thus, for instance, the violence in the trenches of the first World War, the Nazi camps, or the bombing of Hiroshima and Nagasaki were not named as violence by the state either because soldiers were not free to speak of their experience as violence but only as honorific sacrifice; or because the violence was seen as exceptional as in the theory of German *sonder weg*. Another way to think of violence as in the case of the bombing of Hiroshima and Nagasaki, was to render it as surgical violence that was deployed to end other kinds of violence. The second Gulf War makes it clear that the whole realm of excuses and justifications for war are indicative of a certain kind of politics. Thus instead of mirroring state ideologies in drawing boundaries between war, collective violence, and domestic violence, one should see the configurations of these categories in particular events. This means that forms of violence are not simply local events but are deeply inflected by global forces on the one hand, and the practices of the state on the other. This does not mean that we need pay no attention to local logics, but rather that we reconsider locality as made rather than given. Finally, it is Spencer's point that violence and non-violence are coeval—it is our descriptions that treat them as completely separate, for we tend to hide the violence embedded in times of peace and underplay the non-violence through which everyday life is secured even in times of war and collective strife.

If there were but one theme on which I would put a wager as holding a challenge for social sciences worth taking in the new millennium, it would be the question of how to relate knowledge and institutions in the development of these disciplines. An important influence of area studies in the cold war period was to cast India as a space of exception, guarded by gate keeping concepts like caste and hierarchy. Indian scholars and their diasporic South Asian intellectuals over the years have done much to bring the experience of South Asia into social theory more generally. Indian scholars till the seventies were content to do research and teaching in research institutions and universities that were largely supported by the state. This was seen as part of the obligation of the state to provide higher education. Indian intellectuals generally thought of the nation and the state in postcolonial India, as benign forms of collectivities, if lacking in political will to effect reforms with the speed and efficiency that was required. The National Emergency did jolt us out of some of this complacency not only because it demonstrated that freedom of expression could be severely curtailed legally by the government but also because it demonstrated the authoritarian trends within the universities themselves.

The rise of the exclusive Hindutva ideology in the polity and the state's interventions in major research institutions and universities now pose the question about intellectual autonomy in sharp terms. In any case, most social scientists and philosophers are clear that the university as an institution cannot be understood in isolation from the market and the state. What kind of democratic critique can universities generate within these constraints? It is not a question of relevance defined in a narrow sense but the larger question of what kind of institutional mechanisms, material support, and practices of pedagogy will ensure that social sciences retain some measure of autonomy from the state and market. The dispersal of research among different institutional sites such as corporations, NGOs, various ministries of the government, and international agencies in addition to universities requires that we broaden our conception of research. The way that priorities are defined for, say, research in new drugs in the pharmaceutical industry will be presumably different from the priorities that are driven by what Jurgen Habermas called knowledge interests. Similarly global institutions such as the World Bank or World Health Organization are constrained by their conceptions of what are global public goods. These may or may not correspond to public goods defined in other frameworks. NGOs too are not some kind of pure representatives of civil society that represent the voice of conscience—they too have to raise funds for research or advocacy and often define their strategies in relation to global or state priorities. Instead of treating the earlier utopian pictures of universities as the sole repositories of knowledge, it is more useful to think of the tensions and opportunities generated by this proliferation of institutions claiming the legitimacy of their own research ventures. I would suggest that much of this proliferation of knowledge has opened up research on questions that strict disciplinary framings did not allow earlier. But there is also a danger that in the interest of responding to the immediacy of need, or the imperatives of profit, or even the urgency of responding to global or national threats, we could end up by sanctifying data (in the form of numbers, voices, narratives) that do not stand up to serious methodological scrutiny. The answer to my mind is not a rejection of these findings but reframing them in disciplinary perspectives that privilege the long run, recognize the legitimacy of curiosity for driving research, and are respectful but critical of short term solutions offered.

Finally there is the question of ethics. It is clear that science (including social science) cannot provide the picture of limit from within itself. The answer in many universities in the West has been to form Institutional Review Boards that review research projects for ethical implications for human subjects. The model for this review is provided by therapeutic and experimental interventions in medicine while the procedures for review have been inevitably bureaucratized. Some professional bodies such as the American Anthropological Association have tried to device protocols for research in their own disciplines. Some NGOs in India have propagated the principles derived from the practice of medicine, such as the principle of no harm, which seem benign but cannot be translated in any meaningful way in disciplines that generate critique of institutional practices. The situation over all remains unsatisfactory and poses difficult questions that need to be engaged in the light of disciplinary histories and broader questions about the role of knowledge. It is not dramatic revelations about infringements of ethics but attention to the everyday life of disciplines and micro practices of institutions that seem to call for our attention. The hand in handicraft, as a model of thinking, seems to beckon.

I
Conceptual Underpinnings

Social Sciences and the Publics

VEENA DAS

In presenting *The Oxford India Companion to Sociology and Social Anthropology*, I hope for reflection on the processes through which forms of knowledge about Indian society and culture have been generated, as well as the institutional mechanisms for the consolidation of concerns in social science research in the country.[1] My aim in the Introduction is not to summarize the chapters which follow (for these, refer to the sectional introductions) or to trace the history of sociology and social anthropology in India. The latter is the subject of a panoramic opening essay by André Béteille in this volume. What I hope to do is to show the configurations through which the relation between social sciences, public debates, and the imperatives of administration have given a particular shape to the concerns of these disciplines in India.

As is well known, the colonial organization of polity and the establishment of universities, research institutions, as well as governmental institutions for data collection, translation, and the production of texts constituted the contours of colonial modernity and the emergence of disciplines in India in the late eighteenth and nineteenth centuries. The end of colonial regimes and emergence of new nation states provided an important anchor for reorienting the concerns of social sciences in both metropolitan countries and the colonies. It is not surprising, then, that much of social science research in the last fifty years in India has been conducted under the sign of the nation. Further, the end of the Second World War signalled a new division of the world into strategic areas for the pursuit of geopolitical interests. The establishment of Area Study Programs in North American universities was an important source of funding for research on India and had a decisive influence on defining the concerns of these disciplines. Thus a complex pattern of interactions may be discerned between different kinds of geopolitical interests, national aspirations, and intellectual traditions in the colonial period and in the post-War era in the organization of knowledge in the social sciences. All this is in flux today as we see the reorganization of area studies in the West and the emergence of global institutions such as the World Bank, WHO, UNESCO, and UNICEF as well as global foundations (Rockefeller, Ford, McArthur, etc.) as important actors in the generation of knowledge. There is also a powerful diasporic intellectual community with an ongoing relation to the country of origin which has played an important role in not only shaping area studies but also redefining conceptual concerns, especially in the United States. The relations between insiders and outsiders, institutions of state and of civil society, as well as the university and other sites of knowledge production, are also undergoing rapid change in India. Such shifts signal that the authority enjoyed by social sciences to pronounce on society may give way to a scenario in which other forms of knowledge as well as other institutional actors such as non-governmental organizations, media, or market research organizations (to name a few) may compete for legitimacy. Thus the struggle to define the legitimate concerns of social sciences in India today is equally a struggle towards the creation of not only new *sites* but also new *objects* of sociological and anthropological knowledge. I hope that the contributions to this *Companion* reflect not only the consolidation of several fields of study but also name some of the moments in the emergence of novelty.

The Idea of Social Science

A dominant view in the current literature on the history of social sciences sees the rise of social sciences and the formation of modernity as linked events. The dual revolution of industrial and technological practices as also the political practices inherent in the French revolution (with the ensuing waves of democratic demands in European countries) in the late eighteenth and early nineteenth centuries, laid the foundations of the idea of society as both an object of study and of reform (Magnusson et al. 1998; Rabinow 1989). The expression 'moral and political science' came into use in France during the 1760s while 'social science' was coined in the circle around Condercet and subsequently spread to England and Scotland and the German-speaking countries. The institutional changes which took place in the organization of knowledge included the shifting of intellectual work from academies, learned societies, and literary salons to reformed universities and newly created professional schools and research centres. Unfortunately, disciplinary histories as they are taught in the social science faculties today (and not only in India), largely ignore the social and intellectual contexts of the emergence of these sciences. Further, Karl Marx, Emile Durkheim, and Max Weber are considered classics both in sociological and anthropological theory while the work of their predecessors is treated as part of the prehistory and not the intellectual identity of these disciplines (see Magnusson et al. 1998). A tunnel view of history shapes our understanding of the emergence of social science and modernity in which relatively little attention is paid to those ideas which were defeated or simply failed to be realized. In this context, shifting the question from the 'when' of modernity to the 'where' may be of great value—it may help us examine to what extent we may treat modernity not only as a result of institutional changes but also as the functioning ideology of the social sciences which assigns to 'tradition' a place, a modality, and a temporality. Thus the West comes to be seen as the 'natural' home of modernity, while other places are either in the process of being modernized or are waging a struggle against the shackles of tradition. While this particular way of formulating the relation between tradition and modernity has been repeatedly questioned since the eighteenth century,[2] the opposition seems to reinvent itself in new forms. Does this have something to do with the way in which modernity institutes itself in the social sciences and their location in the West?

As part of the functioning ideology of the social sciences, modernity came to be described in classical sociological writings as having certain defining characteristics, namely the key roles of agency, freedom of choice, and moral responsibility as opposed to the shackles of tradition, convention, and authority. However, several scholars have come to question these assumptions in recent years arguing that the specific modern form of polity that took shape during the French Revolution, the modern nation state, did not fulfil the Enlightenment project but rather curtailed it drastically, including its idea of free public spheres and its commitment to cosmopolitanism. According to this view, the classical concerns of social science arose from the constraints to realize the ideals of the Enlightenment traditions rather than as a celebration of these. As a corollary, the standard assumptions about the 'natural' tripartite division—economic activities of the market, political activities of the state, and aggregate social relations of society—had become problematic even as a description of the activities of the state in Europe in the nineteenth century (Wittrock 1998, 2000). It is against the background of these assumptions that the problematic of social sciences in 'other' societies becomes important as a means of comprehending the institutional transformations in European societies and their relation to the project of both understanding and governing the colonies.

It is clear that the new forms of knowledge were part of the colonial project of governance, but these were not mapped on an empty space—the existing systems of knowledge at various levels of society were twined into the colonial projects of rendering the society knowable. In the case of India, there was a period of extensive projects of translation, mapping of legal and social systems, and collection of statistics and innovations in the sites and objects of knowledge in the late eighteenth and early nineteenth centuries. One may recall here that though society came to be defined as the object of expert knowledge with the rise of social sciences, professional understandings could not completely free themselves of the common sense of their times. This was as true for the way that other societies were rendered intelligible as for the manner in which the common sense about 'women' or 'Jews' entered the classic texts of Emile Durkheim (1951) and Max Weber (1978).[3] Thus, it is interesting to see how the project of building social sciences in India, as in other 'new' nations, countered this 'common sense' of western societies presented to them as 'expert knowledge', but it would be a mistake to see the nationalist and other post-colonial projects as producing only reactive knowledge. There were concerns rooted in the processes of social transformation within these countries which also informed the manner in which these subjects developed. Thus, one way to understand the development of sociology and social anthropology in India is to understand the different kinds of stakes that various social actors had in defining the processes through which knowledge was to be produced. A good illustration of this is the role of certain gatekeeping concepts such as caste and communalism which functioned as sociological and anthropological categories for rendering Indian society knowable.

The Role of Gatekeeping Concepts

The difficulty that modern ideology has in providing a sufficient image of social life was the concern of classical sociological theory and provided a major challenge to the French thinker, Louis Dumont, who is perhaps the best known interlocutor of India to the West. Dumont (1971) argued that Indian civilization presented a major contrast to western civilization because of its values of hierarchy and holism (each term implied the other in Dumont's formulation). What was at stake for Dumont was the image of social life in India with its emphasis on holism as it stood in a contrastive relationship to the ideology of individualism in the West (Dumont 1965).

Dumont's characterization of Indian society has been challenged on many grounds—the most important critiques have pointed out that what Dumont saw to be timeless ideology replicated at every level of Indian society and culture, was itself a result of certain practices of classification and enumeration instituted in the context of colonial administration, which gave a dominant place to Brahmanical texts as representative of Indian society (Dirks 1989).[4] What was at stake for Dumont was the representation of India as the 'other' of modern West, so he was much less interested in either the concrete historical processes through which institutions were formed or the contemporary changes in the caste system. The hierarchical relations within an organic whole embodied in the caste system belonged to the order of moral fact for him and provided an image of social life that was embedded in moral relations. Other relations such as those which cut across religious divisions, for example Hindu–Muslim relations, were, at best, relations forged in the market place and at worst were sites for conflict brought about by the emergence of nationalism and the creation of new moralities such as those of nation and citizenship. It is instructive to compare this with the way that caste and communal relations have been studied as part of both the civilizational design in India and contemporary reality not only by Indian anthropologists but also by those scholars who were interested in the implications of these institutions for the development of a democratic polity in independent India. In order to locate this point in the emerging concerns at the end of the Second World War, it would be useful to see how Area Studies Programs developed in the United States on the one hand, and to examine the aspirations of the social sciences in the context of Indian polity on the other.

Area Studies Program: Shaping of South Asian Studies in the United States

The end of the Second World War and the decolonization movements in Asia led to the development of strategic interests in the problems of contemporary South Asia in the United States. Dirks (1998) has argued that it was the conjuncture between Sanskritic scholarship and the strategic concerns of the Second World War which shaped South Asian Area Studies in the US. Despite the long history of Sanskrit studies as part of orientalist scholarship in the departments of a small number of universities in the United States, a new kind of assemblage might be detected after the War in the coming together of Sanskrit scholarship and contemporary concerns. Quoting from a draft document prepared by Norman Brown who held the chair for Sanskrit Studies in the University of Pennsylvania from 1926 to 1966, Dirks shows that a greater investment of resources in contemporary languages, and other contemporary issues, was advocated on the grounds that the War years had demonstrated the inadequacies in information about the 'Orient' and the lack of trained personnel who could handle 'the increased political, business, and cultural relations' between the United States and the emergent post-War regions of influence (Dirks 1998). Major centres of Area Studies were subsequently established at the universities of Pennsylvania, Berkeley, Chicago, Wisconsin-Madison, and Michigan, among others. It would be a mistake, though, to imagine that the scholarly concerns developed in these departments were dictated primarily by strategic interests—the language of interests provided a powerful impetus for universities, government, and foundations to get involved in funding area studies, but the relation between intellectual projects and the articulating of interests was, as in other cases, a complicated one. Edward Said's (1978) critique of Orientalism as an intellectual project and its close affiliation to colonial forms of governance provided a much needed impetus for the emergence of what came to be known as post-colonial theory. However what Said failed to address in his critique was the manner in which profound transformations of the colonies took place due to the exercise of colonial power that radically altered not only institutions but also desires and subjectivities (Dirks 1992; Scott 1997). Nevertheless, it opened a pathway for new readings of the authoritative texts of colonial encounters and created conditions for new alliances between critical literary studies and cultural anthropology. Parallel developments in Indian historiography, anthropology, and sociology showed how Said's arguments needed to be refined for an understanding of the Indian case and also how questions of agency may be addressed in the understanding of India's pasts (Chakrabarty 1992). Some of the most innovative work in this area has emerged in the area of study that conjoins history and anthropology (Guha 1997).

Colonial Constructions

The colonial categories in terms of which Indian society became knowable for governance emerged in the interaction between different kinds of local knowledges, imaginary landscapes of other societies held in the West, and new ideas of governability. While earlier accounts in the form of travelogues and missionary reports were available for the fifteenth and sixteenth centuries and may be seen as providing the prehistory of such disciplines as Indology and ethnology, these did not carry the stamp of official authority (Dharampal-Frick 1995). The categories deployed in these accounts did not thus constitute what Asad (1986) calls 'strong languages' which were consolidated with the penetration of colonial rule. In the context of Indian studies, Bernard Cohn (1987, 1996) tried to show the close nexus between categories of colonial knowledge and colonial rule since the late 1960s and also how social science disciplines in the West had maintained these basic colonial assumptions in the categories they deployed. Although the relation between history and anthropology was foreground in many important studies by Indian sociologists and historians, especially in the Bombay school, there was a somewhat uncritical acceptance of the colonial texts as providing historical sources for the nature of Indian society and culture. There were important exceptions, for example in the challenge posed by Ghurye (1932) to Risley's application of the category of race to caste in early census reports. However, the appeal of history was limited in the writings of Indian sociologists and anthropologists till the 1960s, to showing the continuities of the civilizational categories, especially Hindu categories, in the social life of Indians (see Bose 1971; Kapadia 1955; Karve 1968; Kosambi 1965).[5] Subsequent scholarship both in the fields of history and anthropology became much more critical of the nature of texts that had been used as evidence of an unchanging India. Such concerns consolidated themselves under the rubric of the subaltern school and the whole field of post-colonial theory. I shall return to these themes later.

While the search for the so-called enduring principles of Indian civilization had given the impression of a society which had yet to enter history, the collaboration between history and anthropology led to a shift of focus to a historically grounded understanding of the experience of colonialism and how that had shaped such institutions as caste and communal relationships. The colonial archive thus also became a source for understanding the nature of colonial rule rather than a kind of documentary practice alone. It was used in showing the ruptures in modes of governance and especially the nexus between knowledge and power, the emergence of caste as the trope for Indian civilization, and its use to both legitimize colonial rule and delegitimize indigenous forms of politics as 'pre-political'. The deployment of such categories as 'communal riots' or 'peasant uprisings' served to naturalize these conflicts as based on primordial loyalties and thus convert them into problems of public order rather than as belonging to the realm of politics. The inflection of social science categories by administrative categories (for example, scheduled castes and tribes, communal riots) is used almost as a matter of habit in South Asian scholarship and shows the intimate connection between social sciences and forms of governance.

Enumeration and Classification: The Role of Numbers

Although the predecessor states of the British in India did have apparatuses for counting, classifying, and controlling populations, these were tied to specific needs of the state such as revenue collection or the raising of temporary armies (Appadurai 1996: 114–39). The British colonial state instituted a new way of collecting information in the form of maps, settlement reports, revenue records, statistical information, censuses, enquiry commission reports, compendiums of laws and custom and folklore, to name a few. This new form of governance, or 'rule-by records' and 'rule-by-reports' in the felicitous phrasing of Richard S. Smith (1985) had a decisive influence on the shaping of caste and communal identities in the twentieth century. At the first instance, it may appear odd to suggest that acts of recording that which were seen to be the essential features of Indian society on the ground would lead to major changes in the objects recorded. Much recent research has, however, shown the complex relation between representation in the moral, aesthetic, and political senses—the influence of representation as a linguistic activity on the legal and political processes of representing is now widely acknowledged (see Cavell 1982; Pitkin 1972, 1979). It may be useful at this stage to see how statistical thinking emerged in this period as a new discipline—the impact of administrative concerns on the shaping of social sciences could be seen both in the metropolitan centres and in the colonies.

Following the work of Ian Hacking (1992) and Theodore Porter (1986), it is widely acknowledged now that a distinctive way of thinking through numbers emerged in a period of crucial change between 1820 and 1850 in Europe. As Donnelley (1998) puts it, 'In contrast to the eighteenth century, there was decidedly something new in the use of social or public numbers in the early nineteenth century, so much so that one can think of statistical thinking itself as an innovation of this period.' Hacking (1989) has characterized the early-nineteenth-century period as one of statistical enthusiasm. The collection of statistics moved from a private, amateurish, and ad hoc activity to one that was public, professional, and bureaucratic in orientation. Underlying this move was the conceptual shift from political arithmetic to social statistics: information obtained from numbers was not about the body politic but about the social body. Donnelley (1998) identifies three important changes in this transformation. First, the scale of statistics gathering increased manifold—Hacking (1989) estimates a 300,000-fold increase in the availability of printed numbers in the course of the nineteenth century in Europe. Second, the conceptual framework underlying the collection of statistics underwent a radical change. As techniques of governance were transformed, there was a change in what was counted and what signs, symptoms, and indicators numbers were said to reveal (Asad 1994). Finally there was a change in how numbers could be interpreted since continuous time series replaced sporadic collections of numbers and allowed patterns to be discerned. These patterns revealed a new order of reality which was different from that of individual events. Durkheim (1951), for example, used this method to show how suicide rates belonged to a different order of facts from the individual acts of suicide in any society.

While it is clear that the shift from body politic to the social body led to the novel and fertile idea of 'population' as a system which could be studied as a whole through frequencies of its collective phenomena, this shift owed less to a change in mathematical principles and more to the political innovation in governance seen as the regulation of populations rather than of individuals. Foucault's seminal work (1973) in this area shows how technologies of power, especially the shift from sovereign power to disciplinary power, were central in normalizing the idea of population as an object of study and reform. As discussed earlier, the questions of what is counted and what numbers stand for, owed much to the shifting emphasis on the social body (Buck 1982). While this is not the place to examine this issue in great detail, it is instructive to see how this theme plays out in the construction of populations in the colonies.

In the processes of classifying and enumerating the population, the British did not start with caste as if it were a natural category. In the early phases of colonial rule the emphasis was on cadastral control. Statistics on landownership, tenancy, crop production, and instruments of agricultural production were geared towards standardizing the methods of revenue collection and it was by no means obvious that the caste rather than the village would be the natural unit for the organizing of data. According to Smith (1985) it was only around 1850 that the census in the case of Punjab was transformed from an instrument of tax to an instrument of knowledge. Caste categories which came to be finally used in the census were arrived at after considerable experimentation. Earlier census reports were more pragmatic and localistic in orientation—it was by no means easy to find the principles through which caste names could be standardized on an all India basis. There was considerable tension between the concerns of centrist census officials collating data in an encyclopaedic manner, and the local officials who were concerned in recording the nature of social groups and categories for more practical purposes such as the collection for revenue or the settlement of disputes (Appadurai 1996: 114–39). In order to understand why caste came to occupy such a central place in colonial imagination it is necessary to understand the scientist notions of race during this period.

In shifting to caste as the most natural group around which information regarding Indian society was to be organized, British officials relied on their notions of race and physical types. Risley (1892, 1908) was the most vocal proponent of using anthropometric measures in conducting the ethnographic survey of India because, according to him, anthropometry yielded particularly good results in India by reason of the caste system which prevailed among the Hindus. Marriage, he observed, took place only within a limited circle. He also noted that the differences of physical types which measurement is intended to establish were more marked and more persistent than anywhere else in the world. Relying on such symbolism as that of dark versus light skin colour and the shape of nose and jaw, the category of caste was thus collapsed with that of race. Ghurye (1932) was perhaps the first Indian sociologist to criticize this view of caste and to challenge its political implications. As he noted, the theory of the racial origins of caste provided the basis for the idea of Brahmins as the descendants of Aryan invaders and fed the political processes of the non-Brahmin movements in Maharashtra and Tamil Nadu.

It is not anyone's case that the process of recording caste created this institution ex nihilo. In fact, as Cohn (1984) has argued, what it did was to objectify a particular definition and to freeze the ongoing processes by which caste came to be solidified in the official imagination. It also generated the conception of community as an enumerative community which had a strong influence on processes of political representation. It is important to emphasize the fact that the census, gazetteers, reports, and other such forms of knowledge came to represent the power of official discourse to name and fix the status of caste groups in local mindsets. As an embodiment of official authority, the census became a source for claiming higher status for a particular caste and census commissioners were besieged with petitions challenging a particular status ascribed to a caste. In becoming a source of power at the local level, the census also had to respond to the processes of local politics and, as Smith and others have shown, the collaboration of local-level officials meant that the categories of official discourse could not be seen as completely cut off from the local discourses. Nor could they be seen as neutral records of groups and categories on the ground. In fact the census has continued through this whole century as a political record of the national and regional politics of caste, especially in the context of the policy of caste-based reservations. There were other contexts in which the generation of public numbers became crucial for such activities of the state as the control of epidemics. The detailed statistics on the districts affected by cholera and the districts not affected in Bengal in the nineteenth century, for instance, were to prove crucial for selecting the sites for field testing in 1891 of the first laboratory-produced vaccine in human history, the vaccine against cholera. Thus numbers were not only important as part of the technologies of power but were also seminal in generating ideas about the legitimacy of bio-medical research and forging relations between science and the state.

The transformation of moral and political sciences into what became partially institutional-ized at the end of the nineteenth century as the social sciences thus cannot be understood without taking into account the remarkable conceptual innovations made in response to other areas of expertise such as administration, law, and the needs of the emerging science of bio-medicine. Equally important was the wider configuration of other disciplines, especially orientalist learning and its relation to philology and ethnology. Trautmann (1997) has recently argued for a complex understanding of orientalist scholarship and the distinctive history of the discovery of Sanskrit by Europe. What emerges clearly from his study is that the idea of a common family of languages under the rubric of Indo-European languages created the notion of a kinship between widely dispersed nations and brought into play the relation between language and physical types in defining notions of race. He shows how the influential work of William Jones and the new scholarship gathered under the aegis of the Asiatic Society of Calcutta founded in 1784 was geared towards a Mosaic ethnology—the project being to form a natural defence of the Bible out of materials collected through oriental scholarship. The method of finding etymological connections and reinterpreting Puranic myths in support of Biblical notions of the creation of the world and the dispersal of nations shows that the con-cern with mapping diversities came to be articulated within certain traditions of thought which are parallel to, but not strictly identical with the colonial articulation of interests.

One other aspect of colonial rule deserves mention. Because of the place that India came to occupy in European imagination, especially with the discovery of Sanskrit and the authority of the orientalists, the Pandits emerged as important interpreters of India to the West. Not only did they act as teachers of language and scholarly interlocutors but many were also employed by the East India Company as experts on Hindu law. Derrett and Duncan (1968) showed that at least fifty Sanskrit treatises of law were known to have been produced under the patronage of the British or with their encouragement. As with administrative categories that evolved at the conjunction of conceptual innovations in Europe and local knowledge and strategies, the notions of 'law', 'custom', and 'religion' also took distinctive shape in this period. Although the discovery of Sanskrit came through the route of Persian, the collaboration between the Pandits and their European interlocutors created an image of India as a Hindu country with caste as its basic unit of social organization and cultural distinctiveness. Other strands which went to make up the civilizational fabric, especially the role of Islam and the period of Muslim rule, were not seen as an integral part of India. Thus Hindus and Muslims came to be seen as distinct communities whose interactions were limited to the market place. The distinctive forms of politics came to be defined as communal conflicts and the relations between communities were not seen as made by history but by primordial loyalties and conflicts, subject to endless repetition (Pandey 1990). Thus the vision of India as stabilized in the writing of British historiography and ethnology was that of a country which was pre-political, not yet capable of becoming a nation, and without the resources necessary to be able to enjoy the fruits of liberty and equality. It is not surprising then that the social sciences in India were preoccupied with the nationalist movement and the building of the nation.

Writing Under the Sign of the Nation

The role played by nationalist historiography in challenging the colonial categories with regard to the unchanging nature of Indian society is well known. The earlier generation of economic historians writing in the 1880s (for example Dadabhai Naroji, H.G. Ranade, R.C. Dutt, G.V. Joshi) had challenged colonial theories purporting to explain India's poverty as lying in the character of social institutions in India, by showing the drain of wealth from the colonies to the metropolitan centres and holding colonialism primarily responsible for the tardy industrialization and economic development of the country. The new generation of social scientists who came into academic adulthood, so to say, at the time of Independence also saw an intimate relation between the social sciences and the task of nation building. Thus phrases such as 'unity and indivisibility' of India became part of the vocabulary of social sciences. Amin (1999) has recently analysed the importance of this vision in the articulation of the historian's task through close attention to various presidential speeches to the Indian History Congress. The following is a quotation from the first speech made to the Indian History Congress in 1947:

It is absolutely unnecessary to state that, so far as the historian of India is concerned, the country has always been one and indivisible, and will always continue to be so. The unity of India is one of the fundamental postulates of Indian moral consciousness, and the longing for centralized administration has been one of the most visible and persistent demands of the political spirits of the Indians throughout the ages.[6]

In the context of history, such a nationalist paradigm meant that not only was there a centrality accorded to political and economic history at the expense of social history, but also that many of the debates regarding the periodization of Indian history as well as the interpretations of the past were guided by the needs of the present. As historians became actively involved in such nationalist projects as writing history books for schoolchildren, the emphasis was on the creation of a secular, harmonious vision of India's past. Many of the current debates following the demolition of the Babri mosque, for example, continue to be informed by the needs of the nation. In itself, this is not unique to India—witness the struggles over the representation of the fascist period in history books for schoolchildren in Germany. Further, the intellectual ambience of this period was one in which the new nation states emerging out of nationalist struggles and decolonization movements represented moments of hope. Thus historians, as scholars who could correct the distortions of history introduced by the dominance of colonial historiography, and economists as those who could direct the rebuilding of the nation's economy, had important roles to play. It was not till the 1970s that the dominance of the nation as the proper subject of history came to be questioned, especially through the work of historians who defined their project as that of subaltern history. Before I discuss that development, let me recount the parallel developments in the disciplines of sociology and social anthropology with regard to questions of nation.

I have already pointed out that Risley's race-based theory of caste came under severe questioning in the work of Ghurye who thought that the theories of Aryan origin of Brahmins fed into the political processes of non-Brahmin movements in Maharashtra and Tamil Nadu.

Thus the engagement of sociology and social anthropology in the questioning of colonial representations of Indian polity and society was evident: moreover, social anthropologists such as N.K. Bose, and historians like Kosambi and Rahul Sankrtayayan had worked in close collaboration with Gandhi and the nationalist movement. What distinguished the stance of sociology and social anthropology towards issues of nationalism was first, the preoccupation with the conception of civilization and the resources it provided for building the nation and second, their attempts to add a dose of realism to the utopian constructions of Indian democratic processes by illustrating how grassroots institutions functioned in the new political arenas such as of electoral politics.

Let us first consider the theme of civilization and nation. The discovery of Sanskrit, as mentioned earlier, and the prominent role played by the Pandits in the mediation between Sanskritic traditions and the colonial rulers had nurtured the idea of India as a place where ancient traditions coexisted with contemporary changes. Hancock (1998) has recently documented the important role played by Sanskrit scholars, especially V. Raghavan who was Professor of Sanskrit at the University of Madras, in promoting Sanskrit in independent India as a medium of popular discourse and state ceremony. It was felt that the introduction of Sanskrit as a language in school curricula, and its use in public ceremonies, would promote emotional integration and help to overcome the divisive influence of linguistic and religious diversity. Hancock characterizes this as an attempt to create a new kind of cultural subject as an appropriate citizen of modern India, one who was a 'tradition-infused modern citizen'. This vision of the nation as made out of the resources of the indigenous civilization of course privileged the Hindu traditions and within that assumed the integrating role of Sanskrit as embodying the Great Tradition of Hindu society (Raghavan 1972).

According to Hancock, the collaboration between Raghavan and Milton Singer who was a participant in Robert Redfield's ambitious project on civilization was an important moment in defining this particular vision of nation as a new collective formation based upon the civilizational principles of Hindu society. The position of Brahmins within the civil services and their understanding of themselves as mediators between tradition and modernity gave salience to this project. The distinction between Great Tradition and Little Tradition, then, recognized the diversity of religious traditions even within Hinduism but assumed that these could be blended into a harmonious whole by the assimilationist work which was presumed to have been historically performed by the Pandit traditions of Sanskrit writing. There is little doubt that this was an elitist construction but Hancock's own assumptions about the long association of Brahmanical traditions with Sanskritic Great Tradition mimics the colonial construction of these objects. In fact Sanskrit was not the exclusive language of Brahmins as is witnessed by its use, for instance, in the medieval period by the Jains. However, Sanskrit had been associated before the first millennium with a certain kind of cosmopolitanism and, as Pollock (1996, 1998) has persuasively argued, it had spread from Afghanistan to (the present) Sri Lanka much before the emergence of the nation state. Thus the new collectivity of the nation seems to have drawn from earlier traditions of Sanskrit as the language capable of transcending local and parochial interests. As it turned out, Sanskrit was not able to play this role and India managed to create and preserve its identity by the management of linguistic pluralism by other means, including the recognition of English.

The relation between civilizational values and the project of nation building was articulated very differently in Louis Dumont's writing. In his inaugural lecture on assuming the chair of the sociology of India in Paris in 1955, he initiated the project of establishing a (new) sociology of India which lay at the 'confluence of sociology and Indology' (Dumont 1957). As I have explained earlier, this was hardly a new vision but it was presented as one which would provide the grounds for treating India as having a unity. Further, this unity was not conceived as deriving from its newly emergent status as a nation but from its values of hierarchy embodied in the caste system. Dumont was not unaware of the fact that his assertion that the unity of India lay in the caste system could be construed both as a sociological proposition and a political statement; but he maintained a stance of complete separation between these two positions, creating in the process a curious division between his Indian readers and the modern European reader.

Have not some of our Indian readers found in the affirmation of the basic unity of Indian caste society more than a sociological proposition, something of a kind of political affirmation, not to say a weapon? To clear up all misapprehension it should suffice to recall that the unity to which we have referred not only is not a political unity [sic] but is a religious unity. ... And the course of Indian history as a whole confirms this. Seen from this angle the task of modern Indian statesmen is precisely to replace one sort of unity by the other. From a caste society to the nation the way is long, and the political task will look more arduous the more the nature of the existing unity will be understood (Dumont 1966: 8–9).

The epistemological trap in Dumont's writing here and one which can be detected in a wide range of writing is the assumption of a teleological necessity to the nation's form by some scholars and an essentialist description of what constitutes a nation in others. After all, the nation state is one way among others, along which collective identities have been historically organized and there is no reason to assume that the European experience represents a yardstick by which successes or failures of other experiments are to be decided (Eisenstadt and Schluchter 1998; Wittrock 1998). Dumont's (1966) formulation on the 'whole course of Indian history' confirming that India had opted for a religious unity as against political unity and hence the modern Indian collective identities were against the course of this history, manages to give a seamless unity to the course of Indian history. The problem is compounded by the fact that the processes of colonialism which produced the present by the deep transformations it brought about in the political, economic, and social processes, also projected the results of these transformations as constituting timeless structural principles of Indian society. In the impressive work of Pollock (1998), documenting the changes over a long period of time in the linguistic and literary practices in India, we get an indication of the methods required to overcome these formidable obstacles. As he states it, 'We must attempt to re-conceptualize the key terms of the problematic, culture and power, from within our empirical materials, resisting at once the preconcepts of nationalized, colonized, and orientalized thinking, and even perhaps of normal social science.' Let us briefly review the conceptual innovations suggested by Pollock.

Sanskritization and Vernacularization: Rethinking Culture and Power

As we saw in the earlier sections, much of social science literature has been written under the sign of the nation one way or another. Although the critiques of colonial historiography generated by the subaltern school have questioned both colonial and nationalist historiography (Guha 1997), they have been relatively less successful in explaining to us how we may overcome the obstacles created by the colonial in the creation of epistemological objects. The idea that has gained the maximum currency in recent years of gathering together theory originating from the previous colonies under the general title of post-colonial theory does not address this issue adequately. In Pollock's excellent formulation,

Vernacularization, it seems, most universally signals the protohistory of the nation. The second difficulty is whether we can even get to that history to query it, given the impact—or at least the estimation of the impact—of colonialism. As a generation of brilliant South Asian historians has sought to demonstrate, colonialism effected changes in the economic, social, political, and cultural spheres that produced the present while making it appear to be the past. The development of underdevelopment; the congelation of religious identities and their political mobilization ('communalism'); the rigidification, and for some even the invention of caste; the establishment of a centralized state; the production of the nation, and of 'India' itself—these are all colonial and new but have been presented under the guise of 'precolonial and traditional'. This guise, for its part, is the artifice of the Western knowledge formation called Orientalism, and in view of the scholarship currently available it would appear that the claim often made—that epistemically, Orientalism is untranscendable—is true [Pollock 1998: 43].

Pollock's own research strategy is to take a close look at the literary cultural textual materials in the period roughly between AD 1000 and AD 1500. He finds that in the different parts of South Asia a process of vernacularization of literary texts began to take place so that people began to write in languages that in his words 'did not travel', as relative to Sanskrit that had monopolized the sphere of literary production in the preceding thousand years. Thus he detects an important difference between the literary culture embodied in Sanskrit and the vernacular. He describes Sanskrit as cosmopolitan, because Sanskrit texts circulated from Central Asia to Sri Lanka and from Afghanistan to Annan and thus created a vast cultural ecumene.[7] The vernacular literature produced a regional alternative and a new ideology of language demonstrating that literary texts could be produced in vernacular languages. Pollock sees this development as directly related to the changed definition of sociality. Vernacularization in South Asia (as distinct from Europe) was not related so much to religious change in this period as to new conceptions of kingship and the formation of new collective identities. The impetus towards the production of these texts came from the royal courts, especially in the south. Thus we can see in this process of vernacularization (what some others have called early modernity) the formidable challenges to the unexamined beliefs that inform both our public culture and the social sciences on the nexus of power between Sanskrit and Brahmanism. Further, theories of nation and language which propose that vernacular languages were popularized only after the formation of the nation state (Gellner 1983) or the emergence of print capitalism (Anderson 1983) seem to generalize from very limited historical material.

I am sure that such an enquiry which tries to see the relation between categories of culture and power without a pre-commitment to forms of collective identity considered appropriate under modernity is one way of opening access to India's pasts without becoming mired in colonial categories. In fact, the relation between Sanskritization and vernacularization may prove to be even more complex once the social historian's attention shifts to the transformative period between the twelfth and sixteenth centuries in the different regions in India. In Gujarat, for instance, the production of caste Puranas in this period was an attempt to produce and fix local histories of Brahmin and Bania castes who were losing their pre-eminence in royal courts with the rise of Jain and later Muslim kings or chieftains (Das 1975). Yet this production of locality with which such castes were seen to have primordial connections used Sanskrit and was even parasitical on well-known Sanskrit Puranas, taking the same names and anchoring them to a completely different set of local events. Pollock's (1998) point that regions were produced through particular acts of political will is worth keeping in mind: it serves as an important corrective to the idea of changeless structural principles driving the whole course of Indian history in one direction. If the historian and the literary scholar's craft promise one route to creating new epistemic objects in the study of India, the social anthropologist's and sociologist's craft suggests another strategy. By analysing how grassroots institutions might alter the character of the very institutions that were created in the course of colonial rule, this strategy suggests that although even violent pasts have to be inherited, the institutions that one inherits are made one's own by taking responsibility for them. This was signalled most prominently in the various studies on the role of caste in modern democratic processes.

The decade of the 1950s saw the emergence of full-length monographic studies of caste (Dube 1955) as well as collected essays on village studies, both within the conceptual framework of the notions of great tradition (Redfield 1957) and Little Traditions (Marriott 1950) and Srinivas's (1955b) concern with foregrounding the 'field view' as against the 'book view' of Indian society. While the literary histories of Sanskrit and of the vernacular movement assumed the frame of cosmopolitan and regional levels, as we saw, the anthropological focus of village-level processes yielded the concept of a dominant caste. Srinivas who coined the latter term (perhaps influenced by the concept of dominant tribe in African studies) argued that the ritual hierarchy of caste notwithstanding, the dominant role in village life was played by the landowning peasant proprietor castes who were rarely Brahmins (Srinivas 1955a). The relation between these rich peasant castes and the other castes in the village had the characteristic of patron–client relations. Thus Srinivas argued that the horizontal solidarity of caste expressed by endogamy and commensality was counterbalanced by the vertical solidarity observable at the village level through patron–client relations. However, this very process also created fissions within the village so that factional politics came to be characterized as the typical form of politics in village society (Nicholas 1972). What was interesting was the recognition during this period that the processes of democratic politics and especially electoral politics anchored party politics at regional and national levels to caste and factional politics at the village level (Brass 1964, 1984).

In his presidential address to the Indian Sociological Society in 1957 entitled 'Caste in Modern India', Srinivas had drawn attention to the continuing importance of caste in public life. *The Times of India* of 21 January 1957 (see Srinivas 1962) reflected the opinion of many progressive intellectuals when it commented in an editorial that the role of caste had been greatly exaggerated by Srinivas. Yet the newspapers also expressed the anxiety of many that caste loyalties played a significant role in electoral politics (Béteille 1996a). Over the years it has become a routine matter to calculate electoral alliances on the basis of caste—yet the very processes of politics have also generated new categories such as 'Dalit-Bahujan' or 'Other Backward Castes' (Illaiah 1996) which bear the imprint of their political and judicial origins. Indeed nothing demonstrates better the political plenitude of social scientific categories as the manner in which categories reflecting new alliances between castes or communities have found a way into the vocabulary of the social sciences. An interesting example is the history of the concept of untouchability and its transformations in political and social scientific discourse.

While it could conceivably be argued that some form of caste-based discrimination is to be found in all the legal Sanskrit texts, recent examination of the genealogy of the terms through which untouchability makes an appearance in discourse shows the importance of political and social processes in the negotiation of group identities in democratic societies (Charlsey 1996). The term 'untouchability' is ascribed to Sir Herbert H. Risley and was part of his effort to classify and rank castes in the subcontinent as a whole. While the category *sudra* occurs in the Sanskrit texts, its referents are varied, ranging from kings and powerful landowning castes to castes with extreme disabilities. Prior to Risley, compilers of District

Gazetteers and State Census Reports had experimented with other terms such as depressed classes, depressed castes, *panchamas,* and *pariahs.* The use of the term 'untouchable' in public life owed much to the reformist politics of the early twentieth century. As is well known, Gandhi's politics of reform and the nationalist movement made the abolition of untouchability, not only in law but also in social practice, an important part of his revolutionary message. In 1931, Gandhi adopted the term Harijan (people of god) and substituted it increasingly for other terms in his writings. While the prototypical Harijan was for Gandhi a member of the Bhangi caste who cleaned lavatories and was thus rendered 'unclean', his major political opponent, Ambedkar, of the Mahar caste of Bombay Presidency, was much more interested in forging political alliances between the major agricultural dependent castes, whose low status came from their dependency rather than their 'polluting' occupations. Nevertheless, Ambedkar retained the label 'untouchable' in his politics. A major part of this politics was the attempt of Gandhi to retain untouchables within the fold of Hinduism and Ambedkar's movement to forge a separate identity for them. (Ambedkar, 1946).

The term 'untouchable' was like a *varna* category in that it masked local heterogeneity. Yet its importance lay in the binary division between untouchable and non-untouchable castes, for this division carried the signature of the governmental policy of reservations for untouchable castes. The policy of reservations based on a quota system for broad categories by caste was part of the colonial policy to create allegiances to the state. By 1931, official measures to assist the depressed classes were much under way and lists of castes to be included into the category of untouchables were being compiled and tabulated. Under the Government of India Act of 1935, the term 'depressed classes' was replaced by the apparently technical 'Scheduled Castes'. The history of this concept provides a fascinating glimpse into the imperatives of reservations. Initially untouchability was to be the criterion for the inclusion of castes into the list of Scheduled Castes. Galanter (1972, 1984) has described the difficulties of arriving at a list, given the differences in the south and north of India. The names of the castes that were finally included in the state lists formed a kind of unity only through a 'common relationship their members have with government' (Dushkin 1972: 166).

In 1990 the term *dalit* (lit. the downtrodden) originated among the Buddhists and Scheduled Castes in Maharashtra and has since become the most commonly accepted term in the social science literature and in political discourse. The most interesting feature of this phase of the movement of Dalits is the emphasis not only on political action but also on representation of the experiences of untouchable castes as a critique of caste society. To show the intricate manner in which social science concepts come to have political plenitude is not to delegitimize such a commerce between the processes of politics and the making of social science but rather to show that the very heterogeneity of the actors who come to have voice in the making of social sciences accounts for the direction in which research moves. To analyse these moves purely in terms of a history of ideas misses the important link between institutions and ideas as also the productivity of crisis in moving social science research in new directions. Thus instead of taking *a priori* decisions on what does or does not constitute collective identities in modern democracies or who are the various publics that mediate between the official culture and the domain of the private, we can see how these institutions may themselves bend to the pressures of aligning culture and power in new ways. Fidelity to the present or a self-conscious watchfulness over the traditions within which one writes, offers an opportunity for the sociologist to see the colonial transformation of categories in both public life and social science, and to make attempts to overcome the epistemic obstacles offered by these.

A host of other examples may be found in the provocation offered to sociology and social anthropology by scholars who pointed to the dominance of concepts taken from Hindu society and culture and then assumed to have universal application for all sections of Indian society, including Muslims and Christians (Ahmad 1972). The case for generating an understanding of Muslim communities as located simultaneously within Islam and in the political and cultural context of India was made strongly for instance, by Ahmad (ibid.). Ahmad argued that Indian sociology had been equated with Hindu sociology and proceeded to edit a series of volumes which examined the impact of social space on the cultural practices of Indian Muslims (Ahmad 1976, 1981). It is interesting that this generated a debate as to whether Ahmad was compelled to present a view of Muslims compatible with the demands of the Indian state. One could detect an unconscious inscription of notions of good Muslims versus Muslims who had to compromise their allegiance to Islam because of the demands of a secular state, as if these notions could function as sociological categories (Das 1984; Robinson 1983). Ahmad's intervention was extremely significant, not because sociological and historical works on Islam and on Muslim communities were not available before this but because the implications of using concepts such as Sanskritization and Hinduization[8] for representing an Indian sociology had not been so provocatively theorized before.

The emergence of social movements around issues of environment, gender inequalities, and health (to name a few) have similarly offered important critiques of the disciplines by interrogating notions of normality and pathology around which conceptual distinctions have been organized. For instance, the role of the women's movement in bringing the issue of sexual violence into public discourse has also provided an impetus for rethinking ideas about heterosexuality, reproduction, and sexual geographies in the classic field of kinship and marriage (Uberoi 1996). Similarly, careful demonstrations regarding the widespread misuse of antibiotics and injections have made a simple allegiance to 'people's beliefs' or 'native points of view' in the studies on health and sickness extremely difficult to maintain (Das 1999a; Phadke 1998). These raise important and even fundamental questions about what kind of sociology may be pursued within universities and what relation this is to bear with knowledge produced in other areas such as the women's movement or the environmental movement. This brings me to the final question of this essay: what is it to speak within or outside particular traditions of scholarship?

The Search for Tradition

I suggested in the opening paragraphs of this chapter that modernity functions in many contexts as the ideology of the social sciences. This is not to suggest that there was not, indeed, a profound rethinking on human sociality in the late eighteenth and early nineteenth centuries in Europe but rather, as Wittrock (2000) has argued, it was a different kind of rupture than has been assumed in the representations of modernity in the social sciences. In short, modernity did not institute a complete break with the past, with the fantasy of making the world completely anew by instituting a new relation with the past (contained for Wittrock in the idea of promissory notes of modernity). He asks for a rethinking on modernity in terms of a deeper understanding of its relation to the historical processes—the notion of promise assumes both a binding to the past and the openness of the future for subjects who are endowed with agency.

Wittrock's reformulation raises, then, the question of how we are to understand the relation between modernity as it functions as the ideology of the social sciences and the promissory notes of modernity. The positioning of social sciences in India provides an interesting case for examining this question. Modernization theory as it was formulated in the 1950s (especially in the work of Parsons) ended up presenting the western, especially American, case as providing the yardstick against which all other societies were to be measured. This is not a question of authorial intentionality but of the consequences of the conceptual framework of pattern variables and the acceptance of the threefold classification of human activities into the activities of the state, the market, and the domain of the personal. Given this formulation, it is not surprising that many Indian sociologists and anthropologists thought of modernity either in terms of its failures or in terms of the losses it entailed. Sometimes formulated as a loss of roots (Saran 1977, 1989) or loss of authenticity (Nandy 1999), there was a certain longing for tradition and a feeling of fierce regret at its loss. In many of these formulations there was an acceptance of the claims made on behalf of modernity by the social sciences as a complete break with the past which, as we have seen, is a problematic assumption even for Europe. How far the longing for tradition was a radical fear of the new promissory notes and how much the fear of confronting the pain of a tradition recognizing itself in change, in the possibility of exile, of there being an 'elsewhere', remains to be investigated.

The relation between tradition and the production of truth is most clearly formulated in the work of Gadamer (1981). It has been an abiding concern of the philosopher Stanley Cavell (1982, 1994) who considers the works of Emerson and Thoreau as the founding texts for the claims to philosophy within an American tradition. The inheritance of a tradition, however, has to face many obstacles: one cannot inherit a tradition by birthright as it were. In this context too the assimilation of Indian traditions of philosophy and history as mere mythologies within European traditions of philosophizing (Husserl 1970) has obscured the dense methodological issues on how to make Indian traditions into those which live and breathe in the contemporary context (Mohanty 1992). For the social sciences, these difficulties are compounded by the fact that Indian thinkers, at least according to one contemporary philosopher, had much less interest in theorizing the social than engaging with epistemological issues of the ultimate conditions under which knowledge may be possible (Mohanty 1998). Second, as some contemporary philosophers writing in both Sanskrit and English have argued, the asymmetry between modern (read contemporary) philosophy and the Indian schools is a result of the fact that traditional philosophy has not had the opportunity of interrogating contemporary western philosophy although the conclusions they draw from this may be quite different (see Bhattacharya 1963; Ivekovic 1992; Krishna 1985, 1987; Mukerji 1983).

In the social sciences the call for indigenizing sociology, for building authentic traditions, and for rejecting imported models, is repeatedly made and indeed mirrors some of the anxious discourse in the public culture of India. Occasionally this has led to acrimonious debate as between Saran and Dumont (see Das 1995). At other times the appeal for *swarajya* in the field of science (Uberoi 1968) or experiments with translations between living Pandit traditions and contemporary forms of philosophy (Krishna 1985, 1987) have made scholars realize the great difficulties of recovering one's traditions, especially as living traditions rather than as museum pieces salvaged from extinction. The question of what is one's tradition is itself not easy to define. For example, Madan (1982a, 1982b, 1994) has reflected on this set of questions directly by asking how Indian sociology and anthropology might recover the capacity to write from within its own tradition. But, as his work demonstrates, what defines 'one's own tradition' may not be easy to decipher from a set of textual practices alone. For the generation of social scientists who built sociology and social anthropology after Independence, India is not only the land of karma, caste, and renunciation but also of moral responsibility to the present. Here again the social logic of space is interesting to reflect upon.

In much of the contemporary writing on anthropology in the West (especially in North America), the decolonizing movements are said to have created a crisis for anthropology. In view of the fact that increasingly long periods of fieldwork in other societies are becoming difficult for graduate students of anthropology in American universities at least, there is a 'reflexive turn' and the emergence of anthropology as cultural critique (Clifford and Marcus 1986). Yet so fragmented are the intellectual communities that the major works in this area have never cared to relate these developments to the earlier traditions in countries like India and Brazil (Peirano 1999). Conversely, although Indian sociologists and social anthropologists have engaged in serious social and cultural critique, they have rarely theorized these practices continuing to hold on to an ideology of fieldwork in locally bounded societies as providing the best strategy. It is perhaps the necessary distance from home societies that diasporic communities achieved which gave them the impetus to theorize the notions of circulations, traffic, and flows between local and global domains, and above all the importance of an 'elsewhere' in defining tradition (see especially Appadurai 1996).

I am certain that the first decade of the new millennium will be an important decade of experimentation. Already scholars such as Marcus (1998) have suggested that the traditional emphasis on locally bounded fields be replaced by multi-sited ethnography.[9] Pálsson and Rabinow (1999) similarly suggest that new forms of sociality (especially around biology) will create new communities of interest and that human nature as we have known it may itself be in a process of transformation. While social sciences cannot be neatly divided into bounded national traditions, the experience of place and the micro processes of institutions where knowledge is produced and disseminated will surely orient the discipline in different ways. Madan's (1975) famous formulation on ethnographic work within one's own society as making the familiar strange, marks a palpable tension between tradition as a discipline formulated across different countries and different historical contexts and as located within India. With its long and complex history of movement between a cosmopolitan ecumen and a closure of regions, the traditions of social sciences *in* India and *of* India are poised to enter into new conversations at local, national, and global levels as not just matters of scale but also perspective. It is hoped that by showing how communities of conversation are defining the disciplines of sociology and social anthropology across national boundaries and across disciplines, this *Companion* will also show the close relation between political processes and social theory. For the student of Indian society and culture, whether located in India or elsewhere, I hope that the contributions are adequate testimony to the fact that though Indian scholars have consistently lamented the loss of their own traditions, they have in fact been engaged in the exciting task of establishing, inventing, and moulding these traditions while also learning how to inherit them.[10] Perhaps the search for a ground on which 'authentic' traditions of sociology and social anthropology may be built needs to take into account the simple proposition that the ground is there—right beneath our feet.

ENDNOTES

1. Since abstract ideas often follow concrete trajectories of relationships, it is my pleasure to acknowledge the significant contributions of my colleagues at the Delhi School of Economics, New

School for Social Research, and the Swedish Collegium of Advanced Study in the Social Sciences for the ideas formulated here.

2. See, for example, Asad (1990); Borden (1989); Das (1999a); Holwell (1765–71); Nandy (1999); Singer (1959, 1972) among many others.

3. Consider, for example, the following statements:

'Women's sexual needs have less of a mental character because, generally speaking, her mental life is less developed ... being a more instinctive creature than man, woman has only to follow her instinct to find calmness and peace' (Durkheim 1951: 272).

'With a few devotional practices and some animals to care for, the old married woman's life is full' (Durkheim 1951: 215).

'The Jew, therefore, seeks to learn, not in order to replace his collective prejudices by reflective thought, but merely to be better armed for the struggle. ... Primitive in certain respects, in others he is an intellectual and a man of culture' (Durkheim 1951: 165).

'In all his other dealings, as well as those we have just discussed, the Jew—like the pious Hindu— was controlled by scruples concerning his law', (Weber 1978: 618).

The sharp distinction drawn by Béteille (1996b) between sociology and common sense is much more problematic than he assumes.

4. Burghart (1990) characterized Dumont as a European Brahmin and argued that his theories mimicked the Brahminical categories of time with their effacement of historical process. See also Das (1995: chapter II).

5. The most consistent adherent of the continuity of civilizational categories is Marriott (1990).

6. Presidential Address to the Indian History Congress by Professor Mohammad Habib, December 1947. Quoted in Amin (1999).

7. I have some difficulty with the sharp contrast Pollock makes between Sanskrit and vernacular. While his demonstration of the capacity of Sanskrit to travel is indeed important, its performative traditions were also highly localized. Consider the fact that the extant texts of the one-act plays of Bhasa, based primarily on episodes from the *Mahabharata* were all discovered in Kerala and are likely to have been preserved because of village-level traditions of Sanskrit theatre. I am grateful to Heidrun Brückner for the insight.

8. It must be recognized though that this issue was the subject of heated controversy between Elwin (1960) and Ghurye (1963) with respect to tribal communities.

9. The conceptual move was made in the works of Foucault (1972, 1973) in such notions as dispersed sites and discursive formations (as distinct from discourse).

10. For two of the most interesting formulations on this by scholars who are themselves observers of these processes rather than direct participants, see Ivekovic (1992) and Peirano (1998, 1999).

REFERENCES

Ahmad, Imtiaz. 1972. 'For a Sociology of India'. *Contributions to Indian Sociology* (n.s.). 6:172–8.
———. 1976. *Family, Kinship and Marriage among Muslims in India*. Delhi: Manohar.
———. 1981. *Ritual and Religion among Muslims in India*. Delhi: Manohar.
Ambedkar, B.R. 1946. *Annihilation of Caste*. Jalandhar: Bheema Patrika Publications.
Amin, Shahid. 1999. Alternative Histories: A View from India. (ms.) 52 pages.
Anderson, Benedict. 1983. *Imagined Communities: Reflections on the Origin and Spread of Nationalism*. London: Verso.
Appadurai, Arjun. 1996. *Modernity at Large: Cultural Dimensions of Globalization*. Minneapolis: University of Minnesota Press.
Asad, Talal. 1993. 'The Concept of Cultural Translation in British Social Anthropology'. In James Clifford and George E. Marcus, eds, *Writing Culture: The Poetics and Politics of Ethnography*. Berkeley: University of California Press.

_____. 1993. *Genealogies of Religion: Discipline and Reasons of Power in Christianity and Islam.* Baltimore: Johns Hopkins Press.

_____. 1994. 'Ethnographic Representation, Statistics and Modern Power'. *Social Research.* 6(1):55–68.

Béteille, André. 1996a. 'Caste in Contemporary India'. In Christopher J. Fuller, ed., *Caste Today.* Delhi: Oxford University Press.

_____. 1996b. 'Sociology and Commonsense.' *Economic and Political Weekly.* 31(31–7):2361–5.

Bhattacharya, Kalidas. 1963. *Alternative Stand Points in Philosophy.* Calcutta.

Borden, Carla M. 1989. *Contemporary India: Essays on the Uses of Tradition.* Delhi: Oxford University Press.

Bose, N.K. 1971. 'Some Aspects of Indian Civilization'. *Man in India.* 51(1):1–14.

Brass, Paul R. 1964. *Factional Politics in an Indian State: The Congress Party in Uttar Pradesh.* Berkeley: University of California Press.

_____. 1984. *Caste, Faction and Party in Indian Politics*: (vol. 1) *Faction and Party.* Delhi: Chanakya Publications.

Buck Peter. 1982. 'People Who Counted: Political Arithmetic in the Eighteenth Century'. *Isis.* 73:28–45, 260–78.

Burghart, Richard. 1990. 'Ethnographer and Their Local Counterparts in India'. In Richard Fardon, ed., *Localizing Strategies: Regional Traditions of Ethnographic Writing.* Edinburgh: Scottish Academic Press.

Cavell, Stanley. 1982. *'The Claim of Reason: Wittgenstein, Skepticism, Morality, and Tragedy.* Oxford: Clarendon.

_____. 1994. *Philosophical Passages: Wittgenstein, Emerson, Austin, Derrida.* London: Cambridge University Press.

Chakrabarty, Dipesh. 1992. 'Postcoloniality and the Artifice of History: Who Speaks for 'Indian' Pasts'. *Representations.* 37:1–28.

Charsley, S. 1996. '"Untouchable": What is in a Name?' *Journal of Royal Anthropological Institute'* (n.s.). 2:1–23.

Clifford, James and George E. Marcus, eds. 1986. *Writing Culture: The Poetics and Politics of Ethnography.* Berkeley: University of California Press.

Cohn, Bernard. 1984. 'The Census, Social Structure and Objectification in South Asia'. *Folk.* 26:25–49.

_____. 1987. *An Anthropologist among the Historians.* Delhi: Oxford University Press.

Cohn, Bernard. 1996. *Colonialism and Its Forms of Knowledge. The British in India.* Princeton: Princeton University Press.

Das, Veena. 1975. *Structure and Cognition: Aspects of Hindu Caste and Ritual.* Delhi: Oxford University Press.

_____. 1984. 'Towards a Folk Theology and Theological Anthropology of Islam'. *Contributions to Indian Sociology* (n.s.). 2:293–300.

_____. 1995. *Critical Events: An Anthropological Perspective on Contemporary India.* Delhi: Oxford University Press.

_____. 1999a. 'Tradition, Pluralism and Identity: Framing the Issues'. In Veena Das, Dipankar Gupta, and Patricia Uberoi, eds, *Tradition, Pluralism and Identity: In Honour of T.N. Madan,* 9–23. Delhi: Sage Publications.

_____. 1999b. Public Good, Ethics and Everyday Life: Beyond the Boundaries of Bioethics'. *Daedalus: Journal of the American Academy of Arts and Sciences (special issue on Bioethics).* 128(4):65–98.

Deliege, Robert. 1992. 'Replication and Consensus: Untouchability, Caste and Ideology in India'. *Man: Journal of the Royal Anthropological Institute.* 27:155–73.

Derret, J. and M. Duncan. 1968. 'The British as Patrons of the Sastra'. *Religion, Law and the State in India.* London: Faber and Faber.

Dharampal-Frick, Gita. 1995. 'Shifting Categories in the Discourse on Caste: Some Historical

Observations'. In *Representing Hinduism: The Construction of Religious Traditions and National Identity*. Delhi: Sage Publications.

Dirks, Nicholas B. 1989. 'The Invention of Caste: Civil Society in Colonial India'. *Social Analysis*. 25:42–53.

———, ed. 1992. *Colonialism and Culture*. Ann Arbor: The University of Michigan Press.

———. 1998. 'South Asian Studies: Futures Past'. Paper presented at conference on 'Rethinking Area Studies'. New York. April 24–26.

Donnelly, Michael. 1998. 'From Political Arithmetic to Social Statistics: How Some Nineteenth-Century Roots of the Social Sciences were Implanted'. In Johan Heilborn, Lars Masnusson, and Björn Wittrock, eds, *The Rise of the Social Sciences and the Formation of Modernity: Conceptual Change in Context*. Boston: Kluwer Academic Publishers.

Dube, S.C. 1955. *Indian Village*. London: Routledge and Kegan Paul.

Dumont, Louis. 1957. 'For a Sociology of India'. *Contributions to Indian Sociology*. 1:7–22.

———. 1960. 'A First Step'. *Contributions to Indian Sociology*. 4:7–12.

———. 1965. 'The Modern Conception of the Individual. Notes on the Genesis of the Individual and that of Concomitant Institutions'. *Contributions to Indian Sociology*. 9:13–61.

———. 1966. 'A Fundamental Problem in the Sociology of Caste'. *Contributions to Indian Sociology*. 11:17–33.

———. 1971. *Homo Hierarchicus: The Caste System and Its Implications*. London: George Weidenfeld and Nicholson (original French edition in 1966).

Durkheim, Emile. 1951. *Suicide: A Study in Sociology*. Trans. John A. Spaulding and George Simpson. New York: The Free Press.

Dushkin, L. 1972. 'Scheduled Caste Politics'. In J.M. Mahar ed., *The Untouchables in Contemporary India*. Tucson: University of Arizona Press.

Eisenstadt, Shmuel N. and Wolfgang Schluchter. 1998. 'Introduction: Paths to Early Modernities—A Comparative View'. *Daedalus: Journal of the American Academy of Arts and Sciences (Special Issue on Early Modernities)*. 127(3):1–18.

Elwin, Verrier. 1960. *A Philosophy for NEFA*. Shillong: Government of Assam.

Foucault, Michel. 1972. *The Archaeology of Knowledge*. New York: Harper and Row.

———. 1973. *The Birth of the Clinic. An Archaeology of Medical Perception*. Trans. A.M. Shreidan Smith. New York: Pantheon.

Gadamer, Hans George. 1981. *Reason in the Age of Science*. Trans. Frederick G. Lawrence. Cambridge: MIT Press.

Galanter, Mark. 1972. 'The Abolition of Disabilities: Untouchability and the Law'. In J.M. Mahar, ed., *The Untouchables in Contemporary India*. Tuscon: University of Arizona Press.

———. 1984. *Competing Equalities: Law and Backward Classes in India*. Berkeley: University of California Press.

Gellner, Ernest. 1983. *Nations and Nationalism*. Oxford: Blackwell.

Ghurye, G.S. 1932. *Caste and Race in India*. London: Kegan Paul.

———. 1963. *The Scheduled Tribes*. Bombay: Popular Prakashan.

Guha, Ranajit. 1997. *Dominance without Hegemony: History and Power in Colonial India*. Cambridge, Mass.: Harvard University Press.

Hacking, Ian. 1983. Biopower and the Avalanche of Printed Numbers, *Humanities in Society*. 5:279–95.

———. 1992. 'Statistical Language, Statistical Truth and Statistical Reason: The Self Authentication of a Style of Statistical Reasoning'. In Ernau McMuller, ed., *The Social Dimensions of Sciences*. Nortre Dame: University of Nortre Dame Press.

Hancock, Mary. 1998. 'Unmaking the "Great Tradition": Ethnography, National Culture and Area Studies in India'. *Identities*. 4(3–4):343–88.

Holwell, John Zephaniah. 1765–71. *Interesting Historical Events, Relative to the Provinces of Bengal, and the Empire of Indostan*. 3 vols. London: T. Beckett and P.J. De Hondt.

Husserl, E. 1970. *The Crisis of European Sciences and Transcendental Phenomenology*. Ed. and Trans. David Carr. Evanston: North-Western University Press.

Ilaiah, Kancha. 1996. 'Productive Labour, Consciousness and History: The Dalitbahujan Alternative'. In Shahid Amin and Dipesh Chakrabarty, eds, *Subaltern Studies IX. Writings on South Asian History and Society*. Delhi: Oxford University Press.

Ivekovic, Rada. 1992. 'La modernité en Inde'. In *Orients: Critique de la raison post-moderne*. Paris: Noel Blandin.

Kapadia, K.M. 1955. *Marriage and Family in India*. London: Oxford University Press.

Karve, I. 1968. *Hindu Society: An Interpretation*. Poona: Deshmukh Prakashan.

Kosambi, D.D. 1965. *Culture and Civilization of Ancient India in Historical Outline*. London: Routledge and Kegan Paul.

Krishna, Daya (with assistance from A.M. Ghose and P.K. Srivastava). 1985. *The Philosophy of Kalidas Bhattacharya*. Poona: I.P.Q. Publication No. 9.

———, ed. 1987. *India's Intellectual Traditions: Attempts at Conceptual Reconstructions*. Delhi: ICPR-MB

Madan, T.N. 1975. 'On Living Intimately with "Strangers"'. In André Béteille and T.N. Madan, eds, *Encounter and Experience: Personal Accounts of Fieldwork*. Delhi: Vikas Publishing House.

———. 1982a. 'Anthropology as the Mutual Interpretation of Cultures: Indian Perspectives'. In H. Fahim, ed., *Indigenous Anthropology in Non-western Countries*. Durham, NC: Carolina Academic Press.

———. 1982b. 'Indigenous Anthropology in Non-western Countries: An Overview'. In H. Fahim, ed., *Indigenous Anthropology in Non-Western Countries*. Durham, NC: Carolina Academic Press.

———. 1994. *Pathways: Approaches to the Study of Society in India*. Delhi: Oxford University Press.

Magnusson, Lars, Johan Heilborn, and Bjorn Wittrock, eds. 1998. *The Rise of the Social Sciences and the Formation of Modernity: Conceptual Changes in Context*. Dordrecht: Kluwer Academic Publishers.

Marcus, George E. 1998. *Ethnography through Thick and Thin*. Princeton, New Jersey: Princeton University Press.

Marriott, McKim. ed. 1950. *Village India: Studies in the Little Community*. Chicago: University of Chicago Press.

———. 1990. *India through Hindu Categories*. New Delhi: Sage Publications.

Mohanty, J.N. 1992. *Reason and Tradition in Indian Thought: An Essay on the Nature of Indian Philosophical Thinking*. Oxford: Clarendon.

Mohanty, J.N. 1998. 'Reflections on Practical Philsophy'. S.C. Bose Memorial Lecture. Delhi: St Stephens College.

Mukerji, R. 1983. *Neo-Vedanta and Modernity*. Varanasi: Ashutosh Prakashan Samsthan.

Nandy, Ashis. 1999. 'The Twilight of Certitudes: Secularism, Hindu Nationalism and Other Masks of Deculturation.' In Veena Das, Dipankar Gupta and Patricia Uberoi, eds, *Tradition, Pluralism and Identity: In Honour of T.N. Madan*, 401–21. Delhi: Sage Publications.

Nicholas, Ralph W. 1972. 'Elites, Classes and Factions in Indian Politics'. *South Asian Review*. 6(2):145–53.

Pálsson, Gisli and Paul Rabinow. 1999. 'Iceland: The Case of a National Human Genome Project'. *Anthropology Today*. 15(5):14–18.

Pandey, Gyanendra. 1990. 'The Colonial Construction of "Communalism": British Writings on Banaras in the Nineteenth Century'. In Veena Das, ed., *Mirrors of Violence*. 94–134. Delhi: Oxford University Press.

Peirano, Mariza G.S. 1998. 'When Anthropology Is at Home: The Different Contexts of a Single Discipline'. *Annual Review of Anthropology*. 27:105–28.

———. 1999. 'In Pursuit of Anthropology'. *Indian Social Science Review*. 1(1):153–81.

Phadke Anant. 1998. *Drug Supply and Use*. Delhi: Sage Publications.

Pitkin, Hanna F. 1972. *Concept of Representation*. Berkeley: University of California Press.

_____. 1979. *Wittgenstein and Justice: On the Significance of Ludwig Wittgenstein for Social and Political Thought*. Berkeley: University of California Press.

Pollock, Sheldon. 1996. 'The Sanskrit Cosmopolis, 300–1300'. In Jan E.M. Huben, ed., *The Ideology and Status of Sanskrit*. Leiden: Brill.

_____. 1998. 'India in the Vernacular Millennium: Literary Culture and Polity, 1000–1500'. *Daedalus: Journal of the American Academy of Arts and Sciences (Special Issue on Early Modernities)*. 127(3):41–73.

Porter, Theodore M. 1986. *The Rise of Statistical Thinking, 1820–1900*. Princeton: Princeton University Press.

Rabinow, Paul. 1989. *French Modern: Norms and Forms of the Social Environment*. Chicago: University of Chicago Press.

_____. 1996. *Making PCR: A Story of Biotechnology*. Chicago: University of Chicago Press.

Raghavan, V. 1972. *Sanskrit: Essays on the Value of Language and Literature*. Madras: Sanskrit Education Society (essays written between 1948–50).

Redfield, Robert. 1957. 'Thinking about a Civilization.' In M. Singer, ed., *Introducing India in Liberal Education*. Chicago: University of Chicago Press.

Risley, Herbert H. 1892. *Tribes and Castes of Bengal*. 2 vols. Calcutta: Bengal Secretariat Press.

_____. 1908. *The People of India*. Calcutta: Thacker, Spink & Co.

Robinson, Francis. 1983. 'Islam and Muslim Society in South Asia'. *Contributions to Indian Sociology* (n.s.). 17(1):185–204.

Said, Edward. 1978. *Orientalism*. New York: Vintage.

Saran, A.K. 1977. 'Some Reflections on Sociology in Crisis.' In A.K. Saran, ed., *Crisis and Contention in Sociology*. 85–120. Jaipur: Rawat Press.

_____. 1989. 'Gandhi and the Concept of Politics. Towards a Normal Civilization'. *Gandhi Marg*. 1:6756–757.

Scott, David. 1997. 'Colonialism'. *International Social Science Journal*. (Special Issue on Anthropology— Issues and Perspectives. Sounding Out New Possibilities). 154:517–27.

Singer, Milton, ed. 1959. *Traditional India: Structure and Change*. Austin: University of Texas Press.

_____. 1972. *When a Great Tradition Modernizes: An Anthropological Introduction to Indian Civilization*. Chicago: University of Chicago Press.

Smith, Richard S. 1985. 'Rule-by-records and Rule-by-reports: Complementary Aspects of the British Imperial Rule of Law'. *Contributions to Indian Sociology* (n.s.). 19(11):153–76.

Srinivas, M.N. 1955a. 'The Social Structure of a Mysore Village'. In M.N. Srinivas, ed., *India's Villages*. London: Asia Publishing House.

_____. ed. 1955b. *India's Villages*. London: Asia Publishing House.

_____. 1962. *Caste in Modern India and Other Essays*. Bombay: Asia Publishing House.

Trautmann, Thomas R. 1997. *Aryans and British India*. New Delhi: Vistar Publications.

Uberoi, J.P. Singh. 1968. 'Science and Swaraj'. *Contributions to Indian Sociology*. 11:119–23.

Uberoi, Patricia, ed. 1996. *Social Reform, Sexuality and the State*. Delhi: Sage Publications.

Weber, Max. 1978. *Economy and Society: An Outline of Interpretive Sociology*. 2 vols. Berkeley: University of California Press.

Wittrock, Bjorn. 1998. 'Early Modernities: Varieties and Transitions'. *Daedalus: Journal of the American Academy of Arts and Sciences (Special Issue on Early Modernities)*. 127(3):19–39.

_____. 2000. 'Modernity: One, None, or Many? European Origins and Modernity as a Global Condition'. *Deadalus: Journal of the American Academy of Arts and Sciences (Special Issue on Multiple Modernities)*. 129(1)

Sociology
Concepts and Institutions*

ANDRÉ BÉTEILLE

Sociology is a loosely defined field of study and research in India as in other parts of the world. There are many different approaches to it, and even different conceptions of its scope. If we add social anthropology to it or include it in an extended definition of the subject, the scope is broadened even further. In India, there has been a closer relationship between the two than in many other countries, and this may prove to be a source of their strength. But even here, there is no universal agreement about the relationship. Some regard the two as practically synonymous; others maintain that they stand in a special relationship to each other; and yet others believe that anthropology is no more closely related to sociology than are other cognate disciplines such as history, political science, and economics.

This chapter presumes a close relationship between sociology and social anthropology; such a relationship has existed in the past and is likely to continue into the future. It takes into account the work of social (and also cultural) anthropologists in a way in which it does not take account of the work of historians, economists, and political scientists. While emphasizing the study of Indian society and culture by Indian scholars, it also pays attention to the important contributions of scholars from other countries.

To say that the relationship between sociology and anthropology is a close one is not to suggest that it is free from tension. My own view of it has changed somewhat, partly as a result of changes in the orientations of the disciplines (Béteille 1975, 1993). Under the circumstances, it is difficult to avoid ambiguity of expression in an article of such wide scope. In what follows, I have tried to cover sociology and social anthropology together, hoping that the context will make it clear when I use the term 'sociology' to include both and when I use it to cover the one as against the other. Needless to say, the ambiguity of expression is heightened by the fact that 'anthropology' has several faces of which 'social anthropology' is only one.

Since I have adopted the more inclusive conception of the subject, I would like to stress at the outset the variety of issues and problems that have received attention within it. In one obvious sense, sociology is what sociologists do, although it is not easy to describe succinctly and accurately the results of what they do. More than in most other disciplines, sociologists have to respond to a fluid and changing reality. The sociologist (or social anthropologist) may

*Published earlier in André Béteille, *Sociology: Essays on Approach and Methods* (OUP, 2002) and Veena Das ed., *Oxford India Companion to Sociology and Social Anthropology* as 'Sociology and Social Anthropology' (OUP, 2003).

find that not only have his concepts and methods become out of date, but that the very subject of his investigation has changed its shape within the span of his own professional career.

In a discipline the subject matter of which is itself in a continuous state of flux, it is an advantage to maintain open frontiers. Sociology is not a very old discipline in India, and those who occupied prominent positions in it in the years immediately before and after Independence came to it from a variety of other, older disciplines such as Sanskrit, economics, and political science. They brought with them a variety of different concerns and approaches, and this variety is still reflected in the conceptions of the discipline held by its current practitioners.

While adopting an open and flexible approach to a relatively new and growing subject, it is essential to maintain some sense of the distinctive features of the discipline if a coherent and meaningful account of it is to be attempted. In the broadest sense, sociology and social anthropology deal with social relations, social processes, social structures, social institutions, and social change in all societies comparatively in order to deepen the understanding of each society. Some would say that sociology is at best a subject and not quite—or not yet—a discipline. Nevertheless, it has in the course of time accumulated a body of concepts, methods, and data that, no matter how loosely integrated, gives it a distinctive shape and character.

The main work of interpretation and explanation in sociology is to place human actions and events in the context of the social processes, structures, and institutions within which they occur. Its concern is as much with actions and events as with their social context. Understanding this context requires the formulation of concepts and methods which have to be systematically applied. These concepts and methods are of little value in themselves; their value lies in their use in the collection, arrangement, and interpretation of empirical material. We have today, as a result of sociological enquiry and investigation, a much larger body of reliable data than we had fifty years ago on virtually every aspect of Indian society and culture: village, caste, kinship, religion, economics, politics, and stratification. This abundance of empirical material creates its own embarrassment: it has to be continually sifted through the application of concepts and methods to yield meaningful sociological accounts.

Sociological reasoning is informed by two distinctive tendencies: the search for inter-connections among elements in a given social context, and the comparison and contrast of different social contexts. Sociology is at the same time general and particular in its concerns. Its theoretical aim is general, for it seeks to understand how societies are constituted, how they function, and how they change; at the same time, it must address itself to the facts of each particular society or a section of it. A sociological account, no matter how consistent logically, cannot be adequate unless it is informed by a detailed knowledge of the available and relevant facts.

To describe the data of sociology as particular, and its concepts and methods as general is of course misleading because in any scientific work, the latter have to match the former. In every branch of scholarship, matching concepts and methods with the data is a difficult art in which complete or sustained success is rarely achieved. Anxiety over their mismatch is a perennial feature of Indian sociology, and it gives rise to disagreements that are not always made explicit.

The anxiety referred to above is deepened by the awareness of a disjunction that is in some respects specific to the Indian situation. In the last hundred years or so, a large reservoir of theories, concepts, terms, methods, and procedures has been built on which sociologists in every part of the world draw upon for their work. The tools of sociological enquiry and investigation were initially created by sociologists in England, France, and Germany, and many of the basic ones among them were already in place when the subject began its career in the third and fourth decades of the twentieth century in India. In this regard, India—like other countries in Asia and Africa—had the advantage of the latecomer, as well as its disadvantage.

The advantage lay in the fact that when Indian sociologists began their work in the 1920s and 1930s, they did not have to create anew all the tools of their trade, but found a ready-made stock at their disposal that could be put to use in their work. But this meant two things. One, it stifled, at least to some extent, the creativity and innovation of Indian sociologists on the theoretical and methodological planes, encouraging the lazy habit of applying whatever was readily available to every kind of problem: why, some of them must have asked, try to reinvent the bicycle? Two, it also established a gap on the plane of concepts, methods, and theories between western sociologists and their Indian counterparts. This gap still remains very wide, and some would say that Indian sociologists have failed to be innovative both theoretically and methodologically because of their passive dependence on the work of western scholars.

More serious than the charge of passivity is the argument that concepts and methods in the human sciences, for all their claims to universal validity, are always coloured to a greater or lesser extent by the cultural matrix of their origin and provenance. An uncritical application of these concepts and methods to other and different contexts entails the risk of distorting not only analysis and interpretation, but also the collection and arrangement of empirical material. It is argued that such categories as family, class, and nation do not mean the same things in all places, and when they are turned directly into sociological concepts, they do not fit the reality equally well everywhere.

Beginning with the work of Evans-Pritchard (1962), social anthropologists have become increasingly sensitive to the problem of translating the categories developed in one cultural context for use in a different context. In some ways, the problem of translation has always bedevilled sociologists since they have been unable to devise technical terms that are clearly distinct from the words used in everyday language. It is well known that there is no exact English equivalent for the French term 'sacré' used extensively in the sociology of Durkheim, or the German term 'politik' used similarly in that of Weber. For all that, Anglophone sociologists have more or less successfully adapted these concepts to the requirements of their work.

The problem assumes a different magnitude, and some would say that it becomes qualitatively different, when we move from the western to the Indian context. Here the problem of translation is of a different order, and not merely in the literal sense of the word 'translation'. This may be illustrated by referring to the recent discussion of the concepts 'secular', 'secularization', and 'secularism'. Some have argued that these terms as they are generally used in sociology are the products of the Enlightenment in Europe, and as such they are limited not only in their origin but also in their reach (Madan 1987). It is therefore maintained that even though there might be some indication of 'secularization' in India, the very method of studying the relationship between religion, society, and politics in India is flawed by the application of a perspective that is limited and distorting.

Of course, even those who are troubled most by the distortion caused by the application of western concepts and terms do not themselves wholly desist from drawing upon the common stock of sociological tools for their own work. The question is not simply whether it would be desirable but whether it would be at all possible to do otherwise. Much ground has already been covered by sociologists in India in the last seventy to eighty years; three or four generations of them have built up a cumulative body of information and knowledge; and some of them at least have shown considerable skill in drawing from the common reservoir of concepts and methods, adapting them to their own requirements, and even devising new tools of enquiry and analysis. It would be too much to expect them now to turn their backs on this entire body of work in the hope of creating a whole new approach and discipline. In any case, the main aim of this chapter is not to propose such an alternative even in outline, but to provide a critical account of the existing body of knowledge in sociology and social anthropology as they are understood today.

It is to the credit of sociologists and anthropologists working in India that they have not allowed their genuine concern for alternatives to existing approaches, to seriously interfere with the continuous pursuit of their craft. Three quarters of a century after its inception, sociology in India is now more than merely an individual intellectual pursuit. It is a discipline with a recognized place in universities and institutes of research; it has its own professional associations, national and regional, and its own scholarly journals. The institutionalization of sociology, particularly since Independence, has contributed substantially to the growth and consolidation of the discipline.

Sociology and social anthropology are now taught in many of the post-graduate departments in Indian universities throughout the length and breadth of the country; they are also taught in numerous undergraduate colleges. The two subjects were taught in only a few universities in the pre-Independence period when the size of post-graduate departments was generally small. Given the size and diversity of the country, the quality of teaching and research in the universities is highly uneven. This is aggravated by the rapid and sometimes ill-judged expansion of universities and colleges. Here a certain aspect of the differentiation between the two disciplines may be noted. The first department of anthropology was started in the University of Calcutta in 1922, and initially universities in the eastern region developed departments of anthropology rather than sociology. The first department of sociology was started at about the same time in the University of Bombay; and universities in the western region began in their turn with departments of sociology rather than anthropology. This changed after Independence, but a noteworthy feature of developments thereafter is that attempts to establish departments jointly of sociology and social anthropology have been largely unsuccessful (Béteille 1993).

Apart from the universities, sociological research is actively conducted in several of the institutes of research set up mainly after Independence and now supported by the Indian Council of Social Science Research (ICSSR), such as those in Delhi, Bangalore, and Surat. The Council has been an active promoter of sociological research, although here again the quality of the research has been highly uneven. Shortly after it was set up, the ICSSR commissioned surveys of the research being done in the country in sociology and social anthropology, as well as in other social science disciplines. Even a casual glance at the three volumes that were the outcome of this survey will suffice to give an idea of the range and depth of the research in these fields already in progress by the 1970s (Srinivas et al. 1972).

The growth of centres of study and research has been accompanied by a steady increase in the number and variety of publications by professional sociologists and social anthropologists. Apart from the steady and widening stream of scholarly books, there are professional journals. Reflecting to some extent their differences in origin, background and professional organisation, there are different scholarly journals associated with sociology and social anthropology, although individual scholars publish their articles in some or all of these according to their intellectual interests. The oldest surviving professional journal is *Man in India*, which was started in 1922 and caters to prehistoric archaeologists, physical and cultural anthropologists as well as sociologists. *Sociological Bulletin* began its career just after Independence, in 1951—it owes its special significance to the fact that it is the journal of the Indian Sociological Society, also established in 1951. The other important journal, which has offered its pages to both sociologists and anthropologists, is *Contributions to Indian Sociology* which began publishing in 1957. In addition, there are periodicals, not devoted solely to sociology or social anthropology, in which scholars in these disciplines publish their works regularly, the most notable being *Economic and Political Weekly*.

The publication of *Sociological Bulletin* is one of the two principal activities of the Indian Sociological Society. Its other principal activity is the sociological conference, now held annually every winter. The Society has well over a thousand life members, including more than a hundred foreign life members. Although not every member attends each conference, there is nevertheless a large attendance. Working papers are presented and discussed in small groups, and there are plenary sessions addressed by both individual speakers and panels of speakers.

The Society chooses a particular theme for special attention at each annual conference. Some of the themes chosen for the annual conference in recent years have been: Identity, Equality, and Social Transformation (Mangalore, 1993); Cultural Dimensions of Social Change (New Delhi, 1994); Challenge of Change and Indian Sociology (Bhopal, 1995); and Ecology, Society, and Culture (Kolhapur, 1996). It may be noted that the choice of themes reflects a broad concern with problems and issues that are not merely sociological in a narrow academic sense, but also social in the wider sense: the thrust is to convert social issues into sociological problems. The discussion of the issues inevitably remains inconclusive. Nevertheless, it influences the nature of sociological discourse in the long run. More generally, the annual sociological conference serves to provide unity and continuity to the profession by bringing together sociologists of different generations and from different parts of the country.

II

Before entering into a fuller consideration of the work being done by sociologists and social anthropologists in India, I will briefly discuss some of the basic issues and problems in the light of which this work has to be considered. Here we have to keep in mind the fact that the discipline has grown in India as much through teaching at the postgraduate and undergraduate levels as through research in the restricted sense of the term with the notable exception of Patrick Geddes who lectured briefly on the subject in Calcutta and Bombay around the end of World War I. The teaching of sociology has been conducted from the very beginning by Indians: L.A.K. Iyer and K.P. Chattopadhyay in Calcutta, G.S. Ghurye and K.M. Kapadia in Bombay; and Radhakamal Mukherjee and D.P. Mukerji in Lucknow. Some of the early teachers, though by no means all, were trained in the West, but all of them brought to their teaching and research, the perceptions and concerns formed by their experience as members of Indian society.

Teaching is shaped not only by the perceptions and concerns derived from the teacher's social environment, but also by the books that are used by him. In the early phase, most of the books used by teachers and students were written by European and American scholars who had very little direct experience of the Indian reality. Soon Indian scholars began to write their own books, which they also used in their teaching. The stream of publications by Indian sociologists in the decades since Independence has not driven out books produced in the West; indeed, there are many Indian scholars who now not only publish their books and papers in Europe and America but also write them there in part or in full. The choice of books, in terms of both quality and provenance, remains an important issue in the teaching of sociology in India, and there is considerable variation between universities in what gets chosen. The diversity contributes to the strength and vitality of the subject in India, and also to some of its confusions.

An important concern of students of Indian society and culture is the understanding of the Indian tradition, its unity, integrity, stability, resilience, vulnerability, and capacity for change.

Sociologists address this problem in a particular way through the examination of the present as well as the past. Understanding the past in the present is an important problem for sociologists everywhere, whether of a conservative or a radical persuasion, but the problem is particularly compelling in India because of the richness and depth of its tradition and its continued strength in contemporary life (Shils 1961).

Sociologists and anthropologists, whether Indian or western, have sought to integrate the findings of classical studies with their work on contemporary India much more widely and actively than has been the case with sociological studies of contemporary western societies. Among the outstanding names are G.S. Ghurye, N.K. Bose, Irawati Karve, Louis Dumont, and McKim Marriott. Several prominent members of the first and second generations of Indian sociologists—Benoy Sarkar, G.S. Ghurye, K.P. Chattopadhyay, K.M. Kapadia, and Irawati Karve—were either trained as Sanskritists or well versed in classical literature. They tried to use their familiarity with that literature in their investigation of contemporary forms of family, marriage, kinship, clan, caste, sect, and religion. In European and, even more in American sociology, tradition is a specialized topic of enquiry (Shils 1981): in the sociology of India, it features as a general concern in the study of many different topics.

The real disagreement among sociologists of India is not over the importance of tradition as a subject of study; it is over the possibility—and also the need—of drawing upon tradition to develop a distinctive method for the study of society and culture. This is not the place for examining the merits of the different arguments. Suffice it to say that some would argue that the mismatch between methods and data in Indian sociology arises precisely because Indian tradition is ignored in formulating the appropriate approach to the problems under study. Others would say that tradition can be adequately taken into account by applying to its study, concepts and methods drawn from the common pool of sociological knowledge.

The Indological approach, which has been advocated by such diverse scholars as Louis Dumont (1966) and A.K. Saran (1962), has to be distinguished from the historical approach which seeks to relate contemporary social institutions and processes to their immediate historical settings, especially in the colonial period. Here there are obvious parallels with the historical sociology of such western scholars as T.H. Marshall (1977) and Charles Tilly (1981), although the themes addressed are naturally different. In India, as elsewhere, not all sociological enquiry is equally informed by a historical perspective. Some enquiries pursue an institution (such as the university), an ideology (such as nationalism), or a movement (such as the peasant movement) across a particular stretch of time, and here the work of the historically informed sociologist differs little from that of the sociologically informed historian. Other enquiries focus more specifically on present social arrangements, with only passing attention to the historical context of those arrangements.

While the historical approach in one form or the other has been used by many sociologists, it has been favoured particularly by Marxist sociologists or those under the influence of Marxism. Some of the most influential historians of India have been Marxists, and it cannot be denied that there is some affinity between the materialist interpretation of history and certain influential sociological approaches (Evans-Pritchard 1965: 76–7). A good example of the use of the historical approach from this point of view is the work of A.R. Desai (1959) on the social background of Indian nationalism which has received considerable attention from students of sociology, history, and politics in India. The historical approach has also been widely used by sociologists engaged in the study of agrarian relations.

Sociology in India has benefited above all from the contributions of descriptive and analytical ethnography as exemplified by the work of a long succession of scholars beginning with S.C. Roy and L.A.K. Iyer. As compared to Indology and even history, ethnography was something of a new departure for Indian scholars, and it has remained central to sociological studies of India. Ethnographic enquiry began as a very different kind of intellectual pursuit from Indological or even historical scholarship. Its requirement of field investigation was based on the model of the natural sciences rather than of humanistic scholarship. Whereas Indologists and historians devoted themselves to noble, lofty, and elevated subjects, ethnographers seemed to go out of their way to observe and describe the habits and customs of poor, humble, and illiterate people; before Independence, social anthropologists devoted themselves to a very large extent to the study of tribal communities. Fei Hsiao-Tung (1939), the pioneer of Chinese ethnography, has reported how the whole approach of this work appeared unprofitable, unattractive, and even perverse to the traditional Chinese intelligentsia immersed in the learning of books. Ethnographic enquiry was, if anything, even more alien to the Brahminical than to the Mandarin intellectual tradition.

If sociological enquiry in India is concerned with tradition, it is no less concerned with modernity and modernization. Indeed, the two concerns are closely related, as is evident from the titles of such influential works as *When a Great Tradition Modernizes* by Milton Singer (1972) and *Modernization of Indian Tradition* by Yogendra Singh (1973). These twin concerns with tradition and modernity present important challenges, both empirically and normatively, to sociologists of India, many of whom show a marked ambivalence towards each.

Indian intellectuals were made conscious by their colonial rulers of the fact that theirs was a static, not to say stagnant, society with very little inherent capacity for change: the idea of the Asiatic Mode of Production was, after all, adapted from the writing of James Mill on India. From the beginning of the nineteenth century, under the impact of the colonial encounter, they turned their thoughts to the regeneration and transformation of their society. Some sought to base this regeneration on a modified concept of Indian values while others called for a more radical break with the past. This debate about adapting traditional values to present needs and making a break with the past is an important aspect of the Indian intellectual climate to this day, and it naturally colours the work of contemporary sociologists.

India's Independence in 1947 marks a kind of watershed not only politically but also intellectually. As I have noted, there was a marked expansion in the work of sociologists, accompanying the growth of universities and other centres of advanced study and research. Part of this institutional growth was a response to the perceived need for coping more adequately with the demands of modernization. It will be fair to say that among Indian social scientists in general, the revival of tradition took a back seat in the first two decades of Independence, their sights being set more firmly on the challenges and possibilities of development and modernization. But before long, a kind of disenchantment set in, and just as tradition had been questioned and criticized in the earlier phase, there emerged in the course of time a more sceptical and critical attitude towards modernity.

No matter which institution the sociologist studies in contemporary India—village, caste, temple, factory, laboratory, or hospital—he cannot help observing and recording the changes taking place in it. To some extent this is so irrespective of his attachment to tradition or to modernity as a value. All studies of change are of course made within some kind of framework, explicit or implicit, of description and analysis. There has been much debate in India, as elsewhere, between Marxists and non-Marxists over the adequacy for the understanding of change of the 'structural-functional' framework used extensively by social anthropologists, particularly in their case studies.

The study of social change has often been driven by the urge to give direction to it by analysing its causes and conditions. In the early years of Independence, much hope was placed on the transformation of society through conscious and planned effort. The country had fashioned a new Constitution that set its back on the old hierarchical order. Planners, policy makers, and educators applied themselves to the removal of poverty, illiteracy, superstition, inequality, oppression, and exploitation, and to the creation of a new social order based on equality, justice, freedom, and material prosperity. Naturally enough, Indian social scientists did not wish to fall behind in this exciting venture.

In all this, the lead was taken among social scientists by economists, for it was widely believed then that social change would be driven in the desired direction by economic development. But economic development itself had to be broadly conceived, and in any case it could not be understood or managed without taking into account its social causes and consequences. Hence sociologists and social anthropologists were associated from the beginning, though not as major players, with research on development and change. Such research is conducted at many places, in the universities of course, by agencies of the government, and in autonomous research institutes. The latter were often set up with the specific objective of providing the intellectual tools for analysing and recommending change. This is often evident from their very names: Institute of Economic Growth, named at first Institute for the Study of Social and Economic Growth (Delhi); Centre for the Study of Developing Societies (Delhi); Institute for the Study of Social and Economic Change (Bangalore); Centre for Development Studies (Trivandrum); and Madras Institute of Development Studies (Madras), to name only the prominent ones supported by the Indian Council for Social Science Research.

Before closing this section, I would like to point out two important dilemmas that are an inescapable part of the predicament of the sociologist as an intellectual in contemporary Indian society. The first, to which I have already alluded, relates to the tension between tradition and modernity that is pervasive not only in what the sociologist studies, but also in his own intellectual make-up. Sociological enquiry as we know it, whether in the West or in India, makes some kind of break with traditional forms of knowledge. At the same time, it has to address itself in India not only to traditional social arrangements but also to traditional norms and values. Is the orientation characteristic of modern systems of knowledge adequate for a sympathetic understanding of these norms and values?

This question leads to the second and deeper issue of the relationship between value judgements and judgements of reality in sociological enquiry. This has always been a vexed issue, and nowhere and at no time have sociologists achieved complete consensus on it. There are those who believe that a separation can and should be maintained between the two; there are others who argue that this separation is unnecessary and undesirable, and that it impoverishes both thought and action; and there are still others who say that, although the separation is in principle desirable, it is extremely difficult to maintain in practice. This chapter is written from the viewpoint of the third position (Béteille 1992), although the majority of Indian sociologists would probably like to maintain a closer relationship between facts and values than the present author.

III

Although debates over approach and method continue to be very important, the real progress of sociology and social anthropology has been through the steady flow of substantive studies in a variety of different fields. I will dwell mainly on the work done since Independence, that is during the last 50 years although that work would amount to little without the groundwork prepared during the earlier phase. Even then, the field is vast, and I will deal especially on those areas that have received continuing attention during this period in both research and teaching. I will take account of work done by Indian and foreign scholars in as I believe that their collaboration is a major source of vitality of the discipline.

In entering into empirical social enquiry, Indian sociologists and social anthropologists were moving against the grain of the Indian intellectual tradition whose strength lay in formal disciplines such as mathematics, grammar, logic, and metaphysics rather than empirical disciplines such as history and geography (Béteille 1998).

A major development that began immediately after Independence was the entry by professional sociologists and social anthropologists into village studies. In their earlier empirical work, Indian anthropologists, like anthropologists everywhere, had concentrated on 'tribal' or 'primitive' communities. Village studies today are a continuing source of the deeper and wider understanding of society, economy, and polity in contemporary India. They are significant at more than one level. They are important not only for their substantive findings but also for the grounding they provide to scholars in the craft of their discipline. It is in and through the village that the Indian social scientist began to grasp the significance of what Srinivas has called the 'field-view' as against the 'book-view' of Indian society. The enthusiasm for village studies in the 1960s and 1970s created something like a community of scholars, Indian as well as foreign, who interacted or at least communicated actively with each other over their work. At least among Indian scholars, the distinction between sociology and social anthropology, which remained an obdurate feature of western social science, was largely set aside in the pursuit of this common venture.

From the 1950s into the 1970s, sociology and social anthropology in India were virtually dominated by village studies, having largely displaced the study of tribes amongst whom anthropologists in the pre-Independence period carried out fieldwork. Village studies are still extensively conducted in every region in the country, and they raise a number of important questions regarding the nature of Indian society. Is the Indian village a 'little republic' as was widely believed up until the 1950s? Was it ever a little republic? One study after another showed that the Indian village is not and probably never was an isolated and self-sufficient community of equals. Through their detailed analyses of inequality and of the conflict of interests in the Indian village, sociologists began to question the very idea of community as it applied to the village as a whole.

Part of the impetus for village studies came from the ideas of Gandhi, Tagore, and many others who saw India as a land of villages. Many anthropologists took the position that the village was a kind of microcosm in which the macrocosm of the wider world was reflected in miniature. Few, however, confined their attention exclusively to the village. They examined the networks based on the ties of marriage, kinship, economics, politics, and religion that stretch outward from the village. Not only are new villages being taken up for investigation, some of the old ones too are being restudied (Breman, et al. 1997).

In the wake of Independence, the Indian village occupied the minds of many, and not merely professional social scientists. There were those interested in village studies and the ones interested in village reconstruction; and there was a convergence of interest and collaboration between them. Jayaprakash Narayan presented a document entitled *A Plea for the Reconstitution of Indian Polity* in which the village was given pride of place. The Community Development Programme generated a variety of investigations to which sociologists made contributions;

notable among these was *India's Changing Villages* by S.C. Dube (1960). After the social anthropologists had opened up the village as a field of study, scholars from other disciplines followed. It will not be unreasonable to claim that village studies, more than any other enquiry, brought the work of social anthropologists to the attention of scholars in such diverse fields as political science, economics, demography, history, and geography in the first two decades after Independence.

Closely associated with village studies were studies of caste. Discussions of caste had figured in the writings of Indologists and historians long before the era of village studies. But the 1950s and 1960s witnessed the beginning and consolidation of a somewhat different approach to the study of caste. This new approach lay in the move away from the 'book-view' to the 'field-view' of the subject. Here, the brief essay by Srinivas (1962), 'Varna and Caste' was a turning point. The essay was a trenchant attack on the book-view of caste based on the *varna* model which, according to Srinivas, gave a distorted and misleading picture of the Indian social reality. Srinivas argued that the real operative units of the system were not *varnas* but *jatis* and that these had to be understood in their local and regional contexts, and not in terms of a general and purely formal scheme.

Srinivas's work opened the way for an examination of the dynamics of caste in contemporary India. Caste could no longer be viewed as a harmonious system in which each part maintained itself in its appointed place in an unchanging order. There were fierce conflicts of interest between castes at the village, district, and regional levels. By drawing attention to the enhanced role of caste in democratic politics, Srinivas brought the work of sociologists and social anthropologists to the attention of a wider audience. If it is commonplace among journalists today to speak of Indian politics in terms of caste, they owe something to the work begun by sociologists and social anthropologists in the 1960s.

Close examination of the operation of the system on the ground also showed that the hierarchy of caste was not as rigid and inflexible as it had been assumed to be. The analysis of caste mobility through the process described by Srinivas (1962) as 'Sanskritization' altered the perception of Indian society not only among sociologists and political scientists who study the present but also among historians who study the past.

In India, the best empirical material has come out of qualitative research based on intensive fieldwork, although survey research and quantitative analyses have also made some contribution. This research examines in detail, structure and change in a variety of specific institutional domains—kinship, religion, economics, and politics. We have as a result a much fuller knowledge not only of Indian society and culture in general, but also of the variety of institutions that are their constituent parts.

We may begin with family, marriage, and kinship. Detailed empirical research has altered, and to some extent corrected, some common misconceptions about the contemporary as well as the traditional forms of these important aspects of Indian society. A.M. Shah (1973, 1998) has shown that the Hindu family was often small in size and simple in morphological form even where it was joint in its legal form. I.P. Desai (1964) demonstrated that the 'sentiment of jointness' retains much of its strength even after families have been legally partitioned. Shah has demonstrated through careful analysis of demographic material that the size of the Indian household was on average always relatively small, and that there is little hard evidence to support the view that there has been significant change in the balance of nuclear and joint households from the beginning to the end of the twentieth century. Ramkrishna Mukherjee (1983) has used surveys to analyse the composition of different types of families in contemporary India.

The ties of kinship and marriage extend beyond the family and household, and have been examined through case studies by a number of anthropologists, notably A.C. Mayer (1960) and T.N. Madan (1965). Madan's work examines the ties of the individual not only with his patrilineage but, through bilateral filiation, with a variety of other relatives, near and distant. Not only is the family embedded in the wider kinship structure, but that structure is itself embedded in caste. Irawati Karve (1968) presented the challenging argument that, given sufficient patience and care, it could be shown that each jati was a single genealogical system. Adrian Mayer demonstrated the linkages between caste, subcaste, kindred of recognition, and kindred of cooperation through his field investigation in the Malwa region of Madhya Pradesh.

The work of Srinivas (1952) on the Coorgs was a watershed in the sociological study of religion. It examined in detail the operation of religious belief and practice in the setting of a small and relatively compact community. Following Radcliffe-Brown (1933), Srinivas adopted a structural–functional framework and showed how ritual and belief contribute to the unity and identity of groups at different levels: the household, the village, and the region. But unlike most anthropologists of his time, Srinivas also examined the relationship between local religious belief and practice and the wider universe of a world religion. This study opened the way for examining the interplay between local and wider religious systems. The wider study of Hinduism has led back to the examination of religious texts, now in a perspective enriched by empirical investigations in the field.

The wider study of Hinduism has drawn attention to two important aspects of the relations between religion, society, and politics in contemporary India. These are secularism and communalism, each of which may be viewed in terms of both ideology and practice. Communalism is not an easy subject to study by means of the conventional methods of sociological enquiry, whether through survey research or participant observation. For a long time, it was studied more widely by historians than by sociologists, but the latter have now begun to enter the field where they find much scope for collaboration with the former. Sociologists have been more at ease with secularism, or at least secularization, in the study of which they can have recourse to a much wider body of comparative material in their own discipline.

In the village studies they undertook, some social anthropologists turned their attention to local-level politics, and an empirically grounded political sociology made its beginnings in India during the 1960s. This acquired added impetus from the enthusiasm for the institutions of Panchayati Raj in the country. Political scientists who had till then concerned themselves mainly with national and state politics, also turned their attention to local-level politics, and the convergence of their interests with those of social anthropologists led to some very fruitful collaboration. An outcome of that collaboration was the book *Caste in Indian Politics* edited by Rajni Kothari (1971). Sociologists, social anthropologists, and political scientists have also collaborated for the study of elections.

Sociologists and social anthropologists have studied economic structures and processes, particularly in the rural areas. The traditional village economy of land and grain with its associated crafts and services has been undergoing many changes. *Jajmani* relations are breaking down, and the old relations between patrons and clients are being altered by the cash nexus and the demands of the market (Breman 1974). Economists and anthropologists now discuss and debate with each other the choice of methods best suited to the investigation of these and other problems (Bardhan 1989).

A central problem in Indian society as well as the sociology of India is that of inequality. One of the early village studies (Béteille 1965) addressed itself to class and stratification in an effort to bring together some of the central conceptual and theoretical concerns of classical sociology with the method of intensive fieldwork distinctive of social anthropology. It examined the changing relations between caste, class, and power in a single village, although it also drew attention to the action of external forces in initiating or hastening the change. Similar studies have been and are being conducted in many parts of the country and outside (Gough 1981; Wild 1974).

The more general problem of inequality has been examined in a variety of sociological perspectives of which two are of particular significance. The first of these is best exemplified in the work of Louis Dumont (1966) which has had a far-reaching influence on sociologists in India. In this work, the defining feature of Indian society is seen as hierarchy, itself an aspect of holism; and hierarchy is sharply distinguished from both stratification and class. Hierarchy is conceived by Dumont and his followers in terms of values, and in this conception, status is given primacy over power. Caste is the most striking institutional form taken by hierarchy, although in a more general way, both religion and kinship are also permeated by it. This distinctive approach to Indian society and culture found its fullest expression in the influential journal, *Contributions to Indian Sociology*, particularly in its earlier phase.

A very different, though no less influential, approach to inequality derives its inspiration from Marxian theory, and its exponents have published extensively in *Economic and Political Weekly*. Here the emphasis is on class and material interests rather than caste or hierarchical status. In the study of contemporary India, sociologists continue to disagree on the importance to be assigned to caste and class. The study of class brings together the work of sociologists, economists, political scientists, and historians. The subject can and has been studied at different levels, and sociologists and anthropologists have probably made their best contributions to it by studying it in the context of agrarian relations at the local level. Not all sociologists who study class adopt the Marxian framework, and of course class and caste are often studied together. A number of sociologists have also addressed themselves to the problems of stratification and mobility in relation to the modern occupational structure (D'Souza 1977).

Caste and class are brought together in the study of not only stratification but also politics. I have already alluded to studies of caste politics at various levels by sociologists; these studies tend to be descriptive and analytical and do not generally have any clear or distinctive normative orientation. For Marxists, however, the politics of class is a matter not only of theory but also of practice. Partly as a result of the evidence brought to light by sociologists in the last two or three decades, Marxists are now inclined to pay more attention to caste in their political analysis than before.

The role sociologists assign to caste in politics depends to some extent on their assessment of the significance of collective as against individual identities in Indian society. This is a subject of continuing interest which was sharply posed by Dumont's contrast between India and the West in which India is characterized, on the plane of values, by holism and hierarchy, and the West by individualism and equality (Dumont 1966, 1977). Dumont's categorical assertion that the individual has no place in Indian society has of course been questioned (Béteille 1987; Dumont 1987). At the same time, both sociological investigation and political experience illustrate the continuing importance of collective identities of every kind.

When we examine Indian politics sociologically, we find that caste does not operate alone, but together with a whole family of collective identities based on language, religion, sect, tribe, and so on. The terms 'ethnic group', 'ethnic identity', and 'ethnicity' have been used for referring to their operation, and it is interesting that the word *jati* or *jat* is now widely used in more than one Indian language to refer to the identities not only of caste in the narrow sense but also of language, religion, sect, and tribe. Their constitution and operation are now being increasingly studied by both sociologists and political scientists.

I have described selectively rather than exhaustively some of the areas through whose investigation sociological study and research have grown continuously in the last fifty years. Village, caste, kinship, religion, politics, economics, and stratification may be described as established or core areas because of the length of time over which they have received attention and the number of scholars who attend to them in their teaching as well as research. While work continues to be produced in each of these areas, a number of new areas have come into prominence in the last couple of decades, and some of the most interesting and original work is now being done there.

Among the new developments, pride of place must be assigned to gender studies of which there has been a veritable explosion worldwide, and in India since the 1980s. A good idea of the work being carried out by sociologists in this field may be formed by seeing the interdisciplinary *Indian Journal of Gender Studies* of which the founding editor is a sociologist. It would be fair to say that until only a couple of decades ago, men and women were given unequal attention in all fields of sociological enquiry with the possible exception of family, marriage, and kinship. This has now changed substantially, and women receive far more attention, although still rather less than their due share of it, in every field of sociological enquiry, including economic sociology, political sociology, and social stratification. More important than that, the concern with gender has brought a new perspective into sociology that has enriched not only its data but also its concepts, methods, and theories.

The impetus to the development of women's studies has come from a variety of sources. First, it is a worldwide phenomenon, and the cross-fertilization of ideas across countries and continents has been remarkably quick and effective. But in India, institutional support has also played a part. A turning point in this development was the publication of the influential report, *Towards Equality*, of the Committee on the Status of Women in India (Government of India 1974). Today, women's studies receive active support from both the Indian Council of Social Science Research and the University Grants Commission. The former supports the Centre for Women's Development Studies, and the latter provides special assistance for programmes of women's studies in several universities.

A second relatively new interest that has already made its mark and is likely to extend its influence among sociologists is the study of the environment (Guha 1994). This is an area in which research and policy are closely combined. Sociological research on the environment does not arise from academic interest alone, but is also driven by the active concerns of governments and non-governmental organizations.

Health and medicine are also attracting increasing attention from students of human society and culture. There are innumerable issues in this area, and even to list them would be impossible here. We now understand more clearly, partly through the work of anthropologists, that the very conceptions of health and disease are themselves cultural constructions, at least to a large extent. There are large variations across cultures and within them in real and perceived illnesses, and sociologists and anthropologists play a crucial part in mapping these variations. They also play a part in analysing alternative systems of knowledge and practice in the diagnosis and treatment of disease (see Madan et al. 1980).

There are alternative systems not only of medicine but also of science itself. It is a truism that scientific research is conducted in different ways in different social settings. There are differences in the resources available, in institutional facilities, and in the material and symbolic rewards of scientific work (Visvanathan 1985). Beyond these is the question of the hegemony and authority exercised by science and scientists in the metropolitan centres over their counterparts in the less developed areas; part of the impulse for the sociology of science in India, as for other branches of sociology, comes from the urge for national self-reliance (Uberoi 1978).

We must note that sociology and social anthropology have been criticized everywhere by radicals of various persuasions for their conservatism, and for the bias inherent in their theoretical orientation towards order and stability as against conflict and change. It is undeniable that sociology has had very little success in developing an adequate theory, whereby change and conflict can be explained. Not only that, its conventional methods, whether based on intensive fieldwork on a single site or on survey research on dispersed populations, cannot be adapted easily to every type of enquiry. Inevitably, certain issues and problems, not easily amenable to description and analysis by conventional methods, receive little or no attention from academic sociologists, and becomes a source of disquiet among the consumers of sociology.

Those who observe and experience life in contemporary India are struck by the pervasive violence, both private and public, by which it is marked. Sociologists of the family and political sociologists are beginning to take note of it in their respective studies. But the subject of violence needs to be addressed on its own terms, for it provides challenges and opportunities for sociological enquiry across its entire range. Some interesting work has already emerged as a result of this concern (Das 1990).

IV

Today, the sheer volume and diversity of sociological output would justify the observation that the subject has come of age in India. Has the work of sociology in India acquired a distinctive identity? If such an identity exists underneath the sheer variety of the work being done, it is unlikely that it can be represented by any simple formula.

It should be obvious from what has been described in the preceding section that sociology in India cannot be understood as a simple application of theories and methods developed elsewhere. Nor can its development within the country be explained in intellectual terms alone as the unfolding of a few elementary principles applied successively to the various segments of an external reality. On the plane of ideas, there is the general stock of sociological knowledge on which as I have repeatedly indicated sociologists working in India, both Indian and foreign, have drawn freely and continuously. Beyond this there is a rich and active, though often confusing, intellectual life in India which never ceases to provide stimulus to sociological enquiry. Finally, there is the distinctive experience of a complex and changing society that gives something of its own colour to the studies, no matter how general or abstract, which are based on it.

The Indian experience offers significant material for examining the relationship between facts and values in the study of human society. Sociologists and social anthropologists in India have been influenced, one and all, though in varying degrees, by concepts and methods that are largely of external provenance. These concepts and methods have themselves been shaped, to a greater or lesser extent, by values that are too freely assumed to be universal; to the extent that these assumptions are subjected to critical scrutiny in the course of enquiry and investigation, the scope of sociology is itself enlarged. New concepts and methods do not emerge unless the existing ones are tested through actual enquiry, found wanting, discarded, modified, and replaced.

New insights do not emerge in an empirical science solely from the internal critique of the intellectual apparatus of the discipline. Their emergence also depends on the extent to which new experiences are purposefully and methodically addressed. Every Indian sociologist has a larger life outside the classroom and the study which forces him not only to observe and experience reality but also to judge it. The judgements that are formed by everyday experience and that give shape to it seep into the formulation of his sociological problems. This is true everywhere, and it would be remarkable if the dependence on 'alien' concepts and methods were to insulate the Indian sociologist completely from the concerns and judgements based on everyday experience.

Sociology has developed in different ways in different climes, and it is not uncommon for the discipline to acquire something of the colour of the environment in which it grows. As far back as in the 1930s, Karl Mannheim (1953) wrote two essays in which he contrasted the orientations of German and of American sociology: one of his arguments was that the Americans sought to be more 'scientific' and value-neutral in their sociology than did the Germans.

Sociology has often had a close association with social policy. At the same time, its autonomy as an intellectual discipline may be compromised if it is too narrowly defined as a 'policy science'. Raymond Aron is reported to have observed, somewhat disparagingly, that the trouble with British sociology in the post-War years was that it was too closely concerned with trying to make intellectual sense of the political problems of the Labour Party (Halsey 1987).

Sociology will be greatly impoverished if it chooses as its sole or even its main concern the task of making intellectual sense of the political problems of any party or, indeed, any institution of society, including the state and the church. Indeed, sociology cannot achieve its proper purpose without maintaining some distance from the Church and the state, and from the day-to-day political concerns in general. Commitment to one's own values in the pursuit of sociological research has to be clearly distinguished from partisanship in the cause of the established institutions of society (Béteille 1981). The former fertilizes it, the latter sterilizes it.

In India, the State has not dictated or interfered directly with sociological research, although the Indian Council of Social Science Research, funded by the government, has made weak and, on the whole, ineffectual attempts to establish the priorities of research. State funding has led to research that has been more often critical than approving of the work of governments. Sociologists employed by agencies of the government have made little impact on either teaching or research in their discipline, although an exception may be made of the Anthropological Survey of India.

In India, political parties and sociologists have made very little direct use of each other, and this on the whole has been to the advantage of both. The influence of religious organizations has been equally weak, and sociologists have rarely received financial support from corporate capital or felt inhibited from attacking its interests. For all its many sins, it has to be admitted that Indian society has allowed sociologists to do their work in freedom without any organized interference.

Despite maintaining a distance from the state and party, or perhaps because of it, sociology in India has been marked by a strong moral and even political impulse. Here there is a striking difference between Indian and non-Indian students of Indian society and culture. The former are engaged to a far greater extent, politically and morally, not only in their selection of problems but also in their style of argument than western scholars, whether the latter are anthropologists writing about India or sociologists writing about their own society. At the same time, what is noteworthy about this engagement is more often its vehemence than its focus.

In reviewing the work of Indian sociologists. One is struck by a much greater sense of urgency to make their work socially relevant than in the work of European or American sociologists; some prefer to speak of cultural authenticity in place of social relevance (*Seminar* 1972). This is combined with the persistent criticism from within and outside the discipline that it is enslaved by imported methods, concepts, and theories and is as such remote from the Indian reality. All of this is valid to some extent, for it is true that sociologists in India lean a little too heavily on methods and concepts that were developed in other contexts. It is also true that they are concerned almost single-mindedly with making intellectual sense of the Indian experience; Indian sociologists have paid very little attention in their research, though not in their teaching, to other societies and cultures. However, posing the problem in extreme terms does little to bridge the gap between what ought to be addressed and how it ought to be addressed.

It is necessary to understand and appreciate the impulse to make sociology and social anthropology socially relevant. This impulse can serve to stimulate the most fruitful intellectual work; it can also lead to slipshod, superficial, and unfocused research of no lasting value. To adapt a phrase from Max Weber, research is a slow boring of hard boards, whereas urgent problems call for immediate solutions. Indian sociologists are often impelled to undertake research that is ill-conceived and unproductive, not so much under directives of government or party as from the pressure of public opinion.

The questions that come up for discussion in seminars, conferences, and congresses of sociologists and anthropologists are more likely to be poverty, inequality, and untouchability rather than rates of mobility, forms of rituals or types of marriages. The former are perceived as socially relevant and the latter as merely academic, and the contrast expresses not merely a distinction but also a judgement. Not everybody believes that a choice has to be made between the two, but where such a choice must be made, the bias is in favour of the socially relevant.

Turning a social problem into a sociological one calls for a delicate combination of skills that cannot be conjured into existence by well-meaning sociologists, still less by committees of well-meaning sociologists. And yet, the expansion of the profession and its continuing concern for urgent problems has spawned a large number of such committees to deliberate upon the priorities of research. In the deliberations and recommendations of these committees, the line between sociology and current affairs is easily crossed.

Where sociology merges with current affairs, the craft of sociology suffers. With the phenomenal increase in the size of the profession during the last two or three decades, the problem of maintaining quality in research has become worrisome. After all, sociological research must be not only relevant and meaningful, it must also be technically adequate. In India today, the dilution of technical skills appears to be a larger threat to the identity and character of sociology than its disengagement from socially relevant and meaningful problems. The Indian Council of Social Science Research sponsors programmes of training for research workers, but these have so far been rather narrowly focused on research methodology. The Council is now actively considering proposals to reorganize its training programme to give it a broader base.

Technical skills not only take time and effort to acquire, they cannot be easily applied to a problem simply because it demands urgent social attention. The tendency is to apply common sense to the solution of sociological problems. Many people, including some sociologists, believe that sociology is in any case a form of common sense, embellished more or less by the use of technical vocabulary. But sociology cannot grow as a serious intellectual pursuit unless it disengages itself, at least to some extent, from common sense (Béteille 1996). This does not mean that it should turn its back on common sense and seek refuge in technical virtuosity. It must, on the other hand, place the categories of common sense themselves under critical scrutiny; only then will it be able to contribute to the renewal of common sense, which is perhaps the most significant among its uses.

Is there a sociological mode of reasoning, and has it made any impact on the thinking of persons outside the discipline and the profession? Both of these are questions difficult to answer, the second perhaps even more difficult than the first. But even if no ready answers are available, the questions themselves cannot be set aside as trivial or sterile.

If there is a sociological mode of reasoning, it consists in a patient, methodical, and unremitting effort to relate the actions and ideas of men and women in mutual interaction to the structures and institutions of a complex, amorphous, and changing social reality. The task appears more promising but it is also more challenging when those engaged in it are located within the society whose many faces they seek to understand, interpret, and explain. This task cannot be accomplished by any individual scholar, or even by any single generation of scholars. Indian sociologists have benefited greatly from the work of scholars in other countries, but they must also be mindful of the work of their predecessors, both within and outside the country, for it is only by building on what has already been accomplished that a discipline and a profession can move forward. A major problem in India has been that each new generation of sociologists, while eager to benefit from the work of the best and the most advanced scholars outside the country, seems to work as if it is the first generation of sociologists within the country.

REFERENCES

Bardhan, Pranab, ed. 1989. *Conversations between Economists and Anthropologists.* Delhi: Oxford University Press.

Béteille, André. 1965. *Caste, Class and Power.* Berkeley: University of California Press.

_____. 1975. *Six Essays in Comparative Sociology.* Delhi: Oxford University Press.

_____. 1981. *Ideologies and Intellectuals.* Delhi: Oxford University Press.

_____. 1987. 'Reply to Dumont', *Current Anthropology.* 28(5):672–77.

_____. 1992: 'Religion as a Subject for Sociology'. *Economic and Political Weekly.* 27(35):1865–70.

_____. 1993. 'Sociology and Anthropology'. *Contributions to Indian Sociology* (n.s.). 27(2):291–304.

_____. 1996. 'Sociology and Common Sense'. *Economic and Political Weekly.* 31(35–7):2361–5.

_____. 1998: 'Science and Tradition: A Sociological Perspective'. *Economic and Political Weekly.* 33(10):529–32.

Breman, Jan. 1974. *Patronage and Exploitation.* Berkeley: University of California Press.

Breman, Jan, Peter Kloos, and Ashwani Saith, eds. 1997. *The Village in Asia Revisited.* Delhi: Oxford University Press.

Das, Veena, ed. 1990. *Mirrors of Violence.* Delhi: Oxford University Press.

Desai, A.R. 1959. *Social Background of Indian Nationalism.* Bombay: Popular Book Depot.

Desai, I.P. 1964. *Some Aspects of Family in Mahuva.* Bombay: Asia Publishing House.

D'Souza, V.S. 1977. *Inequality and Integration in an Industrial Community.* Simla: Indian Institute of Advanced Study.

Dube, S.C. 1960. *India's Changing Villages.* London: Routledge and Kegan Paul.

Dumont, Louis. 1966. *Homo Hierarchicus.* Paris: Gallimard.

_____. 1977. *From Mandeville to Marx.* Chicago: University of Chicago Press.

_____. 1987. 'On Individualism and Equality'. *Current Anthropology.* 28(5):669–72.

Evans-Pritchard, E.E. 1962. *Essays in Social Anthropology.* London: Faber and Faber.

———. 1965. *Theories of Primitive Religion*. Oxford: Clarendon Press.

Fei Hsiao-Tung. 1939. *Peasant Life in China*. London: Routledge and Kegan Paul.

Gough, Kathleen. 1981. *Rural Society in Southeast India*. Cambridge: University of Cambridge Press.

Government of India. 1974. *Towards Equality: Report of the Committee on the Status of Women in India*. New Delhi: Government of India.

Guha, Ramachandra, ed. 1994. *Social Ecology*. Delhi: Oxford University Press.

Gupta, Dipankar. 1996. *Context of Ethnicity*. Delhi: Oxford University Press.

Halsey, A.H. 1987: 'Provincials and Professionals: The British Post-War Sociologists'. *LSE Quarterly*. 1(1):43–74.

Karve, Irawati. 1968. *Hindu Society: An Interpretation*. Poona: Deshmukh Prakashan.

Kothari, Rajni, ed. 1971. *Caste in Indian Politics*. New Delhi: Orient Longman.

Madan, T.N. 1965. *Family and Kinship*. Bombay: Asia Publishing House.

———. 1987. 'Secularism in Its Place'. *The Journal of Asian Studies*. 46(4):747–59.

———. et al. 1980. *Doctors and Society: Three Asian Case Studies. India, Malaysia, Sri Lanka*. Delhi: Vikas Publishing House.

Mannheim, Karl. 1953. *Essays in Sociology and Social Psychology*. London: Routledge and Kegan Paul.

Marshall, T.H. 1977. *Class, Citizenship and Social Development*. Chicago: University of Chicago Press.

Mayer, A.C. 1960. *Caste and Kinship in Central India*. London: Routledge and Kegan Paul.

Mukherjee, Ramkrishna. 1983. *Classifications in Social Research*. Albany: State University of New York.

Radcliffe-Brown, A.R. 1933. *The Andaman Islanders*. Cambridge: Cambridge University Press.

Saran, A.K. 1962. 'Review of Contributions to Indian Sociology, no. IV'. *Eastern Anthropologist*. 15(1):53–68.

Seminar. 1972. 'The Social Sciences'. *Seminar 157*.

Shah, A.M. 1973. *The Household Dimension of the Family in India*. New Delhi: Orient Longman.

———. 1998. *Family in India*. New Delhi: Orient Longman.

Shils, Edward. 1961. *The Intellectual Between Tradition and Modernity: The Indian Situation*. The Hague: Mouton.

Singer, Milton. 1972. *When a Great Tradition Modernizes*. Delhi: Vikas Publishing House.

Singh, Yogendra. 1973. *Modernization of Indian Tradition*. Delhi: Thomson Press.

Srinivas, M.N. 1952. *Religion and Society among the Coorgs of South India*. Oxford: Clarendon Press.

———. 1962. *Caste in Modern India and Other Essays*. Bombay: Asia Publishing House.

Srinivas, M.N., M.S.A. Rao, and A.M. Shah, eds. 1972. *Survey of Research in Sociology and Social Anthropology*. Bombay: Popular Prakashan, 3 vols.

Tilly, Charles 1981. *As Sociology Meets History*. New York: Academic Press.

Uberoi, J.P.S. 1978. *Science and Culture*. Delhi: Oxford University Press.

Visvanathan, Shiv. 1985. *Organizing for Science*. Delhi: Oxford University Press.

Wild, R.A. 1974. *Bradstow*. Sydney: Angus and Robertson.

II

Aspects of Social Life

India's Population*

PRAVIN AND LEELA VISARIA

The United Nations estimated the population of the Indian sub-continent (consisting of India, Pakistan, and Bangladesh), on 1 July 2000 as 1299 million, 1.1 per cent higher than 1284 million for China (including Hong Kong).[1] Two of the oldest civilizations of the world together accounted for almost 43 per cent of the world population (6.1 billion) and 53 per cent of the population of the less developed countries (4.87 billion). Since Independence in 1947, the population of India alone, constituting 81 per cent of the population of the subcontinent at that time, has been the second largest in the world, after that of China. It is expected to exceed China's population some time during 2045–6, according to United Nations projections. Such long-run projections are subject to inevitable uncertainty about the validity underlying assumptions; but the general trend is unmistakable. According to the official projections, the Indian population crossed the one billion mark on 11 May 2000; but if allowance is made for the net undercount of population in the 1991 Census, the figure of one billion was reached during 1999. In any case, even compared to China, India is unique in terms of the heterogeneity or diversity of its population, a fact that merits attention in any assessment or discussion about the country as a society, economy, or polity.

DATA BASE

The decennial censuses of India provide reasonably good data on the number, characteristics, and spatial distribution of the people and indicate the magnitude of change during the inter-censal intervals. The vital statistics required to estimate the rate of change of population each year or the number of births and deaths in the country are based on the Sample Registration System (SRS), set up during the 1960s as a partial substitute for the incomplete civil registration. Periodical special surveys and other administrative statistics also help to understand the diverse characteristics of the population.

*The preparation and revision of this chapter has been facilitated by a generous award by the Wellcome Trust to the London School of Economics and Political Science for a four-year research project on 'The Future of India: Population, Human Development and Environment', undertaken by a team of British and Indian scholars, including the authors.

Indian Censuses

The Indian decennial censuses began during 1867–72. Six censuses conducted since Independence have included new questions and have provided more detailed information to help understand the heterogeneity of the population. The task of enumerating the population resident in 588,000 villages and nearly 3700 urban agglomerations (UAs) has, however, become quite difficult. The number of 'enumerators' and their supervisors involved in the 1991 census exceeded about 1.8 million. To limit the costs, the work is assigned to schoolteachers and revenue staff of different states, who get only a token honorarium to cover their incidental costs. As a result, the population data collected by the censuses need to be viewed as only approximations to the reality.

To assess the quality of data, the census authorities have themselves conducted a post-enumeration check (PEC) after each of the six post-Independence censuses. It is difficult to entrust PECs to independent agencies because few of them have the capacity or a large field organization to cover the entire country. The first PEC undertaken after the 1951 Census did not cover the then provinces of Punjab and West Bengal (affected by the large-scale movements of refugees) and was therefore limited to about 81 per cent of the enumerated population. The PECs conducted after the 1951 Census have been better designed.

Census counts can suffer from both omission of persons and from their multiple counting. To illustrate, some persons, particularly those who travel during the enumeration period, may be reported to the enumerators at their usual place of residence by the members of the family and also where they happen to be. But it is also common for the respondents to forget some members of the family, particularly young children aged 0–4 and unrelated members of the household. The enumerators also tend to miss the residents of houses that may be locked or closed at the time of their visit or single-member households. (These problems are particularly important in large urban centres, but they are not altogether absent in villages, when it comes to the count of rural labour households, in which both the spouses and sometimes also the children work outside the home.) On balance, most censuses end up with a net undercount of the population. The PECs try to employ better than average enumerators to revisit a sample of areas and households enumerated earlier and estimate the effect of the omission of entire houses from the enumeration and of the omission or duplication of the residents of the enumerated houses. Besides the issue of coverage, the PECs also try to estimate the errors of content in terms of the reliability of the information recorded by the enumerators at the time of their visit.

The net undercount of population, estimated by the PECs, has been estimated at 1.1 per cent in 1951, 0.7 per cent in 1961, and 1.7 to 1.8 per cent in the last three censuses of 1971, 1981, and 1991. The undercount was clearly higher in urban areas than in rural; and in 1991, the three large metropolitan areas of Bombay, Delhi, and Madras had a net undercount of 4.0 per cent. (For Calcutta, some field problems had evidently raised the net undercount even higher, but the estimates have not been released.)[2] Given the large population, a net undercount of 1.8 per cent meant an omission of 15.5 million persons from the 1991 Census. If allowance is made for the above average undercount of children aged 0–4, the net undercount amounts to 2.1 per cent or 18 million persons. Development plans need to consider the omitted population as well, even though it is a difficult task because of uncertainty about the precise characteristics of the omitted persons.

The problem of undercount is generally more serious for houseless persons. The census authorities make a special effort to count such persons on the last night of the enumeration period, with the help of the police. Further, a few months before the census of population, the census office undertakes 'house-listing' or a census of all houses, when every 'house' is numbered and listed for a subsequent visit.[3] However, the number of 'house-less' persons enumerated in the last four censuses has not exceeded 2.3 million or 0.4 per cent of the total in the 1981 Census. Their share has dropped to 0.2 per cent in the 1991 Census, probably because of the difficulties of achieving a complete count of such persons. (The percentage of the houseless is a little higher in urban areas than in rural; the urban areas also report a much higher excess of males or a higher sex ratio than the average population.) According to the results of the 1991 PEC, persons unrelated to the head of the household faced a much higher risk (more than six times the average) of being omitted from the count. Members of a nuclear family were better enumerated than other members, including the parents.

Yet, compared to our neighbouring countries, such as Pakistan (which could not conduct a regular decennial census in 1971 or 1991 and had to enlist the help of the army for its 1998 census) or Bangladesh (where the net undercount in the census is suspected to be quite high), India has succeeded in achieving reasonably complete census counts. The favourable factors contributing to this outcome are believed to be a relatively small share of the urban population, overall limited mobility of the population, and the generally close links between the enumerators and the population to be enumerated in rural areas.

Some bureaucrats argue that the Indian censuses overcount the population because the respondents try to ensure consistency between their inflated household size according to ration cards (that determine their entitlement from the public distribution system [PDS] and reports to the census enumerators.) However, the PEC results have not changed over the period while the proportion of population receiving PDS supplies has gradually expanded.[4] The extent to which people remember their PDS or ration card details at the time of the census count is also doubtful. Overall, therefore, a net undercount in the census is more likely than an overcount. Further, the magnitude of undercount might, in fact, be higher than is estimated by the PECs, because the latter checks are subject to the same problems as the initial census counts.

Registration of Vital Events

For information regarding the rate of change of population during inter-censal years, the developed countries rely on vital statistics (number of births, deaths, marriages, and divorces) gathered through the civil registration system operated by local authorities. In India, although the Births, Deaths and Marriages Registration Act of 1886 had provided for voluntary registration, several British provinces, which set up birth and death registration systems, had by 1939 passed legislation making registration compulsory. In several provinces, registration was reasonably complete. (A few progressive 'native states' such as Baroda, Cochin, Mysore, and Travancore had also emulated these provinces.) After Independence, the supervision of the activities of grassroots-level government functionaries by their district or taluka-level superiors gradually slackened, and therefore the quality of registration data has deteriorated in many states of the country. The Registration of Births and Deaths Act, 1969, was implemented during April–June 1970 in the major or more populous states and union territories of the country. However, in 1994, only in the five states of Goa, Gujarat, Kerala, Punjab, and Tamil Nadu, were about 90 per cent of the estimated births actually registered; in other states, the figures ranged between a low of 17 per cent in Bihar and a high of about 76 per cent in Karnataka and Maharashtra. The estimate for the country as a whole was 52 per cent. The registration of deaths was even lesser, with a national figure of 46 per cent and with only Goa and Kerala registering about 89 per cent or more of the estimated events (Registrar General 1998a).

Because of the non-availability of reliable vital statistics, a Sample Registration System was developed in the late 1960s to generate annual estimates of the birth and death rates in the rural and urban areas of the different states of the country. In 1994, the SRS covered a sample of about 6 million population (1.1 million households) in 6613 sample units (4420 rural and 2193 urban), where continuous registration by specially appointed informants was supplemented by six-monthly surveys of households. With its follow-up of the same sample of households for about a decade, the SRS has a rich but so far unutilized potential to serve as a quasi-longitudinal survey. The sub-national annual estimates of the SRS can be pooled for a period of three to five years to minimize random fluctuations. (The SRS estimates of birth and death rates form the basis of the number of births and deaths expected to be registered in various states and union territories cited in the preceding paragraph.)[5] Of course, there is no guarantee that the SRS will in fact cover all the vital events in the sample areas. Indirect estimates by Mari Bhat suggest that the undercount of births and adult deaths (of persons aged 5 and over) in the SRS was of the order of 7 and 1 per cent during 1971–81, around 3 and 11 per cent during 1981–91, and 5 and 14 per cent during 1990–7 (Mari Bhat 2000).

National Sample Survey

Changes in other characteristics of the population are assessed through periodical (monthly, quarterly, or annual) sample surveys in different parts of the country. India is fortunate in having a long series of annual surveys conducted since 1950 by the National Sample Survey Organization (NSSO), which has functioned as an autonomous body initially under the Indian Statistical Institute (Calcutta) and after 1970 under the guidance of an independent Governing Council chaired by an honorary non-official social scientist. The NSS surveys have not provided dependable estimates of vital rates because the respondents typically fail to report events such as births and deaths that occurred some time in the past within the reference period of, say, the year preceding the date of survey. This problem of recall lapse is observed quite widely throughout the world. In addition, because of the problem of safety and security of the field investigators visiting households for the survey work, the NSS has to rely mainly on male investigators. Despite these limitations, the NSS surveys have complemented the censuses by providing alternative estimates of the economic characteristics of the population, particularly labour-force participation rates and the level and structure of employment and unemployment, level and nature of migration, and the structure of landholdings. These surveys also help fill in the gaps in our understanding about some of the social groups of India. They are drawn upon at appropriate places in the rest of this chapter.

KEY CHARACTERISTICS OF INDIA'S POPULATION

Size Distribution of Villages and the Level of Urbanization

At the very outset, the important dichotomy between rural and urban areas needs to be considered while discussing the characteristics of the Indian people. The recent archaeological discoveries in Gujarat, Punjab, and Haryana have indicated a considerable spread of urban settlements in the Indian subcontinent; but they were essentially small settlements, at least relative to the large cities of the twentieth century. In any case, the definition of an urban locality has been streamlined since the 1961 Census. A majority of places are classified as urban on the basis of the statutory form of local self-government, such as a municipal corporation, municipal board, cantonment board, a notified area committee, or a Nagar Panchayat. The other census towns have to satisfy the criteria of: minimum population of 5000; density of population of at least 400 per sq. km; and 75 per cent of the male working population being engaged in non-agricultural activities. Towns with a population of 100,000 or more are called cities. The towns and their adjoining 'urban outgrowths' that form a 'continuous urban spread' are designated as 'urban agglomerations' (UAs) (Census of India 1991a).

Of the 4689 towns in 1991, 2987 (64 per cent) were 'statutory' towns and the remaining 1702 were 'census towns'. Further, 3387 towns were not included in any UA while the 381 UAs included 1302 towns. The statutory towns were larger; and they accounted for an estimated 85 per cent of the urban population. The 300 Class 1 cities or UAs with a population of 100,000 or more accounted for 65 per cent of the urban population; and about 33 per cent of all urban residents lived in 23 metropolitan cities with a population of 1 million or more.

According to the census data, the urban population of India has grown faster than the rural, from 79 million in 1961 to 218 million in 1991 or from 18 to 25.7 per cent of the total population of the country. The urban population has grown at the (exponential) average annual rate of 3.2, 3.8, and 3.1 per cent during 1961–71, 1971–81, and 1981–91. The major determinant of urban growth during these three decades was the natural increase of population, rather than the net rural–urban migration (which had accelerated during the 1980s). The reclassification of localities from rural to urban accounted for about 9 to 15 per cent of urban growth over the three decades, but it could become a more important factor in the years ahead. (This decomposition of urban growth does not include the children of the in-migrants born in urban areas among migrants). The important factors responsible for the relatively slower rate of urban growth during 1981–91 (than during the 1970s) seem to be the difficulties of urban housing as well as the growth of rural–urban commutation, facilitated by relatively inexpensive transportation.[6]

Within India, the states of Maharashtra, Gujarat, Tamil Nadu, and Karnataka are more urbanized than the others. However, the rural–urban distinction is difficult to make in Kerala, with its high density of population, where 73 per cent of villages have a population of 10,000 or more and 89 per cent of the rural population lives in these large villages (Visaria 1997b: 266–88).

The rural areas, on the other hand, consist mainly of 'revenue villages' with definite surveyed boundaries, which may include several hamlets. In non-surveyed areas, such as forests, each habitation area with locally recognized boundaries within each forest range officer's beat is treated as a village (Census of India 1998: ix).

At the time of the 1991 Census, the rural population of India lived in 587,000 villages; an additional 47,000 villages were uninhabited. Excluding Jammu and Kashmir, 67 per cent of the inhabited villages, numbering 300,000, were small, with a population of less than 1000 persons; they accounted for only 26.3 per cent of rural population. The average population of a village was 1072. The percentage of small villages was 83 in Orissa, 72 in Assam, 67 in Bihar, and 60 in West Bengal. The north-eastern states too had very small villages. The total number of 'inhabitations' in the country exceeded 1.06 million; about 18.4 per cent of these inhabitations were populated predominantly by the Scheduled Tribes (STs) and another 12 per cent by the Scheduled Castes (SCs), who constitute the disadvantaged groups of India's population (NCERT 1998). The dispersal of population is a key factor that raises the cost of delivery of various services such as education and health and of ensuring their quality.

Size of Population and Growth Rate

Table 1 summarizes the key characteristics of India's population. It goes back to 1901 and reports, for the post-Independence boundaries of India, the size of the population, decennial rate of growth, level of urbanization, the sex ratio as defined by the number of males per 1000 females, and the density of population per sq. km of land area. Although the data relate mainly to the twentieth century, the low rate of decennial growth during 1891–1901 shown against the figures for 1901 reflects the recurrent plague epidemics during 1896–1900 as well as the severe famines of 1896–7 (accompanied by outbreaks of cholera, malaria, and small-pox epidemics) and of 1899–1900.[7] These two famines had reportedly killed nearly 5.15 million and more than 1.0 million persons respectively. Along with the plague epidemics of the decade, they contributed to lowering the average annual growth rate to only 0.3 per cent during 1891–1901.

The decade 1901–11 witnessed a higher population growth than the previous decade, but recurrent famines and epidemics in different parts of the country restricted the growth rate to about six-tenths of 1 per cent. The next decade, with a negligible absolute growth and a virtually zero rate of population growth during 1911–21, was affected by the influenza epidemic (of 1918–19) and its after-effects, which killed about 12.5 million persons or 5 per cent of the total population of the country.

The year 1921 marks a divide between the previous five decades and the subsequent era; the average annual rate of population growth during 1921–51 exceeded 1 per cent. Except for the man-made Bengal Famine during 1943, which is estimated to have caused about 1.5 million deaths, the epidemics and famines during this period were not as deadly as during the previous four or five decades. However, reported growth during the 1940s had been affected by some overenumeration during the 1941 Census (because of the rivalry between the Hindus and Muslims to overstate their numbers, particularly in the then provinces of Bengal and Punjab), and the large-scale refugee migration and the associated excess mortality following the partition of the subcontinent into the two countries of India and Pakistan. Quite likely, even the 1951 Census in the two border provinces of Punjab and West Bengal was adversely affected, although the post-enumeration check was not conducted in these areas and no specific estimate is available. If the 1951 Census suffered from a high undercount, the rate of growth during the 1941–51 decade was understated and that during the 1950s was overstated.

Generally speaking, however, the evident acceleration of the rate of population growth since 1951 is attributed to the decline in mortality resulting from the various programmes initiated during the first and the second Five Year Plans to control mortality and disease. The expected life span of an average Indian has risen markedly (although rather gradually) since Independence from about 32 to an estimated 62–3 years during 1996–2001; it represents a real gain in the welfare of the people.

Post-Independence India has avoided a sharp acceleration of the rate of population growth as was observed in Mexico, Kenya, or even China. In Mexico, the growth rate rose to 3 per cent during 1955–60 and continued above 3 per cent through 1970–5, before declining to 2.7 per cent during the following quinquennium and declining even further thereafter. In Kenya, the growth rate is estimated to have risen from about 2.95 per cent during 1955–60 to 3.8 per cent during 1975–80, and is projected to drop to 2.0 per cent during 1995–2000. In China, the population is estimated to have grown at an average annual rate of 2.6 per cent during 1965–70, before the fertility control measures were initiated which lowered the growth rate to 1.1 per cent during 1990–5 and 0.9 per cent during 1995–2000 (United Nations 1999: 138, 250, 292).

In India, the decennial rate of population growth has remained stable at around 2.1–2.2 per cent during 1961–91. This stability of the growth rate is attributable to a relatively gradual decline in both the death and birth rates. As a result, the increase in density of population has also been rather gradual. The growth rate of population during 1991–2001 is likely to be around 1.9 per cent. However, the large size reached by India's population by 1991 has meant that even with a relatively moderate rate of growth of about 2.0 per cent, the absolute annual addition to its population during the past several years has been nearly 18 to 19 million, higher than in any other country, including China. To understand the dynamics of the observed trend in the rate of growth of population, we turn to the estimates of vital rates or the birth and death rates.

Vital Rates in India

As noted above, the available estimates of annual birth and death rates are based on the SRS and date back to 1971. For the period before 1971, indirect estimates of the average rates for successive decades, based on census data regarding the age distribution of population and the reported rate of inter-censal growth, are available. These estimates make use of the fact that the age distribution of a population is an excellent record of its past demographic history, particularly if it is not exposed to sizeable migration. These estimates are summarized in Table 2.

Death Rates, Infant Mortality, and Longevity

The death rates in India began to decline after 1921 from above 40 per 1000 population to between 30 to 40 during 1921–41 and to even lower values after 1941. Independent scholars have estimated higher death rates of the order of 30 during 1941–51 and 27 per 1000 population during 1951–61, when the official actuarial estimates understated the actual level of mortality (Visaria 1969). For the decades 1971–81 and 1981–91, the difference between the official and independent estimates shrinks to about 1 point per 1000 population (Mari Bhat 1998). For 1995–7, the SRS has reported crude death rates of 9.0, 9.7, and 6.5 for total, rural, and urban India respectively. Even if these recent estimates somewhat understate the mortality level, the true values are unlikely to be more than one point higher.

At the time of Independence, the infant mortality rates (IMR) in the country were around 230–40 per 1000 live births. Even during the decade 1951–61, for which the census actuary used an estimate of 146, based on the NSS survey conducted during 1957–8 in rural India, the actual level of IMR was probably between 180–205.[8] More recent SRS-based estimates of IMR have indicated a drop to about 72 during 1996–8, with 77 in rural India and 45 in urban India.

These important changes are reflected in the estimated longevity or the expected life span of an average Indian. An Indian born during the 1930s and 1940s could expect to live for only 32–3 years; females were at a disadvantage, with an anomalous lower life expectancy at birth. The female disadvantage continued during the 1960s and the 1970s; but in recent years, the average expected life span of an Indian female has begun to exceed that of a male, according to both the SRS-based life tables and independent estimates. The SRS-based life tables for 1992–6 indicate a life expectancy at birth of 60.7 years (60.1 and 61.4 years for males and females respectively). More importantly, the urban males and females enjoyed an advantage of 6.0 and 8.0 years in their life span over their rural counterparts[9] (see Table 3). Females in urban areas had a higher life expectancy at birth (67.7 years) than males (64.9 years), implying an advantage of almost three years; whereas the corresponding advantage of rural females over males was less than a year (a life expectancy of 59.8 and 58.9 years respectively).

There are marked inter-state differences in infant mortality, crude death rates, and the life expectancy of people. In Kerala, boys and girls born during 1992–6 can expect to live on an average for 70 and 76 years respectively. Punjab comes next, with a life expectancy of 66 and 68 years for males and females. At the other end, Madhya Pradesh, Orissa, and Uttar Pradesh have a life expectancy at birth of around 55 to 57 years, with females continuing to have a lower expected life span than males. An important factor responsible for the observed inter-regional differences is the persistent high infant mortality, resulting partly from the relatively low proportion of births occurring in hospitals or receiving attention from a trained birth attendant. The latter differences are partly a result of the paucity of good health infrastructure in states with a low life expectancy at birth. The goal of National Health Policy must be to mitigate these interstate differences and to raise the expected lifespan to the level observed in Kerala and the developed countries.

Birth Rates, Fertility, and the Rate of Natural Increase

Table 2 shows the high birth rates ranging between 45 and 49 (per 1000 population) in the country during 1901–40, dropping to 40–1 during 1941–70 and 27–31 during the decade 1988–98. Beginning 1962–3, on the advice of the Director of Family Planning, a goal of reducing the birth rate from the-then-estimated 40 to 25 over a ten-year period has been pursued through the family planning programme, initiated in 1952 under the First Five Year Plan. The actual decline in birth rate has been far slower and the target year has been moved back repeatedly. The resulting frustration had contributed to impatient efforts in some parts of the country during the emergency period of 1975–7 to introduce 'compulsory sterilization' after the birth of three children (Visaria 1976). The move backfired and the family planning programme received a serious setback, from which it recovered only after about five years. (In fact, the impression of recovery was partly illusory, because it was based on a marked increase in the reported acceptance of reversible methods of contraception, such as IUD and condoms, the numbers of which were exaggerated.)

Among the states, birth rates in Kerala and Tamil Nadu in 1997 were 18–19; in the five states of West Bengal, Andhra Pradesh, Karnataka, Maharashtra, and Punjab, around 22–3; and in Gujarat, Orissa, Haryana, between 26 and 28. The four large northern states of Bihar, Madhya Pradesh, Rajasthan, and Uttar Pradesh continued to report birth rates between 32 and 34. Within all the states, urban birth rates were lower than rural; they generally ranged between a low of 16 in West Bengal and a high of 25 in Rajasthan and 28 in Uttar Pradesh. Even in rural areas, only Haryana and the four northern states reported birth rates between 30 and 35.

The birth rates reported above are crude rates because they are influenced by the age distribution of the population (which changes with decline in fertility). The total fertility rate (TFR) or the average number of births to a cohort of women up to the end of the reproductive period (estimated on the basis of the age-specific rates observed during a given period) is independent of the age composition effects. The TFR as a whole has dropped by over 43 per cent from above 6 in the early 1950s to about 3.4 during 1995–7. If the rural–urban differences in the TFR during the initial period are assumed to be negligible, the urban TFR of 2.4 during 1995–7 is only 40 per cent of the level in the late 1940s and early 1950s.

Among the more populous states, the TFR has dropped to near or below replacement in

Tamil Nadu (2.1) and Kerala (1.8). It is below 3 in six states: Andhra Pradesh, Himachal Pradesh, Karnataka, Maharashtra, Punjab, and West Bengal. States with a TFR of above 4 are Bihar, Madhya Pradesh, Rajasthan, and Uttar Pradesh. In Gujarat, Assam, Haryana, and Orissa, the TFR during 1995–7 was between 3.1 and 3.6. The urban TFR values are subject to greater variability because of the smaller sample size; but they have dropped to below replacement level not only in Kerala and Tamil Nadu but also in Himachal Pradesh and West Bengal; and are between 2.2 and 2.5 in Assam, Karnataka, Andhra Pradesh, Orissa, Punjab, and Maharashtra. These values are below 2.7 and 2.9 in Gujarat, Madhya Pradesh, and Haryana and between 3.2 and 3.9 in Rajasthan, Bihar, and Uttar Pradesh. These changes in TFR values in urban areas are important and are also bound to influence the rural population.

The differences in mortality and fertility noted in the preceding paragraphs imply that the rate of natural increase in states such as Bihar, Haryana, Madhya Pradesh, Rajasthan, and Uttar Pradesh continues to be between 2 and 2.4 per cent per year. It is around 1.1 per cent in Kerala and Tamil Nadu and between 1.4 and 1.6 per cent in several other states. These differences will affect the regional or spatial distribution of our population and therefore also the representation of different states in Parliament. The National Population Policy announced by the Government of India on 15 February 2000 envisages a freezing of the representation of different states in Parliament on the basis of their population at the time of the 1971 Census.

The preceding discussion overlooks the possibility of understatement of the level of fertility because of the under-registration of births in the SRS, as noted earlier. The possibility is real; but it is most unlikely that the estimates do not indicate the broad trend fairly correctly. There is little doubt that a major shift in the level and pattern of child bearing is occurring throughout urban India and somewhat more slowly in rural India. Fertility has declined not only among the better-educated but also among the illiterates and the disadvantaged groups of population. The contributory factors include both a rise in the age at marriage and control of fertility within marriage. We need to examine both these processes in some detail. But before doing so, the anomalous phenomenon of the deficit of women in the population—its magnitude, variations among social and spatial groups, and the determinants—needs to be examined.

Deficit of Women

The Indian population has shown a persistent deficit of women since the first census, conducted in the British provinces in 1881. The deficit has increased progressively, and the sex ratio of the population (males per 100 females) has risen from 103 in 1901 to 108 in 1991, with a minor reversal of this monotonous trend only once in 1981. The absolute size of the deficit of women, relative to the number of men, has risen from 4 million in 1901 to 32 million in 1991. The magnitude of deficit has increased at a faster rate than the growth rate of population (Visaria 1999).

The urban population of India has generally shown a higher deficit of women than the rural population, partly because migration from rural to urban areas is dominated by males. However, since 1961, the deficit of females in urban India has steadily declined from 18 to 12 per cent because of the progressively lower importance of migration as well as lesser sex-selectivity in migration. An increase in the deficit of women was observed between the 1981 and 1991 Censuses only in rural India where the sex ratio rose from 1052 to 1066. The deficit of women is smaller in the southern states (with the sex ratio ranging from 95.6, reflecting a deficit of males, in Kerala to 104 in Karnataka in 1991) than in the northern states of Haryana,

Punjab, Rajasthan, and Uttar Pradesh (with a sex ratio ranging from 110 to 115.6). The other states fall between these extremes.

Interestingly, the deficit of women is the lowest among the STs and the highest among the non-scheduled population. This is because tribal women have enjoyed a fair amount of equality with men. The SCs, on the other hand, have internalized the discriminatory treatment of their daughters from the higher castes. These prejudices seem to be weaker among the predominantly urbanized and more literate and better educated Jains and Christians. The deficit of women is the lowest among Christians and the highest among Sikhs; but it has shown a steady decline in both these groups since 1961. Jains (over 70 per cent of whom lived in urban areas in 1991) and Buddhists also reported lower deficits of women than the two major groups: Hindus and Muslims. The deficit of females used to be higher among Muslims than among Hindus according to the censuses of 1891–1961; but during 1961–71, the deficit rose among Hindus and declined among Muslims. During 1971–81, also, the decline in the deficit was greater among Muslims than among Hindus, so that Hindus began to report a slightly higher deficit than Muslims. Between the 1981 and the 1991 Censuses, the rise in the deficit of women has been a little higher among Hindus than among Muslims.

The three main hypotheses advanced to explain the deficit of women include a greater selective undercount of women, a higher than 'normal' sex ratio at birth, and excess female mortality. The PEC data on the under-count of population do indeed suggest a higher omission of females, particularly widows, from the census count; but the difference is not large enough to explain the deficit of the order of 8 per cent. The recent SRS-based sex ratio at birth of around 110 reflects a higher than normal excess of boys over girls; and many analysts argue that the selective foeticide of female foetuses by pregnant women because of the preference for a son leads to a rise in the sex ratio at birth.[10] However, the reported sex ratios at birth are more likely to reflect the selective omission of female births rather than a genuine rise in the proportion of boys among live births. An important evidence supporting this view is the fact that the sex ratio of children in the ages 0–4, enumerated by the 1991 Census in rural and urban India was only 104.3 and 106. (Census of India 1991a; 1998: 380, Table C–6). The implicit sex ratio of 104.7 among children aged 0–4 in the country as a whole is not consistent with the sex ratio at birth reported by the SRS, unless one postulates even more perverse behaviour among the parents of boys, leading to their neglect and therefore higher mortality. In Punjab and Haryana, however, the sex ratio of the population in the age group 0–4 in 1991 exceeded 110; and female foeticide might be a contributory factor in the reported high sex ratio at birth as well as the deficit of girls in the age group 0–4 in the population enumerated by the 1991 Census.

The observed deficit of females must therefore be attributed primarily to excess female mortality, which has tended to decline in recent years according to the SRS life tables, but which persists, particularly in rural India and in certain states. However, it cannot explain the worsening of the deficit of females between the 1981 and 1991 Censuses. Recent research (some of it by activist groups) has highlighted female infanticide in several parts of the country, particularly Tamil Nadu, Bihar, Haryana, and Rajasthan. It is likely that such callousness and cruelty have not become extinct; and no civilized society can condone them. However, the data relating to the sex ratio of children in the age group of 0–6 available from the primary census abstracts of the 1991 Census do not constitute satisfactory evidence to suspect female infanticide and foeticide because those sex ratios also reflect the effect of errors of age misreporting.

It is also evident that almost 50 per cent of the increase in the deficit of women in India between the 1981 and 1991 Censuses has occurred in the state of Bihar, which accounts for about 10 per cent of the national population. The worsening of the sex ratio between the 1981 and 1991 Censuses is also not corroborated by the data collected during the National Family Health Surveys (NFHSs) from representative samples of households during 1992–3 and 1998–9. A comparison of the age-specific sex ratios of the two censuses suggests that, given the level of mortality reported by the SRS life tables, the 1991 Census has omitted from the count a sizeable number of older women. Therefore, the incomplete count seems an important factor contributing to the observed worsening of the sex ratio (see Mari Bhat 1998).

Marital Status Distribution and Age at Marriage

An important post-Independence change in the composition of the population as regards marital status has been the decline in the incidence of widowhood, because of the decline in mortality. It is not easy to identify this decline in the percentage of widowed men because many of them remarry; but the percentage of widows enumerated by the censuses has declined from 10.8 per cent of all women in 1961 to 6.5 in 1991. As a result, despite population growth of the order of 93 per cent over these thirty years, the absolute number of widows in the country has risen by only 15 per cent from about 23 million in 1961 to 26.5 million in 1991. (The figure for India excluding Jammu and Kashmir was 26.2 million.) (Census of India 1961a: India, Part II C (i), Social and Cultural Tables, Table C–2; Census of India 1991a: India, Part IV-A, Socio-Cultural Tables, Vol. 1, Table C–II.)

The decline in the incidence of widowhood is also partly a result of the rise in the age at marriage and the decline in the proportion of the ever-married among women. The latter has dropped from 57.7 per cent in 1961 to 54.6 per cent in 1991. The age at marriage can be gauged reasonably accurately from the data on the proportion of never-married or the single persons in the population, because the average age of single persons is also the age at which their status was altered to that of the ever-married. Usually, these measures are calculated for persons who marry up to the age of 50. The estimated (singulate) mean age at marriage of Indian women had risen from 13.1 years in 1901 to 15.6 years in 1951 (Agarwala 1962: 238). Over the subsequent forty years, it rose to 16.1 years in 1961 and 19.6 years in 1991. (The mean age at marriage of men has risen from 20.0 years in 1901 and 19.9 years in 1951 to 21.4 years in 1961 and 25.2 years in 1991). (The 1951 data were tabulated for ten-year age groups and, therefore, the estimates for 1951 are not strictly comparable with those for subsequent years. Further, the estimates assume no differentials in mortality related to marital status;[11] and the proportions of never-married in different age groups are assumed to apply to a 'census synthetic cohort'.)

In 1991, rural and urban females, on the whole, married at an average age of 19.0 and 21.3 years respectively, whereas the corresponding figures for males were 24.5 and 27.0 years. Among the states, the age at marriage of females in 1991 varied considerably from a high of 23.9 and 25.8 years in Kerala and Goa to a low of 17.6 and 17.9 years in Rajasthan and Bihar, respectively. Similar differences were observed in the case of males. The female mean age at marriage ranged between 17.1 and 23.5 years in rural areas and between 19.2 and 24.9 years in urban areas. In both cases, the low values were reported by Rajasthan and the high values by Kerala. (Goa, with its heritage of several centuries of Portuguese rule, reported an even higher mean age at marriage than Kerala; and this fact has contributed to the lowest birth rate of 14 according to the SRS and a TFR of 1.9 based on the NFHS for 1992–3 being reported for this small state of 1.2 million population in 1991.)

This rise in the age at marriage is associated partly with a decline in the incidence of child marriage. The Child Marriage Restraint Act (the Sarda Act) of 1929 had initially proscribed marriage of boys and girls before the ages of 15 and 12; but the minimum ages were later revised to 18 and 14. An Act passed in 1978 further raised the minimum age of marriage to 18 for women and 21 for men. (IIPS 1995: 73). Since 1961, the census data on marital status are tabulated only for the age groups 10 and over, so that children aged 0–9 are all assumed to be never-married. However, the 1991 census data reported 3.3 million persons (1.1 million males and 2.2 million females) aged 10–14 to be married, widowed, or divorced. Also, the recent SRS data indicate the age at 'effective' marriage (that is, cohabitation) and in 1994, nearly 21 per cent of the females were effectively married before the age of 18 (the figures were 24 per cent for rural areas and 10 per cent for urban areas) (Registrar General 1997: 28). Despite these violations of the legal provisions, which reflect the difficulties of enforcing laws aimed at social change, the rise in age at marriage seems to be real and has contributed to the decline in fertility and birth rates.

Fertility Rates by Age

As noted in the preceding section, the level of fertility of married women has also dropped considerably over the years, not because of any decline in fecundity or the capacity to reproduce but because of voluntary adoption or use of contraception by married couples. The data show a clear shift in the age pattern of child bearing. Peak fertility now occurs in the age group 20–4 and not in the next age group of 25–9. More importantly, fertility decline is evident in all age groups, but particularly in the ages 30 and above.

The NFHS, conducted in 1992–3 in twenty-five states with a representative sample of 90,000 women aged 13–49, has reported that almost 96 per cent of the respondents knew about a method of contraception, particularly female sterilization. About 41 per cent of the respondent women used a contraceptive method; nearly 89 per cent of them used a 'modern' method. Almost 85 per cent of the users of a modern contraceptive method had adopted female or male sterilization. Only 5.5 per cent of the contraceptors used a reversible method such as pills, IUD, or condoms; their percentage was almost 12 in urban areas but only 3 in rural areas. This difference contributed to a correspondingly higher contraceptive use rate of 51 per cent in urban areas, compared to 37 per cent in rural areas.

Among the more populous states, the level of contraceptive use ranged between lows of 20 per cent in Uttar Pradesh and 23 per cent in Bihar, on the one hand, to highs of 63 per cent in Kerala and 54 to 59 per cent in Maharashtra, West Bengal, and Punjab. The rural–urban difference along the expected lines was evident in Uttar Pradesh and Bihar but not in the states with high contraceptive use rates (IIPS 1995).

Data on the level of use of contraceptives are also available from the service statistics compiled by the Department of Family Welfare regarding the number of acceptors of different methods recruited by the programme functionaries. However, the pressure to achieve the targets about the number of acceptors of different methods of contraception seems to have distorted the data (Visaria et al. 1994). Therefore, greater reliance has to be placed on information obtained by interviewing women in their households.

Some of the important differences in the various characteristics of population are evident with reference to the social categories of SCs and STs and the religious groups. The population size of these categories also needs due attention. Similarly, it is important to examine the characteristics of households, which are the effective or identifiable units of consumption and often also of production, with due attention to the definition of a household, which differs from the sociological category 'family'.

Scheduled Castes and Scheduled Tribes and the Non-Scheduled Population

The Constitution of India has made it obligatory for the census to collect information regarding the number and characteristics of certain special groups of people, whose caste or tribe has been named in statutory lists notified by the President according to Articles 341 and 342 of the Constitution. These lists, first notified in 1950, were modified in 1956 and in 1976. The lists of STs were expanded for the states of Meghalaya and Jammu and Kashmir in 1987 and 1989, respectively. In addition, an amendment of the Scheduled Castes Order in 1990 has recognized the category of SCs among Buddhists (in addition to Hindus and Sikhs) (Census of India 1991d: 6).

The same caste or tribe name of the SC/ST groups sometimes occurs in more than one state. A consolidated list of the number of SCs and STs remains to be compiled. However, a gross count places their number at 1091 and 573 respectively. Almost 16.5 per cent of the enumerated population of the country in 1991 (138.2 million) was classified as belonging to the SCs. The 67.8 million ST persons formed 8.1 per cent of the enumerated population. The SC and ST population is generally backward in terms of its social and economic characteristics with a higher than average proportion of the poor. The STs tend to be concentrated in relatively inaccessible hilly areas and forests, while the SCs are distributed over almost all parts of the country. Both are less urbanized than the rest of the population; only 7 per cent of the STs and 19 per cent of the SCs lived in urban areas in 1991, whereas in the case of the non-scheduled population, the figure exceeded 29 per cent. The deficit of females has been observed to be much less among the STs than among the SCs and the non-scheduled.

In 1991, no group had been listed as a 'Scheduled Tribe' in Punjab and Haryana and in Chandigarh, Delhi and, Pondicherry. Further, in Kerala, Uttar Pradesh, and Tamil Nadu, only between 0.2 and 1.0 per cent of the population was ST, whereas in the other four large states of Andhra Pradesh, Bihar, Maharashtra, and West Bengal, between 6 and 9 per cent of the population was ST. The STs formed 12 to 15 per cent of the population in Assam, Gujarat, and Rajasthan, 22–3 per cent in Madhya Pradesh, Orissa, and Sikkim, 31–4 per cent in Tripura and Manipur, and over 60 per cent in the north-eastern states of Arunachal Pradesh, Meghalaya, Nagaland, and Mizoram, as well as the small union territories of Dadra and Nagar Haveli and Lakshadweep. (No caste had been 'scheduled' in Nagaland, Andaman and Nicobar Islands, and Lakshadweep.)

The revisions of the SC/ST orders, noted earlier, have contributed to some reclassification, which leads to an indication of a faster growth of the population of these groups. Yet the analysts have been concerned about the differentials in fertility and mortality among these groups. The relative poverty of the SC/ST population is presumed to make them suffer from higher than average levels of mortality and morbidity. This is supposed to be compensated for by a higher fertility because of a lower age at marriage as well as the lesser prevalence of the use of contraception. The NFHS of 1992–3 has confirmed that total fertility was highest among the SCs, followed by the STs and the non-scheduled population; but the difference between the highest and the lowest values was only about 19 per cent. Contraceptive use among the SCs and STs was of the order of 33–4 per cent, about 21 per cent lower than among the 'other' population (42 per cent). The IMR, on the other hand, which was also the highest among the SCs, was about 30 per cent higher than among the non-scheduled population, and was intermediate among the STs (IIPS 1995: 97, 148, 214–18). (The available morbidity data based on the NSS of 1995–6 do not suggest higher morbidity among the SCs or the STs than among the non-scheduled; in fact, the reverse is the case. But the reported differences are small and may reflect reporting problems.) (NSSO 1998b: A–11, A–121.) Overall, however, the higher rate of growth of the SC and the ST population seems to be due mainly to the changes in the lists and the basis of their enumeration in 1967, 1976, 1987, and 1990 (rather than a higher rate of natural increase).

Religious Heterogeneity

The Indian population includes followers of six major religions: Hinduism, Islam, Christianity, Sikhism, Jainism, and Buddhism. These six religions account for almost 99.5 per cent of the total population of the country. Between 1961 and 1991, the Muslim population is reported to have grown by 103 per cent, faster than the predominant majority group of Hindus, who have reported a growth of 83 per cent over this period. As a result, the share of Muslims in the total population has risen from 10.7 per cent in 1961 to 12.1 per cent, while that of Hindus has declined from 83.5 to 82.0 per cent. In fact, if the 1991 Census had been conducted in Jammu and Kashmir as well, the number and percentage of Muslims in the country would have shown a slightly higher growth over the thirty-year period.[12]

The primary reason for the faster growth of Muslims has been their higher fertility and somewhat lower mortality. The NFHS data for 1992–3 show the Muslim TFR to be higher (4.4) than the TFR of Hindus (3.3) by 1.1 children; the relative ranking holds among illiterates as well as among women with different levels of education. On the other hand, the IMR among Muslims (77) was about 14 per cent lower than among Hindus (90) (IIPS 1995: 97–9, 214–15). The 1981 census data on children even-born (CEB) and surviving (CS) also indicated higher fertility and lower child mortality among Muslims than among Hindus; the difference in CEB was 0.6 children and mortality up to age 2 was about 20 per cent lower (Census of India 1981: 7 and 11). As a result, the rate of natural increase of Muslim population tends to be higher. The situation is confirmed by the higher proportion of young persons aged 0–4 and 5–14 among Muslims as compared to Hindus in both rural and urban India according to the NSS surveys of 1987–8 as well as 1993–4 (NSSO 1998a: 17). To interpret these facts properly, it is important to remember that almost 36 per cent of the 101 million Muslims enumerated in 1991 lived in Uttar Pradesh and Bihar, the two states with the highest level of TFR. (Hindus resident in these two states formed only 27 per cent of the total population of Hindus in the country.) The levels of literacy and education, as also school attendance rates, continue to be lower among Muslims than among Hindus.

The unrecorded immigration from the neighbouring Bangladesh into the border states of West Bengal, Assam, Tripura, and other north-eastern states also contributes to the faster growth of the Muslim population in the country. The Governor of Assam drew the attention of the President of India to the fact that between 1971 and 1991, the population of Muslims increased by 77 per cent, almost twice as fast as Hindu population (42 per cent) (*Indian Express*, 17 December 1998: 1). According to the Ministry of Home Affairs, Government of India, about 18 million Bangladeshi immigrants live in India, and of them, about 12 million are estimated to be in West Bengal (*The Asian Age* [Delhi edition], 7 February 1999: 2).

The other three religious groups of Christians, Sikhs, and Jains (with a population of 18.8, 16.2, and 3.3 million, respectively, in 1991) have lower values of TFR as well as IMR than either Hindus or Muslims. The level of literacy and education as well as school attendance rates are higher among these smaller religious groups than among Hindus and Muslims.

The other religious groups include the Zoroastrians or Parsis—whose number has declined from 111,800 in 1951 to 71,630 in 1981 and 76,382 in 1991[13]—among whom the mean age at marriage as well as the incidence of non-marriage tend to be very high. The Parsis are a highly urbanized community and have completed the process of demographic transition far ahead of the rest of the Indian population. In fact, the community is concerned about its survival as a distinct group in the country. Despite their very low fertility and a negative rate of natural increase, a complete extinction of Parsis from the country does not seem likely over the next several centuries. Yet, given the high incidence of inter-religious marriages in this highly educated community, the rule that the children of Parsi women married to non-Parsi men cannot become Parsi contributes to the decline in the number of Parsis in the country (Visaria 1974).

Households and their Characteristics

Censuses and surveys typically collect data on households or groups of persons, who commonly live together and eat from a common kitchen, unless exigencies of work prevent any of them from doing so. A household may contain mutually related persons, unrelated persons, or both. Also, there are institutional households which typically include unrelated persons, such as hostels, boarding houses, and jails (Census of India 1998: ix). The censuses since 1971 have enumerated between 245,000 and 292,000 institutional households, a majority of them in urban areas, and their number has declined progressively. The total institutional population (almost 80 per cent of it male) has, however, risen from 2.1 million in 1961 to 4.3 million in 1991 and has constituted between 0.2 and 0.3 per cent of the rural population and between 1.1 and 1.9 per cent of the urban population.

The data on the number of households and their characteristics, according to the censuses from 1961 to 1991, include the number of occupied residential houses (enumerated by the censuses), the number of households per 100 houses, and the density of population per sq. km, separately by rural–urban residence (see Table 4). The faster growth of the urban population as compared to the rural population is evident in each of the indices. Over the thirty-year period, the number of residential houses and households has risen by 183 and 159 per cent in urban areas but only by 66 and 62 per cent in rural areas. In the last two censuses, a large majority of households, except for some 3 to 5 per cent, were enumerated as having a separate residential house; the difference between the two observed in the 1961 and 1971 Censuses, particularly in urban areas, appears to have disappeared, probably because of the decline in the level of rural–urban migration and a change in its pattern, involving less sex-selective movement.

The average size of the household is an interesting variable to examine. Data indicate an increase in the average size of a household from 5.2 in 1961 to 5.5 in 1971; but the subsequent upward change during 1971–81 and a downward change during 1981–91, is visible only in the second figure after decimal point. The average size of both rural and urban households seems to have risen equally between 1961 and 1971 by about 0.33 persons; but thereafter, between 1971 and 1981, the size of urban households rose more than that of rural households. During the ensuing decade, the size of rural households remained static while that of urban households dropped a little.[14]

The NSS data regarding the average size of households do not corroborate the trends suggested by the census data. The average size of both rural and urban households covered by the NSS in its quinquennial surveys tends to be smaller than that of the census households; and a decline in size is evident in both. Interestingly, the NFHS of 1992–3 had reported almost the same average size of urban households (4.5) as the NSS survey of 1993–4 (4.4), but the rural households covered by the NFHS were even larger than those enumerated by the censuses, with an average size of 6.1 (IIPS 1995: 33–7; NSSO 1997a: pp. 16–17). The reasons for these discrepancies require a study at the state level, which is beyond the scope of this chapter. The exclusion of institutional households from the NSS surveys does not seem adequate explanation of the observed differences. A slow decline in average household size can be expected to follow the ongoing decline in fertility as well as the increased splitting or reconstitution of households with changing aspirations regarding life style. Some available evidence on this issue merits a brief review.

The Prevalence of Nuclear Households

While the 1991 Census is yet to publish data regarding the size and composition of households, the 1981 census tables provide some interesting information. They have identified single member households and nuclear households comprising of head and spouse, head and spouse with unmarried children, and head without spouse but with unmarried children. These four categories of households formed 52.5 and 58.9 per cent of all rural and urban households respectively. Chakravorty and Singh (1991) in their paper based on these data also present another category: supplemented nuclear households, consisting of 'head and spouse with or without unmarried children but with other relations who are not currently having spouse'. These households formed about 17 and 15 per cent of the rural and urban households of India. The authors suggest that other relations without a current spouse could be an unmarried brother or sister, or a widowed parent, or divorced, separated or widowed brother or sister. It is not clear whether sociologists would regard such households as different from extended households. However, the evidence suggests that by 1981 at least, extended (or joint) households almost certainly did not form a majority of the Indian households. While the acute shortage of space in most urban houses leads a majority of urban households to become nuclear, the situation in rural areas also does not appear markedly different. (Chakravorty and Singh 1991: 3–4).

Some light on the processes at work in rural India can be shed by looking at the size of households according to their major or main source of income or livelihood. The relevant tables available from the 1987–8 and 1993–4 surveys clearly suggest that the rural labour households, constituting about 38 to 40 per cent of all rural households, were smaller (with 4.6 and 4.5 persons) than average households (with 5.1 and 4.9 persons). The self-employed households working in agriculture or non-agricultural enterprises were larger than average by 12 and 3 per cent respectively in 1993–4 (NSSO 1997a: 18–20, A6). The average size of households rose with a rise in the size of the landholding possessed by a household, from 3.9 for the landless and 6.2 for households with more than 4 hectares (ha) of land. The growth of population and labour force has steadily increased the proportion of small and marginal landholdings on the whole. The percentage of rural households with operational landholdings of less than 2.5 acres (1.01 ha) has risen from 39 in 1960–1 to 63 in 1991–2, whereas the percentage of operational holdings of less than 5.0 acres (2.01 ha) has increased from 62 to 81 (NSSO 1996: 19). As a result, the proportion of rural labour households has also increased; and even in rural areas, the incentive to continue the extended or joint family is likely to have weakened.

Households with Females as their Heads

There is widespread interest in the proportion of all households with female members as their heads. The concept of the 'head of a household' is difficult to communicate to the respondents in a survey or a census; and it is impossible to decide whether the person with the maximum decision-making power is actually reported as the head. The field situation does not permit any debate or discussion with the respondents on the subject and their response has to be accepted without any questioning. Yet the data available from censuses and the NSS surveys need to be explored.

Households with female heads formed 9.4 and 8.1 per cent of the total, according to the censuses of 1971 and 1981 respectively. The figure was a little higher in rural areas (10.6 and 8.2 per cent) than in urban areas (8.8 and 7.6 per cent), respectively, probably because male-dominated out-migration from rural to urban areas led to the spouse being reported as the head of the household. The NSS surveys of 1987–8 and 1993–4 have indicated that about 10 to 11 per cent of all households in both rural and urban areas had females as their heads. The rural–urban difference is negligible and not in the same direction according to the two surveys. More interestingly, households with females as their heads tend to be smaller than the average; and they also have a marked excess of females, with the number of females per 1000 males ranging between 1706 to 1861. About 65 and 62 per cent of the female heads of rural and urban households in 1993–4 were widows; the currently married formed 30 and 18 per cent of rural and urban households with a female head, presumably because the spouse was an out-migrant or temporarily away in search of additional income. About 23 per cent of the female heads in both rural and urban areas were aged 60 and above. Rural households with females as heads also included a higher than average percentage of those not possessing or not cultivating any land. The median monthly per capita expenditure of a rural household with a female as its head (Rs 259) exceeded the average (Rs 250) while the corresponding figures for urban areas were Rs 378 and Rs 404, respectively. These differences are relatively small and do not fully capture the vulnerability of households with females as their heads in our male-dominated patriarchal society (NSSO 1997a: A1–A4, 16–17, A43–A45).

Further research must continue on the various proximate determinants of the level and pattern of living of Indian households. The high proportion of households with females as heads in Meghalaya and Lakshadweep reflects the continued matrilineal nature of the inheritance system in these two small states; but in Kerala, matriliny appears to have disappeared. Prima facie, however, since a majority of female heads of households are widows, the decline in the risk of widowhood, resulting from lower mortality, must decrease the proportion of households with females as their heads. The pattern of male-dominated migration also seems to be changing and therefore must contribute towards the same trend.

Participation in Economic Activity

One of the variables influencing the level of living of a household is the level and pattern of economic activity. An examination of this relationship at the household level would certainly be rewarding, but the present discussion will look at the worker population ratios (WPRs) and sectoral distribution of the workforce mainly on the basis of the data available from the NSS.

The most dependable data on the level and pattern of participation in work in India as a whole are provided by the 1961 Census and the five quinquennial surveys conducted by the NSS almost every five years since 1972–3. The NSS surveys have avoided the underenumeration of the female workforce seen in the censuses of 1971, 1981, and 1991. They also permit alternative estimates of the level of participation in work according to varying concepts of production boundaries. The NSS estimates for states and their regions are subject to a wider margin of error because of their relatively smaller sample, but not the estimates for the country as a whole.

The NSS data suggest a reasonable stability since the early 1970s in the WPRs for rural males at around 54 per cent, for rural females between 32 and 34 per cent, for urban males between 49 and 51 per cent, and for urban females between 13 and 15 per cent. The WPRs for the total population of the country have been stable around 41–2 per cent. Overall, the reported level of employment in the country has not declined despite the substantial growth of population from 439 million in 1961 to 846 million in 1991, and further to an estimated 894 million by 1 January 1994. This seems true of the rural areas as well as of urban areas, where the population has grown more rapidly.

The NSS surveys of 1983, 1987–8, and 1993–4 have reported relatively modest differences in the WPRs of males belonging to ST, SC, and other males, both in rural and urban areas. The WPRs for females, however, have been the highest among ST women, intermediate among SC women, and the lowest among the non-scheduled women. In rural areas, the difference between the WPRs of non-scheduled and SC women was smaller than that between the ST and SC women. In urban areas, however, non-scheduled women reported markedly lower levels of participation in economic activity than either ST or SC women (NSSO 1997b: 23). These differences in the female WPRs reflect the needs as well as the past traditions of the participation of women in economic activities in ST and SC households. The non-scheduled population includes many groups among whom the participation of women in work outside the home is looked down upon, an attitude that has been changing among the urban middle classes with the spread of education.

The WPRs for the population aged 15 and over for the three main religious groups of Hindus, Muslims, and Christians show modest differences among males; but rural Muslim females reported much lower WPRs than their Hindu or Christian sisters. In urban areas, Christian women reported a higher WPR than Hindu women with the difference between the Hindu and Muslim women being relatively modest. These differences are associated with markedly higher levels of literacy and education among Christian women as compared to the non-Christians and in urban areas also among Hindu women relative to Muslim women (NSSO 1998a: 18–21). (The data by religion exclude Jammu and Kashmir, where the 1993–4 survey was limited to only a few districts.) The Muslim tradition of *purdah* probably contributes to their women avoiding participation in work outside the home. However, it is also likely that the region rather than religion determines the extent to which women work and are reported as participating in economic activity (Visaria 1997a).

The overall stability of female WPRs at national level since the 1961 Census suggests that the reported displacement of female workers in several specific activities seems to be compensated by their finding a niche elsewhere in the economy. While the stress and strain involved in such processes need to be recognized and minimized, the macro perspective seems to suggest that the people have somehow managed to find alternative sources of income in the economy. With the well-known slowdown of the growth of employment in the public or the organized sector of the economy, the share of the informal sector and the self-employed in total employment is likely to rise.

Industrial and Status Distribution of Workers

Ever since the dawn of planning in India, a major goal has been to lower the pressure of population on land and agriculture. The emphasis on industrialization has been a logical sequel, implying a goal to encourage a drop in the share of agriculture in both the national income and the workforce. The national income estimates suggest that the share of the national gross domestic product originating in the agriculture sector has dropped from about 48 per cent in the early 1950s to 28 per cent during 1996–7 (Central Statistical Organisation 1998: xxxiv). The share of agriculture in the workforce has, however, not declined at the same pace.

The proportion of workers engaged in the agricultural sector or the primary sector has declined from 76 per cent in 1961 to 65 per cent in 1987–8 and 1993–4. (The fall was about 13 percentage points among male workers and 7 percentage points among female workers.) However, the data for 1993–4 suggest a stability in the share of agriculture in the total workforce at about 65 per cent, the same level as was observed during 1987–8. A similar situation is seen with respect to both the male and female workforce. The data for rural India suggest a slight decline in the proportion of the male workforce in agriculture between 1987–8 and 1993–4 but a slight rise in the share of the female workforce in the agricultural sector. In urban India, the data suggest a steady drop in the proportion of agricultural workers in the workforce, although the figure has remained around 12–13 per cent after 1987–8.

The fall in the proportion of workers in the primary sector since the early 1970s has been accompanied by a compensating gain by the tertiary sector. The secondary sector has not gained, particularly after 1987–8. Its share shows a decline of the order of 1 or 2 percentage points between 1987–8 and 1993–4, both in rural and urban areas and among both males and females. The main contributory factor has been a decline in the share of construction employment in rural areas and a fall in the share of manufacturing employment in urban areas.

Even with a decline in the share of the secondary sector in total employment, the number of workers engaged in manufacturing has increased by 3.3 million from 36.0 to 39.3 million in the country as a whole and by 2.1 million in urban India from 17.4 to 19.5 million between 1987–8 and 1993–4. (The proportion of urban workers in the manufacturing sector has declined by 2.3 and 2.6 percentage points among males and females respectively.) The share of employment in construction has continued to rise in urban areas but not in rural areas, where it had spurted between 1983 and 1987–8, particularly among rural females, because of the employment of a large number of women on the public works started by state governments to ameliorate the effects of a severe drought during the latter year. The share of the urban female workforce engaged in the service sector has risen along with the increase in the proportion of the educated seeking white-collar work among urban women.

Admittedly, the impression based on the 1987–8 data of a considerable slowing down of the growth of agricultural workforce now needs to be modified. Yet there is little doubt that in future, even in rural areas, non-farm work opportunities will have to grow faster than in the past, because the scope for an expansion of the land area under cultivation is virtually exhausted.

With respect to the status or relationship of workers to others in the same enterprise, the data relating to workers of both sexes taken together show a gradual increase in the proportion of casual labourers, from 23 per cent in 1972–3 to almost 32 per cent in 1993–4. This increase was mainly at the cost of the self-employed, whose proportion fell from 61 per cent in 1977–8 to about 55 per cent in 1993–4. The proportion of regular employees varied between 13 and 16 per cent during the period 1972–94 (about 16–20 per cent among male workers and 5–7 per cent among female workers). There has been a decrease in the proportion of regular employees among urban male workers from 51 per cent in the early 1970s to 44 per cent in the 1980s and 42 per cent in the early 1990s. Among rural male workers too, the proportion of regular employees has decreased from 12 per cent to 8 per cent. But among female workers, the share of regular workers has remained stable at 3–4 per cent in rural areas and 25–28 per cent in urban areas (Visaria 2000).

Relations between Urbanization, Industrialization, and Fertility Decline

The theory of demographic transition postulates that fertility decline (which lags behind mortality decline) is generally associated with the processes of urbanization and industrialization, which together lead to modernization, growth of individualism, and changes in the perceptions about the benefits of a large family size. Interestingly, urban India is much closer to the replacement level of fertility than rural India. But if states are to be considered relevant units, the decline in fertility to the replacement level has first occurred not in the state with the highest level of urbanization or industrialization (Maharashtra) but in Kerala, the state with virtually universal literacy and the lowest level of mortality. At the same time, Punjab, the state with the second lowest level of mortality, is not the one with the second lowest level of fertility; it is Tamil Nadu, where mortality is higher than in Kerala, Punjab, and also Himachal Pradesh.

There is no doubt that low mortality helps to lower the desired number of children because of the confidence it generates among parents about the survival of their offspring. However, neither high literacy nor very low mortality is a necessary condition for a sharp decline in fertility. With faster progress towards universal literacy (particularly among females) and a further lowering of infant and child mortality, the wanted fertility can decline and the process of demographic transition or fertility reduction can probably be accelerated.

The central factor influencing fertility behaviour seems to be the aspirations of people about their own life and their children's. Mass media have played an important role in influencing these aspirations. The family planning programme, launched effectively by the government since the mid-1960s, has (despite its many weaknesses) provided the means of controlling fertility. The recent reorientation of the official family planning programme towards reproductive and child health throughout the entire life span of the people augurs well for an improvement in the quality of care provided by the health functionaries. If these functionaries can win the confidence of their target groups and become their counsellors, the unmet need for family size regulation might largely disappear. Simultaneously, the rule of law and the social and economic infrastructure of our small villages need to be strengthened to ensure that the ongoing demographic changes spread throughout the country at an accelerated pace.

The momentum for growth built into the young age distribution of India's population makes it inevitable that even if all Indian couples were to decide immediately to have no more than two children, the rate of population growth would remain positive (or above zero) for the next 50 to 60 years. However, the size of the ultimate total population, at the time when population stabilizes, would be smaller than otherwise if the replacement level of fertility is reached sooner rather than later. Therefore, efforts to accelerate the progress towards the replacement level of fertility certainly need to be pursued.

According to an analysis of the factors contributing to long-term population growth, momentum for growth is likely to account for about 58 per cent of the growth during 1991–2101 (Visaria and Visaria 1996). An ongoing exercise suggests this proportion to be higher, almost 75 per cent (Visaria and Visaria 2000). However, the experience of Kerala and Tamil Nadu also suggests that the expected diffusion of fertility decline might lower TFR below the replacement level. The eventual population may then be lower than is likely to be reached during 2040–50, when India is expected to become the most populous country on planet Earth.

A major uncertainty in assessing the prospective population trends over the next twenty-five years relates to the possible impact of an HIV/AIDS epidemic. In several African countries, the AIDS epidemic which generally affects adults has led to a sharp decline in the expectation of life at birth. There is considerable divergence of views about the extent to which the AIDS infection has already spread in India. The National AIDS Control Organisation (NACO) estimated the number of AIDS-infected persons in India in mid-1998 at 3.5 million. In the states of Maharashtra, Tamil Nadu, Karnataka, Andhra Pradesh, and Manipur, over 1 per cent of the women coming for antenatal check-ups at selected sites have been found to be infected with HIV/AIDS. While the empirical basis and dependability of these estimates is often questioned, the best policy seems to be initiate and implement policies and strategies that would help minimize the spread of the epidemic and its resulting traumatic impact on the people.

Unfortunately, a slowing down of the decline in mortality and rise in expectation of life at birth cannot be ruled out. The United Nations Population Division has estimated that the AIDS epidemic will lower the expectation of life at birth in India by about 1.6 years during 2010–15; and as a result, the total population of India in 2015 would be smaller (than without AIDS) by about 13 million persons. With the help of funds from UNAIDS and USAID, NACO is in the process of launching several programmes to contain the AIDS epidemic and its indirect effects in the form of a resurgence of tuberculosis because of the reduced level of the natural immunity of the AIDS-infected population. The actual course of events will depend on the extent to which our ongoing efforts to restrict the spread of AIDS succeed in achieving their objectives.

ENDNOTES

1. It is not clear whether the population of Taiwan has been taken into account along with China's. According to the 1998 World Population Data Sheet of the Population Reference Bureau, Washington, D.C., the figures for the Indian subcontinent and China (including Hong Kong and Taiwan) would be 1254 and 1271 million, with a difference of 1.3 per cent.

2. With an estimated total population of 846 million, a net undercount of 1.8 per cent of population implies an omission of nearly 15.5 million persons. For the data based on the post-enumeration check conducted after the 1991 Census, see Census of India (1991b).

3. A 'census house' does not necessarily meet the prescribed standards about space or the quality of materials used for the floor, walls, or the roof.

4. In June 1997, a targeted PDS was launched. See Government of India (1999: 67–70).

5. The SRS data for the twenty-six-year period from 1971 to 1996 have been published recently in a singe publication (see) Registrar General, India (1998b). The detailed six-monthly publication called the *Sample Registration Bulletin*, published in July and January each year, has recently been truncated into a four-page summary data sheet to be published in April and October.

6. According to the NSS surveys, over the six-year period between 1987–8 and 1993–4, the number of rural workers reporting an urban workplace had more than doubled from 3.1 to 6.4 million. The relatively smaller counter-flow of urban workers with a rural workplace increased from 0.9 to 1.6 million. The net flow of rural workers with an urban workplace was 4.8 million during 1993–4 and 2.2 million during 1987–8. (See *Sarvekshana* (1990); NSSO (1997a); or *Sarvekshana* (1996)).

7. The famine of 1899–1900 was described as the 'greatest famine recorded' in Indian history up to that time (see Visaria and Visaria 1983).
8. The NSS surveys typically understate the level of infant and child mortality. Yet the census actuary chose to use the NSS-based estimate. If the NSS estimates of death rates were correct, the subsequent SRS-based estimates suggested an implausible rise in mortality. Unfortunately, the official Indian publications continue to cite the IMR of 146 for the decade 1951–61 and understate the gain in IMR and longevity that has occurred since Independence.
9. The expected average length of life of a rural child was 58.9 years, 7.0 years lower than that of an urban child. A rural male and a female child expected to live for 58.5 and 59.3 years respectively, while their urban counterparts could hope to live for 64.5 and 67.3 years (see Registrar General, India 1998c).
10. There is little doubt that the Pre-natal Diagnostic Technique Act, 1994 (Regulation and Prevention Act, 1994), enacted by the Parliament as well as the state legislature of Maharashtra, is violated with impunity throughout the country. However, the availability of these facilities in rural areas is not on the same scale as in urban areas.
11. Several studies in the USA, UK, Netherlands, and parts of Europe have indicated a higher life expectancy (or lower mortality) among married men or women than among the unmarried, widowed, or divorced. Social isolation and loneliness have been noted as contributing to these differences.
12. Similarly, the proportion of Muslims in the Indian population in 1951 is understated as 9.9 per cent and the increase in the share of the community since then is overstated, because the 1951 census was not conducted in Jammu and Kashmir, where 68 per cent of the population enumerated by the 1961 Census was Muslim (Census of India 1961b: iv).
13. The number of Zoroastrians enumerated by the 1971 Census in the country as a whole was 91,266 (Census of India 1971). The 1981 census data on the number of followers of different religions were based on a tabulation according to the religion of the head of the household; and they may not be comparable with previous or subsequent data about Zoroastrians because of the presumed high incidence of inter-faith marriages among them.
14. A.M. Shah, reported a rise in the average size of households by building up a series that included estimates based on the 1951 Census (4.9, 4.7, and 4.8 for rural, urban, and all India) (see Shah 1998: 66).

REFERENCES

Agarwala, S.N. 1962. *Age at Marriage in India*. New Delhi: Kitab Mahal.
Census of India 1951. *Census of India 1954, Paper 6: Estimation of Birth and Death Rates in India during 1941–50*. New Delhi: Government of India.
_____. 1961b. *Paper 1 of 1963: 1961 Census—Religion*. New Delhi: Government of India.
_____. 1971. *Paper 2 of 1972: Religion*. New Delhi: Government of India.
_____. 1981. *Occasional Paper 2 of 1989, Child Mortality, Age at Marriage and Fertility in India*. New Delhi: Office of the Registrar General.
_____. 1991a. *Paper 2 of 1992, Final Population Totals: Brief Analysis of Primary Census Abstract*. New Delhi: Office of the Registrar General. 6.
_____. 1991b. *Paper 1 of 1994, Report on Post-Enumeration Check*. New Delhi: Office of the Registrar General.
_____. 1991c. *Paper 1 of 1995, Religion*. New Delhi: Office of the Registrar General.
_____. 1991d. Series I, India, *Paper 1 of 1992, Final Population Totals*.
_____. 1998. *India: State Profile, 1991*. New Delhi: Office of the Registrar General.
Central Statistical Organisation. 1998. *National Accounts Statistics, 1998*. New Delhi.
Chakravorty, C. and A.K. Singh. 1991. *Household Structures in India* (Census of India, 1991, Occasional Paper 1). New Delhi: Government of India.

Davis, K. 1951. *The Population of India and Pakistan*. Princeton: Princeton University Press.

Government of India, Ministry of Finance. 1999. *Economic Survey*. New Delhi.

International Institute for Population Sciences (IIPS). 1995. *National Family Health Survey (MCH and Family Planning) India 1992–93*. Mumbai.

Mari Bhat, P.N. 1998. 'Demographic Estimates for Post-Independence India: A New Integration'. *Demography India*. 27(1):23–57.

———. 2000. 'Recent Trends in Fertility and Mortality in India: A Critical Reappraisal of Data from SRS and NFHS'. A paper presented at the Millennium Conference of the Indian Association for the Study of Population and the Population Foundation of India, February. New Delhi.

NCERT (National Council of Educational Research and Training). 1997. *Sixth All India Education Survey: National Tables*, Volume I, *Educational Facilities in Rural and Urban Areas*. New Delhi.

———. 1998. *Sixth All India Education Survey: Selected Statistics*. New Delhi.

NSSO (National Sample Survey Organization). 1996. *Operational Land Holdings in India, 1991–92; Salient Features 48th Round (1992)*. Report No. 407. New Delhi.

———. 1997a. *Employment and Unemployment in India, 1993–94: Fifth Quinquennial Survey NSS 50th Round*. Report 409. New Delhi.

———. 1997b. *Employment and Unemployment Situation among Social Groups in India, 1993–94: NSS 50th Round*. Report 425. New Delhi.

———. 1998a. *Employment and Unemployment Situation Among Religious Groups in India, 1993–94: NSS 50th Round*. Report 438. New Delhi.

———. 1998b. *Morbidity and Treatment of Ailments: NSS 52nd Round*. Report 441. New Delhi.

Registrar General, India. 1954. Census of India. *Paper no. 6. Estimation of Birth and Death Rates in India During 1940–50—1951 Census*.

———. 1996. *Population Projections for India and States—1996–2016:* Census of India, 1991. New Delhi.

———. 1997. *Fertility and Mortality Indicators, 1994*. New Delhi.

———. 1998a. *Civil Registration System Newsletter*. Issue 1, April.

———. 1998b. *Vital Rates of India 1971 to 1996 based on the Sample Registration System (SRS)*. New Delhi.

———. 1998c. SRS-Based Abridged Life Tables, 1990–94 and 1991–95. SRS Analytical Studies, Report 1 of 1998. New Delhi.

Sarvekshana. 1990. Special Number. September.

———. 1996. 20 (1, July–Sept.).

Shah, A.M. 1998. *The Family in India: Critical Essays*. New Delhi: Orient Longman Ltd.

United Nations, Department for Economic and Social Information and Policy Analysis, Population Division, 1995. *World Population Prospects: The 1994 Revision*. New York.

———. Department for Economic and Social Information and Policy Analysis, Population Division. 1996. *World Population Prospects: The 1996 Revision, Annex II & III: Demographic Indicators by Major Area, Region and Country*. New York.

United Nations, Department of Economic and Social Affairs, Population Division. 1999. *World Population Prospects. The 1998 Revision, Volume I: Comprehensive Tables*. New York.

Visaria, L. 1974. 'Demographic Transition among Parsis: 1881–1971'. *Economic and Political Weekly*. 9(41–3):19–26.

———. 1999. 'Deficit of Women in India: Magnitude, Trends, Regional Variations and Determinants'. In B. Ray and A. Basu, eds, *From Independence Towards Freedom: Indian Women Since 1947*. 80–99. New Delhi: Oxford University Press.

Visaria, L. and P. Visaria. 1983. 'Population (1757–1947)'. In Dharma Kumar and Meghnad Desai, eds, *The Cambridge Economic History of India,* vol. 2: c. 1757–c. 1970. 530–1. Cambridge: Cambridge University Press.

———. 1996. *Prospective Population Growth and Policy Options for India, 1991–2101*. New York: The Population Council.

———. 2000. 'An Analysis of the Long-Term Population Projections for Various States of India, 1991–2101'. Mimeo.

Visaria L., P. Visaria, and A. Jain. 1994. 'Estimates of Contraceptive Prevalence Based on Service Statistics and Surveys in Gujarat State, India'. *Studies in Family Planning*. Vol. 25, No. 5, September–October 1994.

Visaria, P. 1969. 'Mortality and Fertility in India, 1951–1961'. *Milbank Memorial Fund Quarterly*. 47(1) (Part 1): 91–116.

———. 1976. 'Recent Trends in Indian Population Policy'. *Economic and Political Weekly*. 2 (31–33) (Special Number, August).

———. 1997a. *Women in the Indian Working Force: Trends and Differentials*. Kunda Datar Memorial Lectures, 1993. Pune: Gokhale Institute of Politics and Economics.

———. 1997b. 'Urbanization in India: An Overview'. In Gavin W. Jones and Pravin Visaria, eds, *Urbanization in Large Developing Countries: China, Indonesia, Brazil, and India*. 266–88. Oxford: Clarendon Press.

———. 2000. 'Labour Force in India: Retrospect and Prospect'. Mimeo. A revised version of a paper presented at a Seminar organized by the National Council of Applied Economic Research, New Delhi.

TABLES

Table 1: Key Population Statistics of India, 1901–1991

Census Year	Total Population (million)	Average annual growth rate (percent)	Density (persons per sq. km.)	Sex ratio (males per 1000 females)	Per cent of urban Population
1901	238.3	0.3	77	1029	10.8
1911	252.0	0.6	82	1038	10.3
1921	251.2	N	81	1047	11.2
1931	278.9	1.1	90	1053	12.0
1941	318.5	1.3	103	1058	13.9
1951	361.0	1.3	117	1057	17.3
1961	439.1	2.0	141	1063	18.0
1971	548.2	2.2[b]	178	1075	19.9
1981	683.3	2.2[b]	221	1071	23.3[a]
1991	846.3	2.1	267	1076	25.7

Notes : a) Includes only an estimate for Assam.

b) Growth rate for 1961–71 and 1971–81 take account of the fact that the reference data of the 1971 Census was 1 April, whereas that of the 1981 Census (like the 1951 and 1961 Censuses) was 1 March.

N: Negligible.

Sources : Census of India, 1961, Vol. 1, India, Parts II–A (i) General Population Tables, 1961 and II–C (i), Social and Cultural Tables, 1964;

Census of India, 1971, Series 1, India, Parts II–A (i), General Population Tables, 1975, and II–C (ii), Social and Cultural Tables, 1977;

Census of India, 1981, Series 1, India, Paper I of 1982, Final Population Tables;

Part II-Special, Report and Tables Based on 5 per cent Sample Data, 1984, Part II–B (i), Primary Census Abstract: General Population 1983;

Census of India, 1991, Series 1, India, Paper 2 of 1992, Final Population Totals: Brief Analysis of Primary Census Abstract.

Table 2: Vital Rates per 1000 Population, India 1901–1990

	Birth Rate	Death Rate	Rate of natural increase
1901–10	49.2	42.6	6.6
1911–20	48.1	47.2	0.9
1921–30	46.2	36.3	9.9
1931–40	45.2	31.2	14.0
1941–50	39.9	27.4	12.5
1951–60	40.9	22.8	18.1
1961–70	40.0	17.8	22.2
1971–80	37.8	15.4	22.4
1980–2	33.8	12.3	21.5
1988–90	30.8	10.3	20.5
1991–3*	29.1	9.4	19.4
1994–6*	27.4	8.9	18.5
1996–8*	27.0	9.0	18.0

*Excluding Jammu and Kashmir

Sources: Davis (1951); Registrar General, India (1954); Registrar General, India (1998b).

Table 3: Mortality Indicators for All India 1971–1998

Year	Crude Death Rate			Infant Mortality Rate			Life Expectancy at Birth		
	All	Rural	Urban	All	Rural	Urban	All	Males	Females
1971–5	15.5	17.1	9.8	134	144	83	49.7	50.5	49.0
1976–80	13.8	15.0	8.9	124	134	74	52.3	52.5	52.1
1981–5	11.0	11.9	7.5	90	98	56	55.5	55.4	55.7
1986–90	10.6	11.6	7.3	91	99	59	57.7	57.7	58.1
1991–5	9.5	10.4	6.6	76	83	50	60.0	59.4	60.4
1996–8	9.0	9.7	6.5	72	77	45	61.1*	60.4*	61.8*

Note: Estimates for 1998 are provisional. The state of Jammu and Kashmir is excluded from estimates beginning 1991. *Estimates relate to 1993–7 and are centred on 1995.

Table 4: Salient Features of Households and Population
Enumerated in the Censuses of 1961–1991*

	1961	1971	1981	1991
No. of Occupied Residential Houses (million)				
All-India	78.9	90.8	113.7	147.0
Rural India	65.1	72.7	86.1	107.9
Urban India	13.8	18.1	27.6	39.1
No. of Households (million)				
All-India	84.5	100.5	119.8	152.0
Rural India	68.9	79.6	90.9	111.6
Urban India	15.6	20.9	28.9	40.4
No. of Households per 100 Houses				
All-India	107	111	105	103
Rural India	106	109	105	103
Urban India	113	116	105	103
No. of Households per sq. km				
All-India	26.6	30.6	37.3	49.6
Rural India	21.9	25.2	29.6	38.3
Urban India	404.2	478.7	550.0	631.2
Average Household Size				
All-India	5.2	5.5	5.6	5.5
Rural India	5.2	5.5	5.6	5.6
Urban India	5.0	5.3	5.4	5.3
Density of Population per sq. km				
All-India	138	177	216	267
Rural India	115	148	174	214
Urban India	2050	2505	3002	3370

*Excluding Jammu & Kashmir, which had an estimated population of 7.7 million in 1991.

Ecology and Environment

RITA BRARA

M y aim in this chapter is to draw upon sociological perspectives for an understanding of ecology and environment in India. I should clarify at the outset that I use the terms ecology and environment to refer to the interrelations of human beings, flora, fauna, as well as elements of the physical and natural environment. These interrelations are explored along three dimensions—religious representations, subsistence modes, and the archetypal expressions of the contemporary environmental movement.

The context for ecological and environmental studies was in a sense coterminous with the intellectual orientations (and, later, disciplines) of anthropology and sociology that developed in the wake of the industrial revolution. The gulf separating the scientific representations of nature from its cosmic representations posed a problem for the meaningfulness of cultural representations that anthropologists set out to study. Cultural representations, as Lévi-Strauss (1978) put it, were also thought systems but scientific representations afforded greater mastery over nature and therefore increasingly gained credibility.

While the industrial revolution began in western Europe, it soon gathered a momentum that took the world in its sweep. Lévi-Strauss (1963) speculates that the point of origin of the industrial/scientific revolution is not significant insofar as we recognize that intellectual currents in different parts of the world contributed to the build-up. In his view, what is critical is that this revolution encompassed the globe in a period of about two hundred years. The comparable revolution in his way of looking at anthropology, then, is the neolithic or agricultural revolution that spread over the world in the course of about 5000 years. Differences in cultural representations, however, were not homogenized in its aftermath. Whether we are at the threshold of another revolution—the ecological revolution—is the question that environmentalists are posing now. This domain of ecology is akin to what Foucault describes as the domain of knowledge 'constituted by the different objects that will or will not acquire a scientific status' ([1972] 1992: 182).

Both settled agriculture and the industrial revolution left in their wake forms of knowledge and modes of subsistence that continued unabated from the earlier epochs of human existence. Anthropological time—paleolithic, neolithic, and industrial—approximated with three modes of subsistence in the main—hunting-gathering, agriculture, and industrial labour. Societies and cultures of hunters and gatherers, nomads and peasants were anthropology's object of study as repositories of the human past, as synchronic evidence of humankind's diversity or in another frame, as pre-capitalist social formations. These perspectives, however, overlooked the contemporary aspirations of those who were the focus of anthropological enquiry. They desired precisely those technologies that were the products of the industrial revolution. Such technologies as diesel-operated pump-sets for lifting water, trucks, and motorized boats were seen as rendering prior forms of subsistence viable in an altered global context. There was, evidently, no escaping the fact that the industrial revolution had now affected all peoples. Capitalism and colonization thrived on the new technology which was perceived to be western at first, though gradually, aspects of it were accepted to be of universal significance. As technology explored the world of outer space, a planetary consciousness developed, especially in the West. At present two currents seem to prevail vis-à-vis technology. On the one hand, there is the tendency to push forward and colonize a new frontier—outer space—in the continuing mastery over nature. The cultural imagination of science fiction and children's literature is already replete with earthlings versus creatures from other planets. On the other hand, a parallel tendency is discernible as the other side to the industrial revolution. The increasing vulnerability of the planet and its life forms to the dangers of human proliferation, atmospheric, water and land pollution, and radio-active fall-out has led to a gradual environmentalization of the West and environmentalism as the new cause célebrè. This process has also been fuelled by the recognition of 'life-style' diseases for which science and technology, as yet, have no cure. Scientists, too, increasingly view environmental risk as a parameter to be reckoned with in their enterprise (Beck 1992). Along with scientific investigations, environmentalists retrace their creation myths and ponder whether the Judaeo-Christian outlook on life valorizes the pursuit of mastery over nature (Worster 1977). Such environmentalism, too, can be seen as a particular cultural construction that invites the study of the natural environment as culturally experienced, and as that which human beings perceive, create, and destroy.

In this chapter I delve into the human engagement with nature as it has evolved in the Indian subcontinent. Categories of thought with which we apprehend environmental phenomena are forged by a process of dynamic interaction between cultural residues, in Pareto's (1935) usage, and the natural endowments or resources that people have to deal with at each juncture in their history. Circumventing the enormity of a review that can reckon with particular ecological and environmental contexts in India, I chart a course that will enable me to address questions concerning religious beliefs, modes of subsistence, and the contemporary environmental movement.

This chapter is divided into three parts. Part I deals with the relation of religious beliefs to the environment. The first section discusses religious interpretations of the environment in India while the second reverses the terms of the debate by exploring the environmental understanding of religious beliefs. Part II investigates what I term combinatorial modes of subsistence in India. The first section here seeks to bring out both the potential and the inadequacies of anthropological classifications that dwell on singular modes of subsistence such as hunting and gathering, pastoralism, and settled agriculture. It argues for the notion of a combinatorial mode as a synthetic device for apprehending current and incipient subsistence patterns. The environmental impact of the modes of subsistence is interpreted by deploying the idea of ecological involution in the second section. The embedding of modes of subsistence in wider patterns of occupational culture as well as the culture of the nation state and a global context is outlined in the remaining sections. Part III of this chapter is concerned with environment and the public sphere. It seeks to fathom the new environmental consciousness in India by utilizing the idea of archetypes of environmental representations and struggles—

the Chipko movement, the Citizens' reports on the state of India's environment, and the Narmada anti-dam agitation.

I

Religious Representations and the Environment

All religions offer collective representations of nature which contrast with their scientific representations. As disciplines, anthropology and sociology are concerned with both.

It is challenging to determine the precise manner in which religious beliefs in India are implicated in conceptions of human nature, flora, fauna, space, and time. In this section, I try to work out a trajectory that draws on the paradigm of creation envisaged in the Vedic hymns as a mould or model for ecological and environmental engagement in the life-world that is encoded in a religious world-view. As a model of and for activity in this world (Geertz 1966), the deployment of the Vedic model points towards both the interpretive potential and the complexity of religious beliefs and practices in relation to the natural and the built environment.

If we look at the sociological classics on religion, these prove to be inadequate for a historical or even contemporary understanding of religion in India. Although Durkheim's (1915) study of religion explored its evolution from an anchorage in a totemic clan to an abstract or trans-tribal god, his analysis of religious representations and changes in what constitutes 'the sacred' is insufficient for dealing with subsequent development of religious beliefs and the continuous evolving/transforming of religious traditions, beliefs, and practices. Societal and religious representations were coterminous for Durkheim. But the latter may also tend towards forging distinct religious collectives so that the correspondence between the religious and the social becomes a contest and a matter for empirical enquiry.

By contrast, Weber (1963) focused upon the implications of world religions and particular sects within the latter. However, Weber did not investigate the meanings of 'world religions' for believers of different faiths living in contiguous territory that may have generated an intersubjectivity across particular religions. His concerns were confined to movements within a static characterization of world religions qua world religions; he did not imagine the emergence of new world religions such as tribal religions or Sikhism. But religious beliefs are implicated in conceptions of nature, time, and space, at the dynamic interface of believers in particular social and ecological contexts with the varying centres, orientations, and oral/textual traditions of historic world religions. Further, allowing for the emergence of incipient theodicies enriches comment on the religious interpretations of the environment in India.

In the following two sections, I will take a processual view of religious representations as they have evolved in the subcontinent, and broadly suggest lines of discontinuity with prior conceptions of sacredness. I shall also make a dual attempt to grapple both with the religious as religious or sacred and, therefore, meaningful at its own level and the environmental implications of these beliefs as evident in both the natural and the built environment.

Religious Representations of Man and Nature

Vedic Beliefs

An early formulation of the relation between nature and culture is proffered in the Vedic cosmogonies (1500–2000 BC). What is laid out in the Vedic hymns is an account of the beginnings of the universe that is created out of Prajapati's or cosmic man's sacrifice. All living beings, social classes (*varnas*), plants, and animals, as well as space and time are conceived as emanating from Prajapati's cosmic body.

Smith (1991, 1994) brings out the embodiment, classification, and representation of nature in the Vedas and draws attention to the transformative power of religious beliefs in forging connections across categories—social, animal and vegetable, temporal and spatial. The Brahmin varna is identified as being emitted, first, from the head of Prajapati, the Kshatriya from his chest and arms, and the Vaishya is believed to have generated from his thighs. The classification of the Shudra, as growing out of Prajapati's feet, is integral only to the quadripartite formulation (ibid.).

Trees are said to have been generated from Prajapati's hair and their classification hinges on their use as stakes in sacrifice. The type of wood preferred for a particular rite varies with the varying desire or motive of the sacrificator. The classification of animals, too, relates to the ritual of sacrifice and to their genesis from Prajapati's body. The five animals considered appropriate for sacrifice (*pasus*)—a man, a horse, a bull, a ram, and a he-goat—are domestic and village animals (cf. Das 1983). By contrast, animals and birds in the wild (*aranya*) (see Malamoud 1998) are believed to have been engendered from Prajapati's sweat. Such animals are excluded from sacrifice. Often the cow and antelope are associated with the Brahmin, the horse and the bull with the Kshatriya, the goat and sheep are linked to the Vaishya, and the ass, dog, and crow are related to the Shudra. These connections with different animals, such as the cow, for example, are not invariant within the Vedas. Moreover, the classification of animals also draws on their edibility/inedibility and anatomical and propagative characteristics.

The categorization of time and the articulation of spatial categories is perceived as arising from Prajapati's primal sacrifice. The year is considered identical to Prajapati, a temporal unit that is also substitutable for time past, present, and future (Biardeau 1989). It is often represented as a wheel with three hubs or seasons and twelve spokes or months. The categorization of space is believed to grow out of the utterance—*bhuh* (earth), *bhuvah* (atmosphere), *svaha* (sky), and these represent the three *lokas* (or worlds). These worlds—earth, atmosphere, and sky—are again associated with particular varnas, cardinal directions, beings, deities, seasons, and parts of the day (cf. Smith 1994). The earth is linked to the east, Brahmin, Agni, spring, and the morning. The atmosphere is related to the south, Kshatriya, ancestors, Indra, summer, and the forenoon. The sky is associated with the west, Vaishya, animals, snakes, offspring, and Viswadeva. The cardinal direction of the north is ambivalent and associated variously with water, Shudra, or other classes (Smith 1994).

As a congealed set of representations, Vedic beliefs may be distinguished from a set of what we may call tribal or pre-Vedic religious representations. The distinguishing features of Vedic beliefs lay in the act of sacrifice that was sanctified by Agni, the prohibition on the sacrifice of wild animals, and the centrality of varna or social classes. Vedic sacrifice, Jamous observes, was both a 'specific rite' and a 'model for other rites' (Jamous 1994: 343).

The village as the site of the sacrificial order (Malamoud 1998) contrasted with the sacred terrains and totemic filiations of hunting and food-gathering peoples up to the present times. The *aranya*, moreover, referred to the space outside the *gram* or the village settlement—that is mountains, forested plains, or deserts—along this axis of contrast. Malamoud notes that *aranya* is often translated as 'forest' but 'designates in reality the village's other ... as that which is external to the village' (Malamoud 1998: 76).[1] Non-agriculturists who lived outside the village were described in a derogatory manner by terms such as 'mock-man' and 'dwarf' (Smith 1994).

Later Hinduism

The distance that separates the Vedic from later developments in Hinduism is considerable. How are we as sociologists to make sense of Vedic classifications?

Here two courses seem to be open. One is to view Vedic beliefs as both influential for and ancestral to the subsequent development of religious thought in the subcontinent including its folk strains (Hiltebeitel 1989; Biardeau 1989). The other course (of interest to environmental sociologists) is to regard the Vedic world-view as a product of settled cultivation allowing for the possibility that tribal beliefs of the sacred trace the genealogies of their religion in contradistinction to the Vedic trajectory. (We shall explore this subject in the section on Environmental Interpretations of Religion.)

Turning to the first course, later writers on Hinduism have found it difficult to describe religion in India, whether in contest or accord, as fragment or shift in interpretation, without reference to the Vedas. Vedic symbols and moulds continue to find a resonance in contemporary ethnographic accounts. For example, the four varnas are often believed to have emerged from the original body of Prajapati or Purusha (Parish 1996). On the other hand, it is possible to investigate points of differentiation as well as Vedic beliefs transformed over time generating novel interpretations. Especially because the charting of a historical movement has proved to be intractable for Vedic religion (Biardeau 1989), the Indologist and anthropologists often take recourse to other methods for filling in the missing centuries.

We know that in the intervening centuries, the idea of varna was supplemented by *jati*, a term that referred to the 'natural' species of human beings, plants and animals. Each jati had its associated qualities, occupations, ritual objects, and deities. Local/regional deities, too, had their own *vahans* (vehicles) and associated tree species that were prevalent in their particular environment, such that the same connections were forged between spatial, social, vegetable, and animal categories that were propounded for the varnas in the Vedas. It is as though the Vedas furnished the paradigmatic model and the syntagmatic or lateral spread was codified in the features associated with particular jatis.

The term jati pertained especially to the divisions of the agrarian population of the village (including artisan and service castes) while those outside the village or the world of jati were considered to be outside civilization. The conception of jati entailed the recognition of differences between proximate jatis as well, as when jatis differed from each other by virtue of the crops raised or the fish trapped—in short by the terms of their entwined symbolic and instrumental relationships with nature. The ritualization of difference led to the play of the principles of both division and hierarchy (cf. Dumont 1972; Shah and Desai 1988) but allowed for participation in the inclusive and encompassing rituals at the levels of village and kingdom.

Did the resident jatis of the village come together in the recreation of Prajapati's paradigmatic sacrifice? It is tempting to speculate that although the *jajmani* system was in disarray when first reported (Wiser [1936] 1958) the term *jajman* (Sanskrit: *yajaman*) connotes both the village-level patron and the person who desires to make a sacrifice.[2] The jajmani system may thus have linked the different castes of a village in a sacrificial and religious recreation of the social order that contrasted the order of the village as sacred and civilized, in opposition to those outside it, who were construed as less-than-human or uncivilized. Again, Biardeau (1984) notes that the sacrifice of the buffalo to the goddess during the festival of Navaratri in the rural regions of India still brings all the jatis in the village together during its performance. Typically, the site for resistance within this socio-religious order was distanced from the village (or the king's palace) and, perhaps, it is not a coincidence that the renouncer found his métier in the forest, away from this location.

Does Vedic religion reflect the interests of its Brahminical codifiers? Smith (1994) avers that his commitment to 'western humanism' makes it incumbent on him to take this view. However, it is possible to investigate points of differentiation and discontinuity as Vedic beliefs transformed over time, generating novel interpretations (cf. Heesterman 1993). First, Brahmanism, as Vedic religion is often termed by anthropologists, was time and again resisted in the subcontinent. The challenge was constant in the person of the renouncer and the social formation of the sect that this process engendered (Dumont 1972). The fostering of the now-recognized religions of Jainism and Buddhism affords further evidence of dissent. If the sacrifice of animals was the leitmotif of Vedic times, Jainism and Buddhism opposed, especially, the sacrifice of animals by espousing the value of *ahimsa* (the absence of desire to kill). The continuing development of Jainism reveals the Jain concern for life in all its forms that marks Jain practice to this day (Humphrey and Laidlaw 1994). Again, Buddha noted that the analogy of jati with a natural species was false since jati endogamy was a cultural construct with no basis in nature (Gadgil and Guha 1992).

Over time, the sacrifice of animals lost its pre-eminence among the Brahmins (Heesterman 1993) and liturgy-based worship came to dominate the practice of religion. The eschewing of animal sacrifice is likely to have led to the ascendancy of the cow as a sacred symbol in the period following the challenge from Jainism since the products of the cow (ghee, milk, etc.) came to substitute sacrificial animals in large measure. However, animal sacrifice is still reported from villages, contrary to the prevalent Brahminical practice but paradoxically closer to Vedic ritual (cf. Hiltebeitel 1991, Biardeau 1984).

Second, if we look at the religious representations of nature today it is with the understanding that the Brahmins who disseminated Vedic knowledge did not belong to a monolithic class (cf. Leavitt 1992). The accumulation of knowledge from dispersed locations and environmental contexts helps us appreciate variations within the religious fold. The Brahmins' defence of local custom and the tradition of particular groups often pitted them against the Brahmins of other regions (Trautmann 1981). The dissemination of Vedic views by 'practice-centered genres' (Bauman 1996) of song, verse, dance, and ritual was in active interaction with local non-Brahmins and tribals who influenced regional configurations. The cult of the mother goddess, for instance, was incorporated in Brahminical practice over time.

Biardeau (1984) brings out the association of the *sami* tree in popular ritual and the classical texts. The preferred wood for the sacrificial ritual is sami but it is substituted locally by the *apata* (*Bauhinia tomentosa*) in Andhra Pradesh, to cite an example. Again, in predominantly vegetarian areas, the goddess is offered a pumpkin or a gourd which is stained red in order for it to appear as an animal victim, or elsewhere, the deity is offered a coconut in substitution for a head. Following the developments in later Hinduism, today the sacrificial animals are sometimes set free instead of being killed (Srivastava 1997).

Third, the Vedic discourse has also been appropriated by non-Brahmins who imbued sacrifice with meaning that was relevant in their own contexts—as when the artisans or Vishwakarmis (named after the mythological architect Vishwakarma) construed their work as sacrifice (Brouwer 1995); as with the potters who thought of their creations as analogous with Prajapati's (Cort 1998) or among the Tamils who added their own Veda (Hardy 1995).

The relation of the Brahmins to other Hindus has been complex and multifaceted. Often, Vedic Hinduism is interpreted as exclusively Brahminical (Smith 1994) or Brahminical largely by consensus (Biardeau 1989). Maybe both views underestimate the extent of the strains of both continuity and resistance in a religion that lacked centralized religious institutions for a long part of its history. While devotional (*bhakti*) strains reveal reinterpretations of the Vedic revelation (Hiltebeitel 1989); Sontheimer (1987) shows that cults in Maharashtra draw on the depiction of Rudra in the Vedas, in contradistinction to Shiva as his successor in the Brahminical tradition. In this perspective Vedic beliefs reach out beyond their exclusive characterization as the preserve of Brahmins.

The sacralization of the physical features of the subcontinent was a characteristic accompaniment of the spread of Vedic Hinduism. The Himalayas were the abode of the gods and the Ganges the prototype of the sacred river. Stories from the epics, the Ramayana and Mahabharata, congealed the sacred geography of India (Srinivas 1952). Eck (1983) points out that the religious imagination zoomed in on geographical features because these changed form relatively slowly. Animals associated with deities, often as vehicles, as well as flowers, fruits, and sites connected with the epics were also regarded as embodiments of the sacred.

The planting and worshipping of sacred herbs and trees is still a part of the country's religious landscape (Sarkar [1916] 1972). The *bar* (*Ficus bengalensis*), *peepal* (*Ficus religiosa*), *bilva* (*Aegle marmelos*—with its trifoliate leaf suggestive of Shiva's trident), *neem* (*Azadirachta indica*) and *sami* (*Acacia ferruginea, Prosopis cineraria*), as well as regionally distinctive sacred groves (Chandrakanth and Romm 1991) continue to be planted and maintained in present times. The gods are also offered flowers in worship, varying with the deity and the region. The principles underlying the substitution of ritual offerings in local contexts still need to be ascertained empirically. Cultural motifs predominate but are subject to local alteration—for instance, forms of the Devi (the mother goddess) are offered a red object, often a red flower in the east (oleanders in Nepal; hibiscus in Bengal) whereas in the north-west she is typically propitiated with a red scarf. In this case, the colour takes precedence over the nature of the object, perhaps as a relic of the blood-stained sacrificial victim. However, the vitality of the religious tradition in sacralizing diverse animals, trees, fruits, and flowers is commonly attested.

Apart from flora and fauna, the religious landscape of the country covers an entire array of sacred objects, from unhewn stones to architectural masterpieces. Even where the dominant spaces in a village or town are occupied by large, elaborate temples, simpler shrines are frequent as well. Some deities also have characteristic locations—for instance the temple to the village deity who embodies both malevolent and benevolent aspects is typically located at the edge of the village (Levy 1992).

Religious beliefs also penetrated the building manuals in the sub-continent and so influenced the architectural principles of the built environment. Often, the four corners of any rectangular building—temple or house—are taken to represent the four regions of the cosmos together with their associated beings and qualities (Moore 1989). This aspect has been well brought out in the studies of holy cities (Eck 1983), temples (Kramisch 1976; Waghorne and Cutler 1985) and houses (Beck 1976; Glushkova and Feldhaus 1998). The built environment, here, communicates the meaning of religious beliefs in what Lawrence and Low (1990) term a 'non-verbal language' even while we recognize that specialists and the laity are differentially aware of such significance.

As an example of how religious beliefs are translated into architecture, it may be useful to look at the city of Banaras as portrayed in Eck's (1983) monograph. The city was visualized as resting on the three points of Shiva's trident, which was interpreted by building the city on three hills. This design was intended to accord with the view that in the wake of the cosmic flood Shiva would hold the city atop his trident. While Banaras was conceived as a sacred city, in later periods it was also viewed as the paradigmatic sacred city, inspiring similar designs (Redfield and Singer 1954).

Characteristically, temples are often located at *tirthas*—that is the point at which one crosses a river, metaphorically conveying the conception of a crossing from this world to the next. Again, where the temple is dedicated to a particular deity, that deity is installed in the centre but the other gods of the pantheon are represented in the periphery in a pattern that conveys the polyvocality of the Hindu religious tradition.

The Encounter with Islam

The encounter with Islam and religion as it evolved in India led to the imparting of a name to the Hindu (etymologically, as dwellers on the other side of the Hindukush mountain range). The religion of Islam, too, developed multiple strands of thought and the long contact of believers from both religions entailed the searching of a common ground in beliefs about man, nature, and divinity, on the one hand, and religious separation and distinctiveness, on the other. As is well known, the mystic aspects of Islam had an affinity with the popular and devotional religiosity in India (Madan 1991). This was evident in the offerings proffered by Hindus at the shrines (*mazars*) of *pirs* (spiritual teachers). Or again as in the *akharas* (gymnasia) of Banaras, Ali was conceived as the counterpart of the Hindu Hanuman and a patron of body-building (Alter 1992). Religious hybridity is apparent to this date in the Muslim components of Hindu cults and vice versa (Coccari 1989; Hiltebeitel 1989). For many in the subcontinent, Islamic beliefs were grafted and recast in terms of the pre-existing religious ideas and organization into jatis. This face of Islam has existed both alongside and at variance with other currents historically.

The appreciation of Islam as a world religion with its spiritual centre in Mecca has also been a part of the consciousness of Muslim groups in India. The sacrifice of animals on Id-ul-Fitr was a significant component of the Middle-East tradition that came to be practised in India. Islamic beliefs led to the creation of mosques, burial grounds, and new sacred centres (such as Bahraich, Delhi, and Ajmer) along with those existing outside the sub-continent (such as Mecca and Medina). The successful Muslim invasions of the subcontinent, too, were sometimes ratified by the building of mosques at the same sites where formerly temples had stood. Yet the evidence for a singular interpretation of Islam lacks credibility.

The qualities of Muslim and Hindu religiosity were also locally constructed, drawing on the symbols and practices of both traditions or one or the other, varying at different points in history. At the level of popular belief, certain vegetables—onions and garlic, for example—were classified as Muslim. Pork was taboo for the Muslims and beef for upper-caste Hindus. Patterns of the ritualized killing of animals opposed the Muslim *halal* (conceived as sanctified killing) to the Hindu *jhatka* (one-stroke slaughter). Such issues have scarcely been addressed in the anthropological literature (Ruel 1984). Cardinality, especially the sacredness of the east for Hindus and the direction of Mecca, which happened to be the west for Muslims in the subcontinent, modes of worship (with or without caps), and modes of disposing the dead (burial; cremation) were also deployed in the construction of religious difference (Roy 1994).

From about the middle of the nineteenth century onwards, however, the construction of the 'Muslim' and the 'Hindu' in alterity proceeded apace, derecognizing the schisms within the religious folds. The cow, for instance, came to stand for Hinduism across caste divides. The nationalist consciousness was perceived as Hindu and perhaps contributed towards the spatial separation or Partition into the states of India and Pakistan. That political act is still read with religious overtones and played out in local neighbourhoods by demarcating Hindustan and Pakistan as distinct religious spaces when tension runs high (Mehta and Chatterji 1995).

More recently, trees venerated by Hindus, such as the peepal, have not been planted in mosques. 'Peepli pirs'—a peepal tree and a grave—formerly commemorated Muslim martyrs. Such graves are losing ground as the object of Muslim cults in Rajasthan, for instance, while the renovation of mosques and the accompanying domes and minarets is being accorded greater attention. Simultaneously, Hindu temples are now being constructed by appropriating the space at the base of the peepal tree, especially in towns.

Considering the themes, signs, and objects deployed in the expression of religiosity among Muslims and Hindus, it becomes apparent that interpreting religious difference as theological premise alone is inadequate. Varied elements of the environment—flora, fauna, cardinality, and space—are imbued with a religious significance that is continuously reworked in a plural context of world religions. This ongoing redefinition of the sacred is read as meaningful within a local context of world religions, signs, and symbols.

Environmental Interpretations of Religion

As an ideological pattern of orientations, each world religion has arisen in the context of a specific mode of livelihood and social organization (Weber 1963). If we look at the ecologies of particular religions, it is possible to infer that the equality of men, so stressed by Islam, drew on the nomadic and tribal organization characteristic of the region where it had its genesis (Lindholm 1996). The leitmotif of animal sacrifice, too, probably drew upon a pastoral mode of life (Parkes 1987). By contrast, Vedic Hinduism was evidently the product of a settled mode of animal husbandry and crop cultivation. Its sacred practices, festivals, and rites were imbued with an agrarian spirit and coincided with the rhythms of agriculture. The dispersed and sedentary practice of agriculture, moreover, would have conduced towards the relative autonomy of local practice at village and regional levels.

The centrality of the village as an agrarian and sacrificial site, dividing and bringing together the different social classes, suggests that the early Vedic beliefs arose in a context that produced an agricultural surplus. Gadgil and Guha (1992) speculate that the use of fire for clearing the land for cultivation was legitimized by the emphasis on the sacrificial fire that may have paved the way for inroads into cultivation that was tabooed for hunters and gatherers. An agrarian civilization that allowed for the generation and appropriation of an agricultural surplus would, plausibly, express hierarchical ideologies, compared with the religions of nomadic pastoralists or hunters and gatherers.

The Vedic representations of sacrifice seem to have been consonant with the interests of a ruling class—epitomized by the Brahmin and the king—that was the beneficiary of the agricultural surplus and relied upon its generation. The stress on hierarchy conformed with the division of society into Brahmins and rulers, on the one hand, and agriculturists and those who provided services for agriculture, on the other. The Shudras, ordained to provide the unfree labour, were incorporated as jatis at village level but within the agrarian social order were denoted by terms such as ass and crow. Those outside the pale of the agrarian civilization of the plains on the other hand, were conceived as uncivilized and referred to by terms such as *bhuts* (spirits) and 'mock-men', for instance, till such time as they were acculturated in what may now be described as Hindu religious beliefs.

Animals and quasi-humans may have been good to think with (cf. Lévi-Strauss 1972;

1987) but for whom is a question that now engages sociologists. The religious elite sought to secure the social order through both representations of nature and disciplinary practices (Asad 1983). Along with the royal class, it attempted to naturalize this social regime and propagate its version of civilization. That certain animals were chosen to mark out social categories, too, probably drew on a system of classification that was enunciated in the Vedic period. However, it is only by understanding the dynamic environing of religious beliefs rather than as static, textual prescription that we can attempt to comprehend both the resilience and the resistance vis-à-vis the enunciated classificatory system down to the present. These ideological conceptions, too, were transformed as religious beliefs evolved in the subcontinent. The engendering and encounter with other world religions led to both the embracing and reconstitution of religious faiths.

As people and territories outside the cultivated plains came under the sway of an agrarian civilization in different periods of history, the inhabitants encountered other world religions including those of Islam and Christianity. Eaton (1985) argues that in Bengal and Punjab, these agrarian entrants took to Islam from a former pre-literate religion during the twelfth to the sixteenth centuries. An analogous argument can perhaps be made for the conversion to Christianity by pre-literate tribal peoples closer to our own times.

It may then be useful to take a processual view of religious practices as they evolve in conjunction with changes in habitat/subsistence practices and in interaction with other religious traditions. At one extreme in India, religious hybridity is discernible, as in the cult beliefs across religious divides referred to earlier. In the middle of the array, the anthropologist can plausibly distinguish elements of a particular religious tradition that are freed from such religious nesting and enter the domain of a people's cultural environment. The incorporation of onions in Indian cuisine is one such example. Architectural forms such as the *haveli*—an upper-class house form common to both Muslims and Hindus—afford another example (cf. Pramar 1987). At the other extreme, the landscape and customs prevalent at the time of a religion's genesis influence what is regarded as sacred by its adherents. The diffusion of such practices has considerably accelerated in the present global context.

What we characterize as world religions today have sites and episodes associated with the nativity and lives of their prophets. The re-creation of this landscape through enactment and the visual arts forms a part of religious practice that interacts with pre-existing religious traditions. For Muslims living outside the Middle East, local practices were gradually influenced by the architectural styles of mosques and the dietary taboos of that region (eating pork, for instance), and their manner of disposing of the dead.

Differing religious traditions, moreover, make demands on and sacralize the natural environment to a greater or lesser extent. The Hindu practice of cremating the dead entails the consumption of vast quantities of wood, to take just one example. Again, religious symbols in India have extensively utilized materials from the natural environment—livestock, trees, and even routes to sacred sites. The practice of religion has led to the nurture of plants, trees, forests, and livestock with sacred associations (Gadgil and Vartak 1998). However, the utilitarian concern of environmentalists with the preservation of sacred groves, for instance, sometimes falls short of fathoming the roots of sacredness and the contexts and contests in which it is embedded.

For environmental sociologists, religious texts, oral narratives, and ritual practices in India enable one to fathom the characteristic flora and fauna and the built environment of a region or a period together with their symbolic associations. The cultural ecology of the sacred cow in India has been a protracted subject for anthropological debate and is periodically re-visited (Harris 1966; Heston 1971; Vaidyanathan et al. 1982). Again, Zimmerman's (1987) textual exegesis has drawn attention to the religious significance of the antelope and shifts in the meaning of terms such as 'jungle' over time. These linguistic shifts, Dove (1994) suggests, reflect the changing 'ecological reality' of the region. Aspects that may appear incidental to religious concerns are evidently relevant from an environmental perspective.

Lastly, whether the life of animals is conceived as different from or akin to human beings, is still a live question for bio-ethics, environmental studies, and religious beliefs (Smith and Doniger 1989). In this regard what particular religions have to offer may be of value to both students of comparative religion and environmentalists. While all religions are anthropocentric, their eschatological premises are distinct and entail diverse implications for behaviour vis-à-vis the plant and animal world.

II

COMBINATORIAL MODES OF SUBSISTENCE

In this part of the chapter, I start by delineating modes of subsistence that ecologically oriented anthropologists have long worked with (Ellen 1994), drawing attention to both their strengths and limitations. I argue that a unitary mode of subsistence, such as hunting and gathering or pastoral transhumance, is an inadequate depiction of how livelihoods are obtained contemporarily, and I propose the idea of 'combinatorial' modes of subsistence that combine incipient forms and practices. The second section attempts to capture the impact of combinatorial modes of subsistence upon the environment by using the idea of ecological involution. The third section briefly explores the embeddedness of local modes of substinence in wider occupational and religious cultures and the final section seeks to view these modes in the context of the nation state and increasing globalization. Though the focus is on the contemporary period it may be necessary, at times, to elucidate the argument by reference to the past.

Modes of Subsistence

What is striking in India today is the sizeable and growing population of men, women, and children who derive their subsistence in close interaction with nature, using a variety of tools, techniques, technologies, and habitats. This subsistence takes the shape of garnering, harvesting, fishing, hunting, domesticating, and/or snaring flora and fauna for domestic use, barter, and/or sale; transforming the natural environment with both simple and mechanized technologies, to yield foodgrains and other vegetative produce; artisanal activity that draws on both the produce of nature and manufactured items, as in the production of items such as cloth and pots or dwellings that use plastic sheets and thatches; and participation in both the natural economy and the state/industrial sector, (as when the husband works in an office and the wife looks after the cattle and/or forages for fuel). This listing is suggestive. The modalities and strategies on the ground are multi-dimensional, drawing on the specific, local potential and context, the division of labour and specialization along the lines of class, caste, age, and gender as well as the seasonal and declining availability of flora, fauna, water, forage, fossil fuels, and other inputs.

Overarchingly, the milieux of subsistence involve working with and upon nature. The central problematic for us is to think of categories and concepts that enable us to express this diversity as well as its ecological consequences.

A mode of subsistence is a useful, analytic device that enables us to apprehend collective practices in relation to a nature-based economy (Ellen 1994). By inquiring into the specific types of labour entailed in practices upon nature; the levels of technology; and the acquisition of skills through socialization and apprenticeship in particular ecological contexts, we can develop the material aspects of a subsistence mode. The cosmology characteristic of a mode of livelihood also invites study. However, what is of greater significance at present is the preponderance of combinatorial modes of subsistence. The divergence from a former collective tradition entails that the meaning of the new combinations cannot be expressed other than as fragments of a cosmology. The delineation and synthesis of combinatorial modes can address both individual and household strategies that diverge from or conform along lines of gender, age, and group tradition, and thus enable subsistence. I shall also try to clarify why combinatorial modes of subsistence do not easily fit into the classification of hunters and gatherers, nomadic pastoralists or agriculturists, and industrial workers.

Hunting

The ethnographic accounts of anthropologists draw attention to the distinctive, if obvious, ecological contexts in which inhabitants seek a livelihood: hunting and food gathering with or without cultivation in forests; fishing in coastal, riverine or other water-rich areas; pastoralism in mountains, hills, and deserts; and agriculture in fertile valleys and plains. At a level beyond the descriptive, anthropologists also distinguish hunters and gatherers as a stage in human history (Ehrenfels 1952) as a type of society stressing immediate rather than deferred exchange (Woodburn 1982); as a mode of subsistence enabling economic specialization in marginal environments (Fox 1969); as specifying the activity of an encapsulated population in a post-agricultural world (Woodburn 1988); and as societies characterized by the ethic of sharing (Bird-David 1990).

At one extreme in India, we find hunters and gatherers closest to the anthropological pure type among the Sentinelese of the North Sentinel Island (in the Andaman Islands group). The Sentinelese contact with the population outside the island is limited even today to the biannual visits of officials by boat. We still do not know what the Sentinelese call themselves (Pandit 1994). What we do know is that they live by trapping fish and other marine produce, hunting and gathering, and are still separated from other islands by a sea that is not navigable by country boats. So far the Government of India has been prevailed upon to restrict its contacts, although this strategy is reviewed periodically.

The Jarawas of the North Andaman Islands, again, continue to hunt, gather, and fish as a way of life (Sarkar 1990; Awaradi 1990). However, the resettlement of the Bangladesh refugees on these islands has led to the construction of the Andaman Grand Trunk Road, making inroads into what the Jarawas view as their territory (Awaradi 1990). The incursions of other inhabitants and the state continue to be resisted by the Jarawas through the use of bows and arrows with near-deadly effect.

The Andamanese and the Onges, who were formerly hunters and gatherers, are now sedentarized and live in state-supervised enclaves. The dramatic decline in the numbers of both the Andamanese and the Onges (Myka 1995), in the face of the encounter with the outside world, has kept the question of what the state should do (and should not do) alive for the Jarawas and the Sentinelese.

Hunting, gathering, and fishing that excludes any form of agriculture is probably characteristic of the Sentinelese and the Jarawas alone. It is plausible to visualize these groups as constituting a society, albeit one affected by the state. However, it may be pertinent to note that the island economies of the Andamans were particularly conducive to impenetrability and the reliance on marine foods complemented hunting (cf. Pandya 1993). On the mainland, however, combinations of hunting, gathering and swidden cultivation, along with wage work, are prevalent.

The idea of what constitutes a hunting and gathering society for groups whose members are in regular contact with contractors, state functionaries, peasants, members of state legislatures, and other outsiders is more indeterminate. Often, those who relied more on hunting and gathering in the past were identified as hunting and gathering tribes but this classification is problematic in the contemporary context given the fact that the latter, too, now practise agriculture and seek out wage labour. The notion of distinctive forms of in-group and out-group sociality may be of greater heuristic value than the conception of a society here (cf. Strathern 1991). Furthermore, the clubbing of hunting and gathering as a single form of subsistence is adequate only for conceptualizing subsistence at the level of households, since within the domestic unit it is primarily the men who hunt and largely the women who gather.

Second, hunting also exists as an opportunistic strategy for groups that have not been identified as hunters and gatherers. For instance, in the mountainous regions of Nepal and Ladakh, hunting is resorted to by pastoralists who transhume with their flocks. This practice enables them to ward off predators on domestic flocks but the game is subsequently consumed. Again, in the agricultural mainland as well, hunting is the forte of nomadic groups such as the Bagariyas and Kalbelias in Rajasthan and the Phasepardhis in Maharashtra (Gadgil and Malhotra 1994). Their services are hired by agriculturists to snare birds and mammals who destroy the cultivated crops. Such hunting may be viewed as an adjunct of agriculture but, nevertheless, leads to the depletion of wild life. The Rajputs, again, continue to hunt game such as rabbits and blackbuck, now with guns (Fisher 1997), both as traditional sport and for delicacy meats. Both former and new entrants to hunting, trap or hunt birds and animals for produce that has a market—skin, fur, feather, musk, and other animal produce.

More often than not, hunting now forms a part of a set of subsistence practices. However, it would be an error to overlook the importance of hunting for those tribes for whom it was a way of life. The diminution of the fauna itself (in the face of agricultural extensification) certainly contributed to their impoverishment. The empirical evidence suggests that the territorial rights of former hunters and gatherers were not adequately cognized and this derecognition contributed to their decline and immiserization. Their increasing recourse to agriculture was spurred as the state's land policies veered towards a conception of either private agrarian rights or exclusive state control over forests, without an appreciation of subsistence that was enabled by customary and combinatorial practices of hunting, gathering, and cultivation.

Pastoral Nomadism

The same arguments, in fact, extend to pastoral nomads who are not found anywhere in the subcontinent as a pure type subsisting without any cultivation. Members of pastoralist groups now engage in agriculture apart from practising pastoral transhumance. This is the contemporary picture even where their group names may suggest a tradition of pastoralism, as with the Gujjars or Yadavs, or where their oral narratives may attest such practices until the recent past, as among the Gaddis of Himachal Pradesh (Bhasin 1990) or the Raikas of Rajasthan (Srivastava 1997; Kavoori 1999). Here, again, while private fields are deployed for agriculture, the forage resources of a wider range are utilized for pasturage in a seasonal cycle. As with hunting and gathering, it is the combination of agriculture and pastoral transhumance that makes it viable presently as a form of subsistence (Bhasin 1990).

The trends within part-agriculturists and part-pastoral nomads are as complex and novel as those within the hunters. Groups such as the Jats who were primarily agriculturists and raised livestock for domestic and agricultural use, have now taken to the rearing of smaller animal species and pastoral transhumance alongside agriculture. The shift to smaller species is prompted by the greater economic returns from raising goats for mutton and sheep for wool. As a combinatorial practice, small-animal husbandry dovetails well with one-crop agriculture in areas of uncertain rainfall as in western Rajasthan (Brara 1987). The recent entrants to transhumance speak of the finely honed skills of the traditional nomadic groups, such as the Raikas, and attempt to learn some of their techniques. However, it is by and large the men who transhume with their flocks while the women remain on the farms.

This incipient form of pastoral transhumance avails of the complementary opportunities afforded by changes in the technologies of mobility and agriculture. The truck now affords a means of transporting livestock over long stretches of lean pasturage en route to fodder-rich tracts. Moreover, the pattern of two-crop agriculture enabled by irrigation provides pastoralists with crop stubble in private fields away from home. Such grazing is mutually advantageous as the farmer-hosts benefit from the animal droppings as well.

The new complementarities reinforce the view that while pastoral nomadism of a near-pure type is rare, the viability of a combination of transhumance and agriculture has assumed greater significance. Limits to the pastoral enterprise are increasingly set by the boundaries of a nation state, in contrast to the former natural frontiers such as mountains or a coast. However, the effects of this transformation are mitigated by shared ethnicities across borders, apparent especially in the frontier zones of the north-east, in Kashmir, and along the border of western Rajasthan.

While the practice of transhumance exploits the seasonal availability of water and pasturage in an annual cycle, the migration route itself varies depending on conditions within the nation state and the availability of fodder/water. For instance, the state of Madhya Pradesh sought to close its forests to graziers from the state of Rajasthan (Kavoori 1999). This move was later overruled by the Supreme Court since it infringed upon the citizen's right to move freely within the Indian nation state. But such incidents of resistance to the movement of pastoralists are recurrent.

The number of livestock rearers in the country, however, far exceeds the number of pastoral nomads/transhumans whom anthropologists tend to privilege as a category (Galaty 1981). Most rural inhabitants keep livestock (varying from yaks in mountainous regions to camels in the desert and elephants in forest tracts) that are fed on the vegetative resources of uncultivated lands, in addition to stall feeding. The bullock is still synonymous with Indian agriculture even while the use of tractors gains ground. Livestock (such as cows, buffaloes, hens, pigs, goats, yaks, horses, and asses) are also commonly reared by sedentary agriculturists for various uses—mutton, milk, wool, hides, draught power, etc. From an environmental angle, it is vital to note that the stall feeding of livestock is conceived largely as a supplement to the pasturage that is found in the common lands. The higher- milk-yielding exotic cows (often called *vilaiti*) and the smaller cross-bred livestock are considered to be more expensive to maintain by the vast majority of livestock-rearers who prefer the low-yielding indigenous breeds that can survive on scrub (Brara 1987).

The large numbers of livestock have adverse implications for the vegetative cover of the country that go beyond considering the impact of pastoral transhumance alone. For sedentary villagers, too, it is the combination of animal husbandry and agriculture that provides a viable means of subsistence at present but nevertheless leads to environmental degradation through overdriving. Again, while pastoral nomadism has attracted considerable anthropological research, less emphasis has been placed on the itinerant provisioning of services and entertaining that utilizes animals (Arora and Haldar 1994). The study of the latter may enhance our understanding of combinatorial nomadic and itinerant modes.

As a peninsula, India has a vast coastline that is exploited through maritime pursuits, including the fishing and trapping of a variety of aquatic produce. The streams, rivers, and ponds that dot the countryside furnish additional water bodies for cultivating and harvesting aquatic species. Lately, fishing and pisciculture have been resorted to by agriculturists primarily to augment their cash earnings, while home-grown cereals on private farms constitute the basis of domestic consumption. By and large, indigenous techniques of fishing prevail although the numbers of both mechanized trawlers and diesel-operated boats is rising.

Fishing along the coast is often believed to provide access to the common resource of the sea thereby affording its practitioners an autonomy from hierarchies that are based on the ownership of land. However, Ram (1992) shows that fishing in the commons of the sea is the prerogative of men while women engage in gathering marine produce from the coast and small-time selling. Women thus assume the role of gatherers in modes of subsistence ranging from fishing, hunting, agriculture to the industrial/modern sector.

Settled Agriculture

The practice of agriculture rests upon a combination that utilizes private fields for the cultivation of crops and the resources of a wider range for fodder, fuel, fibre, timber, and medicine. As such, settled cultivation works in conjunction with subsistence afforded by other modes such as gathering, animal husbandry, and artisanship that utilize the commons.

The village is, of course, the characteristic site of agriculture. At the level of the village, cooperation among residents is evident in utilizing the produce of the commons, in allocating water rights (Wade 1988), and in safeguarding the interests of the village as a collectivity vis-à-vis other villages. Traditions of cooperative labour in the village vary with ecological and social contexts but still enable villagers to harness water for irrigation, to take just one example. Mencher ([1966] 1994) notes that the nucleation of villages in Tamil Nadu drew on the construction of a collective water facility while the dispersed character of villages in Kerala accorded with the easy availability of water.

The specific crops grown, methods of cultivation, and levels of technology vary greatly between different ecological regimes and entail diverse modalities in the pooling of labour both within and between households of cultivators. Béteille (1975) observes that the demands on agricultural labour differ significantly between wheat growing and rice cultivation. Agricultural practices also allow for combinations of old and new technologies. At one end of the array, simple devices using human and animal musculature nevertheless require skills that have to be learned, cultivated, and transmitted in the context of specific ecologies. Combinations of part-mechanization, part-manual labour and mixes of indigenous and high-yielding varieties of crops are frequent in the middle. Capital-intensive agriculture using agricultural machinery, high-yielding varieties of crops and trees (often in monoculture), fertilizers, and pesticides characterizes the other end of this spectrum. Defining agriculture as a unitary mode of subsistence in the Indian context, then, is insufficient for an understanding of how livelihoods are obtained and the strategies deployed at the household level.

The greater use of capital-intensive technology, evident in the deployment of fertilizers, canal irrigation, and electricity, or diesel-operated lift-pumps, makes for higher productivity and enables the harvesting of two crops in areas of formerly one-crop agriculture. However, such technology has a negative impact on the environment and human health. The ecological consequences of chemical fertilizers, pesticides, soil salinity, declining yields of crops, and lowered water tables over time are now being addressed. The adverse implications of canal irrigation on human health and the lives of those affected by the displacement caused by gigantic dams are increasingly being documented and their voices are being heard, a subject that this chapter shall return to in Part III.

The legal system in India, as elsewhere, distinguishes the villager's right in arable fields from the rights of villagers over common tracts. What were formerly non-arable tracts, however, have been continuously depleted or taken over by the state for commercial extraction or plantations. This aspect of the country's record has been well documented by environmental historians for the colonial period (Grove 1995; Grove 1998; Grove et al. 1998; Guha and Arnold 1995; Tucker 1988).

In the post-colonial era as well, the codification of private rights in land through a settlement, under conditions of a rising population, facilitated the appropriation of the commons by the state or led to its privatization, affecting the interests of the users of the commons as commons (Singh 1986). Such privatization was often ratified in law by recourse to legal and illegal means by villagers who had the wherewithal to use the law courts to their advantage. The processes of state-abetted agricultural extensification, moreover, did not consider that uses other than agriculture were vital to modes of subsistence based upon the produce of the commons (Jodha 1986).

Moreover, combinations of swidden cultivation and hunting or animal husbandry and dryland agriculture required more extensive tracts for their viability but this aspect was overlooked in the legislation concerning land rights (Jodha 1986). Strikingly, the laws of the modern state conduced toward the recognition of private rights in arable tracts (although circumscribed by rules that made them less than absolute) and the investiture of the non-arable commons in the state. Collective and customary rights, intermediate between the state at one extreme and the private landholder at the other, were not adequately cognized in the statutory laws and proved to be deterimental for the users of the commons (Brara 1989, 1992).

Ecological Involution

The implications of a growing density of human beings and animals that live on the natural resource base and deploy what are here termed combinatorial modes is succinctly expressed by the notion of 'ecological involution'. I adapt the term ecological involution from Geertz's ([1963] 1968) well-known conception of 'agricultural involution'. Geertz drew on Goldenweiser's (1936) insights into involution in order to denote the 'overdriving of an established form in such a way that it becomes rigid through an inward over-elaboration of detail' (Geertz 1968: 82). The suggestion of rigidity is lacking in Goldenweiser's formulation. As he puts it (writing on Maori art): 'What we have here is pattern plus continued development. ... The inevitable result is progressive complication. ... This is involution. ... Being hemmed in on all sides by a crystallized pattern, it takes the function of elaborateness' (Goldenweiser 1936, quoted in Geertz 1968: 81).

As a concept, ecological involution allows us to express and apprehend the characteristic pattern of closely working the land surface for fuel, flora, and fauna by staying attuned to its daily/weekly possibilities instead of the formerly seasonal dimensions. Similarly, the existing water sources are now exploited at greater depths and longer distances. In the metropolises, too, atmospheric pollution spirals and intensifies due to a rising number of old automobiles and polluting industries. As such, the notion of ecological involution enables us to communicate the involutional utilization of time, labour, and space (residential, arable, and non-arable) in rural and urban areas.

The processual aspects of ecological involution may be illustrated by drawing on a village study in Rajasthan (Brara 1987). The effects of both agricultural intensification and agricultural extensification lead to ecological involution at the village level. Boserup ([1976] 1988) argues that the use of technological inputs is stimulated by the need to support larger numbers on the same farm but agricultural intensification is only one of the consequences of the increasing pressure on land. The reduction in the size and duration of fallows is the first impact of agricultural intensification. However, since capital is scarce, agricultural intensification by technological improvements can be afforded only by a few households who then mine the groundwater for irrigation by investing in pump-sets for lifting water. Households with ample labour still have to combine agriculture with the extraction of the resources of the commons for pasturage, fibre, timber, etc., for their subsistence.

The strategy of agricultural expansion is also pursued by villagers. It often takes the form of encroachment in the commons through the process of illegal cultivation, largely by households who can later influence the bureaucratic machinery. Such encroachment, in turn, leads to a compression of a greater number of livestock users on denuded pastures. Its involutional aspects are apparent in the landscape of the commons.

To take the example of a village study in Rajasthan, (Brara 1987) the exploitation of the preferred trees, at first, is followed by the utilization of the less-desirable trees till a point is reached when there are hardly any young trees in the commons. Continuous grazing precludes the shrubs from attaining their potential heights. The ephemeral rain-fed grasses/sedges come to constitute the chief component of the understorey, in contrast with the former perennial grasses. However, it is important to note that even this vegetation is vital to the users for their subsistence.

Instead of private *khejri* (*Prosopis cineraria*) trees, the khejri trees of the commons are now pruned annually and no longer yield the pods that were a valuable food item. The use of this species in the commons shows a movement from the utilization of its optimal portions to sub-optimal parts while it still continues to be closely worked.

At the same time, territorial boundaries are increasingly drawn around the pastures so as to close their access to neighbouring villagers while within the village the number of its users (especially the less-landed households) vastly increases. This is precisely what we seek to grasp as involution that has both social and ecological consequences.

The pursuit of animal husbandry gains ground as its expansion can utilize the commons and additional labour at the household level, in contrast to the relative constancy of agricultural requirements. The labour required for grazing, moreover, is adequately provided for by older members and children while the able-bodied adults work at agriculture or seek other employment. The lack of employment avenues, in fact, contributes to the overdriving of animal husbandry but makes subsistence possible.

The waning of ritual/caste taboos against the rearing of livestock today, and further, the profitability of the enterprise, lead to its practice by members of diverse caste groups, thus compounding the effects of involution. Over time a shift is discernible from the larger species of livestock to the smaller species that can be sustained under the deteriorating forage conditions.

At the same time, nomadic pastoralism that was formerly the forte of specialist castes/tribes in Rajasthan, for instance, is now practised by Jats and Rajputs as well. As a consequence, seasonal forages in uncultivated tracts, such as forest stretches, now have to reckon with larger numbers of graziers. Further, the transhumant graziers are increasingly permitted shorter halts in the villages since villagers allow them the right to passage but not the now-scarce pasturage.

For agriculturists, ground water for irrigation has to be pumped from continuously declining depths thus increasing the salinity of the soil and an increase in the energy expenditure on pumping. In some villages in Rajasthan, the incidence of salinity has compelled farmers to desist from irrigation or to let the irrigated land remain fallow for the subsequent cycle. Elsewhere, farmers are shifting to salinity-resistant crops or other combinatorial subsistence modes that vary with local configurations. However, alternatives to agro-pastoral livelihoods are few and while there is elaboration and change within the system, there is scarce transformation of the basic design.

The utilization of forests shows the same trends. Often, the selective felling of trees has been followed by clear felling (Gadgil and Guha 1992). Agricultural extensification, as in the forest tracts of Bastar in Madhya Pradesh, entails competition in the use of land between sedentary rice cultivators and the Koitors who practise shifting cultivation (Savyasaachi 1991). The latter practice is rendered less productive as the land : man ratio worsens. The extension of the agricultural frontier here does not imply that the land is unencumbered by other uses such as gathering, swidden cultivation, or hunting. In the presence of pre-existing human users and uses, the effects are again competitive.

An involutional turn at the level of the region is evident when graziers from other states are barred entry into forests outside the states where they reside (Kavoori 1999). At the same time, forests are mined for new commodities, for worse ore and timber, new medicinal substances, and foliage by new groups of users. In the wake of increasing extraction, the forms of resistance often take the shape of ethnic or religious movements to safeguard the particular concerns of social groups.

Aspects of urban involution, too, are not unrelated to what happens in rural areas. The migration of rural labour to the towns and cities often entails that while men work for wages, the women continue their quest for fuel, fodder, and water, albeit in changed circumstances. The grazing of livestock in urban parks, again, sets off an involutional chain as green reserves come to be barricaded from opportunistic but, nevertheless, subsistence uses. Since dwelling spaces extend to pavement shelters and slums (Smailes [1969] 1986), the Indian town/city can support a large population. The number of persons per dwelling unit, too, is high (ibid.). At the same time, common pavements are also utilized as shop extensions (sometimes for the storage of hazardous chemicals) and as work spaces for a variety of pursuits ranging from tailoring to itinerant entertaining. Such pursuits, however, are scarcely feasible without involving state functionaries who turn a blind eye to these illegal uses; but the involutional spiral continues.

The concentration of polluting factories in or near cities, along with an increasing number of old and new automobiles, contributes to the spiralling atmospheric pollution that is now beginning to tell on the health of urban dwellers (Mukul 1997). But here, again, lacunae in the implementation of regulatory laws belie their effectiveness in the face of diverse and competing rationalities.

The process of ecological involution, then, evidently arises from the elaboration of a largely nature-based mode of subsistence and the lack of a highly capital-intensive technological transformation. In this sense it has its basis in a slow-moving economy that participates only gradually and selectively in the time and space of the industrial world.

Combinatorial Modes and Culture

Combinatorial modes of subsistence are the products of human culture and involve a physical regimen of the body and knowledge that has to be acquired in a specific context to enable human subsistence from nature. The transformation of nature through the specific qualities of labour makes it difficult to conceive of subsistence as the generic or behavioural value-addition by a population. To pose the question of who does what and why is to introduce the idea of a societal division of labour. Its meaningfulness, however, is premised on the beliefs of a particular culture.

The cultural metaphors of livelihood in India continue to draw upon the vast repertoire of caste orientations. Different jatis have distinctive techniques for exploiting nature. To cite some examples: jatis differ from proximate jatis by their manner of casting a fishing net (Deb 1996), the type of livestock raised or animal hunted (Gadgil and Malhotra 1994), the type of agriculture practised (cereal farming or vegetable growing), or the variety of fibre used for basket making (Gadgil and Guha 1992). Such specialization often fosters *in situ* knowledge in the specificity of a particular habitat that is codified in life-worlds and local dialects rather than textual traditions. Grove (1995) attempts to show that the knowledge of flora gathered by the toddy-tappers in Kerala contributed to taxonomical advances in botany during the colonial period.

Gadgil and Malhotra (1994) observe that in certain tracts of Maharashtra each jati exploits a distinctive ecological niche while lineages within a jati exercise territorial jurisdiction over demarcated tracts. Thus the Tirumal Nandiwallas hunt the larger animals with the aid of dogs, the Vaidus specialize in snaring small carnivores with the help of squirrels, and the Phasepardhis catch deer and birds (Gadgil and Malhotra 1994). Among the artisan and the service castes as well the right to work in particular territories or for certain lineages is considered heritable and can be alienated only within the caste.

Again, the study of rural settlement sites brings out the close association of ecology, ethnicity, and the knowledge of particular cultivation/pastoral techniques, especially at the time of the founding of villages. For instance, Grover's (1985) study shows that the Jats, Gujars, Kanets, and Rajputs exploited distinctive ecological spaces and created characteristic landscapes and settlement patterns in northern Haryana. The Jats who practised settled farming were located in fertile, flat stretches in the vicinity of water sources. Extensive tracts of low agricultural productivity afforded a satisfactory habitat for the Gujars. Their circular settlements enabled the tethering and stall-feeding of cattle. The Kanets cultivated the hill slopes with sickles. And the Rajputs who had historically obtained their rights to a share of the produce through conquest, often had raised settlement sites underscoring considerations of defence, flood proofing, and higher status.

However, it is also important to recognize that the loosening of the fit between jati and occupation has been a recurrent process in India. The term Jat, for instance, is often appended to a group that takes to agriculture as in the Jat-Balais of Rajasthan. While agriculture was open to several castes in the past as well, the overlap of occupations between different jatis is increasingly attested. For instance, the husbandry of small animals such as goats and sheep is now practised by Jats (Brara 1987; Kavoori 1999) and the formerly nomadic caste groups have adopted settled cultivation (Srivastava 1997). Fishing, too, is increasingly attractive for castes other than those for whom it was a traditional occupation (cf. Deb 1996). The implications of niche expansion need to be studied in order to gauge whether the process is a consequence or a cause of the relaxation of caste taboos along lines of ritual purity and impurity—a change in the form and content of the caste system. The loosening of the fit between caste, occupation, and ritual status also has implications for our understanding of both cultural resilience and change. On the one hand, the loosening of caste taboos fuses groups together as Hindu, Muslim, Dalit, and Adivasi, stressing larger cultural entities than caste. On the other hand, the former hierarchical, cultural connotations of caste are preserved as markers of superior identity, despite changes in the mode of subsistence, as among the Rajputs. Cultural markers of status are abandoned, if they are negative as well. Several members of artisan and service castes today use identities/names that do not reveal their traditional occupation, indicating the extent to which such labelling was an act of power and has been overcome by changes in occupation.

Each mode of subsistence is often thought to generate a characteristic culture. Thus the ethic of sharing is commonly regarded as the leitmotif of hunters. In this vein, their relationship with the environment is conceived as one of kinship to a parent or ancestor who provides the resources for sustenance. Springs, rocks, and other physical features are believed to be animated by the spirit of ancestors whose initial ventures lay out the terrain for collective rights in a certain territory. Now that Adivasis also engage in plantation or wage work, cognizance has to be taken of the altered situation. Bird-David (1992) observes that among the Nayaks of the Nilgiris, it is wage work that is 'incorporated' in their way of life and not vice versa.

However, the situation appears to be more complex when viewed over the span of generations. Some hunters and gatherers take to agriculture and often the collective, 'objectified' name distinguishes a group's identity but allows for various modes of subsistence. Or, again, the group may split itself into two sections with different names or coalesce under a wider appellation as is the case with the Adivasi at present. Sometimes the memory of the past comes to be encapsulated in ritual alone, as among the Santals who mark the onset of the agricultural season with a ritual hunt (Archer 1975). Similarly, Hindus who have taken to the modern professions now follow the formerly agrarian cycle of rites and festivals as a part of their religious practice.

Again, if we consider nomadic pastoralism, it is often averred that this mode of subsistence nurtures an ideology of rugged independence. Ahmed (1983), for instance, suggests that nomadic transhumance can be viewed as an expression of and a preference for an autonomous way of life. While autonomy may be a characteristic of the pastoralist pursuit in the north-west of the subcontinent, Srivastava's (1997) study of the Raikas (who engage in pastoral nomadism in Rajasthan), shows that in the milieu of Hindu beliefs, renunciation is their characteristic mode of religious expression.

Metaphors of agriculture in India frequently draw upon the imagery of sexual symbolism—the earth is considered to be female and fertile and the acts of ploughing and the planting of seeds are viewed as analogous to the male function. New representations of agriculture utilize more contemporary notions as well. The conception of 'hybrid' seeds enables the voicing of a host of novel phenomena within agriculture and social life (Vasavi 1994). The expression 'vilaiti' or western, similarly, enables the articulation of the distinctive qualities of tree species, cross-bred animals, technologies, and cultures that are contrasted with the desi or indigenous.

Combinatorial Modes of Subsistence, the Nation State, and Globalization

The longue duree of human cultures and subsistence patterns is often sought to be understood in terms of contrasts such as simple/complex, pre-industrial/industrial, or by modes of production and their variants. What are the advantages and pitfalls of such characterization for the ecological context of India?

In many ways, it is plausible to characterize India's nature-based economy today as pre-industrial and peasant-oriented but this overlooks the capitalist sector in agriculture and industry. Within agriculture, the panorama is one of many peasants who utilize agricultural machinery, irrigation, and fertilizers in varying degrees and combinations. The products of the industrial revolution, in fact, enable nature-based livelihoods in India to remain viable in transformed contexts not only by a selective mix of tractors and bullocks, for instance, but if we look deeper, by the kaleidoscopic assembly of parts at each level.

The industrial mode feeds into the combinatorial modes of subsistence but the constraints of capital preclude it from constituting its basis and, in this sense, the inhabitants cannot avail of known technologies. On the other hand, to simply argue that industrialization threatens rural livelihoods or is environmentally damaging is to overlook the variety of ways in which the products of the industrial revolution feed into the subsistence strategies of the poor. These emergent modes of subsistence grow out of the larger patterns of national culture. Often, comparisons of the culture of farmers qua farmers or hunters as hunters underestimate the extent to which such groups are affected by the ways of a particular nation state.

At the same time, the sitting of polluting factories and risky technologies fuel public concern (Mukul 1997). The chemical gas leak at Bhopal, again, brought out the extent to which developing countries are vulnerable to the risks of high technology (Srivastava 1987; Das 1995). Again, enclaves of industrial development, in and around cities especially, and their excessive pollution levels reveal an environmental impact that is higher than that of more industrialized countries. Moreover, in the present context of globalization, the relocation of manufacturing in developing countries is likely to intensify environmental degradation in this country.

On the ground, one can locate factories and capitalists who employ industrial workers and use raw materials grown and harvested by rural inhabitants—yarn mills, food-processing industries, etc. Automobiles, agricultural machinery, electronic goods, chemicals, and fertilizers are also manufactured in the country. Yet the capitalists do not have a role, even in the economy, that is on par with the state in India which controls from its commanding height—no less significant than the role of the state in the former socialist economies. The capitalists are viewed as being licensed by the state which is perceived as the chief player here.

The state is also by far the largest employer, landlord, and master of the country's natural resource base. The clout of state functionaries is attested at all levels from the local to the national signifying a continuity in the colonial and post-colonial systems of government. It constitutes a new form of domination based on the construction of rules as instruments of control.

New forms of law that derecognize customary and collective rights over nature by sanctioning alternative uses affect subsistence patterns with the stroke of a pen, rendering them illegal and vulnerable to the dragnet of law-enforcement agencies. Most conflicts over the resources of nature are, first and foremost, directed against the state and constitute the running thread of everyday issues that are protested and resisted. The statutory laws and accompanying rules that claim to be in the national interest, however, often continue to be incomprehensible to the vast majority.

Abraham and Rosencranz (1986) observe that the laws set up for environmental protection follow the practice of other countries closely except for the principle of popular participation. Even when the verdicts of law courts run counter to the policies of the state, as with the phased closure of polluting units, for example, the politician-and-bureaucrat combine succeeds in whittling down the directives on the ground. Punitive action is seldom taken against the law breakers.

People and ecological regimes are evidently embedded in the framework of nation states and the larger frame of globalization in the present times. Even when India's rural inhabitants feature in global debates, it is seldom on their own terms. The West's interest in global biodiversity, sustainable development, or indigenous/ecosystemic people sets an agenda which is sought to be recast in terms of national aspirations and less often by the aspirations that rural or poorer inhabitants may have for themselves. What appears to western anthropologists and environmentalists as the diversity of forms of livelihood that draw on nature is often perceived as inequality vis-à-vis contemporary modes of subsistence in the West. It is in this context that spokespersons for the environmentalist cause in India make out a case for eco-justice in global fora. But whose definitions prevail in the hierarchy of environmental discourse, continues to be a moot issue.

III

ENVIRONMENT AND THE PUBLIC SPHERE

My attempt in this part of the chapter is to outline a sociological perspective to some of the environmental issues that resonate in public life, academia, and activist circles. The gamut of posers on the environmental movement is captured in questions such as the following. Is there an environmental movement in the country? Is it a new social movement? Can it be characterized in the singular? What are its discernible characteristics, ideologies, and objectives? Who are its leaders and what is their praxes? To whom is the struggle directed against? In what manner are we to apprehend its linkages with the global environmental movement as well as its distinctiveness in the Indian milieu?

The trajectory of a singular environmental movement in India may be difficult to draw as multi-sited events constitute the environmental discourse. Again, what are termed the 'new social movements' (Melucci 1980, Habermas 1981) worldwide are believed to garner support along lines of 'personal and moral conviction' and not class per se (Touraine 1984). An understanding of environmental struggles and initiatives can improve our appreciation of both the old and the new dimensions of the environmental movement as a social movement in the Indian context (cf. Guha 1992).

Here I shall focus upon three archetypes of environmental representations and struggles in India. These are the collective struggles against interventions that jeopardize subsistence from nature, considering the Chipko movement as archetype; the role of voluntary bodies in the environmental effort, especially the initiative of the Centre for Science and Environment; and finally the Narmada anti-dam agitation as epitomizing the rising resistance to the construction of large dams.

Chipko as Archetype

Collective action and struggle to retain control over the use of natural resources critical to subsistence is commonly attested in a variety of locations all over India contemporarily, as in the pre-Independence period (Gadgil and Guha 1993, Rangarajan 1996, Grove et al. 1998). Its expression assumes a range of forms, from contravening statutory laws to spontaneous outbursts that Scott (1986) succinctly characterizes as 'weapons of the weak'.

One such struggle over a resource and its meaning occurred in 1972 when women in the Garhwal region hugged trees to prevent them from being felled by a sports-goods contractor licensed by the state. This resistance was effective in restraining tree felling locally and it later captured the environmentalist imagination worldwide. The Chipko movement became an archetype for an environmental form of resistance to the felling of trees both in India (Buchy 1996) and abroad, contributing to the building up of an environmental consciousness.

The hugging of trees by women to prevent them from being lopped was first documented among the Bishnois in Jodhpur (Rajasthan). They protested in this manner against agents who were acting on behalf of the ruler of this princely state during the pre-Independence period. On learning of the incident, the ruler revoked his orders. As an intellectual resource, we do not know whether the idea of embracing trees had travelled from Rajasthan or arose spontaneously from a similar cultural soil or 'habitus' in Bourdieu's (1977) sense. The image of a woman embracing a tree as a divine spirit or as she would her child (cf. McCully 1996) is one that men cannot violate with impunity.

The Chipko movement became an object of study as well. The incident has been interpreted from a variety of perspectives—peasant revolts, ecofeminism, and women's subsistence interests. Did the Chipko movement have its roots in the former struggles of the inhabitants of this region to retain control over forests? Guha (1988a) suggests that it is comprehensible as one such flash-point in a continuous line of peasant resistance.

Is the Chipko movement to be understood as an attempt at gender justice? Ecofeminism, a term first coined by the French writer Françoise d'Eaubonne (1974), called attention to the simultaneous subordination of nature and women in the wake of the scientific/industrial revolution. Drawing on her experiences in the Garhwal region, Shiva (1984) offers an Indian rendition of ecofeminism. She argues that the ascendancy of patriarchy in conjunction with colonialism and western science undermined the indigenous thought system that envisaged a cosmic balance of feminine and masculine principles.

The applicability of Shiva's position is evidently inadequate for non-Hindu Indians. The position, however, is untenable because it is simplistic to infer the status of women from the status of deities and cosmic conceptions among the Hindus as well. Beliefs about the malevolent aspects of female sexuality, the sacredness of mothers but the inauspiciousness of widows (Tapper 1979), in fact, represent a cultural male-centred view that cannot easily be reconciled with ecofeminism as promulgated by Shiva (1984).

Evidently, the interests of women, too, are amenable to analysis that employs the conception of class (Agarwal 1992, Shiva and Mies 1993). The concern with gender probed further, however, points to the contradictory interests of women along the axis of power as well, such that the environmental interests of a daughter-in-law and a mother-in-law may not coincide (Jackson 1993). In situations of ambivalent tenure women, too, overexploit forest resources (Kelkar and Nathan 1991). Yet underlying the Chipko movement is an appreciation of the fact that women's interests in the environment arise from a gendered division of labour wherein they are largely responsible for the daily provisioning of fodder, water, and fuel, and Chipko as an archetype draws on this reserve.

Voluntary Bodies and the Environment: Reflexive Praxis

A conglomeration of voluntary organizations and NGOs dispersed throughout the country that act on and reflect upon environmental issues from their particular vantage points forms a bedrock of Indian civil society. Although their 'ecosophies' are diverse they embody the cultural dialogue with global/western ideas and the interface with state policies (Rajan 1997). Gandhian views about man–nature relations and social reconstruction, Marxist initiatives for social change, and the concern with technology appropriate to the country's requirements provide what Guha (1988b) aptly describes as the penumbra of ideological orientations in the Indian context. Since the well-springs of such social action, however, are not necessarily environmentalist, their definitions of the situation often spill beyond or fall short of purposeful environmentalist agendas.

The multiplicity of perspectives and sites notwithstanding, these organizations draw upon the contemporary environmental critique for insights into their own local objectives that are seldom limited to environmental protection per se (cf. Prince et al. 1995). The noted environmentalist, Anil Agarwal, observes that their involvement with socially beneficial environmental practices is what enables one to 'describe this growth—albeit loosely—as the beginnings of an environmental movement' (Agarwal 1994: 347).

The networking of local-level organizations on environmental issues and the documentation of their efforts has, in fact, been facilitated by the Centre for Science and Environment (CSE), spearheaded by Agarwal. The association with already-existing organizations may tend to confirm Touraine's (1984) observation that a social movement has to work with 'relatively permanent cultural forms'. What is of sociological interest here, again, is that the CSE's own position on environmental issues has both shaped and been shaped by the interaction with grassroots organizations.

The CSE, too, debates on the national perspective to environmental issues and the environmental decisions of the Indian state. The CSE's reports on the state of India's environment (Centre for Science and Environment 1982; Agarwal and Narain 1985) in fact generated similar appraisals by citizen's groups in other states.

What is novel is that the CSE, along with other new institutions studying environmental change—the environmental NGOs (I) ENGOs—define the study of the environment in global terms. Their representatives challenge the North's portrayal of environmental issues and seek to make out a case for eco-justice in global fora on matters such as the right to profit from biogenetic resources, for instance.[3] They attempt to reconstitute the terms of the global environmental agenda by drawing attention to the vast majority of Indians who continue to depend upon natural resources for their survival. Subsistence is the foundation for their interventionist efforts much as planetary survival of life forms is the pivotal concern of western environmentalists.

The Narmada Anti-dam Agitation

The displacement of people from the territories that they occupy or utilize by a mandate from the state almost invariably meets with local resistance, regardless of whether it is for the purpose of facilitating wildlife sanctuaries, mining, social forestry, defence sites, irrigation projects, or other public sector undertakings. The record of resistance to displacement in the wake of dam construction is now well documented (Baviskar 1995; McCully 1996, Thukral 1992) but struggles, often violent, against the state's take-over of common and private lands for state projects constitute a recurrent theme of local-level narratives throughout the country.

What is important, then, is to understand why the displacement caused by state projects, that has always been resisted by those who were to be ousted, came to be challenged by environmentalists with regard to the Narmada project. The rural inhabitants who were earlier displaced by the dams were often dependent on the natural resources of these lands and attached to their homeland. However, they had scarcely before been perceived as defenders of the environmentalist interest.

Evidently, the intervening period had witnessed a global decrying of large dams because of the damage caused to the region's flora, fauna, soils, disease profiles, and the enormous social costs of people's displacement. The opposition to the state's take over of lands for the Sardar Sarovar project was, by and large, in consonance with the former pattern of local resistance to the venture except that the environmentalists had joined hands with them. In Madhya Pradesh, especially, Medha Patkar along with local activists and environmentalists, mobilized and organized dissent against the state. The Narmada was often portrayed as a mother to signify a bond with the river that was organic and non-negotiable and the oustees were depicted as disadvantaged indigenous people or Adivasis. The characteristic modes of resistance resonated with forms of non-cooperation including *dharnas* (sit-ins), *satyagrahas* (struggles for the truth), fasts, and marches (Gadgil and Guha 1993). The tools of resistance drew on a repertoire that was fine-honed during the freedom struggle but also generated new modes such as *jal samarpan* or death by drowning. The Narmada was portrayed as a mother in order to signify a bond that is primary—an archetype perhaps characteristic of the collective unconscious (cf. Jung 1968).

The state did not easily compromise its stand on the proposed Sardar Sarovar Dam in the long-drawn-out and, sometimes, violent struggle that questioned the state's claims concerning the resettlement of oustees. However, Patkar and her allies were able to galvanize the environmental NGOs in the West to come to their aid in this cause. Environmental NGOs in the USA exerted pressure on the World Bank to review the resettlement proposals as the Bank had been perceived to be 'environmentally unfriendly' in the past (Kolk 1996). The Independent Review that followed validated local-level apprehensions about resettlement and subsequently the World Bank revoked the financing of the Sardar Sarovar project.

The role of Northern NGOs and the withdrawal of finances for the Sardar Sarovar dam also fuelled thinking about new forms of domination. Doubts were expressed as to whether the NGOs of the North would have as much room for manoeuvre with the North's patterns of consumption that lay behind some of the globe's ecological degradation. Increasingly, the agitations against large dams, like many other social struggles in the country that were directed against the state, forged alliances with like-minded struggles in other countries.

The Narmada Bachao Andolan began by questioning the resettlement of people displaced by the dam and in its evolution had come to question the course of development pursued by the state. The Andolan, under the leadership of Patkar, now cooperates with other like-minded movements that seek to make the Indian state more responsive to the needs of impoverished inhabitants as, for instance, in the struggle for information and transparency in state functioning.

The nature of leadership in such movements is evidently charismatic and moral, evoking the spirit of sacrifice in contrast to what are seen as the self-serving ends of bureaucrats and politicians. However, charisma alone is an inadequate basis for apprehending the transactions between the leaders and other activists and participants in the struggle (Melucci 1996). The 'we', as Melucci puts it, has to be empirically constructed in the course of the struggle and is challenged by other leaders drawn from the movement or outside.

The interest of the Narmada Bachao Andolan activists in sustainable development does not always strike a chord with the Adivasis (Baviskar 1998). The latter also liaise with Adivasi political leaders who promise them economic betterment which is doubted by the activists. Sociologically, the classification of 'indigenous people' in the Indian context is problematic (cf. Béteille 1998) but attractive political capital for the Adivasi leaders who seek the articulation of their interests as Adivasis. The agenda of impoverished inhabitants, however, is not met either by the environmentalist agenda of sustainable development or the actions of the Adivasi leaders.

The agitation is ongoing as new sources of financing the project are sought. The Narmada Bachao Andolan, however, has afforded another archetype of environmental representation and action. Mobilization and resistance against big dams elsewhere in the country are now frequent and widely reported in the media wherever they occur.

In reconstituting the environmental movement in India, my attempt has been to show that certain struggles and events become archetypal and generative—the Chipko, the Citizens' Reports, and the Narmada Bachao Andolan. The archetypes are not exhausted, if one considers, for instance, the ongoing struggles between fishermen and the trawling interests in Kerala (Kocherry and Acharya 1989; Kurien and Thankappan 1994) that are picked up elsewhere on the coast (Dietrich 1989). Again singular events, such as the leakage of toxic gas at Bhopal, also contribute to the momentum of the movement. Yet archetypes are, perhaps, characteristic of a movement that both develops and is developed by environmental struggles that are akin but dispersed at local, national, and global levels.

I have tried to bring out the sense in which these struggles are new yet not new and how their classification as social elucidates some of their characteristics without exhausting their distinctiveness as environmental. Environmentalists, too, tap the reservoir of cultural dispositions in India as they engage with global issues, encounter new forms of global sociality and domination, and work at bringing about a shift in human consciousness with regard to the environment. That shift may be no less vital than what Kuhn (1962) has conceptualized as paradigm shifts or the reconstitution of 'model problems and solutions' (ibid.: p. x) within the scientific community.

As a new term, eco-sociology heralds the concern with planetary ecology and environment in our times, albeit in sociological categories. Sociological/anthropological categories of thought, however, draw their meaningfulness and relevance from locally experienced environments, usages, and dialects that are cognized to apprehend particular life-worlds. The encounter with spatial and environmental contexts beyond the local and the regional, however, does not jettison the job of sociology or social anthropology.

On the contrary, the project of sociology/anthropology contemporarily traverses the local engagement with global languages, including those of science and technology, irrespective of the point of origin. The immediacy of translocal human exchanges and information technology furnish a new context for exploring the ethnographic present.

The unfolding horizons for human beings, whether as instant languages and virtual communities or as irrelevant distant noises call for new tools. It is in this sense that anthropology as the study of humanity in its ever-changing guises and physical environments including that of outer space remains a vital intellectual engagement. Categories of thought in the present are not homogenized with the recognition of the planetary or the industrial or the agrarian, but even now point toward the richness of human variations in relation to nature, the study of which is an anthropologist's act of faith, if not a theoretical premise.

ENDNOTES

1. Malamoud also clarifies that the 'forest, is not a place of dense vegetation (but) perceived as a deserted place, a lacuna between populated areas' (Malamoud 1998: 72).
2. Cf. Dumont (1972) who notes that the word jajman 'comes from the Sanskrit yajaman ... he who has a sacrifice performed' (Dumont 1972: 139).

3. See, in this regard the work of Shiva (1990, 1993) and her colleague (Shiva and Ramprasad 1993) on biodiversity at the Research Foundation for Science, Technology and Natural Resource Policy, Dehra Dun.

REFERENCES

Abraham, C.M. and A. Rosencranz. 1986. 'An Evaluation of Pollution Control Legislation in India'. *Columbia Journal of Environmental Law.* 11:101–18.

Agarwal, Anil. 1994. 'An Indian Environmentalist's Credo'. In R. Guha, ed., *Social Ecology*, 346–84. Delhi: Oxford University Press.

Agarwal, Anil and Sunita Narain, eds. 1985. *The State of India's Environment: A Second Citizens' Report.* New Delhi: Centre for Science and Environment.

Agarwal, Anil, Sunita Narain, and Anupam Misra, eds. 1988. *Hamara Pariyavaran.* (Hindi). Delhi: Gandhi Shanti Pratishthan.

Agarwal, B. 1986. *Cold Hearths and Barren Slopes: The Wood Fuel Crisis in the Third World.* London: Zed Books.

_____. 1992 'The Gender and Environment Debate: Lessons From India'. *Feminist Studies.* 18(1):119–58.

Ahmed, Akbar S. 1983. 'Nomadism as Ideological Expression: The Case of the Gomal Nomads'. *Contributions to Indian Sociology* (n.s.). 17(1):123–39.

Alter, Joseph S. 1992. *The Wrestler's Body: Identity and Ideology in North India.* Berkeley: University of California Press.

Archer, W.G. 1975. *The Hill of Flutes; Life, Love and Poetry in Tribal India: A Portrait of the Santals.* New Delhi: S. Chand and Company.

Arora, Sushil and A.K. Haldar. 1994. 'Economy of the Nomadic Communities of India'. *Man in India.* 74(1):181–91.

Asad, Talal. 1983. 'Anthropological Conceptions of Religion: Reflections on Geertz'. *Man* (n.s.) 18:237–59.

Awaradi, S.A. 1990. *Master Plan (1991–2021) for Welfare of Primitive Tribes of Andaman and Nicobar Islands.* Port Blair: Government of India.

Bauman, Richard. 1996. 'Genre'. In R. Bauman, ed., *Folklore, Cultural Performances and Popular Entertainments: A Communications-centered Handbook*, 53–9. New York: Oxford University Press.

Baviskar, Amita. 1995. *In the Belly of the River: Tribal Conflicts over Development in the Narmada Valley.* Delhi: Oxford University Press.

_____. 1998. 'Tribal Politics and Discourses of Environmentalism'. *Contributions to Indian Sociology* (n.s.) 31(2):195–224.

Beteillé, André. 1975. *Six Essays in Comparative Sociology.* Delhi: Oxford University Press.

_____. 1998: 'The Idea of Indigenous People'. *Current Anthropology.* 39(2):187–92.

Beck, Ulrich. 1992. *Risk Society: Towards A New Modernity.* London: Sage Publications.

Biardeau, Madeleine. 1984. 'The Sami Tree and the Sacrificial Buffalo'. *Contributions to Indian Sociology* (n.s.). 18(1):1–24.

_____. 1989. *Hinduism: The Anthropology of a Civilisation.* Trans. Robert Nice. Delhi: Oxford University Press.

Bhasin, Veena. 1990. Environmental Implications and Economic Development among the Gaddis of Bharmour, Himachal Pradesh, India. *Journal of Human Ecology.* 1(1):5–26.

Bird-David, Nurit. 1990. 'The Giving Environment: Another Perspective on the Economic System of Gatherer-hunters'. *Current Anthropology.* 31(2):189–96.

_____. 1992. 'Beyond "The Hunting and Gathering Mode of Subsistence": Culture-sensitive Observations on the Nayaka and Other Modern Hunter Gatherers'. *Man* (n.s.). 27:19–44.

Boserup, Ester. [1976] 1988. 'Environment, Population and Technology in Primitive Societies.' In D. Worster, ed., *The Ends of the Earth: Perspectives on Modern Environmental History,* 23–80. Cambridge: Cambridge University Press.

Bourdieu, Pierre. 1977. *Outline of a Theory of Practice.* Cambridge: Cambridge University Press.

Brara, Rita. 1987. *Shifting Sands: A Study of Rights in Common Pastures.* Monograph submitted to the Ford Foundation, New Delhi. The Institute of Development Studies: Jaipur.

———. 1989. 'Commons Policy As Process: The Case of Rajasthan'. *Economic and Political Weekly.* 27 Oct.: 2247–54. vol. 24.

———. 1992. 'Are Grazing Lands "Wastelands"? Some Evidence from Rajasthan'. *Economic and Political Weekly.* 22 Feb.: 411–18. vol. 27.

Brouwer, Jan. 1995. *Makers of the World: Caste, Craft and Mind of South Indian Artisans.* Delhi: Oxford University Press.

Buchy, Marlene. 1996. *Teak and Arecanut: Colonial State, Forest and People in the Western Ghats (South India) 1800–1947.* Delhi: Indira Gandhi National Centre for the Arts.

Centre for Science and Environment. 1982. *The State of India's Environment.* New Delhi: Centre for Science and Environment.

Chandrakanth, M.G. and Jeff Romm. 1991. 'Sacred Forests, Secular Forest Policies and People's Actions'. *Natural Resources Journal* 31:740–56.

Coccari, Diane M. 1989. 'The Bir Babas of Banaras and the Deified Dead'. In A. Hiltebeitel, eds, *Criminal Gods and Demon Devotees: Essays on the Guardians of Popular Hinduism,* 251–69. Albany: State University of New York Press.

Cort, Louise Allison. 1988. 'The Role of the Potter in South Asia'. *Proceedings of the South Asia Seminar.* Pennsylvania: University of Pennsylvania.

Das, Veena. 1983. 'Language of Sacrifice'. *Man* (n.s.). 18(1):4–62.

———. 1995. *Critical Events.* Delhi: Oxford University Press.

D'Eaubonne, Francoise. 1974. *New French Feminisms: An Anthology.* Amherst: University of Massachusetts Press.

Deb, Debal. 1996. 'Of Cast Net and Caste Identity: Memetic Differentiation between Two Fishing Communities of Karnataka'. *Human Ecology.* 24(7):109–23.

Dietrich, Gabriele. 1989. 'Kanyakumari March: Breakthrough Despite Break-up.' *Economic and Political Weekly.* 20 May: 1087–8. vol. 24.

Dove, Michael R. 1994. '"Jungle" in Nature and Culture'. In R. Guha, ed., *Social Ecology,* 90–115. Delhi: Oxford University Press.

———. 1996. 'Center, Periphery and Bio-diversity: A Paradox of Governance and a Developmental Challenge'. In Stephen B. Brush and Doreen Stabinsky, eds, *Valuing Local Knowledge: Indigenous People and Intellectual Property Rights,* 41–67. Washington D.C.: Island Press.

Dumont, Louis. 1972. *Homo Hierarchicus: The Caste System and Its Implications.* Paladin: Granada Publishing Ltd.

Durkheim, E. 1915. *The Elementary Forms of the Religious Life:* London: Allen and Unwin.

Eaton, Richard M. 1985. 'Approaches to the Study of Conversion to Islam in India'. In Richard C. Martin, ed., *Approaches to Islam in Religious Studies,* 106–23. Tucson: University of Arizona Press.

Eck, Diana. 1983. *Banaras: City of Light.* London: Routledge and Kegan Paul.

Ehrenfels, U.R. 1952. *Kadar of Cochin.* Madras: University of Madras Press.

Ellen, Roy. 1994. 'Modes of Subsistence: Hunting and Gathering to Agriculture and Pastoralism'. In *Companion Encyclopedia of Anthropology.* London: Routledge and Kegan Paul.

Fisher, R.J. 1997. *If Rain Doesn't Come: An Anthropological Study of Drought and Human Ecology in Western Rajasthan.* New Delhi: Manohar.

Fisher, W.E. ed. 1995. *Towards Sustainable Development? Struggling over India's Narmada River.* New York: M.F. Sharpe.

Foucault, Michel. [1972] 1992. *Archaeology of Knowledge.* Trans. A.M. Sheridan Smith. London: Routledge.

Fox, R.G. 1969: '"Professional Primitives": Hunters and Gatherers of Nuclear South Asia'. *Man in India*. 49(2):139–60.

Galaty, C. 1981. 'Introduction'. In C. Galaty, ed., *Change and Development in Nomadic and Pastoral Societies, 4–26*. Leiden: E.J. Brill.

Gadgil, Madhav and Ramachandra Guha. 1993. *This Fissured Land: An Ecological History of India*. Delhi: Oxford University Press.

Gadgil, Madhav. and K.C. Malhotra. 1994. 'The Ecological Significance of Caste'. In R. Guha, ed., *Social Ecology*, 27–41. Delhi: Oxford University Press.

Gadgil, Madhav and V.D. Vartak. 1998. 'The Sacred Uses of Nature'. In R. Guha, ed., *Social Ecology*, 80–1. Delhi: Oxford University Press.

_____. 1994b. 'Ecological Conflicts and the Environmental Movement in India'. *Development and Change*. 25:101–36.

Geertz. C. 1966. 'Religion as a Cultural System'. In M. Banton, ed., *Anthropological Approaches to the Study of Religion*. New York: Praeger.

_____. [1963] 1968. *Agricultural Involution: The Process of Ecological Change in Indonesia*. Berkeley: University of California Press.

Glushkova, Irina and Anne Feldhaus, eds. 1998. *House and Home in Maharashtra*. Delhi: Oxford University Press.

Goldenweiser, A. 1936. 'Loose Ends of a Theory on the Individual Pattern and Involution in Primitive Society'. In R. Lowie, ed., *Essays in Anthropology Presented to A.L. Kroeber*. Berkeley: University Press.

Grove, Richard H. 1995. *Green Imperialism*. Cambridge: Cambridge University Press.

_____. 1998. *Ecology, Climate and Empire*. Delhi: Oxford University Press.

Grove, Richard, H. Vinita Damodaran, and Satpal Sangwan, eds. 1998. *Nature and the Orient: The Environmental History of South and South-east Asia*. Delhi: Oxford University Press.

Grover, Neelam. 1985. *Rural Settlements: A Cultural-geographical Analysis*. New Delhi: Inter-India Publications.

Guha, Ramachandra. 1988a. *The Unquiet Woods: Ecological Change and Peasant Resistance in the Himalaya*. Delhi: Oxford University Press.

_____. 1988b: 'Ideological Trends in Indian Environmentalism'. *Economic and Political Weekly*. 23(49):2578–81.

_____. 1992. 'Pre-history of Indian Environmentalism: Intellectual Traditions'. *Economic and Political Weekly*. 4 January: 57–64. vol. 27.

_____. ed. 1994. *Social Ecology*. Delhi: Oxford University Press.

Guha, Ramachandra and D. Arnold, eds. 1995. *Nature, Culture and Imperialism: Essays on the Environmental History of South Asia*. Delhi: Oxford University Press.

Habermas, J. 1981. New Social Movements. *Telos*. 49:33–7.

Hardy, Friedhelm. 1995. 'A Radical Reassessment of the Vedic Heritage'. In V. Dalmia and H. von Stietencron, eds, *Representing Hinduism: The Construction of Religious Traditions and National Identity*, 33–50. New Delhi: Sage Publications.

Harris, Marvin. 1966. 'The Cultural Ecology of India's Sacred Cattle'. *Current Anthropology*. 7:51–6.

Heesterman, J.C. 1993. *The Broken World of Sacrifice*. Chicago: University of Chicago Press.

Heston, Alan. 1971. 'An Approach to the Sacred Cow of India'. *Current Anthropology*. 12:191–210.

Hiltebeitel, Alf. 1989. 'Introduction'. In A. Hiltebeitel, ed., *Criminal Gods and Demon Devotees: Essays on the Guardians of Popular Hinduism*, 1–18. Albany: State University of New York Press.

_____. 1991. *The Cult of Draupadi: On Hindu Ritual and the Goddess,* vol. 2. Chicago: University of Chicago Press.

Humphrey, Caroline and James Laidlaw. 1994. *The Archetypal Actions of Ritual: A Theory of Ritual Illustrated by the Jain Rite of Worship*. Oxford: Clarendon Press.

Ifeka, Caroline. 1987. 'Domestic Space as Ideology in Goa, India'. *Contributions to Indian Sociology* (n.s.). 21(2):307–29.

Jackson, Cecile. 1993. 'Environmentalisms and Gender Interests in the Third World'. *Development and Change*. 24:649–77.

Jamous, Raymond. 1994. 'Rites of Ancient India: Outlook for Comparative Anthropology'. *Contributions to Indian Sociology* (n.s.). 28(2):323–52.

Jodha, N.S. 1986. 'Common Property Resources and Rural Poor in Dry Regions of India'. *Economic and Political Weekly*. 21(27):1169–81.

Jung, C.G. 1968. *The Archetypes and the Collective Unconscious*. Princeton: Princeton University Press.

Kavoori, Purnendu. 1999. *Pastoralism in Expansion: The Transhuming Herder of Western Rajasthan*. Delhi: Oxford University Press.

Kelkar, G. and D. Nathan. 1991. *Gender and Tribe: Women, Land and Forests*. New Delhi: Kali for Women.

Kocherry, T. and T. Acharya. 1989. 'Fishing for Resources: Indian Fisheries in Danger'. *Cultural Survival Quarterly*. 13:31–4.

Kolk, Ans. 1996. *Forests in International Environmental Politics*. Netherlands: International Books.

Kramisch, Stella. 1976. *The Hindu Temple*. 2 vols. Delhi: Motilal Banarasidass.

Kuhn, T. 1962. *The Structure of Scientific Revolutions*. Chicago: University of Chicago Press.

Kurien, John and T.R. Thankappan. 1994. 'Overfishing the Coastal Commons: Causes and Consequences'. In R. Guha, ed., *Social Ecology*, 218–43. Delhi: Oxford University Press.

Lawrence, Denise L. and Setha M. Low. 1990. 'The Built Environment'. *Annual Review of Anthropology*. 19:453–505.

Leavitt, John. 1992. 'Cultural Holism in the Anthropology of South Asia: The Challenge of Regional Traditions'. *Contributions to Indian Sociology* (n.s.). 26(1):3–49.

Levy, Robert. 1992. *Mesocosm: Hinduism and the Organisation of a Traditional Newar City in Nepal*. Delhi: Motilal Banarasidass.

Lévi-Strauss, Claude. 1963. *Race and History*. UNESCO: Paris.

———. 1972. *Totemism*. Harmondsworth: Penguin Books.

———. 1978. *Myth and Meaning*. Toronto: University of Toronto Press.

———. 1987. *The View from Afar*. Oxford: Basil Blackwell.

Lindholm, Charles. 1996. *The Islamic Middle East: An Historical Anthropology*. Oxford: Blackwell.

Madan, T.N. 1991. 'Introduction'. In T.N. Madan, ed., *Religion in India*, 1–22. Delhi: Oxford University Press.

Malamoud, Charles. 1998. *Cooking the World: Ritual and Thought in Ancient India*. Delhi: Oxford University Press.

McCully, Patrick. 1996. *Silenced Rivers: The Ecology and Politics of Large Dams*. London: Zed Books.

Mehta, D. and Roma Chatterji. 1995. 'A Case Study of a "Communal" Riot in Dharavi, Bombay'. *Religion and Society*. 42(5):5–65.

Melucci, Alberto. 1980. 'The New Social Movements: A Theoretical Approach'. *Social Sciences Information*. 19(2):199–226.

———. 1996. *Challenging Codes: Collective Action in the Information Age*. Cambridge: Cambridge University Press.

Mencher, Joan P. [1966] 1994. 'Kerala and Madras: A Comparative Study of Ecology and Social Structure'. In R. Guha, ed., *Social Ecology*. Delhi: Oxford University Press.

Moore, Melinda A. 1989. 'The Kerala House as a Hindu Cosmos'. *Contributions to Indian Sociology* (n.s.). 23(1):169–202.

Mukul. 1997. 'Polluting Industries, Environment and Workers' Health: A Case For Intervention.' *Economic and Political Weekly*, 30 August: L37–8.

Myka Frank. 1995: 'Of Adoption and Orphanages: The Bio-cultural Dynamics of Population Decline among the Andaman Islanders'. *Man in India*. 75(1):1–9.

Pandit, T.N. 1994. 'The Hunters and Gatherers of the Bay Islands: Their Survival and Development: An Analysis'. In V. Suryanarayan and V. Sundarsen, eds, *Challenges of Development*. Jaipur: Konarak Publishers.

Pandya, Vishwajit. 1993. *Above the Forest: A Study of Andamanese Ethnoanemology, Cosmology and the Power of Ritual*. Delhi: Oxford University Press.

Pareto, Vilfredo. 1935. *The Mind and Society*. Trans. A Bongiorno and A. Livingston. New York: Harcourt, Brace and Co.

Parish, Steven M. 1996. *Hierarchy and Its Discontents: Culture and the Politics of Consciousness in Caste Society*. Philadelphia: University of Pennsylvania Press.

Parkes, Peter. 1987. 'Livestock Symbolism and Pastoral Ideology Among the Kafirs of the Hindu Kush'. *Man* (n.s.). 22:637–60.

Pramar, V.S. 1987. 'Sociology of the North Gujarat Urban House'. *Contributions to Indian Sociology* (n.s.). 12(2):331–46.

Prince, N., T.M. Finger, and J. Manno. 1995. 'Non-governmental Organisations in World Environmental Politics'. *International Environmental Affairs*. 7(1):42–58.

Rajan, Mukund Govind. 1997. *Global Environmental Politics: India and the North-south Politics of Global Environmental Issues*. Delhi: Oxford University Press.

Ram, Kalpana. 1992. *Mukkuwar Women: Gender, Hegemony and Capitalist Transformation in a South Indian Fishing Community*. New Delhi: Kali for Women.

Rangarajan, Mahesh. 1996. *Fencing the Forest: Conservation and Ecological Change in India's Central Provinces*. Delhi: Oxford University Press.

Redfield, Robert and Milton Singer. 1954. 'The Cultural Role of Cities'. *Economic Development and Cultural Change*. 3:53–73.

Roy, Beth. 1994. *Some Trouble With Cows: Making Sense of Social Conflict*. California: University of California Press.

Ruel, Malcolm. 1990. 'Non-sacrificial Ritual Killing'. *Man* (n.s.). 25:323–35.

Sarkar, Benoy Kumar. [1916] 1972. *The Folk Element in Hindu Culture*. New Delhi: Oriental Books Reprint Corporation.

Sarkar, Jayanta. 1990. *The Jarawa*. Calcutta: ASI and Seagull Books.

Savyasaachi. 1991. 'A Study in the Sociology of Agriculture'. Thesis submitted to the University of Delhi.

Scott, J.C. 1986. *Weapons of the Weak: Everyday Forms of Peasant Resistance*. New Haven: Yale University Press.

Shah, A.M. and I.P. Desai. 1988. *Division and Hierarchy: An Overview of Caste in Gujarat*. Delhi: Hindustan Publishing Corporation.

Shiva, Vandana. 1984. *Staying Alive: Women, Ecology and Survival in India*. New Delhi: Kali for Women.
———. 1990: 'Bio-diversity, Bio-technology and Profit: The Need for a People's Plan to Protect Bio-diversity?' *The Ecologist*. 20(2):44–7.
———. 1993: 'Farmers' Rights, Bio-diversity and International Treaties'. *Economic and Political Weekly*. 13 April: 554–60. vol. 28. no. 14.

Shiva, Vandana and Maria Mies. 1993. *Ecofeminism*. London: Zed Books.

Shiva, Vandana and Vanaja Ramprasad. 1993. *Cultivating Bio-diversity. Bio-diversity Conservation and the Politics of the Seed*. Dehradun: Research Foundation for Science, Technology and Natural Resource Policy.

Singh, Chhatrapati. 1986. *Common Property and Common Poverty: India's Forests, Forest Dwellers and the Law*. Delhi: Oxford University Press.

Smailes, Arthur E. [1969] 1986. 'The Indian City: A Descriptive Model'. In V. Tewari, J.A. Weinstein and V.L.S. Prakasa Rao, eds, *Indian Cities: Ecological Perspectives*. New Delhi: Concept Publishing. pp. 35–51.

Smith, Brian K. 1991. 'Classifying Animals in Ancient India'. *Man* (n.s.). 27:527–48.

_____. 1994. *Classifying the Universe: The Ancient Indian Varna System and the Origins of Caste*. New York: Oxford University Press.

Smith, Brian K. and Wendy Doniger. 1989. 'Sacrifice and Substitution: Ritual Mystification and Mythical Demystification'. *Numen*. 36(2):189–224.

Sontheimer, Gunther-Dietz. 1987. 'Rudra and Khandoba: Continuity in Folk Religion'. In N.K. Wagle, ed., *Religion and Society in Maharashtra*, 1–131. Toronto: University of Toronto Press.

Srinivas, M.N. 1952. *Religion and Society among the Coorgs*. Oxford: Clarendon Press.

Srivastava, P. 1987. *Bhopal: Anatomy of a Crisis*. Massachusetts: Ballinger.

Srivastava, Vinay Kumar. 1997. *Religious Renunciation of a Pastoral People*. Delhi: Oxford University Press.

Strathern, M. 1991. *Partial Connections*. ASA in Oceania. Special Publications, 3. Savage. MD: Rowman and Littlefield.

_____. 1992. 'Parts and Wholes: Refiguring Relationships in a Post-plural World.' In A. Kuper, ed., *Conceptualising Society*. London: Routledge.

Tapper, Bruce Elliott. 1979. 'Widows and Goddesses: Female Roles and Deity Symbolism in a South Indian Village'. *Contributions to Indian Sociology* (n.s.). 13(1):1–31.

Thukral, E.G., ed. 1992. *Big Dams, Displaced People: Rivers of Sorrow, Rivers of Change*. New Delhi: Sage Publications.

Touraine, Alan. 1984. 'Social Movements: Special Area or Central Problem in Sociological Analysis?' Trans. David Roberts. *Thesis eleven*. 9 July:5–15.

Trautmann, Thomas R. 1981. *Dravidian Kinship*. Cambridge: Cambridge University Press.

Tucker, Richard P. 1988. 'The Depletion of India's Forests under British Imperialism: Planters, Foresters and Peasants in Assam and Kerala'. In D. Worster, ed., *The Ends of the Earth: Perspectives on Modern Environmental History*, 118–40. Cambridge: Cambridge University Press.

Vaidyanathan, A., K.N. Nair, and Marvin Harris. 1982. 'Bovine Sex and Species Ratios in India'. *Current Anthropology*. 23:365–73.

Vasavi, A.R. 1994. 'Hybrid Times, Hybrid People: Culture and Agriculture in South India'. *Man* (n.s.). 29(2):283–300.

Wade, Robert. 1988. *Village Republics: Economic Conditions for Collective Action in South India*. Cambridge: Cambridge University Press.

Waghorne, Joanne and Norman Cutler, eds. 1985. *Gods of Flesh, Gods of Stone: The Embodiment of Divinity in India*. Pennsylvania: Anima Books.

Weber, Max. 1963. *The Sociology of Religion*. Massachusetts: Beacon Press.

Wiser, William H. [1936] 1958. *The Hindu Jajmani System*. Reprint. Lucknow: Lucknow Publishing House.

Woodburn, J. 1982. 'Egalitarian Societies'. *Man* (n.s.). 17:431–51.

_____. 1988. 'African Hunter-gatherer Social Organisation: Is it Best Understood as a Product of Encapsulation?' In D. Ingold and J. Woodburn, eds, *Hunters and Gatherers, vol. 1: History, Evolution and Social Change*. Oxford: Berg.

Worster, Donald. 1977. *Nature's Economy: A History of Ecological Ideas*. New York: Cambridge University Press.

Whitcombe, Elizabeth. 1971. *Agrarian Conditions in Northern India: The United Provinces under British Rule, 1860–1900*. Berkeley: University of California Press.

Zimmerman, Francis. 1987. *The Jungle and the Aroma of Meats: An Ecological Theme in Hindu Medicine*. Berkeley: University of California Press.

Social Stratification

DIPANKAR GUPTA

Most generally understood, stratification is about how people are placed in different social categories. Broadly speaking, stratification takes two forms. The first kind of stratification is based on a ranked scale where inequality, of one kind or the other, is the defining factor. There is a second kind of social ordering possible where stratification is not about ranking or inequality. In this case the relevant social categories that separate people are based on conceptions of difference. If inequality is the key feature then the stratificatory system can be characterized as a *hierarchical* one. If *difference* is more important then the various social orders face each other as horizontal and equal blocs. A ranked hierarchy does not make that much sense here.

Inequalities of income or rank quite clearly belong to the hierarchical order of stratification. In fact, for a long time social stratification was only another term for social inequality (see Sorokin 1967). In a ranked hierarchy of wealth there are the rich and the poor, and a variety of people in-between. There could also be hierarchies of power, status, or influence. In a power hierarchy, for instance, those at the top wield the most power while the multitude at the bottom have very little power, if any at all. Similar hierarchies could also be worked out for status or influence. In all such cases we see the geological model of stratification at work, where one layer is placed on top of the other much like the earth's crust.

If instead of power or wealth one takes into account forms of stratification based on difference then the geological model cannot be easily invoked. For example, linguistic differences cannot be placed in a hierarchical order. Looked at closely, neither should differences between men and women be understood in terms of inequality. Sadly, however, such differences are never always allowed to retain their horizontal status. They usually tend to get hierarchized in popular consciousness. This is where prejudice takes over. Men are deemed to be superior to women, certain linguistic groups are held to be less civilized and cultivated than others, and religious bigotry prevails, all because most of us are not conditioned to tolerate difference *qua* difference.

The conceptual need to separate these two orders arises because in the sociology of social stratification attention is directed to the manner in which hierarchy and difference relate to each other. If hierarchy and difference could hold on to their respective terrains then there would be no real need to study stratification as a special area of interest. If it is hierarchy alone that is of interest, then 'social inequality' would be a good enough rubric within which to organize our study. If, on the other hand, it is only difference that is of concern then the tried and tested term 'social differentiation' should do adequately. The term 'social stratification', however, is not a synonym of either social inequality or of social differentiation.

As social stratification is about the way hierarchy and difference continuously act upon each other, we are sensitized to issues of social stability and order, as well as to potentialities for social change. It is because of this dual aspect that social stratification occupies such a central position both in sociology and social anthropology. As will be discussed in the pages to follow, the scope for change and dynamism differs vastly with different kinds of stratification systems.

Social stratification is also of critical academic concern as there are no known societies today that are not stratified in one form or another. One can of course imagine a world where there are no inequalities, but if that world were also to be characterized by sameness then it would certainly be a very boring place to live in. Utopians of all stripes are keen to further an image of a society that knows no hierarchical or class differences. Yet they would baulk at the notion that these societies should be free of differences and variations. In a utopia, differences would not carry traces of hierarchy in them. One could with equal facility, and without prejudice, move from being a fisherman to a poet or from one religious set of beliefs to another.

The real world is vastly different, and that is why utopians tend not to ground themselves in the real. In the real world it is impossible to think of differences without at the same time surreptitiously bringing in hierarchy. Even in the simplest of societies where there are only very rudimentary distinctions between people, there are still rankings of sorts. Men are usually held to be superior to women and cadets and youngsters are under the control of elders; where there are chieftains then the elaboration of hierarchy may get more complex. Yet if we wish to understand how hierarchical orders are disputed and sometimes overthrown, it is necessary to factor the aspect of difference into our analysis. A major contention in this chapter is that hierarchy left to itself emphasizes stability, whereas it is the appreciation of difference that sows seeds of discord within these hierarchical orders.

By the same token, it is precisely in those societies where hierarchies, whether of wealth or of power, are weak that the scope for social change is practically negligible. It is not surprising then that the so-called primitive communities should have been characterized in anthropology as 'cold societies' because they were outside the scope of historical change. When colonialism brought such regions into the ambit of rapid social transformation, they began to develop rigid notions of hierarchy and, concomitantly, a greater degree of alienation based on social difference.

Most contemporary societies, whether developed or developing, present evidence of a higher order of stratification than just between sexes, or between elders or cadets. The question of inequality, of course, looms large in much of our thinking about stratification, but there is also the issue of cultural diversity. Tensions between diverse languages, religions, colours, and sects arise because of the conflicting ways by which each community wants to rank others in real operational terms. Unlike the utopias mentioned earlier, people are not always prepared to let differences flourish for their own sake without hierarchizing and labelling them in terms of good and bad, refined and crude, or civilized and uncivilized.

It should also be kept in mind that the categories employed in the study of social stratification are the creations of the analyst. Sometimes these creations coincide with popular concepts, but most often they do not. For example, the term 'class' is used in everyday language, but a student of social stratification would give it a meaning quite different from its common usage. A sociological treatment of class would differ depending on the scholar's theoretical predisposition—Marxist, Weberian, or functionalist (Ortner 1991: 168).

Even if the sociologist or anthropologist gives a technical meaning to concepts such as class or status, the main material for analysis comes from how people interact with one another and conceive of the divergences in their stations and life-chances. Occasionally, an entire chart of stratification might be based entirely upon how people rank themselves and others (Warner, et al. 1949), but the ultimate choice of categories that the scholar or analyst would employ must be secured by a well-founded theoretical rationale. This holds true whether or not the data comes from subjective and 'warm' facts (such as what people think of each other and of themselves) or from impersonal and 'cold' facts (like the amount of land owned, or money in the bank). The material, in either case, undergoes self-conscious theoretical and analytical transformations at the hands of the sociologist or anthropologist.

Social stratification is not just about categorizing or differentiating people into diverse strata. That would be a purely mechanical exercise, unworthy of conscientious sociological analysis. Though social stratification most obviously stratifies a given population, the principles of stratification tell us a lot more. Properly understood, social stratification provides an analytical basis for comprehending both social order and social mobility. An understanding of social stratification tells us simultaneously about the principles of social stasis and of social dynamics, thus offering a unique window to comprehending the liveliness and vivacity of social reality. To be able to see dynamics in what appears as static ranked order, and, by the same token, to be able to discern order in flux, surely constitute the greatest challenges in any disciplinary pursuit of knowledge.

Natural Differences and Sociological Categories

There are various criteria on the basis of which people are stratified. However, not all of them are of sociological significance. A sure way of testing the disciplinary validity of any kind of stratification is to ascertain the extent to which it tells us about social order and social mobility. If a form of stratification tells us nothing on these counts then it has little relevance for either sociology or for social anthropology. For instance, to distinguish and categorize people on the basis of height or weight or the length of their hair has no sociological salience at all. This should not give the impression that perceived natural differences have no sociological significance. We all know how colour was used as an important aspect of social stratification in apartheid-beset South Africa. Even though racism may have been dismantled as official policy all over the world, and its scientific pretensions debunked repeatedly, the sad truth is that, colour and racial categories still exercise powerful influence over the minds of many. Consequently, race-inspired thinking affects the way people of different colours relate to and interact with one another. This is why distinctions based on popular conceptions of race cannot be ignored in studies of social stratification.

The relationship between natural differences and social stratification is thus not an un-complicated one. There are some natural differences that have no sociological significance, and then there are others that are laden with sociological valency. The fact is that natural differences by themselves do not naturally make for categories of social stratification. If some natural differences, such as colour, are highlighted, it is also true that in the same society there are many other natural differences that are not. The reasons for emphasizing colour as a potent category of stratification do not lie in nature as much as they do in the specific character of the society which considers it to be significant.

The odd thing is that very often there are no natural differences that can be discerned in any tangible fashion, yet members of a society may believe that such differences do in fact exist. The caste system is one such example. Though there is no way by which those in a caste society can actually distinguish unfailing natural markers of difference, they justify caste stratification on the ground that different castes are built of different natural substances (Marriott and Inden 1977).

We have, therefore, two diametrically opposite ways by which nature is forced by culture to act at its behest. In the case of race, a specific physical difference that is on the surface is picked out to substantiate, justify, and perpetuate economic and social inequalities among people. But in caste societies where no natural difference can be discerned by the naked eye, it is imagined that such differences exist and elaborate care is taken so that the substances that constitute each caste do not commingle. Hence the elaborate rules prohibiting inter-caste dining or marriage.

Stratification does not depend solely on real or putative natural differences. Class, status, and power are some of the other axes along which stratification occurs. These could be considered as purely social categories as they are substantiated by markers that have nothing to do with either nature or natural differences. Even so, every sociologist should be sensitive to how these eminently social features tend to be naturalized at popular level. We thus come across seemingly natural justifications as to why poor people deserve to be poor, or why those who follow a different lifestyle have a natural propensity to do so. By acknowledging the persuasiveness of such ideological justifications for social categorizations, we realize the energy that is expended to either maintain or overthrow the status quo. In a later section there shall be occasion to return to this very important aspect of social stratification. For now let us move on to a closer examination of the kinds of strata that social stratification is concerned with.

Hierarchy and Difference: Social Statics and Dynamics

It was mentioned earlier that a test of relevancy for the categories of stratification is the extent to which they contribute to our understanding of social order and change. If this is true then the understanding of social stratification cannot be limited to ranked gradations, whether they be of power, wealth, status, purity, pollution, or colour. This is because such ranks tell us only about order and very little about the potentialities for social mobility and changes within and of that order. To be able to factor this element into the studies of social change it is necessary to think also in terms of differences.

Differences can be said to exist when it is difficult to rank diversities. Wealth, income, status, and even power can be ranked in terms of there being more or less of a single variable. But there are other forms of strata differentiation that cannot be hierarchized or ranked in this fashion. While gradation on the basis of wealth can unambiguously rank the rich and the poor, and even the various degrees of opulence and penury, the same strategy cannot be employed to understand other kinds of stratification. For instance, if an attempt were made to rank different languages, religions, or aesthetic preferences in hierarchical terms then it would not only be incorrect but also offensive to many. Strata of this kind are not amenable to ranking in terms of possessing more or less of a particular attribute. The differences between languages or religions are incommensurable but of logically equal status and thus cannot be measured on a hierarchical scale. For this reason, when attempts are made to hierarchize them, as in sectarian mobilizations, one is immediately alerted to the dimensions of power and prejudice that accompany such drives.

Social stratification thus includes both hierarchy and difference. If one were to talk only of hierarchy then one would be partial to order. If, on the other hand, only differences were to be emphasized then the social imperatives of order would not be appreciated. Instead, change, instability, and dynamism would become the focal points of research. That studies of social stratification are usually conceived in terms of the geographical model (Béteille 1977: 129) has limited our understanding of how stratification systems undergo change, and also of the tensions that exist within any given stratificatory order.

When classes, for instance, are seen along the geographical model then we only observe the passive layering of crust upon crust. Our attention is riveted primarily to the quantitative dimension of variance between different classes. This quantitative factor is premised on a certain kind of unanimity. It is impossible to argue that a person with a lower income belongs to a more affluent class than the person whose income is much higher. There can hardly be disagreement on matters of this kind. Likewise, a manager has more power than the foreman, and the foreman has more power than the worker on the shop-floor. Much as one may find this kind of power hierarchy, its existence cannot be denied.

The fact that such quantitative hierarchizations are possible in some instances sets the tone for the establishment of social order. Once drawn into a system of stratification which employs such quantifiable criteria, there is little scope to challenge hierarchical rankings from within. It would be absurd for workers to say that they have more power than the managers. Likewise, it would be nonsensical for a beggar to claim more wealth than a millionaire. There is a general acceptance by those included within the hierarchy that the positioning accurately reflects the criterion on which the gradations are based. While it is possible to arrive at such a consensus in hierarchies of this kind, it is nevertheless also true that there are often disputes in the relative rankings of grades that are contiguous with one another. This is especially so in the case of rankings with respect to power or status, but not quite as obvious in rankings of wealth. This is primarily because the criterion in the case of wealth is so easily and ostensibly quantifiable.

There can nevertheless be social mobility within a ranked order provided it is one that is allowed for by the hierarchy in question. The gradation based on class in a capitalist society is considered to be one such open system of stratification. Care should be taken not to conflate all class-based hierarchies as belonging to an open system. In feudal societies class boundaries were firm and mobility across them often invited severe reprisals. This is where the distinction between open and closed stratificatory systems becomes relevant.

Open and Closed Systems of Stratification: Variations in Mobility Strategies

In an open system of stratification, mobility is an accepted property of the system. On the other hand, in a closed system of stratification, mobility is strongly discouraged. In such cases ideological wars have to be waged by the aspirants in their bid for upward mobility. In doing so the basis on which low rank was accorded earlier has to be de-legitimized. This would imply that a hitherto low-ranking class must necessarily step out of its location within the ranked hierarchy and energize an ideology of difference in order to justify and legitimize its quest for upward mobility. In an open system of stratification it is possible to move up by simply obeying the internal order of rank differentiation.

Here the hierarchy may be fixed and firm, but individuals can go up or even down the hierarchy. For example, in a modern bureaucratic establishment a person can rise from being a clerk to a manager, a manager to an executive director, and so on. Biographically, there are no reasons why a person cannot aspire to the highest position if the stated qualifications required to fill a position in a hierarchy are satisfied. In a closed system of stratification a person may be strong and brave and yet, because of the accident of birth, not considered a rightful member of the warrior class.

In a closed system of stratification, therefore, ascribed characteristics such as those of caste, colour, or religion are absolutely central. This being the case, it is quite clear that the issue of whether a system of stratification is open or closed also tells us whether this system is one that draws sustenance from quantitative hierarchies or from qualitative differences. In the former there is greater acquiescence within, regarding the hierarchy, and in the latter the hierarchy, or ranked order, is constantly disputed. This is because in an open system of stratification the criterion is indisputable. Even though everyone may want to be rich, a poor person must accept the reality of being poor. A worker may resent being powerless in a factory, but must acquiesce to the fact that those who belong to the category of foreman or manager have a lot more power than he does. Just as everyone may want to be tall and slim, the hierarchy of height and weight cannot be questioned, no matter how we regret our physical shape and size.

In a closed system of stratification, the first principle of distinction is a qualitative one which is then hierarchized. Hierarchization does not come naturally where distinctions are qualitative to begin with. When the differences between the various estates, castes, or races are elaborated there is no scope for movement from one race to the other, or from one caste to the other. Thus when these castes, races, or estates are hierarchized, the criterion of hierarchy has to be imposed from outside and can have no justifications within. The significance of this is not easy to grasp, as there is a pervasive belief that the ordering of estates or races is primarily hierarchical. It is because such a view has been prevalent for a long time that the nature of social mobility between closed and open systems of stratification has not been fully appreciated. Once it is realized that closed systems of stratification are premised on differences first and hierarchy later, one understands why attempts at mobility in such systems are always so strongly ideological in their thrust. It has never quite occurred to most of us that the march of upward mobility in a closed system of stratification must wade through strong headwinds that are built on differences. These differences, once again, are basically incommensurable and unrankable in character.

This point needs to be constantly reinforced if a comprehensive understanding of social stratification is to be arrived at. In a closed system of stratification the hierarchy does not have the complicity of all those who are deemed to be within it. In an open system of stratification, where the basis for the hierarchy is quantitative, one's inclusion at any particular level is above dispute. The only way it is possible to dispute a quantitative hierarchy is to reject it entirely and oppose it in the language of difference. To make the claim of being rich or powerful without actually occupying these positions would only be self-delusionary. But it is always possible to reject the power of the rich or of the powerful by claiming alternative standards of morality, probity, and social order. To do this the language of difference needs to be invoked.

Before we go further down this road, it is necessary to take stock of our earlier claim that stratification must include both hierarchy and difference. This is because it is not just quantifiable ranked order that we are always talking about; very often, ranked orders are imposed on what is inherently incapable of being ranked. The reality is that differences posit logically equal categories whose intrinsic relationship is horizontal in character. To then force them into a vertical hierarchy requires an extraneous agency—which is usually that of political power. Blacks can be characterized as occupying a lower station not because black is an inherently inferior colour, but because in a racist society the White population controls power and uses colour as an ideological weapon of subjugation.

Likewise, in the caste system, or in the division between estates, there is nothing intrinsic in each of these categories that makes them superior to others. Logically, castes such as the Baniyas or Kshatriyas are separate and equal, but it is political power that decides which castes will be superior to which other castes, or which estate shall have precedence over other estates.

We find the justification for including differences and not just hierarchy because it helps us to understand how closed systems of stratification are different from open ones, and how mobilization strategies in one must necessarily diverge from the other. As the divergence between open and closed systems of stratification lies primarily at the level of mobility, the conceptual distinction between hierarchy and difference is crucial. It tells us why mobility is far from routine in closed systems of stratification, but built into open stratificatory systems. It also helps us to be faithful to the *raison d'etre* of different kinds of stratification and at the same time to elucidate their divergent mobility paths.

Open and closed systems of stratification are not always discrete historical stages but can be closely intertwined at the empirical level. This is because in every open system of stratification there is a point beyond which mobility is made extremely difficult. This is often in defiance of the system, and indicates that elements of difference have entered the picture. It is often believed that closed systems of stratification give way to open ones as we move from feudalism to modern industrial capitalist economies. There is no doubt that modern industrial societies are what they are because of the tremendous dynamism and social mobility they allow. Even Marx acknowledged this tremendous liberating role of capitalism. Yet as there are always imperfections in every system as well as attempts to protect one's bailiwick from competition—indeed, as there are always attempts to find security in an insecure world—a closure is constantly sought in what is legally and formally a formal system.

By the same token, closed systems of stratification have also witnessed tremendous upheavals and dynamism, but these have usually gone unnoticed because of the glacial pace of change. In contemporary times, however, this change can no longer be concealed largely because of the dominating forces of modernization and industrialization. That modernization has not only brought machines but, more crucially, changed relations between people, is the reason why the presence of such contemporaneous forces has given a fillip to mobilizations within hitherto closed systems of stratification. The most important effect has been the opening up of the village economy and the concomitant freedom of the lower orders from economic bondage to rural oligarchs or members of the ancient regime.

That modernization and the breakdown of the natural economy have enabled communities, classes, and castes to move out of earlier categories of stratification does not mean that these earlier strata have lost their ideological force or sentimental power. Caste identities are still very strong even as castes are no longer locally confined. Legal justifications for upward caste mobility may be drawn from the liberal language of political democracy, but the emotional charge behind such drives is derived from strong caste loyalties. The fact, however, remains that caste mobility is now much more of a routine affair than it ever was in the past. What one must then pay attention to in any concrete study of stratification is how the open and closed systems interact with each other. This does not deny the fact that one form of stratification is probably dominant at any one point in time of any society. It could well be the case that different sectors of a society may well diverge from one another in this respect. In which case it becomes all the more important to see the interaction between open and closed stratificatory systems and not confine them to separate slots in any empirical investigation.

Caste Mobility: Re-examining the Renouncer

Closed and open systems of stratification are usually exemplified with reference to India and America respectively. Caste in India and the open mobile class structure of America are paradigm cases of the two contrasting systems of stratification. Though the caste system is a prime example of a closed form of an ascription-based system of stratification, it is not as if no mobility had ever taken place in Indian history. But every time it did happen, it aroused a lot of opposition and resentment from the entrenched and powerful castes. The Rajputs and the Gujar Pratiharas between the eighth and tenth centuries, and the Marathas and Jats between the thirteenth and eighteenth centuries, fought their way to the top by conducting a series of wars. Warfare was a route to upward movement in the caste system. Mobility therefore was not a routine thing to be expected, and was even somewhat looked down upon by the privileged sections. When it was not war that served as the impetus for class mobility, it was protest movements of various kind. Some of them were straight caste-based confrontations, but more often a religious sect emerged that promised salvation by breaking caste norms. In each case, the existing social arrangements were threatened and de-legitimized by such attempts at caste mobility.

In the open class system of stratification, mobility is an accepted characteristic of the system. The movement up and down, and even horizontally, does not challenge the ideological basis of the hierarchy, though there may be some resistance to particular individuals making it to a higher grade. This brings to our attention yet another interesting contrast between open and closed stratification. When mobility is an accepted feature of the hierarchy, then it is individuals who move up or down or horizontally within the system. When mobility is not an accepted part of a hierarchy, then it is groups or categories that generally move in unison. This is because in closed systems of stratification hierarchy is forced on to incommensurable differences between communities, castes, races, or religions. To reinforce what was said earlier, in such cases what are logically separate and equal categories are hierarchized by the force of political power. This explains why in such a situation individual mobility will just not do. An individual is not a person in his or her own right but a representative of a larger ascriptive community to which he owes loyalty.

It is often said that Hinduism allows for individual mobility provided one becomes a renouncer (Dumont 1960). Hindu society thus holds a renouncer in the highest esteem regardless of the person's actual caste origin. Though there is something tempting about this postulate there is really a logical obfuscation here. A renouncer does not climb up the caste hierarchy after renouncing the world, but becomes a true 'outcaste', and literally moves over to another world where caste rules do not apply. Indeed the renouncer is deemed to be sociologically dead. On occasions even funerary rites are performed to signify the renouncer's departure from the quotidian world to which he cannot return. Further, by virtue of having renounced, the renouncer cannot influence or prejudice the functioning of the caste order with all its political implications.

But all this is legend and not what is really practised. Renouncers are known to be actively involved in this-worldly affairs and often start movements that promise an alternative social order towards a parallel society. In such situations—quite like the Bhakti saints of medieval

India—renouncers are opposed by those who abide by the rules of caste society The renouncer may have seen the light and may have ambitions to lead a mass of devotees and followers to a caste-free world. But it is not as if the renouncer can lead from the front. Instead in such cases he is a subversive agent.

Alternatively, there is also evidence from both anthropology and history that reveals that the renouncer does not always give up being involved with 'this-worldly' affairs, and, in fact, actually thrives on political patronage. In ancient India the Kalamukha Sannyasins 'claimed Brahman status and took the name of pandita deva, and were often the defenders of the *varnasrmadharma* [the caste order]' (Thapar 1978: 85). The Kapalika sect too had its own patrons that allowed it to survive and win adherents in a hotly contested atmosphere (Thapar 1978: 75). A closer look reveals that these renouncers were technically not renouncers at all, for they often upheld the caste system quite overtly, and, in addition, were tied closely to the ideological premises of politics.

In ancient myths too there are revered sages like Dronacharya and Bhishm Pitamaha who may have had the outward appearances of renouncers but were also deeply implicated in the politics of their times. Perhaps it is also important to distinguish between the renouncer and the ascetic, as Romila Thapar (1978: 64) advises. The ascetic, constantly venerated and lauded in sacerdotal texts and more 'frequently described in literature than encountered in reality' (Thapar 1978), leads a life of loneliness and austerity and is lost to his family, kin, and friends in his search for individual salvation. It is, however, the renouncers who live in collectives and form sects, and it is they who are personages of considerable repute in this-worldly caste society. Such renouncers are also popularly known as *sannyasins*.

If we move from history to anthropology, we again find similar examples of the equivocal nature of renunciation. Richard Burghart successfully pointed out from his anthropological field studies how certain sannyasin sects are integrated within the caste system, and indeed use it as an organizing principle of their monastic life. The Dashnami Sannyasis only recruit the twice-born clean castes to their sects (Burghart 1996: 290). The Ramanandi sect is somewhat more liberated from caste restrictions in that they admit people from all castes to their sect. Within the sect, however, 'caste rules of commensality are observed so that the caste status of the sannyasin is not compromised' (Burghart 1996: 291). In addition, many of these sects are not hostile towards Muslims alone (Burghart 1996: 126), but also carry out violent and hostile campaigns against each other (Burghart 1996:126–8). Surely these so-called men of religion were far from having really renounced the world and all its seductions.

On the other hand the ascetics who live in isolation are so few and so distant that the notion that they have won social acclaim by renouncing caste does not play out in practice. It is true, however, that sannyasin renouncers have tremendous social appeal and prestige. But as they have not really left 'this world' it would be incorrect to say that their elevation occurs because they have opted out of the caste system and all its implications. The fact that the sannaysins and the ascetics have a similar outward appearance has led to a descriptive conflation of the two with rather unfortunate analytical consequences.

Class Mobility in Open Systems of Stratification: The Case of Class in America

In an open system of stratification mobility is always individually accomplished. When a member of the working class enters the managerial level it is not as if the entire family rises up at the same time. In an open system of stratification a single variable must be held in common by all those included in the hierarchy, so that quantitative differences in this variable can be measured in a rank order. If it is land-ownership, then the amount of land owned, from zero acres upwards, is placed in a hierarchy. It should be noticed that the hierarchy in such cases is a continuous one. The gradations do not yield categorical distinctions from within. If we are to separate the lower upper class from the lower upper middle class then it is done on analytical considerations that are not intrinsic to the hierarchy. Thus at one point anybody with 50 acres of land may be termed rich, and on other occasions only 25 acres might allow a person to make the same grade. It all depends on what the analyst would like to do with the gradations, and accordingly distinctions and cut-off points are made within the hierarchy.

Sometimes a continuous hierarchy can be constructed out of a composite of a number of variables, as in the Socio-Economic Status Indexes. Here a variety of factors are considered, like occupation, education, schooling, housing, source of income, in the constitutions of a quantifiable measurable scale. Once weights are attached to each of these variables, such a scale is quite amenable to fine gradations. This is precisely what was accomplished by Lloyd Warner and his associates in a number of studies on social stratification in America. For example, in the classic and oft-quoted work *Social Class in America*, Warner et al. (1949) constructed such a composite index and stratified the sample population into upper class, upper-middle class, lower upper middle class, upper lower class and lower lower class (Warner et al. 1949: 107). One of the persistent criticisms against the Warner school of stratification is that the criterion or criteria for making these class distinctions remain unspecified. For instance, why should there not be a further elaboration of categories to include the lower upper lower class, or a middle upper class and so on. This is not dealt with satisfactorily either by Warner himself or by his academic collaborators. What remains, however, is a continuous scale in which all the respondents who are included possess the identified attributes in greater or lesser quantities.

Composite socio-economic indexes such as the one employed by Warner can lead to disagreement among those studied and also amongst scholars. Disputes arise because the weights given to the variables are never above contestations. For instance, there may be a lot of disagreement regarding what kind of weight should be assigned to diverse occupations. A self-employed plumber may take umbrage if slotted below an office clerk, a shopkeeper may not agree to being placed below a school teacher. It is quite clear then that when such weights are attached to what are inherently different and incommensurable entities, something else is not being grafted from the outside even though the hierarchy has the semblance of continuity. If one were to rephrase the criticism against such socio-economic index studies then it would perhaps be appropriate to say that such studies run into difficulties as differences are being forced into a hierarchy. The end result is therefore bound to be capricious.

If, on the other hand, the hierarchy is established on the basis of a single quantifiable variable, such as wealth, power, or land owned, there is hardly any scope for dissension. A study that emphasizes a hierarchy composed in terms of a factor whose distribution can be seen in terms of more or less cannot be interested in studying social change, though there might be quite an active interest in social mobility, as with Warner et al. (1949). An open system of stratification is ultimately best suited when mobility and class status are plotted, or can be plotted, on a single quantifiable variable. In this case all those in the hierarchy have something in common, though some may have more of it than others. An open system gets complicated once elements of incommensurable differences are superimposed on it.

This tells us why America is seen as such an ideal (almost paradigmatic) case of an open system of stratification. More than the industrially advanced western European nations, America takes great pride in the fact that it has undermined all the privileges and estates of the old world. In America the unencumbered individual is supreme. This makes it the ideal locale for an open system of stratification to exhibit itself. What this also says is that Americans ideologically acquiesce to this system of stratification for they essentially see themselves as being very similar to one another. It is on the basis of this presumed similarity that we can later talk about a graded hierarchy.

Continuous Hierarchies or Discrete Castes: Comparing the Systems

There are other graded hierarchies too which may not have the same kind of popular appro-bation. The caste system is often considered to be a graded hierarchy based on the purity–pollution scale (Dumont 1970). This statement may seem quite unproblematic at first sight, but it conceals many complications. First, the hierarchy that the caste system posits can be seen as uniform and universal provided one takes on the prejudices of the particular caste that is elaborating this hierarchy. The truth is that there is no agreement over who should occupy which position in the hierarchy. It is not as if the Brahmins are universally acknowl-edged in Hindu India to be the most superior community. There are powerful Kshatriya or warrior castes who consider themselves as the most superior castes (Hocart 1945: 31–5; see also Quigley 1993: 3), and belittle both the Brahmin's status and occupation (Gupta 1997: 84–6). Thus, while there is agreement that castes should be hierarchized on the basis of natural substances there is no agreement as to how these supposed 'coded substances' can be quantified along a gradational scale (Marriott and Inden 1977).

At this point it is important to proceed cautiously. To begin with, while there is overall agreement that castes should be hierarchized, there are strong disagreements regarding the positioning of castes (Gupta 1992: 119–30). Even among Brahmins there is no consensus on the relative status of different Brahmin castes (Fuller 1984; Parry 1980: 89–91; Quigley 1993: 62). Further, the scale that is always referred to in the case of the caste system is one based on a putative purity–pollution hierarchy. This scale is itself problematic for it is understood differently in different contexts. When it comes to eating there is a scale of purity that is often observed (Marriott 1959) though here again there is no unanimity between castes regarding who can accept water or food from whom. Usually the implementation of such a hierarchy depends more on political power and less on straight ideological acquiescence (Gupta 1992). When it is not a question of food or inter-dining then the hierarchy of purity is not so much in evidence as the distinction between 'we' and the 'others'. The 'others' in such cases are ranked in order of the degree of distaste from the point of view of the caste in question. In this case it is not a scale of purity that is being invoked but one of pure otherness. In fact it is also possible to say that in such circumstances what is more significant is that the unalterable character of the other be maintained more than anything else. If a gradation of the other occurs it is not from any practical point of view, for neither occupations nor women are likely to be exchanged across caste boundaries.

The reason then why America has an open system of stratification whereas caste India has a closed one is because in the former case there is an ideological acceptance of a certain degree of similarity (Lipset and Bendix 1957), whereas in the latter there is an enormous invest-ment in keeping alive differences. Whenever differences dominate, the system tends to become closed. Contrarily whenever there is agreement over the possession of an attribute that can be quantitatively scaled one can see manifestations of an open system of stratification. Social mobility cannot be fully understood if studies on stratification pay attention to hierarchy only and not differences.

There is yet another advantage in emphasizing both hierarchy and difference while examining social stratification. As a continuous hierarchy in an open system demands and depends upon agreement over a baseline similarity, in that a certain attribute is possessed, to varying degrees, by all in the hierarchy, there is no room for prejudice in the making of the ranked order. When, however, inherently incommensurable differences are placed in a ranked order, we are immediately sensitized to the fact that the ordering is obeying a criterion that is imposed from outside. This imposition can only be an outcome of prejudice. A gross demonstration of this can be seen when sectarians claim that certain languages are inherently superior to others, or that certain religions are more civilized than others. An infinitely more subtle expression of prejudice, but prejudice nevertheless, is found when it is calmly assumed that there is a clear, unanimous caste hierarchy based on the notion of purity and pollution. This ignores the vital reality of castes refusing to accept low status and claiming elevated origins of their own (Gupta 1992). That these non-Brahmanical tales of origin have been ignored in the main has given the impression that castes can unproblematically be placed along a continuous hierarchy.

An open system of stratification is different from a closed system of stratification for a number of reasons. What is most important, however, is that these differences only come to light when a clear distinction is made between hierarchy and difference. In an open system of stratification hierarchy is central, while in a closed system differences dominate. The ranking of logically discrete and incommensurable entities implies real or potential conflict and disagreement. It is this lack of accord that predisposes the stratification system towards a closed character. As differences are emphasized in closed systems of stratification, it is never the individual that is the unit of mobility but the group. For individuals to be mobile there must be agreement on certain baseline similarities between individuals. Further, mobility is found to be justified when individuals acquire a higher quantum of a stated attribute. As the attribute itself is not being changed but is subject to internal gradation, any instance of social mobility does not damage the positions of others in the hierarchy.

A stratification system based on difference may also be ranked and enforced by political power, but any change in ranking in such a system would automatically entail that some other group (or groups) lose status. This is a point that Murray Milner (1994: 29) made very effectively when he said that status hierarchies are zero sum in character. When a group rises in the ranks within a closed system of stratification it must necessarily displace, either in fact or in imagination, the privileged and superior position of some other group or groups. For example, when the Jats or the Rajputs or the Marathas rose to ascendance they displaced the earlier ruling castes in their respective regions. When a Harijan who is disparagingly called a Chamar claims to belong to a Brahmin caste, there is vicarious displacement of the position of the actual Brahmins and other better-off castes in the imaginings of this community that are neither lies, nor pure fabrication. The claim to a superior Brahmin status by Harijans is real as far as this community is concerned, regardless of whether or not it can realize this status in practice. So for Harijans to claim Brahmin status, somewhere in their imaginings the Brahmins who are present must necessarily undergo some status diminution.

In caste conflicts which have been politicized this characteristic is plainly visible. The non-Brahmin movement in both Maharashtra and Tamil Nadu was not simply for the upward mobility of the Maratha or the Mali or the Vellallah or the Thevar or the Gowda castes, but also to undermine the status of Brahmins in these provinces. In feudal societies the aspirations of powerful groups of hitherto subjugated people can be realized only by overthrowing the existing nobility, or by significantly undermining its status.

In an open system of stratification upward mobility does not mean that somebody else must lose status as a consequence. The fact that such movements take place with relative ease is again because the movement is at the level of the individual who is not marked by difference but positioned according to the degree to which the quantifiable attribute that resides within the person has been expressed. Ideologically, such an open system of stratification must assume that people are all equal and that mobility occurs to the extent that people can realize their potentials.

Status and Hierarchy: Impurities in Open Systems of Stratification

In closed systems of stratification it is assumed, on the contrary, that people are inherently different, which is why the notions of the upstart, the *parvenu*, and the social climber have such pejorative connotations. There are times when an open system of stratification is held back by status considerations. Such status considerations are frequently placed in a hierarchy, but this again is a demonstration of prejudice more than anything else. Status distinctions are derived from life-style differences. Even in a modern society where there is relative development of open systems of stratification, it is not as if the issue of difference does not occur at all. Difference manifests itself in these societies in considerations of status. While such status markers do not have the obvious tag of being determined by birth, the qualities demanded are such that they are difficult to attain within a single lifetime. The emphasis now is not so much on the extent of education but on the cultivation of certain dispositions, like taste in music and the classics (Bourdieu 1984). Statuses are marked on the basis of a prejudicial combination of those factors that best reflect the attainments and attributes of the superior communities. As Erving Goffman (1961) perceptively pointed out, an attribute of status snobbery can also be a deliberate and idiosyncratic elaboration of a routine aspect of everyday life. Thus, for example, table manners seem very important, for how one eats a sandwich or pours out tea can indicate the status of a person.

By elevating such routine activities with a certain style that is not generally known or prevalent, a status group can set itself apart as being superior to the rest. Here again it is not a question of gradations. It is hard to grade the styles of eating a sandwich or drinking tea. Either one has the style or lacks it. When dispositions, habits, and manners are cultivated to distance oneself from others, this is not done on a continuous hierarchical scale but one that first emphasizes difference. Given this logic of status distinctions it would be incorrect, and, indeed prejudicial, to talk in terms of 'high' and 'low' culture, or in terms of crude and 'pedigreed culture' (Bourdieu 1984: 56–63). In Bourdieu, for example, what should have really remained as 'distinctions' are suddenly converted into a gradational scale, thus sublating the fact that the variations were based in the first instance on 'differences'. That these differences have now been made to stand in a graded ranked order is not a natural property of the system but has been introduced from without. Academics too are therefore susceptible to such slippages into prejudice. The scope and frequency of such prejudices can be reduced by realizing that hierarchies do not arise naturally out of differences.

In an influential essay, Talcott Parsons (1953) argued that to attribute value to something is to hierarchize it at the same time. The truth of this statement can be gauged in studies of stratification, particularly in the understanding of closed systems of stratification. When a hierarchy is imposed after giving value to a difference then this hierarchy is very different from an open system. In an open system the continuous hierarchy accepts variations in the quantum of a similar attribute among a given population. When status considerations are introduced in an open classificatory system, there is a normative mismatch. This can be exemplified quite starkly by once again taking America as an example.

Race relations in America are governed by status considerations of the kind that should not have been permitted in an open system of stratification. This is the essence of what Gunnar Myrdal once called the *American Dilemma*. On the one hand Americans freely admit that all are equal, which is in line with the declared American valuation of social mobility and an open system of stratification. At the same time there are strong attitudes of intolerance towards the blacks. They are seen by the white population as inferior in culture, taste, and custom. The inability of Americans to resolve this dilemma was the subject of Myrdal's influential work (Myrdal 1962). In many ways the Blacks may have at one point bought into the hierarchy of race by accepting the superiority of the colour white over the colour black. The Blue Vein Society, which existed in Nashville in the first two decades of this century, was an association of light-skinned Blacks who did not allow the darker- complexioned Blacks to be members of that society. The crucial test for admission was whether or not the veins were clearly and visibly blue on a person's wrist (Russel et al. 1992: 24–5). Any person whose skin colour was too dark for the veins to come through in this fashion was denied membership to the association. The fact that such a colour hierarchy was subscribed to by some Blacks makes them that much more accepting of the ideological basis of the gradation by colour. This immediately reveals that those who belong to societies such as the Blue Vein Society (or the Bon Ton Society in Washington) would not protest against colour discrimination.

Just as caste prejudice exists in spite of public declarations to the country, likewise racism lurks in America even though it has been officially disbanded. As long as racism separates the Whites from the Blacks the chances of moving up the colour hierarchy will be severely restricted. The lighter-skinned Blacks may take some pride in their complexions, but as far as colour categories are concerned a Black is always a Black. At one point there was an attempt to quantify it by saying that a person would be legally Black if it could be proved that one-sixty-fourth of his ancestry was Black. This 'one drop rule' was legally quashed in the 1970s but sentiments of this order are quite dominant among the American people. The melting pot has done a good job as far as the White population of America is concerned, but as for the rest the 'mosaic' and the 'salad bowl' still act as lively metaphors.

Caste and Race: Contrasting Examples of Closed Systems of Stratification

Though caste and race are manifestations of closed systems of stratification, it is not as if they are similar to each other. Race is based on phenotypical biological differences, while in the caste system the natural differences are even said to exist in the nature of coded substances that cannot be detected by the senses. But there are more basic differences between race and caste. Though it is considered demeaning for different races to intermarry or even have sexual relations, the notion that a Black person can pollute a White person does not exist. There were, therefore, Black cooks and Black wet nurses even in the ante-bellum South. In India it is inconceivable that a Brahmin, or any one of those who have successfully claimed a twice-born caste status, would ever have a member of an Untouchable community even enter their kitchen, let alone cook or be a wet nurse.

Further, in a racial society one's attachment to a community increases with the level of generality. Thus it did not quite matter in apartheid-practising South Africa if one was French, German, English, or Nordic by birth as long as one was White. Likewise, it did not really make a difference, again in South Africa, whether people came from Namibia, Zambia, or Mozambique—they were all considered Blacks. In other words the fact of belonging to a race grows stronger the wider the net is spread. As particular categories of Blacks are not relevant to particular categories of Whites, it is the distinction between Whites and Blacks that matters most.

In the caste system the logic is, if anything, quite the reverse: different castes have different kinds of interactions with other castes and particular castes have very particular effects on other castes. Contrary to the situation regarding race, the loyalty to one's caste increases the more focalized it gets until it ultimately climaxes at the endogamous *jati* level. Caste categories like Brahmin may excite more passion than the category 'twice-born caste', but the degree of belonging grows as one gets more specific. To belong to a Saraswat Brahmin caste, or to a Maithili Brahmin caste, or to a Kanyakubj Brahmin caste is the ultimate as far as intensity of belonging is concerned in a caste society.

Finally, the manner in which children of mixed marriages are graded in the case of race and caste differs significantly. In a racial society there are terms like mulatto, octoroon, and quadroon that grade the content of White and Black streams in a person of mixed origin. Though a person still remains Black in spite of mixed blood, an octoroon or mulatto is not pushed below the status of the Black parent. In fact such a person may enjoy some advantages over other Blacks purely on grounds of colour. These people of mixed racial origin appear less displeasing to White sensibilities than persons with undiluted Black ancestry. In contrast, in the caste system mixed caste parentage outcastes the child from the caste of both parents. This is why ancient Hindu scriptures like the Manusmriti and the Yagnavalkyasmriti warned against any sexual or marital liaison across castes. These texts clearly state that should such unions produce an offspring, the child will not be of a caste in-between those of the parents, but would be of another caste, far lower than the caste of either parent. This is how these texts justify the existence of the lowly Chamars and Chandals.

The criteria for stratification, whether in an open or in a closed system, have to be socially signified by a number of tangible markers. Though colour and wealth can be considered as features that are easy to identify, they are nevertheless given greater salience through a range of symbolic practices that repeatedly and incessantly underscore the validity of the stratificatory system. It is also true that the less obvious the criteria of stratification, the greater is the symbolic energy spent to make them come to life. Because race differences were quite obvious they did not require too many symbolic markers to signal the divergent statuses and positions within the hierarchy. While we must recall the validity of what was said earlier—that not all natural differences are important for stratificatory systems—it is also true that there is less pressure to mark statuses with ritual/symbolic observances and beliefs if these differences are obvious to the senses. This is probably why it is possible to have a Black cook in a racist society but not an Untouchable in a Brahmin's kitchen. As castes are first differentiated and then capriciously hierarchized on the basis of supposed natural substances that are not tangible to the senses, there is greater stress on ritual and symbolic behaviour in this form of stratification. It is as if the abundance of details in caste distinctions exists to make up for the unconvincing tangible evidence of difference.

Likewise pure differences in wealth need not create barriers between people. The owner–

cultivating Jats and Gujars of western Uttar Pradesh cannot easily be distinguished on the criterion of land owned. A rich Jat (or Gujar) farmer and a poor farmer belonging to the same caste lead identical lifestyles and consume practically the same things (Gupta 1997: 41–4). It is when status considerations overlay economic differences that the economic hierarchy begins to show up in more pronounced form. This again reveals the scope for demonstrating difference through status considerations in what should have been a pure and open gradational hierarchy. Once wealth is used to seal off access by the non-wealthy categories to status goods then status markers stand in for wealth, and differences are created on what was once only a continuous gradation. The fact that status differences supervene upon open hierarchical systems probably tells us that human beings are fallible everywhere. In some places this particular weakness towards creating distance between themselves gets greater encouragement for display than in others. But the tendency to create distinctions and social distance seems to have the status of an anthropological truism.

Protests and their Scope: Beyond Descriptive Sociology

It should be quite clear that though analytical distinctions exist between open and closed systems of stratification, and between hierarchy and difference, no one system of stratification exists in pure form. Open systems of stratification are belied by status distinctions, and closed systems of stratification enforce a hierarchy on what are logically equal and horizontal categories. There seems to be universal sociological resistance to both hierarchical order and to horizontally differentiated utopias. But it is still important to stress these analytical distinctions, for they help us organize our perceptions of how mobility and protest are worked out on the ground. If one were to be unaware of these conceptual distinctions, then open and closed systems of stratification would be simple descriptive categories that appear in historical succession. After all a sociology of social stratification cannot be just a descriptive exercise. It should also provide us with heuristic tools to understand the trajectories of change in different social orders. This in turn should help us grapple with the variations in ambitions, drives, and discontents that exist in different societies.

Keeping this in mind it is worthwhile to examine the scope of protests in different systems of stratification. In an open system of stratification protests can take place on two counts. The first, and more innocuous, variety of protest occurs when for some reason mobility is blocked within the system. This can happen due to a downturn in the business cycle, which leads to retrenchment and recession. In such cases the protest of those who feel their mobility stifled is usually aimed at bad managers and faulty business decisions. This kind of protest may be termed 'economism'. Economism does not challenge the hierarchy, but attacks those who, it is believed, have not played fair by the rules of the extant hierarchical system.

If the open class system is to be challenged at the core then there is no alternative but to step outside the one-dimensional and flat variations of the graded hierarchy and call in a multitude of differences to fuel an ideology of change. The worker is not just somebody who occupies a certain position in the power hierarchy and in the economic hierarchy, (s)he also occupies a social position that has many more aspects to it than can be subsumed by a continuous hierarchy. The agitating workers will now draw upon the diversities in tradition between themselves and their superior classes. Though they acquiesced to a lower ranking on the continuous hierarchical scale, once elements outside the hierarchy are brought in to substantiate the fullness of their being, there is no question of willing subjugation, and an alternative social order seems more possible. Protests of this sort will recall working class traditions, tales of bravery and of sacrifice, homilies and aphorisms of moral probity and virtue, to realize a community, even a fraternity, that is redolent with a multitude of specific characteristics. To build a dialectic that does not return to its starting point in endless rounds of regression, the ammunition for protest must be sought by stepping outside the continuous hierarchy and attaining the gravity of difference. The sliding scale of a continuous hierarchy is far too parlous for sustaining such ambitions.

Perhaps the distinctions Marxists draw between a class in itself and a class for itself can be understood in this light. When a class functions within the ideological framework of the continuous hierarchy then it may be said to function as a class in-itself. When this same class steps out of the quantitative hierarchy and attempts to de-legitimize it, it must necessarily ballast itself by a substantiation of differences. It is only by the consolidation of such attributes of differences that an alternative social order becomes a tangible goal worth striving for. It is on account of building a substantial body of differences that the ideology of change can be symbolically energized. A successful revolutionary movement, or one with a fair chance of success, cannot afford to be unidimensional in character. To be enthused by a vision of an alternative social order, or even of an alternative form of hierarchical ranking (which is admittedly much less ambitious) requires a gathering of differences on a variety of fronts.

In protest movements under closed systems of stratification, such as in caste mobilizations, there seems to be no real alternative but to emphasize differences. The hierarchy in force in such systems of stratification is largely a matter of power, and not so much of ideological acceptance. Mobility in closed systems of stratification was therefore always a major historical event. There was nothing routine about it as is the case with movements up or down a continuous hierarchy. Its relative infrequency, particularly in pre-modern times, is because it took so much to effect social mobility in closed systems of stratification. This often gives the impression to contemporary scholars that there was relative peace in ancient and medieval times. This, however, is just an illusion of distance.

Gradational and Relational Approaches: Stratifying Industrial Societies

It is not as if the deficiencies of seeing social stratification only as a ranked and continuous hierarchy have not been noticed earlier. Quite some time ago Stanislaw Ossowski noted the difference between gradational and relational theories of stratification. In recent years John Goldthorpe et al. (1987) and Erik Olin Wright (1979, 1985) have used the relational scheme of stratification to understand modern classes in industrial societies. Before we posit the advantages of notions of difference, it is necessary to give a quick overview of what Goldthorpe et al. as well as Wright meant by relational theories. Goldthorpe et al. as well as Wright felt that gradational (or hierarchical) theories of stratification lacked explanatory and dynamic capabilities; these theories presented a static and timeless social order. In place of such gradational perspectives Goldthorpe et al. as well as Wright, quite independent of each other, proposed a relational approach. This approach was influenced by Marxist scholarship and its left-wing credentials are quite obvious.

Goldthorpe et al. distinguish between service, intermediate, and working classes in what might seem to be another ranked hierarchy. Goldthorpe et al. dispute such a reading and insist that each of these classes and their subdivisions are relational in character and reflect the tension between classes. The service class consists of high-grade professionals, followed by low-grade professionals and managers in small businesses. The intermediate class is made up of clerical and rank-and-file non-manual employees. In this category they also include small proprietors, self-employed artisans, and supervisors of manual workers. The working class is made up of skilled, semi-skilled, and unskilled manual workers.

The fact that these classes and their constituents are presented in a vertical fashion gives credence to the allegation that this is yet another gradational scheme. To go by Goldthorpe et al.'s own assertions, the class element in their presentation is determined primarily by considerations of the market and their occupational situation. Thus a self-employed artisan would not be at the same level as an employed one. A closer look, however, tells us that there is a quantitative variable that is uniformly present in the making of Goldthorpe's distinctions between the three major classes. The quantitative factor is that of power over one's work process. The service sector has greater control over its own work process as well as that of the other classes, and at the bottom are the manual workers who have no control at all. In between is the independent artisan who is higher than the one who is employed in a factory. In a sense then Goldthorpe et al.'s classes are also gradational, as their hierarchy is determined to a large extent on the uniform variable of power and control over the work process. This is relational too no doubt but hierarchies always posit relations. The grades and ranks within a hierarchy would make no sense on their own. To be rich makes sense only when there are poor people around.

A charitable reading of Goldthorpe et al. would encourage a somewhat different conclusion. The relation between classes that they draw our attention to is not simply a logical relation but a real one in a rather concrete sense. Classes are related in Goldthorpe et al.'s scheme because some classes exercise authority over others in the work process. This is somewhat analogous to the argument that it is not simply a question of there being the rich and the poor as logical necessities, but that the rich exist because it is the poor who make them rich. But do the rich and the poor, or, as in this case, those who control the work process versus those who do not, ever see themselves as embodying differences that are independent of each other? Only then can a class in-itself become a class for-itself. To realize that as a subjugated class one is in the grip of a power hierarchy certainly is a necessary but not sufficient condition for class action— and class action is one of the principal concerns of Goldthorpe et al.

How well does Erik Olin Wright's class map figure in this connection? Wright proceeds on a more markedly Marxist path. The terms that he uses for the various classes, such as bourgeois, petty bourgeois and proletariat, clearly announce his theoretical position. He too makes a composite index of sorts using the variables of ownership or non-ownership of the means of production, and control or autonomy in the production process. We then have a class map with the bourgeois on top, followed by small employees, who are in turn followed by managers and supervisors. After this category we enter the distinctly blue-collar domain with the semi-autonomous wage earners, and finally the proletariat. Wright has amended this map in his later work by clearly postulating a graph based on the quantifiable axes of skills and organizational assets (Wright 1979, 1985).

In Wright we have a combination of hierarchy and difference. The two great polar opposites spanning the extreme ends of his hierarchy are the bourgeoisie and the proletariat. The more capital a bourgeoisie controls the higher his status. On the other hand, the more dependent a worker is on the bourgeois and his managerial class, the lower position on the class map. This situation is not unlike Goldthorpe et al.'s (1987) analysis, though the distinction between bourgeoise and proletariat classes are put in irreconcilable terms. Subsequent elaboration of the class map undoes this irreconcilability to a certain extent, for the two get bridged by the hierarchy of power and control over the production process.

In the final analysis the relational theories provide an alternative to pure hierarchical and gradational approaches to social stratification. For Goldthorpe et al. as well as Wright class is not just occupation, as it was with a host of scholars who followed the lead set by Lipset and Bendix in their classic study *Social Mobility in Industrial Society* (1957). Yet Wright and Goldthorpe et al. fall short because the relational aspects that they so steadfastly emphasize are ultimately compromised by gradational considerations. Nevertheless, they succeeded in presenting a picture of stratification in modern industrial societies, and of the tensions that underlie the relationship between classes. In that sense their contributions are also superior to the earlier works by Lloyd Warner and his team which were primarily descriptive and static in character. But to be able to exploit more fully the potentialities of the relational approach it is necessary to consider it in the light of the distinctions between hierarchy and difference.

Relational approaches can be strengthened if the conception of difference is consciously integrated into them. Differences become salient features of social stratification when logically incommensurable phenomena are forced into a hierarchy. The tension that Wright and Goldthorpe et al. would like us to appreciate can only be underlined once the potentialities for developing differences within different classes are gauged. The sources for substantiating these differences cannot come from the hierarchy of power and supervisory control. When working-class movements react primarily to hierarchies of this sort they only end up, as Marx once put it, fomenting petty bourgeois revolts. While Marxism would posit that little could be gained in a confrontation between managers and big capitalists, or between big capitalists and small capitalists, or between workers and management, such conflagarations occur more frequently than thoroughgoing social revolutions. Though these classes may initially face off against each other because of their divergent positions in the hierarchy, to sustain the tempo of protest, attributes from outside the hierarchy will have to be factored in to give body to the many dimensions of differences between combatants. Only this would allow a variety of nodes of symbolic activity to become simultaneously possible sustaining the imaginings of an alternative order with an alternative hierarchy.

Hierarchy and Difference in Marx and Weber

It is widely acknowledged in contemporary sociology that the contributions of Marx and Weber face each other as theoretical antagonists. While Marx was an advocate of social change, Weber gave more weight to order and to the politics of responsibility. In Weber's understanding Marxists were prone to the politics of commitment, as they did not pay close enough attention to the real interests of people which always emerged from their life chances in the marketplace (Weber 1946). When politics is oriented toward ideologies of commitment then all hell fire and brimstone are let loose. In this commotion the ideologies satisfy their thirst for power while the real needs of the various classes in society remain unmet.

Weber, quite unabashedly, advocated the politics of responsibility. This variety of politics has little room for the ideologue. Greater attention is paid to the real issues of people and how they can be sorted out in a disaggregated fashion depending upon where one's actual empirical interests lie. Unlike the great proletarian revolutions which brought together masses of diverse class backgrounds but under one overarching ideological banner, supposedly led by the working class, the politics of responsibility is a much more modest affair. Weber preferred this kind of politics for its greater fidelity to the observed and defined interests of each social class in the marketplace. These interests were experiential ones and did not have to go through the mutation of a grand ideological operator who sifted the false consciousness from the real.

Though there have been attempts from time to time to place Marx and Weber on the same side, this was clearly not Weber's intention. For our purposes we can see the distinction between them more starkly by casting their divergences in terms of our conceptions of hierarchy and difference. For Marx, a class society was characterized by irreconcilable differences between determinate classes locked into a constitutive contradiction. Thus in a feudal society the basic contradiction was between the feudal lord and the serf. In a capitalist society, likewise, the class struggle is between the capitalist and the proletariat.

For Marx and Marxism it does not really make sense to see these classes in a hierarchy. It is not as if one can gradually become more of a capitalist and less of a worker, or vice versa. As far as the critical element of social contradiction is concerned, capital and labour face each other as objective, structural antagonists. The differences between them are so great that neither wealth nor any other status considerations could diminish them. Therefore, the capital–labour difference is not the same as the distinction between the rich and the poor which can be placed along a hierarchy. The contradictions between capitalists and workers reject any hierarchical ordering because they arise out of extreme difference.

For Weber, in his landmark essay, 'Class, Status and Party', it was hierarchy that was most significant in each of these orders of stratification. Weber argued that class alliances emerged from the hierarchy of the market place. In other words, one's affiliation with a certain class was an outcome of the generosity with which one was treated in the market. It was the market-place that created a hierarchy of success, and it is this that determined the kind of class action which properly informed the politics of commitment. To step outside of this and reach for a communal class action that arraigns a large number of classes along the capital–labour divide would be giving in to the politics of commitment.

Weber also saw notions of status and power along similar lines. Status was determined on the basis of consumption, and power on the extent to which one could effectively exercise control over others. Both status and power are understood hierarchically. Further, Weber insisted that the three axes of social stratification, namely class, status, and power, be seen as independent of one another, even though they cannot always be separated in fact. Nevertheless, for Weber, disputes should first be presented along the specific axes of stratification before their interrelationships are sought. It might also be added that Weber placed greater emphasis on the separation of these axes of stratification than on their mutual interplay.

This is what further separates Marx from Weber. For Marx, power and status are closely related to class. This is what the famous relationship between basis and superstructure is all about in Marxism. Weber's constant exhortation that economics, status, and power dimensions be kept separate was a rebuttal of the Marxian emphasis to see the economic realm as determining, or at least setting the limits of, social action. In Marxism, contradictions, or extreme differences, between workers and capitalists set the conditions for other classes and other hostilities to manifest themselves in capitalist societies. A capitalist society does not just have these two classes, that is, the capitalist and the worker. There are lawyers, doctors, teachers, fitters, mechanics, and so on, as well. Yet Marxists would insist, all these other classes are constrained in their functioning by the basic contradictions of each epoch.

The divergences between Marx and Weber can thus be encapsulated in terms of the manner in which each highlighted questions of hierarchy and difference. Since Weber was drawn closer to hierarchy, his study of class, status, and party privileged order over change. Marx, on the contrary, was a champion of difference. This led him to emphasize change over social order and stability. As has been mentioned earlier, the most crucial class difference for Marx was incapable of being subjected to a hierarchical ordering. The bourgeoisie was not different from the proletariat because the former was rich and the latter poor, or because the former lived a lifestyle full of literary pretensions, while the latter led a much ruder existence. As the capital–labour, or the bourgeoisie–proletariat, contradictions are irreconcilable in nature, these two classes cannot be placed on a graded hierarchical scale.

Looking back from what has been said so far, it is clearly up to us how we learn from the history of sociological theory. Marx and Weber have been emphasized in this section only to drive home the analytical differences between the two that could benefit a contemporary analysis of social stratification. Though Marx elaborated difference more than hierarchy, and Weber hierarchy more than difference, it cannot be said that either of them presented one side to the exclusion to the other. The stylized contrast between Marx and Weber presented here was primarily for analytical purposes.

Stratification is about both hierarchy and difference. If hierarchy strains to establish stability, social differences constantly pose a threat to order. To understand better the dimensions of inequality and the social trajectories they trace, hierarchy and differences must be conjointly examined in any study of social stratification. Only then can such an academic undertaking elucidate the possibilities of change, social mobility, and transformation. To look at hierarchy without difference would impoverish our appreciation of closed and open systems of stratification and with it our ability to position the elements of dynamism in any social order.

REFERENCES

Béteille, André. 1977. *Inequality among Men*. Oxford and London: Basil Blackwell.

Bourdieu, Pierre. 1984. *Distinction: A Social Critique of the Judgement of Taste*. Cambridge, Mass.: Harvard University Press.

Burghart, Richard. 1996. In C. J. Fuller and Jonathan Spencer, eds, *The Conditions of Listening: Essays on Religion, History and Politics of South Asia*. Delhi: Oxford University Press.

Dumont, Louis. 1960. 'World Renunciation in Indian Religions'. *Contributions to Indian Sociology*. 4:33–62.

_____. 1970. *Homo Hierarchicus: The Caste System and its Implications*. London: Weidenfeld and Nicholson.

Fuller, C.J. 1984. *Servants of the Goddess*. Delhi: Oxford University Press.

Goffman, Erving. 1961. *The Presentation of Self in Everyday Life*. Harmondsworth: Penguin.

Goldthorpe, J.H., C. Llewellyn, and C. Payne. 1987. *Social Mobility and Class Structure in Modern Britain*. Oxford: Clarendon Press.

Gupta, Dipankar, 1992. 'Continuous Hierarchies and Discrete Castes'. In Dipankar Gupta, ed., *Social Stratification*. Delhi: Oxford University Press.

_____. 1997. *Rivalry and Brotherhood: Politics in the Life of Farmers of Northern India*. Delhi: Oxford University Press.

Hocart, A.M. 1945. *Caste: A Comparative Study*. London: Methuen and Co.

Lipset, S.M and R. Bendix. 1957. *Social Mobility in Industrial Society*. Glencoe, Illinois: The Free Press.

Marx, Karl and Frederick Engels. 1962. 'Manifesto of the Communist Party'. In Karl Marx and Frederick Engels, ed., *Selected Works*, vol. 1. Moscow: Foreign Languages Publishing House.

Marriott, McKim. 1959. 'Interactional and Attributional Theory of Caste Ranking'. *Man in India*. 39:92–107.

Marriott, McKim and Ronald B. Inden. 1977. 'Towards a Ethnosociology of the South Asian Caste System'. In Kenneth A David, ed., *The New Wind: Changing Identities in South Asia*. Chicago: Aldine Publications.

Milner, Murray. 1994. *Status and Sacredness: A General Theory of Status Relations and an Analysis of Indian Culture*. New York: Oxford University Press.

Myrdal, Gunnar. 1962. *An American Dilemma*. New York: Harper.

Ortner, Sherry B. 1991. 'Reading America: Preliminary Notes on Culture and Class'. In R.G. Fox, ed., *Recapturing Anthropology*. Santa Fe: School of American Research.

Parry, Jonathan. 1980. 'Ghosts, Greed and Sin: The Occupational Identity of the Banaras Funeral Priests'. *Man* (n.s.). 15:88–111.

Parsons, Talcott. 1953. 'A Revised Theoretical Approach to the Theory of Social Stratification'. In R. Bendix and S.M. Lipset, eds, *Class Status and Power: A Reader in Social Stratification*. Glencoe, Illinois: Free Press.

Quigley, Declan. 1993. *The Interpretation of Caste*. Oxford: Clarendon Press.

Russel, Kathy, Midge Wilson, and Ronald Hall. 1992. *The Colour Complex: The Politics of Skin Colour among African Americans*. New York: Anchor Books, Doubleday.

Sorokin, Pitrim. 1967. 'Social Stratification'. In Talcott Parsons, Edward Shils, K.D. Neghle, and J.R. Pitts, eds, *Theories of Society: Foundations of Modern Sociology*, vol.1. Glencoe, Illinois: The Free Press.

Thapar, Romila. 1978. *Ancient Indian Social History: Some Interpretations*. Delhi: Orient Longman.

Warner, Lloyd, Marchia Meeker, and Kenneth Eels. 1949. *Social Class in America*. Chicago: Science Research Associates.

Weber, Max. 1946. 'Class, Status and Party'. In H.H. Gerth and C.Wright Mills, trans. and ed., *From Max Weber: Essays in Sociology*. New York: Oxford University Press.

Wright, Erik Olin. 1979. *Class Structure and Income Determination*. New York: Academic Press.

———. 1985. *Classes*. London: Verso.

The Indian City

Narayani Gupta

URBAN STUDIES

Among the many things for which Patrick Geddes, the first professor of sociology in India, will be remembered is his contribution to the development of urban studies in India. His conversations and writings, above all his admiration for Indian towns, kindled an interest in Indian urban forms among administrators and scholars, ranging from Sanskritists to geographers (Gupta 1988). The Madras Geographical Association from the 1920s, and the Department of Geography at Varanasi in the 1950s, directed research towards the study of individual towns and urbanization (Ramachandran 1988). From the mid-1950s, as part of the massive exercise of building up a database for planners, there was an increase in studies of towns—by economists, demographers, and sociologists (Bose 1973). Urban history, which had academic but little practical value, saw a pioneering venture in 1968 (Gillion) but became a popular subject for research only from the late 1970s. Today the volume of work on urban history is beginning to catch up with that on urban 'problems'. Urban histories have a salutary effect in that they soften the sharpness of the 'traditional'/'modern' binary used by many social scientists. 'Modern' itself means three very different things—a set of values, a revolution in technology, a point in chronology. Similarly, 'traditional' means many different things, but most scholars assume a singular meaning as well as the unchanging character of 'tradition'.

Urban History

Typologies

Urban historians in India have to be wary of two dangers—first, the tendency to follow the periodization into 'ancient', 'medieval', and 'modern' used for much of European history (Thapar 1966). The insidious fusing of these terms with, respectively, 'Hindu', 'Islamic', and 'British' can prompt generalizations which may not be justified. The other danger is that many European or American texts on the city may be treated as canonical—but, to mention some of the best known examples, Fustel de Coulanges' *Ancient City* was only about the Greeks, Henri Pirenne's 'medieval towns' are those of western Europe, and 'modern towns' usually refer only to North America. Some stereotypes are being abandoned—it is now agreed that 'Islamic urbanism' is an over-simplified category (Brown 1986), and also that there is no family resemblance between the 'colonial towns' of North America and those of South Asia (Ross and Telkamp 1985).

Sources

While there is a wide range of material—documents, oral evidence, the built environment—available for the study of urban centres in the last two centuries in India, there is very little for the earlier times. It would be unfair to expect to find the kind of information that one can easily find for contemporary European towns or medieval Indian towns; for example, information about wages, property transfers, or street alignments. It is also important to appreciate that different scholars look for different things in the same town—Sharar's (1975) Lucknow is suffused with *nazakat* (refinement) and nostalgia; for Hasan (1997) it is a town marked by violence; for Llewellyn-Jones (1985) it was an architectural free-for-all; while Oldenburg (1984) directs our attention to the heavy 'ordering' hand of the British after 1858.

Urban and Rural

The predominantly rural and agricultural character of India often makes one forget its five millennia of urbanism. 'There is a view current in some circles of sociologists that the distinction between rural and urban sociology is not meaningful in the Indian context because about 80 per cent of the people live in villages' (Rao 1991). In Europe, economic changes in the last 150 years led to a major revolution. As a result, today an overwhelming proportion of the population lives in urban areas. Such a revolution has not occurred in India, though the relative proportion of town dwellers has been increasing since the 1930s. Bombay, Calcutta and Delhi figure among the largest cities of the world, but their size is explained, like that of many others, as a result of 'urbanization without industrialization'.

Urban Patterns

The pattern of urban settlements—the spacing of cities, medium-sized towns, and small towns ('size' being used to mean that of population, not spatial extent) varies from region to region. The northern plain and eastern India are characterized by a few very large cities, and many small towns and *qasbas* (market towns). Gujarat, Karnataka, and Tamil Nadu have a large number of fairly evenly spaced medium towns; this is also true of late-twentieth-century Punjab and Haryana. Kerala has an unusual landscape of almost continuous urbanism. Andhra and Orissa are markedly under-urbanized. These features are of long vintage—186 of the 216 towns with populations of over one lakh (1981 Census) are historic ones, that is, they are over 200 years old. From the 1950s, there have been official surveys which have repeatedly suggested how urban centres should be spread more evenly across the country, but these suggestions have not met with much success (National Commission on Urbanization 1988).

Classification

Census enumerators and demographers define and grade towns on the basis of population. By the geographers' definition, towns are multifunctional—that is, inhabited by people performing functions that are not primary (agricultural) functions but secondary (industrial) and tertiary (service). In India, Sanskrit and Persian, as well as the vernaculars, have had terms to distinguish different kinds of towns (*rajdhani*, capital; *pattana*, commercial city; *nagara*, town; *shahar*, town; *bandar*, port; *qala*, fort; *qasba*, market town; etc.). Towns can be classified according to their original or chief function—capitals, forts, ports, university towns, temple towns, and hill stations. With the passage of time, the dominant function often changes. Agra began as a capital, but continued as a major commercial *entrepôt*.

Trade

Trade, regional and long distance, has been a rationale for towns since early times. The 'rise' and 'fall' of regimes did not necessarily promote or paralyse trade. In the third and second millennia BC, urban settlements along the Indus linked Afghanistan to Sumer (Ratnagar 1981). When oceanic trade decreased with the decline of Sumer, other transcontinental routes developed, as indicated by sites in the Indus–Ganga interfluve. In the thousand years when Buddhism was dominant (third century BC to eighth century AD), its expansion, marked by monasteries and universities, was linked with that of trade (Ray 1994). As a result, an urban map was spread over much of the subcontinent and central Asia, the towns of which continued to be linked by trade long after Buddhism declined in India. From the ninth century onwards, these ties were reinforced by Islam, when armies, Sufi preachers, and caravans of merchants moved between towns in west and central Asia and India. Guilds of artisans, craftsmen, and traders—strongly bonded families of Marwaris, Chettiars, Bohras, and Parsis—established bases in ports and inland towns (Chattopadhyaya 1994; Champakalakshmi 1996; Ramaswamy 1985). In the eighteenth century, the inroads made by some European trading companies led to a decline in the populations of some towns (described as 'deurbanization'); Surat and Masulipatnam lost merchants to Bombay and Madras (Das Gupta 1979; Subrahmanyam 1993). When the British took over Indian states, towns like Thanjavur, Dhaka, and Murshidabad lost their courts and, therefore, some of their artisans and court gentry. Later, improved highways and the new railway network created new centres and revived older ones (Bayly 1983). From the end of the nineteenth century, with the installation of mechanized factory industries, some towns became much more heavily populated.

Political Power, Culture, Defence

Monumental architecture led to some towns being labelled 'ritual-regal' or 'patrimonial-bureaucratic' (Weber 1966), as 'temple towns' (Geddes 1919) or forts. Most of them were richly multifunctional, and those that became quite deserted were those which were unifunctional, and not on a trade route, like Fatehpur Sikri and Vijayanagara. There were others, like Tamralipti, which succumbed to the forces of nature. Most sites were reused, though at any point of time the actual area under occupation might have been at some distance from older ones. The extant town is no guide to its antiquity, which is gleaned from literary records.

Morphology

Town Size

No schematic model of 'the Indian town' can be prepared, since the size and morphology of each would vary not only with geography but also with the requirements of security, the volume of trade, and the investment by individuals or the sovereign. From the early centuries AD until the eighteenth century there have been redactions of *Vastu shastra* (treatises on the layout of towns and buildings) which must be understood as guide-lines, and not blueprints. Jaipur, established early in the eighteenth century, is often cited as an example of a town built according to Vastushastra. What is more plausible, however, is that Vidyadhar Bhattacharya, who was an astronomer, and Raja Jai Singh, an astrophile, designed a town based on astronomical calculations (Nilsson 1987).

Ecological Models

A rough periodization for Indian towns can be threefold—before the railways, from the 1860s to the 1930s, and from the 1930s onwards, when cars came into use. Pre-railway towns varied in size from 200 to 500 ha, with populations ranging form 1,00,000 to 4,00,000. In the second phase, industries and adventurous migration increased urban density, and there was ribbon development leading out of towns alongside the railway tracks. Once cars came into use, those who could afford them were able to move out of the crowded towns, skirt the jerry-built extensions to shift to well-ordered suburbs. Despite the superficial similarity between present-day Indian cities and American ones (an inner city surrounded by lower-middle-class housing in turn enclosed by upper-class suburbs), it would be inappropriate to apply in India the ecology model of the Chicago sociologists (Park et al. 1925). Gideon Sjoberg had pointed this out in a disarming fashion as early as 1955, 'Anthropologists and sociologists ... must ... recognise that the particular kind of social structure found in cities in the United States is not typical of all societies.' American towns, all less than 300 years old, have no links with older settlements or with villages. Elsewhere, in West and Central Asia, where 'urban'/'sedentary' is the opposite pole to 'nomadic', towns are federations of tribal groupings, not comparable with Indian towns. Indian urban morphology can most usefully be compared to that of European towns, which have long histories and have in many cases grown out of villages or market towns. Most Indian towns were built on slopes or along river banks, important in the centuries of pitched battles and before piped water. City walls were made for security, and were to delineate tax boundaries. Citadels separated from the town by another wall were called *petta-kottai* (town fort) in Tamil.

Neighbourhoods

Mohalla, *para*, and *pol* were the Urdu/Hindi, Bengali, and Gujrati terms for neighbourhoods. Each had usually a single entrance-point, guarded by a gate, and with privacy ensured by culs-de-sac (Doshi 1974; Krafft 1993). Each was inhabited by families linked by kinship, *jati* (sub-caste), or occupation. Their location in relation to the citadel or place of worship was decided by convenience. Relative location did not indicate status (it was often assumed—wrongly—that those of highest social ranks were nearest the citadel). There were no areas specifically cordoned off for any ethnic/religious group, as in European ghettoes. Contemporary maps of the seventeenth or eighteenth century do not indicate any communitarian divisions of urban territory, other than that, not surprisingly, Brahmins were found living near *mandirs* (temples) and *maulvis* near *masjids* (mosques). Beyond the wall lay gardens, orchards, country houses, shrines, graveyards, and *sarais* (rest houses). Soldiers' makeshift camps were usually outside the wall, as were the quarters of weavers or leather workers, who needed running water from rivers or streams. In contrast to the densely built towns of the north, in south India, where the climate was not one of extremes, towns were often open and not walled. Open towns have often been labelled 'Hindu' and densely built ones 'Islamic' because the former appeared to approximate Vastushastra norms and the latter the towns of West Asia. In fact, it was climate rather than religion that decided morphology. Varanasi is similar to 'Islamic' Agra or Shahjahanabad-Delhi, though its profusion of temples and its history made it a 'Hindu' town (Eck 1983). The terms are therefore as inappropriate as it would be to term Paris a 'Christian' city.

Urban Density

From the nineteenth century onwards, as the tight control over the entry and exit of people in towns decreased, and the urban population kept increasing, town walls ceased to be boundaries—the famine-ravaged, the landless, the sharp-witted seeking a fortune, settled either on the periphery or within the towns which seemed to have an elastic quality of being able to accommodate people. The most spectacular example of the town as refuge was the absorption of floods of refugees in Delhi, Lahore, Calcutta, and Karachi during the crisis of Partition in 1947. Increasing density led to degradation of the housing stock, and thus to inner areas becoming the territories of the poor. In earlier days, in such a situation a new quarter would have been laid out, or the old settlement abandoned for a new one adjacent to it (as in medieval Europe). But from the nineteenth century, cartography and the registering of property rights conspired to make towns and villages fixed in space, with definite boundaries. As a result of colonial rule new morphological patterns arose.

Indo-European Towns

In the 1960s and 1970s scholars commonly used the terms 'the colonial town' and 'the colonial port-town' to categorize the Indian urban environment. On examination one finds that there were many 'Indian' elements in the morphology of these ports. The seventeenth-century European coastal settlements began as sturdy forts designed by European engineers. Later, extramural areas were laid out where Indian merchants and weavers could build their houses, as provided by the Peshwas in contemporary Pune. These were often based on the grid pattern. So were the military cantonments later attached to towns annexed by the British, and the 'city extensions' built in the twentieth century (Goodfriend 1989). Extravagant with space, the British lived in spacious garden houses which resembled not homes in Britain but the *havelis* (town houses) of the Indian rich. Many Indians bought land in Madras, Bombay, and Calcutta, and built houses in the wall-to-wall style of the Indian town. Some, however, opted for the garden-house or bungalow favoured by the British. There were many open areas in the British Indian towns which could not be policed effectively, as also vacant stretches on the properties of rich Indians. Here the poorer immigrants settled, either as tenants or as squatters. They built mud-and-thatch clusters—towns-within-towns called *bustees* (small towns) in Calcutta and *cheris* (non-Brahmin neighbourhoods) in Madras. Growing by accretion, Bombay, Calcutta, and Madras became extensive mosaics comprising villages, *agraharams* (originally land given in gift to Brahmins, later connoting Brahmin neighbourhoods near temples), housing estates, garden houses, and dense *mohallas*—clusters (Bose 1968; Kosambi 1980; Neild 1979). These urban conglomerations were spread over a much larger area than older Indian towns.

Real Estate and Town Planning

Colonial governance affected urban morphology in two ways. First, it made the ownership of urban land permanent and transferable. Hitherto, the only way to do this had been to convert property into *waqf* property/land made into a dedicated trust because it was supported by an institution of learning or a place of worship (Malik 1993). Real estate became for the first time a field for investment. This coincided with the trend towards nuclear families, and also with the internationalization of the 'colonial' assumption that one's status was measurable by the size of one's property (King 1976). This explains the new preference by the upper middle class for spacious houses on the outskirts of towns, earlier thought too open. By the 1970s, when civic planning bodies designated neighbourhoods by income (Middle Income/Lower Income Housing) it was accepted by the citizens as natural! Second, British India was given a planning ideology, shaped on the lines of the British Town and Country Planning Act of 1909 and the New York Ordinance of 1916 on 'zoning'—the first advocated anticipating and planning the expansion of towns, the second dividing up towns on the basis of land use, so that an 'industrial zone' would be distinct from an 'institutional' or 'residential' one—totally at variance with the form of Indian towns. The two principles—of demarcating proprietary rights and of zoning—have become the anchors of urban development in India after Independence. What was sought in principle, however, needs to be distinguished from what actually takes place. During colonial rule and to a much greater degree thereafter, the 'best-laid plans' were subverted by squatters. Formal and informal job opportunities act as magnets, and collusion between political operators, officials, and migrants has led to 'colonisation from below' occurring simultaneously with that from above (Bijlani 1986).

Slums

The term 'slum' came into common use in twentieth-century India, and a vast literature has built up around it. One-fifth of the total urban population in 1985 was estimated to be living in slums. Defined by the density of habitation, with implications of poverty, degraded housing stock, and demoralization sliding into crime, this term is used in India without reference to history. It includes historic urban areas, well-organized communities, shanty-towns, and run-down multi-storeyed buildings like Bombay's *chauls* originally used for makeshift homes, later for high-density flats built to house factory workers. This amalgamation of such diverse categories is inimical to any serious proposals for 'urban renewal' that aim to improve the quality of life in over-used areas. Officials find it simpler to resort to expedients like removing or relocating people living in 'slums' (Ali 1995).

Public Areas

In towns, public and private areas coexisted without being rigidly demarcated. 'Public' areas included thoroughfares, gardens, riverbanks, places of worship, and shopping arcades which as in medieval Europe, often shaded off into one another. On the other hand, citadels and palaces had gradations from public to private, demarcated by buildings and their nomenclature. In this layout, there were many cases of imitation by one ruler of palaces they had seen (as the Raja of Amber of Agra) or heard of (Shahjahan of Isfahan) or of practices they had observed (the Marathas of the Mughal court). In Europe there was a striking increase in the seventeenth century in the number of public buildings—town halls, courts, secretariats, museums, and libraries. This occurred in India in the nineteenth century as part of the ideology of the Raj (Metcalf 1989). British New Delhi, a whole city built after 1914 on a baroque plan completely at variance with Indian urban morphology (Irving 1981), later became a model for other capitals (new Patna, Chandigarh, and Bhubaneswar (Kalia 1988, 1994)). Most studies of the built form in India focus on style, patronage, and the political use of architecture (Koch 1991; Meister and Dhaky 1997). From the 1950s there has been a self-conscious quest by many architects for an 'Indian' style (Correa 1985). Few scholars have analysed how town dwellers used buildings or reacted to them—monumental architecture can awaken awe and admiration. Because secular public architecture is relatively new in India, and is associated with government, it often engenders a sense of alienation as town dwellers do not have a sense of pride or of affinity with it (Evenson 1989).

Markets and Streets

Bazaars—neighbourhood, supralocal, periodic—are invariably convivial and animated. Twentieth-century 'planning' seeks to bring order—and monotony—into these by regulating sizes and layout. Modern marketing techniques, which shout to be heard, are fast making shops and their commodities more and more visible, so that window-shopping has become a major leisure activity. Taking advantage of this clientele are those who colonize pedestrian areas by setting out 'pavement shops'; these mark the intrusion of the 'bazaar' into formal shopping precincts. Similarly, streets and *galis* (lanes) have for so long been treated as areas of social interaction and business transactions that it is an uphill task to instil a perception of them as traffic corridors. This problem was faced by European towns in the nineteenth century, and is very common in Asian and African towns today.

Mental Maps

Town- dwellers were familiar with as much of the town as was relevant to their lives. Towns for which vernacular maps are known to have been made (painted, and later printed) are those like Varanasi or Mathura, both of which have a concentration of temples and have therefore been tourist destinations for centuries. Where temple *rath-yatras* (car processions) have more than local significance (like Puri or Madurai) or where the town has a 'sacred geography' (as in Bhaktapur in Nepal or in Ramnagar near Varanasi), the community's sense of the town is more comprehensive (Singh 1953; Gutschow 1993).

Gender in Public Areas

Public areas were largely male territories. Women, jealously guarded, could not venture out except under escort. The degree of protection was proportionate to social status. Until the twentieth century most women did not know much about the town beyond their mohalla, and even today there are many who know far less about the town they live in than about the town where they spent their childhood. In Kolkata for example, even shopping for the household is still the prerogative of men. Elsewhere it is taken care of by the itinerant salesmen who come to the door. In the late nineteenth century Indian women were dismayed when piped water was introduced; this put an end to their only regular out-of-doors activity—the daily walk to the river (the same innovation was resented by African women because it spelt the end of their gossip sessions at the well). Places of worship were areas it was legitimate to frequent, and temples always exuded an air of animation as much as devotion. Other than visiting these, townswomen could not enjoy the role of flaneur.

The Threshold

Between the public and private territories is the wide threshold of the semi-public. Avenues branch off into galis and these into *kuchas* (dead-end lanes), a hierarchy marked by narrowing width and length. The *deorhi/roak*—a raised covered verandah at plinth level marked the area of transition between home and gali. Courtyards, balconies, and roofs also were semi-public areas. In the pre-automobile centuries, social interaction was chiefly in these areas and within a comfortable walking distance from home.

Private Territories

Homes underwent a qualitative change from the mid-nineteenth century onwards. Earlier, personal incomes could not be gauged from people's homes, since they preferred to accumulate wealth in the form of 'portable property'. Many rich merchants lived in disproportionately small houses, often built against or above shops or business premises. There were optimists who built spacious havelis that could accommodate attendants and client craftsmen (Prasad 1998). The poor put together mud-and-thatch houses reminiscent of their village homes (Payne 1977). All homes, big or small, were formally organized so as to ensure privacy, with the *mardana* (men's area) separate from the *zenana* (women's area). In the former, most rooms were multifunctional (Duleau 1993; Pramar 1989) and, in keeping with the climate, furnishings were spare. With a life lived as much 'without' as 'within', the Indian male would not have called his home his castle. For women, the kitchen had a central position, because of the time perforce spent in it and because it was a sphere where they exercised control (Minault 1986). The only women who enjoyed control over the whole establishment were the unorthodox ones— the women whose artistic abilities, wit, and social poise won them grants of property, at the price of being labelled 'nautch-girls' (Lall 1996).

From the nineteenth century, the homes of the well-off in the big towns underwent a change. If the British had gentrified the Bengal hut into the bungalow (King 1984), the rich Indian began to copy elements of British homes in terms of architecture and decor, particularly in rooms where European visitors might be entertained. From early on in the twentieth century, engineers and the controllers of the cement industry began to propagate the concept of 'ideal homes'. Later, 'interior designers' joined them in selling the idea of spacious homes and gardens. Homes also changed because of transformations in the structure and authority of the family. As women got more freedom to control their own time and activities, as well as their homes, the distinction between zenana and mardana disappeared, the kitchen was filled with icons of modern gadgetry rather than objects of ritual worship, the courtyard was appreciated as being trendily 'traditional' rather than as an integral element of lifestyle. From the 1950s, the first generation of Indian architects (as distinct from engineers) began to design homes. The novelty of having a house led to rampant individualism, which became the butt of sarcasm for younger architects (Bhatia 1994). As glossy magazines and television advertisements projected desirable lifestyles, the differences between regions in the subcontinent became blurred.

Civic Governance

Civic amenities also shape lifestyle. As with many institutional changes, the introduction of municipal government in British India after 1861 was seen by many later scholars as something quite novel. Gillion's remarks made in 1968 are representative:

The traditional cities of India ... are viewed in the light of Weberian and Marxist analysis. They are contrasted with the selfgoverning towns of medieval Europe ... [and] appear to be disunited, often ephemeral conglomerations of subjects, dependent on the court, and prevented from free association by caste rivalries.

Going on to analyse Ahmedabad, he expresses surprise. 'Here was a city with a corporate tradition and spirit ... and a history of indigenous financial and industrial activity' (Gillion 1968)—Ahmedabad was not, as he thought, a unique case. Densely populated settlements need regulation to ensure civic harmony and to provide facilities like water, food supplies, and sewerage. The municipalities of the nineteenth century were not a new form of governance— they merely replaced the older *kotwalis* and *panchayats*. With the enlargement of urban settlements after Independence, planning of facilities came to be done at macro level. The volume of reports and studies on these from the 1950s is vast. But it has taken time for the suggestions made in these to be translated into action. Planners and citizens have begun to appreciate that equity demands that urban services be available to all, irrespective of income; that urban facilities should not be subsidized at the expense of rural; that a very high degree of efficiency in maintenance is needed, because of the wear-and-tear of high-density living (Mehra 1991) as well as the hazard of epidemic. Civic sense has to be inculcated since a large proportion of town dwellers are first-generation urbanites, more concerned to fight for their individual rights than to think of a larger, more amorphous 'community'.

Hinterlands

Indian towns have always been cosmopolitan. Since urban consumerism is buoyed by income from land revenue, historians often refer to medieval Indian towns as 'parasitic', a phrase coined by Hoselitz (Habib 1963). This is however to ignore their role as employment generators. Guilds of artisans and builders used to travel over long distances to find employment in towns. Merchants, scholars, and preachers travelled from town to town. The phenomenon of rural people as first-generation urbanites is relatively recent—it is the consequence of agrarian distress, famine, perceived job opportunities in towns, and the sense of the town as a stepping stone to outward mobility. Migration to towns has been in the first instance overwhelmingly male, later followed by families. In Kolkata at any time, only 47 per cent of the population had been born in the city (Raza and Habeeb 1976). Towns' hinterlands could be defined variously. In the pre-railway period it was the area with which a town had mutual dependence. Both before and after the railways were built, one could map the area from which its colleges drew students. After mechanized industries were set up, a 'hinterland' could indicate the regions which provided factory labour. The freemasonry of the poor ensured that no migrant was left to fend for himself, and it was assumed that one's extended kin or jati group would also help one (Banarasidas 1983). Even today, given a choice, newcomers would prefer to live near people of their own language group or 'home town' or village. Their links with the latter, ritualized through annual visits or during the harvest or festive season, gives sustenance, but also dilutes the degree of attachment to the city. Cosmopolitanism is thus an outer veneer on a core of a strong regional identity, which becomes less marked with the second-generation urban dweller.

The Freedom of the City

'City air makes free' was true for India, not in a legal sense as in medieval Europe, but in a more general manner. Towns could provide opportunities and a break with the past. This has been seen over the last hundred years. Immigrants do not have to apprehend the terror of anonymity which haunts Western towns because they are cushioned by jati and kinship support. What *can* generate a sense of alienation is not social exclusiveness, but the inadequacy of civic services, and their mismatch with the glossy advertisements of urban lifestyle. Ascriptive status, as understood until the mid-twentieth century, divided urban dwellers on the basis of the manner of speech, apparel, and social mores. Today, the marker of class divisions is income—proclaimed by life-style and location of home.

Shared Goods and Services

A way in which some countries try to reduce class distinctions and create a sense of citizenship is to invest the public/shared areas with dignity and accessibility. Increased densities have meant that older shared spaces have been whittled away. This makes it imperative that designated public areas be maintained well. Garbage disposal, good lighting, and efficient policing have become important as never before. Structured spaces have been paralleled by structured time, with regimented work patterns and major traffic movements at specific times of the day—which calls for long-term transportation and traffic policies.

Community

Communication

If towns are cosmopolitan, they need a language for communication. Travellers' accounts refer to the many languages heard in Indian towns; *dubashes* (interpreters) were much in demand. There existed numerous hybrid languages like Urdu—the lingua franca of soldiers—developed in Hyderabad and Delhi and Bombaiya Hindi—the link language of Mumbai. The multi-language derivatives of words in many Indian languages tell of the common urban marketplace. At the same time linguists tell us that class differences can be distinguished by the way people employ different registers in the same language.

Patronage

One of the major roles of urban centres was to act as patrons (Sundar 1995). Rulers, aristo-crats, and rich merchants patronized poets, artists and architects, and employed craftspersons. Specific towns came to be identified with particular artistic and literary forms—Maratha Tanjore with Carnatic music, Nawabi Lucknow with Kathak dance, Shahjahan's Delhi with Mughal architecture, the Nizam's Hyderabad with Urdu poetry. Literature and art cut across communitarian divisions and language barriers, reinforcing cosmopolitanism. Urban elites in some cases reinforced jati/sect differences, in others cut across them. Delhi was no more an 'Islamic city' in its culture than it was in its morphology (though it *was* one in the architectural dominance of the Jama Masjid), just as Viajayanagara was more than a 'Hindu city' in its architectural features. The ambit of urban patronage has widened in the last fifty years be-cause of state participation and because of the provision of infrastructure—halls and auditoria. Music and dance earlier contained in courts and temples now have much larger audiences.

Urban Tension

Different urban groups did not always coexist cordially. Though there is no evidence of the kind of street riots that used to occur in medieval Iran, there were instances documented from the eighteenth century of conflict over the use of public areas, particularly the street. 'Left-hand' castes tried to keep out those of the 'Right-hand' in Madras (Roche 1975) and upper-caste Christians challenged the *pariahs* in Pondicherry (Weber 1978)—in both, it would appear that those who protested were taking advantage of the ignorance of the Europeans. Rival groups of Brahmins fought to control a temple in Madras (Appadurai 1981), Shias and Sunnis clashed during Mohurram in Lucknow and Mumbai (Hasan 1997; Masselos 1976) and estab-lished Hindu merchants tried to cut out the newcomer Jains (Gupta 1981). The quarrels were ostensibly over symbols and perceived violations of status/hierarchy. Two generalizations can be made about these episodes which the British called 'riots'—first, as towns became more crowded, codes of conduct earlier honoured were no longer adhered to; boundaries and thresh-olds were no longer held as sacred. As immigrants moved into towns in an unregulated fashion, a proto-proletariat was being created (McGee 1977), that could be recruited for dem-onstrations. Crowds are extraordinarily easy to mobilize in the densely inhabited parts of the towns, where the police would find it difficult to check them (Naidu 1990). Second, public discussion, newspapers, and pamphlets made individuals conscious of an affinity with their own kin and jati groups, or developed loyalties to particular political leaders (Bayly 1975). Linking towns into the chain of larger political associations made for common patterns of behaviour, even copycat riots.

Civic Protest

Towns as battlefield also took the form of protest by citizens against the government. A *hartal*— (literally) to lock one's premises/to down shutters—against a proposed house tax in Varanasi in 1811 (Cohn 1988) followed a time-honoured mode of protest, as did campaigns against merchants hoarding grain, or officials trying to put through a programme of vaccination or of inspecting houses during the plague epidemic in 1898. The high points of the nationalist movement were demonstrations of solidarity in towns (Kumar 1971) which became the models for 'protest marches' and slogan chanting, a marriage of Indian devotional processions and European political demonstrations. After Independence, capital cities were frequently the venue for anti-establishment displays. Delhi has been particularly vulnerable. Tikait's long week of colonizing Delhi's Rajpath in October 1988 and turning it into a rural landscape is a vivid memory (Gupta 1994). These short-term dislocations are different from the other displays of strength—even propagandists have incited pogroms and targeted particular groups for violent actions (Chakravarti and Haksar 1987), or have taken over territories with real-estate value (Patel and Thorner 1995). The establishment is also known to have exercised force, one of the most notorious incidents being the forcible eviction of residents from a 'slum' in Shahjahanabad (Bose and Dayal 1977). Indian towns have not witnessed pitched battles like the class struggles in Paris in 1789 and 1848, but incidents that show how communitarianism can brutalize people en masse are a warning of the frightening situation that can be generated when intolerance is expressed in conjunction with corruption and weak governance.

Images

Many-layered Towns

India has the added distinction of its towns living in several centuries simultaneously. As urban dwellers move from Redfield's 'little communities' to Karl Mannheim's 'mass society', western capitalist patterns of land use coexist with stubbornly persistent older patterns. Kinship groups dissolve into nuclear families. The same individuals patronize both temples and discotheques. Private opulence rises unabashed from a base of public squalor. The obsession with 'countenance' at personal level is matched by indifference to the outward appearance of the public. 'Viewing Indian cities, one might infer Indians to possess, not merely an indifference, but a deep-seated hatred for the physical world. Buildings are often abused in ways that suggest a pent-up rage that might otherwise be unleashed in a frenzy of social destruction' (Evenson 1989). Recently a psychologist predicted that random violence against women might increase, as an expression of frustration and alienation (Nandy 1996). But as against these features of modern urbanism, there is still a sense of the mohalla, poverty is not always synonymous with misery, and the immigrants' bewilderment does not necessarily lead to crippling loneliness or anomie. What is needed is to improve the quality of urban governance for the average town dweller and to generate a sense of the larger community, bigger than the mohalla, smaller than the region.

Urban Images

In most cultures, town and countryside are seen as opposite categories. The sense of a town being a better habitat than a village is widespread: 'The sense of urban superiority papered over material discomforts' (Marcus 1989). The European nostalgia for living in the 'countryside' does not seem strong in India though many writers have described the beauty of the particular rural landscapes of their memory. In earlier days, towns were defined/celebrated in terms of human attributes—brave, strong, beautiful (Ramanujam 1970). Urdu poems in the eighteenth and nineteenth centuries mourned ravaged cities. Today, that sense of specificity and identity is blurred as towns look more like clones of each other—and even toponymy changes with political swings. But it is always possible to hope that, as has happened in other countries, Indian towns will regain their distinctive identities.

REFERENCES

Alam, S.M. and V.V. Pokshishavsky, eds. 1976. *Urbanization in Developing Countries*. Hyderabad.
Ali, Sabir. 1995. *Environment and Resettlement Colonies of Delhi*. Delhi: Har Anand Publisher.
Appadurai, Arjun. 1981. *Worship and Conflict under Colonial Rule: A South Indian Case*. Cambridge: Cambridge University Press.
Banarasidas. 1983. *Adhakathanaka*. Trans. Mukund Lath. Jaipur: Prakrit Bharati Sansthan.
Bayly, C.A. 1975. *The Local Roots of Indian Politics—Allahabad 1880–1920*. Oxford: Oxford University Press.
_____. 1983. *Rulers, Townsmen and Bazaars*. Cambridge: Cambridge University Press.
Bhatia, Gautam. 1994. *Punjabi Baroque and Other Memories of Architecture*. Delhi: Penguin.
Bijlani, H.K. 1986. *Urban Problems*. Delhi: Indian Institute of Planning and Architecture.
Bose, Ajoy and John Dayal. 1977. *For Reasons of State: Delhi under Emergency*. Delhi: Ess Ess.
Bose, Ashish. 1973. *Studies in India's Urbanization 1901–1971*. Bombay: Tata McGraw Hill.
Bose, N.K. 1968. *Calcutta, 1964: A Social Survey*. Bombay: Lalvani.
Brown, Kenneth. 1986. 'The Uses of a Concept: "The Muslim City"'. In K. Brown, M. Jole, P. Sluglett, and S. Zubaida, eds, *Middle Eastern Cities in Comparative Perspective*. 73–81. London: Ithaca.
Chakravarti, Uma and Nandita Haksar. 1987. *The Delhi Riots*. New Delhi: Lancer.
Champakalakshmi, R. 1996. *Trade, Ideology and Urbanization: South India 300 BC to AD 1300*. Delhi: Oxford University Press.
Chattopadhyaya, B.D. 1994. *Making of Early Medieval India*. Delhi: Oxford University Press.
Cohn, Bernard C. 1988. 'Political Systems in 18th Century India: The Banaras Region'. In Barnard Cohn, ed., *An Anthropologist among the Historians, and Other Essays*. Delhi: Oxford University Press.
Correa, Charles. 1985. *The New Landscape*. Bombay: Book Society of India.
Das Gupta, Ashin. 1979. *Indian Merchants and the Decline of Surat c. 1700–1750*. Wiesbaden: Franz Sleiner Verlag.
Doshi, Harish. 1974. *Traditional Neighbourhood in a Modern City*. Delhi: Abhinav Publications.
Duleau, R. 1993. *The Town: ... The House. ... Their Spirit*. Pondicherry: Institute Francais de Pondicherry.
Eck, Diana L. 1983. *Banaras: City of Light*. London: Princeton University Press.
Evenson, Norma. 1989. *The Indian Metropolis: A View Toward the West*. Delhi: Oxford University Press.
De Coulanges, Fustel. 1956. *The Ancient City: A Study of the Religion, Laws and Institutions of Greece and Rome*. New York: Gordon Press.
Geddes, Patrick. 1919. 'The Temple Cities'. *Modern Review*. 25: 3.
Gillion, K.L. 1968. *Ahmedabad: A Study in Indian Urban History*. Berkeley: University of California Press.
Gokhale, B.G. 1988. *Poona in the Eighteenth Century*. Delhi: Oxford University Press.
Goodfriend, Douglas E. 1989. 'The Tyranny of the Right Angle: Colonial and Post-colonial Urban Development in Delhi (1857–1957)'. In Patwant Singh and Ram Dhamija, eds, *Delhi: The Deepening Urban Crisis*. 27–31. Delhi: Sterling.

Gupta, Narayani. 1981. *Delhi between Two Empires*. Delhi: Oxford University Press.

———. 1988. 'The Useful and the Ornamental—Indian Architectural History in the 19th and 20th Centuries'. *Indian Economic and Social History Review*. 25(1):61–77.

———. 1994. 'The Democratization of Lutyens' Delhi'. In C. Asher and T. Metcalf, eds, *Perceptions of India's Past*. 257–69. Delhi: Oxford and IBH Publishing Corporation.

Gutschow, Niels. 1993. 'Bhaktapur: Sacred Patterns of a Living Urban Tradition'. In H. Spodek and D.M. Srinivasan, eds, *Urban Form and Meaning in South Asia*. 163–82. Washington: National Gallery of Art.

Habib, Irfan. 1963. *Agrarian System of Mughal India*. Bombay: Asia Publishing House.

Hasan, Mushirul. 1997. 'Traditional Rites and Contested Meanings: Sectarian Strife in Colonial Lucknow'. In V. Graff, ed., *Lucknow*. 114–35. Delhi: Oxford University Press.

Hoselitz, B.F. 1954. 'Generative and Parasitic Cities'. *Economic Development and Cultural Change* (3:3).

Irving, R.G. 1981. *Indian Summer: Lutyens, Baker and Imperial Delhi*. New Haven: Yale University Press.

Kalia, Ravi. 1988. *Chandigarh: In Search of an Identity*. Delhi: Oxford University Press.

———. 1994. *Bhubaneswar: From a Temple Town to a Capital City*. Delhi: Oxford University Press.

King, A.D. 1976. *Colonial Urban Development*. London: Routledge and Kegan Paul.

———. 1984. *The Bungalow*. London: Routledge and Kegan Paul.

Koch, Ebba. 1991. *Mughal Architecture: An Outline*. Munich: Prestel Verlag.

Kosambi, Meera. 1980. *Bombay and Poona—A Socio-economic Study of Two Indian Cities 1650–1900*. Stockholm: GOTAB.

Krafft, Thomas. 1993. 'Contemporary Old Delhi: Transformation of an Historical Place'. In E. Ehlers and T. Krafft, eds, *Shahjahanabad/Old Delhi*. 65–91. Stuttgart: Franz Steiner Verlag.

Kumar, Ravinder, ed. 1971. *1919: Essays in Gandhian Politics*. Oxford: Oxford University Press.

Lall, John. 1996. *Begum Samru*. Delhi: Roli Books.

Llewellyn-Jones, R. 1985. *A Fatal Friendship: The Nawabs, the British and the City of Lucknow*. Delhi: Oxford University Press.

Malik, Jamal. 1993. 'Islamic Institutions and Infrastructure in Shahjahanabad'. In E. Ehlers and T. Krafft, eds, *Shahjahanabad/Old Delhi*. 43–64. Stuttgart: Franz Steiner Verlag.

Marcus, Abraham. 1989. *The Middle East on the Eve of Modernity*. New York: Columbia University Press.

Masselos, Jim. 1976. 'Power in the Bombay "Moholla" 1904–15'. *South Asia*. 6 (December): 75–95.

McGee, T.G. 'Rural–urban Mobility in South and South-East Asia'. In Abu-Lughod and D. Hay, eds, *Third World Urbanization*. New York: Metheun.

Mehra, Ajay. 1991. The Politics of Urban Redevelopment. Delhi: Sage Publications.

Meister, Michael W., and M.A. Dhaky, eds. 1997. *Encyclopaedia of Indian Temple Architecture*, 2 vols. Delhi: Manohar Publications.

Metcalf, Thomas. 1989. *An Imperial Vision*. London: Faber & Faber.

Minault, Gail. 1986. *Voices of Silence*. Delhi: Chanakya Publications.

Murphey, Rhoads. 1969–70. 'Traditionalism and Colonialism: Changing Urban Roles in Asia'. *Journal of Asian Studies*. 29.

Naidu, Ratna. 1990. *Old Cities, New Predicaments: A Study of Hyderabad*. Delhi: Sage Publications.

Nandy, Ashish. 1996. 'Indian Cities Will Go the Chicago Way'. *Times of India* (7 April).

National Commission on Urbanization. 1988. *Report*. New Delhi: Government of India.

Neild, Susan. 1979. 'Colonial Urbanism: The Development of Madras City in the 18th and 19th Century 217–46'. *Modern Asian Studies*. 13(2).

Nilsson, Sten A. 1987. *Jaipur*. Lund: Magasin Tessin.

Oldenburg, Veena Talwar. 1984. *The Making of Colonial Lucknow 1858–77*. Princeton: Princeton University Press.

Park, R.E., E.W. Burgess, and R.D. McKenzie. 1925. *The City*. Chicago: University of Chicago.

Patel, Sujata and Alice Thorner. 1995. *Bombay*. 2 vols. Bombay: Oxford University Press.

Payne, Geoffrey. 1977. *Urban Housing in the Third World*. London: Leonard Hill.

Pirenne, Henri. 1952. *Medieval Cities: Their Origin and the Revival of Trade*. Trans. from French. Princeton: Princeton University Press.

Pocock, D.F. 'Sociologies: Urban and Rural'. *Contributions to Indian Sociology*. 4:63–81.

Pramar, V.S. 1989. *Haveli: Wooden Houses and Mansions of Gujarat*. Ahmedabad: Mapin.

Prasad, Sunand. 1998. 'A Tale of Two Cities: House and Town in India Today'. In G.H.R. Tillotson, ed., *Paradigms of Indian Architecture*. 176–99. Delhi: Oxford University Press.

Ramachandran, R. 1988. *Urbanization and Urban Systems in India*. Delhi: Oxford University Press.

Ramanujan A.K. 1970. 'Images of the City'. In Richard G. Fox, ed., *Urban India*. Durham: DUPSSA.

Ramaswamy, Vijaya. 1985. *Textiles and Weavers in Medieval South India*. Delhi: Oxford University Press.

Rao, M.S.A. 1991. 'Introduction'. In M.S.A. Rao, C. Bhat, and L.N. Kadekar, eds, *A Reader in Urban Sociology*. Delhi: Orient Longman.

Ratnagar, Shireen. 1981. *Encounters*. Delhi: Oxford University Press.

Ray, H.P. 1994. *Winds of Change: Buddhism and the Maritime Links of Early South Asia*. Delhi: Oxford University Press.

Raza, M. and A. Habeeb. 1976. 'Characteristics of Colonial Urbanization: A Case Study of the Satellitic "Primacy" of Calcutta'. In M.S.A. Rao, C. Bhat, and L.N. Kadekar, eds, *A Reader in Urban Sociology*. 49–69. Delhi: Orient Longman.

Redfield, R. 1973. *The Little Community*. Chicago: University of Chicago Press.

Roche, P.A. 1975. 'Caste and the British Merchant Government in Madras 1639–1719'. *Indian Economic and Social History Review*. 12(4):381–407.

Ross, R. and G.J. Telkamp, eds. 1985. *Colonial Cities*. Leiden: Leiden University Press.

Sharar, Abdul Hakim. 1975. *Lucknow: Last Phase of an Oriental Culture*. Delhi: Oxford University Press.

Singh, R.L. 1953. *Banaras: A Study in Urban Geography*. Varanasi: Nand Kishore and Bros.

Sjoberg, Gideon. 1955. 'The Pre-Industrial City'. *American Journal of Sociology*. 60 (March) 438–45.

Subrahmanyam, Sanjay. 1993. 'The Port City of Masulipatnam 1550–1750'. In Narayani Gupta, ed., *Craftsmen and Merchants: Essays in South Indian Urbanism*. 47–74. Chandigarh: Urban History Association of India.

Sundar, Pushpa. 1995. *Patrons and Philistines*. Delhi: Oxford University Press.

Thapar, Romila. 1966. *History of India*, vol. I. Harmondsworth: Penguin.

Weber, Jacques. 1978. 'Acculturation et assimilation dans les etablissements francais de l 'Inde'. *Mondes et cultures*. 38(2).

Weber, Max. 1966. *The City*. Trans. D. Martindale and G. Neuwirth. London: Free Press.

Migration

MYRON WEINER

INTRODUCTION

Only a small proportion of India's people live outside their place of birth or that of their spouses. Rural-to-urban migration is modest. The majority of India's urban dwellers are locally born, not migrants. Between 1981 and 1991, only 13 million rural dwellers migrated to India's cities and towns, a little more than 2 per cent of India's rural population. Only 3.5 per cent of the total population lives in another state. Less than 1 per cent was born in another country within the region. The number of people of South Asian descent living outside South Asia constitute between 1 and 2 per cent of the population of the subcontinent.

Small as these flows are in percentage terms, the effects on both sending and receiving communities are substantial, and concerns over population movements loom large in Indian political discourse and in India's external relations. The government of Mumbai, for example, has proposed closing the city to migrants in order to arrest the city's high rate of population growth. The governing political party in Assam has pressed for closing the borders with Bangladesh and has threatened secession if the central government fails to halt illegal migration from that country. The Bharatiya Janta Party, India's largest parliamentary party, has called for revising the constitution to eliminate restrictions on the purchase of land in Kashmir so that non-Kashmiris can settle in the state. There has been opposition to the constructions of dams and other development projects that result in forced population displacement. The protection of Indians abroad has been a source of contention between India and Sri Lanka, Myanmar, Nepal, Uganda, and the United Kingdom (UK), and flows of refugees and illegal migrants have been an issue between India and Bhutan and Bangladesh.

This chapter examines the determinants and principal effects of population movements in India and its South Asian neighbours and the political controversies surrounding these flows. It is divided into five sections: migrations into South Asia, a historical overview; emigration from South Asia, both historically and in recent years; international migration within South Asia, particularly the flow of refugees and illegal migrants across national boundaries in the region; internal migration in India, including an analysis of the role of migration in urban growth, rural-to-rural migration, inter-state migration, and forced population displacement. The chapter concludes with a brief discussion of the role of migration in social conflict, both as effect and as cause.

MIGRATIONS INTO SOUTH ASIA

Population movements into the Indian subcontinent, starting in the middle of the second millennium BC and continuing through the nineteenth century, altered the social structure, culture, and political systems of the region and its subsequent historical development. Though the magnitude of these movements and in some instances even their origins are unknown, their legacies were often substantial and enduring. The earliest known population flows consisted of the Aryans, a pastoral people who migrating from Iran through Afghanistan to north-west India starting around 1500 BC and eventually displaced the local Indus valley culture. The principal Aryan deities, Shiva and Vishnu, subsequently became the basis of popular Hindu worship, and Sanskrit, the language of the Aryan religious text, the Rig Veda, was the progenitor of the Indo-Aryan languages of northern India. A thousand years later, in the fourth century BC, Alexander the Great led his Greek army through Persia and Afghanistan into the lower Swat valley of Pakistan and then across the Indus to the Ganges, turning back only when his troops refused to go any further. His legacy was the Greek Bactrian kingdom, extending from Iran through Afghanistan to the upper reaches of the Indus, including portions of the Punjab. Subsequently there were other invasions from West Asia and Central Asia into north-west and northern India: the Scythians (known in India as the Sakas) who replaced the Greeks in Bactria and subsequently occupied the Sind; the Yue-chi (as they were called by the Chinese) from Central Asia, one of whose rulers, Kanishka, patronized Buddhism and extended his power from his capital in Peshawar to Mathura; and Arabs from Baghdad who conquered the Sind and portions of the Punjab in the eight century; Turkish invaders of Afghanistan and north-west India in the eleventh and twelfth centuries who extended their power into Delhi in the thirteenth century; and the Central Asian conquest of northern India by Babur in the sixteenth century and the subsequent consolidation of Mughal rule under Akbar.

An important feature of these invasions is that the invaders became Indian, governed from within India, and were subsequently absorbed into the Indian population. They also displaced existing rulers and imposed or propagated new cultural forms. The arts of Gandhara and Mathura, the Lodi and Mughal gardens, Rajput miniatures, and Indo-Saracenic architecture are among the cultural products of the interaction of local inhabitants with their invaders. Under Turkish and Mughal rule, Persian became the language of administration, large numbers of people in north-western India, the Gangetic plain and Bengal converted to Islam, and Urdu evolved out of Persian and Hindi to become the language of north India's Muslims. Many features of British colonial rule—the system of local administration, land taxation, the state monopoly on salt, the use of an official state language, and the relationship between the British administration and the princely states—were influenced by earlier Mughal practices.

Other migrant communities came not as part of invading armies, but as merchants and traders or as religious minorities in search of protection. The Parsis, for example, fled Islamic rule in Persia and settled in Mumbai and Surat where they became prominent in commerce, finance, industry, and in civic life. Arab traders (known as the Moplah) settled on India's south-west coast. Other small immigrant communities included the Iraqi Jews, Syrian Christians, Armenians, Chinese, and, in recent times, German Jews fleeing Nazi rule.

India's social order of ranked endogamous castes based on conceptions of consanguinity and purity enabled many of the immigrant communities to find a place within the social system without surrendering their community identity. Some of the immigrant communities became Hindu castes while others stayed outside the Hindu social order retaining their cultural practices and often their language. The result was not a process of acculturation or assimilation in which immigrant populations simply adopted the local culture and disappeared as a distinctive community, but rather a process that M.N. Srinivas described as becoming part of the Indian mosaic.

In contrast, the European invaders who came to India from the sixteenth century onwards did not become part of the Indian mosaic. Unlike the earlier invaders, Europeans governed from outside and, with few exceptions, did not permanently settle and become Indian. The opening of the Suez canal enabled British merchants, missionaries, government officials, and military officers to leave their spouses in the UK and to return home on completion of their assignment. While some Portuguese, French, and British spent their lives in India, rarely did their children and grandchildren stay on, except those with Indian wives.

EMIGRATION FROM SOUTH ASIA

The earliest known emigration from the Indian land mass was to nearby Sri Lanka in the last half of the first millennium BC. The migrants, who are believed to have come from north-eastern India, subsequently developed their own Indo-Aryan language (Sinhalese) and converted to Buddhism. Tamil speakers from south India also migrated to Sri Lanka where they retained their language, their Hindu identity, and their caste structure. A succession of Tamil and Sinhalese rulers controlled different parts of the island, and while the two communities were often intermixed, what ultimately emerged was a bifurcated society with two communities of migrant origin, each with its own history, language, religion, and distinctive identity.

Starting in the first century BC, when navigators understood the annual monsoon blowing from the Red Sea to the west coast of India, there was gradual expansion in commercial traffic between Egypt and India, especially from west to east. India traded spices, silks, perfumes, tortoise shells, ivory, pearls, and precious stones, in return for metallic currency. There is, however, no evidence of any significant movement of people in either direction. A substantial sea traffic also developed between India's eastern ports and South-east Asia, or what became known as Greater India. Indian cultural influence penetrated Cambodia, the Malay peninsula, Sumatra, Java, and Bali. The influence was from Brahmin missionaries and traders rather than through any large-scale colonization by Indian migrants. Indian cultural influence was considerably dampened by the Muslim defeat of the sea-faring Tamil kingdom of Vijayanagar in the sixteenth century, and then by the spread of Islam to the entire Malay Archipelago. Again, there is no evidence of any significant flow of migrants from India to Malaysia and Indonesia.

It was not until the nineteenth century that there was a significant flow of emigrants from India. The principal reason for that flow was the establishment of the system of indentured labour. British planters in the colonies, faced with a labour shortage resulting from the abolition of slavery, turned to British India for low-wage workers. Between 1830 and 1916 an estimated one million Indians went abroad (Tinker 1974), mostly as indentured labourers. About half went to the Caribbean to work on sugar plantations, the others to Mauritius, Natal, Malaya, Fiji, and East Africa. Many of the migrants came from western Bihar and eastern UP, regions of famine, land evictions, and unemployment. Contracts provided for return passage after five years, but the bulk of the migrants chose to remain abroad as ex-indentured labourers, selling their labour at higher prices. Their numbers were increased by the arrival of voluntary 'passenger' migrants, usually workers or merchants who paid their own expenses in search of jobs, higher wages, or opportunities for creating businesses. The number of Indians who went abroad was a small percentage of the Indian population, but they often constituted a large percentage of the population of the receiving countries. By 1871, approximately 70 per cent of the population of Mauritius was Indian and by the early part of the twentieth century, half the population of Fiji was Indian. The demography, economy, and in some instances the politics of Trinidad, British Guyana, Malaya, Sri Lanka, and Natal were transformed by Indian immigrants.

By the end of British rule, a considerable proportion of the overseas Indian population had become shopkeepers, professionals, and salaried workers. Though most of the Indian immigrants came with little human capital (in the form of education or specialized skills), they had considerable cultural capital. Their high savings rates, willingness to take risks by starting small businesses, concern for their children's future, work habits, and cohesion were factors in their subsequent high levels of achievement. In this respect the Indian immigrant experience was similar to that of several other global migrant communities such as the Chinese, Jews, Italians, Japanese, and Germans, who were successful almost irrespective of where they settled or how limited their formal education and skills.

When the British empire came to an end, Indian migrant communities were under siege almost everywhere. Several newly independent nationalist-minded regimes sought to repatriate the immigrant communities, whom they regarded as having been imposed upon them without their consent by a colonial government. They hoped to provide more employment opportunities for the native middle classes by nationalizing trade and financial services and for the local labouring classes by nationalizing plantations. Many members of the new governing elites also had a deep distrust of money-lenders and middlemen engaged in trade, and of all 'foreigners'. The government of Uganda pursued the toughest policy by expelling Indians and Pakistanis, including many who were citizens of Uganda. Most settled in the UK and some in Canada, Australia, India, and the United States. Britain had initially declared that its borders would be open to citizens of Commonwealth countries, but with the substantial exodus of Ugandan Asians to the UK, the British government reformulated its immigration and citizenship laws (Mamdani 1981). There was a similar expulsion from Myanmar where a large proportion of the Indians were, as in East Africa, middlemen traders, shopkeepers, and money-lenders. Many, who were of south Indian origin, resettled in Tamil Nadu. The exodus from Sri Lanka was more controlled. The Sri Lankan government disenfranchised the Indian Tamil tea plantation workers and following several years of complex negotiations, the governments of India and Sri Lanka agreed that 525,000 plantation labourers would return to India, 300,000 would be granted Sri Lankan citizenship, and the disposition of the remaining 150,000 would be a matter for future negotiations.

Migrants of Indian origin now form a majority, or are the largest ethnic group, in three countries outside of South Asia: Mauritius, Fiji, and Guyana. (In recent years there has been some emigration of Indians from Fiji, following a coup by the Fiji-dominated military against an Indian-dominated elected government.) In Trinidad and Tobago Indians constitute 40 per cent of the population as against 43 per cent of Blacks, and in Malaysia, Singapore and Sri Lanka they are more than 10 per cent of the total population. Members of the Indian diaspora generally maintain their cultural identity, including norms of endogamy, their religious practices, and in some countries, their language. They have been active in national politics in Mauritius, Guyana, Fiji, and Trinidad and Tobago, although the tendency has been for Indians to first establish themselves in the economy and only later seek political office. In this respect the Indian immigrant community follows a well-established pattern of several other economically successful global migrant communities.

Since 1947 there have been three new migration streams from South Asia: to Great Britain; to the United States; and to the oil-producing countries of the Persian Gulf.

The United Kingdom permitted free immigration for all Commonwealth citizens until 1962 when the Commonwealth Immigrants Act came into force. Though the number of South Asians migrating to the UK was initially small, a chain migration enabled friends and relatives to follow. Even after the legislation was passed, many immigrants from the subcontinent were able to enter. By 1991, people of South Asian origin in the UK numbered 15 million, about half of the non-white ethnic minority population. It should be noted, however, that by the early 1990s over half of the ethnic minorities in the UK were locally born.

Migration to the United States of America from South Asia was made possible with the passage of the 1965 Immigration Act. Every country was allocated 20,000 visas annually, with preferences for individuals with high levels of education and skills for family members. The result has been a steady flow of immigrants from South Asia. Between 1965 and 1992, 548,000 Indians came to the United States and by the mid-1990s the total number of Indians in the United States, including their locally born children, was around 1 million, with major concentrations in Texas, California, New York, New Jersey, and Illinois.

The third emigration stream was to the oil-producing states of the Persian Gulf. With the rise in oil prices in the early 1970s, the Gulf states invested heavily in infrastructure, industries, and education and health services. The Gulf states had unusual demographic and economic profiles for developing countries: small populations, exceptionally low labour-participation rates (with few women in the labour force), high per capita incomes, and labour shortage. To meet the demand for labour, the Gulf states imported immigrant guest workers, particularly from Asia. Though the migrants formed only a small proportion of the labour force of the sending countries, they constituted a large proportion of the labour force in the Gulf. By the late 1980s, foreign workers were 39 per cent of the labour force in Bahrain, 45 per cent in Oman, 71 per cent in Kuwait, 81 per cent in Qatar, and 85 per cent in the United Arab Emirates. The largest number of foreign workers, 1.7 million out of the 3.6 million Asian guest workers in the Gulf states, was in Saudi Arabia. Sixty-three per cent of the Gulf migrants were from Asia, and of these South Asia was the principal source.

All three migration streams were the result of the policies of the receiving countries and in each case such migration chains were established that enabled relatives and friends to join the overseas migrants. There have been a variety of social costs associated with the emigration of males, when wives and children are left behind, but there have also been considerable benefits. The remittances sent by workers in the Gulf countries more than made up for the increased costs of importing oil. Indeed, the remittances from the Gulf countries and from non-resident Indians (NRIs) in the US and the UK, estimated at over US $ 3 billion annually, prevented India from having a balance-of-payments crisis when the country's imports rose faster than its exports. It was not until the early 1990s, when remittances dropped as a result of the Iraqi war, that India experienced a severe financial crisis, so severe that the government was forced to open the economy to foreign investors and initiate a process of economic liberalization. The regions from which the migrants to the Gulf came, most notably Kerala and Goa, experienced a housing boom, a reduction in unemployment, a rise in local wages, and increased investment by families in food, medical care, and education of children (Gulati 1987: WS-45). There has also been a significant flow of technology to India from non-resident Indians in the US and other advanced industrial countries. The expansion of the software industry in Bangalore, for example, has in part been made possible by Indians educated in the US, often holders of green cards who preferred to start their own firms in India rather than take lesser positions in Silicon Valley. As a matter of policy, the Indian government has promoted investment in India by non-resident Indians, a policy supported even by those who are otherwise critical of direct foreign investment. Indian government officials no longer complain of a brain drain. The then Prime Minister Rajiv Gandhi captured the changed mood and said that he regarded Indians abroad as a bank 'from which one could make withdrawals from time to time'.

Though, in the main, the ties between India and the diaspora community in the West have been helpful to India, there has been a downside in the form of support for secessionist movements in Kashmir and in the Punjab by Kashmiri Muslims and Sikhs living in the UK, Canada, and the US. There has also been a flow of money from non-resident Indians to Hindu nationalist organizations within India. Future ties between the Indian diaspora and India depend in part upon whether the locally born children of migrants are completely assimilated into their host countries, whether the present migration stream to the West will continue, and how central to their cultural and political identity do migrants and their descendants continue to regard their homeland?

INTERNATIONAL MIGRATION WITHIN SOUTH ASIA

South Asia has had some of the largest population movements across national boundaries of any region in the world. Approximately 35 to 40 million people have moved between India, Pakistan, Bangladesh, Sri Lanka, Nepal, and Bhutan since 1947, some as economic migrants, and a greater number as refugees. These population movements can be categorized into three types: peoples rejected by governments or by majority ethnic communities engaged in ethnic cleansing; political refugees from repressive regimes; and illegal migrants (Weiner 1993).

The largest single flow within South Asia—and perhaps the largest international flow in world history—took place in 1947 after the partition of India. An estimated six to seven million Muslims moved from India to Pakistan and nearly eight million Hindus and Sikhs moved from Pakistan to India. The massive refugee flows or, as they might be more benignly described, the population exchange, took place under violent conditions. On each side of the border ethnic groups massacred one another, seized property, and forced flight in an effort to create more ethnically homogeneous regions. When the massacres ended—some have put the death toll as high as half a million—and the population flows subsided, Pakistan's Punjab and Sind provinces were almost entirely Muslim, while India's Punjab was almost entirely Hindu and Sikh. In Pakistan the refugees (known as *mohajirs*), mostly Urdu-speaking Muslims from Uttar Pradesh, Bihar, and Gujarat, were initially a powerful political force, forming the core leadership in the national government and in the governing Muslim League as the founders of the new state. Subsequently the mohajirs lost their national political power and were reduced in status to an ethnic minority in the province of Sind where they formed their own political party (known as the MQM) in opposition to the local Sindhi population (Zaidi 1991). In India, the Hindu and Sikh refugees did not become a distinct ethnic or political group, although many of the Hindu refugees became ardent supporters of the anti-Pakistan Jan Sangh (later the Bharatiya Janata Party), and many of the Sikh refugees advocated the creation of an independent Punjab or Khalistan.

Policies of ethnic cleansing forced the exodus of minorities elsewhere in or to South Asia. An estimated 900,000 Indians left Myanmar for India in 1948 and 1949 and in the mid-1960s when the Burmese government nationalized trade, industry, banking, and commerce, thereby depriving Indian middlemen of their property and income. In addition to the Indian tea estate workers in Sri Lanka who lost their citizenship and returned to India, an estimated 200,000 Sri Lankan Tamils fled to India when a civil war erupted over the demand by the Tamils for an independent state. Following the secession of Bangladesh from Pakistan in 1972, nearly 200,000 Biharis who had earlier migrated to what had been East Pakistan were repatriated to Pakistan, but another 300,000 stateless Biharis remained stranded in Bangladesh, denied entry by Pakistan and denied citizenship by the Government of Bangladesh.

There was a flight into Bangladesh of Muslims across the Burmese border, bilingual Bengali and Burmese-speaking descendants of agricultural labourers (known as Rohingya) who had migrated to the Arakan region of Myanmar from Bengal in the nineteenth century when the borders were not clearly demarcated or regulated. In the 1970s, land disputes developed between the Burmese and the Bengali-speaking Muslims. The Burmese government, claiming that many of the Muslims had only recently migrated to Myanmar, refused to provide them with national registration certificates, and frightened unregistered Muslims fled to Bangladesh.

Land disputes also played a role in the flight from Bangladesh to India of the Chakmas, an indigenous non-Bengali-speaking Sino-Tibetan Buddhist tribal community in the Chittagong Hill Tracts (CHT). The CHT had been closed to land purchases by non-Chakmas until 1964 when the Government of Pakistan ended the special status of the region as an 'excluded area'. When thousands of Bengali families settled in the tracts in the late 1970s and early 1980s, and plans were under way to settle another quarter of a million Bengalis, the Chakmas formed the Chittagong Hill Tracts Peoples Solidarity Association which called for regional autonomy, the restitution of all lands taken by Bengali immigrants since the 1970, and a ban on further immigration. When their demands were rejected, the Chakmas launched an armed insurrection and, as the conflict escalated, many Chakmas fled across the border to Tripura and Mizoram.

The largest flight from a politically repressive regime was in 1971 when the military regime in Pakistan refused to permit the Awami League of East Pakistan from forming a national government after it won a majority of seats in elections to the National Assembly. Denied political power, the Awami League sought independence for Bangladesh, and in the ensuing civil war an estimated 8–10 million refugees fled to India, the bulk returning to their homes a year later after Bangladesh became independent. The massive influx of refugees into India was a significant factor in India's decision to invade Pakistan in an effort to 'liberate' Bangladesh and return the refugees.

Another massive refugee flow occurred in South Asia after December 1979 when the Soviet Union invaded Afghanistan. An estimated three million refugees (*mujahiddin* or 'freedom fighters') fled to Pakistan where they were given identity cards, rations, and armed support by the Pakistan government. Though Soviet forces withdrew from Afghanistan in the early 1990s, the war continued as a civil conflict among the various mujahiddin groups. The impact of the Afghan warrior refugees went well beyond Afghanistan. Arms intended for the mujahiddin entered the Pakistan arms markets where they were purchased by ethnic groups in conflict with one another. The 'Kalashnikov culture' turned ethnic disputes between Sindhis and mohajirs in Karachi into armed street battles. Afghan arms and mujahiddin also became an element in the conflict between Kashmiris and the Indian government.

A relatively small flow of refugees from Tibet to India in the 1950s has had large geopolitical consequences for relations between India and China. A protest movement in Tibet, an insurrection, and the suppression of the rebellion by Chinese troops in the late 1950s proved to be a turning point in Indo-Chinese relations. Though India neither armed the refugees nor supported independence or autonomy for Tibet, the Chinese have been displeased by the presence of the Dalai Lama in India and the international recognition that he has received. In an effort to strengthen their control over Tibet, the Chinese military built an access road through the disputed territory of Ladakh; the result was a forward response by the Indian military, and then outright warfare between India and China over both Ladakh and disputed territories in India's north-east.

Apart from politically induced movements, many migrants have illegally moved across the international borders in South Asia in search of land and jobs. The partition of India in 1947, which involved the partition of both Bengal and Assam, did not halt the flow of East Bengalis into Assam for land and employment as agricultural labourers, a flow which had begun in the nineteenth century. As the migration continued, accelerating in the early 1970s, the Assamese became concerned they would be demographically overwhelmed and might lose political control over the state. When the Indian government failed to take adequate measures to seal the borders, a majority of Assamese gave their support to the Ahom Gana Parishad, a political party formed by anti-migrant student leaders who called for the expulsion of Bangladeshis, closed borders, and greater autonomy for the state.

A similar movement against migrants erupted in nearby Bhutan over the presence of Nepalese migrants from eastern Nepal, a region with little arable land and a high population growth rate. As the number of Nepalese migrants increased, the Bhutanese feared that the influx would result in a loss of cultural and political control for them as had already occurred in Sikkim, and that they too would become a minority in their own land. In the late 1980s, the Government of Bhutan adopted measures against the teaching of Nepali in schools, enforced Dzongkha as the official language, proscribed Nepali and Indian dress, and declared that residents of Bhutan who could not prove they came before 1958 must leave the country. The result was a substantial exodus of Bhutanese of Nepali origin into West Bengal and eastern Nepal.

The only legally open borders in South Asia are between Nepal and India under the terms of the Indo-Nepal Friendship Treaty of 1950 and the Tripartite Delhi agreement of 1951. Indians have settled on land in the *terai* and taken jobs in the Kathmandu valley, while many Nepalese have found jobs all over India, especially in the north-east. There has been relatively little opposition to Nepalese presence in India, but there is considerable disquiet in Nepal over the presence of Indians where their numbers, in proportion to the local Nepalese population, are quite large. There are an estimated three to four million Indians in Nepal, and 1.5 million Nepalese in India (Dutt 1981). Critics in Nepal argue that Indians displace local people in the labour market, that 'Indianization' erodes popular commitment to Nepal as a sovereign state and to Nepalese culture, and that Indians have become so numerous that they have become the swing force in Nepal's tug of war between the monarch and political parties.

Notwithstanding the presence of boundaries separating the countries of South Asia, borders are porous. There are few natural boundaries separating one country from another (with the exception of Sri Lanka from India). Boundaries are long, not easily patrolled by the military, and often heavily populated on both sides. In some instances, people on each side of the border share with one another a common language or religion and a sense of common identity, though they are citizens of different countries. Individuals who illegally cross borders can often slip into the local community among friends and relatives, and then find employment. The countries of South Asia do not have any effective systems for identifying their own citizens. Only recently have several countries initiated a system of registration of citizens and in no case is the system yet universal. Agriculturalists and urban employers are not required to check on the legal status of those they hire, and illegal immigrants sometimes have local political allies who can prevent the government from forcing repatriation.

Shortly after independence, governments in South Asia were receptive to refugee flows which they regarded as a kind of 'return' migration or an exchange of populations associated with the process of state formation. However, most of the current international migrations within South Asia are perceived by governments and by many of their citizens as threatening, particularly when migration changes the linguistic or religious composition of the receiving locality. Moreover, even the influx of refugees from the same ethnic or religious community may be regarded with concern if it indicates that the community is being ill-treated in its own country and is likely to become a burden on the host society and government. Thus the influx of Sri Lankan Tamils into south India, Burmese Muslims into Bangladesh, and the Nepalese from Bhutan to Nepal has alarmed the host countries. Host communities have also been at risk when refugees are armed, as was the case with the Afghans who expanded an illegal drug traffic, ran a vast smuggling operation from Afghanistan to Pakistan, and sold arms to local ethnic leaders. Similarly, when the Sri Lankan Tamil Tigers lost the support of the Indian government, they turned against India and assassinated former Prime Minister Rajiv Gandhi.

Looking to the future, one can anticipate two possible scenarios. The countries of the region may open their borders to one another, following the model of Nepal and India, New Zealand and Australia, Germany and Poland, Ireland and Britain, and the countries of the European Union. An alternative scenario is that the states in South Asia may look for improved ways to control entry by strengthening border patrols, introducing identity documents, pressing their neighbours to regulate exit, repatriating illegal migrants, and inducing refugees to return home. This is a more likely scenario though it will make it more difficult to reduce barriers to trade and is likely to strain political relations between states in the region. A third option is that they may do nothing, accepting the illegal flows and the refugees as undesirable but also as uncontrollable, focusing (if at all) on the political management of their domestic consequences.

INTERNAL MIGRATION IN INDIA

Migration and Urban Growth

India has experienced a high rate of urban growth but a low rate of urbanization. This paradox, as we shall see, is explained by the high rate of natural population growth.

In 1995, 240 million people lived in India's urban areas (25.7 per cent of total population), more than the total population of all but the three largest countries of the world (Visaria and Visaria 1995). Several Indian cities are among the world's largest: Mumbai with 12.6 million people, Kolkata with 10.9 million, and Delhi with 8.4 million. According to the Census of India, India's urban population was 62.4 million in 1951, 78.9 million in 1961, 109.1 million in 1971, 159.5 million in 1981, and 217.2 million in 1991. In the last three decades India's urban population has increased by 138 million. Indian cities are characterized by vast squatter settlements; high levels of unemployment; high levels of pollution; inadequate sanitation; shortages of drinking water; a high incidence of disease, malnutrition, and infant mortality; low literacy rates; and much child labour. But little of this can be accounted for by migration.

Though there has been a great deal of urban growth, urbanization (the percentage of population that lives in urban areas) has increased more slowly in India than in many other developing countries or in most of Europe and the United States in the nineteenth century. Only 18 per cent of India's population lived in urban areas in 1961, 19.9 per cent in 1971, 23.3 per cent in 1981, and 25.7 per cent in 1991. In the decade 1981–91 India's urban population increased by 58.7 million, or 36.2 per cent but only 22 per cent (13 million) of the urban growth was the result of rural–urban migration, while 61 per cent was the result of natural increase and the balance because of the reclassification of localities from rural to urban (Visaria 1995). Only a tiny fraction of India's 627 million rural population migrated to urban areas; in fact, the rate of urbanization during 1981–91 was actually lower than in the previous decade.

The low rate of rural–urban migration indicates that India's rapid rural population growth, increased rural land density, deforestation, rural unemployment, low rural wages, and rural poverty have not resulted in a push towards the cities. Indeed, several states with high natural population increases (Rajasthan and Bihar) had low rates of rural–urban migration from 1981 to 1991 and some states with high urbanization rates between 1971 and 1981 had low urbanization rates between 1981 and 1991, without significant changes in their natural population increase. Population density is also not a good predictor of rural–urban migration. Some states with high population densities (Bihar and Uttar Pradesh) have a low level of urbanization, while two less densely populated states (Gujarat and Maharashtra) are the most urbanized. Nor is there any evidence that rural poverty is driving people out of the countryside. Three of India's poorest states—Bihar, Orissa, and Assam—are only half as urbanized as the country as a whole. Only in Andhra Pradesh, Kerala, and West Bengal does migration contribute as much or almost as much to the increase in urban population as does natural population growth, while in Tamil Nadu and Bihar the growth of urban centres is no greater than natural population growth for the state as a whole (Census of India 1991: 58).

The major urban centres that have shown the highest population growth are districts surrounding Delhi, Calcutta, Mumbai, Chennai, and Ahmedabad, areas with substantial industrial and commercial activities. The growth of India's twenty-three metropolitan urban agglomerations with a population of more than one million each was 67.7 per cent during 1981–91, twice that of urban India as a whole. However, the territory of the urban agglomerations for 1991 is not the same as for 1981. For example, the population of Greater Mumbai grew from 8.2 million in 1981 to 12.6 million in 1991 mainly due to the addition of five urban areas to Greater Mumbai. Data from the 1991 Census on the contribution of migration to the growth of the metropolitan areas, as distinct from jurisdictional changes, are not yet available. In many of the largest cities (including Chennai, Calcutta, Kanpur, Nagpur, Jaipur, Lucknow, and Hyderabad) migrants accounted for no more than one-third of the urban population. The 1991 Census reported that there were only a few large cities—Surat, Faridabad, Bhopal, Aurangabad, Ludhiana, and Lucknow—in which migration accounted for as much of the growth as did the natural population increase. The deterioration of many of India's urban centres lies less in migration than in an urban growth that has not been matched by public or private expenditures in power, water, sanitation, and public transportation.

The low rate of rural–urban migration in India, and the high turnover rate, is an indication that urban areas are not expanding rapidly enough economically to provide employment opportunities for India's growing rural population (Bose 1973: 4–8). Opportunities for employment in the cities, even in the informal sector, remain too limited to induce more than a small number of rural dwellers to migrate to them. Many rural dwellers migrate to the cities in search of employment but after a few months, or a year or two, return to their villages. As many as a third of the migrants living in India's urban areas have resided there for less than four years and 15 per cent of the male migrants residing in rural India reported that they last lived in an urban area; these figures indicate that millions of Indians move into and out of cities for short-term employment.

Migrants remit a high proportion of their income to family members in their villages. The social organization of migrants in cities is built around the need to keep expenditures down and savings high by spending as little as possible on housing and consumption. Many male migrants, therefore, live in dormitory-like shacks in densely populated squatter areas—a mode of settlement that accounts for what has sometimes been inaccurately described as the 'ruralization of urban areas'. The inability or unwillingness of many local governments to provide services (such as sanitation, water, electric power, and primary schools) to squatter settlements contributes to their squalid conditions.

The hypothesis that out-migration from rural areas results from a lack of development and that rural development will therefore induce people to remain in place is not supported by evidence from India. Punjab is the most agriculturally developed state in India with a per capita state domestic product almost double the national average—the result of better irrigation facilities, mechanization, fertilizer use, and new farming techniques. The increased demand for agricultural labour during cultivation and harvesting time is met by migrants from rural areas of Bihar and eastern Utter Pradesh. A field survey in Ludhiana and Jalandhar districts of Punjab conducted by the Population Research Centre of Punjab University in Chandigarh found that the rate of out-migration from rural to urban areas has been increasing notwithstanding the increase in income and the growing availability of non-agricultural occupations in rural areas. Indeed, the study reported a high correlation between the growth of the non-agricultural sector and out-migration (Goyal 1990: 73). Rural development, along with an increase in education, has spurred rather than slowed down out-migration.

A similar study conducted in Ratnagiri and Sindhudurg districts of Konkan in Maharashtra, a region with a low level of economic development that is nonetheless a traditional area of out-migration, reports that out-migration is primarily from the relatively well-developed *tahsil* where there are direct transport links to Mumbai (Sita and Prabhu 1989). The evidence from these two studies, and others conducted elsewhere in India, supports findings from developing rural regions elsewhere in the world that improvements in rural education, transportation, and income are a stimulant to rural–urban migration. In case India's economic reforms lead to a significant growth in industrial employment in the next decade or, for that matter, substantial development in rural areas occurs, we can anticipate increased rural–urban migration and a higher urbanization rate.

Rural to Rural Migration

Though the censuses report that nearly 30 per cent of the Indian rural population consists of migrants—a higher proportion of migrants, incidentally, than for most urban areas—the bulk of the migrants are female who have migrated to join their husbands. The high number of females among rural migrants (113.6 million, compared with 32.8 million male migrants) is principally the result of marriage. (Some studies, however, point to substantial numbers of seasonal migrant women workers, see Ray 1982). Caste endogamy, combined with village exogamy, leads most married women in rural areas to change their residences. Marriage migration is typically to nearby villages in the same district or to districts in the same state. Only 6 per cent of India's rural female migrants moved to another state.

Among the nearly 33 million rural male migrants, one of every six has moved to a rural area of another state, more than one out of four to a district within the same state, and more than half have moved within the same district. During the cultivation and harvest seasons there is large-scale migration of agricultural workers, particularly when there are substantial wage differentials between one agricultural region and another. High wage differentials, as for example between East Champaran in Bihar and Jalandhar, a prosperous agricultural district in Punjab, have resulted in an annual migration stream of migrant groups (*tolis*) organized by a *tolidar* as part of a contract labour system, in which the petty contractor finds employment for the group in return for a percentage of the labourer's daily wages. The flows are not because East Champaran has surplus labour or because of seasonal harvesting, but reflects the higher wages that are offered in Punjab. With both Bihari and Punjabi farmers competing for the limited labour supply, wages have risen in both East Champaran and in Jalandhar (Gill 1984; for a similar study in Haryana, see Singh 1993).

Inter-state Migration

More than 95 per cent of all Indians live in the states in which they were born and most have never lived outside their own districts. As noted, Indian women move within or across districts primarily for reasons of marriage, a movement that reinforces community rather than creating cultural diversity. In 1981, only 24 million Indians (3.5 per cent of the population) resided outside of the states of their birth, plus another 7.7 million who originated from neighbouring Pakistan, Bangladesh, Nepal, and other countries. Even when a community attracts migrants from another state for employment, the result need not be greater cultural heterogeneity. Migrants, for example, who move between the Hindi-speaking states generally speak the same language and share similar customs and cultural outlook. India is, by and large, a land of native peoples. Statistically speaking, most of India's men are born, go to school (if they go to school), work, marry, and die in the same community and their wives come from other villages within the district or nearby districts.

The cultural diversity that obviously does exist in most of the Indian states is, with some important exceptions, only marginally the result of contemporary migrations. Religious minorities and tribes are dispersed throughout the country. State boundaries do not coincide with linguistic boundaries and there are numerous linguistic groups that do not have a state of their own. Historic migrations (sometimes hundreds of years ago) have created enclaves of communities that maintain their distinctive identities. And though inter-state migration is statistically small for the country as a whole, a few states (or their cities) do have many migrants from other states or from outside India—namely Maharashtra, Assam, Punjab, West Bengal, Tripura, and Delhi. Telugu- , Bengali- , Kannada- , Marwari- , and Punjabi-speaking communities can readily be found outside their 'home' states.

Chain migrations are readily established wherever a migrant community has an established beach head. Thus there are migration streams from selected districts of Bangladesh into Assam, from selected Konkani- , Tamil- , Telugu- , and Hindi-speaking communities into Mumbai, from coastal Andhra Pradesh to Hyderabad, and from Hindi-speaking districts in Bihar and eastern Uttar Pradesh to particular districts in Punjab.

The movement of people from one cultural linguistic region to another does not necessarily lead to conflict, but such migrations tend to shape a sense of ethnic identity among the migrants and within the local population. Groups that once identified themselves, if at all, on the basis of religion or caste, may become aware of their linguistic identity because of the presence of others speaking another language. Tribes become aware of their distinctiveness when they interact with non-tribals, or with other tribes. The entrance of migrants from another region may lead the autochthonous population to create for itself an identity based on an exclusive claim to its own territory. In short, migration may be an important element in the social construction of an identity.

Material interests play a role in this process. Tribals faced with an influx of immigrants may fear the loss of identity, but they also fear the loss of land and the destruction of their forest reserves; the local middle class may fear that educated immigrants are successfully competing for employment; students may be concerned that they are losing admissions into the university to applicants from other regions; the migration may be sufficiently large so that members of the local community fear they are in danger of losing political control of their local government. The movement of entrepreneurs from one region to another sometimes results in intense competition with local entrepreneurs (Banu 1994).

Resentment against migrants from other regions became a political force in the 1960s and 1970s with the rise of 'sons of the soil' movements, political movements representing indigenous ethnic groups. The economic context for these movements was the slow growth of employment, resulting in increasing competition between the nascent local middle classes and migrants who dominated jobs in the modern sector as government officials, shopkeepers, clerks, and professionals. The 'sons of the soil' movement took a violent turn in Assam, where local Assamese attacked Bengalis, many of whom had migrated illegally from Bangladesh; there were similar anti-migrant movements in Mumbai, Karnataka, and the Chota Nagpur region of southern Bihar. Though violent attacks against migrants have been less common than clashes between castes and religious communities, several anti-migrant political parties have won considerable local support in some states, most notably the Shiv Sena in Maharashtra, the Ahom Gana Parishad in Assam, and the Jharkhand Party in southern Bihar.

India's caste system makes it unlikely that those who migrate from one linguistic region to another will be assimilated into the local community. The ethnic enclaves and ethnic division of labour inherent in most migrations across ethno-linguistic lines is perpetuated in India by the practice of communities marrying within their own castes, since castes are bound by linguistic region. One result is that throughout India there are enclaves of communities that migrated into another region generations ago, who preserve their identity and their language. Migrants may acquire the local language, usually as their second or third language, but marriage to a member of another linguistic community (and hence to another caste) continues to remain uncommon.

The rate of inter-state migration in India is likely to remain low unless the present market-oriented reforms result in a significant growth in disparities in wages and employment opportunities across regions. The prospects of higher lifetime earnings and better career prospects are particularly likely to induce greater mobility among those with high levels of education (Bhat 1993).

Forced Population Displacement

Under the Land Acquisition Act of 1894, amended in 1984, the Government of India can acquire land for public purposes and for companies. This acquisition may be for the construction of multi-purpose irrigation dams, forest reserves, sanctuaries and national parks, mining, and construction of canals, highways and transmission lines. According to the Ministry of Rural Development (1996) no less than 15.5 million people were displaced up until 1985. Some activists put the number of displaced at between 20 and 30 million. Forced displacement differs from other kinds of migration in that migrants are compelled by law to leave their lands and homesteads or are deprived of their livelihood because of the acquisition of common lands. The affected populations are not only those whose lands and homes have been acquired, but also include tenants, sharecroppers, landless labourers, and others engaged in employment or trade within the acquired area.

The traditional government practice has been to pay financial compensation to those who have lost their property, but not to provide compensation to the very large number of others in the community affected by the acquisition of property. Moreover, cash compensation has proven inadequate for the rehabilitation of individuals paid for the loss of property when they are unable to find alternative employment. Many Indian sociologists, anthropologists, and social activists have documented the adverse effects of population displacement. Summarizing this literature Cernea reports that the consequences include landlessness, homelessness, joblessness, marginalization, food insecurity, loss of access to common property assets, increased morbidity and morality, and social disarticulation (Cernea 1996: 1518; for an unusually comprehensive set of studies by Indian scholars see *Economic and Political Weekly*. It is estimated that one-third of those displaced during the last four decades are tribals, for whom dislocation is particularly severe, given the common practice of communal landholding, dependence upon forest lands for livelihood, the non-monetized, non-commercialized nature of many of their economic activities, and the absence of skills for employment in projects (Fernandes and Thukral 1989: 7).

Indian researchers, advocacy groups and non-government organizations, and militant resistance by the displaced have successfully created a public debate over specific projects, in some instances opposing them, in other instances focusing on the need for resettlement and rehabilitation. Opposition to the construction of the Sardar Sarovar Dam on the river Narmada in Gujarat, for example, played a significant role in persuading the World Bank to withdraw its financing, though the project continues with support from the state and central governments and from pro-project beneficiaries. Increasing attention is now being accorded to the rehabilitation of the displaced, besides giving them compensation; developing programmes to restore the living standards and earning capacities of displaced persons; including in rehabilitation programmes all members of the adversely affected community, not only those who lose property; incorporating the financial costs of rehabilitation into a cost–benefit analysis of projects and creating mechanisms for income transfers from beneficiaries to those who have been adversely effected; revising projects so as to minimize dislocation through, for example, lowering the height of proposed dams; paying attention to the relocation of entire communities rather than individuals; and finally, creating a process for population resettlement that includes many of the key social actors such as the affected communities, non-governmental organizations, financial institutions, beneficiaries, agencies that plan and execute projects, and researchers (Cernea 1996: 1515). One result of the public discussion has been the creation of a Draft National Policy for Rehabilitation aimed at 'total rehabilitation' of the displaced, the 'empowerment of project-affected persons', and the 'enhancement of human capital' (Sinha 1996: 1456–7). Though many of the proposals are not likely to be carried out (land-for-land, for example, or collective resettlement), the most promising of the proposals is that the social and economic costs of displacement will be incorporated into the costing of proposed projects, thereby not only increasing the resources for rehabilitation, but also demonstrating that some of the proposed projects that generate displacement are not economically viable and therefore should not be undertaken.

MIGRATION AND SOCIAL CONFLICT

The migratory process is inherently conflictual. Though migration within and across national boundaries is often the result of differential opportunities for employment and higher lifetime income, all too often it is also the result of coercion: attack by one ethnic or religious community against another; involuntary displacement as a result of government acquisition of land; the colonization of one's territory by outsiders; and forced repatriation across national boundaries. Migration theory therefore entails an analysis not only of individual decision making, but also the behaviour of social groups, institutions, and policy makers whose actions impel large numbers of people to move.

Migration also creates social conflict. Even when both migrants and the communities to which they move benefit economically, the consequences are often social and political conflict. Migrants may take jobs that others do not want, bring in new technologies and skills that local people do not have, create new services, reclaim waste lands, or make land more productive, but they may also take jobs from others, make demands upon local transportation, medical facilities and education, speak other languages, engage in social, religious and cultural practices that local people find offensive, and encroach on common lands and on private property. Analysts of migration tend to characterize the hostile responses of local people to migrants as xenophobic, racist, and communal, or the result of political elites appealing to the baser qualities of their constituents. The presumption of such an analysis is that harmonious relations between migrants and natives are normal and conflict exceptional. South Asia's experiences with migration demonstrate that an analysis of migration requires not only an understanding of their economic determinants and consequences, but of the larger social forces that generate coercion and conflict in the sending and receiving communities.

REFERENCES

Banu, Zainab. 1994. 'Immigrant Groups as a Factor in Communal Riots'. *Economic and Political Weekly.* 29(10 September):2408–11.

Bhat, R.L. 1993. 'Internal Migration of Human Capital in India'. *Manpower Journal.* 29(2):1–24.

Bose, Ashish. 1973. *Studies in India's Urbanization 1901–1971.* New Delhi: Tata McGraw Hill Publishing Co. and the Institute of Economic Growth.

Census of India. 1988. *A Handbook of Population Statistics.* Issued for 1991 Census. New Delhi: Registrar General and Census Commissioner, Government of India.

Census of India. 1991. *Provisional Population Totals Rural–Urban Distribution, Series 1, Paper 2 of 1991.* New Delhi: Registrar General and Census Commissioner.

Cernea, Michael M. 1996. 'Public Policy Responses to Development-Induced Population Displacements'. *Economic and Political Weekly.* 31(24):1515–23.

Dutt, Srikant. 1981. ' "Migration and Development": The Nepalese in Northeast.' *Economic and Political Weekly.* 26(24):1053–5.

Economic and Political Weekly. 1996. 21(24). 15 June.

Fernandes, W. and E.G. Thukral, eds. 1989. *Development, Displacement and Rehabilitation.* New Delhi: Indian Social Institute.

Gill, Indermit. 1984. 'Migrant Labour: A Mirror Survey of Jullunder and East Champaran'. *Economic and Political Weekly.* 19(24–5):961–4.

Goyal, R.S. 1990. 'Migration and Rural Development in Punjab: A Study of Inter-Relationships'. *Man & Development.* 12(2):67–76.

Gulati, Leela. 1987. 'Coping with Male Migration'. *Economic and Political Weekly.* 22(44):WS 41–6.

Mamdani, M. 1981. 'The Ugandan Asian Expulsion: Twenty Years After'. *Economic and Political Weekly.* 16:93–6.

Ministry of Rural Development. 1996. 'Draft National Policy for Rehabilitation of Persons Displaced as a Consequence of Acquisition of Land'. *Economic and Political Weekly.* 31(24):1541–5.

Ray, S.N. 1982. *Migrant Women Workers.* Ranchi: Bihar Tribal Welfare Research Institute.

Sharma, S.L. 1989. 'Perspectives on Indians Abroad'. *Sociological Bulletin.* (Special Issue on Indians Abroad) 38(1):1–24.

Singh, R.K. 1993. 'Migration and Economic Development in Haryana'. *Manpower Journal.* 28(4):19–48.

Sinha, B.K. 1996. 'Draft National Policy for Rehabilitation Objectives and Principles'. *Economic and Political Weekly.* 31(24):1453–60.

Sita, K. and K. Seeta Prabhu. 1989. 'Levels of Development and Migration: Caste of South Konkan'. *Economic and Political Weekly.* 14(1):39–41.

Tinker, Hugh. 1974. *A New System of Slavery: The Export of Indian Labour Overseas 1830–1920.* London: Oxford University Press.

Visaria, Leela and Pravin Visaria. 1995. 'India's Population in Transition.' *Population Bulletin.* 50(3).

Weiner, Myron. 1993. 'Rejected Peoples and Unwanted Migration in South Asia.' *Economic and Political Weekly.* 28(21 August):1737–46.

———. 1978. *Sons of the Soil.* Princeton: Princeton University Press.

Zaidi, S. Akbar. 1991. 'Sindhi vs Mohajir in Pakistan: Contradiction, Conflict, Compromise'. *Economic and Political Weekly.* 26(20):1295–1302.

Modernization

SATISH DESHPANDE

Despite our reservations concerning models of tradition and modernity, we find certain contrasts heuristically useful: 'modernity' assumes that local ties and parochial perspectives give way to universal commitments and cosmopolitan attitudes; that the truths of utility, calculation, and science take precedence over those of the emotions, the sacred, and the non-rational; that the individual rather than the group be the primary unit of society and politics; that the associations in which men live and work be based on choice not birth; that mastery rather than fatalism orient their attitude toward the material and human environment; that identity be chosen and achieved, not ascribed and affirmed; that work be separated from family, residence, and community in bureaucratic organizations.

Rudolph and Rudolph (1967)

How can the sociologist be certain that a particular change is part of the process of modernization? Such a difficulty is not merely logico-philosophical, but is inescapable in the actual analysis of empirical processes of change.

Srinivas (1971a)

Unhé bhi to pata chalé ki ham bhi *modern* hain.
(They should also realize that we too are modern.)

Legend painted on the back of a Delhi bus (1996).

Modernization as an overarching theme has helped shape the horizons of Indian sociology and social anthropology. The major concern of this chapter, therefore, will be this general theme and the conceptual apparatus associated with it, rather than the specifics of the historical experience of modernization in Indian society. It will try to tackle questions such as: What has been at stake in the concept and the academic field of modernization? What issues of theory, method, and standpoint has it raised? If our approach to these problems has changed, why has this happened? What is—and should be—the present status of this theme in Indian sociology?

The juxtaposed standpoints of the three epigraphs above provide a preliminary orientation to the terrain on which the vexed question of modernization has been negotiated in India. First, there is the viewpoint of the globally dominant mainstream of (western) social science, comprehensively confident, despite 'reservations', of the content and form of modernity, what it is and looks like. However, even such an unequivocal and detailed description of modernity does not dispel the doubtful unease of the Indian sociologist who wonders whether 'social change in modern India' can be equated with 'modernization'. Yet another contrast is suggested by the voice emanating from everyday life in India at the turn of the twentieth century, a voice confidently affirming its own modernity, concerned only that 'they' also recognize it.

Though they are presented in simplistic terms overstating the contrasts,[1] these standpoints nevertheless supply the major coordinates for mapping the field of modernization studies in India. Alternatively, they can be seen as representing three broad phases in the evolution of research on the theme of modernization in India—a brief initial period of confidence and hope, followed by a long interregnum of ambivalence and anxiety, which shows signs of giving way at the turn of the century to renewed self-assurance and innovation. In the following account, the first section provides a brief overview of the emergence of modernization studies as an academic phenomenon, the institutional—practical forms it took in India, and the major concerns of the dominant strands of research; the second section analyses the uneasy relationship between this theme and Indian sociology: the contextual specificities, the conceptual strategies that these prompted, and the ambivalences and aporias that they led to; and the third section outlines the reasons why the modernization paradigm is no longer viable and explores some of the alternative directions being taken by contemporary social theory.

CONFIDENCE AND HOPE

As the process of becoming or being made *modern*, the broad theme of modernization has been foremost among the originary concerns that shaped the emergent discipline of sociology in the nineteenth century. In the contemporary social sciences, however, the most familiar meaning of modernization is closer to the one given in *The Penguin Dictionary of Sociology*: 'A dominant analytical paradigm in American sociology for the explanation of the global process whereby traditional societies achieved modernity' (Abercrombie et al. 1988: 158). While the theorists of classical sociology—Comte, Marx, Spencer, Durkheim, Tönnies, Weber, and Simmel—were primarily interested in the 'modernization' of the West, the more recent phenomenon of 'modernization theory' is concerned almost exclusively with the transformation of non-western societies. Modernization theory is thus rooted in the confident belief that the new but *non-modern* nations of Asia and Africa (as well as the older nations of Latin America) can, will, and should become modern societies. Such confidence does make modernization seem altogether too 'triumphal' a story by the mores of contemporary social science, a theory of 'the true, the good, and the inevitable' as Appadurai (1997: 11) puts it. But in seeming so, the theory was merely reflecting the spirit of its own age more clearly and intensely than most academic enterprises.

As is well known, modernization theory is the child of a marriage of coincidence between decolonization and the Cold War. The end of the Second World War quickened the process of decolonization and brought a host of new African and Asian nations on to the world stage between the late 1940s and the 1960s. On the one hand, decolonization released new hopes and energies in the new nations and, indeed, across the globe, at a time when boundless faith was being invested in the idea of material progress based on rational–scientific technologies. On the other hand, there was no fundamental change in the socio-political and especially the economic inequalities undergirding the world order. The new nations thus became both the repositories of millenarian agendas of change and progress fuelled by domestic aspirations, as well as potential client states where old and new world powers competed to establish spheres of influence. Added momentum was provided by the fact that decolonization coincided with the most intense phase of the Cold War, and with the almost total hegemony of the United States over the western world. Seen against this background, the emergence and popularity of theories of growth, development, or modernization seems almost inevitable (Myrdal 1970: 8).

Modernization studies were launched in the early 1950s as part of a vast, (and largely United States-sponsored) multi-disciplinary academic project with the overall objective of winning the cold war—both negatively (by preventing the 'slide into communism' of poor Asian, African, and Latin American nations), and positively (by providing socially, economically, and politically viable routes to stable non-communist growth and development). As part of this enterprise, various US federal government institutions (including the military), leading universities, and private philanthropic foundations (notably the Ford and Rockefeller foundations) financed a historically unprecedented volume of social scientific research on the new nations of the Third World (Myrdal 1970: 12–16; Gendzier 1985. esp. Ch. 2). Moreover, nationalism and independence also awakened in the middle class elite of the Third World an intense interest in the development and modernization of their own societies, often translated into state support for research, or at least into willing cooperation with externally sponsored research efforts.[2]

Although it soon came to be dominated by development economics and allied fields, the thirty-year boom (1950s–1970s) in modernization studies affected several disciplines including sociology (especially rural sociology), area studies, political science, and social psychology. Sociology played a particularly prominent role because it provided the most commonly invoked theoretical framework—namely the highly abstract (hence apparently context-free and cross-culturally portable) taxonomic syntheses of Talcott Parsons—and also because of the inevitable importance of rural sociology in studying predominantly rural Third World societies.[3] The major themes taken up by modernization studies included development, the transition from traditional to modern social forms, the aids and obstacles to the emergence of modern political institutions, and the inculcation of (or resistance to) modern values and norms in the individual personality.

Studying Modernization In India

While modernization studies, of course, has been strongly affected by this global background, its history in India is also rather distinctive. Unlike in most other Third World countries, American modernization theory did not dominate the study of social change in India, although it was a prominent and influential presence in the realm of state policy. This difference is due to the combined effect of three factors: the prior involvement of other western scholarly traditions; the presence of a small but relatively well-developed indigenous research establishment; and the hegemonic influence exerted by a long-standing nationalist movement.

As an ancient civilization with a living Great Tradition (rather than a 'decapitated' one, to use Robert Redfield's starkly evocative term),[4] India was no *tabula rasa* for western scholars. The production of systematic knowledge on Indian society based on the pioneering work of orientalist Indologists, colonial administrators and missionaries, and of a recognizably modern kind, developed very rapidly from 1760 onward (see Cohn 1987: 141–71). By the early decades of the twentieth century these varied traditions had already produced a considerable body of works on the arts, sciences, and cultural-religious practices of classical Hinduism; the cultural coherence of Indian/Hindu or aboriginal communities; and regional inventories of castes and tribes detailing their 'customs and manners'. To this must be added the later work of western and Indian scholars trained mainly in the British tradition of a social anthropology, as well as some American anthropologists. The above work consisted largely of ethnographic monographs on village, caste, or tribal communities.[5]

However, this diverse body of largely anthropological work on India did not show deep or sustained interest in social *change,* except in the form of enquiries into the decay or degeneration of traditional practices, institutions, and communities. With Independence, the search for social change became an important item on the agenda of social anthropology in India—so much so, in fact, that some scholars worried that it would eclipse other issues.[6] But even when it was taken up, this search was conducted largely independently of American modernization theory as such, keeping in, perhaps, with the relative indifference towards this theme in anthropology.[7]

The two other reasons for the Indian difference have to be viewed together: the hegemonic status of nationalism in the 1950s, and the existence of institutions that could give intellectual expression to this hegemony.[8] In India, as in most of the non-western world, the themes of modernization, development, growth, and progress were part of the much wider canvas of the colonial encounter, particularly since the latter half of the nineteenth century. They were woven into colonialist narratives of the white man's burden and the *mission civilisatrice*— and also into emergent nationalist narratives of the desire for development thwarted by colonial oppression and economic drain. In the heady aftermath of Indian Independence, the idea of modernization took on the dimensions of a national mission; it became an integral part of the Nehruvian 'tryst with destiny' that the nation had pledged to keep. While Indian nationalism in itself was hardly an aberration (though older than most others in the Third World), India's colonial inheritance of a viable nucleus of western-style academic institutions was unusual, possibly even unique. Like other social institutions of the time, Indian universities and research institutes were also eager to participate in the agendas of the nationalist state, and provided another site for the emergence of modernization studies in India, one marked by an ambivalent attitude towards western scholars and institutions,[9] and by a bias against basic research and towards policy-oriented studies.[10]

An Overview of the Literature

Given the peculiarities of its long pre-history, the study of societal change in India evolved into a much more diverse field of enquiry than that suggested by American modernization theory. The central fact here is the relativization of modernization studies as one paradigm among others speculating on the consequences of the interface between the West and India. Some measure of the extent of this relativization is provided in the distinctive stance of orientalist Indology, the first western scholarly tradition to address Indian society and culture in the late eighteenth and early nineteenth centuries. While it was surely less than egalitarian, this stance still entertained the possibility of a reciprocal relationship, something unthinkable in later models of modernization.[11] However, by the latter half of the nineteenth century and certainly in the twentieth, the Indologists' perspective had been sidelined, and questions of societal change could only be framed within—or against—a firmly Eurocentric intellectual horizon. Nevertheless, the larger question of India's response to western modernity continued to be asked and answered in ways that could not simply be reduced to speculations about the manner in which (or the speed with which) tradition would be superseded.

T.N. Madan has suggested[12] that in Indian sociology and social anthropology, the question of modernity is posed in three major forms. It first appeared in the 1930s in opposition to the Weberian thesis of the other-worldly orientation of Hinduism and its consequent lack of affinity with modern materialist modes of thought. It was then that scholars like Benoy Kumar Sarkar and Brajendranath Seal attempted to foreground the positivistic tendencies in Hindu thought by proposing a 'Hindu sociology' (Sarkar 1985; Seal 1985). The second occasion was the public controversy over the policy to be adopted towards tribal communities—whether they ought to be modernized and 'mainstreamed' or protected and 'preserved'. This debate involved not only the well-known exchanges between Verrier Elwin and G.S. Ghurye, but also engagements with contemporary (1920s–1940s) notions of 'progress' by scholars like D.P. Mukerji and D.N. Majumdar.[13] The third recurrence of this question is, of course, in the post-Independence context of development—an ideology that has dominated world history for several decades.

While these three episodes offer a useful entry point into the history of scholarly engagement with modernity, they are not as helpful in ordering the literature on modernization because the hegemonic sway of the idea of development is such that it dwarfs or subsumes the other two instances. Indeed, if we revert from the broader question of the India–West interface to the more conventional meaning attached to modernization, then the entire literature on the subject—certainly everything written after 1947—is directly or indirectly influenced by the notion of national development.

Given a strong and enduring (but not necessarily unchanging) traditional social system, the modernization question seems to allow for only three elementary outcomes: a) tradition prevails over modernity, absorbing or obstructing it successfully; b) modernity triumphs over tradition, undermining and eventually supplanting it; or c) tradition and modernity coexist in some fashion. One can therefore categorize the literature in terms of these outcomes, and there have been attempts to do so.[14] However, this categorization proves to be lopsided because the first two possibilities were very quickly marginalized in post-Independence India: the massive impact of modernity could not be ignored, nor could the continuing resilience of tradition. Therefore, the bulk of the Indian literature on modernization is concerned with characterizing the nature of the interaction between tradition and modernity, and the long-term trend of this relationship.

Since there is no obvious classificatory scheme available, the following survey of literature is based on an eclectic mix of criteria such as disciplinary location, theoretical perspective, and value orientation. Even so, the field to be covered is vast, given the variety of disciplines (including social anthropology, sociology, social psychology, politics, political economy, and area studies) and theoretical perspectives (such as structural-functionalism, behaviourism, structuralism, Marxism, or evolutionism, not to speak of combinations of these) represented. Moreover, modernization is such a broad theme that almost every author and every work on Indian society addresses it in some sense or the other. The present overview is therefore limited only to work in and around sociology and anthropology that has had a significant influence on the analysis of social change in post-Independence India. These are somewhat imprecise and arbitrary criteria, but unavoidably so.

Social Anthropological Perspectives

Though he refuses the term 'modernization', M.N. Srinivas is among the first and easily the most influential scholar to have written extensively on the question. The *locus classicus* of Srinivas's approach is his book *Social Change in Modern India*, published in 1966, although the major concepts in it had already found mention in his 1952 work on Coorg.[15] Acknowledging the enormity of the enterprise,[16] Srinivas deliberately takes an 'all-India' view of social change, though he relies heavily on the insights garnered during his own fieldwork in Coorg (1940–2) and Mysore (1947–8). For Srinivas, change assumes two major forms: first, the various forms of mobility within the caste system (captured by the concepts of Sanskritization and dominant caste); and second, the wide-ranging process of westernization. (He also adds a chapter on secularization, but the weight of his analysis is undoubtedly borne by the first two areas.)

As is well known, Sanskritization refers to a process that 'seems to have occurred throughout Indian history and still continues to occur' (Srinivas 1971a: 1), by which 'a "low" Hindu caste, or tribal or "other" group, changes its customs, ritual, ideology, and way of life in the direction of a high, and frequently, "twice-born" caste' (ibid.:6) with a view of claiming a higher position in the caste hierarchy. Such claims may, over 'a generation or two' (ibid.), result in some upward mobility,

but mobility may also occur without Sanskritization and vice versa. However, the mobility associated with Sanskritization results only in *positional changes* in the system and does not lead to any *structural change*. That is, a caste moves up, above its neighbours, and another comes down, but all this takes place in an essentially stable hierarchical order. The system itself does not change [Srinivas 1971a: 7, emphasis original].

The concept of a dominant caste, on the other hand, is an attempt to capture the change in the status of some relatively high touchable (*sudra*) castes as a result of their numerical strength, predominant position in the agricultural economy (mainly landownership), and, over time, accumulation of 'western' criteria such as education and government jobs. In other words, this concept points to the rise in the secular status, political power (following adult franchise), and economic power (following land reforms) of some caste groups, which have benefited from the social changes introduced since Independence (Srinivas 1994: 96–115, 4–13).

Westernization refers to the 'changes introduced into Indian society during British rule and which continue, in some cases with added momentum, in independent India' (Srinivas 1971a: 1). Despite being a relatively recent influence, westernization is recognized as 'an inclusive, complex, and many-layered concept' ranging 'from Western technology at one end to the experimental method of modern science and modern historiography at the other', and its different aspects 'sometimes combine to strengthen a particular process, sometimes work at cross-purposes, and are occasionally mutually discrete' (ibid.: 53). Though the upper castes have been particularly active in mediating it, all castes are affected by westernization, which brings about 'radical and lasting changes in Indian society and culture' based on a very wide range of causal factors, including 'new technology, institutions, knowledge, beliefs and values' (ibid.: 46). The changes it effects can often be counter-intuitive, as indicated by the fact that it 'has given birth not only to nationalism but also to revivalism, communalism, "casteism", heightened linguistic consciousness, and regionalism' (ibid.: 55), or that it is linked to Sanskritization in a 'complex and intricate interrelation' (ibid.: 1).

Srinivas's early work on Coorg attracted considerable attention because it was the first social-anthropological study of a complex society with 'high' cultural traditions (as different from the 'simple' or 'primitive' societies that social anthropologists had studied until then). His notion of Sanskritization, and his innovative spatial hierarchy of local, regional, and 'all-India' Hinduism, seemed to offer novel ways of theorizing the relationship between the 'Great' and 'Little' traditions posited by the scholar of the Univeristy of Chicago, Robert

Redfield, and this is how his associate Milton Singer came to study India in the early 1950s. Singer was preceded by another Chicago anthropologist, McKim Marriott who, having been posted in Delhi during the Second World War, decided to build on this experience by carrying out fieldwork in rural north India.

Singer's main work on modernization (Singer 1972, especially Parts 4 and 5) is based on innovative fieldwork—done in three stints in 1954–5, 1960–1, and 1964, in middle and upper class *urban* settings in south India, mainly Madras (Chennai)—and helps complement rural-based perceptions on social change. He focuses on the specific strategies used by urban Indians to manage the simultaneous presence of tradition and modernity in their everyday lives. Thus, *compartmentalization* refers to the strict spatial and temporal segregation of traditional and modern contexts/institutions; *ritual neutralization* is a prophylactic gesture to contain the threat of pollution or other forms of transgression of traditional values in modern contexts such as the workplace; and *vicarious ritualization* refers to a division of labour in which householders unable to perform religious rituals (because of conflicts with their modern occupations) get their wives or professional priests to perform them on their behalf. The main contributions of Marriott relevant here are two concepts namely *parochialization* and *universalization* developed from fieldwork in a north Indian village. The latter is a process whereby elements of the 'little' tradition (customs, deities, and rites) circulate upward to enter the 'great' tradition and thus acquire a more universal status, while the former refers to the opposite process of elements from the 'great' tradition becoming confined to particular local 'little' traditions (Marriott 1955).

The core of the social-anthropological work on the theme of modernization consists of the 'Srinivas–Chicago' body of work and its many critics, elaborators, and interlocutors. Sanskritization in particular has generated a large literature and is the most prominent (some would say the only) concept from the Indian literature to have made an impact on the larger discipline. Numerous studies have appreciated, extended or criticized the concept, mooted the notions of re- or de-Sanskritization, or examined its regional spread.[17] Similarly, the notions of 'great' and 'little' traditions have also elicited further transformations on the basic model, the most important being the presence of multiple traditions (rather than just two) whose significance and modes of inter-articulation are context dependent (Singh 1973: 13–16).

Tradition-identified Perspectives

While the Srinivasian position has attempted to remain neutral regarding the valuation to be placed on the modernization process, a significant minority tendency has not only identified strongly with Indian tradition in a personal–existential sense, but has gone on to fashion a disciplinary agenda sharply critical of the process of modernization and especially the westernized modes of studying it. The best known representatives of this tendency are D.P. Mukerji and A.K. Saran, both of the Lucknow 'school' of Indian sociology, who arrive at this position by very different routes—the former through long engagement with Marxist materialism and its inadequacies, and the latter by way of Hindu religion and metaphysics.

Mukerji's priorities are stated forthrightly in his famous Presidential Address to the first meeting of the Indian Sociological Society in 1955: 'the study of Indian traditions' is the 'first and immediate duty of the Indian sociologist' (Mukerji [1955] 1988: 5). Indeed, he goes further: 'It is not enough for the Indian sociologist to be a sociologist. He must be an Indian first, that is, he is to share in the folk-ways, mores, customs and traditions for the purpose of understanding his social system and what lies beneath it and beyond it' (ibid.: 6). Mukerji argues for indigenous modes of analysis because western concepts fail to capture the complex particularity of Indian society, which 'requires a different approach to sociology because of its special traditions, its special symbols and its special pattern of culture and social actions'. It is only 'thereafter' that there can be a case for studying change, because 'the thing changing is more real and objective than change per se' (ibid.: 15). According to T.N. Madan, Mukerji viewed modernization as 'at once an expansion, an elevation, a deepening and a revitalization' of traditional values and cultural patterns—that is as a kind of self-conscious synthesization of modernity by tradition (Madan 1995: 18). However, this synthesis (and the derivation of indigenous concepts from Hindu philosophy and religion, and from the life of Mahatma Gandhi) is never pursued systematically, but remains at the level of suggestive claims and passing examples, evidence perhaps of the 'self-cancellation' and 'reluctance' attributed to Mukerji (ibid.: 20). A.K. Saran appears to have moved in the direction of Hindu religion and philosophy with a view to exploring their potential for Indian sociology. But again there is a lack of substantial texts (except, perhaps, Saran 1958) where this position is spelt out adequately, and even as sympathetic a commentator as Veena Das is constrained to note that Saran's attitude towards tradition ultimately lapses into nostalgia (Das 1995: 50–4).

This broad position—defined by the triad of tradition identification, anti-modernism, and theoretical indigenism—has exerted disproportionate influence despite its lack of dominance. Though its intellectual reach has always exceeded its scholarly grasp, this tendency continues to attract adherents to its general vicinity, albeit with differing emphases on its three planks. Early exponents include the controversial figure of Verrier Elwin, famous as the anthropologist gone native, while more contemporary versions of different sorts are to be found in the works of Tariq Banuri, T.N. Madan, McKim Marriott, J.P.S Uberoi, Shiv Visvanathan, or (outside sociology and social anthropology proper) Claude Alvares, and especially Ashis Nandy.

Synthetic Overviews

Among the various attempts to synthesize the different perspectives on modernization in India, the most comprehensive and best known is Yogendra Singh's *Modernization of Indian Tradition*. Singh's ambitious theoretical project is to overcome the 'partial focus on social processes' and the 'limitations of the analytical categories used' in previous treatments of change in India, which have rendered them 'narrow and inadequate' (Singh 1973: 1). He identifies commonalities in the earlier perspectives and uses them to fashion his own overarching taxonomic synthesis based on 'unilinear evolutionism in the long run' (ibid.: 23) which distinguishes: a) the micro and macro contexts in which change-producing processes begin and materialize; b) the internal (orthogenetic) and external (heterogenetic) sources of change; and c) the structural and cultural substantive domains within which phenomena are undergoing change. This is said to yield a 'comprehensive as well as theoretically consistent' synthetic theory into which social change in India from the Vedic times to the present can be fitted, including such major epochal changes as the advent of Muslim rule, British colonialism, or Independence.

S.C. Dube's general survey is notable for bringing together the literatures on modernization and development, and also for the fact that it was written well after disillusionment with modernization had set in (Dube 1988). Dube's emphasis is on 'the search for alternative paradigms' (the subtitle of his book), among which he includes 'conscientization', 'affirmative action', and 'institution building'. His survey is oriented towards the practical issues of social policy, as were his two earlier works relevant here, namely the famous book *Indian Village* (Dube 1955), although it does not explicitly address modernization, and the later edited collection

India's Changing Villages (Dube 1958, associated with the Community Development Programme), are both significant studies of social change in rural India.

Gunnar Myrdal's well-known 'institutional approach' to the problem of development in South Asia bases itself on the premise that

[n]ot only is the social and institutional structure different from the one that has evolved in Western countries, but, more important, the problem of development in South Asia is one calling for induced changes in that social and institutional structure, as it hinders economic development and as it does not change spontaneously, or, to any very large extent, in response to policies restricted to the 'economic' sphere [Myrdal 1968: 26].

Easily the largest single work on the subject, *Asian Drama* (Myrdal 1968) was based on a decade-long pioneering effort to collect, evaluate, and synthesize secondary material, from a vast variety of sources, on the political economy of India. Myrdal's overall conclusions were pessimistic because he saw resilient traditional institutions and values as insurmountable obstacles to modernization. By contrast, the institutions of modernity in India—most notably the state—tended to be 'soft', and would therefore, be unable to pursue a modern agenda effectively unless traditional blockages were comprehensively destroyed.[18] However, a contemporary review by a social anthropologist (Madan 1969) notes that Myrdal's social institutions remain underspecified, caste being the only one discussed at some length, though even here the treatment ignores literature offering contrary evidence.

David Mandelbaum's vast and copiously referenced survey of scholarship on Indian society provides a compendium of early work on the theme of change, especially in terms of caste mobility, and religious and tribal movements (Mandelbaum 1970: Parts VII–VIII of vol. 2). Also well known is a two-volume collection on the theme of modernization of underdeveloped societies edited by A.R. Desai (1971). The collection contains more than sixty chapters (mostly previously published) by scholars from across the world writing from diverse perspectives; there are also a few articles written for the collection, among which Inkeles's chapter on the problems of fieldwork in Third World countries and Srinivas's brief queries on modernization are particularly interesting. Myron Weiner's popular collection (originally a series of radio talks on the Voice of America) has also been influential as nine out of his twenty-five contributors have worked on India (Weiner 1966).

Social-psychological Perspectives

The most typical example of American modernization studies in India is perhaps the study by Alex Inkeles and David Smith that examines how 'people move from being traditional to becoming more modern personalities' (Inkeles and Smith 1974: 5) in six developing countries: Argentina, Chile, India, Israel, Nigeria, and East Pakistan (now Bangladesh). Distinctive in looking for attributes of modernity among individuals, the study was based on intensive interviews with a stratified sample of 1000 males in each country, whose responses were measured for their degree of modernization on a composite attitudinal scale developed by the authors.[19] The main findings confirmed the existence of a 'psycho-social syndrome' of modernity as internalized values and attitudes, and manifested in behaviour demonstrating a feeling of personal efficacy, autonomy from 'traditional sources of influence', and openness towards 'new experiences and ideas' (ibid.: 290). The most important causal factor was education, followed by occupation and exposure to mass media; urbanization was found to be unimportant (ibid.: 302–6).

David McClelland and David Winter's study (1964–7) took the form of a training programme (conducted by the Small Industries Extension Training Institute, Hyderabad) for small businessmen from the south Indian towns of Kakinada and Vellore. Based on McClelland's earlier research on the psychology of motivation, the study sought to identify the determinants of the 'need to achieve' with a view to (in the words of their subtitle) 'accelerating economic development through psychological training' (McClelland and Winter 1969).

Other Disciplines and Perspectives

Political science along with rural sociology has perhaps been the most active discipline in modernization theory and has produced numerous studies on 'political development' around the world, largely in response to the intense interest in the politics of the Third World countries during the Cold War. In India, the best-known examples (from the perspective of sociology and social anthropology) would be the works of Rajni Kothari, and Lloyd and Susanne Rudolph. Kothari's classic work (1970) adopts a functional approach towards modernization and focuses on the mutual interaction of tradition and modernity, the specifics of their relationship, the process that it is part of, and their functionality for each other. The Rudolphs' study (1967) attempts to show how modernization in Indian politics changes traditional institutions such that they begin to take on modern roles, the most prominent case being that of caste.

Political economy and Marxism would be next in importance from a sociological perspective. But the work here is very diverse, ranging from (for example) the historical emphasis of Daniel Thorner (1980), through the economics-oriented overview by Pranab Bardhan (1984), to the political theory of Sudipta Kaviraj's (1988) essay on the 'passive revolution'. But the most important Marxist work on the theme of modernization—theorized, however, in terms of the transition from a pre-capitalist to a capitalist mode of production—is that stimulated by the 'mode of production' debate, which tried to ascertain whether and to what extent Indian agrarian relations were capitalist in nature. The decade-long debate produced very sophisticated discussions on the conceptual categorization of 'aberrant' social formations such as India— neither capitalist nor feudal, but with the strong presence of elements of both (Thorner 1982; Patnaik 1990). Some of the theoretical options advocated included semi-feudalism, semi-capitalism, a 'colonial mode of production' and characterizations based on the distinction between formal and real subsumption of labour by capital. Given the valuable contributions that Marxist scholars have made to Indian historiography and political economy, it is a pity that they have, by and large, not ventured very far into the sociological terrain of modernization.[20]

Finally, surveying the institutions sponsoring research, the theme of modernization gives us another perspective to this field. Different kinds of institutional and financial support have been provided to researchers by Indian (Bombay, Lucknow, and Osmania) and foreign universities: Harvard, Chicago, Berkeley, Cornell, and Stanford have been particularly important, while Oxford, the London School of Economics, Stockholm, and McGill have also been involved in facilitating fieldwork or publications (by M.N. Srinivas, S.C. Dube, Gunnar Myrdal, and Yogendra Singh respectively). American private foundations have been very active, led by the Ford Foundation, which has invested heavily in research on change, development, and planning in India (Rosen 1985). The Rockefeller Foundation has also been involved in the early stages, as have the Twentieth Century Fund (Myrdal) and the Carnegie Corporation (McClelland and Winter). Government sources in India have included the Small Industries Extension Training Institute, the National Service Extension Programme, the Community Development Programme, and the Planning Commission. Various organs of the US government have also supported modernization research, including the State Department (which controlled the PL 480 counterpart funds in India and other countries receiving US aid), the US Agency for International Development, and, in at least one instance, the US Air Force (through its Office of Scientific Research which helped with the Inkeles and Smith study (Inkeles 1971: 22, n. 1).

ANXIETY AND AMBIVALENCE

'We may have become weary of the concept of modernization,' writes T.N. Madan, 'but the important question is, have we carefully formulated the reasons for this weariness?' (Madan 1995: 5). Indian sociology does seem to be weary of modernization, not only in the sense of being disenchanted with this theme, but also in the sense of having been exhausted by it— one of the reasons, perhaps, why sociology in India has sometimes looked like a tired discipline (Deshpande 1994). Why has the conceptual pursuit of modernization been so debilitating? Among the better-known answers is the conceptual dead-end of dualism; less well-known are the peculiar disciplinary location of Indian sociology and the problems posed by the abstract generality of the term 'modernization'.

A Discrepant Dualism and its Discontents

The dominant view among students of modern India was that neither tradition nor modernity would be strong enough (at least in the foreseeable future) to completely erase the other. This meant that the search for an adequate summary description of Indian society was transposed into the problem of defining dualism—or characterizing the nature of the relationship between tradition and modernity.

There is, of course, nothing exceptional in this, for dualism is the presiding deity in the conceptual pantheon of modernization not just in India but everywhere in the 'non-West' (Banuri 1990: 40–3). Consider, for example, one of the most famous vignettes in modernization studies—the story of the 'The Grocer and the Chief'—with which David Lerner begins his classic work on *The Passing of Traditional Society* (Lerner 1958: 21–8; subsequent quotations in this paragraph are from these pages). Presented as 'the parable of modern Turkey', this story contrasts two main characters who stand for modernity and tradition. The chief (of the village of Balgat 8 km south of Ankara) is a 'virtuoso of the traditional style'. A prosperous farmer and an imposing personality, he has no unfulfilled ambitions, loves to expound on the values of 'obedience, courage, loyalty', and responds to persistent enquiries about where else he would like to live with a firm 'nowhere'. Balgat's only grocer is described by his interviewer (a Turkish student identified only by the abbreviated name Tosun B.) as an 'unimpressive type' giving 'the impression of a fat shadow', whom the villagers consider to be 'even less than the least farmer'. But the grocer visits Ankara frequently, is fascinated by Hollywood movies, would like to own 'a *real* grocery store' with floor-to-ceiling shelves, and is eager to live in America because it offers 'possibilities to be rich even for the simplest persons'. As if to underline the centrality of this dichotomous model for modernization theory, Alex Inkeles and David Smith present an identical contrast between Ahmadullah, a 'traditional' illiterate farmer from Comilla, and Nuril, a 'modern' metal worker in a Dacca factory, who enact Lerner's Turkish parable all over again—sixteen years later, in Bangladesh! (Inkeles and Smith 1974: 73–83).

The point of recalling these emblematic figures is not to claim that they are absent in India—how could they be?—but to highlight the fact that the *dominant* descriptions of dualism in the Indian literature are different. Simply put, Indian descriptions of dualism seem discrepant because they are relatively more sophisticated than those elsewhere, at least in the early period of modernization studies. The precociously complex analyses of influential scholars like M.N. Srinivas minimize the impact of the cruder models of dualism, even though they are as common in India as elsewhere in the Third World. On the other hand, this means that the aporias of dualism are reached sooner in India, and that more time is wasted in conceptual wheel-spinning because the tradition–modernity dichotomy fails to get a grip on Indian social reality.

The most obvious differences in Indian accounts of dualism have to do with the social units in which tradition and modernity are located, and in their reciprocal articulation. Thus tradition and modernity are not only segregated into two separate personalities as in the Bangladeshi or Turkish tales, but are also apt to occur, in comparable Indian accounts, as integral parts of *the same personality*. For example, M.N. Srinivas mentions meeting the 'driver of a government bulldozer' in his field village of Rampura in 1952, barely two years after Tosun B. met the Turkish grocer and chief on Daniel Lerner's behalf. The bulldozer driver, a Tamil-speaker from Bangalore, was skilled enough to operate his machine and also to 'do minor repairs; but he was not only traditional in his religious beliefs, he had even picked up some black magic, a knowledge usually confined to small groups'. Srinivas reports that 'he saw no inconsistency between driving a bulldozer for his livelihood and indulging in displays of black magic for his pleasure', the 'two sectors being kept completely "discrete"' (Srinivas 1971a: 54–5).

But if such descriptions are more believable and complex than the caricatures of crude dualism, they also place the Indian personality under permanent suspicion of schizophrenia. Here is Srinivas again, speaking this time of the first generation of his own community, South Indian Brahmins, who

took to English education in considerable numbers and entered the professions and government service at all levels. In the first phase of their Westernization, their professional life was lived in the Western world while their home life continued to be largely traditional. (The term 'cultural schizophrenia' comes to mind, but a caution must be uttered against viewing it as pathological.) [1971a: 57][21]

The theme of the coexistence of 'discrete' sectors in a single person, family or other social group is a common one in the literature on modernization in India, and, indeed, in the conversational anecdotes of everyday life.[22] The dualistic-but-unified personality may be described in a wide range of registers—from pathos through pathology to pride. But whatever the tenor of the description, and regardless of the attitude of the person being described, the describer—especially the professional social scientist—is unable to shake off a sense of incongruity which invariably inflects the description. Nevertheless, in the Indian literature, the choice between tradition and modernity is rarely presented as a mutually exclusive 'either/ or', though it is often seen as a morally charged one. In Lerner's description, tradition has no value for the grocer, who wishes only to escape from its parochial constraints; and the chief, though forced to acknowledge the impact of modernity, remains thoroughly immune to it morally. In this parable, 'modern Turkey' is the only transcendent entity capable of subsuming these contrary worldviews, while in the Indian literature the burden of subsumption is felt by social units all along the scale from the national to the individual.[23]

But too much must not be made of such differences. After all, they hold only for the early stage of modernization studies up to the 1960s; there is every reason to presume that anthropological accounts of Third World modernization grew in sophistication over time. Moreover, comparisons of this sort need to consider carefully further questions of detail:

Are the Lerner or Inkeles–Smith type of multi-country survey-based studies comparable with Srinivas's solo ethnography? Is each really representative of the sociological or anthropological work done on the respective field areas?

However, there is another difference that does seem important: the prominence of Indian scholars in the social anthropology of India. In India, the western anthropologist encountered not only natives and 'local counterparts' (Brahmin *pundits*, *gyanis*, or *maulavis*) but also his/her own '*double*', the native anthropologist with comparable western training (Burghart 1990, discussed in Das 1995: 34–41). Such an early and sizeable presence of local scholars is quite unusual among Third World countries, and may well be unique.[24]

Whatever the reasons responsible, the crucial question is whether the presence of Indian researchers made any difference to the descriptions produced. Returning to the comparisons between modernization in Lerner's Turkey and Srinivas's India, a striking difference is now visible. Tosun B., the Turkish graduate student whose field notes caught Lerner's attention and helped produce the parable, is himself outside the frame of reference, or, at best, at its edges. By contrast, Srinivas, the anthropologist with an Oxford degree, is never allowed to forget his Indianness, and is constantly being pulled into the frame of the picture he is painting.[25] Perhaps it is this sustained incitement to self-reflexivity that makes Indian accounts of dualism precociously complex. Indian anthropologists are acutely aware that modernization is happening not just 'elsewhere' but in the 'here and now' that they themselves inhabit.

Whatever the truth of their claim to greater sophistication, Indian accounts of dualism cannot escape the limitations of this mode of theorizing. Modernization—even in its minimalist version of an ongoing interaction of some sort between tradition and modernity—proves to be a conceptual dead end because there is, literally, no exit. A modernizing society is always only a modernizing society: it can no longer call itself traditional, and its modernity is never quite the real thing. In a strange twist on the 'allochronism' (Fabian 1983) that anthropology is accused of, the modernization paradigm evacuates the contemporaneity of such societies, robbing the present of its immediacy and constricting its relations with the past and the future into narratives of loss or inadequacy. It is truly remarkable how this motif of a society, a culture, a history, a politics, or even a personality permanently in a state of in-between-ness—a double-edged failure—recurs across disciplinary contexts.

For example, in anthropology, the 'developing societies' become 'deceived societies as they have had their present transformed into a permanent transition', 'an endless pause' (Madan 1995: 165, 22). In Marxist political economy, (as Mihir Shah puts it in his requiem for the mode of production debate), 'Indian agrarian relations are perhaps destined forever to remaining semi-capitalist' (Shah 1985: PE–66). And Ranajit Guha inaugurates the 'Subaltern Studies' initiative with the announcement that the 'central problematic' of historiography is the 'failure of the nation to come into its own' (Guha 1982: 7). All the various *avatars* of this theme—whether in the garb of a search for modernity, democracy, capitalism, or development—are marked by the anxiety of striving for a norm that is, so to speak, unattainable *ab initio*.

The Ambiguous Inheritance of Indian Sociology

Apart from its difficulties with the barrenness of dualism (which it shared with its siblings in other disciplines), the social-anthropological search for modernization suffered from certain other disabilities peculiarly its own. These had to do with the public image and perceived concerns of social anthropology before and after Independence, and how its disciplinary location differed from that of its neighbours in the social sciences.

The reputation of Indian social anthropology before Independence was an ambiguous one. On the one hand, sections of the nationalist elite approved of orientalist Indology and enthusiastically participated in its celebration of classical Indian/Hindu achievements in literature, philosophy, and the arts. Indeed, Indian-Hindu religio-spiritual traditions and culture were the crucial fulcrum on which nationalist ideology leveraged itself: asserting that India's cultural-spiritual superiority enabled the acceptance of undeniable western economic-material superiority and paved the way for the forging of a nationalist agenda in order to fuse the best of both worlds.[26] But on the other hand, colonialist anthropology met with hostility and resentment because it was perceived as deliberately highlighting the 'barbarity' of Indian culture and its 'customs and manners'.[27] What this means from the specific standpoint of modernization studies is that the 'passing of traditional society' was apt to be viewed with mixed feelings, unlike, say, the transformation of the economy or polity, where the past could in principle be left behind without much soul-searching because there was nothing much there worth salvaging. 'Tradition' was an area of considerable ambivalence because, on the one hand, it contained the well-springs of nationalist ideology, social solidarity, and cultural distinctiveness; but, on the other hand, it was also the source of embarrassing 'social evils', 'superstitions', and other signs of backwardness.

Finally, another aspect of disciplinary location, namely the internal composition of Indian social anthropology, was also relevant. In Indian social anthropology the distinction between sociology and anthropology has been refused at least since Srinivas (that is since the mid-1950s or so). This is an unexceptional refusal in so far as the convention of the former studying 'complex' and the latter 'simple' societies could not really be followed in India and is no longer the rule elsewhere either. However, the well-established Indian practice of referring interchangeably to sociology and anthropology hides the fact that the latter is much better developed here than the former. Because the social anthropology of India was heavily oriented towards 'tradition'—that is towards institutions like caste, tribe, kinship and religion, and towards rural rather than urban society—modernization studies here were also biased in this direction. Had urban sociology, economic sociology, social history, or political sociology been better developed, the content of modernization studies may have been more balanced, with the new and emergent getting as much attention as the old and traditional. As it happened, most studies of modernization in India located themselves in the world of tradition and looked out upon modernity from that vantage point, with its attendant strengths and weaknesses. Indian social anthropology failed to cultivate intensively those methods (such as survey research or quantitative techniques) and research areas (such as industry, the media, or the class structure) of sociology proper which fell outside its usual zone of intersection with anthropology.[28] This in turn affected the manner in which the discipline dealt with the question of modernization, particularly since this question privileges generalization from a macro perspective, something which anthropology is neither theoretically inclined towards nor methodologically equipped for.

The Catholicity of the Concept

Finally, at least part of the difficulty that Indian sociology has had with the theme of modernization has to do with the nature of the term itself, and uncertainties as to what was or was not included within its ambit. It is pertinent to recall here that modernization was introduced into social theory as a very broad, catch-all concept that was considered 'useful despite its vagueness because it tends to evoke similar associations in contemporary readers' (Bendix 1967: 292). As Dean Tipps has written in an important critique already twenty-five years old:

The popularity of the notion of modernization must be sought not in its clarity and precision as a vehicle of scholarly communication, but rather in its ability to evoke vague and generalized images which serve to summarize all the various transformations of social life attendant upon the rise of industrialization and the nation-state in the late eighteenth and nineteenth centuries. These images have proved so powerful, indeed, that the existence of some phenomenon usefully termed 'modernization' has gone virtually unchallenged [Tipps 1973: 199].

This may sound somewhat excessive in the Indian context—the momentous and swift transformations taking place here clearly amounted to more than just 'some phenomenon'. But the question of whether 'modernization' was a useful conceptual basket into which all these varied changes could be thrown did bother Indian scholars sensitive to the 'messiness' of the process.[29] The fact that in modernization theory, this process is 'defined in terms of the goals towards which it is moving' (ibid.: 204) is particularly problematic not only because the directionality of change is difficult to gauge in unilinear terms, but also because this telos is intertwined with conflicting ethical–moral values and claims. The sensitive scholar's instinctive distrust of such treacherous terrain is seen in Srinivas's doubts and queries, expressed in the second epigraph to this chapter: Is all social change to be called modernization? Is modernization the same as westernization?[30] Similar instances can be found in the work of most scholars, and the very existence of many different viewpoints shows that these doubts are not easily settled.

STAKES AND PROSPECTS

Looking back at the literature on modernization at the turn of the century, we cannot but be impressed by the central contradiction that frames it—the remarkable longevity of the theme and its conceptual paraphernalia, despite the very early onset of doubts and disillusionment. What needs did it fulfil, what core concerns did it address that allowed it to live so much of its life on borrowed time? What was at stake in the question of modernization? To answer these questions we must return to the beginning, the word.

Etymological History

The English word 'modernization' inherits the semantic legacy of its ancient Latin root word, *modernus* which has been used in two conceptually distinct but commonly conflated senses: as a generic term that characterizes the distinctiveness of any contemporary era; and as an abbreviation for a specific period in the history of western civilization and the values and institutions associated with it.[31]

In pre-nineteenth century usage, 'modern' appears to have been a pejorative term with strong negative connotations, and we are told that 'Shakespeare invariably used the term in this sense' (Black 1966: 5). However, as Raymond Williams (1983: 208–9) points out, 'through the nineteenth century and very markedly in the twentieth century there was a strong movement the other way, until *modern* became virtually equivalent to improved or satisfactory or efficient'.[32] Although 'modern' still retains its comparative temporal sense of something close to or part of the present, it is interesting to note that, in the last decades of the twentieth century, this sense has been yielding ground to words like 'contemporary' or to neologisms prefixed by 'post', and that the word is no longer unequivocally positive in its connotations.

These recent developments in the career of the word point to a complicated and unequal relationship between its two meanings: the generic one has generally been subordinated, whether surreptitiously or openly, to the specific meaning. The consequences of the ascendancy of the sense connoting western European modernity are acutely felt when we shift from the relatively static noun form to the more dynamic and processual verb form. 'Modernization' entered the English lexicon during the eighteenth century (mainly in references to 'buildings and spelling') when the reversal of the pejorative connotations of the noun form had already begun. By the twentieth century the word had become increasingly common and was 'normally used to indicate something unquestionably favourable or desirable' (ibid.: 208–9). This general connotation of a process of positive change or improvement (particularly with reference to machinery or technology) was inflected—especially when speaking at the macro level about institutions or societies—by the suggestion of a more closed-ended teleological movement towards the European Enlightenment model of modernity. It is in this latter sense that the word enters the discipline of sociology—and vice versa.

The Shadow of the West

The social sciences (especially sociology) are themselves products of and responses to 'modernity' in the specific sense of 'modern' that invokes the era inaugurated by the Enlightenment in seventeenth-century western Europe (Hawthorn 1987). Unlike other attempts to distinguish a modern present from its pasts, modernity is not content with establishing a merely relativistic difference but also claims fundamental superiority. Once claimed, such normative privileges pre-position modernity in a profoundly asymmetrical relationship to all other epochs and cultures.[33]

These claims have, of course, been much more than abstract assertions, having had the status of self-evident truths for most of mainstream social science. Whether in terms of a contrast with the world of 'tradition' (another critical keyword of modern times), or in terms of the coherence of its own multifaceted achievements, there is a formidable array of evidence proclaiming the uniqueness of post-Enlightenment Western European modernity. Some of this evidence is eloquently recounted by the Rudolphs as evident in the first epigraph to this chapter, and forms a long list including the transformation of the human relationship to the natural world; the supremacy of universalistic, utilitarian, scientific-technological rationality; the rise of the individual as the normative agent of social action; the subordination of ascriptive, affect-based communities to impersonal, voluntary associations; the emergence of urban, industrial society and the bureaucratization of social institutions; the revolutionizing of modes of governance with the emergence of democracy, the modern nation state, and its institutional apparatus; and the onset of new and intensified forms of temporality. Also relevant, at a somewhat different level, are the supplanting of God and Nature by Man and Reason as foundational categories, and the consequent predilection for meta-narratives of various kinds, most notably that of Progress.

It hardly needs emphasizing that the ideas and institutions of modernity have wielded enormous material and moral power. Like all other social systems, modernity too has been historically and culturally specific; but it is perhaps the only social system in human history that has had the technological capability, the social organization, and the systemic will-to-power to make so comprehensive an attempt to reshape the entire world in its own image. Colonization is only the starkest form taken by this attempt, beginning with pre-modern Europe itself, through the depopulation and re-settlement of the New World, to the direct or indirect colonial subjugation of the rest of the globe. The mental–moral forms of colonization have been even more profound in their effects: whatever be our attitude towards it, modernity has shaped to an extraordinary degree the ideological frameworks we inhabit, the intellectual tools we use, and the values that we hold dear.

This overgeneral sketch must be immediately qualified and complicated in a number of (sometimes mutually contradictory) ways. Despite the remarkably convergent forces and processes it has unleashed across the globe, modernity has hardly been a single unified entity. Indeed, it is only at the highest level of abstraction that one can speak of something simply called 'modernity'. Not only have disparate, even incompatible, perspectives been produced within its ambit, but modernity itself has spawned oppositional philosophies of various kinds (such as the romanticism of a Rousseau or the nihilism of a Nietzsche). And though it is true that modernity's attempts to colonize the world have been largely successful, this has usually meant not the simple erasure of other cultures or social systems but rather their subjection to sustained pressure. At the same time, modernity has legitimized itself well enough to have transcended to a significant degree its early image of an alien imposition and has acquired, in a wide variety of social contexts, the status of a freely chosen material and moral goal.

It is only against this 'deep background' that one can appreciate the full significance of the idea of modernity outside the West, especially after the birth of modernization theory in the 1950s context of decolonization (as described in earlier pages).

Non-western Predicaments

The stakes in modernization are raised enormously in non-western countries where it is seen as a sort of secular 'theory of salvation' (a phrase attributed to Ashis Nandy in Banuri 1990: 95). The defining condition of non-western engagements with the idea of modernity is, of course, the fact that it is an idea which 'always–already' bears the signs of a prior western presence. Given that even the most amicable routes to decolonization involved some sort of adversarial relationship with the West, this immediately sets up a tension, a predicament. Modernity is the object of intense desire, at the very least because it promises resources with which the marks of colonial subjugation may be erased and equality claimed with the erstwhile masters. It is also the source of extreme anxiety because it seems to threaten any distinctive (non-western) identity—which alone would be proof of true equality rather than mere mimicry. Matters are made worse by two further factors: first, the sense of urgency associated with modernization and change both as a response to late-comer status and because of the release of nationalist energies and aspirations after Independence;[34] second, the realization that most of the intellectual resources with which questions of this sort may be tackled are themselves inseparable from western modernity.

It is this combination of circumstances that produces the long interregnum of scholarly ambivalence and anxiety around the question of modernization. But the transformations initiated by the process of modernization outflank the scholarly mode of posing the question: social history overtakes social philosophy.

As already noted in the preceding pages, modernization has been an omnibus concept, a sort of summary description of epochal dimensions based on an underlying dichotomy between tradition and modernity. If there ever was a time when such an abstract, generalized dichotomy was conceptually useful, it is surely gone now.[35] All the common uses to which it was put— to indicate a division of global society into different spheres, to refer to a similar division within a given society, or to distinguish between past and present—are no longer viable because, today, there are as many similarities as differences across the divide.

'Most societies today possess the means for the local production of modernity', as Appadurai and Breckenridge point out, 'thus making even the paradigmatic modernity of the United States and western Europe (itself not an unproblematic assumption) no more pristine'

(Appadurai and Breckenridge 1996: 1). To continue to refer to non-western or Third World societies as simply 'traditional' is therefore seriously misleading. Similarly, if one were to believe, with Robert Redfield, that '[t]he word "tradition" connotes the act of handing down and what is handed down from one generation to another' and that it therefore 'means both process and product' (quoted in Singer 1975: x), then it is clear that no sharp division can be made between tradition and modernity in the long term. On the one hand, what is modern for one generation will perforce become part of tradition for the next; on the other hand, the product that is passed on cannot possibly exclude the modern. Analytically, it seems futile to think of 'tradition' and 'modernity' as though they were the names of distinct pre-existing objects or fields of some kind; it is more fruitful to think of them as value-laden labels which people wish to attach to particular portions of what they inherit or bequeath. Descriptively, no purpose is served by this contrast after the thorough diffusion and domestication of modernity across every conceivable area of tradition.

However, it would seem that this very ubiquity of modernity has created a new use for 'tradition'—not as a descriptive term, but rather as a 'space-clearing' or 'distinction-creating gesture' (Dhareshwar 1995b: PE108). Tradition of this sort—that is invoked as a sort of claim to difference—is itself a product of modernity, and forms part of the reservoir of resources with which modern adversaries fight each other. Thus, in a very general sense, everything and everyone is modern today, the Taliban as much as Microsoft, velcro and *vibhuti* as much as dowry and debentures. This does not mean, of course, that everyone and everything is the same—just that the traditional–modern axis is unable to tell us anything useful about the very important differences that distinguish contexts, institutions, processes, or relationships.

The non-viability of the high level of abstraction at which terms like tradition, modernity, and modernization have been pitched is underlined by recent attempts to re-examine the self-evident unitary status of most objects to which these terms used to be applied. The nation state is an obvious example: 'fragmentary' perspectives may have their own problems, but it cannot be denied that the taken-for-granted status of entities like 'India' or 'the nation' has suffered serious damage (Pandey 1991; Chatterjee 1994). This breakdown of its objects of reference also serves to evict the concept of modernization from its high perch.

Current Trends

If 'modernization' has lost its analytical–heuristic value as a summary–description of epochal sweep, this is as much due to the internal collapse of the tradition–modernity dichotomy as to the external attacks by dependency theory and world systems theory. But there are as yet no obvious successors, though terms like 'post-colonial', 'post-modern', and lately 'globalization' have been hovering in the wings. However, the most noticeable change in Indian social theory today is the marked increase in confidence *vis-à-vis* the West. (In this, theory seems to have followed social life rather than the other way around, but that is another story.) While such self-assurance was not exactly unknown before, it is probably more widespread and sophisticated, and certainly more ambitious now.[36] Contemporary responses to the demise of the modernization paradigm can take four broad routes.

Downsizing and Avoidance

The most common response has been to avoid the term—modernization is no longer invoked in the grand theory mode. If it is used at all, the scope of the term has been scaled down, and it seems to be returning to the specific technical sense in which it first entered the English language (for example, for buildings, machinery, and spelling). Since it is only at very high levels of abstraction and generalization that the term has proved extravagant, it may still be serviceable in restricted contexts with clear referents, as for example in the modernization of libraries or irrigation systems. However, this does amount to banishing the term from social theory.

Reclaiming the Present

The previous response simply rejects one of the main functions of modernization as a summary–description—a name—for an epoch in which societies previously described as 'traditional' begin to experience rapid change. What gets obscured, however, is that this epoch is a contemporary one, that it constitutes the present of the societies undergoing modernization: the teleological orientation is so strong that descriptions of the journey are overwritten by descriptions of the destination. If modernization studies in general tend to 'evacuate' the present, those within social anthropology are doubly affected because of the discipline's old habit of constructing an 'ethnographic present' in which other cultures are 'distanced in special, almost always past and passing, times' (Clifford 1986: 9). It is not surprising, therefore, that some recent initiatives in this discipline (and elsewhere in the human sciences) have concentrated precisely on the recovery and reconceptualization of contemporaneity. Thus, for example, Veena Das undertakes an anthropology of 'critical events' explicitly in order 'to reflect on the nature of contemporaneity and its implications for the writing of ethnography' (Das 1995: 4); Geeta Kapur confronts the problem of identifying the 'founding equation between history and subject' that might help define the contemporary moment in cultural practice (Kapur 1991: 2805); Madhav Prasad seeks to go 'back to the present' to signal not 'the nation's arrival at some pre-determined telos, but *arrival as such*, arrival in the present as the place from which to find our way forward' (Prasad 1998b: 123, emphasis original); and Vivek Dhareshwar asks what it means to be modern if 'our time' is one where the conditions of intelligibility of 'the key words of our cultural and political self-understanding' no longer hold (Dhareshwar 1995a: 318; 1995b). More generally, these and other such attempts are part of an effort to pay rigorous attention to the historicity of the present without allowing this historicity to be hijacked by the teleology of notions like modernization. As D.P. Mukerji reminds us, it is more important to understand 'the thing changing' rather than 'change *per sé*' (1988: 15).

Exploring Emergent Locations

As outlined in the previous section, Indian social anthropology has until recently been concerned mainly with tradition and how it copes with modernity. This has meant that modernity has been viewed through the frameworks of tradition and has been looked for in its 'traditional' sites, so to speak. These, of course, are not the only or necessarily the most important ones where it is to be found—indeed it is one of the hallmarks of the contemporary era that eruptions (or claims) of modernity may take place in the most unexpected locations. For example, the last epigraph to this chapter, the slogan painted on a bus—'They should realize that we too are modern'—is also the punch line of a mid-1980s television advertisement for sanitary napkins. It is spoken by a mother as she hands a package of napkins to her daughter (who is returning to her in-laws), the connotation being that the napkins will prove to the 'boy's side' that the girl comes from a 'modern' family. That a television advertisement would self-reflexively foreground menstruation in this manner can hardly be anticipated by conventional notions of the 'inner/outer' and 'private/public' domains. Examples of scholarly attempts to systematically explore such unconventional sites where the peculiarities of Indian modernity find expression include recent studies on social aspects of the film form in India (such as Rajadhyaksha 1993 and Prasad 1998a), and new work on the domain of sexuality and its linkages to such varied institutions as the state, the media, the law, and academic disciplines such as demography or anthropology (for example, Uberoi 1996; and John and Nair 1998).

Comparisons across Third World Contexts

For both obvious and less obvious reasons, the lateral contacts among sociologists of non-western countries have been few and largely under the auspices of western institutions. Unfortunately, what Srinivas and Panini said a quarter of a century ago still remains true, including especially their concluding observation:

> Paradoxical as it may seem, the very need to understand Indian society requires from Indian sociologists a commitment to a comparative approach in which the problems, processes and institutions of their society are systematically compared with those of neighbouring countries in the first instance, and later with other developing countries. So far such a comparative approach has been conspicuous by its absence [Srinivas and Panini (1973) 1986].

Though some Indian sociologists have indeed worked on other Third World countries (for example Ramakrishna Mukherjee on Uganda; Satish Saberwal on Kenya; and J.P.S. Uberoi on Afghanistan), the impact on the discipline at large has been negligible. Third World countries have so far only provided the non-western empirical grist for western theoretical mills, as the Brazilian sociologist Mariza Peirano points out: 'The moment we leave behind the frontiers of the country, what here was a theoretical discussion, almost immediately becomes merely regional ethnography' (Peirano 1991: 326). It is only through this kind of cross-cultural comparative work in Third World contexts that we can move beyond tiresome lamentations of western intellectual hegemony to a situation where the specificities of Indian, Turkish, Indonesian, or Brazilian society can finally refuse to be merely 'local colour' and aspire to be part of 'global theory'.[37]

Theory in this sense has long evaded us. Perhaps the story of our long struggle with the theme of modernization will manage to interrupt this evasion.

ACKNOWLEDGEMENTS

Earlier versions of this chapter have been presented in seminars at the Centre for the Study of Culture and Society, Bangalore, and the Department of Sociology, Delhi School of Economics, Delhi University. I am grateful to the participants at both venues, and to Veena Das, Vandana Madan and especially T.N. Madan for helpful comments and suggestions.

ENDNOTES

1. For example, neither faith in modernity nor scepticism towards it are exclusive to western and Indian social science respectively; and 'the West'—howsoever defined—is hardly absent from contemporary Indian social life.
2. These two factors also contributed to the emergence of the multilateral institutional complex built around the United Nations, which also undertook research on modernization and allied issues in the Third World.

3. Ratna Datta (later Ratna Naidu) has attempted to tackle the special vulnerability of sociological categories to the problem of ethnocentrism in her critique of Parsonian modernization theory; her book may well be the only one of its kind by an Indian sociologist (Datta 1971). The heavy involvement of American rural sociologists in modernization studies was not without its ironies; as William Friedland notes, 'The "demand" for rural sociologists to "explain" events in the Third World,' created a paradoxical situation where 'U.S. agricultural social scientists know more about land tenure arrangements and agricultural social relations in Malaysia, Bolivia and the Philippines than they do in Wisconsin, California and Mississippi' (Friedland 1989: 11).

4. Personal communication from Redfield to Singer, May 1956, quoted in Singer (1972: 8).

5. Apart from Cohn's essay cited above, overviews of early work on Indian society and culture are to be found in Kopf 1969; Mandelbaum 1970; Madan 1995 (Ch. 5: 'Images of India in American Anthropology'); Saberwal 1986; and Srinivas and Panini 1986.

6. For example, Louis Dumont felt that the strong desire for change and the state-sponsored drive towards it might force researchers to be less vigilant regarding the *continuities* (or lack of change) in society (Dumont 1964: 10). Similar sentiments were echoed by Ramakrishna Mukherjee in his complaint that the 'modernizers' among Indian sociologists neglected the 'null hypothesis' of 'no change' (Mukherjee 1979: 52). An interesting early discussion of the links among, and the implications of, the community and village studies research; the state-sponsored tendency towards social engineering; and the heavy involvement of western, particularly American, researchers and institutions is to be found in Saran (1958: 1026–32).

7. As Dean Tipps has pointed out, anthropologists—the very people who knew the most about the Third World societies that modernization theory was setting out to study—were typically the least enthusiastic about it (Tipps 1973: 207, see also note 4). This could also be due to the fundamental orientation of classical anthropology towards pre-modern societies, such that modernization seems antithetical to the very raison d'etre of the discipline.

8. Though it is widely recognized that the nation-state is the implicit unit of analysis for modernization theory [for example Appadurai (1997: 9) thinks it has 'ethical' and not just methodological salience], the asymmetrical changes produced by reversing perspective—that is looking at modernization from a particular national context—need more emphasis.

9. George Rosen speaks of the Indian government alternating between 'great sensitivity' and 'undue respect' for foreign scholars and provides useful details (Rosen 1985: 52–4). For example: Douglas Ensminger (the American rural sociologist and consultant, Ford Foundation in India during the 1950s and 1960s, and closely associated with the Community Development Programme) had the kind of direct access to Prime Minister Nehru and the Planning Commission that would have been envied by Indian sociologists, though some economists enjoyed similar status. A.K. Saran points out that after Independence, local scholars may, on the one hand, be enabled to ask uncomfortable questions regarding the desirability of foreign collaboration; but, on the other hand, they may also become much more hospitable to foreign influences, once freed of the moral burden of subject status (Saran 1958: 1028–9, 1031–2).

10. Srinivas and Panini have been very critical of this trend.

> The kind of research that appealed to the administrator was one where he determined the problems to be studied and the scientist was only asked to find clear answers to them in an absurdly short period of time. Social scientists unable to adjust themselves to their newly discovered importance competed with each other for projects. The result was a mass of survey research quickly carried out under the threat of deadlines. It is flattering to think that it answered the administrator's questions assuming, of course, that they had the time, and the inclination to read it [Srinivas and Panini 1986: 38].

On the other hand, sociologists like S.C. Dube supported the trend and associated themselves with it.

11. As Thomas Trautmann (1997, esp. pp. 1–27) has argued, British Indology (and more generally ethnology) between roughly 1780 and 1850 was guided by the relational metaphor of the tree,

rather than the hierarchical metaphor of the staircase—the Indian/Hindu and western European civilizations were thought of as branches of the same larger tree, and Indians (upper caste Hindu north Indians, at any rate) as Aryan kinsmen of the European peoples. And in recording the enthusiasm of the early orientalists for Indian (especially Hindu) traditions, knowledge, and culture in general, David Kopf (1969) has pointed out that they (and their Indian associates) proposed a model of modernization that sharply opposed simple westernization, but wished instead for a confluence of the best in both worlds.

12. Personal conversation, 18 February 1999; however, I must take responsibility for this rendering.

13. See Ramachandra Guha's recent biography of Verrier Elwin (Guha 1999) for a fresh account of this controversy, albeit one strongly sympathetic to its protagonist.

14. Beyond this crude preliminary division there is, of course, considerable scope for distinctions within zones and for overlaps and combinations across zones. For example, A.K. Saran classifies the positions taken by scholars vis-à-vis tradition and modernity: 'those who totally reject Western Civilization and want a return to the traditional principles'; those who 'want a synthesis of the two', further subdivided according to whether they wish this synthesis to be oriented towards modernity or tradition; a final criterion is the basis of the synthesis, leading to a split between those who interpret/justify 'in terms of modern rationalistic-positivistic ideas', and those who adopt a 'value-neutral scientific attitude' (Saran 1958: 1013–14). Milton Singer uses the prognosis of scholars for producing a schema essentially the same as that given here. The differentiation is among scholars who believe: a) that tradition will block modernization; or b) that modernity will eliminate tradition; or c) there will be some form of coexistence (Singer 1972: 245). Compare also Madan's slightly different classification of modernization theories as belonging to either the 'big bang' or the 'steady state' school of thought (Madan 1995: 21).

15. Though it was originally published in 1966, the 1971 University of California Press (fifth printing) edition is used here.

16. 'The subject of social change in modern India is so vast and complex, and an adequate understanding of it will require the collaboration, for many years, of a number of scholars in such diverse fields as economic, social and cultural history, law, politics, education, religion, demography and sociology. It will have to take account of regional, linguistic and other differences' (Srinivas 1971a: 1).

17. The list of works dealing with Sanskritization would be too long to quote here; the best-known overview of early work is that of Yogendra Singh (1973: 5–16; 22–4; 52–9; 194–201) and a recent reassessment has been made by Simon Charsley (1998).

18. In Singer's reading, *Asian Drama* asserts that '"traditional" societies such as India *would not modernize until they had eliminated their traditional institutions, beliefs and values*' (Singer 1972: 245, emphasis added).

19. The sampling scheme included rural cultivators (expected to be the least modern); urban non-factory workers; and new and experienced factory workers (expected to be the most modern). The Indian field director was Dr Amar Kumar Singh of the Department of Psychology, Ranchi University; interviews were conducted between 1964 and 1966 in and around Ranchi (in south Bihar), with both tribal and non-tribal respondents, by trained university students.

20. Modernization theory was particularly shunned by Marxists for its explicitly anti-Marxist origins [in the 'non-communist manifesto' of W.W. Rostow (1960) among others] and its US-sponsored Cold War agendas. While these suspicions were largely justified (see Gendzier 1985), the response remained on macro-theoretical and largely economic ground (through the development of rival perspectives like dependency theory and world systems theory, for example) and did not include independent investigations into the concrete content of social change in post-Independence India. Refer to Lele (1994) for a characterization of modernization studies as a form of orientalism.

21. In a brief later article Srinivas returns to this theme while discussing 'the oft-heard comment that Indians do not have a sense of contradiction, or that it does not have the same emotional and

other implications for them as it has for Westerners' (Srinivas 1971b: 155; page references in this note are to this work). After giving further examples of the Indian talent for tolerating the contradiction between modern and traditional worldviews (including Nehru—publicly contemptuous of astrology, yet pressing his daughter to get a proper horoscope made for his new-born grandson, pp. 155–6), Srinivas distinguishes sources of contradiction found in all cultures (such as role conflict) from those likely to be peculiar to developing societies (such as the compulsion to appear modernized and the very rapid pace of change). He wonders if 'the urge to consistency may become stronger' with further social change, thus accentuating the feeling of contradiction, which in turn 'may be accompanied by increased mental illness' (p. 158).

22. An interesting example is provided by K.N. Raj, a leading Indian economist closely involved with development planning, who recalls that Gulzarilal Nanda, the minister in charge of planning, twice postponed the signing of the First Five Year Plan, insisting on a numerologically auspicious day (Raj 1997: 108).

23. It should be emphasized that what is being marked is a difference in the literatures on modernization at a particular time. No claims are being made about the nature of the social experience of modernization in Turkey, India, or anywhere else; nor is it implied that this difference in the literatures on modernization was a permanent one.

24. A similar situation may conceivably have existed in the South and Central American nations, which were formally independent long before the decolonization of Asia and Africa. A different but well-known instance is that of the Carribbean colonies which, between the 1920s and the 1960s, had already produced a glittering galaxy of writers and intellectuals, including Aimé Césaire, Frantz Fanon, Edouard Glissant, Walter Rodney, Eric Williams, C.L.R. James, and W. Arthur Lewis. But the presence of a sizeable 'westernized' local academic establishment (even if colonial in origin and design) is in all probability peculiar to India. My ignorance of other Third World histories prevents a more informed statement.

25. The last chapter of *Social Change in Modern India,* 'Some thoughts on the study of one's own society', discusses this very subject: 'One of the things that strikes me as I look back on the reception accorded my work outside my country is the repeated reference to my being an Indian sociologist engaged in the study of my own society' (Srinivas 1971a: 147). Srinivas goes on to note that while opinion was divided on whether this was an asset or a liability, his Indianness was invariably remarked upon. For a recent reformulation of his views on this subject, refer to (Srinivas 1996).

26. This in essence is the model of nationalism attributed to Bankim Chattopadhyaya in Partha Chatterjee's (1986) well-known work. Variations on this basic theme can be found throughout the history of Indian nationalism even to this day.

27. In the course of explaining why 'anthropology, unlike economics, political science or history, was unpopular with educated natives in colonial countries', Srinivas recalls Katherine Mayo's (1927) *Mother India* and the notoriety it brought to the discipline, and remembers

   being chased out, in August 1943, of a middle class club in Vijaywada (in Andhra Pradesh) by a fat walking-stick-wielding lawyer who thought I was planning to do a Katherine Mayo on the august culture of the Telugus. I was asking questions about caste, kinship, festivals, fasts and fairs when the angry lawyer lunged at me and said, 'get out, we have no customs' [Srinivas 1992: 133].

28. It is interesting to note that Srinivas began his career in India in the 1950s with the opposite view— that is by advocating the cause of participant observation as a much-neglected method contrary to the popularity of survey research (Srinivas 1994: 14–18). At the end of the century, the shoe would certainly seem to be on the other foot; regardless of the numbers involved, there is a clear mismatch in terms of influence. It would not be easy to cite even *five* survey-based or quantitatively oriented studies that have had a major impact on the misnamed discipline of Indian 'sociology' during the last fifty years.

29. André Béteille has remarked of Srinivas that his strengths lay 'in his sensitive imagination and his

unerring instinct for the ambiguities in a social situation, or what he called its "messiness"' (Béteille 1991: 5).

30. Srinivas himself, as is well known, prefers westernization to modernization. But the reason he provides is curious: namely that modernization implies a value judgement regarding ultimate goals, which social scientists are unable to endorse or reject, whereas westernization is a more neutral term (Srinivas 1971a: 50–2).

31. The generic meaning of 'modern' is considerably older than the specific meaning, and has been traced back to sixth-century Latin usage by the historian (and modernization theorist) Cyril Black, where it was 'a term denoting the quality of a contemporary era' (Black 1966: 5). Raymond Williams also notes that the earliest English meanings of the word 'were nearer our *contemporary,* in the sense of something existing now, just now' (Williams 1983: 208–9, original emphasis).

32. Original emphasis, abbreviations expanded; see also Williams 1989: 31–2.

33. Arjun Appadurai has written that modernity

both declares and desires universal applicability for itself. What is new about modernity (or about the idea that its newness is a new kind of newness) follows from this duality. Whatever else the project of the Enlightenment may have created, it aspired to create persons who would, after the fact, have wished to have become modern [Appadurai 1997: 1].

34. This eagerness to bear witness to change is clearly reflected in Indian sociology at the time, including especially the two classics, M.N. Srinivas's *Religion and Society among the Coorgs of South India* (1952) and S.C. Dube's *Indian Village* (1955).

35. It has been argued for at least the last thirty years that the tradition–modernity dichotomy does not work—for example, refer Gusfield (1967).

36. An interesting illustration is provided by the motif of 'provinciality'. Edward Shils, having been constrained to record the 'sad fact' that 'India is not an intellectually independent country' (Shils 1961: 68), went on to declare that the Indian intellectual's 'fate destines him to provinciality, until his own modern culture becomes creative' (ibid.: 87). But, at around the same time, A.K. Saran's 1962 review of *Contributions to Indian Sociology* had criticized Louis Dumont for having taken 'in the name of science, modernity or objectivity, a firmly provincial standpoint for the study of traditional or tradition-haunted societies' (Saran 1962: 68). However, the real difference is visible in the 1990s: Rabindra Ray is so much 'at home' in the global discipline that he feels compelled to ask why a sociology of India is needed at all (Ray 1990); Dipesh Chakrabarty announces a project for 'provincializing Europe' and returning to it its categories of political modernity 'in the same way as suspect coins return to their owner in an Indian bazaar' (Chakrabarty 1992; 22); and by 1998 Vivek Dhareshwar is unveiling the outline of an all-encompassing meta-theory able to house 'western theories of ourselves', 'our existing theories of ourselves', and 'our meta-theory of western theories' under the same roof (Dhareshwar 1998: 212). These examples are cited merely to illustrate the 'attitude' that Indian scholarship has developed by the 1990s—no claims are being made on behalf of (or against) any of these projects/judgements.

37. Such a comparative perspective must also, as Mariza Peirano points out, prevent our interest in other Third World countries from being restricted to the desire to counter western theories or models, such that, for example, Brazil exists for Indian sociology only in so far as it is the source of dependency theory (Peirano 1991).

REFERENCES

Abercrombie, Nicholas, Stephen Hill, and Bryan S. Turner. 1988. *The Penguin Dictionary of Sociology.* 2nd ed. Harmondsworth, England: Penguin.

Appadurai, Arjun. 1997. *Modernity at Large: Cultural Dimensions of Globalization.* Delhi: Oxford University Press.

Appadurai, Arjun and Carol Breckenridge. 1996. 'Public Modernity in India'. In C. Breckenridge, ed., *Consuming Modernity: Public Culture in Contemporary India*, 1–20. Delhi: Oxford University Press.

Banuri, Tariq. 1990. 'Development and the Politics of Knowledge: A Critical Interpretation of the Social Role of Modernization'; and 'Modernization and Its Discontents: A Cultural Perspective on Theories of Development'. In Stephen Marglin and Frederique Apfel, eds, *Dominating Knowledge: Development, Culture and Resistance*, 29–101. Oxford: Clarendon Press.

Bardhan, Pranab. 1984. *The Political Economy of Development*. Delhi: Oxford University Press.

Bendix, Reinhard. 1967: 'Tradition and Modernity Reconsidered', *Comparative Studies in Society and History*. 9(April): 292–346.

Béteille, André. 1991. *Society and Politics in India: Essays in a Comparative Perspective*. Delhi: Oxford University Press.

Black, Cyril E. 1966. *The Dynamics of Modernization: A Study in Comparative History*. New York: Harper and Row.

Burghart, Richard. 1990. 'Ethnographers and Their Local Counterparts in India'. In R. Fardon, ed., *Localizing Strategies: Regional Traditions of Ethnographic Writings*, 260–78. Edinburgh: Scottish Academic Press.

Cartier-Bresson, Henri. 1987. *Henri Cartier-Bresson: India*. Trans. Paula Clifford. Ahmedabad: Mapin.

Chakrabarty, Dipesh. 1992: 'Postcoloniality and the Artifice of History: Who Speaks for Indian Pasts?'. *Representations*. 37(Winter):1–26.

Charsley, Simon. 1998: 'Sanskritization: The Career of an Anthropological Theory'. *Contributions to Indian Sociology*. 32(2):527–49.

Chatterjee, Partha. 1986. *Nationalism and the Third World: A Derivative Discourse?* London: Zed Books.

———. 1994. *The Nation and Its Fragments: Colonial and Postcolonial Histories*. Delhi: Oxford University Press.

Clifford, James. 1986. 'Introduction: Partial Truths'. In J. Clifford and G.E. Marcus, eds, *Writing Culture: The Poetics and Politics of Ethnography*, 1–26. Berkeley: University of California Press.

Cohn, Bernard. 1987. *An Anthropologist among the Historians and Other Essays*. Delhi: Oxford University Press.

Das, Veena. 1995. *Critical Events: An Anthropological Perspective on Contemporary India*. Delhi: Oxford University Press.

Datta, Ratna. 1971. *Values in Models of Modernization*. Delhi: Vikas Publications.

Desai, A.R. ed. 1971. *Essays on Modernization of Underdeveloped Societies*. 2 vols. Bombay: Thacker & Co.

Deshpande, Satish. 1994. 'The Crisis in Sociology: A Tired Discipline?'. *Economic and Political Weekly*. 29(10):575–6.

Dhareshwar, Vivek. 1995a. '"Our Time". History, Sovereignty and Politics'. *Economic and Political Weekly*. 30(6):317–24.

———. 1995b. 'Postcolonial in the Postmodern; or the Political after Modernity'. *Economic and Political Weekly* (Review of Political Economy). 30(30):PE 104–PE 112.

———. 1998. 'Valorizing the Present: Orientalism, Postcoloniality and the Human Sciences'. *Cultural Dynamics*. 10(2):211–31.

Dube, S.C. 1955. *Indian Village*. London: Routledge and Kegan Paul.

———. 1958. *India's Changing Villages: Human Factors in Community Development*. London: Routledge and Kegan Paul.

———. 1988. *Modernization and Development: The Search for Alternative Paradigms*. New Delhi: Vistaar Publications & Tokyo: The United Nations University.

Dumont, Louis. 1964. 'Introductory Note: Change, Interaction and Comparison'. *Contributions to Indian Sociology* (o.s.). 7(March):7–17.

Fabian, Johannes. 1983. *Time and the Other: How Anthropology Makes Its Object*. New York: Columbia University Press.

Friedland, William H. 1989. 'Considerations on the New Political Economy of Advanced Capitalist Agriculture'. Mss., Santacruz, University of California.

Gendzier, Irene. 1985. *Managing Political Change: Social Scientists and the Third World*. Boulder, Colorado: Westview Press.

Guha, Ramachandra. 1999. *Savaging the Civilized: Verrier Elwin, His Tribals and India*. Delhi: Oxford University Press.

Guha, Ranajit, ed. 1982. *Subaltern Studies I: Writings on South Asian History and Society*. Delhi: Oxford University Press.

Gusfield, Joseph. 1967: 'Tradition and Modernity: Misplaced Polarities in the Study of Social Change'. *American Journal of Sociology*. 72(4):351–62.

Hawthorn, Geoffrey. 1987. *Enlightenment and Despair: A History of Social Theory*. 2nd ed. Cambridge (UK): Cambridge University Press.

Inkeles, Alex. 1971. 'Fieldwork Problems in Comparative Research on Modernization'. In A.R. Desai, ed., *Essays on Modernization of Underdeveloped Societies,* vol. 2, 20–76. Bombay: Thacker & Co

Inkeles, Alex and David H. Smith. 1974. *Becoming Modern: Individual Change in Six Developing Countries*. London: Heinemann.

John, Mary and Janaki Nair, eds. 1998. *A Question of Silence? The Sexual Economies of Modern India*. New Delhi: Kali for Women.

Kapur, Geeta. 1991. 'Place of the Modern in Indian Cultural Practice'. *Economic and Political Weekly*. 26(49):2803–6.

Kaviraj, Sudipta. 1988. 'A Critique of the Passive Revolution'. *Economic and Political Weekly*. (Special Number) 23(27):2429–43.

Kopf, David. 1969. *British Orientalism and the Bengal Renaissance: The Dynamics of Indian Modernization, 1773–1835*. Berkeley: University of California Press.

Kothari, Rajni. 1970. *Politics in India*. Delhi: Orient Longman.

Lele, Jayant. 1994. 'Orientalism and the Social Sciences'. In C.A. Breckenridge and Peter van der Veer, eds, *Orientalism and the Postcolonial Predicament*, 45–75. Delhi: Oxford University Press.

Lerner, Daniel. 1958. *The Passing of Traditional Society: Modernizing the Middle East*. Glencoe (Illinois): Free Press.

Madan, T.N. 1969: 'Caste and Development'. (Review of Myrdal's *Asian Drama*). *Economic and Political Weekly*. 4(5):285–90.

_____. 1995. *Pathways: Approaches to the Study of Society in India*. Delhi: Oxford University Press.

Mandelbaum, David. 1970. *Society in India*. 2 vols. Berkeley: University of California Press.

Marriott, McKim, ed. 1955. *Village India: Studies in the Little Community*. Chicago: University of Chicago Press.

Mayo, Katherine. 1927. *Mother India*. London: Jonathan Cape.

McClelland, David C. and David G. Winter, eds. 1969. *Motivating Economic Achievement*. New York: Free Press.

Mukerji, D.P. [1955] 1988. 'Indian Tradition and Social Change'. (Presidential address to the first meeting of the Indian Sociological Society). In T.K. Oommen and Partha Mukherji, eds, *Indian Sociology: Reflections and Introspections*, 15. Bombay: Popular Prakashan.

Mukherjee, Ramakrishna. 1979. *Sociology of Indian Sociology*. Bombay: Allied Publishers.

Myrdal, Gunnar. 1968. *Asian Drama: An Enquiry into the Poverty of Nations*. 3 vols. London: Allen Lane/Penguin Press.

_____. 1970. *An Approach to the Asian Drama: Methodological and Theoretical Issues*. New York: Vintage Books.

Pandey, Gyanendra. 1991: 'In Defence of the Fragment: Writing about Hindu–Muslim Riots in India Today'. *Economic and Political Weekly*. (Annual Number) 26(11–12):559–72.

Patnaik, Utsa, ed. 1990. *Agrarian Relations and Accumulation: The 'Mode of Production' Debate in India*. Bombay: Sameeksha Trust and Oxford University Press.

Peirano, Mariza G.S. 1991. 'For a Sociology of India: Some Comments From Brazil'. *Contributions to Indian Sociology* (n.s.). 25(2):321–7.

Prasad, Madhav. 1998a. *The Ideology of Hindi Cinema: A Historical Construction*. Delhi: Oxford University Press.

———. 1998b. 'Back to the Present'. *Cultural Dynamics*. 10(2):123–31.

Raj, K.N. 1997. 'Planning: Getting the Economy on Track'. In *India*. (Special supplement issued by *The Hindu* on the 50th anniversary of Independence). August. 107–9.

Rajadhyaksha, Ashish. 1993. 'The Phalke Era: Conflict of Traditional Form and Modern Technology'. In Tejaswini Niranjana, P. Sudhir, and Vivek Dhareshwar, eds, *Interrogating Modernity: Culture and Colonialism in India*, 42–82. Calcutta: Seagull Books.

Ray, Rabindra. 1990. 'And Why an Indian Sociology?'. *Contributions to Indian Sociology* (n.s.). 24(2):265–75.

Rosen, George. 1985. *Western Economists and Eastern Societies: Agents of Change in South Asia, 1950–1970*. Delhi: Oxford University Press.

Rostow, Walt W. 1960. *The Stages of Economic Growth: A Non-Communist Manifesto*. Cambridge (UK): Cambridge University Press.

Rudolph, Lloyd I. and Susanne Hoeber Rudolph. 1967. *The Modernity of Tradition: Political Development in India*. Chicago: University of Chicago Press.

Saberwal, Satish. [1982] 1986. 'Uncertain Transplants: Anthropology and Sociology in India'. Reprinted in T.K. Oommen and Partha Mukherji, eds, *Indian Sociology: Reflections and Introspections*, 214–32. Bombay: Popular Prakashan.

Saran, A.K. 1958. 'India'. In J.S. Roucek, ed., *Contemporary Sociology*, 1013–34. New York: Philosophical Library.

———. 1962. 'Review of *Contributions to Indian Sociology* no. IV'. *Eastern Anthropologist*. 15(1 Jan–Apr):53–68.

Sarkar, Benoy Kumar. 1985. *The Positive Background of Hindu Sociology*. Reprint. Delhi: Motilal Banarasidas.

Seal, Brajendranath. 1985. *The Positive Sciences of the Ancient Hindus*. Reprint. Delhi: Motilal Banarasidas.

Shah, Mihir. 1985. 'The Kaniatchi Form of Labour'. *Economic and Political Weekly*. 20(30):PE 65–PE 78.

Shils, Edward. 1961. 'The Intellectual between Tradition and Modernity: The Indian Situation'. *Comparative Studies in Society and History*. Supplement 1:1–120.

Singer, Milton. 1972. *When a Great Tradition Modernizes: An Anthropological Approach to Indian Civilization*. New York: Praeger.

———. ed. 1975. *Traditional India: Structure and Change*. Jaipur: Rawat.

Singh, Yogendra. 1973. *Modernization of Indian Tradition*. Faridabad, Haryana: Thomson Press.

Srinivas, M.N. 1952. *Religion and Society among the Coorgs of South India*. Oxford: Clarendon Press.

———. [1966] 1971a. *Social Change in Modern India*. Berkeley: University of California Press.

———. 1971b. 'Modernization: A Few Queries'. In A. Desai, ed., *Essays on Modernization of Underdeveloped Societies*, vol. 1 Bombay: Thacker & Co.

———. 1992. *On Living in a Revolution and Other Essays*. Delhi: Oxford University Press.

———. 1994. *The Dominant Caste and Other Essays*. (Revised and enlarged Oxford India Paperback edn). Delhi: Oxford University Press.

———. 1996. 'Indian Anthropologists and the Study of Indian Society'. *Economic and Political Weekly*. 31(11):656–7.

Srinivas, M.N. and M.N. Panini. [1973] 1986. 'The Development of Sociology and Social Anthropology in India'. Reprinted in T.K. Oommen and Partha Mukherji, eds, *Indian Sociology: Reflections and Introspections*, 16–55. Bombay: Popular Prakashan.

Srivatsan, R. 1993. 'Cartier-Bresson and the Birth of Modern India'. *Journal of Arts and Ideas*. 25–6 (December):37–54.

Thorner, Alice. 1982. 'Semi-Feudalism or Capitalism? Contemporary Debate on Classes and Modes of Production in India'. *Economic and Political Weekly*. 17(49):1961–78; (50): 1993–9; and (51): 2061–6.

Thorner, Daniel. 1980. *The Shaping of Modern India*. New Delhi: Sameeksha Trust and Allied Publishers.

Tipps, Dean C. 1973. 'Modernization Theory and the Comparative Study of Societies: A Critical Perspective'. *Comparative Studies in Society and History*. 15(March):199–226.

Trautmann, Thomas R. 1997. *Aryans and British India*. Berkeley: University of California Press.

Uberoi, Patricia, ed. 1996. *Social Reform, Sexuality and the State*. New Delhi: Sage Publications.

Weiner, Myron, ed. 1966. *Modernization: The Dynamics of Growth*. New York: Basic Books.

Williams, Raymond. 1983. *Keywords: A Vocabulary of Culture and Society*. Revised ed. New York: Oxford University Press.

_____. 1989. *The Politics of Modernism: Against the New Conformists*. London: Verso.

III

Religious and Cultural Landscapes

Religions of India

T.N. MADAN

Introductory Remarks, Distributional Patterns

If the term 'religion' may be used to refer to particular aspects of India's cultural traditions, the country can be said to have long been the home of all religions that today have a worldwide presence. Hinduism, Buddhism, Jainism, and Sikhism—the so-called Indic religions—were born here. Christianity, Islam, Judaism, Zoroastrianism, and the Bahai faith arrived here from abroad at different points of time during the last two millennia.

The plurality of religions in India is often obscured by the fact that Hinduism is generally regarded as both the demographically dominant and the culturally characteristic—even hegemonic—religion of the country not only in popular imagination but also by official reckoning—four out of five Indians are Hindus, and they inhabit the length and breadth of the land. From the cultural perspective, anthropologists and sociologists have provided details of the many components of culture and aspects of social structure of the so-called non-Hindu communities that have either been borrowed from the Hindus, or are survivals from their pre-conversion Hindu past, with or without significant alterations.

The foregoing popular view of the cultural scene in India, buttressed by official statistics, needs to be qualified in several respects. Unlike the other religions of India, Hinduism is a federation of faiths which has a horizontal as well as vertical distribution, rather than a single homogeneous religion. Not only do the religious beliefs and practices of Hindus vary from one cultural region of the country to another (say, between Bengal and Maharashtra), Hindu castes in each area are also characterized by similar differences. We will go into the details of such internal plurality among the Hindus in section II below.

Suffice it to note here, first, that Hinduism has a long and eventful history which has resulted in much internal diversity, and second, that there are communities today which are considered Hindu by others but which themselves no longer concur in this judgement. Most notably, the Scheduled Castes of official literature, including the Constitution of the Republic, who have traditionally comprised the bottom rungs of the caste hierarchy, and were called Harijan ('the Children of God') by Mahatma Gandhi (1869–1948), are today by self-description the Dalit ('the Oppressed'). If their claim that they are not Hindu is accepted, the proportion of Hindus in the total population will come down significantly, from four-fifths to two-thirds.

Further, clarification regarding the use of the term 'religion' in the Indian context, anticipated at the very beginning of this chapter, may now be offered. Whether we have the

Indic faiths in mind, or the major religions of non-Indian origin, notably Islam, religion in India is not a discrete element of everyday life that stands wholly apart from the economic or political concerns of the people. To assume so would amount to yielding to the temptation of words. The point is not that the religious domain is not distinguished from the secular, but rather that the secular is regarded as being encompassed by the religious, even when the former is apparently inimical to the latter. The relationship is hierarchical. In other words, religion in the Indian cultural setting traditionally permeates virtually all aspects of life, not through mechanical diffusion, but in an integrated, holistic perspective (see Radhakrishnan 1927).

A second clarification concerns the conception of divinity. The monotheism characteristic of the Abrahamic religions (much more uncompromisingly in Judaism and Islam than in Christianity) is either absent in the Indic religions (as in the case of Buddhism and Jainism), or we find in its place other conceptions, notably an abstract notion of 'Essence' or 'Being' as the source of all that truly exists (the Brahman of Vedantic Hinduism), or polytheism (as in Puranic Hinduism), or the exuberant 'spiritism' of folk Hinduism (see section II below).

The non-theism of Buddhism and Jainism, which was a major scandal in the eyes of the Vedic metaphysicians two thousand years ago, persuaded a modern European scholar of comparative religion, Emile Durkheim (1858–1917), himself born into the Jewish faith, to abandon belief in the divinity as an essential element in the constitution (or recognition) of religion anywhere. Instead he focused on the conception of 'sacred things', that is, 'things set apart or forbidden' that contribute significantly to the constitution of society as a 'moral community'. The notion of sacredness is itself problematic in several respects however, but we will not go into this issue here (see Durkheim 1995).

Finally, it may be noted here by way of clarification, that the notion and word most widely used in India as a synonym for religion, namely, the Sanskrit *dharma* (from the root *dhr*) or its Pali equivalent *dharma*, denotes the ideas of maintenance, sustenance or upholding, steadfastness and moral virtue, rather than the dependent bonding of the human being with supernatural powers conveyed by the term religion, which is of Latin derivation (*religio*, obligation, bond). While a conception of self-sustaining cosmo-moral order is found in all Indic religions—subtle differences of nuance notwithstanding—Islam literally stands for submission to the Will of God, conveyed through his Word as recorded in the Quran, which is to be read repeatedly as an essential act of piety (see section III below). Incidentally, *religio* also denotes reverence.

Keeping the foregoing observations in mind, we will now use the word religion in this chapter without further elucidation or qualification. Let us begin with the demographic picture (on the basis of the 1991 census figures). The Hindus (including most of the Scheduled Castes, who account for 16.48 per cent of the total population) number 688 million, constituting 82 per cent of the total population of about 839 million. (The population in India has crossed 1 billion, but the religion-wise proportions are believed to be the same as in 1991.) Next to the Hindus are the 102 million Muslims (12 per cent), and they are followed by the Christians (20 million, 2.32 per cent) and the Sikhs (16 million, 1.99 per cent). Buddhists (0.77 per cent), Jains (0.41 per cent) and others account for the remaining nearly 2 per cent of the population. Among the 'others' mention may be made of those tribal peoples who adhere to their own traditional faiths—which used to be grouped together arbitrarily as animism under colonial rule—and of the Zoroastrians and the Jews. The total population of the Scheduled Tribes is about 68 million, or 8 per cent of the total population. Although their religion-wise distribution is not available, it is generally known that most of them either follow Hinduism of the folk type or are Christians; only a minority adhere to their ancestral faiths. As for the Zoroastrians and the Jews, they are counted in mere thousands; both are threatened by declining birth rates and assimilation among other religious communities through intermarriage.

State-wise distribution of the religious communities provides a picture of regional dispersal and variation. The Hindus, spread over virtually the entire country, outnumber all the others in the states of Himachal Pradesh (96 per cent), Orissa (95 per cent), Madhya Pradesh (93 per cent), Andhra Pradesh (89 per cent), Gujarat (89 per cent), Haryana (89 per cent), Rajasthan (89 per cent), Tamil Nadu (89 per cent), Pondicherry (86 per cent), Tripura (86 per cent), Karnataka (85 per cent), Delhi (84 per cent), Bihar (82 per cent), Uttar Pradesh (82 per cent), Maharashtra (81 per cent), West Bengal (75 per cent), Sikkim (68 per cent), Assam (67 per cent), Goa, Daman & Diu (65 per cent), Manipur (58 per cent), and Kerala (57 per cent). Similarly, Hindus outnumber all the others in the union territories of Dadra & Nagar Haveli (95 per cent) Chandigarh (76 per cent), and the Andaman & Nicobar Islands (68 per cent). They are the principal minority community in the states of Arunachal Pradesh (37 per cent), Punjab (34 per cent), Meghalaya (15 per cent), Nagaland (10 per cent), and Mizoram (5 per cent), and in the Union Territory of Lakshadweep (5 per cent).

The only other religious community with a perceptible countrywide distribution are the Muslims. They are the majority community in the state of Jammu & Kashmir (64 per cent according to 1981 census) in the extreme north and in the Union Territory of Lakshadweep (94 per cent) in the south. They are the principal minority in the states of Assam (28 per cent) in the north-east, West Bengal (23 per cent) and Bihar (15 per cent) in the east, Uttar Pradesh (17 per cent), Delhi (9 per cent), Rajasthan (8 per cent), and Haryana (5 per cent) in the north, Maharashtra (10 per cent) and Gujarat (9 per cent) in the west, and Kerala (23 per cent), Karnataka (12 per cent), and Andhra Pradesh (9 per cent) in the south.

Christians are the majority community in three north-eastern states, namely, Nagaland (88 per cent), Mizoram (86 per cent) and Meghalaya (65 per cent). They are the principal minority in the states of Manipur (34 per cent), also in the north-east, and Goa, Daman & Diu (30 per cent) in the west, and in the Union Territory of the Andaman & Nicobar Islands (24 per cent) in the south. Sikhs account for 63 per cent of the population in Punjab and are the principal minority in the adjacent state of Haryana (6 per cent) and the Union Territory of Chandigarh (20 per cent).

The state of Arunachal Pradesh in the north-east presents an interesting variation of the general pattern as the followers of traditional (tribal) religions at 36 per cent are about as numerous as Hindus (37 per cent) while Buddhists who account for 13 per cent; Christians (10 per cent) are in the fourth position. The only other places in the country where the Buddhists are a presence in demographic terms are the district of Ladakh (in Jammu & Kashmir), where they account for four-fifths of the population, and the states of Sikkim and Mizoram where their share in the population is 27 per cent and 8 per cent respectively. Jains are concentrated in Rajasthan, Delhi, and the west coast states. Zoroastrians, more generally known as Parsees, four-fifths of whose estimated world population of 120,000 lives in India, are concentrated in the urban areas of Gujarat and Maharashtra. Far fewer than the Parsees are the Jews, who are, however, divided into three distinct groups, namely, the Baghdadi Jews of Calcutta, the Cochin Jews, and the Bene Israeli of Bombay. Only the last named group may be called a community; the other two are really clusters of families.[1]

Before turning to the next topic, we may briefly observe here that, among the countries of South Asia, Sri Lanka shares with India the contemporary plurality of religions more than the other countries do. Although predominantly Buddhist, it harbours sizeable religious minorities, including Hindus, Christians and Muslims. Nepal is more predominantly Hindu, but Buddhists and Muslims also are present, the latter in very small numbers. Bangladesh is predominantly Muslim (85 per cent), with Hindus and Buddhists as notable religious minorities. Pakistan and the Maldives are almost exclusively Muslim and Bhutan is primarily Buddhist.

II. Indic Religions

Vedism and Early Hinduism

The beginnings of religious diversity in India go back to the country's proto-historic past. There is ample material evidence of the existence of elaborate religious activity in the urban centres associated with the Indus Valley or Harappan civilization five thousand years ago, spread over vast areas in north-western, northern, and western parts of the Indo-Pakistan subcontinent. It is reasonable to infer that religious beliefs and rituals of a somewhat different kind must have been present in the rural hinterlands. The city cultures, it is generally believed, were overridden by nomadic Aryan-speaking peoples of central Asian origin, around 1500 BC. They brought in their own religious beliefs and practices, and these focused on the creative and destructive powers of nature. According to this generally accepted view, the Aryans owed little in their religious life to the presumably Dravidian-speaking people they drove out of their homelands.

Scholars who do not accept the general view, but consider the Harappan culture as an unfolding rather than a major break whether wholly internal or aided by a limited migration, maintain that the old and the new cultures coexisted, and that the latter absorbed elements, both religious and linguistic, from the former (see Parpola 1994). Vedic religion and Sanskrit took several centuries to acquire the forms in which they have been handed down to us.

The resultant religion was characterized by internal diversities reflecting social, theological and scholastic divisions. Scholars have written about a state religion, centred in temples, comprising ritual bathing (there is a 'great bath' in the citadel of Mohenjo-Daro), worship of gods and goddesses, and perhaps animal sacrifice. Apart from the public (state) and private (domestic) rituals, differences reflecting clan-based cleavages also seem to have existed (see Possehl 1982). The major source of our knowledge about the religious life of the Aryans, besides the numerous archaeological sites, is the body of sacred literature called the Veda ('knowledge', 'wisdom'), which is believed to be ever-existent *(sanatana)* and therefore lacking any human author *(apaurusheya)*, and stretches over almost a thousand years.

The earliest of the Vedic texts is the Rig, which has been dated no later than 1200 BC (but is perhaps much older). Its ten books of hymns in praise of divinities presumably represent ten family traditions among the Brahmans (rituals specialists) and took several centuries to compose. The Sama and Yajur Vedas extend the scope of the Rig into music and ritual respectively. Finally, the Atharva Veda is believed to represent the absorption of folk religions into the Vedic corpus, resulting in significant changes in it. These religions were encountered by the Aryans as they moved east into the Gangetic valley and adopted more settled ways. Indeed, the valley came to be called the home of the Aryas, Aryavrata. Thus, divinities become devalued and magical spells and rites become ascendant (see Flood 1996; Brockington 1992).

Further, the Vedas became the basis for an immense textual efflorescence, comprising manuals of ritual performances (Brahmanas, Aranyakas), and discursive speculative treatises (Upanishads, also called Vedanta, the culmination of the Veda), all of which bring us close to

300 BC. Schools of Vedic learning and ritual, called 'branches' *(shakha)*, flourished, producing a cultural ambience of, at times, bewildering plurality within the Vedic framework.

But that is not all; Vedism gradually made way for the emergence of what is generally called Hinduism on a subcontinental scale, which brought more texts on more varied subjects into existence, notably the Grihya Sutras, which are guides to the performance of domestic rituals, and the Dharma Sutras, which have social ethics and law as their subject matter. Besides, there are the Shrauta Sutras which are technical treatises on the correct procedures for the performance of Vedic rituals of public significance. The Grihya Sutras have a regional character: a text followed in one part of the country may be unknown in another. The Vedic corpus, considered revealed, is said to be based on *shruti* (that which has been heard) and constitutes the first source of dharma understood as righteous conduct. With the Sutras we come to the second source, namely, *smriti* (that which is remembered), and these texts are credited to human authors.

Later still than the Sutras are the Dharma Shastras which continue with the same themes but in much greater detail. The best known of these texts today is the Manav Dharma Shastra, attributed to a seer called Manu, and therefore also known as the Manu Smriti. It is believed to have been composed between 200 BC and AD 300, which rules out single authorship. What stands out in this and other similar texts is the institutional framework for the conduct of both domestic life and public affairs.

In domestic life the key principles of *varna* (social class) and *ashrama* (stage of life) are adumbrated for the definition of appropriate rituals and worldly affairs. While universal norms *(sarva sadharna dharma)* are not wholly eliminated, but retained as the foundation of all righteous conduct, it is the varna- and ashrama-specific rules that emerge as preponderant. It is thus that Hinduism has been defined as *varna-ashrama-dharma*. Not only the householder, but the kings too, are bound by their respective duties defined in terms of varna and ashrama (see Lingat 1973). As for those who repudiated such divisions, notably the renouncers *(sannyasis)*, even they have been grouped into sects *(sampradayas)* since at least the time of the composition of the Mahabharata (400 BC–AD 400). It is obvious that variant regional, varna (including occupation), and ashrama identities defined the appropriateness of behaviour in particular situations. In view of this Hinduism could only have been a family of faiths and the behaviours that went with them, and the Hindu society, a confederation of communities.

The speculative or philosophical concerns of the Brahmanical tradition, were formulated as different systems of orthodox thought *(jnan)* and termed 'visions' *(darshana)* of life based on the Vedas. Each of these visions, six in number, has its own authoritative texts. The thought or reflection that follows from each position is not exclusive in the manner of the various guides to ritual performance and social behaviour. The 'root' text of each darshana is concerned with extra-referential *(paramarthika)* knowledge, and transactive *(vyavaharika)* knowledge is built upon or grafted into it. Together they constitute what can only be called a complex totality.

The six schools are: (i) Samkhya ('enumeration') which asserts the ontological duality of matter *(prakrti)* and the 'self' *(purusha)*; (ii) Yoga ('joining', 'mixing') which constitutes a pair with Samkhya in terms of its metaphysics; (iii) Mimamsa (Vedic exegesis) which takes a pluralist view of reality; (iv) Vedanta ('culmination of Veda'), grouped with Mimamsa, which denies the reality of the many; (v) Nyaya (logic) and (vi) Vaisesika (dialectics), considered a pair, which deal with logical, ontological, and dialectical issues within an empiricist, pluralist (more precisely atomist) framework (see Hiriyana 1949). The primacy which the monism of Vedanta has enjoyed in contemporary literature on India does little justice to the internal diversities of Brahmanical thought even when dealing with the same issues, or with its method of dealing with them to preclude mutual incomprehensibility.

The foregoing pluralities of scripture, metaphysics, and social organization that are the background of Hinduism and indeed partly constitute it, are characteristic of Brahmanical orthodoxy. This orthodoxy has not remained unchallenged. Indeed, the challenges came from within long before any major external threat materialized. The followers of public Vedic ritual, called the Shrautas (*shruti*, 'revelation'), first yielded space to those who gave precedence to domestic rituals, whether the Smartas (followers of the Smritis or Dharma Shastras) or the Pauranikas (those who organize their religious life on the basis of the Puranas, which are legendary accounts of the doings of gods, goddesses and other supernatural beings as well as human beings like kings and ascetics). The latter two categories of Hinduism are not, however, non-Vedic.

It is the Tantras, texts that are claimed by their followers the Tantrikas to be revealed, that are non-Vedic. Tantric rituals reveal considerable variety, but are generally characterized by secret rituals performed often at special sites such as cremation grounds, and frequently at night. Thus, Tantric rituals that invoke the power of the Supreme Goddess are performed at night in the famous temple of Puri (Orissa), where worship of the Pauranika god Jagannatha (an incarnation of Vishnu, the patron deity of Vaishnavas) and his divine consort is performed publicly during the day (see Marglin 1985). The celebrated yearly 'car festival' *(ratha yatra)* is dedicated to him.

While the worship of Vishnu is combined in the Smartha–Pauranika traditions with that of Devi (the goddess) and Shiva, in some parts of the country, particularly the south, mutually exclusive and often hostile sects have emerged centred on the cults of the two gods. From as early as the fifth century, the Vaishnavas were divided into the sects of Pancharatras and Vaikhanasas. Similarly, the Pashupata, Kapalika, and Kalamukha sects were prominent among the Shaivas (see Lorenzen 1972). Starting in the seventh century, the Vaishnavas and the Shaivas began to generate distinctive liturgical texts called the *samhitas* and *agamas* respectively. Each sect claimed the supremacy of its own deity on the latter's own authority.

In the development of these theistic traditions, from around the closing centuries of the last millennium BC, a number of elements from various sources, including the high Sanskritic and folk religious traditions, fused. Personal devotion to one's chosen deity *(bhakti)*, whether Vishnu in his various incarnations including most notably those of Rama and Krishna-Vasudeva, or Shiva, is a striking characteristic of these cults, and originated in the south and then spread to the north. This devotionalism found expression in emotionally charged poetry particularly among the Vaishnavas from the sixth century onward, and later also among the Shaivites, though the latter's devotion tended to be more austere (see Ramanujan 1973, 1981).

Expectedly, the relationship of the devotee to the deity, whether expressed in human (anthropomorphic) terms or through abstract formulations, constitutes the core of the speculative thought of these religious traditions, ranging from absolute monism *(advaita)*, associated with the name Sankara (*c.* 788–820), to qualified non-dualism *(vishishtadvaita)* of Ramanuja (*c.* 1017–1137) and dualism *(dvaita)* elucidated by Madhva in the thirteenth century. The teachings of the latter two saints combine the metaphysics of the Upanishads with the theism of Vaishnava and Shaiva cults.

Associated with both of these is a third tradition, namely, the worship of the great goddess,

Devi, which emerged virtually independently as the Shakta (from *shakti*, 'power') tradition. Here also the roots go far back in time, perhaps to the Harappan culture, and later developments entail the amalgamation of Puranic, Tantric and folk goddesses and ideas. As Lakshmi, the divine consort of Vishnu, the great goddess is presented as a benign bearer of auspiciousness; as Uma-Parvati, she is the divine consort of Shiva, mother of the universe; and as Durga or Kali, the highest manifestation of divine power, she is the fearsome destroyer of evil and greater than all the male gods through the pooling of whose powers she comes into being. At the village level she appears as the goddess who brings and removes illness and misfortune, such as Shitala, the goddess whose visitations were held responsible for small-pox (see Hawley and Wulff 1996).

The Hindu religious tradition, we have seen, is characterized by strong pluralistic tendencies emanating from various sources and inspirations. It has tended to absorb non-Hindu religious ideas and practices and has dealt with internal dissent through accommodation carried to the furthest extremes. Occasionally, this strategy has failed and resulted in breakaway sects which in the course of time grew into independent religions such as Buddhism and Jainism, adding a new dimension to the religious plurality of India.

Buddhism

The most widely spread religion in Asia today, namely, Buddhism, has adherents in the West also, but it is a minority religion in India, the country of its origin. Named after the title *buddha* ('the enlightened one') of its founder, Gautama (c. 563–483 BC), Buddhism began as a revolt against the Vedic preoccupation with the supernatural, rejecting the beliefs as well as the rituals that went with them. The rejection entailed repudiation of the authority of the Brahmans. Gautama himself belonged to the Kshatriya (warrior) caste and indeed, he was the heir to a kingdom in the Bihar–Nepal area. Following his own awakening to knowledge and wisdom— his enlightenment—the Buddha attracted disciples whom he taught 'the four noble truths' which constitute the fundamentals of all schools of Buddhism (see Harvey 1990).

The first truth of life, the Buddha said, is sorrow (suffering); the second, that the source of sorrow is ignorance and desire; the third, that sorrow can be ended if desire is overcome; and the fourth, that the way to the 'blowing out' *(nibanna)* of both desire and sorrow lies through 'the noble eightfold path'. This path, which is the path of righteousness (dharma, dhamma) consists of the right views, resolve, speech, conduct, livelihood, effort, mindfulness, and concentration.

The Buddha adopted a stance of silence on the issue of the existence of the divinity but denied the Vedic gods any significance in human affairs, and concentrated on human agency. He did, however, retain the root paradigm of karma understood as the doctrine of agency and retribution. It is doubtful that the Buddha thought of himself as anything more than a reformer within the tradition and his teachings as 'a new expansion, not against, but within Brahmanism'. Nevertheless, his teachings were said to be negatory *(nastika)*, repudiating Vedic revelation and the notion of divinity by the establishment and attacked as unforgivably heterodox.

The Buddha originated the idea of the monastic community of monks and nuns *(sangha)*, subject to a rigorous regime *(vinaya)*, as the ideal arrangement for the pursuit of true knowledge. An easier way of life was envisaged for the lay community, with the sangha as their exemplar and refuge. Such was his confidence in this institution that the Buddha did not name a successor nor codify his teachings. He advised resolution of doubts on matters of common concern through discussion and consensus; in the event of failure to reach a consensus the majority view was to be respected. It was thus that the seeds of a plurality of belief and practice among the Buddhists were sown by Gautama himself.

The first great split is believed to have occurred a century after the Buddha's passing at a council of sanghas convened at Vaishali (Bihar) to settle contentious issues concerning monastic discipline and the character of the Buddha's personality. The opposing factions, namely, the orthodox Sthaviras (Elders) and the Mahasanghikas (upholders of the 'Great Community'), reached a temporary truce, but split formally four decades later. While the former held the Buddha to have been an enlightened human preceptor, the latter claimed for him the status of a transcendent being.

The foregoing and other issues continued to cause disagreements. In the process as many as eighteen viewpoints were formalized and collectively referred to as the Hinayana, or the little (or lesser) vehicles (or approaches). One of them, the school of Sthaviras emerged as Theravada (the Way of the Elders) in the second century BC in Sri Lanka, where it is now the state religion. It is the only Hinayana school to have escaped extinction. As for the Mahasanghikas, they were the progenitors of the adherents of Mahayana (great vehicle or approach) Buddhism that is today a major religion in East Asia (China, Japan) and elsewhere.

Mention may also be made of a later development (seventh century) in north India where a convergence of Buddhism and Tantrism occurred, resulting in what came to be called the Vajrayana (thunderbolt vehicle). This in turn spread north into Ladakh (Jammu and Kashmir) and the kingdom of Bhutan (three-fourths of the people there are Buddhists) and Tibet where it absorbed further extraneous elements from Shamanism. In the north-eastern states of Tripura, Mizoram, and Arunachal Pradesh in India there are close to 200,000 Buddhists of the Theravada school.

The presence of the Dalai Lama and settlements of refugees in India since their exile from Tibet in 1959, has enhanced general awareness about Buddhism in its different expressions of doctrine and practice in India. The conversion of large numbers of low-caste Hindus, who call themselves Dalits (the Oppressed) and are generally referred to as Neo-Buddhists, under the charismatic leadership of B.R. Ambedkar (1891–1956), has contributed significantly to the same process. It has, however, explicitly politicized Buddhist identity.

Jainism

Jainism too arose around the same time as Buddhism in the same area (Bihar), for broadly the same reasons, and in a similar manner. But there are significant differences between the Buddhist and Jain visions of life. The terms Jainism and Jain (*Jaina*, follower of the religion) are derived from *jina*, 'the conqueror' (of one's physical self and thus of karmic action). This title was bestowed on prince Vardhamana (599–527 BC)—also called the Mahavira, 'the great hero'—to whom the basic teachings of the faith in their final form are attributed. Actually, he is regarded as the last of a line of teachers called *tirthankara* ('ford maker'), who recovered time and again the perennial 'three jewels' of right faith, right knowledge, and right action. They also founded the Jain community comprising ascetics (monks and nuns) and the laity (householders). It is their community that is considered by the Jains as a spiritual ford (*tirtha*) to help all seekers wash off karma and terminate the cycle of birth–death–rebirth (see Dundas 1992).

Sentiments such as desire, anger, greed, and attachment are the human failings that generate karma (fruit-bearing action). Karma is visualized as material: it contaminates the inner self and is the cause of suffering in one's own life and of injury to other living beings. The Jain ideal therefore is to be forever engaged in self-purification (through the suppression of all bodily appetites) and to assiduously refrain from injury to others (this is the ideal of *ahimsa*, 'non-injury'). Renunciation is highly valued and the final worldly goal for the ascetic is to end one's life through abstinence from food and drink. For laymen, the householder's life, guarded by numerous rules and regulations, is the ideal.

Paradoxical as it may seem, the Jains in actual practice are also very successful merchants, visible in urban centres. Although there are fewer Jains than Buddhists in India, it is they rather than the latter who are the more visible religious community. They share many religious practices including fasts and festivals with the upper-caste Hindus, and are often regarded by the latter as a sect of Hindu society, rather than a separate religious community. Their original atheism and repudiation of Vedic revelation had of course earned them, alongside of the Buddhists, the opprobrium of being heterodox in the judgement of the Brahmans.

Among the Jains themselves heresies and sectarian schisms began to make their appearance even while the Mahavira was alive. According to the mainstream Jain tradition, eight such deviations (*nihnava*, 'concealment' of the true teaching) occurred over a period of six centuries. The last of these resulted in the emergence of a heretical sect. Accounts of this schism are shrouded in rival legends of the so-called mainstream and the breakaway groups, the Shvetambaras (clad in white cloth) and the Digambaras ('clothed by the sky', naked).

The mode of clothing refers to the practices of the ascetics rather than the lay householders, but Digambara nuns do wear clothes; only men remain naked. The Shvetambaras use a bowl to receive food given to them, which they also eat from. Food is important because even those monks who have attained full omniscience (*kevalin*) must eat to survive. The Digambaras do not use a bowl but their cupped hands to receive alms, and it is from the hands so held together that they eat. They insist on absolute non-possession: no clothes and no alms bowls. In their judgement true omniscience means, among other things, that one does not need to eat food anymore. Women are deemed unequal to the demands of total conquest of the passions leading to omniscience and deliverance from the fruits of karma.

The two sects are also separated by the scriptures that each acknowledges. On the fundamentals of Jain faith and knowledge, however, there is no serious difference. Sectarian differences seem to have taken very long to acquire their present rigidity, and regional distribution—Shvetambaras in the north and the west and Digambaras in the south—seems to have contributed to it. The differences notwithstanding, the high value that all Jains place upon non-violence has prevented the two sects from adopting aggressive measures to settle scores. Currently, sectarian conflict among the Jains seems to focus on the issues of ownership of and access to places of worship rather than on matters of doctrine and practice. Regrettably the same cannot be said about other communities.

Sikhism

The beginnings of Sikhism (*sikha*, disciple) early in the sixteenth century followed a major development in the history of religions in India over the previous 800 years, namely, the arrival and growth of Islam. This development is described in the next section, but is mentioned here because it contributed significantly to the making of the new faith. Like Vardhamana and Gautama before him, Nanak Dev (1469–1539), the founder of Sikhism, was an upper-caste Hindu (of the Khatri caste of traders, originally Kshatriyas). From his experience and reflections, he developed an acute dissatisfaction with the ritualism, idol worship, magic, and miracles of the faith into which he was born, and with the stranglehold of the Brahmans over it (see McLeod 1968; Grewal 1990).

Nanak also took a positive view of worldly existence, and of the householder's life and productive labour. He rejected caste distinctions and the traditional ideal of renunciation. Above all he extolled the virtue of a life of religious obedience and devotion focused on an abstract conception of the divinity, and affirming the same through 'name remembrance' (*nam simran*), that is, recitation and singing of hymns. Declaring that there were no true Hindus or Muslims to be found anywhere, he called for a third path comprising moral duty (dharma), human effort (karma), spiritual knowledge, truth, and divine benevolence.

In all this Nanak was carrying forward the medieval Sant tradition of syncretic religious devotionalism, which had given rise to many 'paths' (*panth*) or sects. The disciples who gathered around him and carried forward his teachings after his death came to be called the Nanak Panthis or, later, Sikhs. Some of his followers did not follow all of his core teachings and, like his son who became a renouncer, founded other sects. Other changes and dilutions of dogma and practice, particularly the latter, occurred over the next two centuries, blurring the distinction between Sikhism and caste Hinduism, and rendering the Sikh identity rather 'misty'. Simultaneously, changing historical circumstances—which brought the Jats into the Sikh fold in large numbers, and also created suspicions in the minds of the Muslim rulers about the loyalty of the Sikhs—radically altered the pacifist character of the Sikh community.

The tenth guru of the Sikhs, Gobind Rai (1666–1708), intervened effectively on all fronts—theological, practical, social and political—and created a sharpened sense of identity among the Sikhs by instituting (in 1699) a ritual of initiation (called *pahul*), and laying down norms of conduct including, most visibly, the injunction to retain bodily hair unshorn. He also asked all Sikh men to uniformly substitute Singh ('lion', the caste name of Rajputs) for their various last names; the women were to call themselves 'Kaur' ('lioness').

The institution of these requirements also created unintended divisions among the Sikhs between (i) those who went through pahul and came to be called Amritdhari ('bearers of nectar', the baptismal water); (ii) those who kept their hair and beard and were called Keshdhari (bearers of hair); and (iii) those who affirmed Sikh identity but did not immediately follow the new injunctions, called the Sahajdhari (bearers of the spontaneous, inner light). The first category also called themselves the Khalsa, or the 'pure' and 'the chosen of God', and were to play a hegemonistic role in the second half of the nineteenth century in defining Sikh identity.

A hundred years after Guru Gobind established the Khalsa, a Jat Sikh chieftain, Ranjit Singh (1780–1839) established the Kingdom of Lahore, which did not, however, last long after his death. In the aftermath of the defeat of the Sikhs at the hands of the British in 1846, several reformist movements emerged among the Sikhs. Of these, the most notable were the Nirankari and Namdhari (or Kuka) movements. Both were sectarian in character and acknowledged gurus subsequent to Gobind Singh, who had proclaimed closure of the line of personal gurus. The beliefs of these sects were therefore considered violative of the true Khalsa faith by orthodox Sikhs. The Nirankaris called for a return to the teachings of Guru Nanak who had characterized the divinity as 'formless' (*nirankar*). The Namdharis focused their attention on regenerating the Khalsa as instituted by Guru Gobind. A modernist version of the same effort (namely, Khalsa rejuvenation) was the agenda of the so-called Singh Sabhas which also had a considerable agenda of secular goals. Currently, the Namdharis are not very much in the news, but conflicts between the Nirankaris and the orthodox Akalis have resulted in violence and loss of life. The fundamentalist preacher Jarnail Singh Bhindranwale, who later came into conflict with the government on the issue of Sikh grievances, originally appeared in public (in 1978) as a fierce opponent of the Nirankaris (see Kapur 1986).

From the foregoing account of developments in the long history of Indic religions, it is clear that pluralistic tendencies characterize them all, particularly Hinduism, which lacks a founder or a set of fundamentals of belief and practice or a 'church'. And yet they share a concern with unity in diversity, or the Absolute transcending its myriad expressions. The notions of dharma and karma are key ideas in the metaphysical foundations of each.

III. Christianity and Islam

Christianity

Of the religions that originated outside India but found a home here, Christianity is the oldest. If tradition is to be believed, it was brought to Kerala by the Apostle St Thomas under the auspices of the Nestorian Church. Written records testify to the presence of Christians in India from the sixth century onwards. The Thomas Christians are also known as Syrian Christians for, originally, their liturgy was in Syriac and they acknowledged the jurisdiction of the Syrian Patriarch of the East in Damascus (Syria). Conversions seem to have been made locally among upper-caste Hindus only. The community has remained confined to Kerala. It subscribes to the various fundamentals of Christian faith—such as Immaculate Conception, the divinity of Jesus, and the status of the Bible as revealed scripture—and practice (for example, celebration of the Eucharist).

In the middle of the sixteenth century Jesuit missionaries made Goa their base after it became a part of the Portuguese colonial empire, and spread out to other parts of south India and Sri Lanka and even ventured north. Inevitably, they encountered the Thomas Christians who were asked to sever ties with the Nestorian Church and come under the jurisdiction of Rome. This led to a split among them: while about one-half of the community complied, the rest resisted, and reaffirmed their loyalty to the Syrian Patriarch of Antioch. A long-lasting issue causing dissension among the Thomas Christians as well as the Jesuits was whether missionary activity was to be confined among the upper castes, and whether caste was to be deemed a religious institution and abolished, or only a secular social arrangement and therefore tolerated.

The arrival of the British in India in the mid-eighteenth century had at first no impact on the spread of Christianity as the East India Company in deference to the wishes of the home government did not allow missionary activity. It was only in the early nineteenth century that the British Parliament removed the restriction and chaplains of the Company began to make converts. The Anglican diocese of Calcutta was founded in 1814. To begin with, Anglican chaplains administered to the spiritual needs of the British in India, but an Indian Church had also come into existence by the end of the nineteenth century. A close association of the Church with the State (the colonial dispensation) was a liability and came to be loosened by the 1930s (see Gibbs 1972). Meanwhile, Anglicans, Protestants, and Non-conformist societies had sent out missions, producing a plurality of churches and an interflow between congregations. Thus, some Thomas Christians became Protestants and established the Mar Thomas (Syriac for St Thomas) Church. The majority, however, remained loyal to the Syrian Patriarch, nominally acknowledging his spiritual authority, but otherwise independent. They are known as the members of the Jacobite or Orthodox Church (see Mathew and Thomas 1967; Visvanathan 1993).

In 1947, the year of India's independence, the Anglican, Methodist and other Protestant churches came together to establish the Church of South India. Similar efforts in the north resulted in the establishment of a united Protestant Church in 1970. The predominance of Roman Catholics (nearly 60 per cent) is a noteworthy feature of the Christian community in

India. Also noteworthy has been the search for Indian idioms of expression. Christians of all denominations have retained many of their pre-conversion beliefs, attitudes, and ceremonies, incorporating them into Christianity (see Bayly 1989). Evangelicalism has also remained alive, however, and is indeed a cherished goal. The fundamental right to propagate one's religion, and not merely to profess and practice it, was written into the Indian Constitution (Article 30) to accommodate Christian sentiment on the subject.

Islam

The third and the youngest member of the family of Abrahamic religions, Islam ('submission to the will of God') is dated back to AD 622 when its promulgator, the Prophet Muhammad (AD 571–632) migrated from his native city of Makkah (in Arabia), where he did not receive the support he desired, to Madinah. In the latter city he established the first ever Islamic state. He accommodated resident Jews and Christians in it, since they too were judged to be in possession of books of divinely revealed knowledge and, therefore, entitled to protection.

The fundamentals of religious faith and practice among Muslims ('the submitters') are explicit and universally binding. They must affirm the oneness of God and the status of the Quran ('the text to be read and recited') as the word of God. Besides, they must believe in God's angels and messengers (of whom Muhammad was the most perfect and therefore the last); and in the Last Day, when God will judge the actions of one and all, and despatch the pious to heaven and the sinners to hell (see Rahman 1979).

Moreover, every true Muslim must recite the creed (*kalimah*, 'the word'), which affirms the oneness of God and the finality of Muhammad's prophethood; say daily prayers (*namaz*) at the appointed times; observe the yearly month of fasting by day (*rozah*) to burn away sins; give alms (*zakat*); and, if circumstances allow it, go in pilgrimage to Makkah (*hajj*) so as to be there on Idu'l-Azha. (This day, it is generally believed, commemorates the willingness of Ibrahim [Abraham] to sacrifice his son Ismail [Ishmael] on God's command.) It is noteworthy that Indian Muslims do not include the waging of war (*jihad*) for the extermination of unbelief and the propagation of Islam among the obligations of a Muslim, as is done in many Muslim countries.

Islam is, however, more than the foregoing and similar other fundamentals. Everywhere it incorporates much that is local and pre-Islamic, whether this be in the Arab heartlands or in distant places such as India. Students of Islam have commented on this internal tension owing to its character as a world religion that admits of no variation (for instance, the daily prayers are everywhere said in Arabic) and with its regional, country or national characteristics, for example, the worship of saints and relics which is common in India.

It is widely believed among South Asian Muslims that the Prophet Muhammad had himself wanted to bring the people of India into the universal Islamic community (*umma*). Since Arab traders already had contact with the western seaboard of India from pre-Islamic days (the Mapillas of Kerala were born of mixed marriages of Arab men and Malayali women), they must have been the first carriers of the new faith to the subcontinent. Islam arrived here as a political force in AD 712, when Sind was conquered on behalf of the Umayyad caliphate and incorporated in it. With the new rulers came their advisers on matters concerning Muslim holy law, the *shariah* (see Ahmad 1964; Mujeeb 1967).

The numbers of the immigrants were naturally not large, and they were strangers who knew neither the culture, languages, and religions (Buddhism and Hinduism both were present) of Sind, nor the prevailing system of governance. In the circumstances, native support was necessary, but this in turn entailed a conciliatory attitude towards Indians, which included the assurance that, by and large, there would be few restrictions on non-Islamic religions. In terms of strict Islamic orthodoxy, however, these religions could only be called ignorance (*jahalat*, incorrect belief). The long-term consequence of this initial compromise made for reasons of the State was twofold: first, it laid the foundations of multi-religious polities in which Islam and the Indic religions would coexist, much to the chagrin of the guardians of orthodoxy; second, it sowed the seeds of an Indian Islam, accommodating Indian cultural traits and forms of social organization (notably caste).

From the time of major incursions of political Islam into India, beginning with the invasions of Mahmud, king of Ghazni, in the early years of the eleventh century, two kinds of religious specialists became prominent. These were the *ulama* (doctors of shariah or the holy law) and the Sufis, (mystics in search of direct religious experience). The ulama urged the kings to uphold shariah and be vigilant on behalf of their own religion rather than being tolerant of other misguided faiths. One such outstanding medieval scholar, Zia ud-din Barani (*c.* AD 1280–1360), was of the opinion that the Muslim kings could not be the refuge of Islam unless they completely destroyed unbelief, polytheism, and idolatory. If the kings cannot actually exterminate the unbelievers (because they are so many), they surely should deny them authority and honour, he advised. Such extremist opinions, however, never became general among the ulama or ascendant in the ruling circles. The ulama actually split into two categories: while some of them confined themselves to their specialized duties and kept aloof from statecraft, others opted for a close relationship with the kings. The latter supported the actions of the rulers even when these were grounded in statecraft rather than true faith as interpreted by the ulama.

Islam spread throughout the length and breadth of India, less by the episodic coercion and violence of the kings, and more by the generally peaceful efforts of the ulama and the Sufis. In areas of mass conversion, notably East Bengal (or what is today Bangladesh) and the Kashmir valley, other factors also contributed (directly or indirectly) to the phenomenon. It is noteworthy, however, that at the time of partition in 1947, after 800 years of Muslim rule, no more than a quarter of all the people of India (400 million) were Muslims. In the Gangetic valley, where Muslims provided enormous support to the demand for Pakistan, fewer than two out of every ten Indians professed Islam.

When Islam reached India, it was already marked by divisions of various kinds. According to Muslim tradition, Muhammad himself had prophesized that there would be more sects (*firqah*) in Islam than among the children of Israel, but that they would all be sent to hell by God. Only those who followed his words and deeds, and of his closest companions, would be the ones to be saved (*najiyah*). They came to be called the Sunni (from *sunnah*, customary way of life) or traditionalists, and account for the great majority of Indian Muslims. Their opponents are the Shiahs ('followers'), who came into being following Muhammad's death as the partisans of Ali, the Prophet's cousin and son-in-law, whom they considered the legitimate successor (*khalifah*) and leader (*imam*). It was not Ali, however, but Muhammad's father-in-law, Abu Bakr, who was chosen, resulting in the Sunni–Shiah split which even today leads to violence in both India and Pakistan.

Besides the Shiahs it is the Sufis who are excoriated by the traditionalists. A connection has been sought to be established between the two heterodoxies by claiming Ali as one of the founders of Sufism (*tasawwuf*). According to another view, the Arabian philosophy derived from the teaching of al-Ghazzli (AD 1058–1111) was absorbed into Islam in the form of a mystical theology, but this locates Sufism late in the fifth century of Islam.

Some scholars, including the renowned early medieval historian al-Biruni (AD 973–1048), found similarities between some key ideas of Sufism and the Brahmanical philosophy of Yoga or the magical Tantra. Indeed, it has been suggested that Abu Yazid Tayfur of Iran (d. 874), a key figure in the development of Sufism, may have learned the principles of Brahmanical and Buddhist mysticism from Abu Ali of Sind who himself may have been a convert to Islam. Be that as it may, two general observations can be made. First, a considerable number of Indic elements are recognizable in Sufism in India, but only some of these are pure borrowals, the others being adaptations of classical Islamic Sufi ideas in the Indian cultural environment. Second, Sunni orthodoxy has always frowned upon both Shiahs and Sufis (see Rizvi 1978, 1982). Four major worldwide Sufi orders—namely, Chishti, Naqshbandi, Qadiri, and Suhrawardi—are present in India. Besides, there are numerous local orders of Faqirs and Darveshs: while some of them are seriously devout; the devotion to higher spiritual goals among others who are often given to excesses of various kinds including drug abuse, is highly suspect. Among the former, mention may be made of the Rishi order of the Kashmir valley (see Khan 1994).

Islam was brought to Kashmir, it is generally believed, by the Kubrawi Sufi Sayyid Ali Hamadani late in the fourteenth century, but his efforts seem to have been confined to a small group of neo-converts in the city of Srinagar including the sultan. It was Shaikh Nuruddin (AD 1379–1442), the founder of the Rishi order, who carried the new faith to the masses. His success owed much to not only his amiable disposition and peaceful methods of preaching, but also to his familiarity with and adaptation of prevailing Brahmanical religious ideas and practices (Kashmir Shaivism). His choice of the name Rishi (a Sanskrit word meaning 'seer') for his order is itself revelatory. He adopted vegetarianism for himself and his followers out of his compassion for animals, and thus abjured the universal Muslim practice of animal sacrifice.

While some historians have written of two types of Sufism in Kashmir, the immigrant and the native, or the classical and the folk, others have denied the existence of this dichotomy, pointing out that Sufis of the Suhrawardi order and even the Kubrawis, befriended and eulogized the Rishis. According to the latter, the Rishis' very rootedness in Kashmir's old religious traditions, combined with their exposure to the ideas of classical Sufism made them the ideal agents of the Islamization of Kashmiri masses. It is noteworthy that Nuruddin claimed the Prophet of Islam himself as the real founder of his order, locating himself at least notionally in shariah, the 'highway' of Islam.

It is not the Sufis alone who have contributed to the culture of religious diversity in Indian Islam. The reputedly more stringent ulama have also done so. Thus, in the late nineteenth century three groups of these doctors of the holy law of Islam led sectarian movements, differentiated from one another by big issues (such as matters of belief and law) as well as small (including minutia of everyday life). The most influential of these were the ulama of a famous seminary called the Darul Uloom at Deoband in north India (founded in 1867). Their educational programme too was grounded in the traditional curriculum and thus opposed to the innovations and accommodations of western science that characterized the efforts of the modernists at the Mohammadan Anglo-Oriental College in Aligarh (founded in 1874).

Besides the Deobandis, the two other prominent reformist groups were the Ahl-i Hadis ('people of the tradition') and the ulama of Bareilly popularly known as the Barelwis, who were opposed to both the other groups. In their disputations one or the other of the four recognized schools of Islamic law (Hanafi, Maliki, Shafii, Hanbali) were invoked, but the Hanafi school has always been the dominant one in India.

Finally, mention must be made of the Ahmadiyah sect which was formally proclaimed to be heretical and therefore a non-Muslim minority in Pakistan in 1974. Its founder, Mirza Ghulam Ahmad (1839–1908) was born in Qadiyan, a village in north Punjab. Not trained as a Sufi, he was a law clerk by occupation. He also claimed to be the recipient of divine revelation and therefore the messiah (*mahdi*) promised to the Muslims. Although Ahmad did not dispute the Islamic belief in the closure of prophecy with Muhammad, he asserted that he belonged to a line of secondary prophets. Provoked and influenced by the work of Christian missionaries and the activities of the Hindu revivalist Arya Samaj movement, he organized his response on similar lines, and gathered a considerable following. The sect called Ahmadiyah, or Qadiyani, continues to be recognized as Muslim in India, but it really survives on sufferance.

IV. Religious Pluralism as Ideology

In the previous two sections we described the diversity or plurality of religions in India at two levels. These were, first, the global level, at which the major religions, whether indigenous or of foreign origin, were in focus and second, the intra-religious level at which sectarian or quasi-sectarian movements operate. We have seen that a naïve distinction between pluralist Indic religions and homogeneous (fundamentalist) Indian religions of foreign origin is wholly misleading. It is obvious that whenever a religious community comprises many regional cultural groups and also has considerable numbers, running into millions, internal plurality becomes inescapable. But whatever is present empirically may yet be denied or deprecated ideologically. The question, then, is, has the long history of religious diversity in India produced serious arguments supporting and justifying the phenomenon? In other words, has plurality generated pluralism (see Coward 1987)?

Contemporary ideologues of secularism, understood as religious pluralism, speaking on behalf of or within the Hindu tradition, often claim that pluralism is as old as the oldest Veda. It is recalled that the Rig Veda (I. 164.46) proclaims that 'the Absolute is one, although the sages have given it different names'. Similarly, it is pointed out that the Manu Smriti (II. 14) resolved the problem of conflict between contradictory revelations by laying down that they are all valid and must therefore be respected. Although revelation (shruti) enshrined in the Vedas and other sacred texts is respected, it does not follow that it is widely known among Hindus, like the Bible is among the Christians or the Quran among the Muslims. In the absence of a single core text—the Bhagavad Gita has come to acquire such a position in relatively modern times—or a single founder, or a set of irrefutable fundamentals, or the practice of conversion from other religions, it is not surprising that the Hindu religious tradition has, from its earliest beginnings, been marked by pluralist tendencies. These have been in consonance with the pluralist social organization based on the institution of caste and are essentially inegalitarian in character (see Madan 1997).

Such pluralism as is present has its roots inside the Hindu tradition and is only derivatively applied to other religious traditions. Hinduism tolerates difference by incorporating and hierarchizing it: Buddhism, Jainism, and Sikhism are all considered inferior varieties of Hinduism. Moreover, conflict has not been altogether absent, as the record of the persecution of Buddhists and Jains by various Hindu groups, or of inter-sectarian conflicts between, say, the Shaivas and the Vaishnavas, shows. One can say, however, that the traditional Brahmanical notion of the legitimacy of the right of a group to its own way of life (*svadharma; adhikara bheda*), without conceding that the different ways are of equal merit, is a form of pluralism.

In modern times, the Bengali mystic, Ramakrishna (1836–86) and his renowned disciple

Vivekananda (1863–1902) are credited with promoting the ideology of religious pluralism by word and deed. Ramakrishna was no intellectual, but in his quest for spiritual experience he practised a simplified Islamic life for some time, withdrawing completely from his Brahmanical observances. He also disregarded sectarian differences among the Hindus. Vivekananda formulated an ideology of pluralism, but it was based on tolerance of other religions rather than their acceptance as equals of Hinduism. In fact, within Hinduism itself, he raised Vedanta above all other creeds, calling it the mother of all religions and truer than any other religion. He was explicitly critical of Buddhism and Christianity.

While Bengal witnessed these developments, Punjab was the scene for the flowering of the Arya Samaj movement, founded by Dayananda Saraswati (1824–83) in Bombay in 1874. He not only rejected post-Vedic forms of Hinduism as erroneous, and condemned what he called 'blind faith' (such as idol worship) and 'harmful customs' (such as the practice of caste and gender discrimination), but also denied that Christianity and Islam could be considered divinely inspired religions. He made derogatory observations about them as well as Buddhism, Jainism and Sikhism. The teachings of Arya Samaj represent the exclusivist strand of Vedic Hinduism, anticipate later explicitly fundamentalist developments (notably the thesis of Hindutva, or Hindu identity) and militate against pluralism as an ideology.

In the twentieth century, Mahatma Gandhi (1869–1948) put forward the most explicit formulation of religious pluralism when he announced on 30 May 1913 that, in his opinion, 'the world as a whole will never have, *and need not have* a single religion' (emphasis added) (see Chatterjee 1983). By acknowledging his indebtedness to Christianity and Islam, Gandhi implied that Hinduism could be enriched by incorporating in it some of the truths discovered by other religions. While he maintained that all religions were equally true, he added that because of the limitations of human intellect, they were also equally imperfect. He refused to hierarchize the relationship between different religions, and thus moved in the direction of a genuine religious pluralism.

Islam is, as we have seen, the second major religion of India. Except in Indonesia and Bangladesh, there are more Muslims in India today than in any other country. The attitudes of Muslims to the phenomenon of religious plurality are therefore of great importance for the future of the ideology of pluralism. Given the fundamental Muslim belief that Islam is the most perfect of all divinely revealed religions, and that the Quran is the Word of God, any attempt to project pluralism has to honour these beliefs. A careful reader of the holy book of Islam will find many passages on which an ideology of religious pluralism can be based. To give but one example: 'To you your religion, and to me mine' (109.3).

In the mid-seventeenth century, Dara Shikoh, heir to the Mughal throne, disciple of a Sufi master and a Sanskrit scholar, made a close study of the Upanishads and even translated some of them into Persian. He concluded that they were revealed scriptures anticipating the divine message of monotheism elaborated in the Quran. He described Vedantic Hinduism and Islam as 'twin brothers': for this he was declared a heretic by the ulama, and beheaded on the orders of his brother, the emperor Aurangzeb, who had usurped the succession.

In the twentieth century, the most celebrated effort to argue for religious pluralism on the basis of the Quran itself was made by Maulana Abul Kalam Azad (1888–1958), profound scholar of religion and distinguished political leader. His many-stranded argument focused on, among other issues, the attributes of God and the true nature of divine revelation. He maintained that the manner in which 'divine providence' (*rububiyat*), 'divine benevolence' (*rahmat*), and 'divine justice' (*adalat*) are defined in the Quran, it is obvious that Allah is God of all creation, and that the oneness of humanity is derived from the oneness of God. As for divine revelation, for it to be itself, it must provide guidance to everyone without distinction. Like Dara Shikoh, he detected significant common truths and insights in Islam and Vedantic Hinduism on the foregoing and other key issues. His effort, in the form of an exegesis of the Quran, ran into difficulties with the ulama who detected in it many serious flaws, including an alleged devaluation of the intermediary role of the Prophet and of the importance of formal prayer. In the event, Azad never brought his monumental undertaking to its conclusion (see Azad 1962).

Pluralism as an ideological stance within the Hindu and Indian Muslim religious traditions recognizes and respects plurality, but stresses the oneness of the ultimate goal of different expressions of the religious quest. It is an invitation to coexistence, dialogue and even syncretism. Religious devotionalism (bhakti) of the medieval period in northern India, expressed through 'the voice of the seekers of the truth' (sant vani), was echoed by the ecstatic mysticism of the Sufis. Nanak, the first Sikh guru, was a unique representative of the sant tradition. He sought emancipation from all external formalisms (rituals, customs, social distinctions) through a valorization of the inner spiritual quest. He dismissed the meaningfulness of the prevailing religious distinctions. More than a reconciliation or synthesis, his teaching presented a transcendent third path. The last of the Sikh personal gurus, Gobind, also declared that the true Sikhs or the Khalsa ('the pure' or 'the chosen') would have to be different from both Hindus and Muslims in physical appearance (unshorn and uncircumcised) as well as moral fibre (expressed through a code of conduct beginning with formal initiation or pahul). He too pointed to a higher path transcending not only the divide between Hinduism and Islam, but also the inner polarities of the former (for example, domesticity versus renunciation). Like the Hindu and Indian Muslim perspectives on religious pluralism, the Sikh vision is also hierarchical.

The task of developing a well-argued ideology of religious pluralism on the basis of the religions of India awaits serious and competent attention. The emergence of state-sponsored religious pluralism, summed up in the slogan sarva dharma samabhava (equal respect for all religions), and presented as Indian (in contrast to western) secularism, does not go very far in strengthening inter-religious understanding and appreciation (see Smith 1963; Madan 1997). These values are more profound than a working strategy of passive tolerance and will have to be promoted by men and women of faith themselves. As Gandhi pointed out, the task of the secular state is to leave matters of religion to the people.

Contrary to the assumption of many modernists that religious faith is necessarily exclusive and therefore results in communal conflict, there is considerable historical and ethnographical evidence that the common people of India, irrespective of individual religious identity, have long been comfortable with religious plurality. They acknowledge religious difference as the experienced reality: they do not consider it good or bad. In other words, social harmony, or agreement, is built on the basis of difference.

The traditional elite of the nineteenth century were familiar with this folk pluralism, but considered it as no more than the ignorance of unlettered masses. Today's modernist intelligentsia have opted for the ideology of secularism, which seeks to drive religion into the privacy of people's lives, if not altogether eliminate it. This ideology envisages a pluralism that is a concomitant of structural differentiation in society. Needless to emphasize, the two pluralisms—the people's and the intellectual's—are different in several crucial respects. For example, and most notably, the former is wholly spontaneous—the lived social reality—but the latter is ideological and in that sense self-conscious or constructed; the former is based on a positive attitude towards religion, but the latter is sceptical. Indeed, there is a hiatus between the two pluralisms, but this has not been so far examined with the seriousness it deserves.

ENDNOTES

1. Detailed statistics about the distribution of the population of India by religion and domicile are given in the table below, which is based on the *Census of India 1991, Series I, India, Paper I of 1995: Religion*, pp. xii–xxiii.

Table Religions of India (1991 census)

	Total	Hindus	Mus-lims	Chris-tians	Sikhs	Bud-dhists	Jains	Other	Religion not stated
India	838,583,988	82.41	11.67	2.32	1.99	0.77	0.41	0.38	0.05
Andhra Pradesh	66,508,008	89.14	8.91	1.83	0.03	0.03	0.04	n.a.	0.02
Andaman & Nicobar Islands	280,661	67.53	7.61	23.95	0.48	0.11	0.01	0.09	0.22
Arunachal Pradesh	864,558	37.04	1.38	10.29	0.14	12.88	0.01	36.22	2.04
Assam	22,414,322	67.13	28.43	3.32	0.07	0.29	0.09	0.62	0.40
Bihar	86,374,465	82.42	14.80	–	0.98	0.09	–	0.03	1.67
Chandigarh	642,015	75.84	2.72	0.99	20.29	0.11	0.24	0.01	0.01
Dadra & Nagar Haveli	138,477	95.48	2.41	1.51	0.01	0.15	0.38	20.59	–
Delhi	9,420,644	83.67	9.44	0.88	4.84	0.15	1.00	0.01	0.01
Goa, Daman & Diu	1,169,793	64.68	5.25	29.86	0.09	0.02	0.04	1.67	–
Gujarat	41,309,582	89.48	8.73	0.44	0.08	0.03	1.19	0.03	0.02
Haryana	16,463,648	89.21	4.64	0.10	5.81	0.01	0.21	–	0.02
Himachal Pradesh	5,170,877	95.90	1.72	0.09	1.01	1.24	0.20	–	0.02
Karnataka	44,977,201	85.45	11.64	1.91	0.02	0.16	0.73	0.01	0.08
Kerala	29,098,518	57.28	23.33	19.32	0.01	–	0.01	0.01	0.04
Lakshadweep	51,707	4.52	94.31	1.16	–	–	–	–	0.01
Madhya Pradesh	66,181,170	92.80	4.96	0.65	0.24	0.33	0.74	0.09	0.19
Maharashtra	78,937,187	81.12	9.67	1.12	0.21	6.39	1.22	0.13	0.14
Manipur	1,837,149	57.67	7.27	34.11	0.07	0.04	0.07	0.77	–
Meghalaya	1,774,778	14.67	3.46	64.58	0.15	0.16	0.02	16.82	0.14
Mizoram	689,756	5.05	0.66	85.73	0.04	7.83	–	0.27	0.42
Nagaland	1,209,546	10.12	1.71	87.47	0.06	0.05	0.10	0.48	0.01
Orissa	31,659,736	94.67	1.83	2.10	0.05	0.03	0.02	1.26	0.04
Pondicherry	807,785	86.16	6.54	7.23	–	0.01	0.06	–	–
Punjab	20,281,969	34.46	1.18	1.11	62.95	0.12	0.10	0.01	0.07
Rajasthan	44,005,900	89.08	8.01	0.11	1.48	0.01	1.28	–	0.03
Sikkim	406,457	68.37	0.95	3.30	0.09	27.15	0.01	0.09	0.04
Tamil Nadu	55,858,946	88.67	5.47	5.69	0.01	–	0.12	0.01	0.03
Tripura	2,757,205	86.50	7.13	1.68	0.03	4.67	0.01	–	–
Uttar Pradesh	139,112,287	81.70	17.33	0.14	0.48	0.16	0.13	0.01	0.01
West Bengal	68,077,965	74.72	23.61	0.56	0.08	0.30	0.05	0.67	0.01

REFERENCES

Ahmad, Aziz. 1964. *Studies in Islamic Culture in the Indian Environment*. Oxford: Clarendon Press.
Azad, Abul Kalam. 1962. *The Tarjuman al-Quran*. vol. 1. Ed. and trans. Syed Abdul Latif. Bombay: Asia.
Babb, Lawrence A. 1996. *Absent Lord: Ascetics and Kings in Jain Ritual Culture*. Berkeley: University of California Press.
Baird, Robert D., ed. 1995. *Religion in Modern India*. New Delhi: Manohar.
Bayly, Susan. 1989. *Saints, Goddesses and Kings: Muslims and Christians in South Indian Society*. Cambridge: Cambridge University Press.
Brockington, J.L. 1992. *The Sacred Thread: A Short History of Hinduism*. Delhi: Oxford University Press.
Census of India 1995. *Census of India 1991, Series I, India, Paper 1 of 1995: Religion*. New Delhi: Government of India.
Chatterjee, Margaret. 1983. *Gandhi's Religious Thought*. Notre Dame: University of Notre Dame Press.
Coward, Howard G., ed. 1987. *Modern India's Responses to Religious Pluralism*. Albany: State University of New York Press.
Dundas, Paul. 1992. *The Jains*. London: Routledge.
Durkheim, Emile. 1995. *The Elementary Forms of Religious Life*. Trans. Karen E. Fields, New York: The Free Press.
Flood, Gavin. 1996. *An Introduction to Hinduism*. Cambridge: Cambridge University Press.
Fuller, C.J. 1992. *The Camphor Flame: Popular Hinduism and Society in India*. Princeton, N.J.: Princeton University Press.
Gibbs, M.E. 1972. *The Anglican Church in India, 1600–1970*. Delhi: ISPCK.
Gold, Ann Grodzins. 1988. *Fruitful Journeys: The Ways of Rajasthani Pilgrims*. Berkeley: University of California Press.
Grewal, J.S. 1990. *The Sikhs of the Punjab*. Cambridge: Cambridge University Press.
Halbfass, Wilhelm. 1988. *India and Europe: An Essay in Understanding*. Albany: State University of New York Press.
Harvey, Peter. 1990. *An Introduction to Buddhism: Teaching, History and Practices*. Cambridge: Cambridge University Press.
Hawley, John Stratton and Donna Marie Wulff, eds. 1996. *Devi: Goddesses of India*. Berkeley: University of California Press.
Hiriyana, M. 1949. *The Essentials of Indian Philosophy*. London: Allen and Unwin.
Jones, Kenneth, W. 1989. *Socio-religious Reform Movements in British India*. Cambridge: Cambridge University Press.
Kapur, Rajiv. 1986. *Sikh Separatism: The Politics of Faith*. London: Allen and Unwin.
Khan, Muhammad Ishaq. 1994. *Kashmir's Transition to Islam: The Role of the Muslim Rishis*. New Delhi: Manohar.
Larson, Gerald James. 1995. *India's Agony Over Religion*. Albany: State University of New York Press.
Lingat, Robert. 1973. *The Classical Law of India*. Berkeley: The University of California Press.
Lorenzen, D.N. 1972. *The Kapalikas and Kalamukhas: Two Lost Shaivite Sects*. New Delhi: Manohar.
Madan, T.N. 1997. *Modern Myths, Locked Minds: Secularism and Fundamentalism in India*. Delhi: Oxford University Press.
Marglin, Frederique Apffel. 1985. *Wives of the God-king: The Rituals of the Devadasis of Puri*. Delhi: Oxford University Press.
Mathew, C.P. and M.M. Thomas. 1967. *The Indian Churches of Saint Thomas*. Delhi: ISPCK.
Metcalf, Barbara Daly. 1982. *Islamic Revival in British India: Deoband 1860–1900*. Princeton N.J.: Princeton University Press.
McLeod, W.H. 1968. *Guru Nanak and the Sikh Religion*. Delhi: Oxford University Press.

Mujeeb, Muhammad. 1967. *The Indian Muslims*. London: Allen and Unwin.

Parpola, A. 1994. *Deciphering the Indus Script*. Cambridge: Cambridge University Press.

Possehl, Gregory L., ed. 1982. *Harappan Civilization*. Delhi: Oxford University Press.

Ray, Asim. 1983. *The Islamic Syncretistic Tradition in Bengal*. Princeton N.J.: Princeton University Press.

Radhakrishnan, S. 1927. *The Hindu View of Life*. London: Allen and Unwin.

Rahman, Fazlur. 1979. *Islam*. 2nd edn. Chicago: The University of Chicago Press.

Ramanujan, A.K. 1973. Trans. *Speaking of Siva*. Baltimore: Penguin Press.

_____. 1981. *Hymns for the Drowning: Poems for Visnu by Nammalvar*. Princeton N.J.: Princeton University Press.

Rizvi, Saiyid Athar Abbas. 1978, 1982. *A History of Sufism in India*. vols 1 & 2. Delhi: Munshiram Manoharlal.

Smith, Donald Eugene. 1963. *India as a Secular State*. Bombay: Oxford University Press.

The Laws of Manu. 1991. Trans. Wendy Doniger and Brian K. Smith. New Delhi: Penguin Books.

Uberoi, J.P.S. 1996. *Religion, Civil Society and the State: A Study of Sikhism*. Delhi: Oxford University Press.

Visvanathan, Susan. 1993. *The Christians of Kerala: History, Belief and Ritual among the Yakoba*. Delhi: Oxford University Press.

Sects and Indian Religions

LAWRENCE A. BABB

The English term 'sect' derives its meanings from a specifically European context, and therefore many authorities reject the use of the term altogether in reference to Indian religions (McLeod 1978: 293). Nonetheless, the term can be usefully applied to Indian materials, with some qualification.

Following Ernst Troeltsch (1931: 331–43), social scientists tend to understand a 'sect' as a dissident movement that has split off from a 'church'. A church is a fully bureaucratized religious organization, dominant in its social milieu, that serves as a means of access to the sacred for a lay membership whose affiliation is usually by birth. A sect is a small offshoot of a church. Its relations with the secular world are tense, and recruitment to it—often involving a conversion experience—is voluntary. While sociologists of religion have modified this basic model (Stark and Bainbridge 1985), the church–sect dichotomy remains basic to the concept of sects in the writings of many social scientists. The problem with applying this definition to Indian materials is that India has never had anything remotely resembling a church. Nonetheless, students of Indian religions have long used the term 'sect' to describe certain very important religious groups and communities in India, and we shall continue this usage here.

The sects to be considered in the present chapter belong to Hindu (and to some extent Jain) traditions. As Renou (1968: 91–5) suggests, they tend to be defined by adherence to particular sacred books, the veneration of particular deities, and allegiance to their own philosophical viewpoints. They also typically trace their origins to some ascetic founder. These groups have never claimed the allegiance of the majority of those who are considered 'Hindu'. They have, however, been crucial in the forging and propagation of much of what is called 'Hinduism', and no account of Indian religions can be complete without taking them into account.

Analysis of such groups by social anthropologists has tended to focus on two related issues: the relationship between sects and caste on the one hand, and sects and world renunciation on the other. The views of the French anthropologist, Louis Dumont, have provided the context for much of this discussion.

According to Dumont (1970b), Hinduism is basically a religious/ritual expression of caste relations as modified by the goals and values of world renouncers. He argues that the man-in-the-world—the householder—possesses an identity primarily defined by membership in groups, pre-eminently castes. The renouncer leaves this social world behind; he now pursues his own liberation (*moksa*), and in so doing defines himself as an individual. Of necessity, however, he is an individual–outside–the–world, for the world of caste has no room for the normative (as opposed to the empirical) individual. He is Indian civilization's greatest creative force, a speculator, discoverer, and the inventor of India's great soteriologies. And his religious outlook has provided a civilizational alternative to caste-based (and ascribed) religious values.

In the opposition between those in and out of the world, the Brahmins have been left in a difficult position. As priests, they are settled in society, and the renouncer stands as a living rebuke to this comfortable existence. Orthodox Brahmins have therefore exhibited a 'subdued hostility' to renunciation (Dumont 1970b: 45), which they have always attempted to control. Although Olivelle (1993) has shown that the original system of *āś ramas*—dating from the fifth century BC or shortly after—was not intended to marginalize the renouncer, the later system of 'stages of life' was an obvious attempt to weaken the impact and organizing power of renunciation by relegating it to life's final chapter (Thapar 1982: 296–7). In the end, Brahmins adopted many of the innovations of the renouncers, but also acted as a conservative force.

Sects, for Dumont, are a distinctive product of the renouncer's project. Indian sects (in which category he includes Buddhism and Jainism) are founded by renouncers and tend to retain cores of renouncers. Because renouncers are preceptors not only to each other but to laymen, sects become media for the communication of the renouncer's outlook to the masses. Moreover—and this is a key contention—if the renouncer's values are central to sects, then it follows that sects must exist in a tense relationship with caste. Peter van der Veer (1989: 67) has pointed out that in Dumont's writings the role of 'church' in the usual definition of sect has been usurped by 'caste'. Dumont's view (1970b) is that because they reflect the outlook of renouncers, sects typically reject caste values, or at least do so in principle. But sect and caste nonetheless can and do coexist in a kind of cultural standoff. From the standpoint of the renouncer, caste is tolerable as an essentially worldly concern, having nothing to do with the quest for individual liberation. From the standpoint of the non-renouncer, sect membership is perceived as a fundamentally individual matter, based on personal choice, and thus 'superimposed' on the group status of caste.

As materials surveyed below will show, Dumont's general model works only imperfectly as a way of understanding the dynamics of Indian religions. Nonetheless, Dumont's view of the sect as an expression of the renouncer's values is a useful point of departure for our discussion. Renouncers have indeed played a key role in the development of India's sectarian traditions. Furthermore, by stressing the role of the renouncer we bring into the foreground one of the most important features of sectarian organization in India. Many sects (though not all) are based on a theory of social reproduction that mirrors worldly social structure but also represents a radical alternative to it. This is the principle of disciplic descent (*guru paramparā*).

Indian sects are commonly organized in a way that is strikingly similar to the structure of clans and lineages. The difference is that filiation and succession are not based on parentage but on the dyadic relationship between preceptor and disciple, *guru* and *śiṣya*. As Burghart (1978: 125–7) points out, the typical means by which a person joins a sect is by receiving a distinctive sacred verbal formula (*mantra*) and the person from whom it is received becomes the recipient's guru. The mantra is usually held to have originated with the sect's tutelary deity, often homologized with a human founder, and its passage from generation to generation becomes the basis for a clan-like group, with the tutelary deity in the position of apical ancestor. Such spiritual lineages can be segmented in the same manner as descent groups (Burghart:

134). A religious leader typically emerges as the founder of a sectarian sublineage by writing a commentary on a particular text, and by creating his own doctrines and spiritual method (*sādhanā*).

Disciplic descent thus emerges as a key feature of sects. And because of the great power of the descent metaphor, fictive kinship usually becomes the typical idiom of interpersonal relationships within sects (Gross 1992: 159–60). In its purest form, the guru–śiṣya relationship can be seen as a means of socio-spiritual reproduction employed by those whose manner of life forecloses the possibility of physical progeny. Celibacy, the drawing inward of reproductive power, makes possible reproduction of a parallel but fundamentally different kind.

Sectarian Clans and Lineages

Given the saliency of lineage or lineage-like structures in the organization of Indian sects, any attempt at systematic classification must begin by considering sectarian genealogies. But this can be no simple exercise in religious cladistics, for there is no overarching system in which all sects are embedded; there are, instead, various systems which might be likened to separate 'clans'. Moreover, the line between putative and historical descent is a hazy one. In some cases the analyst can detect lines of historical descent not acknowledged by the traditions themselves. In other cases, and perhaps most, recognized lines of descent are of doubtful historicity. Indeed it has been suggested (van der Veer 1989: 86–7) that, because of the hagiographic character of these genealogies, it is misleading to speak of the 'founding' of such groups at all.

Nonetheless, if we take sectarian descent as our starting point, then we see that most of the sects extant today in non-Muslim South Asia can be linked to—and derive their civilizational legitimacy from—a limited number of great sectarian clans. These clans partake of a general religious culture that is probably best called 'Indic'. Shared elements within this culture include the concept of rebirth, the idea of karmically determined destiny, and the goal of liberation from the cycle of transmigration, itself seen as a concatenation of karmic effects. An admiration for the world renouncer is also a feature of most of these traditions, as are some common modes of worship. The great sectarian clans have flourished within the medium of this culture, but have drawn from, shaped, and transmitted it in their own ways. Thus, the sectarian clans may be said to constitute a structural framework within which important religious 'subcultures' have developed and evolved.

One sectarian clan, usually considered to be separate from 'Hinduism', transmits the traditions known collectively as 'Jainism'. Jain communities consist of a core of initiated ascetics and attached laity. The ascetics belong to various disciplic lineages, all of which trace their descent to Lord Mahāvīra, the last Jina of our era and section of the universe. The great sectarian division among the Jains is between the Digambara and Śvetāmbara lineages, and is based on a point of monastic discipline, namely, whether or not monks should be nude. Within these major lineages there are further subdivisions.

On the Hindu side, it may be said that, from the perspective of the present, the principal sectarian clans are three in number. Historically, the greatest divide is between the Vaiṣṇavas and Śaivas, worshippers of Viṣṇu and Śiva (and their various forms and ancillary deities) respectively. These are not only great clusters of sectarian groups; they are also civilizational categories that for centuries have served to organize much of India's religious life. Another extremely important sectarian clan, one of particular importance from the modern perspective, is that of the poet-saints known as *Sants*. We shall now look at these major sectarian clans in greater detail.

Śaivas

Any account of Śaiva sectarian traditions must begin with the Pāśupatas and the closely related Kāpālika and Kālāmukha sects. These are ancient lineages that, though now extinct, have left important traces in the present. Śaiva Siddhānta is another Śaiva sect with very early roots, but unlike the aforementioned sects, it has survived to the present day. The most important contemporary Śaiva sects are three: the Lingāyats, the Nāth Yogīs, and the Daśnāmīs. Brief descriptions of these traditions follow.

The Pāśupatas (Lorenzen 1972) traced their descent to Lakulīśa, a somewhat obscure figure, held to be an incarnation of Śiva, who was probably born near Baroda during the second century. The Pāśupatas were noted particularly for their defiance of social norms, the purpose of which was apparently to provoke criticism so that the actor's sins could be unloaded on the critic, and also to create social isolation conducive to the cultivation of spiritual detachment (Lorenzen 1972: 187–8). By the Gupta times, there were apparently Pāśupata temples in most of India. The sect was in decline in north India by the eleventh century, but remained stronger in Karnataka.

The Kāpālikas and Kālāmukhas (Lorenzen 1972: 187–8) were closely related to the Pāśupatas. The Kāpālika sect probably originated in south India or the Deccan in the fifth or sixth century. During the next two hundred years it spread northward, but by the fourteenth century it had died out. It was a tantric sect whose presiding deity was Śiva in his fearsome Bhairava form, and it seems highly likely that elements of its beliefs and praxis were absorbed by other tantric sects such as the Nāth Yogīs and the Aghorīs. The Kālāmukha sect flourished in Karnataka during the eleventh to thirteenth centuries, and was probably descended from the Pāśupatas, to whose rituals and beliefs it adhered. It seems to have played some role in preparing the ground for the Lingāyat movement of later times.

Nowadays Śaiva Siddhānta is associated primarily with the Tamil region, but once it was a pan-Indian movement (Davis 1991). It first emerged as a distinguishable division within Śaivism around the ninth century, after which it became conventional to speak of four Śaiva traditions: Śaiva Siddhānta, Pāśupata, Kālāmukha, and Kāpālika. From the tenth century onward, Śaiva Siddhānta priests and ascetics were present in all regions of India, and even in Southeast Asia. The sect enjoyed substantial political backing, and vigorously propagated the Śaiva *āgamas*, the texts on which it based its authority. After the establishment of the Delhi Sultanate in 1206, Śaiva Siddhānta disappeared as an identifiable tradition in the north. The Lingāyat movement had by this time come to dominate the Deccan, with the result that Śaiva Siddhānta became basically a Tamil devotional tradition, to which the earlier poetry of the Nāyanmārs became linked. It remains an important philosophical school today, and its liturgical texts and ritual system are highly influential in south Indian temples. It has also become a vehicle for anti-Brahminism and Tamil nationalism (Ryerson 1983).

The Lingāyat or Vīraśaiva movement is a devotional Śaiva sect consisting of householders formally under the tutelage of an ascetic elite. A dominant community in many areas of northern Karnataka, the Lingāyats are best known for their custom of carrying personal iconic emblems of Śiva, *lingams*, given by their gurus at the time of initiation (Bradford 1985). This sect is often said to have been founded by Bāsava (chief minister to a Jain king) in the twelfth century, but it almost certainly existed before him, and in fact its relationship with preceding traditions is uncertain (Bhandarkar 1965; Nandimath 1979). It is possible that many converts to the sect were adherents of Jainism, then in decline. It is also possible that Lingāyats took over various *maṭhs* (monasteries) of the Kālāmukhas (Nandimath 1979: 6), and indeed the Lingāyats have been seen as a Kālāmukha offshoot (Lorenzen 1972). The Liṅgāyats rejected image worship, and strongly opposed caste and gender discrimination. Nonetheless, caste-like divisions emerged within the sect, a point to which we shall return.

The Nāth Yogīs or 'Jogīs' are an important Śaiva sect that has both ascetic and householder sections, and is prominent in contemporary north India (Briggs 1982; Ghurye 1964). The Nāths are promoters of the idea of physical immortality attained by means of transformation of the body through the 'yoga of force' (haṭhayoga), and in the popular imagination they are associated with occult powers. They are also notable for their humble origins and hostility to caste distinctions. They are sometimes called Gorakhnāthīs after Gorakhnāth, their most prominent spiritual ancestor, and also Kānphaṭā Yogīs because of the slits in their ears. They were probably influenced by tantric Buddhists, and as Ghurye suggests (1964: 128), they might indeed be a later version of the Kāpālikas. They trace disciplic descent from Śiva, whom they consider to be the Ādi Nāth, the 'original master' (nāth). The second Nāth was Macchendra, who is said to have initiated Gorakh, who probably lived between the ninth and twelfth centuries. Some contemporary Nāth Yogīs are peripatetic, while others live in monastic centres, of which the most important is at Gorakhpur; there are, however, many householder Nāths as well.

In connection with the Nāths, mention should be made of the Aghorīs (Gupta 1995; Parry 1985), who resemble both the Nāth Yogīs and Kāpālikas, and who are notorious for their radical defiance of social conventions. They trace their sectarian lineage to Kīnā Rām, whom they regard as an earthly descent, avatāra of Śiva, and who is said to have lived from 1608 to 1779 (Gupta 1995: 135). The leader of their āśrama in Banaras is, in turn, regarded as an avatāra of Kīnā Rām. Eight other monastic centres were established within a 150-mile range of Banaras, but are now in decline. Parry reports that currently there are probably no more than fifteen Aghorī ascetics in Banaras and its vicinity. Although recruitment is in theory open to all castes, Parry found that ascetics are recruited only from upper castes, and Gupta reports that most are of Rājpūt origin. Some Aghorī ascetics have large lay followings. According to Parry, lay followers are mostly upper-caste, middle class individuals who are attracted, often because of some personal crisis, by the Aghorīs' reputation for occult powers.

The elite of the Śaiva ascetics are the ten monastic lineages belonging to the Daśnāmī sect (Ghurye 1964; Gross 1992; Sarkar n.d.; Tripathi 1978). These are said to have been organized in the ninth century by Śaṅkarācārya, probably in recognition of the missionary powers of the renunciant orders of the Buddhists and Jains. As is well known, Śaṅkarācārya established monastic centres in four locations: Badrinath in the north, Puri in the east, Sringeri in the south, and Dvarka in the west. Each of the ten Daśnāmī lineages is assigned to one of these centres, although other Daśnāmī centres exist. Ascetics may either wander or live in such a centre. The Daśnāmīs also have a large lay following. According to Ghurye (1964: 92), Daśnāmī ascetics are drawn from the Brahmin, Kṣatriya and Vaiśya classes (varṇa), whereas Śūdras are relegated to the Nāgā section. The Daśnāmī Nāgās are the naked fighters of the Daśnāmīs. They are organized into centres (the most important numbering six) where they alone are resident (Ghurye 1964: 101–13; Sarkar n.d.: 82–108).

Vaiṣṇavas

The Vaiṣṇava tradition has been somewhat less rigid than the Śaiva in its conception of world renunciation, and has also been more tolerant of non-ascetic sectarian leadership. As van der Veer points out (1989: 75), this subcultural difference is reflected in an important terminological contrast. Śaiva ascetics are generally called Sannyāsīs, a term deriving from *sannyās* (renunciation). (They are also sometimes called Gosāis, although this term has begun to lose its specifically Śaiva denotation). Vaiṣṇava ascetics are called Bairāgīs, a term that derives from *vairāgya* (detachment), a stance that seems to harmonize better with the householder's life than the complete renunciation denoted by the Śaivas' sannyās.

Vaiṣṇavism first becomes historically visible in northern India with the emergence of the theistic Bhāgavata tradition in the second century BC. A later manifestation was the Pañcarātra movement, a devotional tradition whose principal texts date from the fifth to the tenth centuries, and that had a strong influence on subsequent Vaiṣṇava theology and methods of image worship. In south India, a tradition of fervent Vaiṣṇava devotionalism appeared in the poetry of the Āḻvārs from the seventh to ninth centuries, and important innovations in Vaiṣṇava philosophy were introduced by Rāmānuja in the eleventh century. In this southern milieu what are often called the four great 'orthodox' sects of Vaiṣṇavism, emerged.

These four sects all founded by ascetics, are known as the *catuḥ-sampradāya* (Bhandarkar 1965; Ghurye 1964; Gross 1992; Tripathi 1978). They are: the Śrī (or Śrīvaiṣṇava) Sampradāya; the Brahmā (or Mādhva) Sampradāya; the Rudra (or Viṣṇusvāmī) Sampradāya; and the Sanakādi (or Nimbārka) Sampradāya. The Śrī Sampradāya is associated with the doctrines of Rāmānuja (AD 1017–1137), its most illustrious *ācārya*. Basically a householder sect, its greatest importance today is in south India, where it is divided into northern and southern branches (see Appadurai 1981). The founder of the Brahmā Sampradāya was Madhvācārya (AD 1197–1276), who was a Daśnāmī ascetic who shifted his allegiance to Vaiṣṇavism. This order has very few ascetics now, although thee is a monastery at Udipi. The Rudra Sampradāya, originally a purely ascetic order, was founded by the somewhat obscure Viṣṇusvāmī, probably in the thirteenth century. It has few adherents currently, and only two important centres, at Brindavan and Pali (in Rajasthan). The Sanakādi Sampradāya was founded by a Telugu Brahmin, Nimbārka (d. 1162), who settled in Brindavan, which is the location of its most important monastic centre. Currently, its greatest influence is in Rajasthan, Uttar Pradesh, Nepal, and Bengal.

These sects had only a limited direct impact on north India, and even in the south only one of them (the Śrī Sampradāya) remains a strong presence. Nonetheless, they have great cultural importance because they have functioned as a frame of reference within which certain very important later north Indian Vaiṣṇava movements have placed themselves as a means of acquiring a general context in Vaiṣṇava religious culture and a pedigree of Vaiṣṇava sectarian descent. It is not possible to survey the prominent later Vaiṣṇava movements exhaustively in this brief chapter, but three—the Puṣṭimārg, the Caitanya sects, and the Rāmānandī ascetic order—are of sufficient historical and cultural importance to warrant separate discussion.

The Puṣṭimārg (Barz 1976; Jindel 1976; Pocock 1973: 94–121) is a Krishnaite sect with a large following in western India, especially in trading castes, and is a prominent example of a sect lacking a core of full ascetics. The term Puṣṭimārga means the 'path' of *puṣṭi* or 'support' or 'nourishment', and refers to Kṛṣṇa's grace that nourishes and supports the devotee. The sect was founded by Vallabhācārya (AD 1481–1533), a Telugu Brahmin, who—on the basis of divine inspiration from Kṛṣṇa himself—revealed the true identity of an image of Kṛṣṇa that had miraculously appeared atop Govardhan hill in Braj (see Barz 1976: 22–9). At the same time he created the sect's famous conversion formula in which the devotee surrenders all that he possesses—mind, body, and wealth—to Lord Kṛṣṇa.

Vallabhācārya is sometimes held to have belonged to a branch (itself said to have been founded by Nāmdev) of the Rudra Sampradāya (Ghurye 1964: 156–7; also Farquhar 1967: 315–16). This view was probably promoted at one time by the Puṣṭimārg, but nowadays the majority view within the sect is that although Vallabhācārya accepted the ācāryaship of the Rudra Sampradāya (at a late stage of his own career), he was in fact never in need of a guru himself (Barz 1976: 45). Vallabhācārya was a householder (although in 1531 he took ascetic vows), and produced two sons and eight grandsons. Succession to the sect's leadership devolved first to his eldest son, then to his second son, Viṭṭhalnāth, and then to Viṭṭhalnāth's seven sons, whose lines supplied the hereditary leadership of the sect's seven subdivisions (sāt ghar), the most important of which is headquartered at Nāthdvāra. In subsequent years there have been succession disputes and many other vicissitudes (Jindel 1976: 197–205; Pocock 1973: 118–20).

Both resembling and rivalling the Puṣṭimārga is the Svāminārāyaṇa sect (Williams 1984; Pocock 1973: 122–57). This sect, one of the most successful of India's modern religious movements, is principally active in Gujarat where it has a large multicaste following. Its Brahmin founder, Sahajānanda (1781–1829), was initiated by an ascetic named Rāmānanda (not to be confused with the legendary founder of the Rāmānandī sect); he, in turn, was originally initiated as a Śaiva Daśnāmī, but was converted to Rāmānuja's philosophy while on a visit to Srirangam, and is said to have been reinitiated by Rāmānuja in a dream. This group promotes a socially conservative Kṛṣṇa-oriented devotionalism, and although the sect has a strong core of celibate ascetics, its leadership is hereditary in the founder's family.

The Chaitanya movement (Bhandarkar 1965: 82–6; Dimock 1966) emerged in Bengal at about the same time as the Puṣṭimārg was founded. Although the connection is clearly post-facto, this sect (often called 'Gauḍīya') is sometimes said to be a section of Madhvācārya's Brahmā Sampradāya, thus linking it with the catuḥ-sampradāya (Ghurye 1964: 157–61). The movement's founder, Chaitanya (AD 1486–1533), became converted in his early twenties to a highly emotional and demonstrative form of devotion (*bhakti*) focused on the relationship between Rādhā and Kṛṣṇa and emphasizing singing and ecstatic dancing. He later became an initiated ascetic (possibly a Daśnāmī), and spent the remainder of his days at Puri. His earliest and closest disciple was Nityānanda, who was crucial to the organization of the sect, and who was probably strongly influenced by the tantric Sahajiyās (Dimock 1966: 46–53; Dasgupta 1976). Chaitanya sent two other disciples to Brindavan to establish temples there, and later they were joined by four others. These 'Six Gosvāmīs' developed the theology and literature of the Chaitanya movement, and the descendants of one of them (Gopāla Bhaṭṭa, a householder) carry the hereditary leadership of the Brindavan Chaitanyaites. The sect has ascetic orders and also a large lay following in Bengal, Assam, and Orissa.

In 1886, Bhaktivinode Thakur, a city magistrate in the city of Puri and superintendent of the famous Jagannāth temple, established an organization that claimed sectarian descent from the Six Gosvāmīs and was called the Śrī Viśva Vaiṣṇav Rāj Sabhā (on this and what follows, see Judah 1974: 39–45). Later, his son, who had been a college professor, succeeded to the leadership of the group, and in 1918 established the Gaudiya Math Institute and a number of Chaitanyaite missions. In turn, one of his disciples was A.C. Bhaktivedanta Svāmi Prabhupāda, who took ascetic vows in 1959 after a career as a manager of a chemical firm, and journeyed to New York in 1965 where he established the International Society for Krishna Consciousness (ISKCON, better known as the 'Hare Krishnas'). Though now in decline, this sect was once one of the most successful export versions of Hinduism.

Without question the most important Vaiṣṇava sect is the northern ascetic order known as Rāmānandī (also called Rāmāvat), probably the largest ascetic order in South Asia. The sect is dedicated to the worship of Rāma and Sītā, and central to its subculture is the *Rāmcaritmānas*, Tulsīdās's great vernacular rendering of the Rāmāyaṇa. Tulsīdās himself is often said to have

230 HANDBOOK OF INDIAN SOCIOLOGY

been a Rāmānandī (although probably he was not). The sect has important centres in Ayodhya, Chitrakut, and Janakpur (in Nepal), places associated with the Rāma legend.

The sect's putative founder is Rāmānand, whom the Rāmānandīs place in a disciplic genealogy that begins with Rāmachandra; indeed, they consider him to have been an avatāra of the deity. Little, however, is actually known about Rāmānand. His status as the founder of the sect and even his dates are uncertain (Burghart 1978). One authority (van der Veer 1989: 86) will conjecture only that he lived at some time between AD 1300 and 1500. A version of the Rāmānandīs' own account of their origin (van der Veer: 87–9) maintains that Rāmānand was a Kānyakubja Brahmin from Allahabad, and was initiated by a Śrīvaiṣṇava (Rāghavānand, Rāmānuja's fourth successor) in Banaras. However, because he ignored certain rules of purity the Śrīvaiṣṇavas, including his own guru, later denied him commensality. In reaction, he founded his own community in which membership would not be restricted on the basis of caste or sex; indeed, even Muslims were allowed.

If this account is true, then the Rāmānandīs are a branch of the Śrīvaiṣṇavas, and thus spiritual descendants of Rāmānuja. This belief has been long held by the Rāmānandīs themselves, but its historicity is extremely doubtful; in fact, the claim to linkage with the catuh-sampradāya probably arose when the Rāmānandī sect was coming into existence in the sixteenth century as a way of establishing a respectable pedigree (van der Veer: 173). The claim has also been disputed within the order. In an important conclave of Vaiṣṇava ascetics held at Galta in 1713 (to which we shall refer again), Rāmānand was elevated to the same level as Rāmānuja, and in 1921 Rāmānandī ascetics endorsed a newly discovered genealogy in which Rāmānuja does not appear at all (Burghart 1978: 130–2; Pinch 1996: 53–73; van der Veer 1989: 101–7). This view (not held unanimously) appears to have gained momentum because of alleged expressions of southern Śrīvaiṣṇava disdain for northern Rāmānandī ascetics, and has tended to be associated with a liberal view of caste and varna within the sect.

The Rāmānandī sect (Gross 1992; van der Veer 1989) consists of two great sections: a core of *sādhus* and their lay followers. The sādhus act as teachers for laymen. Laymen sometimes seek initiation, thus becoming disciples (śiṣyas) of particular ascetics, who are entitled to their material support. A layman can also become a sādhu by leaving his family and asking a sādhu to become his guru. Initiation is largely the same for sādhus and laymen, but with two important differences. First, the sādhu is pledged to celibacy, whereas the lay initiate is not. Second, although the lay initiate receives a new name, he also retains his old name, whereas the sādhu loses his personal and *gotra* names. To become a sādhu is to enter a new family, that of Rāmānandī sādhus, in which kinship terms are in fact used to express relationships. The Puṣṭimārg and Chaitanyaite sects possess hereditary Brahmin leadership, but nothing of the sort is found in the Rāmānandī sect, which—as van der Veer shows—is essentially a cluster of ascetic lineages and their lay followers. These lineages share identity as Rāmānandīs, a somewhat amorphous religious subculture, and a special relationship with their important centres (especially Ayodhya), but little else.

Three quite different institutionalized religious lifestyles coexist among Rāmānandī ascetics. The Tyāgīs are the hard-core ascetics. Celibate and peripatetic, their organization and praxis are much like those of the Nāth Yogīs (Burghart 1983b). Somewhat more sedentarized than the Tyāgīs are the Nāgās, the fighters, who are organized into 'armies' and 'regiments', and live in fortified temples. The Nāgās apparently arose in imitation of the Daśnāmī Nāgās in order to protect non-military Vaiṣṇavas from other ascetic orders during the great bathing festivals. The most sedentarized are the Rasiks, who practice a 'sweet devotion' modelled on the Kṛṣṇa cults of the Puṣṭimārgīs and the Chaitanyaites. They live in temples headed by live-in gurus; many of these have been previously married, and some have illegal wives.

'Don't ask about caste', egalitarian Rāmānand is said to have said, 'If you love God, you belong to God'. Indeed, in his famous early seventeenth-century *Bhaktamāl*, Nābhādās, himself a Rāmānandī, listed the weaver Kabīr and the cobbler Ravidās among Rāmānand's disciples. Nonetheless, van der Veer's study (1989) shows clearly that caste distinctions are of great importance today in the organization of Rāmānandī ascetics, especially among the highly sedentarized Rasiks. When wandering ascetics become sedentarized, they come under the continuing scrutiny of householders, who care about the caste origin of their gurus. The Rasiks are dominated by Brahmins; in their temples only members of the twice-born varnas are allowed to come into contact with divine images, and Brahmins alone cook in these temples and occupy leadership positions. Indeed, sādhus whose social origin is from low or untouchable castes have had to form their own groups within the larger Rāmānandī order.

Sants

Often mistakenly thought to be cognate with the English word 'saint', the term *sant* derives from *sat*, the 'true' or the 'real', and can be translated as 'one who has realized truth or ultimate reality' (Schomer 1987). When used in reference to sant traditions, the word has had two general meanings. First, it has been used to refer to the thirteenth- to eighteenth-century Vaiṣṇava 'poet-saints' of Maharashtra, who were devotees of the deity Viṭhobā (Viṭṭhal) at Paṇḍharpūr. It has also been used—and this is the sense in which it is used here—to refer to a group of figures from the Hindi-speaking northern region (including Rajasthan and Punjab) who, from the fifteenth century onward, were proponents of a style of devotionalism known as *nirguṇa bhakti*, devotion to the divine being conceived as formless and beyond all qualifications. They were usually of Hindu origin, but some were Muslims. They tended to be from the lower social strata. Mostly poor, uneducated, and unsophisticated, they expressed themselves in vernacular poetry, and their teachings became a rich source of sects.

The Sant tradition has often been said to be a form of Vaiṣṇava devotionalism, but it is clear that Vaiṣṇava influence, though important, is not as deep as was once thought to be the case (Vaudeville 1974, 1987). While Kabīr and Ravidās are often said (following Nābhādās) to have been disciples of Rāmānand, this is certainly factually incorrect. It is true that the Sants often used Vaiṣṇava names for God (Kabīr calls the Supreme being 'Rām'), and their poetry is filled with images drawn from Vaiṣṇava devotional traditions. But the Sant tradition rejects temple and image worship, the idea of divine incarnations, the authority of the Vedas, Brahminical priesthood, distinctions of caste, pilgrimage, and many other features of Vaiṣṇava orthodoxy. Nirguṇa devotion is actually prefigured in Śaivism, and in any case the Sant tradition has multiple sources, including Hindu devotional traditions, Sūfism, and the Nāth Yogīs.

The notion that there is a coherent body of distinctive Sant teachings (*sant mat*) and a common line of spiritual descent among Sants (*sant paramparā*) arose only in the mid-nineteenth century among followers of the Sants themselves. Given considerable impetus by the writings of P.D. Barthwal (1936), this view has also come to be accepted by scholars. Various *sant panths* (loosely, sects) are counted as belonging to the sant paramparā. Although they differ in highly significant ways, their commitment to nirguṇa bhakti and their hostility to Brahminical ritualism provide common ground, as does the strong focus on the figure of the guru as a personal spiritual master. They are, moreover, generally householder traditions, whose leaders have been laymen, not world renouncers.

The Sant tradition acknowledges no single 'founder', but certainly Kabīr (AD 1448/50–1518) was the most illustrious of the early Sants (Vaudeville 1974). Kabīr was an impoverished artisan of Banaras who had no formal education and was apparently a member of the Muslim Julaha (weaver) caste. His verse was sternly iconoclastic, earthy, testy, and direct. His disdain for ritualism, theologies, and sectarian squabbling of all kinds was total; for him the formless divine was completely beyond the limited understanding of particular creeds. Leaving aside Kabīr's deep influence on later Sants, his memory became the focus of a sect cluster, the Kabīrpanth, that has about 2.5 million mostly lower-caste and tribal followers in Madhya Pradesh and eastern Uttar Pradesh (Lorenzen 1987a: 292). It has two main branches, one headquartered at Banaras, and the other with two rival headquarters in the Chhattisgarh region of Madhya Pradesh (Lorenzen 1987a: 290–1). The Kabīrpanth today retains enough of Kabir's egalitarianism for Lorenzen (1987b) to characterize it as a form of 'non-caste Hinduism'.

In addition to Kabīr, three other Sants are usually considered to be among the towering figures of this tradition: Nānak (AD 1469–1539), Ravidās (fifteenth or sixteenth century), and Dādū (1544–1603). Nānak founded the tradition that was later to become Sikhism, arguably not a 'sect' but an important Indian 'religion' with over 13 million adherents. Dādū (Orr 1947) was born a Naddaf (Muslim cotton carder); he founded the Dādupanth, a sect that has both ascetic and lay sections, and is headquartered at Naraina near Jaipur. This sect developed a fighting Nāgā section that played an important role in the history of Jaipur state from the early eighteenth century. Ravidās (Singh 1977; Schaller 1995) belonged to the untouchable caste of Chamars (leatherworkers). His followers have come mainly from north India's lowest castes, especially the Chamar caste, and there is a strong element of social protest in the Ravidās movement. Under the aegis of the All-India Adi Dharm Mission (est. 1957), a temple for his worship is currently being built in Seer Govardhanpur, an untouchable neighbourhood in Banaras.

The Sant tradition underwent a significant revival in the nineteenth century. Under the influence of the relatively obscure Tulsī Sāhib of Hatras (1760–1843), Shiv Dayal Singh (1818–78) of Agra, a householder of Khatri origin, gathered around him a group of disciples who became the nucleus of a new Sant lineage known as Rādhāsoāmī (Babb 1986; Gold 1987; Juergensmeyer 1991). Whether Shiv Dayal Singh actually had a guru is contested within the tradition, but the movement he started clearly belongs within the family of Sant lineages. Subsequently the Rādhāsoāmī movement split into two major branches—one associated with Agra, the other with Punjab—each with various sub-branches. The Punjab branch has made important modifications of sectarian genealogy by promoting the view that Shiv Dayal Singh actually belonged to a specific spiritual lineage traceable to Gobind Singh, the tenth Sikh guru, and thus directly to Nanak.

The Rādhāsoāmī movement has had a special appeal to members of the urban middle class. Its leadership has tended to be socially progressive, and the movement as a whole has taken a generally egalitarian stance on caste. Nevertheless, caste status distinctions are reported to persist at many of the movement's centres (Juergensmeyer 1991: 116–20). The Punjab branch of the movement has been particularly vigorous in expanding its base of support, and has achieved remarkable success in proselytizing outside India (Juergensmeyer 1991: 52–5).

Outside the Lineages

There exist a number of important modern sects—and of course many more less prominent ones—that are not rooted in the classical lineages or traditions, and whose messages have often represented departures, in some cases radical, from sectarian mainstreams. Rammohun

Roy (1772–1833) attempted to synthesize Christian, Islamic, and Hindu traditions in his Brahmo Samaj, but with an emphasis on a recovery of the pure intellectuality of the Upaniṣads. The relatively quick demise of this movement suggests the dangers of excessive departure from established traditions. Rāmakṛṣṇa Paramahaṃsa (1836–86) was possibly initiated into the Puri lineage of the Daśnāmī order (Farquhar 1967: 357). In any case, the Ramakrishna Mission—the creation of his most celebrated disciple, Swami Vivekananda (1863–1902)—represented a new fusion of a Hindu spiritual outlook with an ethic of social service that has been widely admired in India and abroad.

Of all the modern sects, however, it is the Ārya Samāj, founded by Dāyananda Sarasvatī (1824–83), that has probably had the greatest actual impact on Indian society (Jones 1976). Although he himself was initiated into the Sarasvatī lineage of the Daśnāmī order, Dāyananda rejected that heritage, and his Ārya Samāj was essentially a revitalistic movement that attacked image worship and caste discrimination, promoted a return to Dāyananda's version of the pure religion of the Vedas, and supported the idea of active proselytization of non-Hindus. This movement has been enormously successful in north India, especially in Punjab.

Contexts

We now turn to the relationship between sects and their cultural and social contexts. We shall address the issue under three headings: the general relationship between sects and world renunciation; the specific relationship between sects and caste; and the relationship between sects and the authority of the state.

Renunciation

In considering the question of the relationship between sects and the world renouncer, it is useful to return to the issues raised by Louis Dumont. We must first ask about the viability of his radical dichotomization of the renouncer and the man-in-the-world, and here we find a number of problems. Das (1977: 42–51), for example, has argued persuasively that these two poles are mediated by the Brahmin; far from being a force-fed assimilator of ascetic values, the idealized Brahmin actually incorporates both poles. Moreover, there is a sense in which the ascetic, far from being radically opposed to the social order, actually internalizes it by identifying with the sacrificial principle from which society arises (Burghart 1983a: 639). At the level of actual conduct, we find that the line between renouncers, and non-renouncers is often hazy. Among Jains, for example, although there is a sharp boundary between laity and initiated ascetics, lay life is also deeply coloured by ascetic values (Babb 1996; Laidlaw 1995).

Furthermore, and concerning sects specifically, the materials we have surveyed show that Dumont's general model of the sect as centred on a core of world renouncers does not cover all cases. A number of important sects have rejected celibacy as a central ideal (Madan 1987: 9), and in some cases have developed hereditary leadership. Among the Vaiṣṇava lineages the Chaitanyaite tradition and the Puṣṭimārg are obvious examples. On the Śaiva side, the Liṅgāyat sect is a householders' movement. The Sant tradition has tended to emphasize the virtues of householdership. There was once a class of sādhus in the Rādhāsoāmī movement, but this was brought to an end at the turn of the twentieth century, reflecting a commitment to the idea that a male adherent should work to support himself and a family. Uberoi (1991: 327) shows that the Sikh initiation ceremony is precisely a 'renunciation of renunciation' (although there are ascetic orders among the Sikhs).

These considerations should not be allowed to divert us, however, from the fact that the world renouncer does play a special and central role in the world of Indian sects. As noted at the outset of this chapter, the very organization of much of the Indian sectarian world is based on the renouncer's principle of disciplic descent. Furthermore, even householder sects have often begun as renouncer orders or as movements founded by renouncers. Chaitanya's followers established temples, and leadership became hereditary within a Brahmin elite, but he was an ascetic himself. Vallabhācārya, founder of the Puṣṭimārg, appears to have been an initiated renouncer both before and after he produced sons. In addition, even sects completely embedded in a pro-householder ideology often promote renouncer values. The Rādhāsoāmī movement is a householder movement to its core, but its leaders are nonetheless deeply suspicious of sexuality; they allow sex in marriage, but constantly emphasize the need for 'control' (Juergensmeyer 1991: 131–4). And if the Sikhs renounce renunciation, there is also a sense in which the renouncer's outlook is included in a wider synthesis in which polity, householdership, and renunciation are jointly affirmed (Uberoi 1991: 330–2). Finally, sects that are primarily householder movements often have renouncer branches, as we see among the Lingāyats, Kabīrpanthīs, Sikhs, and elsewhere.

It should be noted also that, although full world renunciation has tended to be seen as an option for males, female ascetics are certainly part of the South Asian sectarian world. Among Śvetāmbara Jains, female ascetics (sādhvīs) actually considerably outnumber their male counterparts. In Jain tradition, however, female ascetics are decisively subordinated to male ascetics. The Brahmā Kumārīs are a sect (Śiva oriented, but apparently without older Śaiva lineage connections) of mostly renouncer females with a lay following of male and female householders. This group has explored the potential of world renunciation as a means of pursuing goals that are, in part, feminist (Babb 1986).

Few sects are fully intelligible unless the role of the renouncer is considered, but the renouncer's role is never the end of the matter either. Therefore, instead of seeing sects in their essence as expressions of renouncer values, it seems more useful to analyse them as settings in which renunciation and non-renunciation are often juxtaposed in a complex and sometimes tense relationship. The bedrock fact is that even purely ascetic orders must come into interaction with the world, and in so doing inevitably take something of the world into themselves. The process that van der Veer calls 'sedentarization' (1989: 70–182) seems to be a common trend. Among the Rāmānandīs, the peripatetic Tyāgīs approximate the pure ideal of the world renouncer, but the temple-dwelling Rasiks stick fast to particular places. In the case of the Rasiks, sedentarization has even led to 'domestication': celibacy has been compromised, and succession to leadership has been pushed in the direction of hereditary transmission. The all-important principle of disciplic succession, fundamental to the organization of ascetic orders, seems to fit well with the flux and flow of the peripatetic life, but becomes more difficult to maintain when residence is fixed.

The tension between renouncer and non-renouncer values in sects is dramatically illustrated by the cycles of degeneration and reform that have been characteristic of Jain history in both Śvetāmbara and Digambara traditions. For example, although the ideal of the peripatetic ascetic is central to Jainism, in medieval times a community of sedentary ascetics known as Chaityavāsīs (temple dwellers) appeared among the Śvetāmbaras (Babb 1996; Dundas 1992). They were ousted by a reformist movement in the eleventh century, and these reformers later became the source of a major ascetic lineage known as the Khartar Gacch. Later yet, within this lineage itself (and within others, too) a class of sedentary ascetics called Yatis came to dominate the scene. They, in turn, were pushed into near oblivion by twentieth-century reforms. The Jain case suggests that the ideal of the wandering ascetic—an image of extraordinary power and persistence in most South Asian religious cultures—will probably always be waiting in the wings as a powerful rebuke to those who slide into domesticity while maintaining pretensions to spiritual authority.

Caste

Closely related to the issue of sects and renunciation is the question of how sects relate to castes. If the sect is a distinctive organization of renouncers, and if renouncers are truly external to the system of castes, then—as Dumont's model suggests—the sect is in some sense the simple, polar 'other' of caste. But as we know, reality is more complex than this. Do sects necessarily reject caste? Are sects themselves free of internal caste distinctions? Do reformist sects generally succumb to the influence of caste values in the end (Srinivas 1952: 30)? Does the renouncer sect, as Uberoi eloquently puts it, 'become disheartened or lose the point of its protest, and even end by seeking to re-enter the house of caste through the back door?' (1991: 330). These are some of the important questions that the student of Indian sects must address.

Regarding the question of whether caste is present within sects, it is clear that caste often manifests itself strongly in sects. The Svāminārāyaṇ sect of Gujarat is an example of a sect that has apparently found it easy to coexist with an internal caste hierarchy. Although there has been some weakening of caste distinctions among adherents, the sect's constituent castes have maintained commensal and connubial separation from each other, and sectarian and non-sectarian branches of each caste continue to intermarry (Williams 1984: 147–50). Caste can also be present in ascetic orders. For example, Peter van der Veer's (1989) work on the Rāmānandīs shows clearly that the caste origin of a sādhu is important in determining his status among other sādhus.

Juxtaposing sect, renunciation, and caste, Burghart (1983a: 640–2) has shown that in fact four distinct patterns can be shown to exist in Indian sects. First, sects can combine a strong emphasis on renunciation with a recognition of caste, either in recruitment (such as the Daśnāmī Sannyāsīs), or by recognition within the sect (the Rāmānandīs in later times). Second, a strong emphasis on renunciation can also be combined with castelessness (Burghart suggests the early Buddhists as one example). Third and fourth, sects may also downplay or refuse to recognize the distinction between renouncer and householder, and this can be done in a way that does (the Puṣṭimārg) or does not (the Ravidāsīs) recognize caste.

W.H. McLeod (1978) has proposed that when sect and caste mingle there are three possible outcomes: that the caste divides into sectarian and non-sectarian sections, that the sect actually becomes a caste, or that the sect reproduces the caste system within itself. Examples of each possibility are not hard to find. The Jains of western India illustrate the division of caste by sect, for, as Dumont points out, here we find Hindu and Jain sections of the same castes (1970b: 188). The Satnāmī sect of the Chhattisgarh region of Madhya Pradesh is a sect that is (and in a sense was from the start) a caste (Babb 1972; Grant 1870: 100–03). Founded between 1820 and 1830 by a visionary named Ghāsī Dās (whose teachings were undoubtedly inspired by Jagjivan Dās [1669–1760]), the sect was in essence a mobility movement among Chamars. By the time Ghāsī Dās died in 1850, the Satnāmī sect had in effect become the Chamar caste under a new name.

Although the Lingayat sect of Karnataka rejected caste normally, it is often said to be a sect that actually duplicated the caste system within itself; indeed, Dumont argues that in this case the sect 'replaced Brahminism', becoming a 'reference group' for a caste system distinct from that of the Hindus (1970a: 188–91). From N.J. Bradford (1985) we learn that the Lingayats of northern Karnataka are divided into about eighty endogamous *jātis*. The functional equivalent of the Brahmin varṇa is the class known as Jangamma, who function as priests and preceptors of other Lingayats, and are considered to be embodiments of Śiva himself. The Jangamma, in turn, are divided into two classes. One consists of those who trace patrilineal descent from five putative original Vīraśaiva gurus; they are associated with a hierarchy of maṭhs to which non-Jangamma Lingayats have patrilineally inherited links of 'discipleship'. The other class consists of ascetic gurus whose maṭhs were traditionally situated outside inhabited areas, and who were seen as a class of Lingayat renouncers; discipleship with them was voluntary. Succession to leadership positions among the non-ascetic Jangamma was hereditary; among the ascetics it was by means of guru-śiṣya ties.

According to Bradford (1985: 94–101), in this century the ascetic class has replaced the non-ascetic class as the leadership of the community, reflecting the inability of the more rigidly organized non-ascetics to adjust to rapid social and cultural change. Here, it seems, the renouncer has emerged as the most viable 'agent of transformation' of Lingayat society.

Is it possible for ascetic orders—that is, sects that are not householder oriented—to generate castes or caste-like offshoots? While there is no reason to believe that such a process is inevitable, there are important instances of such castes. For example, there are householder Rāmānandī castes in western India, apparently formed by individuals who were unable to re-enter their castes of origin after lapsing from sādhuhood, and the householder Gosāi castes probably consist of ex–Daśnāmī sādhus (van der Veer 1989: 72).

The householder Nāths (A. Gold 1988, 1992; D. Gold 1996) provide us with perhaps the best example of a caste produced by an ascetic order as a by-product. In Rajasthan, the householder Nāths constitute a middle-ranking, landowning agricultural caste; elsewhere their traditional occupation is often public performance. They are a caste among other castes, but they also possess certain distinctive attributes. They bury rather than burn their dead, as do ascetics generally; they also sometimes serve as gurus to other castes and as priests in some temples and shrines. They have a reputation for special powers, as is befitting their status as Nāths. From the standpoint of non-householder Nāths, the householders are seen as degraded versions of the real thing; the householders, however, see themselves as authentic Nāths.

Of particular interest is the fact that the Nāths distinguish householders from full ascetics in terms of the all-important idiom of descent (D. Gold 1996). Both householder and non-householder Nāths are organized into lineages and sublineages. Nāths speak of a special divine sound, *nād*, which is heard in meditation. Disciplic succession among ascetics is called *nād paramparā*, succession through sound, in reference to the mantra passed from guru to disciple. Hereditary succession among householders, by contrast, is called *bīj paramparā* or *bindu paramparā*. *Bīj* and *bindu* refer to seed or semen, but they are also technical terms of yoga, in effect uniting householder and non-householder Nāths as co-sectarians, while also differentiating them at another level.

Politics

The current spectacle of sādhus making fiery political speeches might strike observers as incongruous at first glance, but in truth India's sects, including the ascetic orders, have always interacted with economic and political structures. It seems highly unlikely that the purely solitary, truly extra-social world renouncer has ever been much more than a civilizational ideal (albeit one of great importance). Even those individuals most committed to the renouncer's path must traffic with the world at some level, and when renouncers themselves form groups, the need to engage in transactions with the wider social world becomes all the more compelling. Such groups must find ways of obtaining material support, and this inevitably requires institutionalizing relationships with lay communities and political powers. They must also compete with one another for disciples, territory, pilgrimage centres, political patronage, and material resources.

The involvement of sects in India's political and economic affairs is dramatically illustrated by the development of militant asceticism (see Ghurye 1964: 98–113; Pinch 1996: 24–30; van der Veer 1989: 130–59). While the exact chronology is unclear, it appears that Nāgā militants first appeared among the Daśnāmīs, and later—probably in self-defence against Śaiva militants— among the Vaiṣṇavas. By the eighteenth century north Indian ascetic orders were deeply involved in trade and professional soldiering, and of course these activities are connected. Ascetics made ideal long-distance traders, in part because of their mobility, and in part because of their ready-made infrastructure of pilgrimage routes and maṭhs (Cohn 1964). The absence of compulsions to engage in conspicuous consumption probably also gave its own impetus to capital formation among these groups. Although Śaiva Daśnāmīs seem to have been the most prominent in trade, Dādupanthīs, Sikhs, and Vaiṣṇava Rāmānandīs were also notable participants. Pre-adaptation to ascetic military organization resulted from the fact that sādhus had borne arms in the course of trade; it is an easy transition from mobile bands of armed sādhu-traders to military formations. Recruitment was aided by the fact that monastic military organization provided a means for men of humble social origin to enter Śaiva and Vaiṣṇava monastic organizations (Pinch 1996: 26).

Once ascetic military formations exist, it is but a short step to the ascetic as hired mercenary, as we see in the case of the Nāgā Dādupanthīs (among others), who became tax farmers for, and defenders of, Jaipur state (Orr 1947: 199–208). When sects serve rulers they ineluctably become involved in affairs of state. A well-known example is Jodhpur state in the nineteenth century (D. Gold 1995). Notoriously, the Nāth Yogīs exercised great power over Maharaja Man Singh, ruler of Jodhpur from 1803 to 1843, who himself had a Nāth guru. At first the Nāths' role was primarily military; later Ayas Dev Nāth, Mān Singh's guru, was actually managing the state's day-to-day affairs. Inevitably, armed ascetics also came into conflict with the East India Company; the result was the series of conflicts in Bengal and Bihar in the late eighteenth century known as 'the fakir and sannyasi uprisings' (A.K. Dasgupta 1992).

One of the most important sectarian legacies in contemporary Indian politics was left by the Rāmānandīs, who flourished more than any other sect during the eighteenth and nineteenth centuries. One important ingredient in later events was a reformist view of caste discrimination. As we know, the Rāmānandīs were and are ambivalent on the matter of caste. Caste organizes the sect in important ways, but legendary Rāmānand himself is associated with a liberal and generous tradition of egalitarianism. The sect's inconsistency on these issues was reflected by events at the famous Vaiṣṇava conference at Galta in 1713 (the same conference at which the organization of Vaiṣṇava Nāgās is said to have been set in place) (Pinch 1996: 61–80). On the one hand, it was decided that Rāmānand's (alleged) female and non-twice-born followers would be ineligible to transmit the tradition (that is, disciplic succession could not emanate from such figures as Kabir). But on the other hand, the conference ratified an egalitarian social vision by removing Rāmānuja from the guru paramparā, a step which ultimately led to the complete severing of links with the traditionalist Rāmānujīs in the early twentieth century. This latter move was representative of a radical sub-tradition within the Rāmānandī fold that could and did provide a highly supportive environment for the later efforts of stigmatized groups to seek social justice.

Another development of great importance occurred among the Rāmānandīs more or less at the same time. This was the emergence of a powerful mythical–historical vision to which the city of Ayodhya was symbolically central. It is important to note that, in fact, the Rāmānandī advent at Ayodhya was relatively late, for they were not actually established there until the eighteenth century. Prior to that, the Daśnāmīs appear to have been the dominant sect in Ayodhya (van der Veer 1989: 142–5). As Pinch has shown (1996: Ch. 2), the myth-history promulgated by the Rāmānandīs centred on the idea of Muslim tyranny as the cause of Hindu decline before the advent of Rāmānand. In this same vision, Ayodhya itself became symbolically central to the cult of Rāma. Rāma and Rāmānand both emerged as hero-saviours of 'Hindu' India.

Interacting with these trends was another, which was not directly connected with the Rāmānandī sect, but was extremely important in intensifying the importance of Ayodhya in the politics of the region. This was the Kshatriya reform movement of the late nineteenth and early twentieth centuries (Pinch 1996: 81–147). Claims to Kshatriya ancestry arose mainly among Kūrmī and Yādav peasants in Bihar and eastern Uttar Pradesh. In a sense, these claims echoed Rāmānandī ambivalence on caste: they arose from a sense of social injustice, but they were finally disharmonic with the egalitarianism of the Rāmānandī radicals (because of the emphasis on Kshatriya pedigrees). But more important, and as Pinch has convincingly argued, they arose within, and were made plausible by, a specifically Vaiṣṇava frame of reference. That is, the claims to Kshatriya identity drew deeply from the resurgent Vaiṣṇava religious culture of the eighteenth and nineteenth centuries, that the Rāmānandīs were so energetic in promoting. In the context of the culture of the time and region, to be Kshatriya was to be Vaiṣṇava, because it was to link one's own group with the genealogies of Ramachandra and Krishna.

This history sheds considerable light on why and how Ayodhya could later be used (though its use was certainly not inevitable) by Hindu nationalists as a means of mobilizing support, and it also helps us understand why, in the upheavals, of the late twentieth century, the Rāmānandīs might turn out to be the 'main actors' at the local level in Ayodhya (van der Veer 1995: 300). By stressing the idea of descent from Vaiṣṇava deities, the Kshatriya reform movement put unprecedented emphasis on the need for physical birthplaces for Ramachandra and Krishna. It also reinforced the myth-model image of Muslim destructiveness, for in this vision of things the Muslims could be portrayed as the destroyers of the sacred lineages to which new claims of affiliation were being made. After the 1940s, the politics of Kshatriya identity waned as the groups in question gradually shifted to an alternative politics of social victimhood. But the historical vision from which Kshatriya reform drew its strength has remained alive to the present day, and has become an important element in the world-view of some Hindu nationalists.

REFERENCES

Appadurai, Arjun. 1981. *Worship and Conflict Under Colonial Rule: A South Indian Case*. Cambridge: Cambridge University Press.

Babb, Lawrence A. 1972. 'The Satnamis—Political Involvement of a Religious Movement'. In J. Michael Mahar, ed., *The Untouchables in Contemporary India*, 143–51. Tucson: University of Arizona Press.

———. 1986. *Redemptive Encounters: Three Modern Styles in the Hindu Tradition*. Berkeley: University of California Press.

Babb, Lawrence A. 1996. *Absent Lord: Ascetics and Kings in a Jain Ritual Culture*. Berkeley: University of California Press.

Barthwal, P.D. 1936. *The Nirguna School of Hindi Poetry: An Exposition of Medieval Indian Santa Mysticism*. Benares: Indian Book Shop.

Barz, Richard. 1976. *The Bhakti Sect of Vallabācārya*. Faridabad: Thompson Press.

Bhandarkar, R.G. [1913] 1965. *Vaiṣṇavism, Śaivism and Minor Religious Systems*. Reprint. Varanasi: Indological Book House.

Bradford, N.J. 1985. 'The Indian Renouncer: Structure and Transformation in the Lingayat Community'. In Richard Burghart and Audrey Cantlie, eds, *Indian Religion*, 79–103. New York: St Martin's Press.

Briggs, George Weston. [1938] 1982. *Gorakhnāth and the Kānphaṭa Yogīs*. Reprint. Delhi: Motilal Banarsidass.

Burghart, Richard. 1978. 'The Founding of the Ramanandi Sect'. *Ethnohistory*. 25(2):121–39.

———. 1983a. 'Renunciation in the Religious Traditions of South Asia'. *Man*. 18(4):635–53.

———. 1983b. 'Wandering Ascetics of the Rāmānandī Sect'. *History of Religions*. 22(4):361–80.

Cohn, Bernard S. 1964. 'The Role of the Gosains in the Economy of Eighteenth and Nineteenth Century Upper India'. *Indian Economic and Social History Review*. 1:175–82.

Das, Veena. 1977. *Structure and Cognition: Aspects of Hindu Caste and Ritual*. Delhi: Oxford University Press.

Dasgupta, Atis K. 1992. *The Fakir and Sannyasi Uprisings*. Calcutta/New Delhi: K.P. Bagchi & Company.

Dasgupta, Shashibhusan. 1976. *Obscure Religious Cults*. Reprint of third edition. Calcutta: Firma KLM Private Limited.

Davis, Richard H. 1991. *Ritual in an Oscillating Universe: Worshipping Śiva in Medieval India*. Princeton: Princeton University Press.

Dimock, Edward C. 1966. *The Place of the Hidden Moon: Erotic Mysticism in the Vaiṣṇava-Sahajiyā Cult of Bengal*. Chicago: University of Chicago Press.

Dumont, Louis. 1970a. *Homo Hierarchicus: The Caste System and Its Implications*. Trans. Mark Sainsbury. Chicago: University of Chicago Press.

———. 1970b. 'World Renunciation in Indian Religions'. In Louis Dumont, ed., *Religion/Politics and History in India*, 33–60. Paris/The Hague: Mouton Publishers.

Dundas, Paul. 1992. *The Jains*. London: Routledge.

Farquhar, J.N. [1920] 1967. *An Outline of the Religious Literature of India*. Reprint. Delhi: Motilal Banarsidass.

Ghurye, G.S. 1964. *Indian Sadhus*. 2nd edn. Bombay: Popular Prakashan.

Gold, Ann. 1992. *A Carnival of Parting: The Tales of King Bharthari and King Gopi Chand as Sung and Told by Madhu Natisar Nath of Ghatiyali, Rajasthan*. Berkeley: University of California Press.

———. 1988. *Fruitful Journeys: The Ways of Rajasthani Pilgrims*. Berkeley: University of California Press.

Gold, Daniel. 1987. *The Lord as Guru: Hindi Sants in North Indian Tradition*. Oxford: Oxford University Press.

———. 1995. 'The Instability of the King: Magical Insanity and the Yogis' Power in the Politics of Jodhpur, 1803–1843'. In David N. Lorenzen, ed., *Bhakti Religion in North India: Community Identity and Political Action*, 120–32. Albany (N.Y.): State University of New York Press.

Gold, Daniel. 1999. 'Nath Yogis as Established Alternatives: Householders and Ascetics Today'. *Journal of Asian and African Studies*. 34(1):68–88. March.

Grant, Charles, ed. 1870. *The Gazetteer of the Central Provinces of India*. 2nd edn. Bombay: Education Society's Press.

Gross, Robert. 1992. *The Sadhus of India: A Study of Hindu Asceticism*. Jaipur and New Delhi: Ravat Publications.

Gupta, Roxanne. 1995. 'The Kīnā Rāmī: Aughars and King in the Age of Cultural Contact'. In David N.

Lorenzen, ed., *Bhakti Religion in North India: Community Identity and Political Action*, 132–42. Albany (N.Y.): State University of New York Press.

Jindel, Rajendra. 1976. *Culture of a Sacred Town: A Sociological Study of Nathdwara*. Bombay: Popular Prakashan.

Jones, Kenneth W. 1976. *Arya Dharm: Hindu Consciousness in 19th Century Punjab*. Berkeley: University of California Press.

Judah, J.S. 1974. *Hare Krishna and the Counterculture*. New York: John Wiley & Sons.

Juergensmeyer, Mark. 1991. *Radhasoami Reality: The Logic of a Modern Faith*. Princeton: Princeton University Press.

Laidlaw, James. 1995. *Riches and Renunciation: Religion, Economy, and Society among the Jains*. Oxford: Oxford University Press.

Lawrence, Bruce B. 1987. 'The Sant Movement and North Indian Sufis'. In Karine Schomer and W.H. McLeod, eds, *The Sants: Studies in a Devotional Tradition of India*, 359–73. Berkeley: University of California Press.

Lorenzen, David N. 1972. *The Kāpālikas and Kālāmukhas: Two Lost Śaivite Sects*. Berkeley: University of California Press.

———. 1987a. 'The Kabir-Panth and Social Protest'. In Karine Schomer and W.H. McLeod, eds, *The Sants: Studies in a Devotional Tradition of India*, 281–303. Berkeley: University of California Press.

———. 1987b. 'Traditions of Non-caste Hinduism: The Kabir Panth'. *Contributions to Indian Sociology* (n.s.). 21(2):263–83.

Madan, Triloki N. 1987. *Non-Renunciation: Themes and Interpretations of Hindu Culture*. Delhi: Oxford University Press.

McLeod, W.H. 1978. 'On the Word *Panth*: A Problem of Terminology and Definition'. *Contributions to Indian Sociology* (n.s.). 12(2):287–95.

Nandimath, S.C. [1942] 1979. *A Handbook of Vīraśaivism*. Revised version of 1942 edition. Delhi: Motilal Banarsidass.

Olivelle, Patrick. 1993. *The Āśrama System: The History and Hermeneutics of a Religious Institution*. New York: Oxford University Press.

Orr, W.G. 1947. *A Sixteenth-Century Indian Mystic: Dadu and His Followers*. London: Lutterworth Press.

Parry, Jonathan P. 1985. 'The Aghori Ascetics of Benares'. In Richard Burghart and Audrey Cantlie, eds, *Indian Religion*, 51–71. New York: St Martin's Press.

Pinch, William R. 1996. *Peasants and Monks in British India*. Berkeley: University of California Press.

Pocock, David F. 1973. *Mind, Body and Wealth: A Study of Belief and Practice in an Indian Village*. Totowa (N.J.): Rowman & Littlefield.

Renou, Louis. 1968. *Religions of Ancient India*. First Schocken edition. New York: Schocken Books.

Ryerson, Charles A. 1983. 'Contemporary Śaivism and Tamil Identity: An Interpretation of Kunrakkuṭi Aṭikalār'. In Fred W. Clothey and J. Bruce Long, eds, *Experiencing Siva: Encounters with a Hindu Deity*, 177–88. New Delhi: Manohar Publications.

Sarkar, Sir Jadunath n.d. *A History of Dasnami Naga Sanyasis*. Allahabad: Sri Panchayati Akhara Mahanirvani.

Schaller, Joseph. 1995. 'Sanskritization, Caste Uplift, and Social Dissidence in the Sant Ravidās Panth'. In David N. Lorenzen, ed., *Bhakti Religion in North India: Community Identity and Political Action*, 94–119. Albany (N.Y.): State University of New York Press.

Schomer, Karine. 1987. 'Introduction: The Sant Tradition in Perspective'. In Karine Schomer and W.H. McLeod, eds, *The Sants: Studies in a Devotional Tradition of India*, 1–17. Berkeley: University of California Press.

Singh, Darshan. 1977. *Sant Ravidas and His Times*. Delhi: Kalyani Publishers.

Stark, Rodney and William Sims Bainbridge. 1985. *The Future of Religion: Secularization, Revival, and Cult Formation*. Berkeley: University of California Press.

Srinivas, M.N. 1952. *Religion and Society Among the Coorgs of South India*. Oxford: Oxford University Press.

Thapar, Romila. 1982. 'The Householder and the Renouncer in the Brahmanical and Buddhist Traditions'. In T.N. Madan, ed., *Way of Life: King, Householder, Renouncer*, 273–98. New Delhi: Vikas Publishing House.

Tripathi, B.D. 1978. *Sadhus of India: The Sociological View*. Bombay: Popular Prakashan.

Troeltsch, Ernst. 1931. *The Social Teaching of the Christian Churches*. 2 vols. Trans. Olive Wyon. London: George Allen & Unwin Limited.

Uberoi, J.P.S. 1991. 'Five Symbols of Sikh Identity'. In T.N. Madan, ed., *Religion in India*, 320–32. Delhi: Oxford University Press.

van der Veer, Peter. [1988] 1989. *Gods on Earth: The Management of Religious Experience and Identity in a North Indian Pilgrimage Centre*. Reprint of 1988 edition, Athlone Press. Delhi: Oxford University Press.

———. 1995. 'The Politics of Devotion to Rama'. In David N. Lorenzen, ed., *Bhakti Religion in North India: Community Identity and Political Action*, 288–305. Albany (N.Y.): State University of New York Press.

Vaudeville, Charlotte. 1987. 'Sant Mat: Santism as the Universal Path to Sanctity'. In Karine Schomer and W.H. McLeod, eds, *The Sants: Studies in a Devotional Tradition of India*, 21–40. Berkeley University of California Press.

———. 1974. *Kabīr*. vol. I, Oxford: Oxford University Press.

Williams, Raymond B. 1984. *A New Face of Hinduism: The Swaminarayan Religion*. Cambridge: Cambridge University Press.

Performances

HEIDRUN BRÜCKNER AND ELIZABETH SCHÖMBUCHER

PERFORMANCES IN THE SOCIAL SCIENCES

The term 'performance' encompasses a wide range of cultural events, from various theatrical performances, performing arts, or the performance of an oral text, to a number of rituals and, eventually, to any speech event. The inclusion of plural events under a single concept of 'performance' is the result of a changing methodological approach in the social sciences. Emphasis has shifted from studying social institutions or texts, to actors and their creative potentiality. Since Milton Singer's (1972: 64), often-quoted statement that religious and cultural performances should be viewed as 'the elementary constituents of the culture and the ultimate units of observation' the 'performance approach' has been further developed by various social scientists. Whereas some performance theorists such as Victor Turner (1982) and Richard Schechner (1985) take theatrical performances on stage and the theatrical potential of social life as their starting point, others, such as Baumann and Briggs (1990), apply the term 'performance' in a linguistic sense to any speech event, whether artful and elaborated or just everyday verbal interaction. According to the latter approach, language (or rather speech) is not only seen in its referential or indexical function, but any use of language is interpreted as 'social action' in which 'things are done with words' (Austin 1962). For speech act theorists, such as Austin, the elocutionary force of an utterance is not simply a product of its referential content, but depends on various conditions of the whole performance of the utterance, such as the setting, the intentionality of the speaker, his status and authority, and the conventions that are followed by the participants (Austin 1962).

Both the theatrical and the linguistic approaches open up new perspectives in the interpretation of culture. Cultural performances, such as rituals, ceremonies, carnival and theatre, but also performances in the linguistic sense, so-called speech events, can be seen as interpretations of social life by the actors themselves (Turner 1982). In a sense, culture is encapsulated within these discrete performances (Bell 1992) and is then exhibited to the participants as well as to outsiders. Each performance is a highly structured event which enables the observer to get an encompassing view of it (Singer 1972: 64). A cultural performance is a 'stage', meaning that space and time are specified, the sequence of events fixed, participants, performers and audience and specific roles assigned to. Similar characteristics apply to speech events. The use of language is seen as a communicative process in which it is not just the 'text' with its poetic or aesthetic qualities, that is of importance—the ethnography of speaking has now established several other important criteria for analysing speech events. For the interpretation of the meaning of a linguistic performance, it is important to consider, in addition to the content of the speech event, the sender as well as the receiver of linguistic utterances, the mode of transmission, and the scenario of the communication (Hymes 1962).

However, it is not as easy for the outsider to read a public performance just like a text, as, for instance, Geertz (1972) and Singer (1972: 64) propose. The most crucial aspect in the performance approach, the shift from the study of texts to the analysis of texts in contexts, leads to another problem. Who is going to define 'context'? What should be included? What can be excluded? To avoid reifying 'context' by describing everything that surrounds a set of utterances and seems adequate for selection by the analyst, Baumann, and Briggs (1990: 69) demand that one should 'study the textual details that illuminate the manner in which participants are collectively constructing the world around them'. The shift should not only be towards studying texts in context, but 'Towards achieving an agent-centered view of performance' to show how performers and audiences contextualize their text (Baumann and Briggs 1990: 69). Baumann and Briggs's demand for contextualization in the sense of an agent-centred view of performance leads to a number of aspects which have to be included in the study of a performance. Despite the risk of reifying, they shall be summarized here.

The Setting

The setting of a performance includes time and space as well as the course of events and the persons involved. Each cultural performance is set apart from day-to-day social life by time and space. Many rituals and theatre performances are on the occasion of seasonal festivals which are celebrated according to a fixed calendar. But even in occasional rituals, certain preconditions regarding time have to be followed. Moreover, time is defined as extraordinary by the very fact that a ritual or theatre performance takes place in it. The possibilities for defining space as extraordinary are manifold. The stage in a theatrical performance, or the temple in the case of a ritual, is easily recognized as distinct or demarcated space. However for social dramas in Turner's (1982) sense or in less elaborated ritual events such as possession mediumship or spirit possession, for instance, space has to be created—be it the open space for the negotiation of a conflict before an audience of neighbours and relatives, or the sacred space which can be created by purification in any house before inviting the deity to enter the body of the medium for a possession séance.

The course of events of a performance is supposed to be fixed, despite the variations caused by an individual performer. It can be remembered and at the same time anticipated by the participants and audience. This applies to ritual, theatre and the performance of oral texts. To be efficacious, certain parts of a ritual may not be omitted, whereas others are more open to individual changes by the performer. Albert Lord (1964: 16f) has already emphasized the interaction between performers and audience in oral composition. Not only do the length and complexity of an oral composition depend on the reaction and feedback of the audience, so do the composition's poetic and artistic qualities. But even if the performance is shortened and some parts are omitted, its overall character must be recognized as the same. The evaluation of the artistic and communicative competence of performers by the audience is crucial for the estimation and impact of a performance. The persuasiveness and effectiveness of ritual performances depend especially on the evaluation by an audience.

Several persons—organizers, participants, performers, and audience—are involved in each performance. The success of a performance depends on their adherence to the rules. After deciding to hold a performance, the organizers have to proceed according to conventions. Kapferer (1983) has shown that in Sri Lanka, the decision to hold the ceremony of the great demon of the cemetery, Mahasona, is postponed by the relatives as long as possible (mostly due to financial and organizational problems). But when finally organized, a fixed procedure has to be followed. Certain persons have to be invited, specific food has to be cooked, the space for the ritual has to be prepared, and ritual specialists (exorcists) have to be invited to perform the ritual.

The Textual Dimension

Until recently, Indology was preoccupied with the study of written texts, and textual criticism, distinguishing layers of texts, etc., with a priority placed on questions of chronology, the oldest parts or versions of a text being considered the most important ones. Less attention was paid to the performative uses to which texts are put. Indian texts themselves seem to presuppose, from the earliest times, an awareness of context including the dimension of performance. These two central concepts, context and performance, have also begun to attract attention in text-oriented South Asian studies. As long as texts such as the Vedas plural existed only through their oral performance they were not permitted an isolated existence—except in the form of 'mental texts' in the minds of those who memorized them. Living people and social rules of authorization of transmission were essential for the continued 'life of a text' (Lutgendorf 1991). Only when texts started being 'reduced' to writing could they begin to exist on their own—although manuscripts were the property of an owner—for longer than the life-span of a human being 'entitled' to know them. Their transmission began to depend on scribes and their patrons and on the text being considered important enough to be copied.

Contemporary Indian culture is probably unique in its variety of coexistent types of transmission ranging from exclusively oral to exclusively written/printed with a wide spectrum of the most fascinating combinations. These include parallel transmission—orally, as manuscript and in print with ritual priority on orality (Veda); or conversely, oral tradition assigning a quasi-iconic value to the written text, the physical presence of the manuscript or printed book playing an important role in the oral performance (Blackburn 1988; Lutgendorf 1991). The study of the interaction of various oral and written traditions that have also been labelled 'folk', 'popular' or 'classical' was initiated by Stuart Blackburn and A.K. Ramanujan in their study of folklore in 1986. Other more recent approaches with special reference to theatre will be discussed below.

A PHENOMENOLOGY OF CULTURAL PERFORMANCES

We have divided our exposition into two major sections, one on ritual performances, another on the range of performances based on epic and puranic texts and culminating in theatrical performances. In many instances, no sharp borderline can be drawn between ritual and theatrical performances—theatre often being placed in a ritualized setting and religious ritual often displaying theatrical features of dramatization. Moreover, in western avant-garde theatre of the early decades of the twentieth century there have been attempts to 'ritualize' theatre in order to explore new dimensions of meaning. Fresh efforts at 're-ritualization' have been made in the 'performance-art' of the 1960s and 1970s. Since the 1980s the intercultural dimension has gained increasing importance in theatre and performance studies (Schechner 1983; Fischer-

Lichte 1990; Marranca and Dasgupta 1991). As in the social sciences, in theatre studies too, the concept of 'performance' has helped widen the field. Scholars like E. Fischer-Lichte extend the notion of theatricality to include all types of 'staging' of reality. She speaks of a theatricalization of everyday life brought about by the new media and by a 'new orality'. Against this background, the distinctions made in the following sections are to be understood as attempts to organize the material rather than as classificatory categories in their own right.

Ritual Performances

Vedic Ritual

Indian culture has preserved detailed accounts and prescriptions for the performance of texts from the earliest times. Vedic sacrificial ritual of the first millennium BC is perhaps the best documented ancient ritual performance. Various genres of meticulously transmitted Vedic literature contain liturgical texts, performance manuals and interpretations of ritual acts. The major form to which they refer are the large public *śrauta* rites. There are strict rules concerning the consecration of a certain space, the fixing of a particular time, the appointment of proper ritual specialists and the duties of the patron. They are performed in a temporarily sanctified and purified open space, the sacrificial ground, to be abandoned after the performance of the rituals. They take place at fixed times of the year such as certain new- and full-moon days, or in larger time-cycles or at special occasions such as the consecration of a king or his becoming a universal ruler (*cakravartin*) by successfully conducting the horse-sacrifice (*aśvamedha*).

The Vedic texts relate to the performances from several complementary angles and jointly provide a comprehensive picture of a sacrificial performance. The oldest groups of texts, collected in the *Rigveda*, consist of hymns to the deities to be used as invocations during the rituals; the *Yajurveda* contains sacrificial formulas (*yajus*) to be pronounced in the course of the sacrificial rites; the *Sāmaveda* preserves the melodies in which the texts of the *Rigveda* are to be chanted. In the performance, each of the three Vedas is taken charge of by a priestly specialist. The *hotar* (*Rigveda*) recites verses from the *Rigveda* to praise the gods and to invite them to descend invisibly onto their seats of honour on the sacrificial ground. The *udgātar*, the 'singer' (*Sāmaveda*) accompanies the preparation and offering of the sacrificial items with his chants. The *Adhvaryu-priest* (*Yajurveda*) actually performs the sacrificial acts, murmuring prayers and sacrificial formulas from the *Yajurveda*. The most basic of these formulas consist of statements such as 'this for Agni', 'this for Indra' which accompany the act of throwing or pouring offerings such as grain or clarified butter into the sacrificial fire; that is, the performative act is provided meaning by the accompanying speech act. The latter can also be a more elaborate or explicit statement of the purpose of the act. The fourth major officiant, the Brahman priest, has to know all the Vedas and supervises the entire performance. If the slightest mistake is committed, he has to set it right by reciting special formulas. He later came to be associated with the fourth Veda, the Atharvan, a collection of magical texts. Both, the sāma- and the yajurvedic text collections are arranged liturgically, that is, in the sequence in which they are to be used during the major sacrificial rites.

There are several more genres of Vedic texts focusing on the same performances, such as the ancient prose texts called the Brāhmanas that provide explanations and interpretations of the meaning, reason, and purpose of ritual acts or of implements and materials used in them. Chronologically, these texts were followed by the composition of performance manuals, the *Śrauta-Sūtras*, which—in aphoristic brevity—sketch the sequence of the sacrificial performance. Providing further differentiation for this elaborately documented 'science of sacrifice', most of the textual genres referred to were transmitted in various 'recensions' of different 'schools'. We can even study variations in the performance of the major sacrificial rituals of Vedic times.

The texts also refer to patronage because the patron (and sometimes his wife, see Jamison 1996) is central to the performance. There are hardly any references, though, to the eventual presence and function of a wider audience and response to the rituals. We know that according to later prescriptions, women and Śūdras were prohibited from even merely hearing the Vedas. Most information about the social setting can be gleaned from the descriptions of royal rituals such as the royal consecration, the *rājasūya*, studied by Jan Heesterman (1957), which continued to be performed by Hindu kings. There is also evidence for the legitimating social and political function of the horse-sacrifice in Vedic as well as later times. In spite of the existence of printed editions and manuscripts, for the practitioners of Vedic religion, oral transmission in a teacher–student setting is still the valid mode of continuing the tradition. Access to training in Vedic texts and practices is strictly controlled and regulated and has until recently been limited to twice-born males, usually Brahmans. Apart from its liturgical use in the major sacrifices, the recitation of Vedic texts has, since classical times, also been part of various Hindu religious ceremonies. The most 'private' mode of performance is the *svādhyāya*, the individual practice of reciting the texts for purposes of memorization.

Ritual Performances in Predominantly Oral Cultures

The second set of ritual performances on which we want to focus here used oral texts not written down within the respective traditions themselves, but recorded only by scholars.[1] Out of the vast range of ritual performances, we have selected the possession rituals using the performative paradigm to study such rituals that opens up a vastly different perspective from that gained by a 'textural' approach. Various forms of possession rituals are widespread in south Asia. They include possession states in which divine or demonic beings are incorporated in human beings, whether to endanger the cosmic order (spirit possession), or to announce the causes of misfortune, illness, etc. (divinational possession), or to be worshipped and give blessings to their devotees (theatrical possession). Outside observers are generally awed by the often-spectacular performances in which the possessed person acts rather menacingly while incorporating a furious spirit or a goddess in all her rage. For a long time, the interpretation of possession rituals was dominated by the altered state of consciousness of the possessed person, who subsequently was supposed to act in an idiosyncratic way, pathologically or under social stress (Claus 1984). Possession was analysed and interpreted with western psychopathological concepts or under the presupposition of socio-economic marginality. An interpretation of possession as cultural performance, however, brings the description closer to the events experienced by the people themselves. Possession rituals may be very simple, with minimal performative features, or they may be highly elaborated theatrical events. Examples from both ends of this range shall be quoted here.

Among the Vāḍabalija, a Telugu-speaking fishing caste on the coasts of Andhra Pradesh and Orissa, female media (*bhakturālu*) can become possessed by a goddess who can then be approached by her devotees. These rituals of divinational possession appear unspectacular when compared to the Teyyam cult in Kerala with its elaborate theatrical features. A closer look, however, reveals a planned and structured performance in both cases. In both possession rituals, time and space cannot be selected at random, but have to be in accordance with ritual requirements. Whereas among the Vāḍabalija, the goddess can be invited to come into her human vessel throughout the year, but only on the days of the week when she is worshipped, in Kerala, the deity possesses its devotees only during the annual Teyyam festival. In both cases, the medium, as well as the space where the ritual is to take place, have to be ritually purified. In Kerala, possession usually takes place at the shrine; among the Vāḍabalija, it takes place in the house of the medium or of any devotee, after the house has been ritually purified. The medium who is going to be possessed, as well as the impersonator in the Teyyam cult, are devoted to one specific deity. Just before the possession, they reinforce their devotion by worshipping the deity and by fasting. These necessary preparations are followed by the invocation, a text spoken or sung by another ritual specialist (a non-Brahmanic priest) in which he pleads with the god or goddess and convinces him or her 'to come to his or her innocent children only for one hour', thus creating the divine presence (Schömbucher 1994a: 126). The invocational text consists of a number of fixed, stereotypical lines, 'formulaic speech' in the sense of Parry and Lord (Lord 1964; Freeman 1993: 123; Schömbucher 1994b: 45). They are interspersed with parts that display the individual style of the speaker.

After a successful invocation, the deity announces its temporary presence through the medium, who is now in trance, beginning to recite the divine words. Among the Vāḍabalija, the divine presence is created in a rather unspectacular way, by the medium falling into trance and the goddess announcing her presence. In Teyyam rituals, possession marks the end of a process of transformation. Outwardly, the Teyyam dancer dons a specific costume and puts on make-up. The process of getting possessed is completed by the gazing into a mirror, the final step, when the performer perceives his image as that of the deity (Freeman 1993: 123). The divine speech differs from ordinary speech in a number of linguistic and paralinguistic features. Among the Vāḍabalija, the text is sung; it consists of lines of approximately the same length with the same beginnings and endings. Linguistic devices such as parallelism and repetition throughout the text guarantee the fluidity of the recitation. The semantic structure follows certain rules. The recitation begins with the greeting of other deities, according to their status in the divine hierarchy. This introductory greeting also has stabilizing qualities for the medium's trance. A change of melody and longer lines mark the beginning of the section in which the deity refers to individual problems of the devotees present. The divine answer to specific human problems is again interspersed with 'formulaic' passages in which the goddess's power is praised and in which events of its biography are recited. The end of the séance is announced by the deity with the words 'I am leaving'. In Teyyam rituals, the performance is more rigidly structured and has other theatrical elements besides the recitation of the text. After the onset of possession, 'the Teyyam performers commence a series of dance steps which are carefully rehearsed and executed to the sets of changing rhythms kept by the drummers' (Freeman 1993: 127). Despite a certain amount of textual improvising during Teyyam possession, there are long passages which are memorized and used by the performers to praise the deities, to narrate their story of origin and to give blessings to the devotees.

The meaning of possession rituals as they exist among the Vāḍabalija is usually derived from the divinational character of the text. Human problems are interpreted and explained by a divine entity, who also proposes the solution (which has to be interpreted again by the audience). However, another meaning lies behind the divinational dimension of the text, although this seems to be the dominant part in a possession ritual. A comparison with the theatrical performance of the Teyyam cult shows similar, though less elaborate, performative patterns. Besides solving problems, possession rituals create time and space for worship and communication with the deities. This is confirmed by the fact that the audience consists of persons 'who ask' and persons 'who sit' (cf. Schömbucher 1994a: 125). The worship of a deity by the audience occurs during its presence in the house and body of the medium. Offerings (coconuts, bananas, incense, *kumkum*, money) are made by the persons who ask, just as if they were worshipping the deity at the temple. As a further advantage, the persons in the audience get to know the problems in their neighbourhood, how they are dealt with, and how to avoid similar difficulties. The efficacy of a possession ritual depends not only on the recitation of the text, but also on the mode of life of the medium and on how well the deity comes onto the body. A further important presupposition is the belief among the performers and the audience that the divine presence can be created by humans (Freemen 1993: 126).

Theatrical Performances

Considering the immense range of performance traditions in south Asia, it is often difficult to differentiate between strictly theatrical and non-theatrical forms. If—as has been common in the West up to recently—we start from the notion of a dramatic text consisting of dialogues, soliloquies, etc.—rendered in direct speech by actors impersonating particular characters, then a form like the Kathakali dance theatre of Kerala would not be theatre since the actors do not speak. The minimal definition of theatre offered by Fischer-Lichte is perhaps more helpful: A impersonates B while C is looking on. Furthermore, Hansen, referring to Abrahams, stresses 'the acting out of the story, so that make-up, costumes, and movement visually represent the narrative events to the audience' (1992: 54). Probably the largest arena of public performances emerged from the Sanskrit epics—and the Purāṇas following a few centuries later—which were presented by bards and narrators in a variety of ways. From about the tenth or eleventh century onwards, renderings of the epics were often based on vernacular versions. The modes of performance ranged from the delivery of portions of the text by a teller or singer to full-fledged theatrical performances of episodes which might also include ritual possession of actors in certain peak scenes.

We want to discuss this range of performance genres as well as the range of theatre proper by using two major sets of examples, one from a north Indian Rāmāyaṇa tradition, the other from a group of forms from south India based on the epics as well as the Bhāgavata Purāṇa. Since most of the theatrical performance traditions to be sketched here share features with classical Sanskrit drama and its theory of performance as first elaborated in the *Nāṭyaśāstra* (approximately second century), a few remarks about the classical traditions of the first millennium AD are in order. The texts of the available classical plays such as the ones by Kālidāsa (fifth century) are multi-lingual, which to some extent reflects, albeit in a stylized way, regional and social linguistic diversity. Most of the dramas are court-dramas centring on the love of a king for a young princess or nymph, or on political intrigues involving a minister (or both in combination). Themes are often taken from the epics. The king and his minister speak Sanskrit, the female characters speak Śauraseni Prakrit and may have verses in Mahārāṣṭrī Prakrit, low-class males speak Māgadhī Prakrit. There are two interesting exceptions: female ascetics and highly educated courtesans may also speak in Sanskrit; the jester (*vidūṣaka*) who is a Brahman and the king's companion speaks Śauraseni like the noble ladies, and not Sanskrit as may be expected. The plays all have prologues in which a stage-manager (*sūtradhāra*) introduces the audience to the play and usually also to the playwright and the performance context.

The joint evidence of the information contained in Sanskrit theoretical treatises such as the *Nāṭyaśāstra* and the *Daśarūpa* (approximately tenth century) on the one hand, and of the hints contained in the prologues and stage directions of the dramas themselves, on the other hand, suggests that classical Indian theatre was radically non-naturalistic and non-illusionistic and made hardly any use of props and scenery. It assigned at least as much importance to the subtleties of histrionics, especially the mimic expression of emotions, music and dance as to the verbal delivery of a fixed text. The most important concept developed in the *Nāṭyaśāstra* and elaborated in the tenth century into a comprehensive aesthetic theory by the Kashmiri author Abhinavagupta is the concept of *rasa* (lit. 'taste', 'essence'). The dramatic depiction of eight, later nine, emotional states (*bhāva*) such as love, mirth, anger, and sorrow are meant to evoke the aesthetic experience, the 'tasting', of the erotic, the comic, the furious, the pathetic, etc. in a refined form presupposing an audience of connoisseurs. In the course of the second millennium, the aesthetics of rasa originally developed for the theatre came to be generalized and extended to the appreciation of all the arts as well as to religious experience of the bhakti type.

This should be kept in mind while turning to our first example, a Rāmāyaṇa performance tradition of north India. Its literary base is Tulsidās's sixteenth-century Hindi retelling of the Sanskrit epic, the *Rāmcharitmānas*. Lutgendorf (1991) distinguishes four performance genres: individual recitation of the text in homes; public recitation by professional reciters; public exposition by professionals (*kathāpravacana*); and full dramatic enactment in the Rāmlīlā dramas. The notion of *lila* or divine play has most recently been discussed in Sax (1995).

In contradistinction to the Vedas, access to these texts is not restricted or controlled. Puranic recitation has probably served as a model for public recitation. All types of performances, such as reciting the entire text in particular portions within a certain number of days, are considered religious activities and are sometimes equated in terms of merit with Vedic rituals. Both reciting and listening are considered equally meritorious. Lutgendorf (1991) gives detailed descriptions of various 'rites of recitations'. In spite of printed texts being available, including cheap editions, *kathā* exposition of the text is still the most important mode of transmission. Lutgendorf defines it as 'systematic-recitation-with-exposition', a 'slow, systematic, storytelling recitation, interspersed with prose explanations, elaborations, and homely illustrations of spiritual points' (115). He considers environment itself as constitutive of the act of katha (118). Based on Bonazzoli, he points out that there had similarly been two basic categories of Purāṇa expounders, 'those who simply recite texts with little or no elaboration and those who translate texts into the vernacular or otherwise comment on them' (124–5). The tradition of public exposition thus provided a living commentary in which the audience might also participate (126).

The Rāmlīlā

Perhaps the most complex performance genre of the Rāmāyaṇa–*Rāmcharitmānas* tradition is the Rāmlīlā, performed over a large area of north India in various settings and with varying patronage (royal, temple-monastery, mercantile, neighbourhood). Generally, the Rāmlīlā stagings use different locations between which the performers and the audience have to move. In the tradition patronized by the mahārājas of Benares (since the eighteenth century) these locations extend over several square miles and include a number of permanent structures. Lutgendorf explains: 'The *Rāmlīlā* is outdoor and peripatetic not because latter-day patrons could not afford to construct theaters but because the pageant came to express notions of cosmography and pilgrimage that aim at reclaiming and transforming the mundane world' (1991: 255). According to Schechner (1983), the 'performance text' (in the sense of the entire *miseenscène*) consists of three main 'texts': the Rāmcharitmānas recited by a Rāmāyaṇi-specialist seated at the back of the audience; the dialogues (*saṃvāda*) spoken on stage by child actors (*svarūpa*); and the 'spectacle'. There is constant alternation between dialogues and recitation. The dialogues translate and elaborate Tulsidās's text. They are controlled by adult experts, the *vyāsas*, who direct the performance on stage and whisper the text of the dialogues into the ears of the role-players. The staging is iconographic, especially when at the end of the daily performance portion, lights are waved (*āratī*) (in front of the five svarūpas, the four brothers, and Rāma's spouse, Sītā) as if they were statues (*mūrti*) of the divine heroes of the play. The performance at Rāmnagar is a 31-day event timed during the Dussehra period in September–October. The daily performances alternate between stasis and motion including processional performance (Schechner 1983: 254). The action is 'both physical and narrative'. The actual movement of the characters is itself a decisive part of the story (Schechner 1983: 259). There is also audience participation in that the audience may be considered at certain times of the story as the population of Ayodhayā, etc. The svarupas and the other actors are non-professionals who receive a basic training for some time before the annual performances.

The points to be noted are: recitation of the basic text becomes part of the theatrical performance as well and the theatrical performance on stage is non-illusionistic. There is no attempt to hide that the svarupas in their dialogues are just repeating a text transmitted by the vyāsas. At the same time, the svarūpas are in fact icons of the divine heroes they impersonate and are worshipped as such. Costume, make-up and especially the crowns worn by the svarūpas play an important role.

Classifying Theatrical Performances

The bardic traditions of rendering Sanskrit epics also have their counterpart in vernacular oral epic traditions found all over the subcontinent (see Blackburn et al. 1989). Like the renderings of the Sanskrit epics and their vernacular telling, oral epic and other narrative traditions exist in a variety of performance genres and subgenres and in different contexts, including entirely different social settings and modes of patronage. Kathryn Hansen (1992), discussing parameters of the 'folk' and 'classical', suggests 'that instead of looking internally to textual strategies, themes, or codes as determinatives, we give consideration to the sources of a tradition's authority, its modes of reproduction, and its relation to dominant social groups'. On this basis she proposes a three-part definition of the 'classical':

First, a textual authority must be present that legitimizes and governs the art form ... . Second, this textual tradition must be studied and passed on by trained specialists ... who control reproduction of the art form. Third, the producers, performers, and their institutions must be supported by a dominant social group. In pre-modern times, courts and temples most frequently acted as patrons; nowadays sponsorship comes from government agencies, corporations, and cultural institutions constituted from elite groups. (p. 44)

Hansen's aim is to locate the Nauṭanki theatre of north India studied by her as an 'intermediate' theatre between the folk and the classical stressing that these terms should not be used in an essentialist way.

Using her approach, the Rāmnagar variety of the Rāmlīlā just discussed would also occupy an 'intermediate' position displaying both folk and classical elements. A more comprehensive attempt at locating the multitude of Indian theatre traditions has been made by Richmond, Swann, and Zarrilli (Richmond et al. 1990).[2] They distinguish the tradition of classical Sanskrit theatre, continued to some extent in the Kūṭiyāṭṭam theatre of Kerala, from five other traditions: the 'ritual' ones such as the Teyyam of Kerala; the 'devotional' ones, such as Rās Līlā and Rāmlīlā, the 'folk-popular' ones, such as Nautaṅki and Tamāśa; the traditions of dance-dramas and dramatic dances, such as Kathakali and Chau; and, finally, the traditions of 'modern' theatre. In this scheme, Rāmlīlā figures as a devotional tradition which Swann distinguishes from the folk-popular in the following way: 'Devotional forms in addition to their dramatic significance have a symbolic, holy meaning conveyed through spectacle, mimetic action, dialogues and the like. Folk-popular forms focus their concern on the mundane life of human beings rather than on the gods' (1990: 239). This would also be a way to distinguish more clearly between forms such as the Rāmlīlā and the Nautaṅki. Summarizing his observations on the folk-popular forms discussed by him, Swann lists a number of resemblances

which mark them as being of and for the common people: (1) They integrate in varying proportions vocal and instrumental music, dance, and mimetic action. (2) All of them give a significant place to the comic sentiment and many of them have stock comic figures. (3) They show evidence of having originated as open-air performances, open to whomever wishes to attend. (4) While staging is simple, costume may be simple or elaborate. (5) Although the forms may vary in their position in the sacred–profane continuum, all are set within the sacred context, as indicated by some form of religious preliminary. (1990: 246)

Terukkūttu

Among the south Indian set of examples we want to discuss now, the Terukkūttu ('street-play') of Tamil Nāḍu has been labelled 'ritual' theatre by Zarrilli (1990: 309). Like the Rāmlīlā of Rāmnagar, Terukkūttu is based mainly on a vernacular telling of a Sanskrit epic, here a Tamil version of the Mahābhārata. It is part of a large-scale performance setting covering an entire village and extending over a period of twenty days. It constitutes three levels of performance, the first one being recitation of the epic text by professionals termed *piracankam* (Skt. *prasanga*) and comparable to the recitations of the Rāmāyanis during the Rāmlīlā; the second one is dramatic enactment proper, the Kūttu (cp Terukkūttu); and the third one is ritual enactment (Hiltebeitel 1988: 135). Although these appear to be the same components that we encountered in the Rāmlīlā, their spatial and temporal distribution and weightage differ considerably. In the variety studied by Frasca (1990), who is our major source, the Terukkūttu performance is part of the cult of the goddess and Mahābhārata heroine Draupadī during whose annual festival rituals, core scenes from the Tamil Mahābhārata are recited and enacted with a number of other rituals in synchronicity. Epic recitation is a daily, independent feature all through the twenty-day festival. From the tenth to the eighteenth day, the recitations are complemented by the enactment of the same scenes in the Terukkūttu performance mode which uses its own texts for the episodes. From the tenth to the last day there are also large-scale ritual enactments constituting the third level of rendering the Mahābhārata events and partly involving some of the actors (Frasca 1990: 170–1, Fig. 42). Thus, Frasca observes, the marriage of Draupadī is performed thrice: as described in the recitation of the prasanga; as staged by the Terukkūttu actors; and as a ritual in the temple performed by priests (1990: 147).

The dramatic enactment of the Terukkūttu uses stylized make-up, song, dance, rhythm, narrative prose, and intonation (Frasca 1990: 5, Fig. 1). Music and third-person narrative are delivered by musicians and singers at the back of the stage, dance and first-person dialogue by the actors in front. There is a clown who figures mainly at the beginning of the performance. An important feature of the staging are the curtain entrances of the individual characters, also found in other south Indian theatre forms. A small curtain is held up by two stage hands. Behind it the character makes his appearance creating suspense until the curtain is removed. He then shows artistic and energetic dances while the narrative is being sung by the singers. According to Frasca, these curtain entrances are the most intensive sequences of a performance. It is here that the actors and members of the audience may also lapse into possession during peak scenes (Frasca 1990: 10). These sequences alternate with dramatic enactment by the performers using first-person speech, that is, speaking directly as the characters. The improvised prose dialogues are called *vacanam*. The predominance of the ritual frame and the feature of sometimes violent ritual possession would justify labelling Terrukkūttu as ritual theatre rather than bhakti-oriented devotional theatre. Its village base, communal patronage and comparatively low degree of codification and control of transmission would make it appear, at the same time, folk-popular rather than classical.

Yakṣagāna

The folk-popular elements link Kūttu to the performance tradition in neighbouring Karṇāṭaka state, the Yakṣagāna, which could also be labelled a 'dance-drama'. Zarrilli (1990: 308) argues that the dance-drama is distinguished by being overtly dramatic and by giving primary or equal emphasis to dance when enacting a scripted drama or dramatic story: In his words, '... movement and choreography are determined by dramatic context—pure and interpretative dance elements are subsumed within and shaped by the drama (*nātya*) ... Movement supports and fills out the playing of roles in the drama. In Yakṣagāna,[3] third-person narrative and sung dialogue by background singers alternates with impromptu dialogic sequences spoken by the actors as characters. Traditionally, themes have been taken from Kannaḍa versions of the Mahābhārata, the Rāmāyaṇa, and the *Bhāgavata Purāṇa*. The oldest known texts of the plays are preserved in manuscripts dating back to the sixteenth century. They are called prasanga and contain only the texts sung and recited by the singer–director–stage-manager, termed Bhāgavata, this name pointing back to a tradition of recitation and exposition of the *Bhāgavata Purāṇa*. Speech by the actors and the clown is not fixed in writing but improvised.

Yakṣagāna is performed in fields after the harvest or in open spaces near temples or estates. The performance area is marked off by four decorated poles creating a square or rectangular temporary stage. Although there is no ritual framing comparable to Terukkūttu, performances are often sponsored in fulfilment of religious vows and many troupes are entertained by temples in the coastal region of Karṇāṭaka, some of them looking back on a continuous tradition of nearly 200 years. The one-night performances commence with the worship of Gaṇapati in the greenroom and later on stage. The preliminaries include a dance by two young boys representing god Krṣṇa and his brother Balarāma, followed by another dance by two cowgirls or milkmaids from the entourage of the god. They are impersonated by males as there are no females among the performers. A clown and his troupe of youngsters also figure in the preliminaries. The clown returns to the stage at various points for comic interludes, sometimes functioning as messenger of the hero.

The performance structure of the play proper, the prasanga, is similar to Terukkuttu. It involves certain entrances alternating with impromptu dialogues that elaborate the sung or recited portions. In addition, the Bhāgavata questions the character about his identity and purpose, giving him a chance to introduce himself. The main themes and the highlights of the performances are battles displaying forceful male dances, and marriages, often as parts of the same play.

Kathakali

Further down the west coast in Kerala, Yakṣagāna shares its martial and heroic character with Kathakaḷi. In Kathakali, too, the story is told in third-person narrative by singers standing at the back of the stage. But, in contradistinction to Yakṣagāna, the actors translate the story heard in the linguistic code into highly stylized gestural and mimical codes. They never speak. Both, verses in narrative third-person Sanskrit (*ślōka*) and dialogue portions (*pada*) in the regional language, Malayālam—usually written in first person as if the actor were speaking— are delivered by the singers (Zarrilli 1990: 326–7). By divorcing the speaking and singing of the text from the acting, the actor–dancer is freed for the vigorous choreography and complex gestural interpretation of the text (Zarrilli 1990: 318). There is no clown or jester in Kathakali. The plays are based on dramatizations of stories drawn by playwright-composers first from the Rāmāyaṇa, then the Mahābhārata and later from the *Bhāgavata Purāṇa* (Zarrilli 1990: 315), that is, from the same sources as in Yakṣagāna. By incorporating 'some of the more virtuosic dramatic techniques of Kūṭiyāṭṭam, including its emphasis on face, hand, and eye gesture' (Zarrilli 1990: 317), Kathakali became more 'classical' and rasa-oriented although it remained highly popular. Patronage, too, originally came from the highest ranks of society (Zarrilli 1992) and the patrons were connoisseurs who often contributed to the refinement of the form.

Kerala can also boast of the only surviving performance tradition of classical drama in India, the Kūṭiyāṭṭam theatre, dating back to at least the eleventh century AD. The transmission of performance techniques and performance texts has been exclusively in the hands of Cākyār actors and Naṅṅyār actresses.[4] In Kūṭiyāṭṭam ('acting together') the aesthetics of rasa was developed to utmost subtlety by an extreme emotional elaboration of individual scenes and passages. Thus, in this acting style the rendering and interpretation of a single stanza may take far more than an hour. Only individual acts of dramas are performed, taking several nights. The multilingualism of Sanskrit drama is multiplied by including Malayālam trans- lations of Sanskrit and Prakrit passages by the vidūṣaka, the jester. His lengthy learned and humorous discourses add an epic element to the staging. They may also be presented inde- pendently in a purely male subgenre called Kūttu. The Naṅṅyār actresses, on the other hand, have their own female subgenre of mono-acting, the Naṇṇyār Kūttu, in which dance plays a major role. Performances of all three types were restricted to the temple theatres of Kerala until the 1970s and depended on royal or princely patronage of these temples. The audience consisted of Brahmans, princes and landed nobility, and castes of temple-servants (*ambalavāsin*). After Independence (1947) and as with Kathakali and other traditional forms, patronage has started shifting to the state and there often is 'a disjuncture between social and artistic roles in the ranks of the patrons' (Zarrilli 1992: 121).[5]

Summary: Theatrical Performances

The major features of all theatrical performances addressed here are: (1) An 'epic', non- illusionistic performance style making little use of props and scenery but emphasizing the performance, costume and make-up of the actor; in several forms an alternation between sung third-person narrative and dialogue by the actors; sometimes the figure of a director or stage- manager on stage during the performance; (2) a high degree of elaboration in terms of acting style, preliminaries, translation process between languages as well as from linguistic to other codes, leading to a minimum performance time of one full night and extending up to twenty

(Terukūttu), thirty-one (Rāmlīlā) or even forty-one nights (the longest Kūṭiyāṭṭam performance); (3) training of actors for certain role types (*vēṣa*), generally no group rehearsals; (4) a religious performance context; and (5) a rural or temple economic base.

Modern Indian Theatre

In contrast to the traditional forms of theatre, modern Indian theatre is profane, urban and commercial (ticketing system) with a standard performance duration of two to three hours.[6] It developed in the nineteenth century under the impact of the British colonial power and the English education introduced by the latter. Modern drama first followed European as well as ancient Indian models. Since the 1960s—and along with the reception of Brecht's 'epic' theatre, itself inspired by Asian techniques—regional forms of traditional drama were rediscovered by modern Indian playwrights and directors and made fruitful for their own work. At the same time, members of the international, mainly Euro-American theatre, scene developed the notion of intercultural performance (Marranca and Dasgupta 1991). They were attracted by the subtleties of Indian traditional and ritual theatre forms. Directors like Peter Brooks successfully staged a full night production of the Mahābhārata in European and American capitals, integrating various features of traditional Indian renderings of the epic (Varadpande 1991; Marranca and Dasgupta 1991; Hiltebeitel 1992). At present, we witness in India the simultaneous existence and flourishing of the entire range of performances sketched here.

Conclusion

It has generally been postulated that cultural performances attempt to communicate meaning (Peacock 1990: 208), and that they are of a reflexive character. More recently, aspects of agency have been stressed: cultural performances are not only said to communicate meaning but also to have the potential to change society and to be events where critique might be expressed or where different versions of culture could be negotiated. As Schieffelin noted: '(t)he central issue of performativity, whether in ritual performance, theatrical entertainment or the social articulation of ordinary human situations, is the imaginative creation of a human world' (Schieffelin 1998: 205). Through the various performances, life is interpreted, identity is created, and individual crises explained and mastered.

The most important result of studying cultural performances is the insight that the textual dimension cannot be considered exclusively in the interpretation of performances. For one reason, the text is often incomprehensible to the participants. Formalization, poetic language, and the unusual referential content of language give staged speech an esoteric character which distinguishes it from day-to-day speech, but which also makes it less accessible to both audience and performers. It seems to be precisely its esoteric character that makes staged speech effective, even if its meaning is not perceivable. According to Tambiah (1968), the efficacy and power of ritual lie in the textual, symbolic, and cosmological representations that the performative character—repetition, conventionality and stereotype—establishes. Frequently, the language of healing is incomprehensible—even to the patients. We may conclude that 'meaning' is more than mere words and action. Meaning does not derive from the text, not even from the text in context, but from the text in performance.

This has perhaps become most evident in our sketch of theatrical performances in which south Asian cultures create polyphone, aesthetically stylized, idealized projections of themselves to reconfirm and celebrate their multifaceted identities.

ENDNOTES

1. The situation is the reverse of the the Vedic one: performances without descriptions and recorded texts instead of descriptions without performances but abundant collections of texts.
2. cp also Varadpande (1991) who discusses a wide range of performance genres based on the Mahābhārata. Gargi (1991) and Varadpande (1992) place 'epic' theatre in the context of classical and folk forms.
3. Information on Yakṣagāna is based on Karanth (1975) (new edition 1997) and Ashton and Christie (1977).
4. Note that there are no female performers in any of the other traditions discussed here, that is, Rāmlīlā, Terukkūttu, Yakṣagāna and Kathakali. Female characters are also impersonated by male performers.'
5. Government agencies have also begun to look after the more artistic of the theatrical rituals thereby causing a move from ritual to 'art'.
6. Popular traditional forms like Kathakali and Yakṣagāna have also begun to be performed commercially in town halls and tents against entrance fee. Full-night performances are complemented by three-hour productions, also shown when touring abroad.

REFERENCES

Ashton, M. and B. Christie. 1977. *Yakṣagāna*. Delhi: Abhinav Publications.

Austin, John L. 1962. *How to do Things with Words*. Oxford: Oxford University Press.

Baumann, Richard and Charles L. Briggs. 1990. 'Poetics and Performance as Critical Perspectives on Language and Social Life'. *Annual Reviews of Anthropology*. 19:59–88.

Bell, Catherine. 1992. *Ritual Theory, Ritual Practice*. New York: Oxford University Press.

Blackburn, Stuart. 1988. *Singing of Birth and Death: Texts in Performance*. Philadelphia: University of Pennsylvania Press.

Blackburn, Stuart, et al. 1989. *Oral Epics in India*. Berkeley: University of California Press.

Blackburn, Stuart and A.K. Ramanujan. 1986. *Another Harmony: New Essays on the Folklore of India*. Berkeley: University of California Press.

Claus, Peter J. 1984. 'Medical Anthropology and the Ethnography of Spirit Possession'. *Contributions to Asian Studies*. 18:60–72.

Fischer-Lichte, Erika, ed. 1990. *The Dramatic Touch of Difference*. Tübingen: Gunter Narr Verlag.

Frasca, A. 1990. *The Theatre of the Mahābhārata: Terukūttu Performances in South India*. Honolulu: University of Hawaii Press.

Freeman, J. Richardson. 1993. 'Performing Possession: Ritual and Consciousness in the Teyyam Complex of Northern Kerala'. In H. Brückner, L. Lutze and A. Malik, eds, *Flags of Fame: Studies in South Asian Folk Culture*. 109–38. Delhi: Manohar Publishers,

Gargi, Balwant. 1991. *Folk Theatre of India*. Calcutta: Rupa and Co.

Geertz, Clifford. 1972. 'Deep Play: Notes on the Balinese Cockfight'. *Daedalus*. 101:1–37.

Hansen, Kathryn. 1992. *Grounds for Play: The Nauṭaṅkī Theatre of North India*. Berkeley: University of California Press.

Heesterman, Jan. 1957. *Rājasūya: The Ancient Indian Royal Consecration*. S-Gravenhage: Mouton and Co.

Hiltebeitel, Alf. 1988. *The Cult of Draupadī*. Chicago: The University of Chicago Press.

———. 1992. 'Transmitting Mahābhāratas. Another Look at Peter Brook'. *The Drama Review*. 36 (3, Fall): 131–59.

Hymes, Dell. 1962. 'Ethnography of Speaking'. In T. Gladwin and W.C. Sturtevant, eds, *Anthropology and Human Behavior*, 13–53. Washington, D.C.

Jamison, Stephanie W. 1996. *Sacrifice Wife/Sacrificer's Wife. Women, Ritual and Hospitality in Ancient India.* New York: Oxford University Press.

Kapferer, Bruce. 1983. *A Celebration of Demons. Exorcism and the Aesthetics of Healing in Sri Lanka.* Bloomington: Indiana University Press.

Karanth, Shivaram. 1975. *Yakṣagāna.* Mysore: Institute of Kannada Studies, University of Mysore. New edition 1997, IGNCA and Abhinav Publications.

Lord, Albert B. 1964. *The Singer of Tales.* Cambridge, Mass. Harvard University Press.

Lutgendorf, Philip. 1991. *The Life of a Text.* Berkeley: University of California Press.

Marranca, B. and G. Dasgupta. 1991. *Interculturalism and Performance.* New York: Raj Publications.

Peacock, James L. 1990. 'Ethnographic Notes on Sacred and Profane Performance'. In R. Schechner and W. Appel, eds, *By Means of Performance. Intercultural Studies of Theatre. and Ritual,* 208–20. Cambridge: Cambridge University Press.

Richmond, Farley et al. 1990. *Indian Theatre: Traditions of Performance.* Honolulu: University of Hawaii Press.

Sax, William S., ed. 1995. *The Gods at Play: Lila in South Asia.* New York: Oxford University Press

Schechner, Richard. 1983. 'Ramlila of Ramnagar: An Introduction'. In Richard Schechner, ed., *Performative Circumstances from the Avant Garde to Ramlila,* 238–88. Calcutta: Seagull Books.

———. 1985. *Between Theater and Anthropology.* Philadelphia: University of Pennsylvania Press.

Schieffelin, Edward L. 1998. 'Problematizing Performance'. In F. Hughes-Freeland, ed., *Ritual, Performance, Media,* 194–207. London and New York: Routledge.

Schömbucher, Elisabeth. 1994a. 'When the Deity Speaks: Performative Aspects of Possession Mediumship in South India'. In J. Kuckertz, ed., *Jahrbuch fur musikalische Volks- und Völkerkunde,* band 15, 124–34. Eisenach: Karl Dietrich Wagner.

———. 1994b. 'The Consequences of not Keeping a Promise: Possession Mediumship among a South Indian Fishing Caste'. *Cahiers de Littérature Orale.* 35:41–64.

Singer, Milton. 1972. *When a Great Tradition Modernizes: An Anthropological Approach to Indian Civilization.* London: Pall Mall Press.

Tambiah, Stanley. 1968. 'The Magical Power of Words'. *Man.* (n.s.). 3:175–208.

Turner, Victor. 1982. *From Ritual to Theater: The Human Seriousness of Play.* New York: Performing Arts Journal Publications.

Van Baumer, R. and J. Brandon. 1981. *Sanskrit Drama in Performance.* Honolulu: University of Hawaii Press.

Varadpande, M.L. 1991. *Mahabharata in Performance.* Delhi: Clarion Books.

Varadpande, M.L. 1992. *History of Indian Theatre: Loka Ranga, Panorama of Indian Folk Theatre.* Delhi: Abhinav Publications.

Zarrilli, Phillip. 1990. 'Kathakali'. In Richmond et al., eds, *Indian Theatre: Traditions of Performance,* Ch. 10, 315–57. Honolulu: University of Hawaii Press.

———. 1990. 'Dance-Drama and Dramatic Dances' (Introduction). In Richmond et al., eds, *Indian Theatre: Traditions of Performance,* Honolulu: University of Hawaii Press.

———. 1992. 'Patronage in Kathakali Dance Drama'. In Joan, L. Erdman, ed., *Arts Patronage in India: Methods, Motives and Markets,* 91–142. New Delhi: Manohar Publishers.

Public Culture

ARJUN APPADURAI

INTRODUCTION

The sociology of India since the 1950s has been dominated by one of two major interests. The first pertains to overarching ideologies of civilization, of tradition, and of cultural genius. The second has been a preoccupation with the workings of caste, ritual, and rank at the village level. A few important works have sought to bridge these two strands (Béteille 1983; Dumont 1970; Ghurye 1953; Madan 1987, 1994; Marriott 1955; Singer 1972; Srinivas 1971; Saran 1989). But on the whole they have proceeded in parallel until recently. This dual focus has meant that certain spaces, institutions, careers and practices have fallen outside the disciplinary gaze. Such spaces include streets, bazaars, and restaurants. Neglected institutions include the state, legal, and non-governmental organizations. Careers and occupations, such as those of bus conductors, grain dealers, truck drivers, and stock-brokers have been paid scant attention. And such practices as life insurance, blood donation, well irrigation, and moneylending, have received little sustained analysis. Many of these interstitial practices, spaces, and institutions span villages and cities, isolated communities and state organizations, informal and formal occupational strategies. They are neither about the Indian village—as such—or about Indian civilization, conceived as an integrated cultural design. There have been some prescient calls to attend to these intermediate phenomena (Cohn and Marriott 1958; Breman 1985; Shah 1988) but the response, until recently, has been scant. Even where such studies have been conducted, they have been empiricist or institutional, rarely placing them within a wider framework of cultural analysis or criticism.

The concept of public culture can be an illuminating way to bring such interstitial phenomena into the mainstream of a renewed sociology of India. This project has implications for the academic division of labour, the epistemology of disciplines and the terms of the relationship between sociology and other fields as they define their methods and produce their objects of study in India. These implications are taken up in the conclusion of this essay. To examine how public culture works in India, it is necessary to take stock of the context in which the popular and the public constitute a consequential zone of cultural practices and to ask how our current interest in these practices has been formed.

From Popular to Public Culture

While the term 'popular culture' has a clear set of referents and associations, 'public culture' is a newer conceptualization. Popular culture draws our attention to the everyday practices of ordinary people and, as a category, emerged in the social history of Europe as an antidote to the study of elites, of grand events, and of official sources and perspectives. Building on these European precedents, scholars working on South Asia have made important contributions to the study of public ceremonies and rituals (Freitag 1989a), of dramatic and performance traditions (Schechner 1983), of oral traditions of narrative (Raheja and Gold 1994), and of leisure and its varied forms (Kumar 1988). Prior studies of popular culture were often descriptive accounts of specific traditions, practices, and cultural forms, and the perspective of these studies tended towards the 'salvage' mode, seeking to record cultural practices that appeared to be in the process of disappearing.

The best studies of popular culture, however, made two important contributions. First, they provided a counterpoint to the overwhelmingly structural preoccupations of the bulk of the ethnography of India since 1950. Where most social anthropologists (and many culturally oriented sociologists) were concerned with kinship, caste, and ritual as parts of a complex structural whole, the best studies of popular culture opened our eyes to activities and values— sometimes aesthetic, sometimes religious, sometimes ludic—which could not be directly or mechanically tied to social reproduction, rank or status. In other words, these activities were expressive, and what they expressed was often the life-worlds of specific castes, occupational groups, regional groups, and micro-audiences, outside the encompassing structures of work, rank, and power. Going as far back as the texts from the British colonial archive these expressive formations were seen as cultural emblems of social groups, but such texts and their modern equivalents tended to be segregated from studies engaging the dynamics of rank, status, and reproduction. For this reason, much of the work on Indian popular culture has tended to create the image of a gap between everyday life and the requirements of livelihood and social hierarchy. Inadvertently, the objects of such research seemed to be set apart as being either about bread or about circuses.

Starting in the mid-1980s, the study of popular culture began to witness a shift away from a strict interest in the expressive practices of specific subcultural groups and to recognize that popular cultural expressions are inevitably tied to contests over power, value, and meaning. This period coincided with a waning interest in the study of caste as a technical subject and a related decline in studies of kinship, rank, and stratification among younger anthropologists working on India. The reasons for this shift are complex: in part, it was a response to a global drift away from studies of kinship and social organization in anthropology as a discipline; there was also a recognition that the study of rural India, especially at the village level, needed to include wider networks of regional, state, and national processes and policies; and finally there was a growing sense that the study of larger forms of turbulence in Indian society and politics required fresh approaches to caste, class and identity.

Signs of this shift towards a more politically sensitive understanding of popular culture, away from a narrower civilizational or expressive focus, are to be found in studies of the links between Hindu nationalism and popular culture (A. Kapur 1993a; Lutgendorf 1990), of film and other popular media (Krishen 1991), of sexuality (Kakar 1989), gender politics (O'Hanlon 1994) and of education and science as cultural fields (Thapan 1991; Uberoi 1984; Visvanathan 1985). These studies were largely independent of the new developments in history and historiography that came out of the Subaltern School and certain historically oriented anthropologies developed principally in the United States, which sought to place indigenous cultural formations in the perspective of the *longue durée* (Appadurai 1981, 1988; Breckenridge 1978; Dirks 1987; Freitag 1989b; Kumar 1988; Prakash 1990; Presler 1987; Price

1988). Today, however, the line between these various streams of cultural criticism is frequently blurred.

Two scholars who inspired these multiple streams of work were themselves anthropologically oriented historians: Bernard Cohn and Ranajit Guha, both of whom had established overlapping ways of theorizing popular practices, colonial knowledge and the working of state powers and official archives (Cohn 1985; Guha 1983). It is worth remarking that these works were also responses to the critiques of knowledge advanced in the West by Foucault (1981) and Said (1978), and in India by Nandy (1987) and Uberoi (1978, 1984) among others. These latter works had deeply weakened the claims of existing forms of humanist anthropology and colonial knowledge and had thus exposed the epistemological price extracted by the very way in which the human sciences had constructed their objects, both in the West and beyond. After these trenchant epistemological critiques had taken some of the high ground, the anthropological study of India as the paradise of hierarchy unbound, could no longer proceed in the manner of a normal science.

Culture and the State

The zenith of a folkloristic, rather than a critically grounded approach to popular culture can be seen in the many books and catalogues that accompanied the Festival of India in 1986, where scholars from India and the West combined to produce a dazzling display of ethnological accounts, exhibits, and performances calculated to show the unity-in-diversity of Indian popular culture. Although a few such works showed an admirable interest in the political contexts of Indic cultural forms (Borden ed. 1989), the majority tended to be marked by the rhetoric of preservation and celebration. Already underpinned by the massive investments of the Indian state and subject to intense criticism and debate in India, the 'exhibitionary complex', (Bennett 1988) associated with the Festivals of India overseas and the cultural apparatus of 'Apna Utsav' performances throughout India, marked the transition to a marked politicization of cultural identities in India in the middle to late 1980s, notably during the tenure of the late Rajiv Gandhi as prime minister.

It is possible to make two observations about this period, with the benefit of hindsight. First, this intense nationalization and commodification of popular culture by the Indian state accompanies an aggressive effort by the same regime to advance the cause of economic liberalization, privatization, mass media, and high technology, thus radically opening Indian markets, consumers and audiences to global forces and resources. Second, the efforts to nationalize Indian culture in the second half of the 1980s provided the facade beneath which another drama was taking shape: the mobilization of new forms of cultural nationalism by the forces of Hindutva.

By the late 1980s and the early 1990s, when it also became clear that Rajiv Gandhi's policies had come at a high cost in terms of pressures to accept stiff doses of structural adjustment meted out by the international lending agencies (A.N. Das 1992), the study of popular culture (often de facto of Hindu culture) began to be placed in a stronger framework of critical analysis. It became increasingly apparent that many popular forms, especially the televisual propagation of the epics, were part and parcel of the explosive growth in the power of the Bharatiya Janata Party (BJP), the Vishva Hindu Parishad (VHP), and the many organizations of the Sangh Parivar, particularly in the Hindi belt. More recent studies of Indian popular culture show the impact of the destruction of the Babri Masjid in Ayodhya on 6 December 1992, and have sought to account for the relationship between Hindu popular cultural practices and the massive victories of the BJP in state and national elections (Nandy ed. 1995; van der Veer 1994; Pandey ed. 1993); of the cultures of violence unleashed during this period (Kakar 1995); and of the relationship of the Ramjanmabhoomi movement to wider transformations in electoral politics, mass media (Farmer 1996; Rajagopal 1994), and ideologies of economic nationalism (Deshpande 1993). The awareness that popular energies and quotidian cultural forms could be annexed for the purposes of larger and more violent national politics was not entirely lost on anthropologists and sociologists (Manuel 1993; van der Veer 1994; Fox 1996).

This awareness is especially marked in two recent edited collections (Ludden ed. 1996; Pandey ed. 1993) which place anthropological and sociological understandings of Hindu nationalism in the context of studies from art history (Davis 1996; A. Kapur 1993a), economic and social history (Sarkar 1996) and political science. More than many other individual essays and studies, these two collections (which involve collaborations mainly between scholars based in the United States and in India) demonstrate that narrowly folkloric or culturological accounts of popular culture, especially in its Hindu forms, implied an innocence on the part of the analyst that is no longer sustainable.

Overseas Perspectives and Views from India

While the co-optation of 'Indian' culture and civilization by the forces of the Hindu right from the late 1980s onwards made it impossible to divorce the study of popular culture from its broader political context, there were developments in Britain and in the United States going back to the early 1980s which were also important in creating the need for a more critical, contextual, and globally oriented account of popular culture. These developments fall under the broad rubric of 'cultural studies' which recently acquired the status of a publicly recognized field in India (*Seminar* 1996; Niranjana et al. 1993). This field has been regularly enriched by critical and theoretical work emanating out of Indian diasporic intellectuals and experiences (Bhabha 1994; Mohanty 1991; Mani 1987; Spivak 1987) who have helped shape its interest in hybridity, border identities, multiculturalism and feminism. The most recent example of this cross-pollination, in which resident and non-resident Indians continue to shape central debates in cultural studies, is a special issue of the journal *Critical Inquiry* that contains a number of Indianist contributions in its discussion of 'borders' (*Critical Inquiry* 1997).

The emergent zone of traffic between cultural studies, area studies, and ethnography was marked by the emergence of the journal *Public Culture* in 1988. In the years since it was founded, this journal has helped to define 'public culture' as an aspect of culture which pays special attention to debate and contestation, to national inflections of cultural forms and to the globalization of cultural institutions and images. While it appears to be just another cultural studies journal produced by the academic industry in the United States, this journal was animated by the wish of the founder-editors to engage with the alternative modernities of societies such as India, which appeared to fall between the cracks of a rurally oriented anthropology and a past-oriented cultural history. The specific urge to develop a framework to deal with Indian modernity from a cultural point of view was a central part of the motivation behind its founding. Over the years the journal has retained a strong interest in Indian phenomena and cultural debates, and has helped to create a comparative context for the discussion of Indian advertising (Srivatsan 1991), cinema (Krishen 1991), diaspora (Ghosh 1989), epics (Richman 1995), historiography (Chakrabarty 1992), and politics (Chatterjee 1990). An entire issue of the journal in the 1990s was in fact devoted to debate surrounding a controversial work of cultural criticism (Ahmad 1992) and included essays by several Indianists. At the same time, two volumes published by scholars associated with the work of *Public Culture*, Breckenridge and van der Veer eds. 1993) sought to illuminate the diverse ways in which major cultural forms in contemporary India encode themes of nation and violence, state culture and sub-dominant practices, spectacle and commodity, expenditure and leisure.

Public culture emerges, in this body of work, as a way of looking at India as one site, among others, where western modernity is being translated, interrogated, and contested, as Indian traditions of some antiquity encounter the complex forces of colonialism and the political economy of the postcolonial order. In this view, culture no longer implies consensus; traditions are subject to multiple appropriations and deployments; class becomes a site for cultural consumption as well as production; and the state is a key player in virtually every domain of cultural expression. Public culture, looked at this way, encourages the study of the relationship between minority and majority cultural forms; of the relationship between national and global cultural economies; and of the relationship between forms of identity politics and cultural assertion to transformations in space, media, and the market. In this context, it is worth noting the coincident foundation of *Public Culture* in the United States and *The Journal of Arts and Ideas* based in India, the latter with a strong focus on the visual arts and a wider concern with cultural analysis and criticism.

By its nature, the study of Indian public culture does not permit the segregation of leisure from work, of politics from kinship, and of the marketplace from the temple and the voting-booth. Two other recent studies can be seen as illuminating the dynamics of public culture regarded in this manner. The first, a collection of essays by Veena Das, invites old concepts to 'inhabit unfamiliar spaces' and to acquire 'a new kind of life' (1995a: 1). These unfamiliar spaces are those of the Partition, of kinship strained by the struggle between national systems of honour, of the discourse of Sikh militants in the 1980s and of the suffering and the pain of the victims of industrial–ecological disasters. In this book, Das poses a series of critical questions about the relationship between the state, communities, and the individual, showing how law and cultural norms are mobilized at each of these levels, and further showing how contemporary events can benefit from an anthropological perspective on the discourses of law, suffering, terror, and communal mobilization. Das's essays may be seen as eminent examples of studies in public culture, for every one of the topics she explores involves fundamental cultural contests over meaning, value, and power. In developing her argument, Das is able to show that the legal and bureaucratic order of the modern nation-state suffuses the lives of individuals and communities in ways that affect the deepest matters of kinship and honour, self and the other. From another perspective, Das's book may be seen as a formative contribution to what may be called the 'ethnography of the state', in which she joins a wider anthropological interest (Feldman 1991; Taussig 1997) in studying what has recently been called the 'social poetics of the nation-state' (Herzfeld 1997).

The second book to offer a conceptual approach to the phenomena of public culture is a recent collection of essays which explores the relationship between culture and colonialism (Niranjana et al. 1993). This collection, much more within the cultural studies tradition, is centrally preoccupied with issues of literary, cinematic, and photographic representation, and contains a series of glimpses of the ways in which Indian visual practices and institutions, as well as more traditional forms such as the novel, bear the definite mark of the colonial encounter. Though the essays deal with a wide range of cultural practices and forms, the collection is unified by an approach to modernity which sees Indian culture 'not as some kind of organic whole ... but as "ways of struggle"' (1993: 2).' Thus the emphasis is on 'the materiality of culture, the connections between culture and ideology, and the intersections of culture, knowledge, and power in the colonial and post-colonial contexts' (1993: 7). Here the overlaps with Das's approach to 'critical events' and the concern of a growing group of analysts with transnational flows, alternative modernities, and the debates which constitute public culture are evident.

If there is one major tendency which unites these diverse approaches to public culture in India, it is a concern with the new visual order, which encompasses billboards and photographs, calendars and posters, films and television, spectacles and performances, all in a manner which links aesthetics to politics, representation to contestation, seeing to believing. There is a growing coincidence of interests between scholars studying theatre (A. Kapur 1993b), film (Prasad 1993; Pandian 1992; Rajadhyaksha 1987; Vasudevan 1995), television (Rajagopal 1994, 1996; V. Das 1995b), photography (Pinney 1990; Srivatsan 1991), and traditional forms of pictorial art (G. Kapur 1995; Thakurta-Guha 1992). All these scholars are interested, to a significant extent, in relating problems of representation to problems of violence, community, identity, and modernity. Though some of this work is mostly concerned with the internal structure of visual texts and genres, and with highly theoretical issues of spectatorship, aura, and authorial style, a growing body of studies is concerned with the social medium in which these visual objects circulate and with the ways in which audiences, fan clubs, journalists, and political parties interpellate themselves into this visual field (S.V. Srinivas 1996; Dickey 1993; Vasudevan 1996; A. Kapur 1993a; Babb and Wadley 1995).

In some ways, therefore, the conditions for the study of public culture in India are now relatively well defined, and cultural analysts working on Indian material have been in the forefront of defining the parameters of this field. In a context where modernity and its everyday expressions had largely been seen through western epistemologies and exemplified in cosmopolitan ethnographies, studies of Indian phenomena have sparked important cross-cultural exercises in the study of public culture. Furthermore, the worldwide search for critiques of western knowledge, forms and regimes has been led by thinkers from India such as Nandy and Uberoi, along with counterparts from Africa, Latin America, the Middle East, and East Asia. New historiographies of everyday forms of subaltern practice and agency have been inspired by historians working principally on Indian colonial materials. Recent contributions to the 'high' theory of diaspora, hybridity, intertextuality and narrativity have been suffused with Indian voices and approaches; international feminist scholarship has been enriched and interrogated by feminist scholars working in and from India. Also, some of the richest work to revise earlier Eurocentric models of nationalism and its postcolonial expressions have been led by work on Indian nationalism. In addition, path-breaking work on cinema, ethnic violence, women's fiction, popular science, and a host of other public cultural phenomena has been shaped by contributions from India. From a broad interdisciplinary perspective, work on India has suffused the richest recent developments in cultural studies, art criticism, film studies, political philosophy, and development studies. A glance at such journals as *Alternatives, Lokayan, Journal of Arts and Ideas, Public Culture*, and the *Economic and Political Weekly* substantiates this interdisciplinary claim. But the contributions of social anthropologists and sociologists to this burgeoning field of interdisciplinary inquiry have so far been limited in number and scope, and in a sense, high theory has outstripped the empirical study of Indian public culture. In the remainder of this essay, I shall make some programmatic suggestions for conceptualizing a specifically ethnographic and sociological contribution to the study of public culture in India. What follows is thus less an inventory and more a prospectus.

The Politics of Space

The study of space is hardly new in the cultural sociology of India. Many village studies have examined land and soil, boundaries and house forms, regions and sacred sites. But the study of rural space as a product and medium of human activity and as a context for agency and conflict has been less well attended as regards rural India. Likewise, there is a large literature in sociology, urban planning and social work on cities, slums, urban renewal plans and migration. But this literature, which is dominated by demographic, structural and aggregate phenomena does not have a strong cultural dimension.

Consider the ethnography of motion and travel. While we know about the large-scale logistics of roads, railways, trucking and other forms of 'life on the move', we have few sustained ethnographic glimpses of these phenomena, and those few concern pilgrimage as a cultural form. These studies offer only a tantalizing glimpse of what an ethnography of Indian transportation could say about public culture. We need answers to questions like the following: How is the growing trade in domestic tourism organized at both national and regional levels? Who are the entrepreneurs behind this industry? Where are its drivers, guides, and promoters recruited from? How localized is this traffic and when does it bring together consumers from different regions and classes in common spaces-in-motion? How do ordinary Indian travellers conceptualize the relationships between leisure, pleasure, and devotion in these journeys?

Another set of questions having to do with space is especially pertinent to cities. As many Indian cities undergo massive demographic change, occupational and linguistic groups from regions which previously did not occupy common urban space are thrown together in volatile economic and political circumstances. In cities like Surat, Mumbai, Hyderabad, and elsewhere, the dynamics of labour and capital combine with mass-mediated propaganda and severe shortages of living space and jobs to create conditions of considerable social friction. We need to link the work on change in the cities of such regions to other studies of cultural style and labour circulation. Thus, in the case of Gujarat, a politically potent brand of public culture studies could seek to link recent work on cloth and clothing among rural *jatis* (Tarlo 1996) to the first-rate work on labour circulation (Breman 1985), and these to what is known about urban demographics, communal violence, and reservation politics in Gujarat. Political messages, sartorial conventions, circulating sites of employment and anxiety about economic opportunities create a volatile landscape of desire, fear, and violence in which cultural styles and political mobilization may be seen in a single framework. Such linkages can also be explored in other parts of India, where similar glimpses of work, cultural style, and political identity are available in the form of unfinished puzzles.

Closer still to the everyday life of cities, we know less than we should about the growth of all sorts of houses, colonies, and squatter settlements, which characterize a growing number of Indian cities. This spatial explosion occurs along a complex continuum ranging from the upmarket complexes of suburban housing being built by mega-developers (with a substantial eye to overseas purchases by non-resident Indians) to the ad hoc arrangements of street-dwelling indigents or proletarians, always at risk of natural or political destruction. Linking these economically diverse real estate markets, notably in a city like Mumbai, are a complex network of real estate developers, politicians, speculators, and hoodlums, who operate in a shadow world of licences, pay-offs and physical violence, to protect those who pay and to evict or blackmail those who cannot. In Mumbai during 1992–3, there was clearly a complicated nexus that linked the excesses of municipal violence against street vendors and their illegal structures to the larger politics of organized crime and communal politics, and thus fed into the brutal violence of December 1992 to January 1993 which followed the destruction of the Babri Masjid in Ayodhya. This episode has been thoroughly documented in the recently published report of the Srikrishna Commission.

The line between spaces of traffic, commerce, and leisure has become completely blurred in many Indian cities. We need to ask about the everyday pressures, for many pedestrians, of walking on the road, avoiding cars, scooters, bullock-carts, and bicycles because footpaths are either non-existent or fully occupied by vendors of consumer goods. Such commerce, itself a vital component of the informal economies of many cities, in turn generates large amounts of unaccounted income which flows into circuits of street expenditure on (often prohibited or smuggled) goods and services, ranging from *paan* and prostitutes to video cassettes and fake Nike sneakers. What is the sociology of expenditure in these street settings? How do the cross-ethnic links that characterize these daily transactions connect to the sudden paroxysms of communal violence which periodically segregate ethnic groups? How does this micro-economy of street expenditures and sales tie into the service economy generally, through the provision of food and related services to the lower level employees of large corporations and offices? In terms of taste, lifestyle, and social aspirations, how do these spatial logics link lumpen consumption to the upscale lifestyles of film-stars, crime lords, and corporate chieftains? As citizens navigate these immensely crowded spaces, characterized by many kinds of cash transactions, ad hoc structures, and ethnically inflected occupational niches, how do the cross-cutting ties of work and commerce resist the essentializing and segregating discourses of right-wing media propaganda? How do the rhythms of amity and enmity interact in cities where residence, work, and transport throw culturally distinct groups into constant contact? What is called for here is a series of close studies of the relationships between street commerce, real estate markets and their controllers, and various kinds of criminalized practice. Such studies, from a variety of urban settings, would tell us a great deal about the pathways and nerve centres which guide the journey of rumours, weapons, gangs, and money in the urban cartography of ethnic violence.

Finally, such studies of the dynamics of lived space, especially in cities besieged by migrants from diverse communities and regions, could build a perspective from the ground upwards of what various groups valorize as national space, national boundaries, and national monuments (such as the Babri Masjid). The spatialities involved in these contexts are of course different, but the perspective of public culture might allow us to mediate the relationship between the everyday spaces of work, residence, and worship and the more overdetermined sites of national honour and ethnic purity. As communal parties and other radical voices increasingly cast the net of 'national space' over specific sites and monuments in particular cities and localities, the sense of national honour is localized, and cityscapes become both icons and indices of ethnonational identity and purity. These cartographic transpositions need intense empirical investigation, and the traditional strengths of cultural sociology in India, in the study of temples, pilgrimage sites, village gods, religious routes and the like, could be revitalized and extended to illuminate these new spatial worlds. In this way, we might begin to develop a sociological sense of the links between property and territory, a vital (and unfulfilled) requirement for understanding the political economy of communalism. These ethnographic accounts would complement the initiatives already taken in the realm of studies of the discourses surrounding community, identity, and honour in the India of the last two decades.

Cultures of Commerce

The preceding consideration of new ways of looking at space and its production in contemporary India implies collateral perspectives on media and visual culture, as well as on commerce and consumption. There have of course been some studies of commercial communities, market processes, and consumption by anthropologists of India. But these have rarely tied commerce to wider forms of cultural politics nor have they usually linked sociological issues to those of culture. Today, as the whole of Indian society comes to be more explicitly tied to the global economy, as Indian labourers and professionals increasingly travel to overseas markets, as major new class fractions and fragments enter the political arena in cities, small towns and villages, we need to re-examine the cultural dynamics of commerce. The public culture of commerce raises a wide range of questions which social anthropologists could engage with.

What are the ways in which commoditization has transformed rural and urban life? How exactly have changing consumption patterns, material aspirations, and marriage markets affected the politics of dowry (including the pattern of domestic violence and dowry death)? What sort of ties between commerce, trade, and group identity provided the context for the mobilization of Rajput hyper-masculinity in the celebrated *sati* death of Roop Kanwar? In so far as a significant number of Indians (about 15–20 per cent of the population, according to most estimates) have the capacity to spend some money on modern consumer goods, what determines their attachment to these goods? Who are the groups that most profit from the flow of urban goods to rural areas?

Answers to these, and related questions, might supply an ethnographic dimension to the vital question of the class and caste composition of many new social movements, ranging from anti-reservation movements and Hindu nationalist parties to farmers' movements and backward caste coalitions. The salience of commerce and consumption to the study of these social formations (which have transformed the culture of politics throughout India in the last half century) is that the 'world of goods' serves as a system of public signals of both solidarity among groups (Douglas and Isherwood 1979) and of difference between groups (Bourdieu 1984). In a state like Uttar Pradesh, it will be hard to understand the complex links between *mandir* and *mandal* (popular ways of referring to communalism and caste politics respectively) until we have a fuller sense of the solidarities that have emerged in and through the marketplace and the world of commodities.

By extension, as has recently been suggested by several sociologists (Rajagopal 1996; Deshpande 1995), there are definite ties between economic globalization, the pressures of structural adjustment since the early 1990s and the rise of the Hindu right. On the one hand, new forms of consumption and new commercial classes have turned to Hindu revival as keys to national welfare as opposed to older ideologies of *swadeshi* (economic autonomy) and Gandhian simplicity. On the other hand, the ideologies of liberalization and those of Hindu revival seek, as Rajagopal has suggested, to restore national competitiveness and cultural revival in linked idioms. But understanding the links which may account for the paradoxical mutuality of open markets and cultural closure requires a closer examination of the ideologies and practices of various emerging classes, both of their leaders and their members. Thus, the openness of the Shiv Sena leadership in Maharashtra to multinational companies like Enron with a parallel hostility to the Pakistani cricket team and to other forms of cultural invasion are not easy to interpret. They demand a nuanced sense of how certain castes and classes view market processes, of how they disarticulate economic cosmopolitanism from territorial nativism, and of how they understand the cultural markedness of different forms of capital. This nuanced approach to commerce and capital requires the ethnographic and textual strengths of social anthropology and sociology.

Such an approach will provide one other bridge between everyday practices and identities and the larger political and cultural solidarities that characterize Indian society and politics today. Even when viewed from the classical perspective of caste studies, the structure and ethos of commercial castes has been studied less than those of other groups. The result, with a few exceptions, is that the intervillage, regional, and state-level links that often characterize commercial castes have tended to fall out of the picture, reinforcing the stereotype of the isolation of the Indian village. Likewise, this gap has made it difficult to create a useful dialogue between social anthropologists and economic historians, on problems in the history of capital formation, marketization, and monetization. Finally, the relatively scant attention paid to the cultural dynamics of contemporary commerce in India has meant that a large gap has developed today between the sociology of commerce and various Indological contributions to the study of debt, livelihood and market norms in ancient India.

To treat commerce and commodification as a part of public culture in India opens the prospect of breaking certain artificial disciplinary boundaries that segregate economic forms from cultural forms. Further, this angle on commerce offers the prospect of grounding cultural practices in the material world while recognizing that consumption (and production) take place in regimes of value that are historically and culturally inflected. As considerations of life style (hence of commodities and consumption) increase in their importance as indices of rank, the study of commerce from a public culture perspective is sure to contribute a valuable dimension to the general study of new forms of stratification.

Mass Mediation and Public Life

Neither space nor commerce can be engaged without a focused concern with the workings of mass media. To appreciate this argument, one need only notice the place of advertisements on streets and highways throughout India. I have suggested earlier that we already have a good deal of insight into specific developments involving television and film, advertising and photography, music and theatre, among other forms of mass mediation. We also have the beginnings of important insights into the links between mass media and religious nationalism (van der Veer 1994; A. Kapur 1993a; Rajagopal 1994, 1996) and between the logic of public debate and the discourses of terror and revival (V. Das 1995a; Vasudevan 1996). What we need now is to build on our knowledge of audiences and mass-mediated messages to see media as part of a broader circulatory logic in which images, messages, experiences, and desires are interactively moving. Such a picture of circulation is not available in western theories and studies of mass media, except in partial and highly contested fragments. India, with its saturation by mass media (especially through film, but also through radio, television and newspapers) and its diversity of languages in which mass mediation operates, is a spectacular field for studying publics which are divided by different media genres and by the varied languages and contexts within which media messages circulate. Here then is an opportunity to complicate both the monoglot and middle-class-centred approach of Habermas (1989) to the western bourgeois public sphere and to complicate the unilinear assumptions about print, capitalism and nationalism proposed by Anderson (1983). The variety of languages, genres, contexts, and registers which constitute the circulatory field of mass media in India offers a unique opportunity to examine the multiple rationalities that might drive print-based nationalisms as well as the multiple cultures of reception that might shape media environments in India. A deeper ethnographic grasp of such processes of differentiation and divergence might throw valuable light on what has been widely seen as a new pattern of regionalization in Indian politics, in which the politics of the centre does not predict or determine regional outcomes. Such regional political patterns are not likely to be understood by looking at electoral data and the strategies and statements of elites alone. They will certainly require a close examination of the nature and composition of reading and viewing publics, as well as of the forms of mediation which they enjoy and appropriate.

In thus approaching mass-mediated forms and processes as part of a wide, interactive field of circulation, anthropologists and sociologists would surely add a new dimension to the classical issue of 'text and context' that exercised the minds of some of the finest social scientists of India in the 1950s and 1960s, such as Milton Singer and M.N. Srinivas. More importantly, the approach to mass media sketched here is not likely to replicate some of the folkloristic drawbacks of earlier approaches to popular forms and events, which tended to see them mainly as expressive insignia of particular social categories and subcultures, elements of an unspecified Indian mosaic. This earlier view was perfect grist for the operations of the cultural apparatus of the *state,* which inevitably prefers static formulae about unity and diversity.

The critical, contextual, and conjunctural approach to mass media suggested here tends to redirect our attention to the broader contours of cultural politics in contemporary India. In this view, the analysis of mass media would draw our attention back to 'critical events', in Veena Das's usage, to new understandings of space and spatiality (in which everyday and imagined spaces could be connected) and of commerce (by looking at new relationships between buying and being in the age of structural adjustment). Mass mediation, as an object of analysis in a public culture perspective, holds the promise of shedding new light on the ways in which desires, fantasies, and the life of the imagination work in contemporary India.

That India is now a media-saturated society is widely accepted. But the cultural implications of this fact are not well understood. Thus an important component of the way in which elites and poorer classes in India form their pictures of power, status, and the economy eludes us. By extension, the context in which different individuals and groups respond to efforts to mobilize them are only hazily understood, and an important dimension of many new social movements (involving the environment, Dalit politics, and liquor consumption, for example) remains elusive. If the cultural sociology of India is to contribute seriously to the understanding of such forms of mobilization, the study of mass media as part of a broader field of communications and transactions cannot be postponed.

Conclusion

The points of entry into public culture discussed here—space, commerce, and mass media— do not constitute a closed list. There are other areas of vital relevance to public culture and its study—science, environment, technology, labour—to name just a few. All of them could be seen as the province of specialists in fields beyond anthropology and sociology—such as history, economics, mass communication, and political science. But the idea of public culture—culture viewed as a zone of debates and contestation—certainly offers sociologists and anthropologists both an opportunity and a justification for studying these complex objects. In this way, some of what is contemporary about India can be illuminated by some of what is contemporary about anthropology. In taking up these challenges, the social life of modernity in India will not remain a study of derivations, oddities, and spectacles and the social life of anthropology will not remain confined to stereotyped debates about rural, traditional or hierarchical India. On the other hand, a robust view of Indian public culture should return us to the perennial problems of caste, family, and class, enriched by a sharper grasp of state policies, new economies, emergent classes, and incipient social movements.

As India approaches the turn of the century, and celebrates a half-century of independence, it seems appropriate to ask how far we have moved from the basic principles, assumptions and interests of colonial sociology. In so far as village life is still studied in isolation from wider regional and national forces, in so far as cultural forms still tend to be viewed ethnologically and folkloristically, and in so far as the study of the state and nation still remains relatively distant from the study of everyday life, the answer to this question is: not far enough. Attention to the phenomena of public culture, in the manner implied throughout this essay, might be one important part of engaging with the realities of the last few decades.

A further bonus of such an engagement will surely be to redraw the terms of the relationships between social anthropology, sociology and the neighbouring fields and disciplines involved in the study of India. It is not easy to predict what form these relationships might take. But it is not difficult to see that the cultural politics of contemporary India do not comfortably fit into a division of fields which was produced by Europe in the nineteenth century. In the reconfiguration of the cultural sciences that will surely occur in the next few decades, critical cultural analysis of public culture phenomena could be one way in which the sociology of India retains its leverage. By extension, the probability will increase that places like India will generate not just alternative modernities, but alternative sociologies as well.

ACKNOWLEDGEMENTS

I am grateful to Carol Breckenridge and Veena Das for critical readings of an earlier draft of this chapter. While I have not been able to respond to all their queries, they have certainly helped me to sharpen my arguments and avoid some errors of interpretation.

REFERENCES

Ahmad, Aijaz. 1992. *In Theory: Classes, Nations, Literatures*. London; New York: Verso.

Anderson, Benedict R. 1983. *Imagined Communities: Reflections on the Origin and Spread of Nationalism*. London; New York: Verso.

Appadurai, Arjun. 1981. *Worship and Conflict under Colonial Rule: A South Indian Case*. Cambridge, UK; New York: Cambridge University Press.

_____. 1988. 'How to Make a National Cuisine: Cookbooks in Contemporary India'. *Comparative Studies in Society and History*. 30 (1):3–24.

Babb, Lawrence A. and Susan Wadley. 1995. *Media and the Transformation of Religion in South Asia*. Philadelphia: University of Pennsylvania Press.

Bennett, Tony. 1988. 'The Exhibitionary Complex'. *New Formations*. 4:73–102.

Béteille, André. 1983. *The Idea of Natural Inequality and Other Essays*. Delhi: Oxford University Press.

Bhabha, Homi K. 1990. *Nation and Narration*. London; New York: Routledge.

_____. 1994. *The Location of Culture*. London; New York: Routledge.

Borden, Carla, ed. 1989. *Contemporary Indian Tradition*. Washington, D.C.; London: The Smithsonian Institution.

Bourdieu, Pierre. 1984. *Distinction: A Social Critique of the Judgment of Taste*. Cambridge, MA: Harvard University Press.

————. 1995. *Consuming Modernity: Public Culture in a South Asian World*. Minneapolis: University of Minnesota Press.

Breckenridge, Carol A. 1977. 'From Protector to Litigant: Changing Relations between Hindu Temples and the Raja of Ramnad'. *Indian Economic and Social History Review*. 14(1):75–106.

Breckenridge, Carol, A. and Peter van der Veer, eds. 1993. *Orientalism and the Postcolonial Predicament: Perspectives on South Asia*. Philadelphia: University of Pennsylvania Press.

Breman, Jan. 1985. *Of Peasants, Migrants, and Paupers: Rural Labour Circulation and Capitalist Production in West India*. Delhi: Oxford University Press.

Chakrabarty, Dipesh. 1992. 'The Death of History: Historical Consciousness and the Culture of Late Capitalism'. *Public Culture*. (2):47–66.

Chatterjee, Partha. 1990. 'A Response to Taylor's "Modes of Civil Society"'. *Public Culture*. 3(1):119–34.

Cohn, Bernard S. 1985. 'The Command of Language and the Language of Command'. In Ranajit Guha, ed., *Subaltern Studies IV: Writings of South Asian History and Society*, 276–329. Delhi: Oxford University Press.

Cohn, Bernard S. and McKim Marriott. 1958. 'Networks and Centres in the Integration of Indian Civilization'. *Journal of Social Research*. 1:1–9.

Critical Inquiry. 1997. Special issue: *Front Lines/Border Posts*. 23(3).

Das, Arvind N. 1992. *India Invented: A Nation in the Making*. New Delhi: Manohar Publications.

Das, Veena. 1995a. *Critical Events: An Anthropological Perspective on Contemporary India*. Delhi; New York: Oxford University Press.

————. 1995b. 'On Soap Opera: What kind of Anthropological Object Is It'? In Daniel Miller, ed., *Worlds Apart: Modernity through the Prism of the Local*, 169–89. London: Routledge and Kegan Paul.

Davis, Richard H. 1996. 'The Iconography of Rama's Chariot'. In David Ludden, ed., *Contesting the Nation: Religion, Community and the Politics of Democracy in India*, 27–54. Philadelphia: University of Pennsylvania Press.

Deshpande, Satish. 1993. 'Imagined Economies: Styles of Nation-Building in Twentieth Century India'. *Journal of Arts and Ideas*. 25(6):5–35.

————. 1995. 'Communalising the Nation-Space: Notes on Spatial Strategies of Hindutva'. *Economic and Political Weekly*. 30(50):3220.

Dickey, Sara A. 1993. *Cinema and the Urban Poor in South India*. Cambridge: UK; New York: Cambridge University Press.

Dirks, Nicholas B. 1987. *The Hollow Crown: Ethnohistory of an Indian Kingdom*. Cambridge, UK; New York: Cambridge University Press.

Douglas, Mary and Baron C. Isherwood. 1979. *The World of Goods: Towards an Anthropology of Consumption*. New York: Basic Books.

Dumont, Louis. 1970. *Homo Hierarchicus: An Essay on the Caste System*. Chicago: University of Chicago Press.

Farmer, Victoria. 1996. 'Mass Media: Images, Mobilization and Communalism'. In David Ludden, ed., *Contesting the Nation: Religion, Community, and the Politics of Democracy in India*, 98–118. Philadelphia: University of Pennsylvania Press.

Feldman, Allen. 1991. *Formations of Violence: The Narrative of the Body and Political Terror in Northern Ireland*. Chicago: University of Chicago Press.

Fox, Richard. 1996. 'Communalism and Modernity'. In David Ludden, ed., *Contesting the Nation: Religion, Community, and the Politics of Democracy in India*, 235–49. Philadelphia: University of Pennsylvania Press.

Foucault, Michel. 1981. *Power/Knowledge: Selected Interviews and Other Writings, 1972–1977*. New York: Pantheon Books.

Freitag, Sandria B. 1989a. 'State and Community: Symbolic Popular Protest in Banaras's Public Arenas'.

In Sandria Freitag, ed., *Culture and Power in Banaras: Community Performance and Environment, 1800–1980*, 203–28. Berkeley: University of California Press.

———. 1989b. *Collective Action and Community: Public Arenas and the Emergence of Communalism in North India*. Berkeley: University of California Press.

Ghosh, Amitav. 1989. 'The Diaspora in Indian Culture'. *Public Culture*. 2(1):73–8.

Ghurye, G.S. 1953. *Indian Sadhus*. Bombay: Popular Book Depot.

Guha, Ranajit. 1983. *Elementary Aspects of Peasant Insurgency in Colonial India*. Delhi: Oxford University Press.

Habermas, Jürgen. 1989. *The Structural Transformation of the Public Sphere*. Cambridge, MA: MIT Press.

Herzfeld, Michael. 1997. *Cultural Intimacy: Social Poetics in the Nation-state*. New York: Routledge.

Kakar, Sudhir. 1989. *Intimate Relations: Exploring Indian Sexuality*. Harmondsworth: Penguin.

———. 1995. *The Colours of Violence*. New Delhi; New York: Viking.

Kapur, Anuradha. 1993a. 'Deity to Crusader: The Changing Iconography of Ram'. In Gyanendra Pandey, ed., *Hindus and Others: The Question of Identity in India Today*, 74–109. New Delhi; New York: Viking.

———. 1993b. 'The Representation of Gods and Heroes: Parsi Mythological Drama of the Early Twentieth Century'. *Journal of Arts and Ideas*. 23–4:85–107.

Kapur, Geeta. 1995. 'When was Modernism in Indian Art'. *Journal of Arts and Ideas*. 27–8:105–26.

Krishen, Pradip. 1991. 'Knocking at the Doors of Public Culture: India's Parallel Cinema'. *Public Culture*. 4(1):25–42.

Kumar, Nita. 1988. *The Artisans of Banaras: Popular Culture and Identity, 1880–1986*. Princeton, NJ: Princeton University Press.

———. ed. 1994. *Women as Subjects: South Asian Histories*. Charlottesville: University Press of Virginia.

Ludden, David E., ed. 1996. *Contesting the Nation: Religion, Community, and the Politics of Democracy in India*. Philadelphia: University of Pennsylvania Press.

Lutgendorf, Philip. 1990. 'Ram's Story in Shiva's City: Public Arenas and Private Patronage'. In S. Freitag, ed., *Culture and Power in Banaras: Community, Performance and Environment, 1800–1980*, 34–61. Berkeley: University of California Press.

Madan, T.N. 1987. *Non-renunciation: Themes and Interpretations of Hindu Culture*. Delhi; New York: Oxford University Press.

———. 1994. *Pathways: Approaches to the Study of Society in India*. Delhi; New York: Oxford University Press.

Mani, Lata. 1987. 'Contentious Traditions: The Debate on Sati in Colonial India'. *Cultural Critique*. 7:119–56.

Manuel, Peter L. 1993. *Cassette Culture: Popular Music and Technology in North India*. Chicago: University of Chicago Press.

Marriott, McKim. 1955. *Village India*. Chicago: University of Chicago Press.

Mohanty, Chandra T. 1991. 'Under Western Eyes: Feminist Scholarship and Colonial Discourses'. In Chandra T. Mohanty, Ann Russo and Lourdes Torres, eds, *Third World Women and the Politics of Feminism*, 51–80. Bloomington: Indiana University Press.

Nandy, Ashis. 1987. *Traditions, Tyranny, and Utopias: Essays in the Politics of Awareness*. Delhi; New York: Oxford University Press.

———. ed. 1995. *Creating a Nationality: The Ramjanmabhumi Movement and Fear of the Self*. Delhi: Oxford University Press.

Niranjana, Tejaswini, P. Sudhir, and Vivek Dhareshwar, eds. 1993. *Interrogating Modernity: Culture and Colonialism in India*. Calcutta: Seagull Books.

O'Hanlon, Rosalind. 1994. *A Comparison between Women and Men: Tarabai Shinde and the Critique of Gender Relations in Colonial India*. Madras; Oxford: Oxford University Press.

Pandey, Gyanendra, ed. 1993. *Hindus and Others: The Question of Identity in India Today*. New Delhi; New York: Viking.

Pandian, M.S.S. 1992. *The Image-Trap: M.G. Ramachandran in Film and Politics*. New Delhi; Newbury Park: Sage Publications.

Pinney, Christopher. 1990. 'Classification and Fantasy in the Photographic Construction of Caste and Tribe'. *Visual Anthropology*. 3(2–3):259–88.

Prakash, Gyan. 1990. *Bonded Histories: Genealogies of Labor Servitude in Colonial India*. Cambridge, UK; New York: Cambridge University Press.

Prasad, Madhava. 1993. 'Cinema and the Desire for Modernity'. *Journal of Arts and Ideas*. 25(26):71–86.

Presler, Franklin A. 1987. *Religion Under Bureaucracy: Policy and Administration for Hindu Temples in South India*. Cambridge, UK; New York: Cambridge University Press.

Price, Pamela. 1988. 'Ideology and Ethnicity under British Imperial Rule: "Brahman", Lawyers, and Kin-Caste Rules in Madras Presidency'. *Modern Asian Studies*. 22:151–78.

Raheja, Gloria G. and Ann G. Gold 1994. *Listen to the Heron's Words: Reimagining Gender and Kinship in North India*. Berkeley: University of California Press.

Rajadhyaksha, Ashish. 1987. 'The Phalke Era: Conflict of Traditional Form and Modern Technology'. *Journal of Arts and Ideas*. 14–5:47–78.

Rajagopal, Arvind. 1994. 'Ram Janmabhoomi, Consumer Identity and Image-based Politics'. *Economic and Political Weekly*. July 2:1659–68.

———. 1996. 'Communalism and the Consuming Subject'. *Economic and Political Weekly*. February 10:341–8.

Richman, Paula. 1995. 'Epic and State: Contesting Interpretations of the Ramayana'. *Public Culture*. 7(3):631–54.

Said, Edward W. 1978. *Orientalism*. New York: Pantheon Books.

Saran, A.K. 1989. 'Gandhi and the Concept of Politics: Towards a Normal Civilization'. *Gandhi Marg*. 1:675–727.

Sarkar, Sumit. 1996. 'Indian Nationalism and the Politics of Hindutva'. In David Ludden, ed., *Contesting the Nation: Religion, Community, and the Politics of Democracy in India*, 270–93. Philadelphia: University of Pennsylvania Press.

Schechner, Richard. 1983. *Performative Circumstances, from the Avant Garde to Ramlila*. Calcutta: Seagull Books.

Seminar. 1996. Special issue: *Cultural Studies*. No. 446 (October).

Shah, A.M. 1988. 'The Rural–Urban Networks in India'. *South Asia*. 11(2):1–27.

Singer, Milton B. 1972. *When a Great Tradition Modernizes: An Anthropological Approach to Indian Civilization*. New York: Praeger.

Spivak, Gayatri Chakravorty. 1987. *In Other Worlds: Essays in Cultural Politics*. New York: Methuen.

Srinivas, M.N. 1971. *Social Change in Modern India*. Berkeley: University of California Press.

Srinivas, S.V. 1996. 'Devotion and Deviance in Fan Activity'. *Journal of Arts and Ideas*. 29:66–83.

Srivatsan, T. 1991. 'Looking at Film Hoardings: Labour, Gender, Subjectivity and Everyday Life in India'. *Public Culture*. 4(1):1–23.

Tarlo, Emma. 1996. *Clothing Matters*. Chicago: University of Chicago Press.

Taussig, Michael T. 1997. *The Magic of the State*. New York: Routledge.

Thakurta-Guha, Tapati. 1992. *The Making of a New 'Indian' Art: Artists, Aesthetics and Nationalism in Bengal, c. 1850–1920*. Cambridge: Cambridge University Press.

Thapan, Meenakshi. 1991. *Life at School: An Ethnographic Study*. Delhi; New York: Oxford University Press.

Uberoi, J.P.S. 1978. *Science and Culture*. Delhi: Oxford University Press.

———. 1984. *The Other Mind of Europe: Goethe as a Scientist*. Delhi; New York: Oxford University Press.

Vasudevan, Ravi S. 1995. 'Film Studies, New Cultural History and Experience of Modernity'. *Economic and Political Weekly.* 30(44):2809.

_____. 1996. 'Bombay and Its Public'. *Journal of Arts and Ideas.* 29:44–65.

Veer, Peter van der. 1994. *Religious Nationalism: Hindus and Muslims in India.* Berkeley: University of California Press.

Visvanathan, Shiv. 1985. *Organizing for Science: The Making of an Industrial Research Laboratory.* Delhi; New York: Oxford University Press.

IV
Family, Childhood, and Education

IV

The Family in India

PATRICIA UBEROI

INTRODUCTION

A review of scholarly writings in the field of Indian family and kinship studies suggests that the field is not, at least at present, a well-integrated one. One of the problems is that the subject is partitioned between several different social science disciplines whose protocols, problematics, theoretical foci, and practical concerns are all rather different: Indology, law, anthropology, sociology, psychology, psychiatry, economics, demography, human geography, and social work. In particular, the 'metropolitan' division of labour between the *anthropology of kinship* and the *sociology of the family* in terms of theories, methods, and preoccupations has been faithfully reproduced in the textbooks commonly used in Indian colleges and universities, notwithstanding a widespread sentiment against differentiating anthropology and sociology in the Indian context.[1]

Second, there has been an immense amount of empirical data collected under the aegis of the Census of India and other socio-economic survey instruments, but this vast material has only intermittently been brought under sociological scrutiny. Indeed, much of it is deemed unsuitable for testing sociologically meaningful hypotheses (see Shah 1999a). Third, the sociology of Indian family and kinship has focused more on kinship *norms* than on pathology, deviance, and breakdown. For this reason it has largely failed to inform or to confront the practical challenges of social activism and public- policy intervention.

This chapter does not deal directly with these issues of disciplinary boundary maintenance, but approaches them indirectly, through a critical reviewing of the single question that has dominated sociological discussion of the Indian family as well as public discourse in India. This is the question of the future of the 'traditional' Indian joint family or, more precisely, the question of whether or not the joint family has been breaking down as a result of the processes of modernization. At one stage this issue seemed to have been satisfactorily resolved (or was it just wished away?) by the privileging of the supposedly more precise notion of 'household' over the more fuzzy-edged concept of 'family', but in retrospect it appears that gains in definitional precision have unduly restricted the range of questions that can be asked and the issues that can be addressed. I believe that there is a pressing need now to recover 'the family' as an integrated object of study and, by this means, to reclaim for the disciplines of sociology and anthropology themes that have been sidelined by the one-sided focus on questions of household type and composition. Ironically, in thus retracing the trajectory of an intellectual debate, this chapter has itself been shaped and constrained by the very preoccupation it sets out to critique. Some indications of the hiatuses in the present account and a number of suggestions towards a renewal of the field are made, however, by way of conclusion.

THE FAMILY IN INDIA

India occupies a special place in the comparative sociology of the family as a textbook case of the working of a 'joint family system' (see Goode 1963: Chapter 5; and 1964: 48–51). Nonetheless, few questions have been as confused, or as confusing, as that of the Indian joint family: its definition; its composition; its functions; its history; and, of course, its future trajectory. The ideal of the Indian joint family has long been an important ingredient in national self-imaging as the social institution that uniquely expresses and represents the valued aspects of Indian culture and tradition;[2] thus it has become rather difficult to separate fact from value, behaviour from norm and indeed, to talk dispassionately about the subject at all. This is more so since the joint family and its supporting value system (often termed 'familism', as distinguished from 'individualism') are widely believed to be under threat from alien values and an alien way of life.

Historically, the concept of the 'Indian joint family' was the product of the engagement of British colonial administration with indigenous systems of kinship and marriage, notably with respect to the determination of rights in property and responsibility for revenue payment. Seeking to understand the principles of Indian legal systems, the British turned to the Hindu sacred texts, the Dharmashastras (see Kane 1930–62), or parallely, for the Muslim population of the subcontinent, to the Shariat and the rulings of Muslim legalists (see Mulla 1972). This approach, retrospectively termed the 'Indological' approach to Indian family studies (see Shah 1973: 124–5), confirmed the 'joint family' as the typical and traditional form of family organization in India, located it within the discursive domain of the law, and defined its special features.

An important influence in putting the Indian family on the map of comparative family studies and in shaping the Indological approach to the Indian joint family was the pioneering work of Henry Sumner Maine (1822–88), Law Member of the Council of the Governor-General in India from 1862 to 1869. Relying on the classical textual sources of Hindu law, read along with contemporary ethnographic and administrative reports, Maine projected the Indian joint family as a living example of the earliest or 'ancient' form of the human family whose outlines could also be discerned in the legal system of ancient Rome as well as in Celtic and Slavic survivals of earlier forms of social organization (Maine [1861] 1972). Maine termed this type of family the 'patriarchal family' for the reason that it was constituted by a group of persons related in the male line and subject to the absolute power (*patria potestas*) of the seniormost male member. In Maine's understanding, the patriarchal family functioned as a sort of a 'corporation', existing in perpetuity, whose living members were coparceners in a joint estate. Family property was divided equally among sons before or after the death of the ascendant; alternatively, the undivided family might expand over several generations to become an organized and self-regulating 'brotherhood of relatives', the 'village community', that Maine believed to be a characteristic South Asian form of social organization. Maine proposed that this ancient form of social organization, based on the principle of 'status', would in due course evolve through several stages into one based on 'contract', with the patriarchal joint family being replaced by the monogamous conjugal family unit of the contemporary western type, associated with the individual ownership of property and linked to the power of testation (Maine [1861] 1972).

Many of the early generation of Indian sociologists identified the patriarchal joint family of the Sanskrit legal and sacerdotal texts as the 'traditional' form of the family in India. In a discursive environment shaped by the force of 'cultural nationalism', they regarded the joint family as a unifying civilizational ideal that had been 'very widely held by all Hindus—the rich as well as the poor, the learned as well as the lay, the city men as well as the village folk' (Prabhu [1940] 1955: 5). This viewpoint was vigorously propounded in the writings of the Sanskritist/sociologist G.S. Ghurye who, in his erudite *Family and Kin in Indo-European Culture* (1955), claimed an Indo-European pedigree for the Indian joint family. By implication, of course, he also excluded from this venerable heritage the structurally quite different subcontinental culture of Dravidian kinship, the kinship practices of non-Hindu communities, and a wide range of non-Brahmanic usages.

Reconciling the unitary Sanskritic heritage with the empirical variety of contemporary Indian family and kinship practices was a problem that several of Ghurye's students at the Sociology Department of Bombay University sought to address explicitly (see, esp., Kapadia 1955). For instance, following the general line of Lewis Henry Morgan (1871), Irawati Karve sought to link Indian kinship systems, through the structure of their vocabularies of kinship terms, to the major subcontinental language groups and sub-linguistic areas. By these criteria she identified four main types of kinship organization in India: (i) an Indo-European or Sanskritic type in the north, where kinship practices were essentially continuous with those described in classical Sanskrit sources; (ii) a Dravidian type in the south; (iii) a mixed 'central' zone between the two; and (iv) a geographically non-contiguous Austro-Asiatic type (of Mundari and Mon-Khmer linguistic affiliation) in the East (Karve 1953: Chapter 1). Counterbalancing this heterogeneity, Karve then proposed three *unifying* factors through the subcontinent: (i) the all-India institution of caste, notwithstanding its many regional variations (Karve 1953: 6–10); (ii) the patrilineal or matrilineal 'joint family' (which she defined as 'a group of people who generally live under the same roof, who eat food cooked at one hearth, ... hold property in common and ... participate in common family worship and [who] are related to each other as some particular type of kin' [Karve 1953: 10]); and (iii) the Sanskritic heritage, wherein one may find descriptions of almost all the kinship practices still found throughout the subcontinent (Karve 1953: 28). In Karve's formulation, then other words, the Hindu joint family had a positive role to play as a unifying force beneath the enormous variety of Indian kinship systems, as well as being an important instrument of social and economic security (Karve 1953: 301). It was another matter that, particularly in its northern variant (in continuity with the classical model), it was very hard on women: a price to be paid, perhaps, for the greater goal of civilizational continuity and unity.

THE MODERNIZATION THESIS

The conviction that the traditional Indian joint family system was in the process of breaking down gained currency following early British censuses which revealed that, empirically speaking, this type of family structure was by no means as prevalent as the strength and persistence of the ideal would have led one to expect (Shah 1973: 125–6). The Indological training of many of the first generation of Indian sociologists predisposed them to think likewise. However, the idea gained social scientific legitimacy in the post-World War II period when theorists of 'modernization' identified the Anglo-American nuclear family, focused on the conjugal couple, as the family type best adapted to the requirements of a modern, industrial society.

The most influential contribution to the sociology of the family in the post-War period was that of the eminent American sociologist and social theorist, Talcott Parsons, whose theory of family socialization and interaction was an important constituent in his structural-functional and comparative theory of society and social change (esp. Parsons [1949] 1959; Parsons and Bales 1955). Parsons was responding to the widespread post-War perception that the rising divorce rate, declining birth rate, and changes in sexual morality portended the imminent breakdown of the American family. To the contrary, he asserted that such changes were indicative of the stresses of a period of 'transition', and not signs of a trend to dysfunction and disorganization per se (Parsons and Bales 1955: 4). According to Parsons, American society was presently witnessing the culmination of a long-term process of the 'isolation', 'differentiation', and 'specialization' of the nuclear family as a bounded sub-system of society. This was the inevitable result of the logic of the modern occupational system with its emphasis on mobility and individual performance: 'As the occupational system develops and absorbs functions in society', Parsons wrote, 'it must be at the expense of the relative prominence of kinship organization as a structural component in one sense, and must also be at the expense of what previously have been functions of the kinship unit' (Parsons and Bales 1955: 12).

Complementing the isolation and loss of function of the nuclear family in modern societies, according to Parsons, was the enhanced emphasis on both the parental and the conjugal bonds (the latter, paradoxically resulting in increased strain on the institution of marriage). Now 'stripped down' to its elementary structural characteristics and 'root' functions, the contemporary American nuclear family afforded a unique empirical example of the 'minimal structural and functional essentials' of the human family as a special type of small social group (Parsons and Bales 1955: 354). That is, in its elementary structure, the family comprised four basic roles differentiated along the two axes of generation and of sex—father, mother, male child, female child—the differentiation of generation amounting to a differentiation in terms of power, and the differentiation of sex to a differentiation between 'instrumental' and 'expressive' functions.

There is something both candid and narcissistic about Parsons' formulation: candid in its recognition that the functional stability of the American nuclear family was dependent on a supposedly 'naturally' given generational hierarchy of authority and sexual division of labour, narcissistic in that the family pattern thus valorized within an evolutionary theory of societal development was both ideally and empirically typical of the white American, middle class family (father as breadwinner, mother as housekeeper), delegitimizing other family patterns (see Morgan 1975: 40–8). Writing in the 1950s, Parsons had clearly not envisioned that the 'transition' of the American family would be a continuing and open-ended process. A combination of demographic factors (declining birth and death rates), variations in sexual and conjugal arrangements (for example, gay and lesbian marriages, the legal recognition of live-in arrangements), as well as the impact of new reproductive technologies of motherhood and fatherhood, have since changed the face of the American family, even its white middle class variant. Moreover, with the introduction of programmes of economic liberalization, governments worldwide have begun to review the costs of their welfare programmes, seeking to restore to families the burden of care (of the young, of the aged, of the invalid, and the handicapped) that the modern state and its agencies had assumed during several decades of welfarism or socialist construction. The declaration of a UN International Year of the Family in 1994 was an indication of a growing and worldwide sense of crisis in the institution of the family, precipitated by the downsizing of welfare programmes, as are continuing appeals for the reinstitution of 'family values', marital fidelity, and premarital continence. In many countries this conservative backlash, targeted especially against the sexual emancipation of women, has also been associated with anti-western xenophobia and with the rise of religious fundamentalisms (see Hasan 1994; Jayawardena and de Alwis 1996).

Focusing on the typical family pattern of white, middle class Americans as the most 'advanced' type of kinship organization, functionally adapted to the requirements of modern industrial society, Parsons himself had little interest in *other* modes of family life except insofar as these served to validate his general theory (see Parsons and Bales 1955: Chapter 6). But his functionalist perspective on family organization, albeit slightly modified, was assimilated into the 'development' literature of the 1950s and 1960s, notably through the influential writings of William J. Goode (see 1963 and 1964).

Goode's *World Revolution and Family Patterns* (1963) is an ambitious comparative survey of modern changes in the family in five different areas of the world (the Arab world, Sub-Saharan Africa, India, China, and Japan), set against the background of the historical evolution of the family in the modern West. According to Goode, the process of industrialization is bound to bring critical pressures to bear on traditional family structures as increased physical and social mobility separates individuals from larger kin groups and as functions formerly performed by the kin group are taken over by other social agencies. Allowing that the actual patterns and directions of change would differ (depending on the characteristics of the traditional kinship and family systems concerned), Goode nonetheless concluded that *all* societies the world over were in the process of moving towards the same end, that is towards the institutionalization of what he termed the 'conjugal family' form:

It is clear ... that at the present time a somewhat similar set of influences is affecting all world cultures. *All of them are moving toward industrialization, although at varying speeds and from different points. Their family systems are also approaching some variant of the conjugal system* [Goode 1963: 368, emphasis added].

In presenting the comparative evidence from the five different societies of his study, Goode had found the Indian case to be particularly problematic (Goode 1963: Chapter 5). First, as he candidly admitted, there was in fact no conclusive evidence that the majority of Indians had *ever* lived in extended families in the past (notwithstanding ideals to the contrary),[3] nor that Indian families were at present moving decisively towards a conjugal family pattern. Second, to the extent that there appeared to have been some changes in this direction (for instance increased emphasis on the husband–wife bond as against that of mother and son; a higher level of contact between a married woman and her natal family; a decline of patriarchal authority in the family; greater freedom of choice of marriage partner), these changes could not plausibly be attributed to the impact of industrialization per se, since they had in fact preceded any significant level of industrialization. Nevertheless, and remarkably in the face of the paucity of his evidence, Goode remained convinced of the historical inevitability of a global revolution in family patterns towards the conjugal pattern presently exemplified by the West. As he wrote in the conclusion to his monumental survey,

In this investigation, we have, in a very deep sense, pointed to both the present and the future while attempting to make a sociological analysis of the past half-century: As an illustration, in suggesting that various of these family changes are now taking place in India and the Arab world, we are pointing in effect to data that *will* appear, behavioral patterns that *will* become more pronounced, attitudes that are emerging but *will* become dominant in the future. ... We are suggesting that processes are at work which will lead to the changes indicated [Goode 1963: 379, emphasis in original].

Needless to add here, perhaps Goode's conjugal family pattern was projected not merely as an 'ideal type' in the neutral Weberian sense of the term but, on balance, as a morally superior social and political ideal which (like capitalism as an economic system) institutionalized the individual's 'freedom' to 'choose', and offered people 'the potentialities of greater fulfilment, even if most do not seek it or achieve it' (Goode 1963: 380).

Two further aspects of Goode's reading of the Indian data on the modernization of the family might briefly be noted. First, Goode observed that in India, *ideological* change (expressed, for instance, in progressive legislation or in the opinions of the educated elite) was far ahead of *behavioural* change, which remained relatively slow. Second, reflecting on the resilience of traditional Indian family patterns, Goode suggested that these family patterns are not merely dependent variables, changing in response to the exogenous impact of industrialization, but that they 'embody or express most of the factors that have impeded India's social development' (Goode 1963: 203). This is a hypothesis that, in one form or another, has had a long history, notwithstanding the lack of sound empirical evidence to support it.[4]

Oft-cited as a refutation of Goode's thesis is Milton Singer's (1968) study of the family histories of nineteen Madras industrialists. While Singer had indeed found some inter-generational changes (in residence, household size and composition, occupation, and educational levels) which he speculated might functionally be associated with urbanization and industrial entrepreneurship, he also noted an inter-generational persistence of joint family living in many cases, the constant interactions of both nuclear and joint families with their relatives in villages, the continued sense of joint-family obligations even on the part of those actually living in nuclear families, and the continuity of aspects of family occupation (for instance continuity in the professions of trade and business) despite new educational specializations (Singer 1968: 436–8). Singer interpreted his findings as indicating the potential of the Indian joint family for 'structural adaptation' to new circumstances (Singer 1968: 444). This type of joint family organization, he concluded, is not only compatible with the development of modern industry, but may even constructively *assist* the establishment of a modern industrial enterprise (Singer 1968: 445).

As a number of critics have pointed out, the value of Singer's study was compromised by his failure to define with precision the concepts of 'nuclear' and 'joint' family and his conflation of 'family'—a genealogical construct—and 'household'—a residential and/or commensal arrangement of persons who are mostly (if not invariably) kin. In retrospect, however, one can appreciate the importance of Singer's principle of 'structural adaptation' as a way of reconciling *both* persistence *and* change in the realm of Indian family and kinship.

HOUSEHOLD VERSUS FAMILY

The lack of uniform operational definitions of the concepts of 'joint' (or 'extended') and 'nuclear' ('conjugal' or 'elementary') family, and the conflation of 'family' and 'household' were not confusions peculiar to Milton Singer's work. On the contrary, they were, and still remain, widely prevalent in studies on the Indian family in the discipline of sociology as well as in other social sciences. Under the circumstances, one wonders how the sociologist can be expected to answer the only question that anyone seems to want to ask of the Indian family: 'Is the joint family disintegrating?', and what general conclusions can be built on such shaky foundations.

Two sociologists in particular, A.M. Shah and Pauline Kolenda, working independently along rather similar lines, have contributed significantly to clarifying the conceptual issues involved in assessing trends in the composition of the Indian family. In a series of articles from 1964, now collected in *The Family in India* (1998), and in his earlier monograph on *The Household Dimension of the Family in India* (1973), A.M. Shah had sought to spell out the features of what he considered a properly 'sociological' approach to the Indian family (as distinct from the 'Indological' or 'legal' approach that had earlier prevailed). Shah's clarification had two distinct aspects. First, following M.N. Srinivas's emphasis on field-based, as against text-based, approaches to the study of Indian society, he stressed the importance of the empirical observation of kinship *behaviour* (in the 'field') as the proper basis of sociological generalization. He also cautioned against the methodologically dubious procedure whereby present ethnographic realities are posited against an ideal picture of family life derived from normative and prescriptive textual sources, and conclusions drawn therefrom on the nature and direction of social change (Nimkoff 1959).[5] Second, in line with current sociological usage, Shah recommended that the object of study should be what he called the *household* 'dimension' of the family, the household being defined as the strictly commensal and co-resident group. This focus discounts the features of 'coparcenership' and ritual corporateness that had defined the Hindu joint family in the Indologically oriented literature (Lardinois 1992).[6]

Substituting the commensal and co-resident 'household' group for the more imprecise and polysemous term 'family', the question, 'Is the joint *family* disintegrating?' is rephrased as, 'Is the joint *household* disintegrating?'. This question is supposedly more amenable to empirical verification—that is so long as comparable time-series data are available—but unfortunately, neither family nor household data have hitherto been elicited with uniform definitions in mind. However, Shah urged, meticulous attention to methodological questions, the judicious use of data sources, and a cautious approach to generalization can enable the sociologist to monitor longitudinal trends, at least in patchwork manner. Moreover, as time goes by there will be further opportunities for anthropologists and sociologists to restudy communities that they themselves or others had earlier studied, an exercise that is by now well under way (see Epstein 1973; Ghurye 1960; Kessinger 1974; Kolenda 1987: Chapter 3; Shah 1973: 86–93; 1998: Chapter 7; Wadley and Derr 1988).

Several household-classification schemes have been devised by sociologists to enable them to capture with greater precision the multiple forms of household composition and the dynamics of household change in India. Of these, the scheme that has had widest currency (in its original form, or somewhat modified) is the twelve-type classificatory scheme proposed by Pauline Kolenda in her pioneering 'Region, Caste and Family Structure: A Comparative Study of the Indian "Joint" Family', based on an analysis of twenty-six post-1949 ethnographic studies and household censuses (Kolenda 1968).[7] The scheme has proved pragmatically useful for highlighting aspects of household composition that tend to be obscured in the dichotomous classification of households into either joint/extended or nuclear/elementary types. For instance, by a dichotomous classification, the commonly encountered domestic group composed of a widowed mother or father along with a married son, his wife, and children, is classified by some analysts as a joint household (depleted), and by others as a nuclear household (supplemented): depending on the scheme adopted, the relative proportions of joint versus nuclear households in the population under study will be skewed accordingly (Kolenda 1968: 373ff; see also Vatuk 1972: 59–63). Again, a simple joint/nuclear categorization obscures the phenomenon of single-person households, a household type which may be of both sociological and practical interest.[8]

It is no easy matter to sum up the burden of the empirical research that has been conducted on patterns of household composition and change in India. A number of observations may be hazarded, nonetheless, with the caution that they are more in the nature of the deconstruction of well-entrenched stereotypes than a positive input into remapping the field:

(1) The joint household is rarely the statistically predominant form of household; nuclear households are usually more numerous.[9] However, even with the majority of *households* being nuclear in composition, the majority of *persons* in a population might still reside in joint or supplemented nuclear families.[10]

(2) Overall, the proportion of joint over nuclear households does not appear to be *decreasing*. The average size of the household has actually been increasing over the last century and a half (see Shah 1998: 66; also Orenstein 1961) and, while there is no direct correlation between household size and household type, there is every likelihood that proportions of joint households have been increasing as well. Indeed, such an outcome would appear inevitable given population growth, increased longevity, greater pressure on land and housing, the usual norms of household formation, and the preponderant rule of patri(viri)local residence, the absence of state-run social services, economic development and the accumulation of assets, and an overall encouragement in the wider political culture to the Sanskritization of custom. It is pertinent to note in this context that some longitudinal studies (in rural settings) have registered increase in *both* nuclear *and* joint household types over time, accompanied by a decline in households of other types (sub-nuclear or supplemented nuclear, for instance [see Kolenda 1987: Ch. 3; Shah 1973: 88–93; Wadley and Derr 1988]). The demographic fact of increased life expectancy may be the simple key to this latter type of change.

(3) Despite the predominance of nuclear households, many or most people would experience living in several different types of households. Households, like individuals, have a 'life-cycle' of development as individual life courses web in complex ways with trajectories of household expansion, fission and replacement, and with wider socio-economic forces. This is the phenomenon that anthropologists have termed 'the developmental cycle of the domestic group' (see Fortes 1962; Freed and Freed 1983; Gould 1968; Robertson 1991: esp. 11–16, 31–6; Vatuk 1972: 64–9; and from a demographer's angle, Raju 1998).

(4) A 'stem family' form (of parents residing with a married child), structurally if not developmentally similar to the classic pattern of Europe or Japan, may be an emerging pattern of family organization and an important social mechanism for care of the elderly. (Statistically, widowed or widower parents are frequent 'supplements' to the nuclear household [see Vatuk 1972: 64–72; also Shah 1999 (b)].

(5) Rural households tend on average to be larger than urban households (5.59 to 5.33 members respectively in 1991 [see Shah 1998: 66]); parallely, joint households are more numerous in rural than urban areas (Shah 1998: 74). However, it would be premature to accept these findings as supporting the proposition that urbanization *leads to* nuclearization, at least not without a very careful monitoring of longitudinal trends. Such composite figures may only conceal the complexity and heterogeneity of the processes involved. For instance, India has had a long history of urbanism, and probably a relatively high proportion of persons in the old cities live in joint households. On the other hand, while new migrants to the towns and cities may come initially as individual workers and then establish nuclear families, the passage

of time combined with the governing principles of household formation and the pressures of urban living may well encourage the development of joint households in due course. Similarly, while the lifestyles and occupational mobility of the professional middle classes may discourage joint-household living, another section of the urban middle class (for instance those engaged in business enterprise) may prefer to maintain joint households along with their joint business and property interests.[11] Such communities may also be the social reference groups in urban centres.

(6) There appear to be significant *regional* differences in the prevalence of joint households. Utilizing a combination of census data and anthropological field studies from the first decade after Independence, Pauline Kolenda had shown that the joint household is strongest through a contiguous belt across north India, and weakest in south India. This mapping coincides in its broad outlines with the distinctions that have been made between north and south Indian kinship systems, centring around marriage practices (Karve 1953; see also Bhat 1996; Dyson and Moore 1983).[12] In sum, Kolenda's work suggested that regional patterns may be more consistent than some of the other factors that have been hypothesized to correlate with preference for joint or nuclear households, for instance caste status or landownership (Kolenda 1968; also Basu 1992; Raju 1998; Vatuk 1972: 69).

(7) Notwithstanding nuclear-household *residence*, there is strong and generalized commitment to joint-family *values* and *norms* of kinship behaviour (see Desai 1964). While urban nuclear families may be relatively isolated from close kin, perhaps translating neighbourhood relations into a kinship idiom instead (see Sharma 1986; Vatuk 1972), in the village context individual households may well live under the same roof as close kin, or in adjacent houses (see Raju 1998). Property and ritual observances may be common, and codes of conduct (for instance a woman's veiling herself before senior affines) will apply as in the case of a regular joint household. Similarly, through much of India (especially north India) the norm of household formation follows the pattern whereby brides are initially recruited into the households of their husbands' patrilineal kin ('patri[viri]local residence'), although the young couple may move out of the joint household and set up separate residence in due course of time.[13]

While the work of Kolenda, Shah, and others has succeeded in nailing the myth of the ongoing 'disintegration' of the Indian joint household, an enormous amount of research still remains to be done to chart the dynamics of the household life cycle and the complex processes of family change in the South Asian region. Kolenda's data in the studies cited (1967, 1968, and 1989) is derived from ethnographic monographs and surveys of the first decade after Independence, and from the 1961 Census of India. Since the 1970s, some regions of the country have begun to register fertility decline, indicating significant changes in traditional family-building strategies. However, the task of monitoring these processes in all their heterogeneity—over regions, castes, classes, and communities, and through individual life cycles—has barely begun.[14]

RECOVERING 'THE FAMILY'

Privileging the concept of 'household' over that of 'family' has no doubt introduced a welcome precision into scholarly discussion on the Indian family and has enabled more rigorous comparative studies of households across cultures and over time (Netting et al. 1984). At the same time, the exercise has also been self-limiting, if not actually self-defeating. Driven by the one-point agenda of pronouncing authoritatively (one way or another) on the fate of the Indian

joint family in modern times, inquiry has been largely restricted to quantitative and morphological aspects of household form/composition at the expense of the more ineffable dimensions
of family life and relationships.[15] It has excluded address to the other reality of the family as
a property-sharing or ritual unit *distinct from* the strictly co-resident or commensal group
(Lardinois 1992), as well as investigation of the economics of the household as a unit of
production, distribution, and consumption. Overemphasis on the household does not allow
speculation on the role of the family in the organization of human reproduction, in the socialization of citizens, or in the provision of welfare—questions which are mostly left to other
disciplines to address. The emphasis on household discounts as sociologically irrelevant the
ubiquity of ideals of joint-family living that may be fervently ascribed to *even when* the
individuals concerned actually live out some or the greater part of their life courses in nuclear
households (see Desai 1964). Perhaps the time has now come to backtrack to the point from
where sociologists of the Indian family had set out on their quest for greater precision,
replicability, and general methodological rigour through the conceptual distinction of family
and household, and to begin a more broad-based reconstruction of the field of Indian family
and kinship studies.

Such an enterprise would include, but also go beyond, what has been described as a shift
of focus in Indian family and kinship studies in the 1990s, from 'structure' to 'process' (see
Wadley 1998: 119ff.). It might involve, for instance: (i) taking a new and critical look at revisions
of the history of the family in Europe and North America (e.g. Goody 1990; Laslett 1972;
Robertson 1991; Wall et al. 1983), and in other regions as well, themes so far taken up, if at
all, mainly by social demographers (see Das Gupta 1995); (ii) a re-engagement with the now
relatively disfavoured functionalist and structural-functional approaches to family and kinship
in social anthropology and in Parsonian sociology, short of endorsing their status-quoist and
sexist assumptions;[16] (iii) openness to insights from the 'cultural' approach to kinship studies
as a means of understanding both the ideology of the joint family and, more generally, the
nature of indigenous conceptions of relatedness (Schneider [1968] 1980); (iv) recognition of
the structural implications of marriage alliance in determining the role of the family in the
wider kinship system; (v) exploration of the political economy of the household—both the
intrahousehold distribution of resources and the imbrication of the household economy within
the wider national and global economies; (vi) consideration of the relations of contradiction and
collusion between state, community, and household (see Agarwal 1988; Risseuw and Palriwala
1996); and (vii) a general openness to insights from other disciplines, taking back on board
themes that have been largely marginalized in recent sociological research on the family in
India.

This is a rather formidable agenda, and this chapter can only hope to indicate and comment
on some general trends and hiatuses in the existing literature. As suggested earlier, some of
these are the product of the informal division of labour between sociology and anthropology on
the one hand, and between these disciplines and social work on the other. In many instances,
as will be evident in the discussion that follows, one finds that the writings of feminist scholars
have provided a bridge across these conventional disciplinary divides, and suggested new
emphases and directions.

Kinship Ideology

Anthropologists studying primitive societies have had long-standing interest in indigenous
theories of procreation—what are often called 'descent' or 'procreative ideologies' in

anthropological parlance—linked, in particular, to the functioning of unilineal descent groups and justifying the rights and duties associated with membership in such groups. In the South Asian context, where kinship systems are largely (though by no means exclusively) based on patrilineal descent, such ideas are seen as the foundation of a pervasive 'patriarchal' ideology which rationalizes the differential access of men and women to the material and symbolic resources of society.

An influential input into this mode of thinking in the Indian context has been Leela Dube's paper (1986) on the ubiquitous South Asian procreative metaphor of 'seed and earth': man is the active principle, providing the 'seed' of the child's future identity, and woman merely the passive 'field' in which this seed is sown and nurtured (also Misri 1985). This theory of the unequal contribution of the sexes to the process of reproduction, Dube argues, 'provides the rationalization for a system in which woman stands alienated from productive resources, has no control over her labour power, and is denied rights over her offspring' (Dube 1986: 44; and 1997: esp. Chapter 3). By contrast, she observes, some of India's matrilineal communities have had quite different theories of procreation, along with their different understandings of women's entitlement (Dube 1986: 32–3, 51n.).

Other feminist writers have pursued this reasoning further, seeking correlations between the descent principle and a number of other features of the system of kinship, marriage, residence, and succession, along with other indicators of women's status and 'bargaining power' (see Agarwal 1994; 1997), as has Dube herself in a recent comparative study of gender and kinship in South and South East Asia (Dube 1997). The connections thus made between the principle of patrilineal descent, its expression in a masculinist procreative ideology, and aspects of the 'secondary' status of women in south Asian society are both insightful and compelling, and of wide ramification through diverse domains of social life including public administration and law (see Agarwal 2000; Kapur and Cossman 1996: Chapter 2; Uberoi 1996a: Chapter 14). But this is clearly not the whole story. Dube's own paper shows that the status of the mother is *also* a significant component of the child's identity, since placement in the caste hierarchy is ultimately a function of the status of *both* parents, not of the father alone (see Das 1976; Hershman 1981: 129–33; Hsu 1963; Misri 1985; Tambiah 1975; Yalman 1963). The special status of motherhood in Hindu society is therefore not merely an extension of the mother's role as father's wife or ancestress, but derives from cultural understandings of the unique 'natural' bond that exists between mother and child in consequence of the mother's 'sacrifice' in bearing and nurturing the child with her blood and milk (see Das 1976; Madan 1983: 105). Also, as Louis Dumont and others have demonstrated (Dumont 1983b; Kane 1930–62: II, 1, 452ff.; Trautmann 1981: 246–71), the important concept of 'sapinda' in Hindu kinship reckoning is not exclusively agnatic, but varies from an exclusively agnatic orientation in the context of oblations to ancestors, to a modified patrilineal emphasis in the context of birth and death pollution and inheritance rights, to a more even-handedly cognatic emphasis in the exogamous rules governing marriage.

In fact, the problem is not only with the rather uncomfortable fit between metropolitan kinship theory and ethnographic evidence from the non-western world but, it has been suggested, with the theory itself. In particular, the so-called 'descent' approach to kinship studies within the structural-functional tradition is problematic in several respects that have been highlighted in the anthropological literature, including from the perspective of the 'alliance' and 'cultural' approaches (see Uberoi 1995). It is to the latter—that is the 'cultural' approach—that I draw attention immediately, reserving for later some comments on the relevance of 'alliance' theory (see section entitled 'The Family in the "System" of families').

In his pathbreaking *American Kinship: A Cultural Account* (1980 [1968], David Schneider had set out to describe the 'meaning' of American kinship as a 'system of symbols' independent of the anthropologists' usual classificatory inventory of principles of descent, residence, inheritance, succession, etc.[17] Proceeding from analysis of the American kinship terminology, Schneider had characterized the cognitive universe of American kinship in terms of an opposition of relations by 'blood' (conceived as 'natural', permanent, and substantive), and different types of relations 'by marriage', that is, relations of a more contingent character, governed by an express 'code of conduct' and conceived as based in 'law' or 'culture' rather than in 'nature'.

In a patchy sort of way, different scholars have picked up and elaborated on different strands of Schneider's work in the Indian context. Inden and Nicholas, for instance, have looked at the principles of classification of relatives in the culture of Bengali kinship and the codes of conduct that these relations require, augmenting this analysis with consideration of the symbolic structure of Hindu rites of passage (*samskaras*) which work to ritually transform the person through successive stages of the individual life-cycle (Inden and Nicholas 1977). A number of chapters in Ostor, Fruzzetti, and Barnett's collection, *Concepts of Person* (1983), link the idiom of kinship in north and south India to constructions of personhood and, in particular, to caste identity. T.N. Madan (1983) has looked at the Kashmiri Pandits' ideology of householdership and its relation to their sense of community, while John Gray (1995: Chapter 2) has similarly argued that understanding the dynamics of the Nepali household as an institution must begin with an appreciation of the meaning of 'householdership' in the Nepali worldview. The Nepali household, he argues, is a 'structure of consciousness' before it is a group of persons or a set of shared functions.

In a rather different idiom, Margaret Trawick (1996) has elaborated on the meaning of 'love' in the culture of Tamil kinship—not merely the contrast of 'erotic', 'conjugal' love versus non-erotic 'consanguineal' love that Schneider (1968) proposes in the context of American culture, but love (Tamil, *'anpu'*) construed as the multiple and contradictory attributes of 'containment', 'habit', 'harshness', 'dirtyness', 'humility', 'simplicity', 'servitude', the 'reversal' of normal social hierarchies, 'confusion' (Trawick 1996: Ch. 4)! Others see the culture of South Asian kinship as an instance of a more encompassing ontology that is reflected in many different domains: architecture, medicine, religion, law, land, and labour relations, etc. (see Daniel 1984; Marriott 1990; Osella and Osella 1996).

From the viewpoint of the discussion here of the 'ideology' of the Indian joint family as a component of the wider kinship system, one of the most interesting inputs has been Veena Das's essay on Punjabi kinship (1976). Punjabis, she says, acknowledge the strong emotional bonds arising from the 'natural' sexual relation of husband and wife, and the 'natural' procreative relation of parent (especially mother) and child, but they insist that these emotions must be kept—socially speaking—'backstage', to be 'sacrificed' and transcended in the interests of the manifest solidarity of the patrilineal joint family (see also Trawick 1996: Chapter 4). In these terms, the joint family might be defined not so much as a specific type of household formation, but as an *ideology* and *code of conduct* whereby the relations of husband and wife and parent and child are expected to be subordinated to a larger collective identity. This ideology finds constant affirmation in the world of Indian popular cinema.

In fact, kinship 'ideologies' (ideas about how the family is constituted and how it functions) inform public discourse in many domains, including administration and the law, and are embedded in many provisions of public policy (see Agarwal 2000; Kapur and Cossman 1996: Chapter 2). Similarly, culturally embedded ideas of sexuality and procreation are seen to inflect judgements on points of Hindu personal law that are formally phrased in the quite different legal idiom of marriage as 'sacrament' versus marriage as 'contract' (see Uberoi 1996a: Chapter 14). Or judgements in rape cases disclose the pervasive cultural assumption that the violent 'sexualization' of a virgin girl devalues her currency as an object of exchange between men, and renders her effectively unmarriageable (see Das 1996).

With the studies just cited, one shifts from rural or village India to the 'modern' sector of Indian society, focusing on the urban middle and upper-middle classes whose self-image and concepts of person are projected on to the national canvas as *the* Indian culture of kinship. There remains, still, much scope for the continuation and refinement of the cultural approach, with reference to other ethnographic regions of the subcontinent as well as to the kinship ideology of the lower caste, tribal, and marginalized groups of Indian society of whose concepts of personhood one as yet knows very little (but see Khare 1984; Moffatt 1979).

The Social 'Functions' of the Family

Aside from the insights afforded by the cultural approach to family and kinship studies, it would be worthwhile to recall some features of the functionalist perspective on the family that are routinely rehearsed in most elementary texts on the family (see Goode 1964: Chapter 1; Murdock 1949: esp. Chapter 1).[18] In reviewing the current literature on these dimensions of Indian family life, it will be clear that sociologists/anthropologists have relinquished much ground to other disciplines. The suggestion is that this ground should now be reclaimed.

Biological Reproduction

Foremost among the family's social functions is its role as the usual and legitimate site of biological reproduction. Human fertility is both determined by and impacts upon family values and structures in the wider context of society and culture, but the complex mechanisms of this reciprocal action remain the subject of academic controversy. For instance, in an influential early article (1955), Kingsley Davis had speculated that the dysfunctional levels of fertility that presently characterize certain underdeveloped and agrarian societies, such as India, are linked to the prevailing type of family organization (that is unilinear descent groups and joint households). In such systems, Davis observed, the nuclear family of procreation is able to share the burden of child raising with a wider kin group. Consequently, the age of marriage tends to be quite young, and numerous offspring, especially male offspring, are viewed as a positive asset to the group, providing security to the parents in their old age when few other means are available (Davis 1955: 34–7).[19]

Considering their common focus on the reproductive functions of the family, one might have expected that anthropologists/sociologists and social demographers would be in constant dialogue. Regrettably, this has not usually been the case. In fact, sociologists have sometimes been quite dismissive of survey research methods applied to the sensitive area of human reproduction (a particular target has been the knowledge-acceptance-practice [KAP] focus of the early family planning surveys), and have insisted that reproductive behaviour can only be viewed in the wider context of culture and social structure (Srinivas and Ramaswamy 1977). For their part, demographers have been impatient with the ethnographic detail of micro-level fertility studies, and have questioned the generalizability of such studies to the wider canvas of regional or national population planning.

The position has changed somewhat since the 1980s, however, particularly with the more nuanced elaboration of a *regional* perspective on Indian demographic behaviour and family patterns (Raju et al. 1999; Singh 1993). A number of important studies (see Agarwal 1994; Basu 1992; Bhat 1996; Dyson and Moore 1983; Kolenda 1987: Chapter 2; Miller [1981] 1997, to cite just a few) have now demonstrated considerable consistency between demographic variables such as fertility rates, household size, sex ratios, sex-differentiated infant and child mortality, and women's age at marriage, and the regional patterns of kinship organization described by anthropologists, particularly the north/south contrast (Karve 1953; Trautmann 1981: esp. Chapter 3). These different patternings of kinship organization are seen to correlate with different degrees of 'female autonomy' (as measured by proxy variables such as the mean distance between natal and conjugal homes; freedom of divorce and remarriage; literacy rates; work participation rates; and women's inheritance rights), and with different degrees of 'son preference'. In general, the north Indian region (the states of Gujarat, Rajasthan, Uttar Pradesh, Madhya Pradesh, Punjab, and Haryana) is strongly masculinist on most measures; the south (the states of Kerala, Tamil Nadu, Andhra Pradesh, Karnataka, and Maharashtra), much less so; while the eastern region (Bihar, West Bengal, and Orissa) lies in between, with mixed characteristics. These differentials also correspond, more or less, with the success or otherwise of state-sponsored measures of population control, though there are some notable exceptions to the pattern which merit close attention, and trends of change which promise to reverse long-established patterns (see Bhat 1996; Harriss-White 1999; *Public Report* 1999; Visaria 1999).

For their part, some sociologists have sought to test demographic hypotheses through intensive participant observation fieldwork at micro-level (a good recent example is Patel 1994), while others have used large-scale survey methods to confirm trends that are perhaps less obvious when viewed close up. Notable here is Monica Das Gupta's study (1987) of sex-differentiated child morbidity and mortality levels in a micro region of rural Punjab that had been intensively studied in the 1950s. Her work demonstrates the greatly impaired survival chances of higher birth order girls (as compared to their brothers and to first-born girls), despite the overall economic development of the region and significant declines in both fertility and mortality. She links this disparity with sex-differentiated access to food and clothing and, most crucially, medical attention. Revealingly, and disconcertingly, this disparity is shown to be inversely related to mothers' educational levels.

The collaboration of social demographers and anthropologists/sociologists has been stimulated by the urgent need for population control, but this narrow focus has produced some distortions and blind spots as well. First, notwithstanding recent changes in international population-control policies, the emphasis of research and intervention has been, until very recently, quite one-sidedly on *female* reproductive behaviour. (This emphasis appeared especially compelling following the politically disastrous promotion of male sterilization during the national Emergency in India [1975–7].) Second, focus on population magnitudes has tended to marginalize address to the social implications of the new reproductive technologies (NRTs) now patronized by the middle and upper-middle classes. The important exception here has been the linked practices of amniocentesis and sex-selective abortion, which have attracted much public attention (if not equally serious scholarly address) as pathological indicators of the strength of Indian son preference (Visaria 1999: 90–1). But there are several other dimensions to the NRTs which deserve greater sociological scrutiny for the light they throw on Indian kinship ideologies and family-building strategies, and for the connections they demonstrate between economic development, class formation, and the exaggeration of some traditional features of Indian family organization. This may be another, and rather more malign, dimension of the 'adaptive' capacities of the Indian family that Milton Singer (1968) had alluded to. That is, traditional pathologies may be exaggerated, not eliminated, by processes of modernization and economic development.

Sexuality

Sexuality is one area where the disciplinary division of labour between sociology and anthropology is revealed most clearly. Considering the intimate connection between procreation and sexuality, it is remarkable that, after the pioneering work in this area of the redoubtable G.S. Ghurye (1973: Chapters 9 and 10), sociologists for the most part seem to have scrupulously avoided investigating Indian sexuality.[20] There is no Kinsey Report, no Hite Report, and no monitoring of changing sexual practices except from the very narrow perspective of conjugal procreative behaviour in the context of population control. Anthropologists, on the other hand, seem to have no such compunctions: in fact, exoticizing the sexual practices of object societies is a conspicuous sign of their 'othering' enterprise. Expectedly, then, the significant inputs into the study of sexuality have come from anthropologists, along with psychologists and psychoanalysts, social historians (particularly those influenced by the work of Michel Foucault), and social workers dealing with sexual pathologies, incest, and domestic violence. Latterly, feminist researchers, too, have broken their self-imposed silence to address male and female sexuality as a major topic of both theoretical and practical concern (John and Nair 1998; Uberoi 1996a). Some of this work is referred to in the brief discussion that follows.

First, there, is the suggestive anthropological writing on 'procreative ideologies', already referred to, and the inputs of some psychologists and psychoanalysts who have sought to explore the oedipal tension of the mother–son relation in India, usually counterposed against the sexual dynamics of the conjugal relation (see Carstairs 1957; Kakar 1981: Chapter 3; and 1989; Nandy 1980). In addition to this, one may also note the continued reference to an 'Indological' or 'Sanskritic' model of conjugal sexual relations whereby sexuality is deemed legitimate only for the production of male offspring to continue the ritual offerings to ancestors: and not, primarily, for the production of pleasure. Otherwise, sexual activity for males is perceived as a source of sin, impurity, and danger which is likely to impair both physical well-being and spiritual development (see Allen 1982; Kapadia 1955: 159–60; Misri 1985; Prabhu [1940] 1995: 240–1).

A second exploration of sexuality may be found in the quite extensive anthropological literature on Hindu life-cycle rituals—particularly those of marriage, childbirth and, most conspicuously, female puberty (see Dube 1988; 1997; Good 1991). In many communities through south Asia, a girl's menarche is marked by a series of rituals which simultaneously celebrate her attainment of fecundity and marriageability while underlining her state of impurity and vulnerability and dramatizing the danger she now poses to her natal kin (see Bennett 1983: Chapter 6; Good 1991: Chapter 7; Kapadia 1995: Chapter 5; Yalman 1963). Once again, however, the richness of the ethnography of the 'traditional' sector of Indian society is in no way matched by comparable work on the urban and more 'modern' sector, and one is left to speculate on where and whether a girl's coming of age in the contemporary urban milieu is stigmatized or celebrated, ritually marked or unmarked, or transformed into some other idiom, secular or 'medicalized', through agencies such as the multinational pharmaceutical companies.

290 HANDBOOK OF INDIAN SOCIOLOGY

Yet another trend may be found in the recent critical literature, for the most part by 'Subaltern' historians and feminists, which has begun the process of reassessing the last century and a half of Indian social reform (see Nair 1996; papers in Hasan 1994; Kapur 1996; John and Nair 1998; and Uberoi 1996a). As is well known, Indian social reform efforts were largely concentrated on two issues: the removal of untouchability and the improvement of the social condition of women. A major emphasis of this latter project involved community and state interventions to regulate female sexuality inside and outside of marriage in line with upper-caste, Sanskritic norms and/or Victorian standards of propriety. Deconstruction of the discourse of social reform shows that both the nationalist and the reformist agendas, even on such questions as the abolition of *sati* and female infanticide or the raising of the Age of Consent, were more ambiguous and complex than superficial appearances and received opinion might suggest (Uberoi 1996a: Introduction). Particularly problematic was the process of the codification of customary and religious law, and interventions into the 'reform' of matrilineal systems of kinship and marriage (see Dube 1997; Nair 1996: Chapter 6; Saradamoni 1996), which often, in fact, placed new and untoward restrictions on women's freedom of action.

Finally, on the theme of sexuality, it is likely that the AIDS crisis will increasingly focus attention on aspects of Indian sexuality, beyond procreation, both inside and outside of marriage (see Bharat 1999). Indeed, the effect of this new and now donor-driven orientation, proceeding impatiently from research to policy recommendations, has already been felt, though to date more in social work than in anthropology/sociology proper.

Socialization

Following on from the family's role as the site of biological reproduction is its role as the first, the so-called 'primary', agency of socialization. After initial enthusiasm during the 1950s, when the study of child socialization practices was linked with the comparative study of personality types and political cultures (Minturn and Hitchcock 1963), sociologists/anthropologists appear to have almost abandoned the study of child socialization to the disciplines of psychology, psychoanalysis, and child development (see Kakar 1981). Indeed, with the exception of a paper by Urvashi Misri (1985) on the Kashmiri Pandit understanding of the child and of childhood, sociologists have not reflected particularly on the cultural meaning of the concept of 'childhood' in the Indian context (Ariès 1962; Erikson 1950; Robertson 1991: Chapter 7).[21] The Pandits, according to Misri, see the child as both an individual with his or her own unique *karma,* and as a sharer in the inherited bodily substance of father and mother. Childhood is a process of separation of the child from divinity, with the child's loss of innate sacredness and purity being matched by the incremental attainment of adult community identity through successive rites of passage (*samskaras*).

Contrariwise, and in a more secular mode, Krishna Kumar points to the traditional continuity between the world of the child and the adult world (Kumar 1993; also Kakar 1981: esp. Chapter 4 and Appendix). Kumar suggests that contemporary social processes have brought about a new distantiation of the child and adult worlds in urban India as children's schooling on the one hand, and adult work schedules on the other, now structure childhood and adolescent experience. Obviously, too, the 'invention' of Indian childhood is being reinforced for the middle classes by the new post-liberalization consumerism, which has identified childhood and adolescence each as a distinctive life stage—and consumer market segment (for the latter, see Butcher 1999)!

Krishna Kumar's work has succeeded in bringing under examination the cultural practices of the Indian urban middle classes whose obsessive concern with their children's education, employment, and marriage instances the modern family's critical role in the reproduction of class status. Similarly, André Béteille has argued (1991) that in contemporary India it is the institution of the family (rather than the traditional caste group) that now ensures the social placement of the younger generation—through arranging school and college admissions, professional training, and employment opportunities.[22]

There is one aspect of the process of child socialization that *has* received considerable attention from sociologists/anthropologists. This is the process of socialization of the girl child and her internalization of feminine gender identity through a variety of social mechanisms (Das 1988; Dube 1988; Minturn 1993: esp. Chapter 12; Minturn and Hitchcock 1963). One of the important mechanisms of sex-role socialization is the sex-differentiated allocation of family resources (see later discussion). Another is the series of life-cycle rituals, particularly those of puberty (already mentioned) and of marriage (Dube 1988 and 1997; Fruzzetti [1982] 1990; Good 1991; Hanchett 1988). In the north Indian patrilineal kinship system, in particular, a young girl is made aware early on that she will 'belong' after her marriage to another family, a family of strangers, and that, except in the greatest adversity, her rights, responsibilities and entitlements will pertain in that family.

As in all societies, the process of maturation involves the internalization of gendered codes of bodily deportment (see Das 1988) and of social space. Sex segregation is strongly, if unevenly, marked throughout much of South Asia where *purdah* (the veiling and seclusion of women) is practised to greater or lesser extent among Hindus as well as (albeit in different form) among Muslims (see Mandelbaum 1988; Minturn 1993: Chapter 3; Papanek 1982; Sharma 1978; Vatuk 1982). Women's relative seclusion and their inability to access the public domain on equal terms with men have been identified as important impediments to their economic independence and betterment (see Agarwal 1994: 268–70, 298–311, 458ff.; Sharma 1980: 3–7, 201–2).

Welfare

A major function of the family is that of care and nurturance—of the young, the handicapped, the sick, the unemployed, the aged. Indeed, in some 'biologistic' explanations, the care of the helpless infant and the protection of the pregnant and lactating mother are the very *raison d'être* of the human family as a social institution concerned with the reproduction of the species (see Fox 1967: esp. Chapter 1). As remarked earlier, in the upper income 'developed' societies, and especially in the erstwhile socialist states, many of these functions had been taken over by agencies of the state. However, the dismantling of socialist regimes and policies of liberalization have created a crisis of welfarism worldwide, stalling the aspiration for comprehensive social welfare in developing countries and restricting the state's commitment to areas of dire distress, or to sectoral investment in programmes which conspicuously further other developmental goals.[23] Perhaps this explains why the agency for initiating and prosecuting social-welfare schemes has been substantially relocated from the state to international organizations on the one hand, and to non-governmental organizations (NGOs) on the other (Risseeuw and Palriwala 1996; Uberoi 1996b).

In public discourse in India, problems in the delivery of welfare are often construed as evidence of a crisis in the *family*, rather than, for instance, a failure of state planning or a lack of political will. Thus it is widely believed that the Indian joint family is a type of family organization perfectly adapted to providing the maximum degree of security to its members (see Kapadia 1955: 248–51; Karve 1953: 301), but that this function has been seriously impaired by the expansion of an 'individualistic' ethos (Sharma 1989), and by new socio-economic trends such as occupational and spatial mobility, and the enhanced participation of women in some sectors of the workforce. This is all a matter of speculation. In fact sociologists tell us very little about how families cope with severe stress, about the ways in which familial care supplements or substitutes care provided by the community and the state and, in general, about the principles of the Indian moral economy in normal and abnormal times (but see Greenough 1982; Khare 1998). In consequence of the disciplinary division of labour between the theoretical and the applied sciences, such questions have not been a prominent focus of the sociology of the Indian family, and are largely left to social workers to address (Bharat and Desai 1991).

Feminist writers have been at the forefront of efforts to investigate the familial and extra-familial resources that households draw on to cope with adversity, whether these be the normal ups and downs of everyday life, or situations of extreme distress (Risseeuw and Palriwala 1996). At the same time, they have been wary of accepting at face value, the valorization of the family as an efficient instrument of care, perceiving here a convenient rationalization of the state's withdrawal from welfare responsibilities and its shifting of this burden to families (or rather, to *women*, who are the major care givers in the context of the family [Uberoi 1996b]). Similarly, they have critiqued the presumption that altruism is the governing principle of family relations, highlighting gender asymmetries in the allocation of family resources and bringing the issue of domestic violence prominently on to the public agenda (Karlekar 1998, and this volume).

The duality of the family as at once the site of oppression and violence and a 'haven in a heartless world' has been graphically illustrated in recent writing on the Indian Partition (Das 1995: Chapter 3). While male family members often took the lead in persuading their female kin to commit suicide for the sake of family honour, or themselves executed their own womenfolk, families also rallied to provide shelter and sustenance to victims and, wherever possible, to cover up the history of their women's abduction during those traumatic times. Similar stories could no doubt be told of the survival strategies of families in other situations of extreme distress and deprivation (Bharat and Desai 1991).

Production, Distribution, and Consumption

As noted, the distinction between 'family' and 'household and the definition of the household as the co-resident and commensal group were analytical refinements introduced to deal with two conceptual problems. The first is what one might term an 'enumerative' problem, arising from the fact that a house (as a material structure) might contain several distinctly demarcated social groups ('hearths') (see Madan [1965] 1989; Rao 1992; Shah 1998). The second is the confusion arising from the 'Indological' definition of the family as a property-sharing group. That is, as a result of the often uneven and staggered processes of family partition, the kinship group constituted by shared property interests might be smaller, or more likely larger, than the co-resident/commensal domestic unit. Ethnographers describe many cases where hearth-group units are separate, but where landed property continues to be jointly cultivated and the proceeds shared (see Madan [1965] 1989; Parry 1979; Raju 1998). That is why many sociologists had, *contra* the 'Indological' approach, discounted relations in property as defining features of 'household' membership. (Of course, the criterion of commensality in the definition of the household *does* imply a certain sharing of budgeting and consumption [Agarwal 1994].) Nonetheless, there has been a well-developed and continuing tradition in social anthropology which attends to the 'domestic group' as a unit of ownership, production, consumption, and distribution, as well as of reproduction (see Gray 1995; Madan [1965] 1989: Chapters 7 and 8; Mayer 1960), and this emphasis has now been strengthened by the important work of several feminist scholars (see Agarwal 1994; Sharma 1980).

Crucial to the familial organization of production is the sexual division of labour, both within the household itself and between the private realm of the household and the world outside. Feminist scholars, particularly those operating within a Marxist framework, have seen women's confinement to the domestic, reproductive sphere, their inability to access the public domain on equal terms with men, and the 'naturalization' of this arrangement at the ideological level ('woman's place is in the home') as the historical and contemporary source of women's subjection. They have particularly taken issue with those traditions in sociology/ anthropology, and some earlier feminist writings (such as of Michelle Rosaldo 1974), that have placed the opposition of the private and the public realms at the centre of kinship theory (see Moore 1988: 21ff.; Yanagisako and Collier 1987). Following the suggestive lead of Jack Goody and S.J. Tambiah (Goody 1976; Goody and Tambiah 1973), feminist social scientists have recently sought to explore connections between the sexual division of labour in the household and the wider political economy, the structure of property rights, the nature of marriage payments (bride wealth or dowry), the frequency of divorce and remarriage, sexual permissiveness, restrictions on women's movement in public space (especially the institution of purdah), and modes of production in different ecological environments (see Agarwal 1994).

An outstanding example of the empirical investigation of the hypothesized connection between women's work (particularly their participation in agricultural labour) and their overall social status is Ursula Sharma's comparative case study of women's economic roles in a village in Himachal Pradesh, where women participate actively in paid and unpaid agricultural work, and one in Punjab, where women have been increasingly withdrawn from the agricultural labour force (Sharma 1980). Though the Himachali women were publicly more visible, Sharma concluded that they did not *on this account* have conspicuously more domestic or extra-domestic 'social power' than their Punjabi counterparts.[24] She attributed this to a complex of social structural and cultural factors, but especially to women's effective exclusion from inheritance rights in land in both states (notwithstanding the formal provisions of the Hindu Succession Act of 1956), and their ultimate economic dependence on their male kin. Additionally, even where women did have title to property (in inherited land, in dowry goods, or in wages), Sharma stressed, this property was rarely—given cultural and social structural constraints— under their own control and management.

The measurement of women's socio-economic status in terms of the rate of their partici- pation in the workforce is a somewhat problematic issue which one need not go into at this point, except to note that these measures fail to capture and account for the quantum and value of women's unpaid labour and their productive work in the domestic sphere, in home- based industry, and in reproducing class status through what Hanna Papanek has aptly termed 'family status production work' (see Papanek 1989). This latter aspect of women's work has also been addressed by Sharma in the course of a study of the economic roles of employed women and housewives in an urban centre of north India (Shimla, Himachal Pradesh) (1986). As in the rural study already mentioned (Sharma 1980), Sharma found that neither ownership of property nor monetary earnings *in themselves* could ensure women's economic indepen- dence, since their control over these resources was constrained by generational and sexual asymmetries of power within the household, and by social codes of feminine deportment. In any case, without reciprocal adjustments by their male kinsmen, women's participation in the labour force, for the most part, resulted in their shouldering the 'double burden' of unpaid housework and paid employment (see Kapur 1970; Karlekar 1982: Chapter 5).

The economic and political role of the household as an intermediary unit between the individual and the state is prominently acknowledged in public policy and administration, public goods and services being routinely allocated to the household as if it were a single unit of consumption. Similarly, the household is seen as a self-regulating administrative unit, whose individual members are identified in terms of their relations to the household 'head' (usually assumed to be the seniormost male member), who is their representative in the public domain and whose authority over other members is questioned only in the event of exceptional abuse of power.

These commonplace assumptions have been challenged recently—at the theoretical level within economics, as well as on pragmatic and ethical (equity) grounds. For instance, economist Amartya Sen (1983) has urged interrogation of commonplace assumptions on the nature of the household as an economic institution, arguing for its recognition as an arena of both cooperation and conflict, of the mutual 'bargaining' over resources, in which some members are structurally so placed that they are likely to get the worst end of the bargain. In the context of the Indian family, Sen points to gender as a major basis of disadvantage, affecting notions of entitlement and access to land, food, education, and medical attention, and severely compromising the life chances of females vis-à-vis males, differentially through the life course (Das Gupta 1995; Kynch and Sen 1983; also Drèze 1990; Papanek 1990). This approach has been further elaborated by Bina Agarwal (1994: 53–71; and 1997) who, like Ursula Sharma (1980), has stressed that it is particularly their restricted access to *land* as the major productive resource in South Asia that has placed the greatest limits on women's bargaining position in the family.

Though the assumption of the 'unitary' household is not one that sociologists/ anthropologists have been wont to make (as noted, Parsons had maintained that the modern nuclear family was a basic and functional unit of society *precisely because* of its generational hierarchy of authority and sexual division of labour), the economists' linking of the political economy of the household and the wider society with reference to the goal of distributive justice has been an important corrective to the status quoist assumptions of functionalist anthropology/sociology (see Morgan 1975: 95ff. and Chapter 5), as well as to the gender blindness of neoclassical economics.

Family Roles and Relationships

Though the analysis of family roles and relationships finds little place in discussions of change in household composition, descriptions of both normative expectations and behavioural patterns have been, and rightly continue to be, a mainstay of anthropological, sociological, and social psychological writing on the family (for excellent examples, see Bennett 1983; Das 1976; Ross 1961; Trawick 1990). Apart from interviews, surveys, and the participant observation of family-interaction patterns, sociologists and others have found in literature, the arts, the contemporary mass media and 'folklore' rich sources of data, albeit to be used with caution and sensitivity to the constraints of genre. In particular, folklore and women's genres have provided important insights into cultural norms, as well as evidence of vigorous critiques of these same norms from the viewpoint of the disadvantaged (see Chowdhry 1994; Raheja and Gold 1996: esp. Chapter 2; Srinivas 1942).

Among the issues that have dominated cross-cultural research especially on changes in family, the relative priority accorded to different dyadic relationships is of special interest. It has been proposed, for instance, that the family system of (patrilineal north) India is based on the father–son relationship, while that of North America is based on the conjugal relation (see Inden and Nicholas 1977). Others have argued that Indian kinship emphasizes the mother–son bond over that of husband and wife (Kakar 1981: Chapter 3; Nandy 1980) or of father and son (Hsu 1963). Still others argue that seen from the viewpoint of women, the overriding opposition is between a woman's role as daughter/sister (that is patrilineal kinswoman) and her role as wife (Bennett 1983; Karve 1953; Minturn 1993: Chapter 2); or that functions of sexuality and procreativity have been dichotomously projected on to the complementary social roles of the wife *versus* the 'other woman' as in the feminine role structure of Indian popular cinema [see Uberoi 1997]; and so on.

Certainly, most observers would agree that the introduction and valorization of the ideal of companionate and romantic marriage over the last century has simultaneously focused attention on the conjugal bond and given rise to cultural conflict over the 'meaning' of marriage and of wifehood. Feminist historians and historically minded sociologists have taken the lead in exploring this theme, using a variety of data sources, from public debates on legal reform to the arts and mass media (e.g. Sarkar 1993; papers in Uberoi 1996a).

As Talcott Parsons might have predicted, the new emphasis on the conjugal relationship and on values of romance and companionship within marriage has put the conjugal relationship under extra strain, directing the sociologist's attention to issues of domestic violence and marital discord and breakdown. Some of the most sensitive and suggestive ethnography of Indian marriage and family relations is to be found in studies by psychologists and psychoanalysts (e.g. Kakar 1989), and by social workers who seek to understand the cultural and social ambience in which 'violence is the form assumed by sexual love in a conjugal context', where antinomies of 'suspicion and sexual love', 'possession and desire', 'authority and affection' intersect in the husband's oftentimes brutal impress on his wife's body (Geetha 1998).

THE FAMILY IN THE SYSTEM OF FAMILIES

The academic and public focus on 'the family' as the prioritized object of study tends to obscure two important facts. The first is the empirical *variety* of family forms, of which, as noted, South Asia presents a great number. From this perspective, to speak of *the* Indian family is to assign normative value to only one of these many types (that is the patrilineal joint family of the northern type). The second is the fact that 'the family' pertains only in the context of what one might term a *system* of families. It does not, indeed cannot, exist in itself. How such a system is to be intepreted, however, is the subject of much debate and the basis of theoretically opposed positions in the sociology/anthropology of family and kinship. For instance, in A.R. Radcliffe-Brown's structural-functional anthropology, 'the basic unit on which the kinship system is built' is the 'elementary family', consisting of a man, his wife and their children, and comprising the 'three basic relationships' of (i) parent and child, (ii) siblings, and (iii) husband and wife as parents of the same child or children (Radcliffe-Brown 1950: 51). Each member of the elementary family connects with a member of another elementary family in a second-order relationship (for example, mother's brother) and each again in a third-order relationship (for example, mother's brother's son), and so on: 'This interlocking of elementary families creates a network of ... genealogical relations, spreading out indefinitely' (Radcliffe-Brown: 52).

A not dissimilar perspective was proposed by Talcott Parsons who stressed that every individual is, uniquely, a member of *two* different conjugal families: that into which he was born, called the 'family of orientation', and the 'family of procreation' founded by his marriage (Parsons 1959: 242ff). These two conjugal families comprise 'the inner circle of the kinship structure', each member of which is a connecting link with another conjugal family (Parsons 1959: 245).

A very different orientation has been suggested, however, by the French anthropologist, Claude Lévi-Strauss. In his model, the basic unit of kinship is not the 'naturalized' elementary family but the 'family' of a brother-sister pair, the sister's husband and their child—or, more parsimoniously, the relationship of brothers-in-law. This elementary structure derives from the universal prohibition of incest. As Lévi-Strauss put it,

The prohibition of incest establishes a mutual dependency between families, compelling them, in order to perpetuate themselves, to give rise to new families. ... For incest prohibitions simply state that families (however they should be defined) can only marry between each other and that they cannot marry inside themselves [Lévi-Strauss (1956) 1960: 277, emphasis added].

Supplementing the social function of the incest taboo, many societies also prescribe certain categories of kinsfolk as desirable marriage partners, setting up by this means intricate systems of marital 'exchange' (see Lévi-Strauss (1956) 1960: 279ff.; and [1949] 1969; Trautmann, this volume). Thus marriage is not (as it may appear from a commonsensical contemporary western perspective), primarily an arrangement between two *individuals*. It is an 'alliance' between two *families*, which is typically perpetuated into the next generation in the special relation of the mother's brother to his sister's children and perhaps, through further marital alliances, indefinitely.

As is well known, south Indian kinship is structurally distinct from north Indian kinship, having 'positive', not merely 'negative', rules of marriage. But in either case, as Louis Dumont in particular has argued (1966), it is the relationship of *affinity* (i.e. of marriage) that ultimately structures the kinship system. Expressed and consolidated in conventional patterns of gift giving and rules of kinship etiquette, Hindu marriage institutes a hierarchical relationship between 'wife-takers' (superior) and 'wife-givers' (inferior). In this way the kinship system of South Asian Hindus engages with the caste system, for each marriage not only links individuals and families, but also reproduces the hierarchy of Hindu caste society.

The 'alliance' perspective has been of singular importance in transforming the under-standing of Indian family and kinship and its many varieties, and in rendering the institution of 'arranged marriage', so called, in a new, and rather less exoticized, light. That is, arranged marriage is not merely an expression of the authority of seniors over juniors in the family, but is essential to the reproduction of the family as a system of kinship *and* affinity embedded within the wider structure of caste. Needless to add, it also reproduces communitarian separateness.

CONCLUSION AND NEW DIRECTIONS

In reviewing the current state of Indian family and kinship studies, this chapter took as its starting point the single question that has dominated professional and popular discourse on the Indian family: namely the fate of the joint family in modern times. In particular, it has followed one trajectory of this debate in the sociological literature—the redefinition of the object of study as the co-resident/commensal household. This gesture, though it introduced new rigour into sociological studies of changes in family composition, has had little impact on the terms and direction of public discourse. This itself, perhaps, suggests a challenge: Is it not possible for the sociologist of the family to engage in a more constructive way with people's own understanding of their family life, rather than simply dismissing this understanding as the empirically unfounded product of cultural nostalgia? Second, the focus on household composition as the aspect of family that can be empirically *quantified* has been self-limiting. There is certainly a need for continued investigation of changing patterns of household formation, composition, and dispersion—over different regions, castes, communities, and classes in India. Apart from any other justification, this is intimately connected to public policy in several domains. But this should not become a pretext for ignoring the more ineffable aspects of family life and relationships and the wide range of functions that households/families typically perform.

This chapter has attempted to briefly survey the literature on these other dimensions of family life, underlining that these are areas where sociology and anthropology need to plumb their own disciplinary resources and histories as well as to engage actively with other social sciences. This does not imply acceptance of the idea that the family is functional, consensual, and homeostatic. On the contrary, sociologists need to confront (and not to abandon to psychology and social work) the dysfunctional and pathological aspects of family life, to recognize the family's capacity for adapting to changing circumstances, and indeed to acknowledge that questions of justice, human rights, distributional equity, directed social transformation, and policy formulation *are* the professional business of sociologists in general, and sociologists of the family in particular.

Third, in following the trajectory of the debate on the modern fate of the Hindu joint family, this chapter has, like the participants in that debate, colluded in the equation of *the* Indian family with the Hindu patrilineal joint family. It has thus marginalized consideration of the kinship patterns of non-Hindu and tribal communities, of communities following principles of matrilineal or bilateral descent, and of groups for whom the joint family is neither the cultural ideal nor an empirical preference (see Singh 1993). Some writers argue that *regional* patterns of kinship overwhelm communitarian differences (Agarwal 1994), but in general the perception of the Indian family that prevails, among sociologists and the wider public, is a generalized and hegemonic Indo-Aryan/north Indian one. This returns us to our earlier discussion of the mindset of the earlier generation of Indian sociologists, and our observations on the important role of the family as the trope for community and nation.

A broadening of the agenda for sociological studies of Indian family and kinship suggests going beyond head counting and genealogical reckoning to engaging in methodologically eclectic and unconventional ways with new sources of data—literature, the arts, popular culture, and mass media (see Wadley 1998: 123), with the data sources of the public domain (law, politics, public administration [Agarwal 2000; Uberoi 1996a: Chapter 14]), and with historical records of various types. These are sources that sociologists have so far scarcely tapped.

The sociology of the Indian family, I have suggested here, seems to have been trapped in a debate which is no longer productive of new insights. It has also fallen victim to its own narcissistic preoccupations, in the sense that there is very little engagement with contemporary theoretical challenges in family and kinship studies, such as they are, nor much openness to insights from cross-cultural and historical research. This is ultimately impoverishing. South Asian ethnography in the past was simultaneously shaped by, and itself contributed to shaping, the evolutionist and diffusionist theories of the pioneers of family and kinship studies in anthropology and sociology—Henry Sumner Maine, Lewis Henry Morgan, and W.H.R. Rivers

(See Uberoi 1993: 7–20); it provided grounds for the exploration of the integrative social function of religious belief and ritual in relation to different levels of social organization (Radcliffe-Brown 1952); it afforded illustration of the structurating principles and inbuilt tensions of matrilineal kinship systems (Gough 1959; Radcliffe-Brown 1950: 72–82; Schneider and Gough 1961); it furthered the testing and elaboration of the alliance approach to kinship studies (Lévi-Strauss [1949] 1969; Dumont 1968 and 1983a; see Uberoi 1993: 20–31), as well as of the cultural approach in vogue during the 1970s (Inden and Nicholas 1977; Schneider [1968] 1980; Ostor et al. 1983); and it provided a well-documented instance of the impact of 'modernization' on the family in developing countries (Goode 1963: Ch. 5). Indian ethnography also substantiated the case for instituting a conceptual distinction between the 'family' as a genealogical construct and the 'household' as a residential-commensal unit in the context of historical and cross-cultural research on household dynamics (Wilk and Netting 1984; Carter 1984).

But that is all in the past: a legacy. For the present, I believe, there is urgent need for renewal.

ENDNOTES

1. I have possibly exaggerated here the opposition of the anthropology of kinship and the sociology of the family in the western academy to make this point. Certainly, pioneers of new or synoptic perspectives in the sociology of the family have often sought to bolster their claims to theoretical universality by reference to the data of comparative ethnography (see Goode 1964; Parsons and Bales 1955: Chapter 6; or latterly Robertson 1991). At the same time, anthropologists have intermittently sought to bring their distinctive perspectives and methodologies to bear on family, kinship, and marriage in advanced, industrial societies, or on ethnic communities within these societies (see Bott 1957; Firth et al. 1970; Schneider [1968] 1980). Nonetheless, the metropolitan distinction between the anthropology of kinship and marriage and the sociology of the family has been perpetuated in the syllabi of Indian universities, notwithstanding the overlapping disciplinary affiliations of many Indian anthropologists and sociologists.

2. The three social institutions commonly held to characterize 'traditional' Indian society are the caste system, the village community, and the joint-family (Kapadia 1955: 233; Karve 1953: Introduction). Of the three, it is the family which has been viewed most positively in both public and sociological discourse (see Béteille 1991). Attitudes to the caste system and village community have been more ambiguous, indeed, often hostile. On the latter, see Jodhka 1998.

3. In retrospect, it seems somewhat odd that the criterion for establishing an 'ideal type' of Indian family pattern should be seen to depend on the demonstration that *the majority* of persons, or of families, statistically conform to the pattern.

4. For a summary of views on this question, see Madan (1976).

5. This is not to say that such sources are irrelevant, for they indicate ideals of family life that continue to command prestige in Hindu society. Shah, in fact, finds a role for such ideals through M.N. Srinivas's concept of 'Sanskritization', that is the social process whereby lower-caste groups attempt to raise their status in the caste hierarchy by adopting the more 'Sanskritized' kinship (and ritual) practices of higher-caste groups such as a ban on widow remarriage.

6. Shah's definition of the household is more problematic than is apparent at first sight, combining as it does the three features of (i) kinship relationship, (ii) co-residence, and (iii) commensality. In practice, anthropologists have often found it difficult to decide, for instance, whether a family member residing in the city but maintaining his village household and returning there frequently should or should not be counted as a member of the village household (perhaps even its 'head'). Census and National Sample Survey (NSS) definitions of the household have focused on features of residence

and commensality, and have therefore included servants, sometimes even 'visitors', in their definition of the household. For a useful discussion of conceptual problems in different definitions of the household (the disciplines of anthropology/sociology, the Census, and the NSS), see Rao (1992).

7. The twelve types are as follows: (1) *nuclear family*, a couple with or without unmarried children; (2) *supplemented nuclear family*; (3) *sub-nuclear family*; (4) *single-person household*; (5) *supplemented sub-nuclear family*; (6) *collateral joint-family*; (7) *supplemented collateral joint-family*; (8) *lineal joint-family*; (9) *supplemented lineal joint-family*; (10) *lineal-collateral joint-family*; (11) *supplemented lineal-collateral joint-family*; and a residual category, (12) *other*. See Kolenda (1987: 11–13) and A.M. Shah's perceptive critique of this scheme (1973: 220–5).

8. For instance, a high or rising proportion of bachelor households may indicate a situation of migration or social upheaval, the bachelor household in one place being matched by a female-headed household in another; or it may indicate a situation provoked by imbalances in the sex ratios and consequent distortions in the marriage market. Or, should the single persons be widows, one may be confronting a category of extreme social and material deprivation that demands active intervention (e.g. Chen 1998; Drèze 1990). On the other hand, a marked increase in spinsterhood would indicate a major change in one of the most persistent features of Indian family life—the near universality of marriage for Indian women (see Raju et al. 1999: 80).

9. All-India figures for 1981 (using a dichotomous classification) indicate a slightly higher proportion of nuclear over joint families in both urban and rural areas (see Shah 1998: 74).

10. Kolenda calculates that with 30 per cent of more joint families in a population, over 50 per cent of persons would reside in such households (1968: 390).

11. In this connection, it is pertinent that M.S. Gore's study (1968) of families of the Aggarwal business community in and around Delhi was unable to demonstrate significant differences in family size and composition between the rural and urban sample families, though he did report *attitudinal* differences on several counts, correlating with respondents' educational levels (cf. Vatuk 1972: esp. Chapters 3 and 7). See Abbi (1969) and Shah (1973: 204–7) for critiques of this well-known study.

12. To the usual distinction Kolenda has added some further points of difference: (i) differing cultural norms as to the appropriate timing of household partition (Kolenda 1967); (ii) differing degrees of what she calls women's 'bargaining power' in the family, as reflected in such features as women's relative freedom of divorce and remarriage, the institution of bridewealth versus that of dowry, and stronger ties with the wife's or the husband's kin (Kolenda 1967); (iii) for certain areas of rural Rajasthan which have registered unusually high proportions of joint households, traditions of young adolescent marriage related to region-specific customs such as sibling- and collateral-set marriages and multiple marriages (Kolenda 1989); and (iv) dependence on the joint family as a labour unit which is both a 'work team' and a 'well team' (Kolenda 1989). These and a number of other factors, including women's rights of inheritance to landed property, have been explored more consistently by Bina Agarwal in a major study of the geography of women's land rights through South Asia (1994). See also Raju et al. (1999) for a demographer's presentation of some of these factors.

13. The timing of this 'nuclearization', and the possible factors which facilitate or impede it, is the subject of a useful demographic study by K.N.M. Raju (1998). See also the detailed analyses of cases of household partition in Madan ([1965] 1989) and Parry (1979).

14. See, however, the important paper by P.N. Mari Bhat (Bhat 1996) on the regional distribution of joint families in the context of fertility limitation, based on data from the 1991 Census and the 1981 Census household tables; also S. Raju et al. (1999).

15. See Bharat (1996) for a social psychologist's self-critical discussion and assessment of the various 'measures' of aspects of family life that psychologists have devised or adapted for the Indian context.

16. For a critique of structural-functionalism in family studies, see Morgan (1975: Chapter 1, esp. 40–8).

17. This is, of course, a rather crude summary of a much more complex position, but it is not necessary to address these other aspects here.
18. This is not to disregard the heterogeneity of approaches classed as functionalist, nor to discount their several well-publicized limitations. D.H.J. Morgan (1975: Chapter 1) has summed up these limitations as emphasis: (i) on function more than dysfunction (whether for the individual or for society); (ii) consensus more than conflict; and (iii) stability rather than change.
19. There is probably much to commend Davis's formulation, which appears to be supported by macro-level data (see Bhat 1996), though its empirical corroboration at micro level has not actually been conclusive (see, for example, Patel 1994: 66). One reason for this, as Davis, himself had pointed out in the article referred to, is that nuclear households in India are often located in very close proximity to the larger kin group, so that fertility decisions are *still* likely to be influenced by the extended family, regardless of the formal type of family/household organization. See also Raju (1998).
20. An interesting exception here is Promilla Kapur's study of the life histories of Indian 'call-girls' (Kapur 1978).
21. Recent focus on the phenomenon of child labour and the 'rights of the child' has, however, drawn attention to the need for engagement between social scientists and policy makers on the concept of childhood. See Burra (1995); also Nieuwenhuys ([1994] 1999).
22. To these mechanisms for reproducing class identity, Béteille might have added the importance of strategies of matchmaking in recruiting influential affines. For an early reflection on the family's role in the social reproduction of class status, see Ross (1959).
23. For instance, providing old-age care or raising women's educational levels may be proposed as a means towards the achievement of population limitation, rather than as desirable social goals in themselves (see Uberoi 1996b).
24. More recent research has, however, confirmed a remarkable enhancement of women's 'capabilities' (education, literacy, health) in Himachal Pradesh, if not compared to neighbouring Punjab/Haryana, at least compared to other states of the 'northern' zone of kinship (See *Public Report* 1999).

REFERENCES

Abbi, Behari. 1969. 'Urban Family in India: A Review Article'. *Contributions to Indian Sociology* (n.s.). 3:116–27.

Agarwal, Bina. 1988. *Structures of Patriarchy: State, Community and Household in Modernizing Asia.* New Delhi: Kali for Women.

_____. 1994. *A Field of one's Own: Gender and Land Rights in South Asia.* Cambridge: Cambridge University Press.

_____. 1997. '"Bargaining" and Gender Relations: Within and Beyond the Household'. *Feminist Economics.* 3(1): 1–51.

_____. 2000. '"The Family" in Public Policy: Fallacious Assumptions and Gender Implications'. Ninth Lecture NCAER Golden Jubilee Seminar Series, National Council of Applied Economic Research, New Delhi.

Allen, Michael. 1982. 'Introduction: The Hindu View of Women'. In Michael Allen and S.N. Mukherjee, eds, *Women in India and Nepal.* 1–20. Canberra: Australian National University.

Ariès, Philippe. 1962. *Centuries of Childhood: A History of Family Life.* New York: Alfred Knopf.

Basu, Alaka. 1992. *Culture, the Status of Women and Demographic Behaviour: Illustrated with the Case of India.* Oxford: Clarendon Press.

Bennett, Lynn. 1983. *Dangerous Wives and Sacred Sisters: Social and Symbolic Roles of High-caste Women in Nepal.* New York: Columbia University Press.

Béteille, André. 1991. 'The Reproduction of Inequality: Occupation, Caste and Family'. *Contributions* to *Indian Sociology.* 25(1):3–28. (Reprinted in Patricia Uberoi, ed., 1993 *Family, Kinship and Marriage in India.* Delhi: Oxford University Press: 435–51).

Bharat, Shalini, ed. 1996. *Family Measurement in India.* New Delhi: Sage Publications.

———. 1999. *HIV/AIDS Related Discrimination, Stigmatisation and Denial in India: A Study in Mumbai and Bangalore.* Mumbai: Unit for Family Studies, Tata Institute of Social Sciences.

Bharat, Shalini and Murli Desai, eds. 1991. *Research on Families with Problems in India: Issues and Implications.* 2 vols. Bombay: Tata Institute of Social Sciences.

Bhat, P.N. Mari. 1996. 'Contours of Fertility Decline in India: A District Level Study Based on the 1991 Census'. In K. Srinivasan, ed., *Population Policy and Reproductive Health*, 96–117. New Delhi: Hindustan Publishing Corporation and Population Foundation of India.

Bott, E. 1957. *Family and Social Network.* London: Tavistock.

Burra, Neera. 1995. *Born to Work: Child Labour in India.* Delhi: Oxford University Press.

Butcher, Melissa. 1999. 'Parallel Texts: The body and television in India'. In Christiane Brosius and Melissa Butcher, eds, *Image Journeys: Audio-visual Media and Cultural Change in India*, 165–96. New Delhi: Sage Publications.

Carstairs, G. Morris. 1957. *The Twice-born: A Study of a Community of High-caste Hindus.* London: Hogarth Press.

Carter, Anthony J. 1984. 'Household Histories'. In Robert McC. Netting Richard R. Wilk and Eric J. Arnould, eds, *Households: Comparative Studies of the Domestic Group*, 44–53. Berkeley: University of California Press.

Chen, Martha Alter, ed. 1998. *Widows in India: Social Neglect and Public Action.* New Delhi: Sage Publications.

Chowdhry, Prem. 1994. *The Veiled Women: Shifting Gender Equations in Rural Haryana, 1880–1990.* Delhi: Oxford University Press.

Daniel, E. Valentine. 1984. *Fluid Signs: Being a Person the Tamil Way.* Berkeley: University of California Press.

Das, Veena. 1976. 'Masks and Faces: An Essay on Punjabi Kinship'. *Contributions to Indian Sociology.* 10(1):1–30. (Reprinted in Patricia Uberoi, ed. 1993. *Family, Kinship and Marriage in India.* Delhi: Oxford University Press, 198–224).

———. 1988. 'Femininity and the Orientation to the Body'. In Karuna Chanana, ed., *Socialisation, Education and Women: Explorations in Gender Identity*, 193–207. New Delhi: Orient Longman.

———. 1995. *Critical Events: An Anthropological Perspective on Contemporary India.* Delhi: Oxford University Press.

———. 1996. 'Sexual Violence, Discursive Formations and the State'. *Economic and Political Weekly.* 31(35–7):2411–23.

Das Gupta, Monica. 1987. 'Selective Discrimination against Female Children in Rural Punjab, India'. *Population and Development Review.* 13(1):77–100.

———. 1995: 'Life Course Perspectives on Women's Autonomy and Health Outcomes'. *American Anthropologist.* 97(3):481–91.

Davis, Kingsley. 1955. 'Institutional Patterns Favouring High Fertility in Underdeveloped Areas'. *Eugenics Quarterly.* 2: 33–9.

Desai, I.P. 1964. *Some Aspects of Family in Mahuva.* Bombay: Asia Publishing House.

Drèze, Jean. 1990. *Widows in Rural India.* London School of Economics, Development Economics Research Programme Discussion Paper Series, no. 26.

Dube, Leela. 1986. 'Seed and Earth: The Symbolism of Biological Reproduction and the Sexual Relations of Production'. In Leela Dube, Eleanor Leacock, and Shirley Ardener, eds, *Visibility and Power: Essays on Women in Society and Development*, 22–53. Delhi: Oxford University Press.

———. 1988. 'On the Construction of Gender: Hindu Girls in Patrilineal India'. In Karuna Chanana, ed., *Socialisation, Education and Women: Explorations in Gender Identity*, 166–92. New Delhi: Orient Longman.

Dube, Leela. 1997. *Women and Kinship: Comparative Perspectives on Gender in South and South-East Asia*. New Delhi: Vistaar Publications.

Dumont, Louis. 1966. 'Marriage in India. The Present State of the Question, III. North India in Relation to South India'. *Contributions to Indian Sociology*. 9:90–114.

———. 1968. 'Marriage Alliance'. In D. Sills, ed., *International Encyclopaedia of the Social Sciences*. 10:19–23. New York: Macmillan and Free Press.

———. 1983a. *Affinity as a Value: Marriage Alliance in South India with Comparative Essays on Australia*. Chicago: University of Chicago Press.

———. 1983b. 'The Debt to Ancestors and the Category of *Sapinda*'. In Charles Malamoud, ed., *Debt and Debtors*, 1–20. Delhi: Vikas Publishing Hase.

Dyson, Tim and Mick Moore. 1983. 'On Kinship Structure, Female Autonomy and Demographic Behavior in India'. *Population and Development Review*. 9(1):35–60.

Erikson, E.H. 1950. *Childhood and Society*. New York: W.W. Norton.

Epstein. T.S. 1973. *South India: Yesterday, Today and Tomorrow*. London: Macmillan.

Firth, Raymond, James Hubert, and Anthony Forge. 1970. *Families and their Relatives: Kinship in a Middle-class Sector of London*. London: Routledge & Kegan Paul.

Fortes, Meyer. 1962. 'Introduction'. In Jack Goody, ed., *The Developmental Cycle in Domestic Groups*, 1–14. Cambridge: Cambridge University Press.

Fox, Robin. 1967. *Kinship and Marriage: An Anthropological Perspective*. Harmondsworth: Penguin Books.

Freed, Stanley A. and Ruth S. Freed. 1983. 'The Domestic Cycle in India: Natural History of a Will-o'-the-wisp'. *American Ethnologist*. 10(2):313–27.

Fruzzetti, Lina M. [1982] 1990. *The Gift of a Virgin: Women, Marriage and Ritual in a Bengali Society*. Delhi: Oxford University Press.

Geetha, V. 1998. 'On Bodily Love and Hurt'. In Mary E. John and Janaki Nair, eds, *A Question of Silence: The Sexual Economies of Modern India*, 304–31. New Delhi: Kali for Women.

Ghurye, G.S. 1955. *Family and Kin in Indo-European Culture*. Bombay: Oxford University Press.

———. 1960. *After a Century and a Quarter*. Bombay: Popular Prakashan.

———. 1973. *I and Other Explorations*. Bombay: Popular Prakashan.

Good, Anthony. 1991. *The Female Bridegroom: A Comparative Study of Life-crisis Rituals in South India and Sri Lanka*. Oxford: Clarendon.

Goode, William J. 1963. *World Revolution and Family Patterns*. London: Free Press of Glencoe.

———. 1964. *The Family*. Foundations of Modern Sociology Series. Englewood Cliffs, NJ: Prentice-Hall.

Goody, Jack. 1976. *Production and Reproduction: A Comparative Study of the Domestic Domain*. Cambridge: Cambridge University Press.

———. 1990. *The Oriental, the Ancient and the Primitive: Systems of Marriage and the Family in the Pre-industrial Societies of Eurasia*. Cambridge: Cambridge University Press.

Goody, Jack and S.J. Tambiah. 1973. *Bridewealth and Dowry*. Cambridge: Cambridge University Press.

Gore, M.S. 1968. *Urbanization and Family Change*. Bombay: Popular Prakashan.

Gough, E. Kathleen. 1959. 'The Nayars and the Definition of Marriage'. *Journal of the Royal Anthropological Institute*. 58(5):826–53.

Gould, H.A. 1968:. 'Time Dimension and Structural Change in an Indian Kinship System'. In Milton Singer and C. Bernard Cohn, eds, *Structure and Change in Indian Society*, 413–21. New York: Wenner-Gren Foundation.

Gray, John N. 1995. *The Householder's World: Purity, Power and Dominance in a Nepali Village*. Delhi: Oxford University Press.

Greenough, Paul R. 1982. *Prosperity and Misery in Modern Bengal: The Famine of 1943–44*. New York: Oxford University Press.

Hanchett, Suzanne. 1988. *Coloured Rice: Symbolic Structure in Hindu Family Festivals*. Delhi: Hindustan Pubulishing.

Harriss-White, Barbara. 1999. 'Gender-cleansing: The Paradox of Development and Deteriorating Female-life-chances in Tamil Nadu'. In Rajeswari Sunder Rajan, eds, *Signposts: Gender Issues in Post-Independence India*, 124–53. New Delhi: Kali for Women.

Hasan, Zoya, ed. 1994. *Forging Identities: Gender, Communities and the State*. New Delhi: Kali for Women.

Hershman, Paul. 1981. *Punjabi Kinship and Marriage*. Delhi: Hindustan Publishing Corporation.

Hsu, Francis L.K. 1963. *Clan, Caste and Club*. Princeton, N.J.: D. Van Nostrand.

Inden, Ronald B. and Ralph W. Nicholas. 1977. *Kinship in Bengali Culture*. Chicago: Chicago University Press.

Jayawardena, Kumari and Malathi de Alwis, eds. 1996. *Embodied Violence: Communalising Female Sexuality in South Asia*. New York: St Martin's Press. *Contextualising Women's Sexuality in South Asia*. New Delhi: Kali for Women.

Jodhka, Surinder S. 1998. 'From "Book View" to "Field View": Social Anthropological Construction of the Indian Village'. *Oxford Development Studies*. 26(3):311–31.

John, Mary and Janaki Nair, eds. 1998. *A Question of Silence? The Sexual Economies of Modern India*. New Delhi: Kali for Women.

Kakar, Sudhir. 1981. *The Inner World: A Psychoanalytic Study of Childhood and Society in India*. Delhi: Oxford University Press.

——. 1989. *Intimate Relations: Exploring Indian Sexuality*. New York: Viking/Penguin.

Kane, P.V. 1930–62. *History of Dharmasastra*, 5 vols. Poona: Bhandarkar Oriental Research Institute.

Kapadia, K.M. 1955. *Marriage and Family in India*. London: Oxford University Press.

Kapadia, Karin. 1995. *Siva and Her Sisters: Gender, Caste and Class in Rural South Asia*. Boulder, CO: Westview Press.

Kapur, Promilla. 1970. *Marriage and the Working Woman in India*. Delhi: Vikas Publishing House.

——. 1978. *Life and World of Call-girls in India: A Socio-psychological Study of the Aristocratic Prostitute*. Delhi: Vikas Publishing House.

Kapur, Ratna. ed. 1996. *Feminist Terrains in Legal Domains: Interdisciplinary Essays on Women and Law in India*. New Delhi: Kali for Women.

Kapur, Ratna and Brenda Cossman. 1996. *Subversive Sites: Feminist Engagements with Law in India*. New Delhi: Kali for Women.

Karlekar, Malavika. 1982. *Poverty and Women's Work: A Study of Sweeper Women in Delhi*. Delhi: Vikas Publishing House.

——. 1998: 'Domestic Violence'. *Economic and Political Weekly*. 33(27):1741–51.

Karve, Irawati. 1953. *Kinship Organization in India*. Poona: Deccan College Monograph Series.

Kessinger, Tom G. 1974. *Vilyatpur, 1848–1968: Social and Economic Change in a North Indian Village*. Berkeley: University of California Press.

Khare, Ravindra S. 1984. *The Untouchable as Himself: Ideology, Identity and Pragmatism among Lucknow Chamars*. Cambridge: Cambridge University Press.

——. 1998. 'The Issue of "Right to Food" among the Hindus: Notes and Comments'. *Contributions to Indian Sociology*. 32(2):253–78.

Kolenda, Pauline. 1967. 'Regional Differences in Indian Family Structure'. In Robert I. Crane, ed., *Regions and Regionalism in South Asian Studies*, 147–228. Durham, South Carolina: Duke University Press. (Reprinted in Kolenda 1987: Chapter 2).

——. 1968. 'Region, Caste and Family Structure: A Comparative Study of the Indian "Joint" Family'. In Milton Singer and Bernard Cohn, eds, *Structure and Change in Indian Society*, 339–96. New York: Wenner-Gren Foundation. (Reprinted in Pauline Kolenda, *Regional Differences in Family Structure in India*, 1987. Jaipur: Rawat Publications, Chapter 1.)

——. 1987. *Regional Differences in Family Structure in India*. Jaipur: Rawat Publications.

——. 1989. 'The Joint Household in Rural Rajasthan: Ecological, Cultural and Demographic Conditions for its Occurrence'. In John N. Gray and David J. Mearns, eds, *Society from the*

Inside out: Anthropological Perspectives on the South Asian Household, 55–106. New Delhi: Sage Publications.

Kumar, Krishna. 1993. 'Study of Childhood and Family'. In T.S. Saraswathi and Baljit Kaur, eds, *Human Development and Family Studies in India: An Agenda for Research and Policy*, 67–76. New Delhi: Sage Publications.

Kynch, Jocelyn and Amartya Sen. 1983. 'Indian Women: Well-being and Survival'. *Cambridge Journal of Economics*. 7:363–80.

Lardinois, Roland. 1992. 'Family and Household as Practical Groups: Preliminary Reflections on the Hindu Joint Family'. In K. Saradamoni, ed., *Finding the Household: Conceptual and Methodological Issues*, 31–47. New Delhi: Sage Publications.

Laslett, Peter. 1972. 'Introduction: The History of the Family'. In Peter Laslet and R. Wall, eds, *Household and Family in Past Time*, 1–89. Cambridge: The University Press.

Levi-Strauss, Claude. [1956] 1960. 'The Family'. In Harry L. Shapiro, ed., *Man, Culture and Society*, 261–85. 2nd ed. New York: Galaxy Books.

———. [1949] 1969. *The Elementary Structures of Kinship*. London: Eyre & Spottiswoode.

Madan, T.N. 1976. 'The Hindu Family and Development'. *Journal of Social and Economic Studies*. 4(2): 211–31. (Reprinted in Patricia Uberoi, ed., *Family, Kinship and Marriage*, 1993. Delhi: Oxford University Press: 416–34).

———. 1983. 'The Ideology of the Householder among the Kashmiri Pandits'. In Akos Ostor, Lina Fruzzetti and Steve Barnett, eds, *Concepts of Person*, 99–117. Delhi: Oxford University Press.

Madan, T.N. [1965] 1989. *Family and Kinship: A Study of the Pandits of Rural Kashmir*. 2nd ed. Delhi: Oxford University Press.

Maine, Henry Sumner. [1861] 1972. *Ancient Law*. London: Everyman edition.

Mandelbaum, David G. 1988. *Women's Seclusion and Men's Honor: Sex Roles in North India*. Tucson: University of Arizona Press.

Marriott, Mckim. 1998. 'The Female Family Core Explored Ethnosociologically'. *Contributions to Indian Sociology* (n.s.). 32(2):279–304.

———. 1990. *India through Hindu Categories*. New Delhi: Sage Publications.

Mayer, Adrian C. 1960. *Caste and Kinship in Central India: A Village and its Region*. London: Routledge & Kegan Paul.

Miller, Barbara. [1981] 1997. *The Endangered Sex: Neglect of Female Children in Rural North India*. Delhi: Oxford University Press.

Minturn, Leigh. 1993. *Sita's Daughters: Coming out of Purdah. The Rajpur Women of Khalapur Revisited*. New York: Oxford University Press.

Minturn, Leigh and John Hitchcock. 1963. 'The Rajputs of Khalapur, India'. In B. Whiting, ed., *Six Cultures: Studies in Child Rearing*. New York: Wiley.

Misri, Urvashi. 1985. 'Child and Childhood: A Conceptual Construction'. *Contributions to Indian Sociology*. 19(1):115–32.

Moffatt. Michael. 1979. *An Untouchable Community in South India: Structure and Consensus*. Princeton: Princeton University Press.

Moore, Henrietta. 1988. *Feminism and Anthropology*. Minneapolis: University of Minnesota Press.

Morgan, D.H.J. 1975. *Social Theory and the Family*. London: Routledge & Kegan Paul.

Mulla, D.F. 1972. *Principles of Mohamedan Law*. 20th ed. Bombay: N.M. Tripathi.

Murdock, George Peter. 1949. *Social Structure*. New York: Macmillan Company.

Nair, Janaki. 1996. *Women and Law in Colonial India: A Social History*. New Delhi: Kali for Women.

Nandy, Ashis. 1980. 'Woman *versus* Womanliness in India: An Essay in Cultural and Political Psychology'. In Ashis Nandy, ed., *At the Edge of Psychology: Essays in Politics and Culture*, 32–46. Delhi: Oxford University Press.

Netting, Robert McC., Richard R. Wilk, and Eric J. Arnould, eds. 1984. *Households: Comparative and Historical Studies of the Domestic Group*. Berkeley: University of California Press.

Nieuwenhuys, Olga. [1994] 1999. *Children's Lifeworlds: Gender, Welfare and Labour in the Developing World*. New Delhi: Social Science Press.

Nimkoff, M.F. 1959. 'The Family in India: Some Problems Concerning Research on the Changing Family in India'. *Sociological Bulletin*. 8: 32–8.

Orenstein, H. 1961. 'The Recent History of the Extended Family in India'. *Social Problems*. 8:341–50.

Osella, Filippo and Caroline Osella. 1996. 'Articulation of Physical and Social Bodies in Kerala'. *Contributions to Indian Sociology*. 30(1): 37–68.

Ostor, Akos, Lina Fruzzetti, and Steve Barnett, eds. 1983. *Concepts of Person: Kinship, Caste, and Marriage in India*. Delhi: Oxford University Press.

Papanek, Hanna. 1982. 'Purdah: Separate Worlds and Symbolic Shelter'. In H. Papanek and G. Minault, eds, *Separate Worlds: Studies of Purdah in South Asia*, 3–53. Delhi: Chanakya Publications.

———. 1989. 'Family Status-production Work: Women's Contribution to Social Mobility and Class Differentiation'. In Maitreyi Krishnaraj and Karuna Chanana, eds, *Gender and the Household Domain: Social and Cultural Dimensions*, 97–116. New Delhi: Sage Publications.

———. 1990. 'To Each Less than She Needs, from Each More than She Can Do: Allocations, Entitlements, and Value'. In Irene Tinker, ed., *Persistent Inequalities: Women and World Development*, 162–81. New York: Oxford University Press.

Parry, J.P. 1979. *Caste and Kinship in Kangra*. Delhi: Vikas Publishing House.

Parsons, Talcott. [1949] 1959. 'The Social Structure of the Family'. In Ruth Anshen, ed., *The Family: Its Function and Destiny*. Revised ed., 241–74. New York: Harper.

Parsons, Talcott and Robert F. Bales. 1955. *Family, Socialization and Interaction Process*. Glencoe, Ill: The Free Press.

Patel, Tulsi. 1994. *Fertility Behaviour: Population and Society in a Rajasthan Village*. Delhi: Oxford University Press.

Pillai, S. Devadas. 1997. *Indian Sociology through Ghurye: A Dictionary*. Mumbai: Popular Prakashan.

Prabhu, Pandharinath H. [1940] 1995. *Hindu Social Organization: A Study in Socio-psychological and Ideological Foundations*. 4th ed. Bombay: Popular Prakashan.

Public Report on Basic Education in India. 1999. Delhi: Oxford University Press.

Radcliffe-Brown, A.R. 1950. 'Introduction'. In A.R. Radcliffe-Brown & Daryll Forde, eds, *African Systems of Kinship and Marriage*, 1–85. London: Oxford University Press.

———. 1952. 'Foreword'. In M.N. Srinivas, ed., *Religion and Society among the Coorgs of South India*, 5–9. Oxford: Clarendon Press.

Raheja, Gloria Goodwin and Ann Grodzins Gold. 1996. *Listen to the Heron's Words: Reimagining Gender and Kinship in North* India. Delhi: Oxford University Press.

Raju, K.N.M. 1998. *Family and Household Functions: A Demographic Study*. Bangalore: Sunrise Publications.

Raju, Saraswati, Peter J. Atkins, Naresh Kumar, and Janet G. Townsend. 1999. *Atlas of Women and Men in India*. New Delhi: Kali for Women.

Rao, N.J. Usha. 1992. 'Gaps in Definitions and Analysis. A Sociological Perspective'. In K. Saradamoni, ed., *Finding the Household: Conceptual and Methodological Issues*, 49–74. New Delhi: Sage Publications.

Risseeuw, Carla and Rajni Palriwala. 1996. 'Introduction: Shifting Circles of Support'. In Rajni Palriwala and Carla Risseeuw, eds, *Shifting Circles of Support: Contextualising Gender and Kinship in South Asia and Sub-Saharan Africa*, 15–47. New Delhi: Sage Publications.

Robertson, A.F. 1991. *Beyond the Family: The Social Organization of Human Reproduction*. Cambridge: Polity Press.

Rosaldo, Michelle Z. 1974. 'Woman, Culture and Society: A Theoretical Overview'. In Michelle Z. Rosaldo and Louise Lamphere, eds, *Woman, Culture and Society*. Stanford: Stanford University Press.

Ross, Aileen D. 1959. 'Education and Family Change'. *Sociological Bulletin*. 8:39–44.

Ross Aileen D. 1961. *The Hindu Family in its Urban Setting*. Bombay: Oxford University Press.

Saradamoni, S. 1996. 'Women's Rights and the Decline of Matriliny is Southern India'. In Rajni Palriwala and Carla Risseeuw, eds, *Shifting Circles of Support: Contextualising Gender and Kinship in South Asia and Sub-Saharan Africa*, 133–54. New Delhi: Sage Publications.

Sarkar, Tanika. 1993. 'Rhetoric against Age of Consent: Resisting Colonial Reason and Death of a Child Wife'. *Economic and Political Weekly*. 27(36):1869–78.

Schneider, David M. [1968] 1980. *American Kinship: A Cultural Account*. 2nd. ed. Englewood Cliffs, N.J.: Prentice-Hall.

Schneider, David M. and E. Kathleen Gough. 1961. *Matrilineal Kinship*. Berkeley: University of California Press.

Sen, Amartya. 1983. 'Economics and the Family'. *Asian Development Review*. 1(2):14–26.

Shah. A.M. 1973. *The Household Dimension of the Family in India*. Berkeley: University of California Press.

———. 1998. *The Family in India: Critical Essays*. Delhi: Orient Longman.

———. 1999a. 'The family in the Census of India'. *Sociological Bulletin*. 48(1–2):235–7.

———. 1999b: 'Changes in the Family and the Elderly'. *Economic and Political Weekly*. 34(20):1179–82.

Sharma, Ursula. 1978. 'Women and Their Affines: The Veil as a Symbol of Separation'. *Man*. 13:18–33.

———. 1980. *Women, Work and Property in North West India*. London: Tavistock.

———. 1986. *Women's Work, Class and the Urban Household: A Study of Shimla, North India*. London: Tavistock.

———. 1989. 'Studying the Household: Industrialisation and Values'. In John N. Gray and David J. Mearnsm, *Society From the Inside Out: Anthropological Perspectives on the South Asian Household*, 35–54. New Delhi: Sage Publications.

Singer, Milton. 1968. 'The Indian Joint Family in Modern Industry'. In Milton Singer and Bernard Cohn, eds, *Structure and Change in Indian Society*, 423–52. New York: Wenner-Gren Foundation.

Singh, K.S., ed. 1993. *An Anthropological Atlas* (Anthropological Survey, *People of India*, vol. 11). Delhi: Oxford University Press.

Srinivas, M.N. 1942. *Marriage and Family in Mysore*. Bombay: New Book Company.

———. 1952. *Religion and Society among the Coorgs of South India*. Oxford: Clarendon Press.

Srinivas, M.N. and E.A. Ramaswamy. 1977. *Culture and Human Fertility*. Delhi: Oxford University Press.

Tambiah, S.J. 1975. 'From Varna to Caste through Mixed Unions'. In Jack Goody, ed. *The Character of Kinship*. Cambridge: Cambirdge University Press.

Trautmann, Thomas R. 1981. *Dravidian Kinship*. Cambridge: Cambridge University Press.

———. 1987. *Lewis Henry Morgan and the Invention of Kinship*. Berkeley: University of California Press.

Trawick, Margaret. 1996. *Notes on Love in a Tamil Family*. Berkeley: University of California Press.

Uberoi, Patricia, ed. 1993. *Family, Kinship and Marriage in India*. Delhi: Oxford University Press.

Uberoi, Patricia. 1995. 'Problems With Patriarchy: Conceptual Issues in the Engagement of Anthropology and Feminism'. *Sociological Bulletin*. 44(2):15–221.

———. 1996a. *Social Reform, Sexuality and the State*. New Delhi: Sage Publications.

———. 1996b. 'The Family in Official Discourse'. In *Second Nature: Women and the Family*. *India International Centre Quarterly*. Winter: 134–55.

———. 1997. 'Dharma and Desire, Freedom and Destiny: Rescripting the Man-woman Relationship in Popular Hindi Cinema'. In Meenakshi Thapan, ed., *Embodiment: Essays on Gender and Identity*, 145–71. Delhi: Oxford University Press.

Vatuk, Sylvia. 1972. *Kinship and Urbanization: White Collar Migrants in North India*. Berkeley: University of California Press.

———. 1982. 'Purdah Revisited: A Comparison of Hindu and Muslim Interpretations of the Cultural Meaning of Purdah in South Asia'. In H. Papanek and G. Minault, eds, *Separate Worlds: Studies of Purdah in South Asia*, 54–78. Delhi: Chanakya Publications.

Visaria, Leela. 1999. 'Deficit of Women in India: Magnitude, Trends, Regional Variations and

Determinants'. In Bharati Ray and Aparna Basu, eds, *From Independence towards Freedom: Indian Women since 1947*, 80–99. Delhi: Oxford University Press.

Wadley, Susans S. 1999. 'Anthropology'. In Joseph W. Elder, Edward C. Dimock, Jr., and Ainslie T. Embree, eds, *India's Worlds and US Scholars*. 111–37. Delhi: Manohar/American Institute of Indian Studies.

Wadley, Susan and Bruce W. Derr. 1988. 'Karimpur Families Over Sixty Years'. *South Asian Anthropologist*. 9(2):119–32. (Reprinted in Patricia Uberoi, *Family, Kinship and Marriage in India*, 1993. Delhi: Oxford University Press, 393–415)

Wall, Richard, Jean Robin, and Peter Laslett, eds. 1983. *Family Forms in Historic Europe*. Cambridge: Cambridge University Press.

Wilk, Richard R. and Robert McC. Netting. 1984. 'Households: Changing Forms and Functions'. In Robert McC. Netting, Richard R. Wilk and Eric J. Arnould, eds, *Households: Comparative Historical Studies of the Domestic Group*, 1–28. Berkeley: University of California Press.

Yalman, Nur. 1963. 'On the Purity and Sexuality of Women in the Castes of Ceylon and Malabar'. *Journal of the Royal Anthropological Institute*. 93(1):25–58.

Yanagisako, Sylvia Junko and Jane Fishburne Collier. 1987. 'Toward a Unified Analysis of Gender and Kinship'. In Jane Fishburne Collier and Sylvia Junko Yanagisako, eds, *Gender and Kinship: Essays toward a Unified Analysis*, 14–50. Stanford: Stanford University Press.

Domestic Violence

MALAVIKA KARLEKAR

INTRODUCTION: DEFINITION OF VIOLENCE[1]

This section focuses on violence against women and girl children in the home with an emphasis on physical acts of abuse and neglect. Though domestic violence is the specific context, the growing ubiquity of gender-specific violence in public spaces is evident from statistics and the discourse on rape and sexual harassment at the workplace (Das 1996; Agnes 1993; Krishna Raj 1991; Pati 1991; PUDR 1991; Samuel 1992; S. Sarkar 1994; T. Sarkar 1991; Sunder Rajan 1993). The sexual violation of women in times of political, communal, and ethnic strife has led to innovative analyses based on archival research, life stories, and narrative techniques (Bhasin and Menon 1994; Butalia 1993, 1998; Das 1990; Das and Nandy 1986; Menon and Bhasin 1998; Sarkar and Butalia 1995), encouraging an interrogation of established representations of major events such as Partition and, more recently, religious strife. There is also some discussion of sex workers and of aberrant events such as *sati* (widow immolation), witch-hunts, stripping and shaming of women—particularly those from the lower castes, often as punishment for their community's transgressions (see Vyas et al. 1996 for a comprehensive guide to material available).

The present chapter, however, does not go into a discussion of such forms of violence and while it is well established that psychological (Carstairs 1983; Ghadially 1987; Kakar 1983) and indeed symbolic (Bondurant 1965; Bourdieu 1977) manifestations of violence are as widespread, these are by and large, beyond the scope of this chapter. Though the discussion on entitlements does touch upon attitudes and stereotypes which result in denial and neglect, in the Indian context there is urgent need to spend far more time and resources on the mental-health aspect of violence. This has so far been an area largely neglected by government and police agencies, voluntary organizations, and researchers. In part the neglect can be explained by the overall social attitude of suppressing—if not ignoring—factors which reflect on the inner life of individuals and families and cannot easily be classified as an 'illness'. An alarming finding of the latest World Development Report (1993) was that, globally, rape and domestic violence account for about 5 per cent of the total disease burden among women in the age group of 15–44. Disease is defined as both, physical as well as non-physical ailments. It need hardly be pointed out that these figures possibly represent only a fraction of actual violence-induced psychological and somatic disorders. As the focus is on the household, the term domestic violence is preferred to family violence: the former helps focus on the physical unit of the home rather than the more amorphous context of the family, even though the underlying world-view may be that of the larger familial and kin group.

An overview of studies in a communication paper circulated by Anveshi, Research Centre in Women's Studies in Hyderabad (1995), shows that while there is no gender difference in severe mental disorders such as schizophrenia and manic depression, twice as many women than men are afflicted with common mental disorders such as anxieties, phobias, and obsessive-compulsive behaviour. The paper concluded that when mental illness has a biological basis, the prevalence was the same across genders; however 'where mental illness has a psycho-social basis, women are far more frequently ill than men' (Anveshi 1995: 2). In other words, there is a strong correlation between women's life situations and their mental and physical health (see Davar 1995).

There is also limited recognition of the fact that a physical act, catastrophic event, or violent abuse can result in a range of symptoms known generically as post-traumatic stress disorders (PTSD). Evidence proves that the impact of these disorders can often be far greater and last much longer than the act or event itself. A report on global mental health (Desjarlais et al. 1995) point out that PTSD is a 'persistent response', and one that can impede the functioning of some of those exposed to a particular trauma. As an instance, it may be worth pointing out that in India, the 'possession' of women by malevolent spirits is socially and culturally accepted; elaborate procedures for exorcism—which are often violent in nature— bring into focus the woman or girl, who as a victim of this particular affliction, is expected to behave in ways which violate conventional norms of appropriate conduct. (see Kakar 1983 for a discussion of feminine possession). This state of possession, often caused by severe familial, social, and sexual abuse and trauma, may be classified as part of the PTSD syndrome.

Quite apart from the silence around the non-physical acts of aggression, such as verbal abuse and denial of food, education, and care, there is surprisingly little material available in the form of books or academic essays or papers on the entire issue of violence against women in India; despite the fact that a battery of statistics and reports made available by official sources and the media reinforce the view that this form of gendered violence is fast becoming a feature of daily living in contemporary India, it has yet to become a priority area of research. Further, of what is available, about half relates to violence within the family (Vyas et al. 1996). In Patricia Uberoi's ([1994] 1995) opinion, this silence is explicable by a certain hesitance in subjecting the family and its intimate relationships to scrutiny; at the same time, if there is any data base on the nature and kind of violence that goes on behind locked doors, it has become available largely due to the activities of NGOs, those in the women's movement and the police.[2]

Uberoi feels that though the 'family is also a site of exploitation and violence ... sociologists appear to eschew issues of social pathology, at least in regard to the family' ([1994] 1995: 36). This is because the family is 'a cultural ideal and a focus of identity', its inviolability as an institution being reaffirmed by an environment which limits interaction and discourse between the professional academic and the activist. The situation is compounded by the fact that familial concern with propriety, honour (*izzat*), and reputation makes it difficult for those researchers interested in investigating violence within the home to gain access to those perceived as victims. Thus it is hardly coincidental that a large percentage of available data on violence against women locates the family as a major cause of oppression and subsequent ill health and loss of identity. The Anveshi paper noted that 'all our analyses point to the fact that marriage and the family are necessary stressors in the cause of mental illness among Indian women' (Anveshi

1995: 3–4). It thus becomes necessary to 'pay attention to the violence of everyday life' (Das 1997).

Put simply, violence is an act of aggression, usually in interpersonal interaction or relations. It may also be aggression of an individual woman against herself, such as suicide, self-mutilation, negligence of ailments, sex determination tests, food denial, and so on. Basically, then, violence brings into question the concept of boundary maintenance (Nedelsky 1991) and a sense of self as well as a perception of another's autonomy and identity. It implies that when the body— and indeed the self—is vulnerable to violation, individuals have a very different notion of 'what is one's body and what is done to one's body' (Litke 1992: 174). Indian scholars in the field of women's studies have emphasized the dynamics of power and powerlessness involved in a violent act. It is a coercive mechanism 'to assert one's will over another, to prove or to feel a sense of power' (Litke 1992: 174).

Given that violence is not limited to any single group, 'it can be perpetuated by those in power against the powerless or by the powerless in retaliation against coercion by others to deny their powerlessness' (Poonacha 1999). Further, Govind Kelkar (1991) situates violence against women 'in the socio-economic and political context of power relations'. He feels that the view that violence is 'an act of illegal criminal use of force', is inadequate and should include 'exploitation, discrimination, upholding of unequal economic and social structures, the creation of an atmosphere of terror, threat or reprisal and forms of religio-cultural and political violence' (Kelkar 1991: 1).

This wide definition of violence finds resonance in a hierarchical society based on exploitative gender relations. Violence often becomes a tool to socialize family members according to prescribed norms of behaviour within an overall perspective of male dominance and control. The family and its operational unit, the household, are the sites where oppression and deprivation of individual psyches and physical selves are part of the structures of acquiescence: often enough, those being 'moulded' into an acceptance of submission and denial are in-marrying women and children. Physical violence, as well as less explicit forms of aggression, are used as methods to ensure their obedience. At every stage in the life cycle, the female body is both the object of desire and of control (Thapan 1997b; Karlekar forthcoming).

The Indian family, its forms, structure, and functions have been important areas of study. Debates on definitions and concepts which continue, are by no means free of contradictions (Desai 1980). Relevant areas of concern relate to whether the basic family unit is joint or nuclear in structure (Desai 1980; Desai 1964; Gore 1968; Shah 1964, 1973, 1988), and how to distinguish between the family and the household. These have direct bearing on the status of women, not only in terms of the number and quality of relationships to which they have to adapt and the distribution of functions and roles, but also with regard to the allocation of resources. All these aspects can be, and indeed are, areas for differences of opinion. Clearly a joint or extended family imposes certain emotional and physical burdens on the daughter-in-law, at the same time it provides much-needed support in child rearing and care (Gore 1968; Karlekar 1982; Kasturi 1990).

The fact that in most parts of India, women enter as strangers into an already structured world of consanguineally related men generates its own tensions and conflicts in loyalties and commitments. The exceptions are castes such as the Tamil–Brahmins which practice cross-cousin and maternal uncle-niece marriages. In fact, according to M.S. Gore, the two main causes of strain in the joint family are the evolution of a strong conjugal relationship and 'the difficulty of socialising the women members into developing a community outlook and a sense of identity with the family groups' (Gore 1968: 25). In the present context, conflicting identities are particularly significant for an understanding of the external dynamics of a group united on the basis of blood, and living together with those from other families. They raise, for instance, the question of whether, for any analysis on women's status, the household is more relevant or the family.

There is no simple answer to this question, particularly as 'the very attempt to distinguish between family and household in India, if not elsewhere too, goes hand in hand with establishing a relationship between the two' (Shah 1983: 34). By and large, households 'are task-oriented residence units' while families are 'kinship groupings that need not be localised' (Netting et al. 1984: xx). To put it somewhat simplistically, the household implies a physical structure, goods and services held in common, and a core membership. On the other hand, the family is more amorphous, spread over time and space, characterized by a 'developmental process' (Shah 1983:4) in roles and relationships. A household is the operational unit which functions broadly within the parameters of a family and kinship ideology; this would include rules of marriage, residence, property ownership, roles and functions determined according to age and gender. As Rajni Palriwala writes, 'While the household forms the grid for a major part of women's activities and interpersonal relations, various facets of kinship provide necessary cultural and social structural contexts' (Palriwala 1990: 17). In other words, these contexts provide the ground, so to speak, for a working out of family ideologies around specific roles and expectations.

There are, as Veena Das (1976) has commented in the context of Punjabi kinship, certain moral rules which influence the trajectory of individual lives. It can be argued that these moral rules operate to maintain a certain gender-biased order internal to families and kinship systems. In arguing that the family more than the caste system is responsible for reproducing inequalities within society, André Béteille feels that entire families work towards 'transmitting its cultural and social capital to its younger members, despite psychological failures of many kinds' (Béteille 1998: 440). Clearly, moral rules of a family do operate with an eye to a shoring up on, as well as acquisition of, Bourdieuan capital; however, what Béteille overlooks is that embedded in this very process is a gender-based inequality. In looking at the role of the family in socialization, Béteille has glossed over the inequality that is often institutionalized between the 'older' and 'younger members'. This inequality is embedded in oppressive structures of a family ideology committed to an age and gender hierarchy which is worked out within a household. Who shall have access to which scarce resource of capital is thus determined by the gender as well as age of the family member. As will be clear soon, the girl child is often the victim of such discrimination as families devise coping mechanisms on resource sharing. However, there is a tendency to perceive domestic violence only in terms of inter-spousal violence: in a study among professionals—paediatricians, general physicians, and psychiatrists—dealing with victims of domestic violence, as well as a sample of the victims themselves, researchers from the Delhi-based Multiple Action Research Group (MARG) found that 'by the large, there appeared to be no clear understanding of "domestic violence". Each case is treated symptomatically even if it traced to violence in the family' (MARG 1996: 25). Thus violence against children and the aged was hardly perceived as instance of domestic violence. Studies that speak of discrimination against the girl child or the old grandparents in terms of the food and nutrition they receive, would view this as the physical impact of deprivation; rarely would it be regarded as an act of violence. If there are meagre data on violence against the elderly, there are even less on abused single women and men in families. Using the life cycle approach, the following section argues that at every stage, there is discrimination and violence, particularly against girl children and later women within the household, either natal or conjugal. With age, problems are compounded as increased dependency, illness, and fatigue arise. Finally, it also suggests that despite the ubiquity of violence, micro-studies may well point to the emergence of alternate discourses which question a dominant familial ideology in many ways.

VIOLENCE IN THE NATAL HOME

Female Foeticide and Infanticide

A major gain from the women's movement has been the emergence of a rich storehouse of information and data on women at every stage of the life cycle-exposure of the prevalence of the acts of foeticide and infanticide being a case in point. While both these methods of dealing with unwanted daughters go back in history, is the misuse of medical tests for female foeticide and increasing incidence of infanticide in parts of the country where it was once unknown are of recent origin. Apart from the medical issues involved, there are important ethical questions being raised: if abortions are legal, why are different standards applied to sex-determination tests which may or may not be used to influence sex-selective abortions? How can one combat the logic of those who argue that it is better to avoid the suffering imposed on unwanted girl babies by not allowing them to be born (Padmanabhan 1993)? In a democratic society, why should the state interfere in the right of couples to decide whether they want girls or not?

This is particularly so in India where abortion (medical termination of pregnancy or MTP) is a form of birth control actively encouraged by the medical establishment. In a well-argued article where she places the Indian debates around abortion and female foeticide in the wider context of the rights discourse, Nivedita Menon points out that

there is a profound philosophical incoherence involved in arguing for abortion in terms of the right of women to control their bodies and at the same time demanding that women be restricted by law from choosing specifically to abort female foetuses. It is essential that feminists should avoid being forced to counterpose the rights of (future) women to be born against the rights of (present) women to have control over their bodies [Menon 1996: 374].

In other words, feminists and concerned citizens have to acknowledge that in asking for women to have the right to control their bodies, they have to accept for caveat that women may themselves work against future generations of their gender. However, those who want to make a distinction between a gender-neutral abortion and abortion induced following sex-selective tests, argue that the latter actively works against equality and the right to life for girls.

Keeping these arguments in mind, a discussion of the violence of female foeticide and infanticide follows, arguing that how women control their bodies is often the manifestation of a dominant ideology which valorizes the male child. While some studies have seen the discrimination against female children to be validated by economic functions (see Miller 1981 for an analysis of region-wise differences on son and daughter preferences in the context of their productive roles in the family), other studies point to a far more deep-seated yearning for the male child, who, among other things, facilitates the passage of a Hindu to the next world. (Prabhu [1940] 1995)

Female foeticide has become popular with the spread of amniocentesis, a medical technique evolved to discover birth defects. A part of the test involves establishing the sex of the foetus. Introduced in 1974 at a leading government-run hospital in New Delhi, the new technology was quickly appropriated by medical entrepreneurs. A spate of sex-selective abortions followed.

Though a series of government circulars from 1977 onwards conveyed the ban on the tests, 'the privatization and commercialization of the technology' was well under way within a few years of its introduction (Mazumdar 1992).

A case study from a hospital in a city in western India conducted from June 1976 to June 1977 revealed that of the 700 women who sought prenatal sex determination, 250 were found to have male foetuses and 450 females. While all the male foetuses were kept to term, 430 of the 450 female foetuses were aborted (Ramanamma and Bambawale 1980). According to Kuntal Agarwal, 'amniocentesis tests and female foeticide have been prevalent since 1977, but have become popular (only) since 1982 and thereafter small towns and cities are also experiencing their effect' (Agarwal 1988). A field study conducted by Dr Sanjeev Kulkarni of the Foundation for Research in Community Health (1986) brought to light the fact that in the 1980s, five thousand amniocentesis tests were carried out annually in Bombay for determining foetal sex. Eighty-four per cent of the gynaecologists contacted by him admitted to having performed the amniocentesis tests for sex determination. Of these, seventy-four per cent had started performing the tests since 1982 and only a few cases of genetic defects were detected. The overwhelming majority of 'patients', most of whom were of middle or upper class status, came merely to obtain information about the sex of the foetus. Many women who came for the tests already had at least two daughters. Several clinics were run under the guise of maternity homes, clinical laboratories, and family health centres, and costs ranged from Rs 70 to Rs 600. Thirty per cent of the doctors believed that their patients came to them under some kind of pressure. At the same time, there is also evidence that women often took the decision on their own (Juneja 1993). It is a moot point whether mothers-to-be genuinely believed that girls were burdensome or whether they were socialized into such a world-view.

Today there are clinics throughout the country and 'Gujarat topped the list with SD clinics spreading even in small towns' (Ravindra 1993). Despite the efforts of women's organizations, voluntary groups, and the media to the contrary, sex-determination (SD) tests are becoming increasingly common.

A far more pernicious manifestation of an ideology which devalues girl children is the recent resurgence of female infanticide. In 1870, the British government in India outlawed infanticide (see Kasturi 1994; Pakrasi 1970 and Panigrahi 1972, for discussions of the practice), but over a century later, there are alarming reports of baby girls being murdered in areas where the custom did not previously exist. In a study in the 1970s, based on a study of historical records, Barbara Miller had noted that 'female infanticide in nineteenth century India was practiced primarily in the higher social groups of the North, though this point is debatable' (Miller 1981: 55). The author relate this practice to the control and distribution of property and variations in the tradition of dowry. Further, fieldwork and analysis of census data, led her to conclude that there was a distinct son preference in the north, related to inheritance patterns as well as to sex-related work roles. Today, the growing number of incidents of female infanticide from the south fly in the face of well-argued research results of social scientists who have been concerned over these issues. What has happened in the years between?

The obvious answer readily proffered is the all-pervading menace of dowry and the concomitant negative attitudes towards girl children. What is particularly disquieting is the spread of dowry among communities which practised bride price or bride wealth, and where, historically, women had a high status, such as, for instance, among the Mizos and the Kallars of Tamil Nadu. The obsessive hold of Sanskritization is evident among the prosperous sections of the Kallar community which is seen to 'claim comparability with upper caste culture' (Devi

1991; Mazumdar 1992). Social sanction and legitimization of infanticide are surely important in communities where the poor fear dowry, and the rich, a fragmentation of property.

In a study of twelve villages of K.V. Kuppan Block, North Arcot, Ambedkar district of Tamil Nadu state, which began in September 1986 and continued for four years, it was found that of a population

of 13,000 there were a total of 773 births recorded, involving 759 live births of which 378 were male and 381 female. Further, among the cohort of live born infants, 56 died in the period of two and a half years and of these there were 23 males and 33 females. ... Of these deaths, 19 were confirmed infanticides (which were all female infanticides).

The research further indicated that the villages in which 'female infanticide occurred are less "developed" in terms of urban linkages, services and education than the non-infanticide villages' (George, et al. 1992: 1153).

A recent study done by the Community Service Guild of Madras in collaboration with Adithi, a Patna-based organization for the development of rural women with a branch in Chennai, shows that in Salem district of Tamil Nadu, female infanticide is rampant (Venkatachalam and Srinivasan 1993). Though the study covered Christians, Hindus, and Muslims, the practice of female infanticide was found only among Hindus. Of the 1250 families in the sample—most of whom were Goudas with a few Naickers, Vanniars, and Chettiars—covered by the study, 606 had only one girl child and 111 admitted that they had done away with the unwanted girl child. Equally alarming was the fact that 476 respondents said that 'they would have to commit female infanticide when more than one female child was born to them' (Venkatachalam and Srinivasan 1993: 26). Most women said that they had killed their babies under pressure from their husbands: 'Women said that sometimes the men would beat them up insisting on the murder of new born daughters' (Venkatachalam and Srinivasan 1993: 53).

A detailed study of juvenile sex ratios and data from Primary Health Centres (PHC) in Tamil Nadu (Chunkath and Athreya 1997) established two additional facts: analysis of juvenile sex ratios may lead to surprising conclusions as well as provide the data for a longitudinal assessment of the prevalence of female infanticide. For instance, for the 1991 Census, the three districts of Dharmapuri, Salem, and Madurai accounted for forty-one out of the forty-six blocks in Tamil Nadu, with a juvenile female sex ratio of less than 900 to a 1000. Further, as is evident from a study of earlier census reports, this sharp decline is of fairly recent origin. The authors concluded that 'this would be true of female infanticide as well' (Chunkath and Athreya 1997: WS-22). Analysis of PHC data also corroborated this observation.

Poverty, alcoholism among men, ignorance of family planning, and cost of dowry are the possible causes of this practice of infanticide, and there is scattered evidence to suggest that it is more prevalent in other parts of India than is readily acknowledged. At the same time, while instances of infanticide are indicative of negative attitudes towards girls, a certain caution needs to be exercised before extrapolating on the likely spread of this social malaise; it is also useful to keep in mind Chunkath and Athreya's observation that birth order also determines the fate of a girl child; analysis of household data where female infanticides had occurred in 1995 showed that 'the first female infant is, in a majority of cases not a victim of female infanticide (Chunkath and Athreya 1997: WS-28), the second girl child would often escape, and it was the third girl who was invariably the victim.'

The Abused Child

An area in which there is little available research is that of child abuse within the home. This includes sexual aggression, beating, as well as extracting hours of labour from children who should be in school or at play. Nonetheless, nearly all available studies have shown that children are victims of substantial abuse of a physical, psychological, and emotional nature (MARG 1996). In part, this abuse is caused by the life situation of families, where, for instance, children become part of the labour force due to poverty. Recent studies have shown that, in absolute terms, child labour is on the increase, particularly for those who work as marginal workers. For girls the expansion has been dramatic in both rural as well urban areas (Chaudhuri 1996). Neera Burra (1995) has divided child labour into four categories—those who work in factories, workshops, and mines; those who are bonded; street children; and children who form part of the familial labour force. Working in inhuman conditions often for a pittance, children are abused at work and within homes where their earnings become the property of their parents. Not unexpectedly, then, child labour has become an emotive issue resulting in a sense of moral outrage in the international community and the concomitant boycott of products using this form of labour; however, banning child labour is a simplistic response to a much deeper problem, which lies embedded in structures of power, availability of alternatives and schooling, as well as the overall immiseration of at least a third of the population (see Raman forthcoming, for a discussion of the issue). For those children who do not work for a wage but contribute to the family workforce, leisure, education, and anything remotely regarded as the rights of the child need to be defined keeping in mind the cultural specificities of notions of childhood, play, learning, and consequently exploitation and abuse.

Apart from the physical burden of working before the body is ready for it, children are often enough subjected to beatings and lashings in a range of situations. Amarjit Mahajan and Madhurima (1995) have argued that punishment per se does not constitute violence; however, when an act of punishment involves substantial injury, it is no longer legitimate punishment but violence against a defenceless child. In a study carried out in a village in Haryana, 200 children in the age group 7–14 years were interviewed. The majority came from landless families, and 97 per cent of fathers in this category said that they punished their children as against 83 per cent of the landowners; interestingly, both sets of fathers preferred physical punishment. However, the reasons for punishment were different: 72 per cent of the landowners punished the children for non-compliance with family norms and standards of discipline; for the landless, the major concern was with unwillingness to work—for 'when the child shirked work, he was given severe punishment' (Mahajan and Madhurima 1995: 86). It was also this category of children who were injured more often in the course of punishment. Most parents, irrespective of their background, felt that there were positive consequences associated with beating. On the other hand, the study found that routinely abused children started hating their parents, became more obstinate, and a few even ran away from home.

In a 1982 study of a 1000 victims of child abuse, Dave et al. (1982) found that 81 per cent could be classified as victims of physical abuse, 7 per cent of what the authors call physical neglect, 9.3 per cent of sexual abuse, and 2.7 per cent of emotional abuse. None of these categories can be treated as exclusive and it is important to note that studies of this kind are extremely difficult to undertake, particularly so in the area of sexual relations where the overall attitude of secrecy and suppression that governs any discussion or reference to sex, makes it difficult to come to definite conclusions on the extent of sexual abuse of children. Yet, of the available figures, of almost 10,000 reported rapes in 1990, an alarming 25 per cent are of girl children below the age of 16, and about a fifth are of those under ten. A recent analysis done by the Crimes Against Women Cell, Delhi Police, points out that of the 381 rape cases registered between January and August 1997, 270 or almost 75 per cent of the victims were in the age range 7–18 years. Only 57 of the rapists were unknown to the victims. Most were immediate neighbours; ten girls were raped by their fathers; and three by step fathers (*The Pioneer*, 29 September 1997).

Such alarming figures are indicative not only of the sexual vulnerability of the girl child in and around her home, but also of a social climate which encourages her violation. In an interesting presentation at a seminar on child rape organized by the National Commission for Women (NCW) in New Delhi, in October 1992, Sobha Srinath from NIMHANS, Bangalore pointed to an important, though perhaps little thought about, fact: a young child below the age of ten need not always be aware that her sexual violation is in fact qualitatively different from thrashing and abuse: it is only with the onset of puberty that she becomes aware of her sexuality. In fact, in an environment where physical contact, both affectionate and abusive, by relatives of both sexes is not uncommon, child rape needs to be viewed a little differently from the rape of a post-pubertal girl.

Not unexpectedly, families rarely talk about the rape of their young daughter; when the rapist is a father or a brother, the chances of reporting are even lower. Members of voluntary organizations said that a mother would often suppress and wish away the event, not only because of a sense of shame and outrage, but also out of fear of reprisals from her husband, son, or other relatives (NCW Seminar, October 1992, personal observations). Interestingly, in 1992–3, there were eight cases of rape and molestation reported by mothers to the Crime against Women Cell in Delhi; officials at the Cell pointed out that this was a significant development as hardly any such instances were reported earlier. At the same time, wives expected the police to merely caution their husbands, filing a case against them would be unheard of (Wadhwa 1993). If there is a silence around the sexual violation of the girl child in the family, this is equally true of cases of sodomy and abuse of the male child.

Inequality in the Household

The prevalence of a dominant ideology which confines girls and women to definite roles and obligations leads to their devaluation and discrimination in a range of areas. The basic assumption is that girls are inferior, physically and mentally weak, and above all sexually vulnerable. In a society which lays so much stress on purity and pollution, various oppressive structures—including early marriage—are encouraged so as to confine the physical mobility of girls and women. A declining sex ratio (929 women to 1000 men according to the Census of 1991) would suggest endemic female mortality and morbidity (Agnihotri 1997; Deshpande 1991; Irudaya Rajan et al. 1991, Mazumdar 1992, Reddy 1991) caused by consistent neglect and sustained discrimination, both manifestations of violence and oppression.

In this context, the notions of expectations and entitlements are particularly important. An entitlement (Papanek 1990; Sen 1983, 1987) represents the right to a share of resources such as health care, nutrition, education, and material assets, as well as to parental attention and interest. The distribution of these resources is usually in keeping with a family ideology and can be seen in intra-household allocation of resources. Evidence indicates that girls and women are usually far less privileged than boys in access to material resources (Basu 1989; Batliwala 1983; Gopalan and Chatterjee 1985; Gulati 1978; Kumari 1989; Minocha 1984; Sen and Sen

Gupta 1985). However, these often vary according to the birth order of the girls, and, as mentioned already, it is often the case that excess female child mortality is more common in families which already have a daughter (Das Gupta 1987; Das Gupta and Chen 1995).

Rural health surveys in north India show that women and girls are ill more often than boys and men. At the same time a study of records at medical institutions (Batliwala 1983) reported that there was only one woman user to every three men who use hospital facilities. Hospital records (Kynch and Sen 1983) indicate a similar pattern of crises-related admissions. A recent study of 1853 persons who came to a general health facility found that 193 (10.4 per cent) had psychological problems. Most were women in the age group 16 to 45 years, who had come to the facility from a far greater distance than those with physical disorders. For a majority of this group, 'the cause of stress lay in personal and family life' and specifically, for 10 per cent, marital and sexual reasons were the cause of distress (Srinivasa Murthy, 1992). It would be fairly safe to hypothesize, then, that while a sizeable percentage of women's health problems lie rooted in familial dynamics and tension-ridden relationships, more often than not women tend to get treated for physical disorders.

The fact that forms of discrimination in food exist in upper caste, middle class homes as well, indicates that factors other than scarcity are crucial. Further, the ailments of boys and men are more likely to get treated, or if women do get attention, much less is spent on their ailments (Dandekar 1975). In an analysis of state- and district-level data, Sunita Kishor found that 'a critical manifestation' of discrimination against girl children 'is the under-allocation of medicine and food' (Kishor 1995: 48). Making a distinction between survival rates and discrimination, she points out that while the former seems to rise with the socio-economic status of the household, there is not enough evidence to suggest that discrimination declines with higher status: observations from the field show that upper caste, upper-middle-class families, discriminate against girls with respect to the access they have to higher education, as well as in matters such as protein intake, games and extra- and co-curricular activities (Karlekar 1987).

Other data (Das Gupta 1987; Kumari et al. 1990) indicate a definite bias in feeding boys milk and milk products and eggs, while both boys and girls have equal access to cereal and vegetables. Taboos associated with giving girls meat, fish, and eggs which are regarded as hot food, are fairly widespread (Dube 1988, Kumari et al. 1990). In Rajasthan and Uttar Pradesh, it was usual for girls and women to eat less, and usually after the men and boys had eaten (Kumari et al. 1990). Greater mobility outside the home provided boys with the opportunity to eat sweets and fruit from saved-up pocket money or from money given to buy articles for food consumption (Khan et al. 1986). In case of illness, it is usually boys who are given preference for receiving health care (Chanana 1990; Das Gupta 1987; Desai and Krishna Raj 1987; Kanhere 1987; Mankekar 1985). In fact, a study in rural Punjab established that there were wider sex differentials in access to medical care than in food allocation: more was spent on clothing for boys than for girls, which had an effect on morbidity (Das Gupta 1987). Thus familial views on what should be a girl's expectations take precedence over the right to greater individual entitlement and, on the whole, reinforce her growing sense of marginalization, powerlessness, as well as vulnerability. Here again ethnographic studies would be useful in furthering an understanding of the dynamics of feminine socialization, availability of resources, and patterns of oppression. For instance, apart from the usual indicators of caste, class, religion, and so on, observations from the field on availability of resources, and infrastructure such as PHCs, schools, and hospitals would show whether their existence appreciably influences girls' access to a better quality of life. Also, size of family, differences of attitudes towards children on the basis of birth order, spacing between siblings and, age of the mother, may also influence attitudes towards allocations not only between boys and girls but among female siblings as well.

Violence in the Conjugal Home

Marriage continues to be universally regarded as essential for a girl, in India, irrespective of class, caste, religion, and ethnicity, as control of her sexuality and its safe transference into the hands of the husband is given prime importance. Concern over the conduct of the sexually vulnerable girl is important cause of early marriage. According to the Census of 1991, about 30 per cent of women in the ages group 15–19 were married; as the official age for marriage is 18 for girls, it is possible that a large percentage of these marriages were of under-age girls. Though the age of marriage is rising gradually, it is important to note that girls are barely out of their teens when they leave their natal homes for another unknown residence. The exception is the familiarity characterizing cross-cousin marriages. Subsequent expectations and relationships impose a considerable load on those who are as yet girls, ill-equipped to adjust to a totally new environment, and a set of unfamiliar relationships. For, in India, marriage establishes a network of interacting individuals: it is rarely only a highly personal relationship between a man and a woman (see Das 1976 for a discussion of *biradari*).

The persistence of a dominant family ideology which enjoins a strict sexual division of labour and age and gender hierarchy means that young wives have to invest a considerable amount of time and energy in forging new relationships, not all of which are caring or accommodative. These take precedence over all other relationships in the natal home. Nothing describes the transient nature of a girl's brief life in her parent's home or her inherent worth better than the north-Indian saying that a girl is *paraya dhan* or another's wealth. It not only establishes the very notion of belonging but also that, a girl is wealth (dhan) which belongs ultimately elsewhere (paraya).

Is wealth the same as property? What does the concept of women as wealth mean? It can be argued that both property and wealth involve ownership, control, and right of disposal. They also imply the capacity to generate more assets, if properly utilized. Clearly, such an understanding is more comprehensible in the context of physical goods and immovable assets. In the case of human resources, it would include intangibles such as skills, education, reputation, and physical attributes as well. In the traditions of marriage for most of India, 'the bride is a vehicle for the passage of valuables from her own kin to that of her husband' (Hirschon 1984: 11). The unequal nature of the marital relationship sanctified by significant gift exchanges, rituals, and expectations establishes the parameters of subsequent intra-familial behaviour patterns.

Based on her field data from Papua New Guinea, anthropologist Marilyn Strathern has argued, 'If women are passed between groups of men, equated with the wealth that flows between them, then they must be treated as objects themselves. As objects they must be a form of property' (Strathern 1988: 163). But, she asks, what about their personhood and their capacity to assert their identities? She points out that 'the definition of personhood is not tied up with the manipulation of things' (Strathern 1988: 144). Strathern's position is worth taking note of in the context not only of dowry but the present-day ramifications of the system, namely the violence and even physical annihilation associated with this form of gift giving. The very notions of personhood and identity are under threat from familial power structures where the in-marrying woman's sense of self is constantly assailed. Of course, with age and gain in status within the family as the mother of sons and, ultimately, a mother-in-law, a distinct identity emerges. In fact, it is an identity which, in the popular imagination, is often linked to oppression of new female entrants to the family. Bollywood has had an important role to play in the stereotyping of the evil mother-in-law and the oppressed, submissive daughter-in-law.

Within this framework of matrimony and affinal relationships, many women attempt to negotiate space for themselves, to assert their personhood. The capacity to do so is dependent on a range of factors such as age, maternal status, and position in the hierarchy of senior or junior daughters-in-law. It is also often enough the case that intra-couple discord (which may later escalate into a dowry-related demand and expectation syndrome) is over roles, their performance or otherwise, and a woman's quest for her identity. It is this which distinguishes inanimate wealth/property from an animate being who may be the reason or vehicle for transactions, but nonetheless resists being treated in the same manner as a disposable commodity. That, often enough, a woman loses out is a symbol of the unequal power play within the home.

An important part of the power relationship between spouses and indeed their families, relates to dowry and its ramifications. In the Indian context, the preference for structural asymmetry between the two families and the consequent burden of gift giving on the bride's family strengthens inequality. Anthropological studies, particularly of north-Indian marriage and kinship patterns, indicate that hypergamous unions establish a permanent asymmetry in gift giving and prestations. Here the notion of property in marriage acquires another meaning: not only is the in-marrying girl viewed as the property of her husband if not of the conjugal family, but also, the event marks the unequal flow of goods and even property between the two kin groups (Dumont 1975; Goody and Tambiah 1973; Madan [1965] 1989; Sharma 1984; Stri Kriti Samiti 1984; Patnaik and Sadual 1988; Ranjana Kumari 1989; Uberoi [1994] 1995; Vatuk 1975; Verghese 1997). Based on her fieldwork in north-India, Ursula Sharma has argued persuasively that dowry, or what the bride's family gives to the groom's family at the time of hypergamous marriages, is 'a concrete form of property in which members of the household, both men and women, have different kinds of interest and over which they have different kinds of control' (Sharma 1984: 62). Important for later analysis is the communal aspect of dowry, nor is it a one time transaction: ritual occasions, festivals, and indeed any minor pretext result in more demands being made on the daughter-in-law's family.

In India, there is a tendency to club most marital violence under the overall heads of 'dowry', 'dowry deaths', and 'dowry violence'. This categorization glosses over the other causes of violence which pervade the familial context. However, to argue that dowry is not always the cause behind marital discord is not to ignore the fact that it is one of the major factors responsible for domestic violence. While keeping this fact in mind it is necessary to work towards a fuller understanding of the institution of dowry and its impact on inter-family relationships. Madhu Kishwar (1986) feels that oppression of wives for bringing inadequate dowry is one more excuse for using violence against them: in other words—and in fact evidence from other countries has indicated as much—even without the additional 'attraction' of dowry, interspousal violence is endemic. She has also pointed out that dowry payments in themselves do not transform girls into burdens but rather 'dowry makes daughters "burden-some" only because daughters are unwanted to begin with' (Kishwar 1986). For instance, middle class parents who save to pay lakhs as capitation fees for sons in medical or engineering colleges do not view them as burdensome; but similar sums set aside for daughters' marriages are regarded differently.

Though it is difficult to be categorical on the background of those either harassed or killed for dowry, it is clearly a phenomenon on the increase among all social categories. In a study of dowry victims in Delhi, Ranjana Kumari (1989) commented that 'dowry has become inseparably interlinked with the general status of women in our society'. Her study shows that in a sample of 150 dowry victims, one-fourth were murdered or driven to commit suicide, and more than half, i.e. 61.3 per cent, were thrown out of their husband's house after a long-drawn-period of harassment and torture. Dowry-related killings followed two patterns. First the young brides were either murdered or forced to commit suicide (18.4 per cent) when their parents refused to concede to continuing demands for dowry. Second, the murders were committed also on the pretext of 'complex family relations'. Extramarital relationships were alleged in 52.6 per cent cases of death. It was also discovered that the conflicts intensified because of the refusal by young brides to yield to overtures made by father-in-law, uncle-in-law or brother-in-law. There were also cases where wives alleged that the husband was impotent.

In 69.3 per cent cases, parents sent their daughters back to the husbands while being fully aware of the torment they were undergoing. Of these, 77.9 per cent returned only to be deserted and 11.5 per cent to be murdered. In 72 per cent of cases, parents were more willing to put thousands of rupees in the hands of a man who tortured their daughter than to spend even a fraction (10 per cent) of the dowry to train the girl to survive independently, because they did not consider independent survival of women as respectable. Ranjana Kumari also found dowry giving and taking to be universal across caste, religion, and income groups. However, she observed that 'while desertion and harassment cases are more among higher income groups, middle income groups show higher dowry death rates'. She also found that only 5 per cent of marriages were love marriages while 11 per cent were inter-caste. The rest had married according to the prevailing social norms of 'arranged' matches (see Ranjana Kumari 1989: 88–91 for this discussion; see also Mahajan and Madhurima 1995; Sinha 1989).

There is no satisfactory explanation for why the system of dowry is growing and indeed spreading to communities where it earlier did not exist. Nonetheless, its role in perpetuating violence within the home is substantial. Of particular relevance is the fact that dissatisfaction over dowry payments and subsequent prestations result in abuse of the wife not only by her husband but by other affines as well. This, however, is not the only reason for ill-treatment of married women. Apart from ill-health and stress, a violent home environment can led to a total psychological remoulding such as the internalization of deception, manipulative techniques, and feigning. It can also lead to anticipation and provocation, a macabre expectation of the inevitable (see Agnes 1988; and Kakar 1990, for perceptive interpretations of inter-spousal violence).

Thus wife abuse, a practice shared with many other cultures, acquires a different connotation in Indian society due to the institution of dowry. Here, the term 'abuse' includes physical as well as non-physical acts. There is enough evidence to suggest that such abuse often receives wider familial sanction. It is institutionalized in various forms that range from inhumanly long hours of labour, often within and outside the home, food denial, neglect of ailments, and verbal abuse by affines to physical violence by the husband and sometimes other family members. In this context, it is important to note the growing number of cases being registered under section 498A of the Indian Penal Code (IPC, 1983) which indicts a husband or relative of the husband for cruelty against a wife. For instance, all-India police data under this head that are available from 1989 onwards record a steady increase: from 11,803 cases registered in 1989 cases went up to 15,949, or by 37.5 per cent in 1992. As entire families and indeed the state become involved in the ramifications of inter-spousal disputes, the incidence of these events continues to spiral upwards, occasionally with macabre outcomes: personal communications with police officials indicated that the unnatural deaths of wives were on the increase each year.

Abuse of wives and wife beating—or in more extreme cases wife battering—is the most common form of abuse worldwide irrespective of class, religion, community, and in the case of India, caste background (Bogard 1988; Chen 1922a; Cheung and Law 1990; Dong Xing 1995; Finkelhor et al. 1983; Gelles 1980; Gelles and Loseke 1993; Hoff 1990; Jahan 1994; KWDI 1993; Strauss 1980; Walker 1983). In India, studies have correlated childhood abuse, alcoholism, unemployment, and poverty with the growth of this malaise (Ahuja 1987; Kaushik 1990; Mahajan and Madhurima 1995; Sinha 1989; Sood 1990). It has also been argued that it is not a woman's dependence which makes her particularly vulnerable: a wife in a high-status job may be beaten more than her unemployed neighbour (Pawar 1988). Battered women are also seen as lacking self-esteem and self-confidence and being apathetic and nervous (Kaushik 1990).

In an interesting study of the impact of wife beating on the women themselves as well as on other members of the family, Vijayendra Rao (1995) found that in three multi-caste villages in the southern state of Karnataka, only 22 per cent women claimed to have been abused by their husbands. In fact, during fieldwork, two women were hit by their husbands; but, in response to a question, the very same women did not say that they had been abused. The researcher concluded that it was only if the beatings were very severe that women perceived of themselves as being abused: the odd slap or blow was regarded as routine husband-like behaviour. There was wide societal tolerance for wife abuse, which was even considered justifiable under certain circumstances: 'Disputes over dowries, a wife's sexual infidelities, her neglect of household duties, and her disobedience of her husband's dictates are all considered legitimate cause for wife-beating' (Rao 1995: 11). Observations during fieldwork for a project on domestic violence also confirmed a high degree of acceptance of male violence: it was only when the torture became unbearable or death appeared imminent that most women appeared willing to speak out (Karlekar et al. 1995).

In a detailed discussion of wife abuse, Flavia Agnes (1988) has convincingly rebutted the popular myths which surround the phenomenon of wife beating in India, such as middle class women do not get beaten; the victim of violence is a small, fragile, helpless woman belonging to the working class; and the wife beater is a man who is frustrated in his job, an alcoholic, or a paranoid person, aggressive in his relationships. Nor is it true that so-called loving husbands do not beat their wives or that women provoke men to beat them. Yet many of these myths seem to pervade the analysis of wife beating and feminine expectations in Indian society.

For instance, based on an analysis of cases which had come to the Delhi-based women's organization Saheli, it was evident that wife beating was common among all social classes as it 'is a reflection of the power relationship between a husband and wife', which mirrors a woman's secondary social status (Saheli 1988:1) However, the pattern of violence differs from one class to another, with the whole neighbourhood being witness when a slum-dweller beats his wife while a middle class professional's physical oppression of his spouse is extremely private in nature.

Like child rape within the family, another area about which little is known and which is hardly discussed is that of marital rape: in India. Despite some thinking along these lines by feminists and legal experts, there has as yet been no amendment in law to include sexual violence as rape within marriage. The only exception is if the wife is below 16 years of age. Though figures on marital rape as well as other sexually demeaning and violent acts are difficult to obtain, discussions[3] with counsellors working with abused women indicated that a very large percentage of their clients were tortured with forced sexual intercourse.

Feminine socialization which stresses docility, compliance, and shame predisposes a wife to accept a range of physical behaviour from her spouse, where, without doubt, her sexual satisfaction is of little consequence. On the basis of her fieldwork among upper-middle-class and middle-class women in Delhi, all of whom had contracted 'so-called "love" marriages', Meenakshi Thapan (1997) concludes that women had internalized notions of the perfect female body and of femininity; consequently, they were often complicit in the mechanisms of oppression, particularly those aspects which dealt with physical and sexual attractiveness. However, that such psychological and physical oppression can equally develop into a site for resistance—a point not addressed by Thapan—is discussed later. It would not be too extreme to hypothesize that much male physical violence in marriage is related to sexual activity: detailed interviews and discussions at the women's shelter for battered women[4] quite often led to admission of sexual excesses; when a woman resisted, she was beaten; or if she did not satisfy her husband's demands (which could quite often be perverse in nature), the outcome was physical abuse. It is indeed ironical that for long, the family, viewed as an individual's ballast against the world, becomes the arena for legitimate physical and mental oppression of women. While the legal and police systems have, after 1975, become more receptive to certain excesses, much remains unstated, invisible and repressed.

The Ageing Person within the Home

With a decline in rates of mortalities there are a growing number of aging people in families and households. In a recent demographic study of the aged, Kumudini Dandekar (1996) has concluded that in a rural population of about 640 million, about 45 million or 7 per cent are above 60; half of this population is poor and at least 10 per cent of those above 60 are helpless and in the category of requiring financial support. While there is little information on attitudes and behaviour of younger family members towards the elderly, a few studies have established that a situation of dependency on the younger generation results in neglect and in some cases, ill-treatment and different forms of violence against older people, in particular, women. For instance, neglect of ailments by family members which is quite common, is extremely demoralizing for the aged (Shankardas 1997).

Researchers in the West have tried to make a distinction between active and passive neglect while others have viewed neglect and abuse differently (see Mahajan and Madhurima 1995). Reluctance to speak of their trauma and a concern with the family's reputation or *izzat* coupled with a dependence on others has meant that 'elder abuse becomes known to the authorities through a third party' (Mahajan and Madhurima 1995: 106).

While in India, institutionalization of the elderly is virtually unknown, there is evidence that households are increasingly disinclined to invest scarce resources on those whom they feel will have little to contribute to a family's success and mobility (personal observations during fieldwork for various projects on the position of women in India). A report brought out by the women's organization Karmika (quoted in MARG 1996: 18–19), characterized the habitual scolding, nagging, non-communication, as well as feigned ignorance about their needs and ailments as informal violence; this form of violence, argued the report could be 'sometimes worse than physical injury' (MARG 1996: 18).

In a study of 749 elderly working-class persons in the districts of Haryana of whom 369 were men above 60 years of age and 380 women above 55, Mahajan and Madhurima found that over 30 per cent of all respondents 'admitted that quite often or sometimes they were abused by family members' (Mahajan and Madhurima 1995: 120). Further enquiries indicated that inability to work, lack of finances, and failing health accounted for ill-treatment. Interestingly, the level of satisfaction among women was higher than among men. Aging siblings, some of whom may or may not have married, old couples who have to rely on one another, and destitutes are other categories of the elderly about whom very little is known.

The position of the aged in rural areas and situations of in chronic poverty is a much neglected area of study. During a recent field trip to households suffering from severe food shortages in Madhya Pradesh, Veena Das encountered two very old women who existed on the margins of society: as widows and destitutes, they did not figure in the welfare measures instituted by the local-level bureaucrats, and were paid scant attention by the villagers. She concludes that the preponderant emphasis on the married woman in the reproductive cycle has led almost to an effacement of other categories such as the elderly, the never married, and the disabled (Das 1997). In fact, before the declaration of the Year of the Girl Child a few years ago, not much was known about female children either.

Irrespective of their geographic location, little is known about the treatment and neglect of the elderly who have lost their spouses. A recent study of widows established that 'of the poor in India, widowed women are in all likelihood the most disadvantaged, both socially and economically' (HIID-WIDER Workshop 1992: 1). Not only do widows and their lot slip through the net in discussions on poverty, but also little is known about their treatment within families. In a study of north-Indian widows, Martha Chen and Jean Drèze observed that marginalization, social as well as physical, was usual and the widow 'remains highly vulnerable to neglect' resulting in poor health and high mortality rates (Chen and Drèze 1995: 283). Importantly, the widow who headed her own household which included an adult son had the lowest mortality risk. Extrapolating from these data, we can conclude that food discrimination, inadequate health care, lack of living space, and excessive expectations as far as domestic work is concerned make the widow's situation extremely tenuous. When these are combined with lack of access to property and assets, it is not difficult to envisage the overall situation of denial and deprivation they face.

Increase in domestic workload, loss of self-respect, as well as tendency to neurosis was observed in a study of 350 widows in Haryana which also found that most felt that survival and accommodation were major problems (Sandhya 1994). In a study which probed the entire question of violence against widows, Mukesh Ahuja (1996) found that of the 190 widows interviewed in Jaipur city, the most common complaint was that of verbal abuse from their in-laws; such behaviour ranged from sarcastic comments to scolding, shouting, and humiliating remarks in the presence of others. A large percentage said that they had been denied access to their husbands' assets. While 12.5 percentage said that they had been physically beaten by their in-laws, another 15 percentage said that their children too were beaten and ill-treated (Ahuja 1996: 88). Of the twenty-nine women who had grown-up children, fourteen reported abusive behaviour by their sons and daughters-in-law.

Sexual vulnerability of the widow is a prevalent though little- discussed and-acknowledged fact of their existence. Twenty-six of Ahuja's respondents said that they had been victims of sexual attacks; well over 60 per cent said that the assailants had been affines while the rest had been molested by neighbours, employers, or friends' brothers (Ahuja 1996: 93). A woman's physical and sexual vulnerability is accentuated in times of social and political stress, communal disturbances being a case in point. Recounting their experiences at a centre at Tilak Vihar in west Delhi, activists spoke poignantly of the sixty young Sikh widows they were trying to rehabilitate after the holocaust of November 1984, following the assassination of Prime Minister Indira Gandhi. The typical familial response of 'settling' the widow was to marry her to a brother-in-law, in itself an old practice. The results were often disastrous as 'very few have been able to resist the onslaught of these cruel societal norms' (Srivastava 1989: 65). Those who had the courage to resist faced social and familial ostracism as well as 'drunken beating and exploitation or worse at the hands of their men' (Srivastava 1989: 65). Prostitution was encouraged by affines even as the women were trying to piece together their lives. Thus, despite the will to survive, 'the stringent codes of conduct of Indian society crushes them again into keeping the family's interest and name and fame above their own and their children's hope for a better life' (Srivastava 1989: 64). Clearly then, widowhood exposes a woman to new forms and networks of exploitation and violence.

Conclusion

The ever-present fact of violence, both overt and covert, physical and non-physical has over-whelming influence on feminine identity formation. A child's sense of self is greatly dependent on how others think, feel, and behave towards her. This fundamental difference in identity formation between the sexes has deep roots in the socialization processes, resource allocation within families, the impact of external influences such as mass media, pornography, and the educational system. While identity, notions of self, roles, and obligations are worked out fairly early in a woman's life, no stage of her life-cycle is without change and questioning of received norms. Thus feminine identity and a woman's position within the family continue to be open to modification, depending on her situation in the life-cycle. What is important in this context is that these modifications are often determined by the collectivity: individual self-expression is repressed and subjugated and the anger at being violated is internalized.

There is clearly much more that needs to be understood about the Indian family and its internal dynamics. For instance, to pin all violence against the girl child on the fear of dowry appears a convenient rationalization, shrouding a range of motivations. Is it to be assumed that dowry giving is such a widespread and prevalent practice as to influence every parent who goes in for female foeticide, abortion, or infanticide? While, in the absence of adequate data, it is difficult to be categorical, there is clearly a need to further investigate the family's strategies for survival and mobility as well as how dependency of the young, the housewives, and the elderly conditions responses to these conditions. It is clear that far from being a refuge from the outside world, the family is complicit in processes and mechanisms of socialization, many of which are oppressive if not extreme in nature.

The validity of field studies in filling the gaps in knowledge has been stressed more than once in this chapter. These would not only enhance the data base on various phases in the female life cycle, but would also help in gauging the voices of resistance. Whether it is the covert activities of Bangladeshi housewives who find innovative ways of hiding a part of their earnings; the systematic putting away of a measure of grain by village women in the Bankura district of West Bengal; or the uninhibited account of a battered wife narrated to a police official, women are finding ways of challenging the established familial hierarchy, based on male domination and control (personal observations).

Despite the ubiquity of violence against women, both within the home and in public spaces, the celebration of individual experiences has led to the emergence of alternate discourses where the 'truth' and validity of established structures, norms, and roles are called into question. In order to appreciate how individual experience may become the ground for alternative discourses to emerge it is necessary to see the family and its individual members in an emerging context with many players in the field: an interface between them, the state, the law, and the women's movement becomes increasingly relevant (see Agnes 1995; Gandhi and Shah 1992; Kapur and Cossman 1996; Kumar 1993; Nair 1996). As retelling and reinterpretation become the sites for differing realities, it is clear that contemporary understandings of domestic violence will need to interrogate a familial ideology based on unity and patriarchal dominance in a manner that does not valorize victimhood alone but takes note of agency and resistance as well.

ENDNOTES

1. Much of the work on this section is based on the introductory chapter in 'Violence against Women—Domestic Violence', unpublished report of a study by Malavika Karlekar with Anuja Agarwal, Maithili Ganju, and Meena Mukherjee, Centre for Women's Development Studies, New Delhi, undertaken for the Government of India, 1995. However, I have added more material and my later perceptions owe a lot to discussions with Veena Das. I am grateful to her for useful suggestions as well as for help in locating additional references.
2. It is a global fact official police data, in particular statistics, deal with crime rather than with the much more pervasive phenomenon of violence. One reason for this variance is that the police data on crime are based on complaints and cases registered, which in turn depend on willingness to report and police receptivity to acts as crimes against women as well as the inclination to investigate these. It would not be an exaggeration to state that crime figures are merely the proverbial tip of the iceberg.
3. Some cases have been discussed in 'Violence against Women—Domestic Violence'. On the basis of the study a workshop was held in 1995 and its report entitled 'No Safe Spaces—Report of a Workshop on Violence against Women' by Malavika Karlekar et al. (1995), was circulated.
4. See Karlekar et al. (1995: Chapter 3).

REFERENCES

Abraham, Margaret. 1995. 'Ethnicity, Gender and Marital Violence: South Asian Women's Organization in the United States'. *Gender and Society.* 9(4):550–68.

Agarwal, Kuntal. 1998. 'Survival of Females in India'. Paper presented at International Conference of Women, Development and Health, Michigan State University, Michigan.

Agnes, Flavia. 1988. 'Violence in the Family: Wife Beating'. In Rehana Ghadially, ed., *Women and Indian Society: A Reader*, 151–66. New Delhi: Sage Publications.

———. 1993. 'The Anti-Rape Campaign: The Struggle and the Setback'. In Chaya Datar, ed., *The Struggle against Violence*, 99–150. Calcutta: Stree Publications.

———. 1995. *The State, Gender and the Rhetoric of Law Reform*. Bombay: RCWS, SNDT Women's University.

Agnihotri, Satish Balram. 1997. 'Unpacking Juvenile Sex Ratios in India'. Paper presented at a UNICEF-UNIFEM-UNDP-SDC Conference on Ending Violence against Women and Girls in South Asia. Kathmandu, 21–4 October.

Ahuja, Mukesh. 1996. *Widows: Role Adjustment and Violence*. New Delhi: Vishwa Prakashan.

Ahuja, R. 1987. *Crimes against Women*. Jaipur: Rawat Publication.

Anveshi. 1995. 'Women in India and Their Mental Health'. Communication paper.

Basu, A.M. 1989. 'Culture and the Status of Women in North and South India'. In Singh et al. eds, *Population Transition in India*. Delhi: B.R. Publishing Corporation.

Batliwala, S. 1983. 'Women in Poverty: The Energy, Health and Nutrition Syndrome'. Unpublished paper.

Béteille, André. 1998. 'The Reproduction of Inequality: Occupation Caste and Family'. In Patricia Uberoi, ed., *Family, Kinship and Marriage in India*, 435–51. Delhi: Oxford University Press.

Bhasin, Kamala and Ritu Menon, eds. 1994. *Against all Odds: Essays on Women, Religion and Development in India and Pakistan*. New Delhi: Kali for Women.

Bograd, M. 1988. 'Feminist Perspective on Wife Abuse: An introduction'. In K. Yllö and Bograd, eds, *Feminist Perspective on Wife Abuse*, 11–25. Newbury: Sage Publications.

Bondurant, Joan. 1965. *Conquest of Violence: The Gandhian Philosophy of Conflict*. Berkeley and Los Angeles: University of California Press.

Bourdieu, Pierre. 1977. *Outline of a Theory of Practice*. Cambridge: Cambridge University Press.

Burra, Neera. 1995. *Born to Work: Child Labour in India*. Delhi: Oxford University Press.

Butalia, Urvashi. 1993. 'Community, State and Gender: On Women's Agency during Partition'. *Economic and Political Weekly*. 28(17):12–24.

————. 1998. *The Other Side of Silence: Voices from the Partition of India*. New Delhi: Viking.

Carstairs, M. 1983. *Death of a Witch: A Village in North India 1950–1981*. London: Hutchison.

Chanana, Karuna. 1990. 'Structures and Ideologies: Socialisation and Education of the Girl Child in South Asia'. *Indian Journal of Social Science*. 3:53–71.

Chaudhuri, D.P. 1996. *A Dynamic Profile of Child Labour in India 1951–1991*. New Delhi: ILO.

Chen, Martha A. and Jean Drèze. 1995. 'Widowhood and Well-being in North India'. In Monica Das Gupta et al., eds, *Women's Health in India: Risk and Vulnerability*, 245–88. Delhi: Oxford University Press.

Chen, R. 1992. 'Marital Violence in Taiwan: Characteristics and Risk Factors'. *Journal of Sociology*. 21:123–60.

Cheung, F.M. and J.S. Law. 1990. 'Victims of Sexual Assault: A Summary of the Crime Victimization Surveys of 1978, 1981 and 1986'. In F.M. Cheung, R.G. Audry, and R.C. Tam, eds, *Relevance on Rape and Sexual Crime in Hong Kong*, 1–18. Hongkong: The Hong Kong Institute of Asia Pacific Studies. CUHK.

Chunkath, Sheela Rani and V.B. Athreya. 1997. 'Female Infanticide in Tamil Nadu: Some Evidence'. *Economic and Political Weekly*. 32(17) (26 April): Review of Women's Studies, WS 22–9.

Dandekar, K. 1975. 'Has the Proportion of Women in India's Population been declining?' *Economic and Political Weekly*. 10(42):1663–7.

————. 1996. *The Elderly in India*. New Delhi: Sage Publications.

Das, Veena. 1976. 'Masks & Faces: An Essay on Punjabi Kinship'. *Contributions to Indian Sociology* (n.s.). 10(1):1–30.

————, ed. 1990. *Mirrors of Violence: Communities, Riots and Survivors in South Asia*. Delhi: Oxford University Press.

————. 1996. 'Sexual Violence, Discursive Practices and the State'. Paper presented at the International Conference on Gender Perspectives in Population, Health and Development in India. 12–14 January.

————. 1997. 'Gender Sensitivity: Research and Action'. Presentation made at the National Assembly of Voluntary Organizations, Indian Social Institute, New Delhi. 2–4 October.

Das, Veena and Ashis Nandy. 1986. 'Violence, Victimhood and the Language of Silence'. In Veena Das, ed., *The World and the World*. New Delhi: Sage Publications.

Das Gupta, Monica. 1987. 'Selective Discrimination against Female Children in Rural Punjab, India'. *Population and Development Review*. 13(1):77–100.

Das Gupta, Monica and Lincoln Chen. 1995. 'Overview'. In Monica Das Gupta, L. Chen and T.N. Krishnan, eds, *Women's Health in India—Risk and Vulnerability*, 1–18. Bombay: Oxford University Press.

Datar, C. 1993. *The Struggle against Violence*. Calcutta: Stree Publications.

Davar, Bhargavi. 1995. 'Mental Illness among Indian Women'. *Economic and Political Weekly*. 30(45):2879–86.

Dave, A.B., et al. 1982. 'Child Abuse and Neglect (CAN), Practices in Drug Abuse in a District of Madhya Pradesh'. *Indian Paediatrics*. 19:905–12.

Desai, A.R. 1980. *Urban Family and Family Planning in India*. Bombay: Popular Prakashan.

Desai, I.P. 1964. *Some Aspects of Family in Mahuva*. New Delhi: Asia Publishing House.

Desai, Neera and Maithreyi Krishna Raj. 1987. *Women and Society in India*. New Delhi: Ajanta Books.

Desjarlais, Robert, Leon Eisenberg, Bryon Good, and Arthur Kleinman. 1995. *World Mental Health: Problem and Priorities in Low-Income Countries*. New York: Oxford University Press.

Desphande, A. 1991. 'Census Underlines Anti-women Bias'. *The Telegraph*, 24 March.

Dong, Xing. 1995. 'Study of Domestic Violence'. *Sociology and Research* (third issue).

Dube, Leela. 1974. *Sociology of Kinship: An Analytical Survey Literature*. Bombay: Popular Prakashan.

Dube, Leela. 1986. 'Seed and Earth: The Symbolism of Biological Reproduction and Sexual Relations of Production'. In Leela Dube, Eleanor Leacock, and Shirley Ardner, eds, *Visibility and Power: Essays on Women in Society and Development*, 22–53. Delhi: Oxford University Press.

———. 1988. 'Socialisation of Hindu Girls in Patrilineal India'. In K. Chanana, ed., *Socialisation, Education and Women*, 168–92. New Delhi: Orient Longman.

Dumont, L. 1975. 'Terminology and Prestations Re-visited'. *Contributions to Indian Sociology* (n.s.). 9(2):197–215.

Finkelhor, David, Richard Gelles, Gerald T. Hotaling, and Murray A. Strauss, eds. 1983. *Dark Side of Families: Current Family Violence Research*. Beverly Hills: Sage Publications.

Gandhi, Nandita and Nandita Shah. 1992. *The Issues at Stake*. New Delhi: Kali for Women.

Gelles, Richard. 1980. 'Violence in the Family: A Review of Research in the Seventies'. *Journal of Marriage and Family*. 42(4).

Gelles, K. and D.R. Loseke. 1993. *Feminist Controversies in Family Violence*. New Delhi: Sage Publications.

George, Sabir, Abel Rajaratnam, and B.D. Miller. 1992. 'Female Infanticide in Rural South India'. *Economic and Political Weekly*. 27(22):1154–6.

Ghadially, Rehana, ed. 1987. *Women in Indian Society*. New Delhi: Sage Publications.

Goody, Jack and Stanley J. Tambiah. 1973. *Bridewealth and Dowry*. Cambridge: Cambridge University Press.

Gopalan, C. and Meera Chatterjee. 1985. 'Gender Bias in Health and Nutrition Care'. *NFI Bulletin*. 8(4).

Gore, M.S. 1968. *Urbanization and Family Change*. Bombay: Popular Prakashan.

Gulati, Leela. 1978. *Profiles in Female Poverty*. New Delhi: Hindustan Publishing House.

HIID-WIDER. 1992. Proceedings of the Workshop on 'Widows in Rural India'. 2–5 March, New Delhi.

Hirschon, Renee. 1984. *Women and Property—Women as Property*. London: Croom Helm.

Hoff, Lee Ann. 1990. *Battered Women as Survivors*. London: Routledge.

Jahan, Roushan. 1994. *Hidden Danger: Women and Family Violence in Bangladesh*. Dhaka: Women for Women.

Juneja, R. 1993. 'Women should also be Punished for Foeticide'. *Pioneer*. 11 August.

Kakar, Sudhir. 1983. *Mystics, Shamans and Doctors*. Delhi: Oxford University Press.

———. 1990 *Intimate Relations: Exploring Indian Sexuality*. Delhi: Oxford University Press.

Kanhere, Usha. 1987. *Women and Socialisation: A Study of Their Status and Role in Lower Castes of Ahmedabad*. Delhi: Mittal.

Kapur, Ratna and Brenda Cossman. 1996. *Subversive Sites: Feminist Engagements with Law in India*. New Delhi: Sage Publications.

Karlekar, Malavika. 1982. *Poverty and Women's Work*. New Delhi: Vikas.

———. 1987. 'Education'. In Desai and Krishnaraj, eds, *Women in India*, Delhi: Ajanta Press..

———. 1998a. Review of Henrietta Moorea. 1995. *A Passion for Difference: Essays in Anthropology and Gender*. Cambridge: Polity Press; and Review of Meenakshi Thapan, ed. 1997. *Embodiment: Essays on Gender and Identity*. Delhi: Oxford University Press (for the Nehru Memorial Museum and Library). *The Book Review*. 22(1–2):10–3.

_____. 1998b. *Breaking the Silence and Choosing to Hear: Perceptions of Violence against Women.* New Delhi: Sage Publications.

Karlekar, Malavika, Anuja Agarwal, and Maithali Ganjoo. 1995. 'No Safe Spaces'. Report on a Workshop on Violence against Women. New Delhi: Centre for Women's Development Studies.

Kasturi, Leela. 1990. 'Poverty, Migration and Women's Status'. In Veena Mazumdar, ed., *Women Workers in India*, 3–169. New Delhi: Chanakya.

Kasturi, Malavika. 1994. 'Law and Crime in India: British Policy and the Female Infanticide Act of 1870'. *Indian Journal of Gender Studies.* 1(2): 169–93.

Kaushik, Sunanda. 1990. 'Social and Treatment Issues in Wife Battering: A Reconsideration'. In S. Sood, ed., *Violence against Women*, 23–34. Jaipur: Arihant Publications.

Kelkar, Govind. 1991. *Violence against Women in India: Perspectives and Strategies.* Bangkok: Asian Institute of Technology.

Khan, et al. 1986. *Health Practices in India.* Bombay: Operations Research Group.

Kishor, Sunita. 1995. 'Gender Differentials in Child Mortality—A Review of Evidence'. In M. Das Gupta et al. eds, *Womens Health in India: Risk and Vulnerability*, 19–54. Bombay: Oxford University Press.

Kishwar, Madhu. 1986. 'Dowry to Ensure her Happiness or to Disinherit her?' *Manushi.* 34:2–13.

Krishnaraj, Maitheryi. 1991. *Women and Violence: A Country Report. A Study sponsored by UNESCO.* Bombay: RCWS, SNDT Women's University.

Kulkarni, Sanjeev. 1986. *Pre-natal Sex Determination Tests and Female Foeticide in Bombay City.* Bombay: The Foundation for Research in Community Health.

Kumar, Radha. 1993. *The History of Doing.* New Delhi: Kali for Women.

KWDI. 1993. *A Study on the Prevention and Future Directions of Domestic Violence.* Seoul: Korean Women's Development Institute.

Kynch, J. and A. Sen. 1983. 'Indian Women: Well-being and Survival'. *Cambridge Journal of Economics.* 7(3–4).

Litke, Robert. 1992. 'Violence and Power'. *International Social Science Journal.*

Madan, Triloki N. [1965] 1989. *Family and Kinship: A Study of Pandits of Rural Kashmir.* Bombay: Asia Publishing House.

Mahajan Amarjit and Madhurima. 1995. *Family Violence and Abuse in India.* New Delhi: Deep & Deep Publications.

Mankekar, Purnima. 1985. *The Girl Child in India: Data Sheet on Health.* New Delhi: UNICEF.

Mazumdar, Veena. 1992. 'Aminocentesis and Sex Selection'. Paper Presented at WIDER, Helsinki.

Menon, Nivedita. 1996. 'The Impossibility of "Justice": Female Foeticide and Feminist Discourse on Abortion'. In Patricia Uberoi, ed., *Social Reform, Sexuality and the State*, 369–92. New Delhi: Sage Publications.

Menon, Ritu and Kamala Bhasin. 1998. *Borders and Boundaries: Women in India's Partition.* New Delhi: Kali for Women.

Miller, Barbara. 1981. *The Endangered Sex.* Ithaca: Cornell University Press.

Minocha, Aneeta. 1984. 'Mother's Position in Child Feeding and Nutrition: Some Sociological Consideration'. *Economic and Political Weekly.* 12(48):2045–8.

Mitchell, Juilet. 1963, *Women's Estate.* New York: Random House.

_____. 1974. *Psychoanalysis and Feminism.* New York: Penguin.

Multiple Action Research Group (MARG). 1996. *Within Four Walls—A Profile of Domestic Violence.* New Delhi: MARG.

Nair, Janaki. 1996. *Women and Law in Colonial India: A Social History.* New Delhi: Kali for Women.

Nedelsky, Jennifer. 1991. 'Law, Boundaries and the Bounded Self'. *Representations.* Spring.

Netting R. McC., R.A. Wilk and E.J. Arnould et al. eds. 1984. *Households: Comparative and Historical Studies of the Domestic Group.* Berkeley: University of California Press.

Padmanabhan, M. 1993. 'Outlawing Sex-determination, No Solution'. *Pioneer.* 22 September.

Pakrasi, Kanti B. 1970. *Female Infanticide in India*. Calcutta: Temple Press.

Palriwala, Rajni. 1990. 'Introduction'. In Leela Dube and Rajni Palriwala, eds, *Structures and Strategies: Women, Work and Family*, 15–55. New Delhi: Sage Publications.

Panigrahi, Lalita. 1972. *British Social Policy and Female Infanticide*.

Papanek, Hannah. 1990. 'Socialization for Inequality: Issues for Research and Action'. *Samya Shakti*. 4–5:1–10.

Pati, Biswamony. 1991. 'Women, Rape and the Left'. *Economic and Political Weekly*. 21(5):219–20.

Patnaik M.M. and M.K. Sadual. 1988. 'The Problem of Dowry, Domestic Violence and Legal Literacy in India'. Paper Presented at the Fifth National Conference on Women's Studies on Religion, Culture and Politics.

Pawar, M.S. 1988. 'Women and Family Violence: Policies and Programmes'. *Social Change*. 8(3):26–40.

People's Union of Democratic Rights. 1991. *Custodial Rape*. New Delhi: The Union.

Poonacha, Veena, ed. 1999. *Women and Violence*. Bombay: SNDT University.

Prabhu, P.H. [1940]. 1995. *Hindu Social Organization: A Study in Socio-Psychological and Ideological Foundations*. Bombay: Popular Prakashan.

Rajan, Irudaya et al. 1991. 'Decline in Sex Ratio: An Alternative Explanation?' *Economic and Political Weekly*. 26(51):2963–4.

Raman, Vasanthi. Forthcoming. 'A Question of Child Rights'. *Indian Journal of Gender Studies*. 5(1).

Ramanamma, A. and U. Bambawale. 1980. 'The Mania for Sons: An Analysis of Social Values in South Asia'. *Social Science and Medicine*. 14B:107–10.

Ranjana Kumari. 1989. *Brides are not for Burning: Dowry Victims in India,* New Delhi: Radiant.

Ranjana Kumari, et al. 1990. *Growing up in Rural India: Problems and Needs of Adolescent Girls*. New Delhi: Radiant Publishers.

Rao, Vijayendra. 1995. 'Wife-beating in a Rural South Indian Community'. Research Memorandum no. 143. Center for Development Economics, Williams College, Mass, USA.

Ravindra, R.P. 1993. 'The Campaign against Sex Determination Tests'. In Chhaya Datar, ed., *The Struggle against Violence*. 51–98. Calcutta: Stree Publications.

Reddy, P.H. 1991. 'Perpetual Gulf in Male–Female Ratio'. *Deccan Herald*. 4 May.

Saheli. 1988. 'Wife Battering: Creating Choices for Individual Women, the Role of Government and Issues Facing the Women's Movement'. Paper Presented at the National Workshop on Family Violence against Females. 15–18 Feb. New Delhi.

Samuel, Hazel. 1992. 'Report of the Seminar on Harassment of Women in the Workplace'. *Vikasini*, 7(1).

Sandhya. 1994. *Widowhood—A Socio-Psychiatric Study*. New Delhi: Mohit Publications.

Sarkar, Lotika. 1994. 'Rape: A Human Rights versus a Patriarchal Interpretation'. *Indian Journal of Gender Studies*. 1(1):69–92.

Sarkar, Tanika. 1991. 'Reflections on Birati Rape Cases—Gender Ideology in Bengal'. *Economic and Political Weekly*. 21(5):215–8.

Sarkar, Tanika and Urvashi Butalia. 1995. *Women and the Hindu Right*. New Delhi: Kali for Women.

Sen, A. 1983. 'Economics of the Family'. *Asian Development Review*. 1(2).

———. 1987. 'Gender and Cooperative Conflicts'. Harvard Institute of Economic Research. Discussion Paper No. 1342.

Sen, A. and S. Sengupta. 1985. 'Malnutrition of Rural Children and Sex Bias'. In Devaki Jain and N. Banerjee, eds, *Tyranny of the Household*, 3–24. New Delhi: Shakti Books.

Shah, A.M. 1964. 'Basic Terms and Concepts in the Study of Family in India'. *Indian Economic and Social History Review*. 1(3):1–36.

———. 1973. *The Household Dimension of the Family in India*. Delhi: Orient Longman.

———. 1983. 'Issues in Family Studies: Some Notes'.

———. 1988. 'The Phase of Dispersal in the Indian Family Process'. *Sociological Bulletin*. 37(1–2).

Shankardas, Mala Kapur. 1997. 'The Plight of Older Women: Victims of Domestic Violence'. In Kalyan

Baghi ed., *Elderly Females in India: their Status and Suffering*, 79–88. New Delhi: Society for Gerontological Research and Help Age, India.

Sharma, Ursula. 1984. 'Dowry in North India: Its Consequences for Women'. In R. Hirschon, ed., *Woman and Property: Women as Property*, 62–74. London: Croom Helm.

Sinha, Niroj. 1989. *Women and Violence*. New Delhi: Vikas Publishing House.

Sood, Sushma. 1990. *Violence against Women*. Jaipur: Arihant Publishers.

Srinivasa Murthy, R. 1992. 'Mental Health'. In *State of India's Health*. New Delhi: VHAI.

Srivastava, Jaya. 1989. 'The Widows of November 1984'. In Pramila Dandevate et al., eds, *Widows Abandoned and Destitute Women in India*, 63–7. New Delhi: Radiant Publishers.

Strathern, Marilyn. 1988. 'Out of Context: The Persuasive Fictions of Anthropology'. *Current Anthropology*. 28(3).

Straus, M.A. 1980. 'Sexual Inequality and Wife Beating'. In Straus and Hotaling, eds, *The Social Crisis of Husband-Wife Violence*. Minneapolis. University of Minnesota Press.

Stri Kriti Samiti. 1984. 'On the Dowry Question'. Unpublished paper presented at the Second National Conference on Women's Studies. 9–12 April, Trivandrum.

Sunder Rajan, Rajeshwari. 1993. 'Life after Rape'. In Rajeshwari Sunder Rajan, ed., *Real and Imagined World: Gender, Culture and Postcolonialism*, 63–82. London: Routledge.

Thapan, Meenakshi ed. 1997a. *Embodiment: Essays on Gender and Identity*. Delhi: Oxford University Press.

_____. 1997b. 'Femininity and its Discontents: Woman's Body in Intimate Relationships'. In Meenakshi Thapan, ed., *Embodiment: Essays on Gender and Identity*, 172–93. Delhi: Oxford University Press.

The Pioneer. 29 September 1997.

Uberoi, Patricia [1994]. 1995. 'Introduction'. In Patricia Uberoi, ed., *Family, Marriage and Kinship in India*, 1–44. Delhi: Oxford University Press.

Vasanthi Devi. 1991. *Socio-Economic Context of Female Infanticide. A Study of Usilanpatti, Taluk in Tamil Nadu*. Madras: Madras Institute of Development Studies.

Vatuk, S. 1975. 'Gifts and Affines in North India'. *Contributions to Indian Sociology* (n.s.). 9:155–96.

Venkatachalam, R. and Viji Srinivasan. 1993. *Female Infanticide*. New Delhi; Har-Anand Publications.

Verghese, J. 1997. *Her Gold and Her Body*. 2nd ed. Ghaziabad: Vikas Publishing House.

Vyas, Anju, Naheed Mohsini, and Madhushree. 1996. *Voices of Resistance, Silences of Pain: A Resource Guide on Violence against Women*. New Delhi: Centre for Women's Development Studies.

Wadhwa, S. 1993. 'Incest Cases Pose Challenge for Authorities'. *The Pioneer*. 16 August.

Walker, L.E. 1979. *The Battered Woman*. New York: Harper and Row.

_____. 1983 'The Battered Women Syndrome Study'. In D. Finkelhor et al., ed., *Dark Side of Families: Current Family Violence Research*, 31–48. Beverly Hills: Sage Publications.

World Development Report. 1993. *Investing in Health*. New York: Oxford University Press.

The Paradox of Child Labour
and Anthropology*

OLGA NIEUWENHUYS

In relating the child labour debate to the observed variety of children's work patterns, this chapter reveals the limits of current notions such as labour, gender, and exploitation in the analysis of this work. Particularly in the developing world, most work undertaken by children has for a long time been explained away as socialization, education, training, and play. Anthropology has helped disclose that age is used with gender as the justification for the value accorded to work. The low valuation of children's work translates not only into children's vulnerability in the labour market but, more importantly, in their exclusion from remunerated employment. I argue that current child labour policies, because they fail to address the exclusion of children from the production of value, paradoxically reinforce children's vulnerability to exploitation.

The Paradox of Child Labour

Irrespective of what children do and what they think of what they do, modern society sets children apart ideologically as a category of people excluded from the production of value. The dissociation of childhood from the performance of valued work is considered a yardstick of modernity, and a high incidence of child labour is considered a sign of underdevelopment. The problem with defining children's roles in this way, however, is that it denies their agency in the creation and negotiation of value. Illuminating the complexity of the work patterns of children in developing countries, recent anthropological research has begun to demonstrate the need to critically examine the relation between the condemnation of child labour on the one hand and children's everyday work practice on the other. The emerging paradox is that the moral condemnation of child labour assumes that children's place in modern society must perforce be one of dependency and passivity. This denial of their capacity to legitimately act upon their environment by undertaking valuable work makes children altogether dependent upon entitlements guaranteed by the state. Yet we must question the state's role—as the evidence on growing child poverty caused by cuts in social spending has illuminated—in carrying out its mission.

This chapter is divided into three parts: (a) a discussion of the theoretical perspectives

*First published in *Annual Review of Anthropology*. 1996. 25:237–51. Permission for reprint is gratefully acknowledged.

adopted by development theory as it has dealt with poverty and child labour, (*b*) an assessment of the contribution of anthropology to the child labour debate, and (*c*) a discussion of the need of future research based on the idea of work as one of the most critical domains in which poor children can contest and negotiate childhood. First, in the section on Approaches to Children's Work, I argue that from its inception the notion of child labour has been associated with factory work and hence was limited to western countries. The interest in children's work in the developing world can be traced back to theories of socialization, a preoccupation with population growth, and unfair economic competition. The section on Children's Work and Anthropology probes the paradox of the market impinging upon locally accepted forms of child work without transforming it into 'child labour'. Here, I discuss how anthropologists have criticized the simplistic views of child labour espoused by western development experts. Approaches to children's work undertaken from the anthropological perspective highlight the very complex interplay of gender and age in determining a child's work allocation. Third, in the section The Negotiation of Childhood, I propose to enlarge the notion of children's exploitation to include the more mundane aspects of work. Finally, I outline the direction future research should take to enable us to understand not only how children's work is negotiated and acquires its meaning but children's own agency therein.

Approaches to Childrens' Work

The recent concern with child labour draws on a shared understanding among development experts of how, from the mid-nineteenth century onward, western industrial society began to eliminate through legislation the exploitation of children. However, historians still debate more deep-seated reasons for the nineteenth-century outcry in Western Europe and the United States against child labour, which is probably as old as childhood itself. For instance, Nardinelli (1990) has questioned the assumption that this outcry was inspired, as some authors have argued (see Fyfe 1989; Thompson 1968; and Walvin 1982), by the brutal treatment of children working in factories. Besides humanitarian reasons, Nardinelli (1990) argued that there was a desire to protect initiatives to mechanize the textile industry from the uncontrolled competition of a labour force composed almost entirely of children. Another equally important reason was the fear of political instability created by a youthful working class not to be disciplined by the army, schools, or the church (Minge-Kalman 1978; Nardinelli 1990; Weiner 1991; Weissbach 1989). While some believe compulsory education was the single most important instrument leading to the elimination of child labour (Fyfe 1989; Weiner 1991), others have argued that changes in the perceived roles of children (Walvin 1982; Zelizer 1994) and the increase in family income (Nardinelli 1990), played a more decisive role.

Progressive state legislation has marked the major steps of child labour abolition in the West. However, while such legislation defined child labour as waged work undertaken by a child under a certain age, it also established the borderline between morally desirable and pedagogically sensible activities on the one hand, and the exploitation of children on the other. While condemning the relatively uncommon forms of waged labour as exploitation, it sanctioned a broad spectrum of other activities, including housekeeping, child minding, helping adults for no pay on family farms and in small shops, domestic service, street selling, running errands, delivering newspapers, seasonal work on farms, working as trainees in workshops, etc. In contrast with child labour, these activities were lauded for their socializing and training aspects (Davin 1982; Walvin 1982).

The distinction between harmful and suitable—if not desirable—work as defined by western legislation has become the main frame of reference of most contemporary governmental and bureaucratic approaches to children's work. Many countries in the world have now either ratified or adopted modified versions of child labour legislation prepared and propagated by the International Labour Organization (ILO) (ILO 1988, 1991). The implications are far-reaching. Legislation links child labour quite arbitrarily to work in the factory and excludes a wide range of non-factory work. It therefore sanctifies unpaid work in the home or under parental supervision, regardless of its implications for the child. In the words of an ILO report:

We have no problem with the little girl who helps her mother with the housework or cooking, or the boy or girl who does unpaid work in a small family business. ... The same is true of those odd jobs that children may occasionally take on to earn a little pocket money to buy something they really want [see ILO 1993].

Many of the odd jobs mentioned here, as in the case of helping on the family farm or in shops and hotels, though strictly not prohibited, are felt by both children and the public at large to be exploitative. Legislation also selects chronological age as the universal measure of biological and psychological maturity, and it rejects cultural and social meanings attached to local systems of age ranking (La Fontaine 1978). More specifically, it denies the value of an early introduction to artisanal crafts or traditional occupations that may be crucial in a child's socialization (see section on The Negotiation of Childhood). Finally, legislation condemns any work undertaken by a child for his/her own upkeep—with the notable exception of work undertaken to obtain pocket money. The denial of gainful employment is the more paradoxical in that the family and the state often fail to provide children with what they need to lead a normal life (Zelizer 1994). These are some of the reasons why the industrial countries, despite much lip service to the contrary, have not succeeded in eliminating all forms of child work (Challis and Elliman 1979; Herpen 1990; Lavalette 1994; Lee-Wright 1990; Mendelievich 1979; Williams 1993).

Given the factory origins of the notion of child labour, it is hardly surprising that children's work in the erstwhile colonies caused no concern. Most colonial administrations passed factory acts excluding children under 14 from the premises soon after they had been passed at home. However, these laws carried only symbolic value. The colonies were merely seen as sources of cheap raw materials and semi-manufactured goods produced by rural villagers, while the factory system of production was energetically discouraged. The administration's main preoccupation was that the local rural population—men, women, and children—continue to find in the old forms of subsistence the means of surviving while delivering the agricultural goods necessary to maintain the colonial revenue (Nieuwenhuys 1993; White 1994).

This may explain why in the West social activists expressed outrage about child labour at home, while anthropologists romanticized the work of rural children in the colonies as a form of socialization well adapted to the economic and social level of pre-industrial society (Mead and Wolfenstein 1955; Whiting 1963; for a critique see Hull 1981). Engrossed with the intricacies of age ranking and passage rites, anthropologists seldom hinted at what this meant in terms of work and services required by elders from youngsters (Van Gennep [1908] 1960). The high premium put on the solidarity of the extended family as the corner-stone of pre-capitalist society overshadowed the possibility of exploitation occurring within the family or the village.

This perception changed with the identification in post-War development theory of population growth as the main obstacle to the eradication of poverty in the new nations of the Third World. Celebrated as an antidote to poverty during the colonial period, children's work contributions to the family economy came to be perceived as an indicator of poverty, if not its cause. In the 1960s and 1970s, a burgeoning literature on the 'population explosion' tried to show that the fast-growing numbers of poor children—non-workers with escalating expectations— were to be held responsible for consuming the developing world's scant resources (Dore 1982; Eisenstadt 1956). These allegations often masked the fear that the mounting frustrations of youngsters would 'fester into eruptions of violence and extremism' (McNamara 1968) and thereby threaten the stability of the post-War world order (Michaelson 1981; Schrijvers 1993). Large-scale foreign-funded research programmes were introduced in high-fertility countries to induce poor couples to control births. However, resistance to birth control was unexpectedly staunch. By the mid-1970s, research began to provide clues that the poor desired a large family because children represented an important source of free labour (Michaelson 1981). Mamdani's seminal work on the importance of children's work contribution for the reproduction of the peasant household in the Green Revolution areas of the Punjab cast an entirely new light on high fertility by suggesting that India's peasants needed many children to meet their labour demands (Mamdani 1972, 1974, 1981).

Mamdani's research inspired a fresh approach to children's work in terms of its utility to the peasant household. During the 1970s, anthropologists carried out extensive and painstaking time-allocation and family-budget studies to show that even young children were contributing to their own sustenance by undertaking a whole range of activities in the subsistence sphere of the peasant economy (Hull 1981; Marcoux 1994; Mueller 1975; Nichols 1993; White 1975). The ensuing debate on the determinants of high fertility in peasant economies showed, however, that the claim that poor peasants' desire for children would be inspired by their value as workers was premature (Datta and Nugent 1984; Vlassoff 1979; 1982; Vlassoff and Vlassoff 1980; White 1982). Caldwell's (1976, 1981, 1982) work on Nigeria and India was particularly influential in mapping the wider setting of children's historical, social, and cultural roles (Caldwell 1976, 1981, 1982). Research on intra-household relations also questioned the concept of the household as an unproblematic unit, highlighting the outspoken inequality that exists not only between males and females but between seniors and juniors (Elson 1982; Folbre 1994; Jain and Banerjee 1985; Schildkrout 1980, 1981). Another criticism of the 'cost–benefit' analysis has been its exclusive focus on decision making at the level of the household; it ignores the larger context in which the actions of its members occur (Goddard and White 1982, Rodgers and Standing 1981; Wallerstein et al. 1982).

In spite of such criticism, the neoclassical belief that child labour is essentially a problem of household economics has continued to be espoused in the studies of child labour published under the auspices of international agencies such as the United Nations International Children's Educational Fund (UNICEF), the World Health Organization (WHO), and the ILO following the International Year of the Child in 1979 (Bequele and Boyden 1988; Black 1995; Bouhdiba 1982; Challis and Elliman 1979; Fyfe 1989; Mendelievich 1979; Myers 1991; Rimbaud 1980). Similar views are expressed in the documents produced by international charities devoted to the welfare of children such as the International Catholic Bureau, Save the Children, Defence of Children International, Anti-Slavery International (for overviews, see Boyd 1994; Bureau of International Affairs, US Department of Labor 1994; Ennew 1994). Typical of these publica- tions is a moral preoccupation with abolition through legislation and a zealous belief in the desirability of extending western childhood ideals to poor families worldwide. Their merit lies essentially in having staked out child labour as a new and legitimate field of global political and academic concern. As aptly stated by Morice and Schlemmer (1994), the continuous reference to (western) moral values, however, all too often not only supplants scientific analysis but may at times mask its very need. The emerging picture is one of conceptual confusion, in which ill-grasped notions from diverse analytical fields are indiscriminately used. The most glaring confusion is undoubtedly the one between the moral oppression and the economic exploitation of children (Morice 1981; Morice and Schlemmer 1994; Nieuwenhuys 1993). Reference to broad and ahistorical causes of the oppression of children such as poverty, illiteracy, backwardness, greed, and cruelty fail to go beyond the mere description of oppression and ignore the historical and social conditioning of exploitation (Sahoo 1995).

As a global solution to eliminate child labour, development experts are now proposing a standard based on the sanctity of the nuclear family on the one hand and the school on the other as the only legitimate spaces for growing up. If this becomes a universal standard, there is a danger of negating the worth of often precious mechanisms for survival, and penalizing or even criminalizing the ways the poor bring up their children (Boyden 1990; Cunningham 1991; Donzelot 1977). This criminalization is made more malevolent as modern economies increasingly display their unwillingness to protect poor children from the adverse effects of neoliberal trade policies (Amin 1994; Cornia et al. 1987; Fyfe 1989; Mundle 1984; Verlet 1994).

Children's Work and Anthropology

Children's lives have been a constant theme in anthropology. However, in-depth studies of their work remain few and have been inspired, as I have argued, by a critical concern with the neoclassical approach to the value of children. Two main areas of research have elicited anthropologists' interest: the family context of work and the relation between socialization, work, and schooling.

One of the leading themes of economic anthropology has been the conceptualization of work and its cultural meanings. The growing numbers of publications on child labour in the developing world have invoked renewed interest in the family context of work. Central to some of the most notable studies has been how children's work is constrained by hierarchies based on kinship, age, and gender, a constraint that results in its typically rural, flexible, and personalized character. Rather than a widespread form of exploitation, child employment is mostly limited by the free-labour requirement of families that is satisfied by giving children unremunerated and lowly valued tasks (Céspedes and Zarama 1994; Dube 1988; McEwen 1982; Melhuus 1984; Reynolds 1991; Wyers 1986).

Considering the low cost of children's labour, it is indeed surprising that employers do not avail themselves more fully of this phenomenal source of profit. Despite more than 100 million children in the age bracket 5 to 15 living in abject poverty in India, for example, a mere 16 million are employed, the vast majority of whom are teenagers who work in agriculture. About 10 per cent are employed by industries, largely producing substandard if not inferior products for the local market (Gulrajani 1994; Kothari 1983; Nieuwenhuys 1993).

There is more and more evidence that poor children who are not employed perform crucial work, often in the domestic arena, in subsistence agriculture, and in the urban informal sector (Campos et al. 1994; Gangrade and Gathia 1983; Marcoux 1994; Mies and Shiva 1993; Moerat 1989; Mutiso 1989; Nieuwenhuys 1994; Oloko 1991; Reynolds 1991; Salazar 1991). Theories explaining underdevelopment in terms of the persistence of precapitalist labour relations provide some clues about why these children are not employed (Martin and Beittel 1987; Meillassoux 1983; Southall 1988). The crucial aspect of underdevelopment in these theories is the unequal exchange realized in the market between goods produced in capitalist firms, where labour is valued according to its exchange value, and goods produced by the peasantry and the urban informal sector, where the use value of labour predominates. The latter group is paid only a fraction of its real cost because households are able to survive by pooling incomes from a variety of sources, undertaking subsistence activities and using the work of women and children to save on the costs of reproduction (Wallerstein et al. 1982). The unpaid work of children in the domestic arena, which turns them into 'inactives', is seen as crucial for the developing world's low labour cost rationality.

The reasons children are more likely than adults to be allotted unpaid work in agriculture or the household can be gauged by the work of feminist researchers that highlights how ideologies of gender and age interact to constrain, in particular, girls to perform unpaid domestic work (De Tray 1983; Dube 1988; Nieuwenhuys 1994; Oppong 1988; Reynolds 1991; Schildkrout 1980; 1981; Wyers 1986). The ideology of gender permits the persistence of an unequal system in which women are excluded from crucial economic and political activities and their positions of wives and mothers are associated with a lower status than men (Dube 1988; Folbre 1986; Jain and Chand 1979; Scheper-Hughes 1987). The valuation of girls' work is so low that it has been 'discovered' by feminist anthropologists making a conscious choice to include housework and child care in their definition of work (Folbre 1986; Jain and Banerjee 1985; Jeffrey et al. 1989; Schildkrout 1980; Sen and Sengupta 1985). Girls are trained early to accept and internalize the feminine ideals of devotion to the family (Bellotti 1981; Kakar 1981). The role of caretaker of younger siblings has not only the practical advantage of freeing adult women for wage work, it also charges girls' work with emotional gratifications that can make up for the lack of monetary rewards (Leslie and Paolosso 1989; Myers 1992).

Elson (1982) has argued that seniority explains why children's work is largely valued as inferior: Inferiority is not only attached to the nature of the work but to the person who performs it as well. Poor children are not perceived as workers because what they do is submerged in the low status realm of the domestic. The effect of seniority is not limited to the control of children's work within the nuclear family. Anthropologists have also uncovered how children's work plays a cardinal role in the intricate and extensive kinship and pseudo-kinship patterns that are at the core of support systems in the developing world. While servicing the immediate household is young children's mandatory task, poor children coming of age may also be sent to work as domestics and apprentices for wealthier kin (Caldwell 1982; Kayongo-Male and Walji 1984; Morice 1982; Salazar 1991). For the parent-employer, this is a source of status and prestige (Caldwell 1982). The widespread African practice of fostering the children of poorer (pseudo-)relatives is just one example of the intricate way family loyalty and socialization practices combine to shape how poor children are put to work. Another example is the practice among the poor in some areas of India of pledging their children's work against a loan. Although the object of much negative publicity, the practice is seen by parents as a useful form of training, a source of security, and a way of cutting household expenditures (Gangrade and Gathia 1983; ILO 1992; Nieuwenhuys 1994). Old crafts such as carpet weaving, embroidery, silk reeling, artisanal fishing, and metal work lend themselves to protracted periods of apprenticeship in which a child is made to accept long hours of work and low pay in the hope of becoming master (Kambargi 1991; Morice 1981; Vijaygopalan 1983). While often exacting, children may experience apprenticeship or living in another household as valuable, particularly if it helps them learn a trade or visit a school. Children's valuation of the practice is nevertheless ambiguous, and they may prefer employment to servicing their kin (Fyfe 1989; Lee-Wright 1990; Nieuwenhuys 1994; Salazar 1991; Sinha 1991; White 1994).

There is a persistent belief, which finds its origins in the neoclassical approach, that schooling is the best antidote to child labour (Fyfe 1989; Weiner 1991). However, one consequence of the personalized character of children's work patterns is that this work is often combined with going to school. Reynolds' (1991) study of the Zambezi Valley describes how Tonga children need to work in subsistence agriculture while attending school simply to survive. Insecurity about the value of diplomas and marriage strategies is among the reasons girls in Lagos, Nigeria, spend much out-of-school time acquiring street-trading skills (Oloko 1991). In Kerala, India, where attending school is mandatory, children spend much time earning cash for books, clothes, and food (Nieuwenhuys 1993). Around the world children undertake all kinds of odd jobs, not only to help their families but to defray the fast-rising costs of schooling, be it for themselves or for a younger sibling (Bekombo 1981; Boyden 1991; Hallak 1990; La Fontaine 1978). However, children may also simply dislike school and prefer to work and earn cash instead (Kambargi 1991; White 1994).

Although to some extent schools and work can coexist as separate arenas of childhood, schooling is changing the world orientation of both children and parents. Among the most critical effects is the lowering of birth rates, which has been explained by the non-availability of girls for child care (Caldwell et al. 1985; Myers 1992). Another explanation, inspired by the neoclassical approach of balancing children's costs against the returns, is related to what Caldwell (1981) has called the 'intergenerational flow of wealth.' This notion suggests that schooling increases the costs of child rearing while reducing children's inclination to perform mandatory tasks for the circle of kin. The traditional flow of wealth from juniors to seniors is thus reversed. Perhaps of greater importance, schooling—despite the heavy sacrifices it may demand—provides children with a space in which they can identify with the parameters of modern childhood. It makes possible negotiations with elders for better clothes and food; time for school, homework, and recreation; and often payment for domestic work (Nieuwenhuys 1994). The proponents of compulsory education have also argued that literate youngsters are likely to be more productive later in life than uneducated ones, who may have damaged their health by early entrance into the labour market (Weiner 1991). For Purdy (1992), schooling reinforces the useful learning imparted by parents at home and may, for some children, be the only useful form of learning.

Schools are also said to have a negative impact. Illness, lack of support at home, or heavy work make poor children's performance often inadequate and repetition and dropping out common. Competition in the classroom helps breed a sense of inferiority and personal failure in poor children, turning their work assignments into a source of shame. The high costs of schooling, including the need to look respectable in dress and appearance, incites poor children to engage in remunerative work, which contradicts the belief that compulsory education would work as an antidote to child labour (Burra 1989; Fyfe 1989; McNamara 1968; Weiner 1991).

In the past few years, non-governmental organizations (NGOs) concerned with children have been encouraged to develop low-cost solutions to address the problem of child labour. The solutions are based on a combination of work and school and recognize the need of poor children to contribute to their own upkeep. The approach has gained support within the ILO, the organization that until recently was the most staunch defender of prohibition by legislation (Boyd 1994; Espinola et al. 1987; Fyfe 1994; Gunn and Oslas 1992; ILO/Government of Germany 1991). The poor quality of the education imparted, the heavy demands of studying after work, and above all the fact that they leave untouched the unjust social system that perpetuates children's exploitation are among the most problematic aspects of NGOs' interventions (Boyden and Myers 1995).

The articulation of gender, age, and kinship plays a cardinal role in the valuation of poor children's work and is instrumental in explaining why some work is condemned as unsuitable and some is lauded as salutary. Hierarchies based on gender, age, and kinship combine to define children's mandatory tasks as salutary work and condemn paid work. By legitimizing children's obligation to contribute to survival and denying them their right to seek personal gain, these hierarchies effectively constrain them to a position of inferiority within the family. It is then not so much their factory employment as their engagement in low-productivity and domestic tasks that defines the ubiquitous way poor children are exploited in today's developing world.

Anthropology has sought to explain the apparent inability of the market to avail itself more fully of the vast reservoir of cheap child labour by pointing out that the free-labour requirements of poor families are satisfied by giving children lowly valued tasks. This explanation questions child labour studies' conceptualization of the exploitation of poor children. Employment is clearly not the only nor the most important way children's work is exploited: child work contributions to the family are instrumental in its subsistence and in the production of goods that reach the market at prices far below their labour value. The moral assumption that poor children's socialization should occur through the performance of non-monetized work excludes this work from the same economic realm that includes child labour; it is as much a part of children's exploitation. This fact seriously questions the premises of modern childhood discussed in the next section.

The Negotiation of Childhood

Irrespective of what they do and what they think about what they do, the mere fact of their being children sets children ideologically apart as a category of people excluded from the production of value. The dissociation of childhood from the performance of valued work has been increasingly considered a yardstick of modernity. International agencies and highly industrialized countries now turn this yardstick into a tool to condemn as backward and undemocratic those countries with a high incidence of child labour (Bureau of International Affairs, US Department of Labor 1994). The problem with this way of defining the ideal of childhood, however, is that it denies children's agency in the creation and negotiation of value.

The view that childhood precludes an association with monetary gain is an ideal of modern industrial society (De Mause 1976; Zelizer 1994). Historians highlight the bourgeois origins of this ideal and question its avowed universal validity not only across cultures but across distinctions of gender, ethnicity, and class (Ariès 1973, 1980; Cunningham 1991; Donzelot 1977; Hoyles and Evans 1989). Some have argued that this ideal is threatened at the very core of capitalism and may be giving way to more diversified patterns of upbringing or even to the 'disappearance of childhood' (Evans 1994; Postman 1982). The current debate over children's rights is symptomatic of the discredit bourgeois notions of parental rights and childhood incompetence seem to have suffered (Archard 1993; Franklin 1986; Freeman 1983; Purdy 1992; Vittachi 1989). The exposure of child abuse in the western media during the 1980s and 1990s has, in this line, been explained as a display of excessive anxiety sparked by the growing fragility of personal relationships in late-modern society that cannot but also affect childhood. Late-modern experiences of childhood suggest that the basic source of trust in society lies in the child. Advances in children's rights or media campaigns against child labour or sex tourism would point to a growing sanctity of the child in late modernity (Jenks 1994). This sanctity, however, is essentially symbolic and is contradicted by actual social and financial policies, as borne out by the harshness with which structural adjustment programmes have hit poor children in developing countries and caused a marked increase in child mortality, morbidity, illiteracy, and labour (Amin 1994; Cornia et al. 1987; Folbre 1994; Fyfe 1989; Graham-Brown 1991; Mundle 1984). Under these conditions it is no wonder that, as noted by Jenks (1994), late-modern visions of childhood are now increasingly split between 'futurity' and 'nostalgia'.

As childhood becomes a contested domain, the legitimacy of directing children into economically useless activities is losing ground (Zelizer 1994). The need to direct children into these activities is linked to a system of parental authority and family discipline that was instrumental in preserving established bourgeois social order. The price of maintaining this order is high, because it requires, among other commitments, money to support the institutions at the basis of the childhood ideal, such as free education, cheap housing, free health care, sports and recreation facilities and family welfare and support services. Developing economies will unlikely be able to generate in the near future the social surplus that the maintenance of these institutions requires. As the neoliberal critique of the welfare state gains popularity, wealthy economies also become reluctant to continue shouldering childhood institutions. It is interesting to note that with the retreat of the state, the market itself has begun to address children as consumers more and more, explicitly linking their status to the possession of expensive goods, thereby inducing poor children to seek self-esteem through paid work (White 1994). Working children find themselves clashing with the childhood ideology that places a higher value on the performance of economically useless work. Although working for pay offers opportunities for self-respect, it also entails sacrificing childhood, which exposes children to the negative stereotyping attached to the loss of innocence this sacrifice is supposed to cause (Black 1995; Boyd 1994; Bureau of International Affairs, US Department of Labor 1994; Challis and Elliman 1979; Fyfe 1989; Myers 1991).

Rethinking the paradoxical relation between neoliberal and global childhood ideology is one of the most promising areas for research. Research should especially seek to uncover how the need of poor children to realize self-esteem through paid work impinges upon the moral condemnation of child labour as one of the fundamental principles of modernity. In stark contrast with what happened in the nineteenth-century West, the future may very well see employers, parents, children, and the state disputing the legitimacy of this moral condemnation. Women, in particular, as they expose the construction of gender roles as instrumental in their discrimination in the labour market, are likely to be girls' foremost allies in contesting modern childhood's ideal of economic uselessness (Folbre 1986, 1994). The ways children devise to create and negotiate the value of their work and how they invade structures of constraint based on seniority are other promising areas of future anthropological research. This type of research is even more relevant in that it may not only enrich our knowledge of children's agency but may prove seminal in understanding the process by which work acquires its meaning and is transformed into value.

REFERENCES

Amin, A.A. 1994. 'The Socioeconomic Impact of Child Labour in Cameroon'. *Labour Capital Society*. 27(2):234–49.

Archard, D. 1993. *Children, Rights and Childhood*. London: Routledge.

Ariès, P. 1973. *L 'Enfant et la Vie Familiale sous l'Ancien Régime*. Paris: Seuil.

———. 1980. 'Motivation for Declining Birth Rates in the West: The Rise and Fall of the Role of the Child'. *Population Development Review*. 6(4):645–50.

Bekombo, M. 1981. The Child in Africa: Socialisation, Education and Work.

Bellotti, E.G. 1981. *Dalla Parte delle Bambine, l'Influenza dei Condizionamenti Sociali nella Formazione del Ruolo Femminile nei Primi Anni di Vita.* Milano: Feltrinelli.

Bequele, A. and J. Boyden, eds. 1988. *Combating Child Labour.* Geneva: International Labour Organization.

Black, M. 1995. *In the Twilight Zone: Child Workers in the Hotel, Tourism and Catering Industry.* Geneva: International Labour Organization.

Bouhdiba, A. 1982. *Exploitation of Child Labour: Special Report of the Subcommittee on Prevention of Discrimination and Protection of Minorities.* New York: United Nations.

Boyd, J. 1994. 'Introduction: Child Labour Within the Globalizing Economy'. *Labour Capital Society.* 27(2):153–61.

Boyden, J. 1990. 'Childhood and the Policy Makers: A Comparative Perspective on the Globalization of Childhood'. In A. James and A Prout, eds, *Constructing and Reconstructing Childhood: Contemporary Issues in the Sociological Study of Childhood.* 184–215. London: Falmer.

Boyden, J. 1991. Working Children in Lima. In *Children of the Cities*; London, Zoo Books.

Boyden, J. and W.E. Myers. 1995. *Exploring Alternative Approaches to Combating Child Labour: Case Studies from Developing Countries.* Florence: UNICEF/Innocenti Occasional Paper 8.

Bureau of International Affairs, US Department of Labor. 1994. *By the Sweat and Toil of Children: The Use of Child Labor in American Imports.* Washington, D.C.: US Department of Labor.

Burra, N. 1989. *Child Labour and Education: Issues Emerging from the Experiences of Some Developing Countries of Asia.* Paris: UNESCO-UNICEF.

Caldwell, J.C. 1976. 'Towards a Restatement of Demographic Transition Theory'. *Population Development Review.* 2(4):321–59.

———. 1981. 'The Mechanisms of Demographic Change in Historical Perspective'. *Population Studies.* 35:5–27.

———. 1982. *Theory of Fertility Decline.* London: Academic.

Caldwell, J.C., P.H. Reddy and P. Caldwell. 1985. 'Educational Transition in Rural South India'. *Population Development Review.* 11(1):29–51.

Campos, R., M. Raffaelli and W. Ude. 1994. 'Social Networks and Daily Activities of Street Youth in Belo Horizonte'. *Child Development.* 65:319–30.

Céspedes, B.S. and M.I.V. Zarama. 1994. Le travail des enfants dans les mines de charbon en Colombie. *Travail Capital et Société* 27(2):250–69.

Challis, J. and D. Elliman. 1979. *Child Workers Today.* Middlesex: Quartermaine.

Cornia, G., R. Jolly, and F. Stewart, eds. 1987. *Adjustment with a Human Face*, vol. 1, *Protecting the Vulnerable and Promoting Growth.* Oxford: Clarendon.

Cunningham, H. 1991. *The Children of the Poor: Representations of Childhood since the Seventeenth Century.* Cambridge, MA: Blackwell.

Datta, S.K. and J.B. Nugent. 1984. 'Are Old-age Security and the Utility of Children in Rural India Really Unimportant?' *Population Studies.* 38:507–9.

Davin, A. 1982. 'Child Labour, The Working Class Family, and Domestic Ideology in 19th-Century Britain'. *Development Change.* 13(4):663–52.

De Mause, L., ed. 1976. *The History of Childhood.* London: Souvenir.

De Tray, D. 1983. 'Children's Work Activities in Malaysia'. *Population Development Review.* 9(3):437–55.

Donzelot, J. 1977. *La Police des Familles.* Paris: Minuit.

Dore, R. 1982. *The Diploma Disease, Education, Qualification and Development.* London: Allen & Unwin.

Dube, L. 1981. 'The Economic Roles of Children in India: Methodological Issues'. pp. 179–213.

———. 1988. 'On the Construction of Gender in India, Hindu Girls in Patrilineal India'. *Economic and Political Weekly.* 30 April:WS11–24.

Eisenstadt, S.N. 1956. *From Generation to Generation, Age Groups and Social Structure.* New York: Free Press.

Elson, D. 1982. 'The Differentiation of Children's Labour in the Capitalist Labour Market'. *Development Change*. 13(4):479–97.

Ennew, J. 1994. *Street and Working Children: A Guide to Planning*. London: Save the Children.

Espinola, B., B. Glauser, R.M. Oriz and Cartzosa S. de Ortiz. 1987. *In the Streets: Working Street Children in Asunciòn: A Book for Action*. Bogotà: UNICEF.

Evans, D.T. 1994. 'Falling Angels? The Material Construction of Children as Sexual Citizens'. *International Journal of Children's Rights*. 2:1–33.

Folbre, N. 1986. 'Hearts and Spades: Paradigms of Household Economics'. *World Development*. 14(2):245–55.

———. 1994. *Who Pays for the Kids?* London/New York: Routledge.

Franklin, B., ed. 1986. *The Rights of Children*. Oxford: Blackwell.

Freeman, M.D.A. 1983. *Rights and Wrongs of Children*. London/Dover: Pinter.

Fyfe A. 1989. *Child Labour*. Cambridge: Polity Press.

———. 1994. 'Educational Strategies for Street and Working Children'. Presented at Conference on the Street Child. Psychoact. Subst.: Innov. Coop., World Health Organization, Geneva.

Gangrade, K.D., and J.A. Gathia, eds. 1983. *Women and Child Workers in the Unorganized Sector, Non Government Organization's Perspective*. Delhi: Concept.

Goddard, V.B. and White, eds. 1982. 'Child Workers Today'. *Development Change*. 13(4):465–78.

Graham-Brown, S. 1991. *Education in the Developing World, Conflict and Crisis*. London/New York: Longman.

Gulrajani, M. 1994. 'Child Labour and the Export Sector: A Case-study of the Indian Carpet Industry'. *Labour Capital Society*. 27(2):192–215.

Gunn, S.E., and Z. Ostas. 1992. 'Dilemmas in Tackling Child Labour: The Case of Scavenger Children in the Philippines'. *International Labour Review*. 131(6):629–46.

Hallak, J. 1990. 'Setting Educational Priorities in the Developing World'. In *Investing in the Future*. Paris: UNESCO/Internal Institute for Educaction Planning, Perganion Press: pp. 303.

Herpen, A. 1990. *Children and Youngsters in Europe: The New Proletariat? A Report on Child Labour in Europe*. Brussels: Centre for European Studies/European Trade Unions Commission.

Hoyles, M., and P. Evans. 1989. *The Politics of Childhood*. London: Journeyman.

Hull, T. 1975. *Each Child Brings Its Own Fortune: An Enquiry into the Value of Children in a Javanese Village*. Canberra: Australian National University.

———. 1981. 'Perspectives and Data Requirements for the Study of Children's Work'. pp. 47–80.

International Labor Organization (ILO). 1988. *Conditions of Work Digest: The Emerging Response to Child Labour*, vol. 7(1). Geneva: International Labor Organization.

———. Government of Germany. 1991. *International Programme of the Elimination of Child Labour (IPEC)*. Geneva: International Labor Organization.

———. 1991. *Conditions of Work Digest, Child Labour Law and Practice*, vol. 10(1). Geneva: International Labor Organization.

———. 1992. *Children in Bondage: A Call for Action*. Geneva: International Labor Organization.

———. 1993. *World of Work*. June 6–7. Geneva: International Labor Organization.

Jain, D. and N., Banerjee, eds. 1985. *Tyranny of the Household: Investigative Essays on Women's Work*. Delhi: Shakti.

Jain, D. and M. Chand. 1979. 'Rural Children at Work: Preliminary Results of a Pilot Study'. *Indian Journal of Social Work*. 40(3):311–22.

Jeffery, P., R. Jeffery and A. Lyo. 1989. *Labour Pains and Labour Power, Women and Childbearing in India*. Delhi: Manohar Publishers.

Jenks, C. 1994. Child Abuse in the Post-Modern Context: An Issue of Social Identity. In *Childhood Global Perspect* 2(3):111–21.

Kakar, S. 1981. *The Inner World, A Psycho-Analytic Study of Childhood and Society in India*. Delhi: Oxford University Press.

Kambargi, R. ed. 1991. *Child Labour in the Indian Subcontinent, Dimensions and Implications*. Delhi: Sage Publications.

Kayongo-Male, D. and P. Walji. 1984. *Children at Work in Kenya*. Nairobi: Oxford University Press.

Kothari, S. 1983. 'There's Blood on Those Matchsticks, Child Labour in Sivakasi'. *Economic and Political Weekly*. 13(27):1191–202.

La Fontaine, J.S. 1978. *Sex and Age as Principles of Social Differentiation*. London: Academic.

Lavalette M. 1994. *Child Employment in the Capitalist Labour Market*. Aldershot, UK: Avebury.

Lee-Wright, P. 1990. *Child Slaves*. London: Earthscan.

Leslie, J. and M. Paolosso. 1989. *Women, Work and Child Welfare in the Third World*. Boulder, CO: Westview.

Mamdani, M. 1978. *The Myth of Population Control, Family, Caste and Class in an Indian Village*. New York: Monthly Review.

––––––. 1974. 'The Ideology of Population Control'. *Concerned Demogr*. 4:13–22.

––––––. 1981. 'The Ideology of Population Control. pp. 39–49.

Marcoux, R. 1994. 'Des inactifs qui ne chô ment pas: une réflexion sur le travail des enfants en milieu urbain du Mail'. *Travail Capital et Société* 27(2):296–319.

Martin, W.G. and M. Beittel. 1987. 'The Hidden Abode of Reproduction: Conceptualizing Households in Southern Africa'. *Development Change*. 18:215–34.

McEwen, S.A. 1982. 'Changes in the Structure of Child Labour Under Conditions of Dualistic Economic Growth'. *Development Change*. 13(4):537–50.

McNamara, R. 1968. *The Essence of Security: Reflections in Office*. London: Hodder & Stoughton.

Mead, M. and M. Wolfenstein, eds. 1955. *Childhood in Contemporary Cultures*. Chicago: University, Chicago Press.

Meillassoux, C. 1983. 'The Economic Basis of Demographic Reproduction: From the Domestic Mode of Production to Wage Earning'. *J. Peasant Stud. 11(1):50–61*.

Melhuus, M. 1984. 'Cash Crop Production and Family Labour: Tobacco Growers in Corrientes, Argentina'. In *Family and Work in Rural Societies: Perspectives on Non-wage Labour*. London: Tavistock.

Mendelievich, E., ed. 1979. *Children at Work*. Geneva: International Labor Organization.

Michaelson, K.L., ed. 1981. *And the Poor Get Children: Radical Perspectives on Population Dynamics*. New York: Monthly Review.

Mies, M. and Vandana Shiva. 1993. 'The Impoverishment of the Environement: Women and Children Last'. In eds, *Ecofeminism*. M. Mies and Vandana Shiva, 70–91. London: ZED.

Minge-Kalman, W. 1978. 'The Industrial Revolution and the European Family: The Institutionalization of Childhood as a Market for Family Labour'. *Comparative Studies in Society and History*. 20:456–63.

Moerat. F. 1989. *A Study of Child Labour with Regard to Newspaper Vendors in the Cape Peninsula*. Cape Town: University of Cape Town.

Morice, A. 1981. The Exploitation of Children in the 'Informal Sector': Proposals for Research. 131–58.

––––––. 1982: 'Underpaid Labour and Social Reproduction: Apprenticeship in Koalack, Senegal'. *Development Change*. 13(4):515–26.

Morice, A. and B. Schlemmer. 1994. La mise au travail des enfants: une problématique à investir. *Trav. Cap. Soc*. 27(2):286–94.

Mueller, E. 1975. The Economic Value of Children in Peasant Agriculture. Presented at Conf. Popul. Policy, Resour. Fut.

Mundle, S. 1984. 'Recent Trends in the Condition of Children in India: A Statistical Profile'. *World Development*. 12(3):297–308.

Mutiso, R. 1989. *Housemaids in Nairobi: A Review of Available Documents on the Subject of Female Domestic Workers in Nairobi*. Nairobi: Undugu.

Myers, R. 1992. *The Twelve Who Survive: Strengthening Programmes of Early Childhood Development in the Third World*. London/New York: Routledge.

Myers, W.E., ed. 1991. *Protecting Working Children*. London: ZED Books/UNICEF.

Nag, M., B. White and R.C. Peet. 1978. 'An Anthropological Approach to the Study of Economic Value of Children in Java and Nepal'. *Current Anthropology*. 19(2):293–306.

Nardinelli, C. 1990. *Child Labour and the Industrial Revolution*. Bloomington, IN: Indiana University Press.

Nichols, M. 1993. 'Third World Families at Work: Child Labor or Child Care?' *Harvard Business Review*. January/February: 12–23.

Nieuwenhuys, O. 1993: 'To Read and Not to Eat: South Indian Children between Secondary School and Work'. *Children Global Perspective*. 1(2):100–9.

_____. 1994. *Children's Life-worlds: Gender, Welfare and Labour in the Developing World*. London/New York: Routledge.

_____. 1995: 'The Domestic Economy and the Exploitation of Children's Work: The Case of Kerala'. *International Journal of Children's Rights*. 3:213–25.

Oloko, B.A. 1991. Children's Work in Urban Nigeria: A Case Study of Young Lagos Traders. 24–45.

Oppong, C. 1988. 'Les femmes Africaines: des épouses, des mères et des travailleuses'. In *Population et Sociétés en Afrique au Sud du Sahara*. Paris: Harmattan.

Postman, N. 1982. *The Disappearance of Childhood*. New York: Delacorte.

Purdy, L. 1992. *In Their Best Interests? The Case against Equal Rights for Children*. Ithaca/London: Cornell University Press.

Reynolds, P. 1991. *Dance Civet Cat: Child Labour in the Zambezi Valley*. London: ZED.

Rimbaud, C. 1980. *52 Millions d'Enfants au Travail*. Paris: Plon.

Rodgers, G. and G. Standing, eds. 1981. *Child Work, Poverty and Underdevelopment*. Geneva: International Labor Organization.

Sahoo, U.C. 1995. *Child Labour in Agrarian Society*. Jaipur/Delhi: Rawat.

Salazar, M.C. 1991. 'Young Workers in Latin America: Protection of Self-determination?' *Child Welfare*. 70(2):269–83.

Scheper-Hughes, N., ed. 1987. *Child Survival*. Dordrecht: Reidel.

Schildkrout, E. 1980. 'Children's Work Reconsidered'. *International Social Science Journal*. 32(3):479–90.

Schrijvers, J. 1993. *The Violence of Development*. Utrecht: International Books; Delhi: Kali for Women (Inaugural address).

Sen, A., and S. Sengupta. 1985. Malnutrition in Rural Children and the Sex Bias. 3–24.

Sinha, S.K. 1991. *Child Labour in Calcutta: A Sociological Sutdy*. Calcutta: Naya Prokash.

Southall, A. 1988. 'On Mode of Production Theory: The Foraging Mode of Production and the Kinship Mode of Production'. *Dialectical Anthropology*. 12:165–92.

Stadum, B. 1995. 'The Dilemma in Saving Children from Child Labor: Reform and Case-work at Odds with Families' Needs'. *Child Welfare*. 74(1):20–33.

Thompson, E.P. 1968. *The Making of the English Working Class*. Harmondsworth, UK: Penguin.

Van Gennep, A. [1908] 1960. *The Rites of Passage*. Chicago: University of Chicago Press.

Verlet, M. 1994. 'Grandir à Nima (Ghana): dérégulation domestique et mise au travail des enfants. *Travail Capital et Société*. 27(2):162–90.

Vijayagopalan, S. 1993. *Child Labour in the Carpet Industry: A Status Report*. Delhi: NCAER.

Vittachi, A. 1989. *Stolen Childhood: In Search of the Rights of the Child*. Cambridge: Polity Press.

Vlassoff, M. 1979. 'Labour Demand and Economic Utility of Children: A Case Study in Rural India'. *Population Studies*. 33(3).

_____. 1982. 'Economic Utility of Children and Fertility in Rural India'. *Population Studies*. 36:45–60.

Vlassoff, M. and C. Vlassoff. 1980. 'Old Age Security and the Utility of Children in Rural India'. *Population Studies*. 34(3):487–99.

Wallerstein, I., W.G. Martin and T. Dickinson. 1982. 'Household Structures and Production Processes: Preliminary Theses and Findings'. *Review*. 5(3):437–58.

Walvin, J. 1982. *A Child's World: A Social History of English Childhood 1800–1914*. Harmondsworth, UK: Penguin.

Weiner, M. 1991. *The Child and the State in India: Child Labour and Educational Policy in Comparative Perspective*. Princeton, NJ: Princeton University Press.

Weissbach, L.S. 1989. *Child Labour Reform in Nineteenth Century France: Assuring the Future Harvest*. London: Baton Rouge Louisiana University Press.

White, B. 1975. 'The Economic Importance of Children in a Javanese Village'. In M. Nag, ed., *Population and Social Organization*. 127–46. The Hague: Mouton.

_____. 1982. 'Child Labour and Population Growth in Rural Asia'. *Development Change*. 13(4):587–610.

_____. 1994. *Children, Work and 'Child Labour': Changing Responses to the Employment of Children*. The Hague: Inst. Soc. Study. (Inaugural address). Development and Change. 25:849–78.

Whiting, B.B., ed. 1963. *Six Cultures: Studies of Child Rearing*. New York: Wiley.

Williams, S. 1993. *Child Workers in Portugal*. London: Anti-Slavery Institute.

Wyers, J. 1986. 'Child Labour in Brazilian Agriculture'. *Critical Anthropology*. 6(2):63–80.

Zelizer, V. 1994. *Pricing the Priceless Child, The Changing Social Value of Children*. Princeton, NJ: Princeton University Press.

Patterns of Literacy and their Social Context

JEAN DRÈZE

INTRODUCTION

India's proverbial diversity applies in particular to literacy and education. At one end of the scale, remaining uneducated is almost unthinkable for the Tamil Brahmin, or the Bengali Kayasth, or the Goan Christian. At the other end, literacy rates in 1981 were as low as 2.2 per cent among the Musahars of Bihar and 2.5 per cent among the Kalbelias of Rajasthan (for women, the corresponding literacy rates were below one per cent).[1]

For those who are at the receiving end of these massive inequalities, educational deprivation is a many-sided burden. It affects their employment opportunities, reduces their health achievements, exposes them to corruption and harassment, and generally undermines their ability to participate successfully in the modern economy and society. Indeed, literacy is a basic tool of self-defence in a world where social interaction often involves the written media, and the same can be said of numeracy and other skills acquired in the process of basic education. As Anand Chakravarti notes in a recent study of agricultural labour in Bihar, 'lack of education is a factor of overwhelming significance in emasculating the capacity of labourers in general to cope with the conditions of existence imposed upon them'.[2]

Literacy and education are also essential for the practice of democracy. If democracy is interpreted in the narrow sense of electoral participation, then widespread education is not a pre-condition for it.[3] But if it means sustained, informed, and equitable participation in democratic institutions (electoral campaigns, public debates, village panchayats, the legal system, and so on), then universal elementary education is clearly central to the democratic project. The exclusion of a large majority of the population from effective political participation is a crippling limitation of Indian democracy.

To illustrate, consider the current debate on economic reforms. While this debate superficially appears to be lively and inclusive, it actually involves a tiny fraction of the population. As several recent surveys have shown, most Indians do not even know that economic reforms are taking place.[4] People can hardly be expected to have a view on this matter, let alone take

This chapter was written before the 2001 census, and also before the publication of the 'Public Report on Basic Education in India' (PROBE Team, 1999). These and other recent studies have further enhanced our understanding of the literacy situation in India, and they also point to significant progress in this field in the 1990s. However, the basic issues discussed in this chapter retain their relevance.

active steps to oppose or support the reforms, if they have no awareness of what is going on. The recent public debate on India's achievements and failures after fifty years of independence has been no less elitist. The 'common man' (not to speak of the common woman) was nowhere to be seen, except in R.K. Laxman's refreshing cartoons.

This article focuses on the most elementary aspect of formal education, namely literacy. It begins, in the next section, with a brief recapitulation of the literacy situation in India today. We then proceed to examine various causes of educational deprivation among the disadvantaged sections of the population. Specific social disparities, relating in particular to caste and gender, are discussed in the penultimate section. This is also the occasion to note Himachal Pradesh's outstanding experience of educational advancement, which illustrates the mutually reinforcing effects of social equality and universal literacy. The last section presents some concluding remarks.

THE LITERACY SITUATION IN INDIA

At the time of the 1991 census, India's average literacy rate (defined as the proportion of literate persons in the age group of 7 and above) was 52 per cent. This is, of course, much higher than the corresponding figure of about 18 per cent at the time of independence, and vastly higher than India's literacy rate at the beginning of the twentieth century—around 5 per cent. Yet, the literacy situation in India remains unimpressive from several perspectives.

First, India has not done particularly well in comparative international terms. Here, a comparison with China is particularly relevant.[5] Careful examination of recent literacy rates in the older age groups suggests that, in the late 1940s, India and China had similar levels of literacy (see Figure 1). Today, however, China is far ahead of India, and even has literacy rates comparable to those of Kerala in the younger age groups. Comparisons with other east Asian countries, too, put India in a rather unfavourable light. Even in sub-Saharan Africa, average literacy rates are higher than in India (especially among women), according to World Bank data.[6]

Second, India still has a major problem of widespread illiteracy in the younger age groups, which has been largely resolved in many other developing countries. The issue is not just that a large number of Indian adults are non-literate, because they did not get a chance to go to school many years ago; even today, millions of children are deprived of that opportunity. Nearly half of all adolescent girls, for instance, were unable to read and write in 1991.

Third, there are sharp disparities of literacy rates between different sections of the population. The gender gap is particularly striking (Table 1). Important differences in literacy achievements also exist between rural and urban areas as well as between different regions and communities.[7] When these contrasts are considered together, the chances of being literate vary enormously between different social groups, from close to 100 per cent for urban males in Kerala to less than 5 per cent for scheduled-caste women in rural Rajasthan.

In assessing India's record in this field, it is useful to supplement literacy data with information on years of schooling. While 'total literacy' has become a focal point of public policy, it should be remembered that the Indian constitution directs all states to achieve much more: free and compulsory education for all children until the age of 14.[8] This roughly corresponds to eight years of schooling. In 1991, the proportion of adults who had actually completed eight years of schooling was as low as 30 per cent, with an even lower figure (16 per cent) for women.[9] Mean years of schooling were estimated at 2.4 years, compared with 5 years in China, 7 years in Sri Lanka, and 9 years in South Korea.[10]

In short, despite much improvement in the literacy situation since Independence, a sharp contrast remains between constitutional goals and practical achievements. It is no wonder that, in a recent poll of Delhi residents, 88 per cent of the respondents agreed with the statement that 'our country's biggest failure has been in the field of education'.[11]

CAUSES OF EDUCATIONAL DEPRIVATION

In order to understand why so many Indian children do not go to school, the first thing to recognize is that sending a child to school on a regular basis requires a great deal of effort, especially in underprivileged families. There has to be money for books, slates, fees, clothes, and other expenses. The child has to be freed from full-time domestic chores or other work requirements. He or she needs attention and encouragement in the morning, at the time of preparing to go to school, and perhaps help with homework. The parents have to be convinced that what the child learns is worthwhile. The child may have to overcome the fear of a hostile reception from teachers or fellow pupils. Last but not least, the interest of the child in learning has to be sustained. This whole chain of efforts is only as strong as its weakest link. The fact that leaving school is, for practical purposes, an irreversible step adds to the fragility of the schools' attendance process.

Three specific obstacles have been much discussed in the literature: low parental motivation; economic deprivation; and the poor quality of schooling. Each of these is briefly considered below.[12]

Parental Motivation

It is often asserted that Indian parents have little interest in education. This view has been particularly influential in official circles, where it provides a convenient rationalization of the state's failure to achieve universal elementary education in a reasonable time frame.[13] The myth of parental indifference, however, does not survive close scrutiny. Indeed, there is much evidence that an overwhelming majority of parents today, even among deprived sections of the population, attach great importance to the education of their children. To illustrate, one recent survey of the schooling situation in India's most educationally backward states found that the proportion of parents who considered it 'important' for a child to be educated was as high as 98 per cent for boy and 89 per cent for girls.[14] Further, educational aspirations were highly consistent with the constitutional goal of universal elementary education: only a small minority of respondents, for instance, aspired to fewer than 8 years of education for their sons or daughters. Only 3 per cent of parents were opposed to compulsory education at the primary level.

This is not to deny that lack of parental motivation may be an issue in specific contexts. Parental commitment to female education, in particular, is still rather inadequate in many areas (we shall return to the possible roots of this gender bias). And even parents who state that education is 'important' may not always translate that interest into practical efforts to send their children to school on a regular basis. Yet, it is important to take note of the generally positive disposition of most parents towards elementary education, and in particular, of the consistency between parental aspirations and the constitutional goal of eight years of education for all children.

It is also worth noting that parental attitudes towards education are far from immutable, and can be positively influenced through various means. For one thing, educational *aspirations* are not independent of the *opportunities* that people have (or perceive that they have). Attitudes towards education, especially female education, are also strongly influenced by cultural norms, role models, public discussions, and related factors. Indeed, educational aspirations and schooling decisions have a significant 'social' dimension. For instance, educational aspirations among parents and children of disadvantaged castes are bound to be influenced by *other* people's perceptions of the importance of education for the 'lower castes'. Ultimately, the task to be faced is not just to consolidate the motivation of individual parents, seen as isolated decision-makers, but to build a social consensus about the centrality of elementary education for every child's upbringing. The possibility of making rapid progress in that direction has been well illustrated in recent years in the context of the Total Literacy Campaign and related initiatives.[15]

Economic Deprivation

Poverty makes it harder to send a child to school in at least two ways. First, poor families sometimes depend on child labour for their survival. Second, poverty makes it harder to meet the direct costs of schooling.

Child labour is often seen as the main obstacle to universal schooling in India. In recent years, the movement against child labour has been particularly active in highlighting this problem. According to the Coalition Against Child Labour (1997), for instance, India has more than 60 million child labourers, working 12 hours a day on average. As one of the leading spokespersons of this movement recently put it, 'How can we make our country fully literate when 60 million of our children are engaged in full-time jobs as child labourers?'[16]

These figures may have some useful shock value, but their accuracy is another matter. In fact, studies of the time utilization of Indian children point to a very different assessment, namely that full-time workers account for a small proportion of out-of-school children.

To illustrate, Table 2 shows the distribution of children aged 5–14 by activity status according to the 1991 census. As the second column indicates, only 10 per cent of all out-of-school children in this age group were counted as 'workers' by the census enumerators.[17] Like all labour-force participation data, these figures have to be taken with a pinch of salt. It is quite likely, in particular, that domestic work is under-counted in these estimates. Recent research, however, has tended to corroborate the notion that productive work (*including* domestic work) accounts for only a small share of the overall time utilization of out-of-school children.[18] Bearing in mind that school hours are short and that schools are closed for about half of the days in the year in most Indian states, the proportion of children whose work activities are incompatible with that of the school is likely to be small.

It is also important to bear in mind that, when children work instead of going to school, the direction of causation need not run from child labour to non-attendance. In many cases, it is the other way round: drop out children take up productive work (of their own choice or through parental pressure) as a 'default occupation'. One recent case study of working children in Calcutta finds that two thirds of these children 'work as they have nothing else to do as the schools are not very attractive and teaching conditions are poor' (CINI-ASHA 1996). Similarly, Karin Kapadia (1997) observes that in rural Tamil Nadu 'it is very commonly the case that children are put to work by their parents to "keep them out of trouble" because they have dropped out of the hugely uninspiring (and underfunded) school system'.

In short, the role of child labour as an obstacle to universal schooling has often been over-emphasized. This is not to deny that India does have a serious problem of child labour, or to dismiss the vital role of the movement against child labour. The point is that it would be a mistake to regard child labour and educational deprivation as two sides of one coin, and even more of a mistake to see a simple causal link running from the former to the latter.[19]

Turning to direct costs, there is much evidence that elementary education in India is quite expensive, even in government schools. While the Constitution of India directs all states to provide 'free education', this term seems to have been interpreted by most state governments in the narrow sense that there should be no fees. A more pertinent interpretation is that elementary education should not involve any expenditure for the parents. In that broader sense, elementary education in India is far from free. According to one recent survey, sending a child to a government primary school in rural north India costs around Rs 360 a year on average, at 1996 prices.[20] This may look cheap, but poor parents are likely to differ. An agricultural labourer in Bihar, for instance, would have to spend more than a month's earnings each year just to keep two children in such a school.

School Quality

As we noted earlier, sending a child to school on a regular basis demands a good deal of effort, especially in poor families. The willingness of parents to make that effort depends a great deal on what they perceive to be getting in return. If there is little activity in the classroom, or if the child does not make any progress, the game may not seem worth the candle. Similarly, the willingness of the child herself to make the effort of going to school often depends on whether the classroom activities stimulate her interest. Thus, the quality of schooling has an important influence on school attendance. Indian schools, however, leave much to be desired, particularly in rural areas.

The low quality of schooling has many aspects. To start with, the infrastructure is grossly inadequate. At the time of the sixth All-India Educational Survey (1993), 27 per cent of primary schools in India had only one classroom (if any), 21 per cent had a single teacher, and more than 60 per cent had at most two teachers.[21] It is hard to see how minimal teaching standards can possibly be achieved in schools where a single teacher handles children belonging to five different grades in a single classroom.

Second, low levels of teacher accountability have seriously undermined the effectiveness of the schooling system. Parents have no means of keeping the teachers on their toes, and the formal inspection system is a poor substitute for their vigilance. Since teachers have permanent posts, with salaries unrelated to performance, they have little incentives for exerting themselves. The accountability problem has been further enhanced by the collective political power of the teaching profession.[22]

Third, teaching methods in Indian schools are often stultifying. This is so even in urban middle class schools, as the recent report on the 'burden of learning' (Government of India 1994) clearly illustrates. In rural schools, the problem tends to take a different form (for example, lack of teaching activity, rather than over-exacting curriculum), but with a similar result, namely that the interest of the child is not sustained. Lack of class-room activity, non-comprehension of what is taught, fear of beating or humiliation, and social discrimination in the classroom are common causes of child discouragement.

In the light of these and other aspects of the low quality of schooling, it is not surprising that pupil achievements are abysmally low.[23] Nor is it difficult to understand why parents and children often lose patience with the schooling system.

Discussion

We have focused on three distinct reasons why children might be out of school: inadequate parental motivation, economic deprivation, and the low quality of schooling. It is difficult, of course, to arrive at a precise assessment of the relative importance of these factors. In many cases, when a child drops out of school, some combination of these influences is at work. Further research is required to go much beyond this general statement.

Meanwhile, a few basic conclusions can be drawn. First, single-focus explanations (highlighting one particular cause of educational deprivation and ignoring the others), which are common in public debates, do not survive close scrutiny. Second, as far as male education is concerned, parental motivation is very high in most social groups. The main problem here is not lack of motivation, but the fact that the abysmal quality of schooling discourages parents and children from making the effort required to achieve regular school attendance. Third, in the case of female education, there is, in some circumstances, an additional issue of low parental motivation (on which more below). Fourth, there is growing evidence that child labour is not a major general obstacle against regular school attendance, even though work burdens do have an adverse effect on schooling opportunities for specific categories of children.

In a sense, these findings are good news. If it were the case that parents are not interested in education, or that children from poor families are too busy to go to school, there might be good grounds for concern about the possibility of universalizing elementary education in a reasonable time frame. Contrary to this diagnosis, there is every reason to expect parents and children to respond positively to public initiatives aimed at facilitating their involvement in the schooling system. That expectation is amply confirmed by recent experience.

EDUCATIONAL DISPARITIES

As noted in the introduction, schooling opportunities in India are highly unequal. At one end of the scale, the offspring of the urban elite are likely to reach prestigious university colleges, with a good prospect of further studies abroad. At the other end, a girl born in a poor family in rural Rajasthan has a slim chance of entering (let alone completing) primary school. These educational disparities, which *contribute a* great deal to the persistence of massive inequalities in Indian society, also largely *derive* from more fundamental inequalities such as those of *class*, *caste*, and *gender*. This section explores some of these connections.

Gender Bias

It is possible to link the neglect of female education in India (especially in the northern region) with specific social practices that create deep asymmetries between male and female education. Prominent among these social practices are the gender division of labour and the kinship system.

The gender division of labour confines many adult women to household work (and some family labour in agriculture). It is arguable that literacy and education are no less useful in these activities than in, say, white-collar employment. There is overwhelming evidence, for instance, that maternal education has a strong positive influence on child health.[24] The benefits of female education at home, however, are often less clearly perceived, and less strongly valued, than the economic returns to male education (for example, in terms of better employment and higher earnings). Hence the common statement, 'what is the point of educating our daughter, in any case after she grows up she will be cooking *rotis*?' (quoted in Senapaty 1997).

The kinship system, in many parts of India, involves the separation of an adult woman from her parents after her marriage, when she joins her husband's family. This implies that educating a daughter is of little benefit from the point of view of parental self-interest (with one qualification, discussed below). The situation is very different in the case of sons, since educated sons are expected to get better jobs and to look after their aged parents. This may seem like a cynical view of parental motivation for education, but there is much evidence that employment opportunities and old-age security do play a major role in schooling decisions.[25] The fact that educating a daughter does not bring any tangible benefits to her parents, and is no less costly than educating a son, may well be the most important cause of gender bias in schooling opportunities.

Aside from these basic problems, various other considerations discourage Indian parents from sending their daughters to school. For instance, parents are often reluctant to let their daughters wander outside the village. This prevents many girls from studying beyond the primary level, given that upper-primary schools are often unavailable within the village. Similarly, many parents rely on their elder daughters to look after young siblings (here again the gender division of labour is at work).

Against this background, the really interesting question is not so much why Indian parents show little interest in female education (that is relatively easy to understand), but rather why so many of them do send their daughters to school. One answer is that they do so out of concern for their daughters' well-being. This is certainly plausible, yet this explanation does not really help to understand variations in female school attendance between social groups and over time.

A complementary explanation is that, as the level of *male* education rises in a particular community, parents develop more positive attitudes towards female education. One specific reason for this arises from the relationship between female education and marriage prospects. Indian men often expect their spouse to be a little less educated than they are themselves, without the gap being too large. In a community with low levels of male education, a relatively well-educated daughter is often considered as a burden, because she may be difficult to marry.[26] In communities with high levels of male education, however, *uneducated* daughters may become a liability, for the same reason. In such communities, education is often considered (up to a point) to improve a daughter's marriage prospects.[27] Given that a daughter's marriage is often regarded as the overriding goal of her upbringing, these links between female education and marriage prospects are likely to have a significant influence on schooling decisions.

The notion that female literacy in India is largely a by-product of male literacy may seem depressing. However, we are talking here of historical patterns, not of what can be achieved today through public action. As far as the latter is concerned, there is much evidence that public campaigns can have a strong influence on social attitudes towards female education, and reduce the gender gap in school opportunities. The experience of the Total Literacy Campaign, in districts where it has received active support from the local administration and popular organizations, is quite encouraging in this regard.[28] Even in India as a whole, the gender gap in literacy has narrowed quite rapidly in recent years, and is likely to narrow further in the near future.

Caste and Tribe

The fact that literacy rates among disadvantaged castes (particularly the 'scheduled castes') are much lower than average is well-known. What is less clear is why this contrast happens to be so sharp and resilient, even when different castes share the same schooling facilities. Economic deprivation among the disadvantaged castes helps to explain this pattern, but there is much evidence of a strong caste bias in literacy rates even at a given level of income.[29]

This bias has several possible roots. First, the traditional upper-caste view that education is not appropriate for the 'lower' castes continues to have some social influence. This view is bound to reduce the educational aspirations of children from the disadvantaged castes, and the parental and social support they receive in pursuit of these aspirations.

Second, there may be objective differences in economic and other returns to education for different castes. For instance, an educated boy from an upper-caste family with good social connections often has better chances of finding a well-paid job than a low-caste boy with similar educational qualifications.[30]

Third, children from disadvantaged castes are still discriminated against within the schooling system. Blatant forms of caste-based discrimination (for example, denying school facilities to certain castes) have by and large disappeared, but more subtle forms of discrimination remain widespread. Some examples include discrimination against scheduled-caste settlements in the location of schools, teachers refusing to touch low-caste children, children from particular castes being special targets of verbal abuse and physical punishment by the teachers, and low-caste children being frequently beaten by higher-caste classmates.[31]

These causes of educational deprivation also apply, in many cases, to tribal communities. Tribal education, however, has also raised some further issues. One of these is the relevance of modern education, including literacy, to tribal children. On this, a common view is that tribal communities do not really 'need' modern education, or that they consider it as irrelevant. A variant of this theme is that tribal people have their own 'mode of knowledge', which modern education threatens to destroy. Another variant is that interest in education is inherently low among tribal communities.[32]

Little evidence, however, has been produced to substantiate the view that the educational needs and aspirations of tribal children are fundamentally different from those of other children. Of course, the school curriculum and teaching methods should be sensitive to the culture of tribal children—indeed of *all* children. But recognizing this basic pedagogical principle (and the fact that it is routinely overlooked in the schooling system today) is not the same as dismissing the relevance of modern education for tribal children. That dismissive view is far from widespread among tribal communities themselves, judging from the fact that tribal children have often taken to schooling like duck to water in areas where well-functioning educational facilities have been made available to them—notably in the north-eastern region, in the tribal districts of Himachal Pradesh, and in parts of southern Bihar and eastern Madhya Pradesh. The tremendous response of tribal communities in Madhya Pradesh to the 'education guarantee scheme' initiated in 1997 is another case in point.

These positive experiences suggest that the basic cause of educational deprivation among tribal communities is not so much a fundamental lack of interest in education on their part, as the dismal state of schooling facilities in most tribal areas. Until recently, for instance, single-teacher schools were the norm in these areas (when no schools existed at all). The general problem of official neglect of elementary education has tended to take an extreme form in tribal areas, partly due to the political marginalization of tribal communities in most Indian states.

Some Regional Contrasts

Regional contrasts in literacy largely follow familiar patterns that also apply to many other indicators of 'social development' in India (see map): Kerala is far ahead; the southern states, with the notable exception of Andhra Pradesh, fare better than the northern region; and the large north Indian states (Bihar, Madhya Pradesh, Rajasthan, and Uttar Pradesh) lag behind all others. Explaining these broad regional contrasts would call for historical enquiry of a kind that cannot be attempted in this short paper.[33] The weight of the historical legacy is evident from the fact that similar regional patterns already applied at the time of independence, and even much earlier.

Historical legacy is much less of an explanation for another (relatively little noticed) aspect of India's literacy map, namely the impressive achievements of the Himalayan region. Much of that region was considered as an underdeveloped backyard fifty years ago. Today, most Himalayan districts have literacy rates well above the all-India average, especially in the younger age groups.[34] Within the region, an outstanding case of successful expansion of literacy is Himachal Pradesh.

Starting with similar levels of literacy as, say, Bihar or Uttar Pradesh in the early fifties, Himachal Pradesh has virtually caught up with Kerala within forty years (see Figure 3). In 1991, literacy rates in the 10–14 age group in Himachal Pradesh were as high as 95 per cent for males and 86 per cent for females. And in 1992–3, 91 per cent of all children in the 6–14 age group were attending school (International Institute for Population Sciences 1995: 56).

In several respects, the experience of literacy expansion in Himachal Pradesh in recent decades is even more impressive than that of Kerala. First, the transition from mass illiteracy to near-universal primary education has taken place over a much shorter period of time in Himachal Pradesh. Second, educational expansion in Himachal Pradesh has been based almost entirely on government schools, with relatively little contribution from private schools, missionary organizations and related institutions. Third, Himachal Pradesh has an unfavourable topography; in particular, villages are scattered over large areas with poor connections (in sharp contrast with Kerala, where settlement patterns have been favourable to the expansion of public services in rural areas). Fourth, child labour used to play an important role in Himachal Pradesh's economy, partly due to the dependence of many households on environmental resources and also (in the case of girls) to the fact that a high proportion of adult women work outside the household.

The foundations of this success have not been fully explored, and this is not the place to do so. Let me just mention one contributing factor which might be of interest to sociologists and social anthropologists: the relatively equal social structure of village communities in Himachal Pradesh (or for that matter in many other parts of the Himalayan region). This observation refers in particular to the absence of sharp inequalities of land ownership (the incidence of landlessness, for instance, is very low in Himachal Pradesh); to the relatively narrow social distance between different castes; and to the high participation of women in social life outside the household.[35] This is not to say that hill villages are 'egalitarian'. Nevertheless, the divisions of class, caste and gender that have been so pernicious elsewhere in north India tend to be less pronounced in this region. In particular, these social divisions do not preclude a strong sense of collective interests at the village level.[36]

There are several reasons why the absence of sharp social disparities might be expected to facilitate the spread of education. First, social equality is conducive to the emergence of consensual social norms on educational matters. Elsewhere in north India, it is perfectly possible for children of one caste to go to school while children of another caste—in the same village— are deprived of that opportunity. In fact, contrasts of this type are necessary to sustain the inegalitarian social order. In Himachal Pradesh, by contrast, the notion that schooling is an essential part of every child's upbringing has acquired the character of a widely-shared social norm.

Second, social equality is likely to facilitate cooperative action for the provision of local public services, including schooling facilities. To illustrate, parents in Himachal Pradesh often cooperate to repair the village school, a rare event in other north Indian states (Bhatty et al. 1997). Their collective vigilance has also played an important role in preserving the accountability of the schooling system.

Third, the absence of sharp social disparities can help to ensure that the demands made on the state by local communities and their representatives are oriented to basic social needs. In highly inegalitarian states such as Bihar and Uttar Pradesh, village leaders act as powerful intermediaries between the state and the people, and routinely use state resources as instruments of patronage and individual gain (Drèze and Gazdar 1997). In Himachal Pradesh, village leaders are more likely to clamour for collective facilities such as roads, electricity, drinking water and primary schools.[37]

These remarks are not intended to 'explain' Himachal Pradesh's success on their own. Other factors, such as rapid economic growth and a high level of central-government assistance, have also contributed. The preceding line of enquiry, however, does seem to be worth pursuing, especially because it helps to explain the rapid progress of education not only in Himachal Pradesh but also in other parts of the Himalayan region.

CONCLUDING REMARKS

From this account it should be clear that literacy achievements in India depend crucially on the social context: the gender division of labour, the kinship system, caste-related norms, economic entitlements, and so on. The statement is perhaps trivial, but it is worth noting that the overwhelming context-dependence of literacy achievements conflicts with the notion of elementary education as a basic right of all citizens.

As this book goes to press, the results of the 2001 census are putting the literacy situation in India in a fresh light. On the one hand, the basic patterns identified in this chapter (including the fundamental connection between educational deprivation and social inequality) continue to apply. On the other hand, there is evidence of accelerated progress towards universal elementary education in the 1990s. Literacy rates and school participation have substantially improved, the gender bias in educational achievements has narrowed, and some of the 'laggard' states (notably Rajasthan and Madhya Pradesh) are rapidly catching up.

Consolidating and extending these achievements calls for wider acknowledgement of elementary education as a fundamental right of all citizens. There has been some positive changes in this respect in recent years. The notion that every child has an inalienable right to learn is much more widely accepted today than it was (say) ten years ago, when the main focus of attention was on the pros and cons of 'compulsory education'. As things stand, the right to education is nowhere near being realized, but the 1990s have demonstrated the *possibility* of rapid progress in this field—a possibility that remains to be seized in full.

ENDNOTES

1. K.S. Singh (1993), pp. 658 and 966.
2. Anand Chakravarti (1997), p. 359.

3. Indeed, recent election studies conducted by the Centre for the Study of Developing Societies indicate that voter turnouts are, if anything, *lower* than average among relatively well-educated sections of the population (Yogendra Yadav, 2000).

4. See for example, Yogendra Yadav (1996) and The World Bank (1996). Those who claim some knowledge of the reforms often turn out, on further probing, to have something else in mind. Some respondents, for instance, believe that economic reforms are about the introduction of cooperative farming, or about the recent wave of corruption in high places (Yogendra Yadav, personal communication).

5. For a more detailed comparison, see Drèze and Loh (1995).

6. See for example, *World Development Report 1997*, pp. 226-7.

7. P.N. Tyagi (1993) provides useful data on regional and social disparities in literacy rates.

8. Indian Constitution, Directive Principles, Article 45. The target date for this goal (1960 according to the constitution) has been postponed again and again. The latest target date is 2005.

9. Calculated from unpublished 1991 census data.

10. *Human Development Report 1994*, p. 146.

11. *Sunday Times* (New Delhi), 21 September 1994, p. 24. In another recent poll of youth in major cities (reported in *The Times of India*, 15 August 1997), the respondents were asked to identify 'the most important thing in life'. 'Knowledge' was the most frequent answer (48 per cent of all responses), far ahead of 'love' (20 per cent), not to speak of 'money' (18 per cent).

12. For a more detailed examination of the evidence, see Kiran Bhatty (1998).

13. This tradition was already well established during the colonial period. Some observers went so far as to argue that active resistance to education was common: 'It may be stated generally that among the mass of people there is no desire for learning. The Jats as a body are not only illiterate but actually opposed to education, and in Jat villages thriving schools are very seldom to be found.' (Government of India 1922: 111). Interestingly, the same Jats now seem to have a passion for education, and are even deeply involved in the teaching profession (Craig Jeffrey, personal communication based on ongoing field work; see also Jeffery and Jeffery 1994).

14. See Bhatty *et al.* (1997).

15. See particularly Ghosh *et al.* (1994), who report that 'tremendous enhancement of demand for primary education and enrolment of children in primary schools have been noticed in many literacy campaign districts' (p. 23).

16. Kailash Satyarthi, quoted in *National Herald*, 2 January 1997.

17. For a detailed discussion of this pattern, see D.P. Chaudhri (1996).

18. See D.P. Chaudhri (1996), National Council of Applied Economic Research (1996, 1997), Preet Rustagi (1996), Rukmini Banerji (1997), Kiran Bhatty et al. (1997), Arup Maharatna (1997), R. Nagarajan (1997), National Sample Survey Organisation (1997), among others; also Manabi Majumdar (1998).

19. Such a causal link may however apply to specific categories of children, such as children of migrant labourers and eldest daughters in poor families.

20. See Bhatty *et al.* (1997). This figure is broadly consistent with independent estimates of the costs of schooling based on recent surveys by the National Council of Applied Economic Research and the National Sample Survey Organisation. On the latter, see also Tilak (1996), and the survey reports cited there.

21. Calculated from National Council of Educational Research and Training (1997). The schooling infrastructure has improved in recent years, but it remains completely out of line with the constitutional goal of universal education until the age of 14 (see for example, Kiran Bhatty et al. 1997).

22. Teachers, for their part, often complain about their difficult work environment, their low status in the administrative hierarchy, and the heavy burden of non-teaching duties. These complaints are frequently justified, and teachers do need better support. Enhanced accountability and improved support are best seen as complementary requirements of higher teaching standards.

23. In some schools, many pupils are still unable to read or write even after four or five years or schooling (Bhatty et al. 1997; Kapadia 1997). On pupil achievements, see also Govinda and Varghese (1993) and Sharma (1998), among others.

24. See Murthi et al. (1995), and the literature cited there.

25. See for example, Caldwell *et al.* (1985), Kashinath Bhoosnurmath (1991), Jeffery and Jeffery (1994), Bhatty et al. (1997), and the literature cited in Bhatty (1998).

26. Caldwell et al. (1985), for instance, note that in rural Karnataka some parents are worried that education 'would make daughters unmarriageable', because a woman 'must be married to a male with at least as much education'. For similar observations elsewhere, see also Committee on the Status of Women in India (1974:74), A. Almeida (1978:264), Seetharamu and Ushadevi (1985), van Bastelaer (1986:61), Khan (1993), among others.

27. See for example, Jeffery and Jeffery (1994), Jejeebhoy and Kulkarni (1989), Minturn and Kapoor (1993), Ursula Sharma (1980).

28. See particularly Ghosh et al. (1994).

29. See Drèze and Sharma (1998), Jayachandran (1997), Labenne (1995).

30. Caste-based reservation policies have probably reduced this advantage, without eliminating it. On the relationship between positive discrimination and investment in 'human capital', see Coate and Loury (1993); also Montgomery (1995) and the literature cited there.

31. For some illustrations, see Shami (1992:26), Varma (1992), Bashir et al. (1993:20-21), Lata (1995:32), Sinha and Sinha (1995), Drèze and Sharma (1998), Mehrotra (forthcoming).

32. Under the title 'why tribal children may not like school', for instance, the World Bank highlights the findings of a recent study of primary education in Andhra Pradesh, according to which 'a third of the children of school age did not attend school, preferring instead to spend their time moving freely around, swimming in ponds and streams, catching fish, climbing trees, hunting birds, collecting berries, riding on buffaloes, etc.' (World Bank 1997: 137). This rosy picture undoubtedly applies to some children, but it is only a small part of the overall story of tribal exclusion from the schooling system.

33. For an early interpretation of these regional patterns, see Rudolph and Rudolph (1972); also David Sopher (1980).

34. It is also worth noting that, according to one recent World Bank survey, literacy rates in the younger age groups in Nepal are now considerably higher than in the large north Indian states. In other words, Nepal seems to fit in the general pattern of rapid educational progress in the Himalayan region (bearing in mind that literacy rates in Nepal used to be extremely low, even by South Asian standards).

35. On these aspects of village communities in Himachal Pradesh and the neighbouring Uttar Pradesh hills, see Berreman (1972), Parmar (1979), Guha (1989), Saraswat and Sikka (1990), Sax (1991), Sikka and Singh (1992), Moller (1993), Keith-Krelik (1995), and Bondroit (1998), among others. These studies are best read along with similar studies for other regions, since the point being made here is not that local social inequalities in Himachal Pradesh are unimportant, but rather that they are *less* significant than in many other parts of India.

36. The sense of village community, so weak elsewhere in India (Dumont 1980), appears to be quite strong in the hill region. Institutions and rituals such as village festivals, village deities and even village pilgrimages help to consolidate these bonds. See for example, Sax (1991), chapter 2.

37. Prof. N.S. Bisht (Department of Economics, Himachal Pradesh University), personal communication based on first-hand experience in Himachal Pradesh and Uttar Pradesh.

REFERENCES

Almeida, A. 1978. 'The Gift of a Bride: Sociological Implications of the Dowry System in Goa'. Université Catholique de Louvain, Louvain-la-Neuve, Belgium. Mimeo.

Baland, Jean-Marie and Platteau, Jean-Philippe. 1995. 'Does Heterogeneity Hinder Collective Action?' Discussion Paper No. 146, Centre de Recherche en Economie du Dévelopment, Université de Namur, Belgium.

———. 1997. 'Wealth Inequality and Efficiency of the Commons'. Discussion Paper No. 193, Centre de Recherche en Economie du Dévelopment, Université de Namur, Belgium.

Banerji, Rukmini. 1997. 'Why Don't Children Complete Primary School? A Case Study of a Low-Income Neighbourhood in Delhi'. *Economic and Political Weekly.* 32(32):9 August.

Bashir, Sajitha, et al. 1993. *Education for All: Baseline Survey of Three Districts of Uttar Pradesh, India.* Vol. 2. New Delhi: New Concept Consultancy Services.

Berreman, Gerald D. 1972. *Hindus of the Himalayas: Ethnography and Change.* 2nd ed. Delhi: Oxford University Press.

Bhatty, Kiran. 1998: 'Educational Deprivation in India: A Survey of Field Investigations'. *Economic and Political Weekly,* 33(27):1731–40.

Bhatty, K., A. De, J.P. Drèze, A.K. Shiva Kumar, A. Mahajan, C. Noronha, A. Rampal, Pushpendra and M. Samson. 1997. 'Class Struggle'. *India Today.* 13 October.

Bhoosnurmath, Kashinath. 1991. 'People's Perception of Importance of Education: A Field Experience in Dehradun District'. *The Administrator.* 36.

Bondroit, Marie-Eve. 1998. 'Les Aspects Economiques et Culturels Liés a l' Education des Filles en Inde'. M.A. dissertation, Faculté des Sciences Economiques, Université de Namur, Belgium.

Caldwell, J.C., P.H. Reddy and P. Caldwell. 1985. 'Educational Transition in Rural South India'. *Population and Development Review.* 11(1):29–51.

Chakravarti, Anand. 1997. 'Social Power and Everyday Class Relations: Agrarian Tansformation in North Bihar'. Delhi School of Economics. Mimeo. To be published as a monograph.

Chaudhri, D.P. 1996. *A Dynamic Profile of Child Labour in India, 1951–1991.* New Delhi: International Labour Organization.

CINI-ASHA. 1996. 'Our Present Day Understanding of Child Labour Issues'. *The Administrator.* 16:169–74.

Coalition Against Child Labour. 1997. 'Public Hearing on Child Labour: Reference Kit'. Document prepared for the 2nd National Convention of Child Labourers. 30–31 March 1997. New Delhi.

Coate, S. and G. Loury. 1993. 'Will Affirmative-Action Policies Eliminate Negative Stereotypes?' *American Economic Review.* 83:1220–40.

Committee on the Status of Women in India. 1974. *Towards Equality.* New Delhi: Ministry of Education and Social Welfare.

Drèze, Jean, and Amartya Sen. 1995. *India: Economic Development and Social Opportunity.* Delhi and Oxford: Oxford University Press.

———. eds 1997. *Indian Development: Selected Regional Perspectives.* Delhi and Oxford: Oxford University Press.

Drèze, Jean and Haris Gazdar. 1997. 'Uttar Pradesh: The Burden of Inertia'. In Jean Drèze and Amartya Sen, eds, *Indian Development: Selected Regional Perspectives.* 33–128. Delhi and Oxford: Oxford University Press.

Drèze, Jean and Jackie Loh. 1995. 'Literacy in India and China'. *Economic and Political Weekly.* 11 November. 30(45) 2868–78.

Drèze, Jean and Naresh Sharma. 1998. 'Palanpur: Population, Society, Economy'. In P. Lanjouw and N. Stern, eds, *Economic Development in Palanpur Over Five Decades.* 3–113. Delhi and Oxford: Oxford University Press.

Dumont, Louis. 1980. *Homo Hierarchicus.* Revised ed. Chicago: University of Chicago Press.

Ghosh, A., U.R. Ananthamurthy, A. Béteille, S.M. Kansal, V. Mazumdar and A. Vanaik. 1994. 'Evaluation of Literacy Campaigns in India'. Report of an independent Expert Group appointed by the Ministry of Human Resource Development. New Delhi: Ministry of Human Resource Development.

Government of India. 1922. *District Gazetteer of the United Provinces of Agra and Oudh. Meerut*. Vol. 4. Comp. and ed. H.R. Nevill. Delhi.

Government of India. 1987. 'Social and Cultural Tables'. *Census of India 1981, ser. 1 (India), pt. IV-A.* New Delhi: Office of the Registrar General.

Government of India. 1994. *Learning Without Burden: Report of the National Advisory Committee appointed by the Ministry of Human Resource Development*. New Delhi: Ministry of Human Resource Development.

Govinda, R. and N.V. Varghese. 1993. 'Quality of Primary Schooling: An Empirical Study'. *Journal of Educational Planning and Administration*. 1.

Guha, Ramachandra. 1989. *The Unquiet Woods: Ecological Change and Peasant Resistance in the Himalaya*. Delhi: Oxford University Press.

International Institute for Population Sciences. 1995. *National Family Health Survey 1992–3*. Bombay: IIPS.

Jayachandran, Usha. 1997. 'The Determinants of Primary Education in India'. M. Phil. thesis, Department of Economics, Delhi School of Economics.

Jeffery, Patricia, and Roger Jeffery. 1994. 'Killing My Heart's Desire: Education and Female Autonomy in Rural North India'. In Nita Kumar, ed., *Women as Subjects: South Asian Histories*. 125–7. London: University Press of Virginia.

Jejeebhoy, S. and S. Kulkarni. 1989. 'Demand for Children and Reproductive Motivation: Empirical Observations from Rural Maharashtra'. In S.N. Singh, eds, *Population Transition in India*. 107–21. New Delhi: B.R. Publishing.

Kapadia, Karin. 1997. 'Emancipatory Processes in Rural Tamil Nadu Today: An Anthropological Study of Discourse and Practice Relating to Rights'. Research proposal, International Institute of Asian Studies, Amsterdam.

Keith-Krelik, Yasmin. 1995. 'Development, for Better or Worse: A Case Study on the Effects of Development on the Social and Cultural Environment of Spiti'. Unpublished dissertation, Department of Politics, University of Newcastle-upon-Tyne.

Khan, Sharukh R. 1993. 'South Asia'. In E. King, and A. Hill, eds, *Women's Education in Developing Countries: Barriers, Benefits and Policy*. Baltimore: Johns Hopkins University Press.

Labenne, Sophie. 1995. 'Analyse Econométrique du Travail des Enfants en Inde'. M.Sc. thesis, Department of Economics, Université de Namur, Belgium.

Lata, Divya. 1995. 'An Assessment of Early Child Care and Education Programmes Supported by SCF in India'. New Delhi: Save the Children Fund (UK). Mimeo.

Maharatna, Arup. 1997. 'Children's Work, Activities, Surplus Labour and Fertility: A Case Study of Six Villages in Birbhum'. *Economic and Political Weekly*. 32(7):363–69.

Majumdar, Manabi. 1998. 'Child Labor as a Human Security Problem: Evidence From India'. Harvard University: Harvard Center for Population and Development Studies. Mimeo.

Mehrotra, Nidhi. (Forthcoming), 'Primary Schooling in Rural India: Determinants of Demand'. Ph.D. thesis, University of Chicago.

Minturn, Leigh and Swaran Kapoor. 1993. *Sita's Daughters: Coming Out of Purdah, The Rajput Women of Khalapur Revisited*. New York: Oxford University Press.

Moller, Joanne. 1993. 'Inside and Outside: Conceptual Continuities from Household to Region in Kumaon, North India'. Ph.D. thesis. London School of Economics.

Montgomery. 1995. 'Affirmative Action and Reservations in the American and Indian Labor Markets: Are They Really That Bad?' University of Maryland, College Park. Mimeo.

Murthi, M., A.C. Guio and J.P. Drèze. 1995. 'Mortality, Fertility and Gender Bias in India: A District Level Analysis'. *Population and Development Review*. 21(4):745–82.

Nagarajan, R. 1997. 'Landholding, Child Labour and Schooling'. *Journal of Rural Development*. 16(2):193–217.

National Council of Applied Economic Research. 1996. *Human Development Profile of India. vol. II: Statistical Tables.* New Delhi: NCAER.

National Council of Applied Economic Research. 1997. 'Time Utilization of Children'. (provisional tables). MIMAP project. New Delhi: NCAER.

National Council of Educational Research and Training. 1997. *Sixth All-India Educational Survey.* New Delhi: NCERT.

National Sample Survey Organisation. 1997. 'Economic Activities and School Attendance by Children in India'. Revised Report No. 412 (based on the 50th round, 1993–4). New Delhi: NSSO.

Parmar, H.S. 1979. 'Subsistence Economy of Rural Himachal Pradesh: A Case Study of Three Small Villages'. *Economic Affairs.* 24(10–12):249–55.

PROBE Team. 1999. *Public Report on Basic Education in India.* New Delhi: Oxford University Press.

Rudolph. S.H., and L.I. Rudolph, eds. 1972. *Education and Politics in India: Studies in Organization, Society, and Policy.* Cambridge, MA: Harvard University Press.

Rustagi, Preet. 1996. 'The Structure and Dynamics of Indian Rural Labour Market'. Ph.D. thesis, Centre for Economic Studies and Planning, Jawaharlal Nehru University.

Saraswat, S.P., and B.K. Sikka. 1990. *Socio-economic Survey of an Affluent Village in Himachal Pradesh (A Study of Village Kiari in District Shimla).* Shimla: Agro-Economic Research Centre, Himachal Pradesh University.

Sax, W. 1991. *Mountain Goddess: Gender and Politics in a Himalayan Pilgrimage.* New York: Oxford University Press.

Seetharamu, A.S., and M.D. Ushadevi. 1985. *Education in Rural Areas: Constraints and Prospects.* New Delhi: Ashish Publishing House.

Senapaty, Manju. 1997. 'Gender Implications of Economic Reforms in the Education Sector in India: Case of Haryana and Madhya Pradesh'. Ph.D. dissertation, University of Manchester.

Shami, N. 1992. 'Socio-Economic Survey of Village Patna Khurd'. Mussoorie: Lal Bahadur Shastri National Academy of Administration.

Sharma, Rashmi. 1998. 'Universal Elementary Education: The Question of "How"'. *Economic and Political Weekly.* 27 June. 33(26):160–47.

Sharma, Ursula. 1980. *Women, Work and Property in North-West India.* London: Tavistock.

Sikka, B.K. and D.V. Singh. 1992. 'Malana: An Oldest Democracy Sustainability Issues in Village Economy (Himachal Pradesh)'. Himachal Pradesh University, Simla: Agro-Economic Research Centre. Mimeo.

Singh, K.S. 1993. *The Scheduled Castes.* New Delhi: Oxford University Press.

Sinha, Amarjeet, and Ajay Sinha. 1995. 'Primary Schooling in Northern India: A Field Investigation'. Centre for Sustainable Development, Lal Bahadur Shastri National Academy of Administration, Mussoorie. Mimeo.

Sopher, David, ed. 1980. *An Exploration of India: Geographical Perspectives on Society and Culture.* Ithaca, NY: Cornell University Press.

State Statistical Bureau. 1985. *1982 Population Census of China.* Chinese edition. Beijing: Population Census Office.

Tilak, J.B.G. 1996. 'How Free is Free Primary Education in India?' *Economic and Political Weekly.* 31(5):275–82.

Tyagi, P.N. 1993. *Education for All: A Graphic Presentation.* 2nd ed. New Delhi: National Institute of Educational Planning and Administration.

UNICEF. 1997. *The State of the World's Children 1997.* Oxford and New York: Oxford University Press.

van Bastelaer, Thierry. 1986. 'Essai d'Analyse des Systèmes de Paiements de Mariage: Le Cas de l'Inde'. M.Sc. thesis, Facultés des Sciences Economiques et Sociales, Universite de Namur, Belgium.

Varma, Jyotsna. 1992. 'Lanka Kachuara: A Village Divide'. Lal Bahadur Shastri National Academy of Administration, Mussoorie. Mimeo.

Visaria, P., A. Gumber and L. Visaria. 1993. 'Literacy and Primary Education in India, 1980–81 to 1991: Differentials and Determinants'. *Journal of Educational Planning and Administration*. 7:13–62.

World Bank. 1996. Background papers on economic reforms and rural poverty. Prepared for the 1996 *Country Economic Memorandum*. Washington DC: World Bank.

World Bank. 1997. *Primary Education in India*. Washington, DC: World Bank.

Yadav, Yogendra. 1996. 'The Maturing of a Democracy'. *India Today*. 31 August.

_____. 2000. 'Understanding the Second Democratic Upsurge'. In F. Frankel, R.Z. Hasan, and R. Bhargava, eds., *Transforming India: Social and Political Dynamics of Democracy*. Oxford: Oxford University Press.

TABLES

Table 1: Educational Achievements in India, 1991

	Female	Male	Persons
Literacy rate (%)			
Age 7+	39	64	52
Age 15–19	55	75	66
Mean years of schooling (age 25+)	1.2	3.5	2.4
Median years of schooling[a] (age 6+)	0.0	4.8	2.5
Proportion of adults (age 20+) who have Completed 8 years of education (%)	16	44	30

[a]1992–3.

Sources : Census of India 1991; International Institute for Population Sciences (1995), Table 3.9; *Human Development Report 1994*, p. 147. The literacy rates in the 15–19 age group have been calculated from unpublished 1991 census data, kindly supplied by the Office of the Registrar General; similarly with the proportion of adults who have completed eight years of education (strictly speaking, this refers to the completion of 'middle school and above').

Table 2: Child Work and School Attendance, 1991
(number of children aged 5–14 in different activity groups)

	Attending school (000s)	Not attending school (000s)	Total (000s)
Workers[a]	497 (0.5)	10,788(10.2)	11,285 (5.4)
Non-workers	103,762 (99.5)	94,938(89.8)	198,701(94.6)
Total	104,259	105,726	209,986

[a] Both 'main' and 'marginal'.

Source : Census of India 1991, Social and Cultural Tables, Part IV, Table C-4. Figures in brackets are percentages of the column total.

V
Economic and Political Life

Agrarian Structures and Their Transformations

SURINDER JODHKA

All economic activity is carried out in a framework of social relationships. Production is organized socially, markets function as social institutions, and consumption patterns are shaped by social norms and cultural values. Agriculture is no exception. The institutional framework of agricultural production determines how and by whom land is cultivated, what kinds of crops can be produced and for what purpose, how food and agricultural incomes can be distributed, and in what way or on what terms the agrarian sector is linked to rest of the economy/society.

However, agrarian structures and their transformations have not been the major concern of sociologists and social anthropologists. Western sociology, since the days of its classical traditions, has remained preoccupied with the study of social life in urban-industrial societies. As Shanin rightly points out, in its most fundamental self-image, the western capitalist world defined itself as a 'world without peasants'. The division of societies into 'modern' and 'backward' in the evolutionist schema of early social theory also meant that conceptually the agrarian populations, or the peasants, were reduced to an unspecified part of the mixed bag of 'remainders of the past' (Shanin 1987: 468).

In their search for 'pure' and 'primitive' cultures, early practitioners of social anthropology— the discipline that was supposed to study 'pre-modern' societies—invariably chose the pre-agrarian 'tribal/folk communities' for their field studies. Even when they began to look at the 'village', they viewed it as a closed, unchanging community of 'ascriptive groupings' organized around a normative belief system that essentialized it into an 'oppositional other' of the western type of modern urban societies (Inden 1990).

It was outside the mainstream western tradition of social sciences, in peripheral eastern and central Europe, that the 'agrarian question' became important on the political and intellectual agenda. The famous debate between the populist thinkers led by the Russian economist Chayanov (1987) on the one side, and the Marxist class analyses of the Russian countryside by Lenin (1899; 1908) along with Kautsky's work on the 'agrarian question' (Banaji 1976) on the other, laid the foundation of what later came to be known as 'agrarian studies'.

Though the 'Russian debate' during the early twentieth century made substantial contributions to the field, 'agrarian studies' could really take off only after the Second World War. The emergence of the 'new states' following decolonization during the post-War period played an important role in changing the research agenda of the social sciences. The most characteristic

—

feature of the newly emerged 'Third World' countries was the dependence of large proportions of their populations on a 'stagnant' agrarian sector. The struggle for freedom from colonial rule had also developed new aspirations among the 'masses' and the 'elites' of these societies. In some of these struggles, the peasantry had played a crucial role. Thus the primary agenda for the new political regimes was the transformation of their 'backward' and stagnant economies. Though the strategies and priorities differed, 'modernization' and 'development' became common programmes in most Third World countries. It was in this historical context that 'development studies' emerged as one of the most important areas of interest in the global academy.

Since a large majority of the populations in Third World societies were directly dependent on agriculture, understanding the prevailing structures of agrarian relations and working out ways and means of transforming them emerged as important priorities within 'development studies'. Western political interest in the rural inhabitants of the Third World and the growing influence of modernization and development theories also brought with them a good deal of funding for the study of peasant economies and societies (Silverman 1987: 11). It was at this time that the concept of 'peasantry' found currency in the discipline of social anthropology. At a time when primitive tribes were either in the process of disappearing or had already disappeared, the 'discovery' of the peasantry provided a vast new field of investigation to the discipline of social anthropology (Béteille 1974b: 40).

As distinct from the isolated 'primitive communities' of tribal society, peasant communities were defined as 'part societies with part cultures' (Krober 1948). Redfield (1965) argued that peasant societies had similarities all over the world. He particularly emphasized their attachment to land and the pursuit of agriculture as a way of life. Peasant societies, unlike tribal communities, also produced a surplus that was generally transferred to a dominant group of rulers in the city (Wolf 1966:4). Thus peasant society could not be seen as self-sufficient and isolated, for it was the surplus produced by peasants that partially supported the activities of rulers.

Corresponding to the idea of the peasantry having something generic about it, Shanin offered an 'ideal type' of peasant society with the following features. First, the peasant family was the basic unit of production and consumption in a multidimensional social organization. Second, land husbandry was the major means of livelihood. Third, there was a distinct traditional culture linked to the way of life of peasant communities. Fourth, an elite living outside the community dominated the peasantry (Shanin 1987: 3–5).

Whereas peasants were by definition pre-modern and hence were primarily seen as 'subject matter' for social anthropologists, or later for those in 'development studies', 'rural sociology' had come into existence in the United States much before peasant studies became popular. The civil war in the late nineteenth century and the ensuing 'farm crisis' saw the emergence of farmers' organizations demanding federal aid to solve the problems of rural areas afflicted by severe depression. Rural sociology, as an applied discipline, came into existence essentially in response to this crisis (Newby 1980: 10).

The main concern of 'rural sociology' came to be the understanding and diagnosing of the social and economic problems of farmers. More emphasis was placed on issues such as the internal structures of 'community life' and the changing composition of rural populations (Schwarzweller 1984: xi) than on their relationships with land or the social aspects of agricultural production. Theoretically, rural sociology remained caught up in bipolar notions of social change, where 'rural' often got defined as the opposite of 'urban'. 'Rurality' was conceptualized as an autonomous sociological reality (Bonnano 1989). The identification of 'rural sociology' with 'rural society' has also raised questions about its relevance in the western context where no rural areas were left anymore and almost the entire population had become urbanized (Friedland 1982: 590).

In response to these critiques of rural sociology, a new sub-discipline of sociology emerged that operated largely within the functionalist paradigm and was preoccupied with the study of the community life of rural people. This sub-discipline, known as sociology of agriculture, focused its attention on understanding and analysing the social framework of agricultural production and the structures of relations centred around land (Friedland 1989). It raised questions about how and on what terms the agrarian sector was being integrated into the system of commodity production and about the unequal distribution of agricultural incomes and food among the different social categories of people (Friedland 1989; 1984). The sociology of agriculture also distinguished itself from 'peasant studies' on the grounds that its focus was on capitalist farming, where the production was primarily for the market, not on peasants producing for their own consumption by using family labour. Thus, it claimed more kinship with the tradition of the 'political economy' of agriculture or 'agrarian studies'. At the methodological level, historical inquiries became as relevant as ethnographic/empirical studies. This conceptual shift during the early 1970s also helped in bringing sociologists working on agrarian issues in the western countries closer to those concerned with agrarian transformations in the Third World.

This chapter is an attempt to look at the Indian agrarian context broadly from the perspective of the 'sociology of agriculture'. Though the focus is on the contemporary agrarian scene, I approach it from a historical perspective.

THE INDIAN CONTEXT

The Indian agrarian context occupies special status, both in the social scientific literature on India and in the literature on agrarian societies in general. However, unlike studies on caste, kinship, village community, or, more recently, gender, study of agrarian relations did not occupy a central position in Indian sociology. Though some sociologists, particularly those working on developmental issues, were writing on agrarian issues, it was with the publication of André Béteille's *Studies in Agrarian Social Structure* in 1974 that 'agrarian sociology' gained professional respectability within the two disciplines.

'Peasant studies', in a way, arrived in India with 'village studies'. The vastly influential collection of essays, *Village India*, edited by Marriot (1955) with its emphasis on 'little communities' and 'great communities' was brought out under the direct supervision of Robert Redfield. It is therefore interesting to see Béteille's (1974b) critique of the assumption that the village in India could conceptually be equated to peasant communities in Europe. Béteille pointed out that the Indian village was characterized by a baffling variety of land relations and a complex hierarchy of ownership rights over land. By defining 'little communities' not in relation to land but through other social institutions, such as kinship, religion, and the social organization of caste, there was a shift away from looking at the rural population in relation to agriculture and land (there were some notable exceptions to this broad trend such as Bailey 1958; Gough 1955; Mukherjee 1971). Caste hierarchy came to be defined in terms of ritual or social interaction over institutions of commensality and marriage. Nearly universal acceptance of functionalism among the social anthropologists of the 1950s made them overemphasize the need to understand what produced social order. Even when they found evidence to show that neither the village nor the caste system was an unchanging reality, it was not reflected in the overall picture of the village that they presented (Jodhka 1998). There was a perceived dualism in thinking on caste and class. Studies of land and agriculture came to be associated with the domain of economics while the sociologist/social anthropologist specialized in caste (Béteille 1974a: 7–34).

Much before village studies were initiated by professional anthropologists during the early 1950s, social life in the Indian village and its agrarian structures were extensively documented by colonial ethnographers, though, as with many other practices of colonial historiography, the accounts were written in a manner that justified colonial subjugation of India (Cohn 1987: 212). Along with the earlier writings of James Mill, Charles Metcalfe's notion of the 'Indian village community' set the tone for much of the later writing on rural India. Metcalfe, in a celebrated remark, stated that:

the village communities are little Republics, having nearly everything they want within themselves, and almost independent of foreign relations. They seem to last where nothing else lasts. Dynasty after dynasty tumbles down; revolution succeeds revolution; Hindu, Pathan, Mughal, Mahratta, Sikh, English are masters in turn; but the village communities remain the same [quoted in Cohn 1987: 213].

This construction emphasized the fact that these communities were harmonious, relatively isolated, and, above all, unchanging, thus blocking from view the impoverishment caused by colonial policies. Perhaps the most critical element of this construct was the assumption about the absence of private ownership of land; land was thought to be owned by the village community collectively. Since there had been no private rights over land, the British believed that there would have been no significant economic differentiation in the Indian village.

Later historical research in different regions of pre-colonial India has convincingly shown that this was at best a superficial understanding of the Indian village. Since land was in abundant supply, there was no sale or purchase of land in most parts of the Indian countryside. However, not everyone had equal rights of cultivation or claims over land produce: these were instead based upon custom or upon grants made by the king (Neale 1962: 21). Irfan Habib, writing on the Mughal period, points out that these rights could even be purchased and sold (Habib 1963: 154). 'The village did not hold its land in common. Common were its officials and servants' (Neale 1962: 21).

Historians have also gathered enough evidence to show that claims that the Indian village was internally undifferentiated, self-sufficient, and stable were incorrect. According to Irfan Habib, during the Mughal period of Indian history

economic differentiation had progressed considerably among the peasantry. There were large cultivators, using hired labour, and raising crops for the market, and there were small peasants, who could barely produce food grains for their own subsistence. Beyond this differentiation among the peasantry, there was still sharper division between the caste peasantry and the 'menial' population (Habib 1982: 247).

Dharma Kumar also argues that there was a sizeable population of those who primarily worked as agricultural labourers in pre-colonial south India and generally belonged to some specific caste group (Kumar: 1992).

The village was linked to the central authority through the revenue bureaucracy. Land revenue worked as the dominant mode of surplus appropriation during 'medieval' times. Mughal authorities discriminated between the classes of landowners while fixing the revenue demands.

The larger landholders, such as *zamindars*, headmen or a favoured community, were required to pay less per unit (Kumar 1992: 239–40).

Pre-colonial agrarian relations were also not free of conflicts and tensions. Whenever the revenue demands became unbearable, the typical response of the peasantry was to flee en masse to other territories where conditions were more conducive to land cultivation (Habib 1963; Moore 1966: 332). There were also instances of the peasantry revolting against local rulers. Most of these revolts, however, were unorganized, inspired by some religious ideology or a millenarian dream (Dhanagare 1983: 29).

The notion of the '*jajmani* system' was also popularized by the colonial enthography. It tended to conceptualize agrarian social structure in the framework of exchange relations. In its classical construct, different caste groups specialized in specific occupations and exchanged their services through an elaborate system of division of labour. Though asymmetry in position of various caste groups was recognized, what it emphasized was not inequality in rights over land but the spirit of community. For instance, Wiser argued, 'Each served the other. Each in turn was master. Each in turn was servant. This system of inter relatedness in service within Hindu community was called the Hindu Jajmani system' (Wiser 1969: xxi). Central to such a construction of exchange is the idea of 'reciprocity' (Gouldner 1973: 173–220) with the implicit or explicit assumption that it was a non-exploitative system where mutual gratification was supposed to be the outcome of the reciprocal exchange (Bhattacharya 1985: 114–15).

How far is this construct correct? Later research has questioned the assumption that jajmani relations were non-exploitative. On the contrary, it has been argued that the dominant landlords used the system of hereditary obligations and occupational duties to perpetuate and legitimize the local variety of pre-capitalist/feudalistic relations (Beidelman 1959:6; Djurfeldt and Lindberg 1976:42). Moreover, what was projected as a pan-Indian reality that had been in practice since antiquity was only a local system confined to northern parts of India with a rather short history (Mayer 1993).

AGRARIAN CHANGES DURING COLONIAL RULE

Apart from theories on the Indian village produced by the colonial empire, British rule also had far-reaching material effects on the Indian countryside. It may however be relevant to stress that although British colonial rule had a significant impact on the village economy, the initial representation of the village as having been unchanging and static in earlier periods does not stand up to historical scrutiny.

After having established its political supremacy, the colonial regime initiated the task of reorganizing local society in a framework that would make governance easy and manageable. This process began with the introduction of new property rights in land. The first, and historically the most controversial, was the Permanent Settlement introduced in Bengal in 1793. Under this the intermediary zamindars (the tax-collecting officials in the earlier regime) were granted ownership rights over lands from which they previously only had the rights to collect revenues. Moore argues that apart from simplifying things, the colonial rulers saw in the local zamindars a counterpart of the 'enterprising English landlord', who, they believed, had the capacity to 'establish prosperous cultivation' if provided with secure and permanent ownership rights over land (Moore 1966: 345). Others have argued that the Permanent Settlement also had politico-strategic implications, for in the landlord the British rulers saw a possible support base in local society (Desai 1976: 39).

At least during the initial years, for the peasantry the new system just meant an increase in revenue demands. The additional economic burden also weakened the 'traditional' structure of patron–client relations between the zamindars and the local tenants, leading to a disintegration of what Scott calls 'the moral economy of the peasantry' (Scott 1976). Contrary to the expectations of the colonial rulers, Permanent Settlement accelerated and intensified the trend towards 'parasitic landlordism' (Moore 1966: 346). By the middle of the nineteenth century the entire area under Permanent Settlement was in a state of crisis.

Learning from the Bengal experience, the colonial regime tried a new arrangement in the regions of Madras, Bombay, and Berar. This came to be known as the *ryotwari* system. Under this, the actual landholders (*ryots*) were given formal proprietary rights. The ryot in theory was a tenant of the state, responsible for paying revenue directly to the state treasury, and could not be evicted as long as he paid his revenue (Baden-Powell 1892: 126). Stokes argues that the growing influence of Utilitarian philosophy in England during the time also produced distaste for landlordism and led to the introduction of new systems of revenue assessments (Stokes 1978).

Another variety of land settlement known as *mahalwari* or *malguzari* was introduced in the United Provinces, Punjab, and the Central Provinces. Under this, the village was identified as the unit of assessment. As such the mahalwari system was not very different from the ryotwari. Effective ownership of the cultivated land was vested in the cultivator here as well, but the revenue was collectively paid by the village. A villager of 'good social standing' was generally given the responsibility of collecting the revenue from individual cultivators and paying the assessment on behalf of the village.

Despite differences in arrangement, the patterns of change experienced in land relations were more or less similar in most parts of the empire. Though the new settlements changed the formal structures of authority, the colonial policies also reinforced and revitalized older, 'quasi-feudal' structures which for the peasant meant 'not less but in many cases more intensive and systematic exploitation' (Guha 1983: 7). The new land revenue systems also forced the peasants to become increasingly involved with the market, even when they did not have the capacity to produce surplus.

Commercialization of Agriculture

The expression 'commercialization of agriculture' is used to describe two related processes: first, a shift in the agrarian economy from production for consumption to production for the market; and second, a process where land starts acquiring the features of a commodity and begins to be sold and purchased in the market, like other commodities.

Though it grew both quantitatively as well as qualitatively during British rule, production for the market was not an entirely new phenomenon for Indian agriculture. As Habib points out, the big peasants during the Mughal period produced cash crops such as cotton, tobacco, and sugar cane (Habib 1982). However, these markets were generally local in nature and the demand for such things was limited. Establishment of colonial rule changed the entire scenario. The laying of the railways and the opening of the Suez canal made the Indian village a part of the global market.

The Industrial Revolution in England around the same time generated fresh demands for some specific agricultural products required as raw material in the new industries. The manifold increase in the land revenue at the same time compelled the peasantry to shift to crops that had better market value, which effectively meant switching over from food crops to cash crops. According to one estimate, in Rayalseema region of southern India, the area devoted to food crops declined from 78.2 per cent in 1901–4, to 58.2 per cent in 1937–49, while at the other end it increased from 17.0 per cent to 30.1 per cent for cash crops during the same period (Satyanarayana 1991: 57). Similarly, from the state of Punjab a large proportion of food and non-food crops began to be exported. While there was a rapid increase in the agricultural production of the region from 1921 onwards, the per capita output of food crops experienced a decline. According to the estimates made by G. Blyn for the entire country, exportable commercial crops grew more than ten times faster at 1.31 per cent annually, compared to only 0.11 per cent increase per annum for foodgrains from 1894 to 1947. He also estimated that per head availability of foodgrains declined by 25 per cent during the inter-War period. This decline was highest in Bengal, Bihar, and Orissa at 38 per cent, while the relatively prosperous state of Punjab also saw a decline of 18 per cent (Blyn 1966).

One obvious consequence of this shift in cropping patterns and a growing involvement of the peasantry in the market was a significant increase in the vulnerability of local populations to famines. Forced commercialization of agriculture disintegrated the traditional systems of food security. India experienced a number of serious famines, particularly during the second half of the nineteenth century and the first half of the twentieth century. According to an estimate, 3.5 to 4 million people (one-tenth to one-eighth of the total population of the region) perished during the 1876–8 famine in parts of southern India (Kumar 1982: 231).

Similarly Bengal was transformed from a prosperous region to a region with frequent famines. In one of its worst famines during 1943–4, nearly 3.5 million people died. Though the official reports and 'inquiries' by colonial rulers attributed these famines to scarcity of food due to crop failures, the per capita availability of food in Bengal in the year 1943 was not substantially different from the previous year and there were no widespread crop failures in 1942 (Sen 1976; Greenough 1982).

According to Sen (1976) it was not the scarcity of food but the changes in the 'exchange entitlements' that caused the 1943 Bengal famine. The year 1942–3 saw unprecedented inflation, mainly resulting from War expenditure, and the absolute level of prices moved rapidly upward. But the prices of different commodities did not move in the same way. While food prices went up, wage rates, particularly of rural unskilled labour, remained low. This was reinforced in certain regions of Bengal by a direct decline in employment arising from loss of agricultural activity due to cyclonic destruction, making the exchange entitlements worse for certain groups. While some classes benefited from the incomes newly created by the war economy, others faced higher prices of food without a corresponding rise in their monetary incomes and therefore starved (Sen: 1976; 1977). Greenough adds that there were also some cultural patterns specific to Bengal which explain the selective starvation and death during the famines. There was cultural acceptance in Bengali society of 'abandoning' those dependents who were deemed inessential for the reconstitution of family and society in the post-crisis period and of protecting those whose survival was held essential for the future (Greenough 1982: 265).

Commodification of Land

While the new land settlements conferred formal and transferable/alienable rights over land, the growing revenue demands and the increasing market orientation of agricultural production created conditions under which land began to acquire the features of a commodity. The new administrative and judicial system also introduced laws against defaults of legal dues that included default of rent, revenue, and debts. The moneylender, who until then lent keeping a peasant's crops in mind, began to see his land as a mortgageable asset against which he could lend money. Further, an increase in population during the nineteenth century made good-quality cultivable land scarce.

Apart from an absolute increase in population, colonial rule also led to what has been called the 'de-industrialization' of the Indian economy. Displacement of the native rulers after the conquest of India by the East India Company resulted in a sudden and almost complete collapse of old urban handicrafts in the absence of patronage. The influx of cheap machine-made goods from England after the Industrial Revolution hastened this process. Economic ruination of urban and village artisans increased the pressure on land considerably (Gadgil 1933). The net result was an ever-growing burden of debt for a majority of peasants.

Indebtedness as such was not an entirely new thing for the Indian peasant. Moneylenders as a distinct social category had always been a part of village social life. In most regions, they existed as a separate caste group. Whenever the peasant's stocks finished, he could go to the *sahukar* (moneylender) for a loan of grain. The local sahukar was also the customary source for peasants who generally needed an occasional loan. He was more of a functional category, a 'crude balance wheel to even out periods of scarcity and prosperity' (Moore 1966: 358). He evaluated the creditworthiness of a particular peasant on the basis of his ability to pay back, and decided on how much could be advanced to a particular peasant. The prevailing system of credit was perhaps close to what Weber conceptualized as 'neighborhood help' (Weber 1978: 361).

As land became both scarce and transferable, and the economic environment began to change, the moneylender started advancing much more than before, provided the peasant was willing to offer his land as guarantee against a possible default. At this stage rich landowners also entered the credit market, more with the intention of usurping the lands of smaller peasants than to earn interest. Thus began the process of 'land alienation'.

Land alienation was a pan-Indian development irrespective of the system of revenue settlement: zamindari, ryotwari, or mahalwari (Dhanagare 1983). This impoverished the small and, often also, the middle peasant, and strengthened the position of big landowners and moneylenders in rural society. The professional moneylender generally did not evict the peasant from his land. If the peasant could not pay back his loan, the moneylender asked for the transfer of ownership rights over land while the peasant continued cultivating land, but as a tenant of the moneylender. Where moneylenders were also landlords, the indebted peasant could end up being a landless labourer. Thus tenancy as well as landlessness grew significantly in most parts of the British empire. According to one estimate, out of the total population of male agricultural labourers in the state of Punjab, the proportion of those coming from peasant and landowning castes went up from 0.8 per cent in 1911 to as much as 29.7 per cent in 1931 (Bhattacharya 1985: 136). Similarly, in the case of Orissa, Bailey argues that once a market in land developed, peasants began to sell their lands whenever they were faced with a 'contingent need' (Bailey 1958).

Peasant indebtedness and land alienation acquired such gigantic proportions that even the colonial administrators began to see this as 'a problem' (Darling 1947; Thorburn 1983). Reports on growing discontent among the peasantry from different parts of the empire added to their worries. The Deccan riots of 1875 only confirmed these apprehensions. Colonial rulers responded to the growing unrest in the countryside by passing legislations such as the Deccan Relief Act of 1879 and the Punjab Alienation of Land Act of 1901. The main thrust of these legislative measures was to stop the transfers of agricultural land to members of non-agricultural castes. However, in the absence of any significant change in the revenue structure or in the overall politico-ideological framework of colonial rule, these legislative measures hardly brought any relief to the peasantry. For the poor peasants the only difference these measures made was that they now had to depend more on the credit of the richer landowners from the cultivating castes. The discontent among the peasantry continued to grow and expressed itself in a series of revolts and protest movements, particularly during the first half of the twentieth century.

The study of these movements became quite popular in the 1970s and 1980s. While scholars such as Desai (1979), Gough (1979), and Dhanagare (1983) explored these mobilizations from the conventional perspectives of social movements and Marxist class analysis, the famous 'Subaltern Studies' pioneered by Guha (1982) raised the issue of the relationship between peasant mobilizations and the nationalist movement. These studies questioned the dominant historiographies of the colonial period, which tended to subsume the politics of the peasantry within the broader framework of the nationalist struggle led by middle-class elite, thereby erasing the question of the agency of the subaltern classes. Guha argued for a perspective that gave autonomy to peasant consciousness and looked at the 'politics of the people' independently of the domain of elite politics.

The question, 'What did the agrarian policies of the colonial rulers do to the Indian village?' has most frequently been raised by Marxist scholars. Marx himself had almost celebrated the colonial conquest of India, which he thought would break the earlier stagnant system and help private property relations, and hence contradictions, to grow in Indian society. Though guided by its own 'vilest' self-interest, Marx argued that British rule was responsible for 'causing a social revolution in Hindustan' (Marx 1959: 18). Some later Marxists have also argued that high indebtedness of the peasantry, forced commercialization of agricultural produce, land alienation, and increasing domination of rich landowners and moneylenders over tenants and peasants was a specific form of 'the primitive accumulation of capital' which, in the ultimate analysis, led to 'a formal subsumption of labour under capital' (Alavi 1990; Fox 1987).

More popular has been the thesis of 'conservation-dissolution', which is that while colonial rule destroyed some of the local pre-capitalist structures, it also preserved many. As Patnaik argues, colonial rule 'broke down' the earlier structures without 'reconstituting' them, and 'bourgeois property relations' developed without a corresponding 'development of capitalist relations of production' in Indian agriculture (Patnaik 1990: 41). In certain cases, colonial rule in fact introduced semi-feudal relations to perpetuate itself. 'Unlike its parent mode of production in the West, distinguished historically by its continuous expansion of the productive forces, the mode of production installed in the colonies reduced the entire process of production to an immense super exploitation of the variable capital' (Banaji 1990: 126). The colonial West reinforced 'backward relations of exploitation' and transmitted to its colonies the pressures of the accumulation process in the metropolis without unleashing any corresponding expansion in the forces of production (Banaji 1990: 126). Alavi also argued that colonial or 'peripheral capitalism' was not the same as 'metropolitan capitalism'. While it was an integrated process of development in the West, 'peripheral capitalism brought about a disarticulated form of generalized commodity production' because the surplus generated in agriculture was reinvested not in the local economy but in the metropolitan centres (Alavi 1990: 170). Though with a different emphasis, Guha too argued that the fusing of landlordism and usury by colonial rule made a possible development of capitalism difficult both in agriculture and in industry. However, unlike Alavi, Guha emphasizes that the composite apparatus of dominance over peasantry and their subjection to the triumvirate—*sarkari* (of the state), *sahukari* (of the moneylender), and *zamindari* (of the landlord)—was primarily a political fact (Guha 1983: 8).

AGRARIAN CHANGES AFTER INDEPENDENCE

In many ways, independence from colonial rule in 1947 marked the beginning of a new phase in the history of Indian agriculture. Having evolved out of a long struggle against colonial rule with the participation of the people from various social categories, the Indian state also took over the task of supervising the transformation of its stagnant and backward economy to make sure that the benefits of economic growth were not monopolized entirely by a particular section of society. It is with this background that 'development' emerged as a strategy of economic change and an ideology of the new regime.

However, even though the political system had changed in a very fundamental sense, at a micro level the structures that evolved during colonial rule still continued to exist. The local interests that had emerged over a long period of time continued to be powerful in the Indian countryside even after the political climate had changed. Speaking at the Delhi School of Economics in 1955 after his extensive trips to different parts of independent India, Daniel Thorner was among the first to conceptualize this fact. He argued that the earlier structure of land relations and debt dependencies, where a small section consisting of a few landlords and moneylenders (who usually belonged to the local upper castes) were dominant, continued to prevail in the Indian countryside. The nature of property relations, the local values that related social prestige negatively to physical labour, and the absence of any surplus with the actual cultivator for investment on land ultimately perpetuated stagnation. 'This complex of legal, economic, and social relations uniquely typical of the Indian countryside served to produce an effect' that Thorner described as 'a built-in depressor' (Thorner 1956: 12). Thorner's formulation was, in a sense, symptomatic of the way in which agrarian issues began to be framed in the context of development studies and modernization of agriculture debates.

Land Reforms

The 'agrarian question' had also been an important topic of discussion for leaders of the Indian freedom movement, starting with Ranade and Dutt, who extensively wrote and debated on how Indian society and economy ought to be reorganized after independence from colonial rule (see Joshi 1987). The 'land question' had become one of the most hotly debated topics during the final years of the struggle for Independence.

Land reforms also became a question of considerable academic interest and debate in the discourse about planning and development. They were viewed as necessary for initiating modernization in agriculture. While there was a general agreement that the prevailing agrarian structures, marked by absentee landlordism and semi-feudal relations of production, needed to be reorganized, two extreme positions were taken on the following crucial questions: 'What kind of agrarian reforms are required and which would work the best?' and 'Is there an economic logic behind land reforms?' The competing answers to the latter question came to be known as the 'farm size-productivity' debate.

The first view was that of the 'institutionalists', who argued that the way out for Indian agriculture lay in a radical reorganization of land-ownership patterns that would not only democratize the village and revive the independent 'peasant economy', but also increase the productivity of land. Thus the slogan, 'land to the tiller' (Thorner 1956; Herring 1983). They also argued that smaller-sized holdings gave higher productivity (see Herring 1983: 239–67). The second viewpoint argued against the redistribution of land on the grounds that it was both unviable, as not enough land was available for everyone, and that it worked against the logic of 'economics'. The modernization of agriculture, it was argued, required landlords' reorientation. They needed to be motivated to cultivate their own land with wage labour and using modern technology. The land reforms, according to them, would only divide the land into 'unviable holdings', rendering them unfeasible for the use of modern technology (Bauer and Yamey 1957; Lewis 1963). Speaking from a very different position, some Marxist scholars also argued against the 'institutionalists' who reminded them of the neo-populist Narodanics of Russia. They thought that the argument in favour of small farms emanated from the Chayanovian logic of the peasant economy, which was in their view historically untenable (Patnaik 1972).

However, the process of agrarian reforms is inherently a political question (Ghose 1984:6) and not a purely technical or economic one. The choices made by the Indian state and the actual implementation of land reforms were determined by the 'politics' of the new regime rather than by the theoretical superiority of a particular position. The Indian state chose to reorganize agrarian relations through redistribution of land, but not in a comprehensive and radical manner. Joshi described it as 'sectorial or sectional reforms' (Joshi 1987: 56). The Government of India directed its states to abolish intermediary tenures, regulate rent and tenancy rights, confer ownership rights on tenants, impose ceilings on holdings, distribute the surplus land among the rural poor, and facilitate consolidation of holdings. A large number of legislations were passed by the state governments over a short period of time. The number of these legislations was so large that, according to Thorner, they could be 'the largest body of agrarian legislations to have been passed in so brief a span of years in any country whose history has been recorded' (Thorner 1956: 14).

The actual implementation of these legislations and their impact on the agrarian structure is, however, an entirely different story. Most of the legislations had intentionally provided loopholes that allowed the dominant landowners to tamper with land records by redistributing land among relatives—at least on papers—evicting their tenants, and using other means to escape the legislations. In the absence of a concerted 'political will' (Joshi 1976), land reforms could succeed only in regions where the peasantry was politically mobilized and could exert pressure from below (Radhakrishanan 1989).

Despite overall failure, land reforms succeeded in weakening the hold of absentee landlords over rural society and assisted in the emergence of a 'class of substantial peasants and petty landlords as the dominant political and economic group' (Bell 1974: 196). In a village of Rajasthan, for example, though the 'abolition of *jagirs*' (intermediary rights) was far from satisfactory, it made considerable difference to the overall landownership patterns and to the local and regional power structures. The Rajputs, the erstwhile landlords, possessed much less land after the land reforms than they did before. Most of the village land had moved into the hands of those who could be called small and medium landowners. In qualitative terms, most of the land began to be self-cultivated and the incidence of tenancy declined considerably (Chakravarti 1975: 97–8). The fear of losing land induced many potential losers to sell or rearrange their lands in a manner that escaped legislation (Byres 1974).

However, it was only in rare cases that the landless labourers living in the countryside, most of whom belonged to the ex-'untouchable' castes, received land. The beneficiaries, by and large, belonged to middle-level caste groups who traditionally cultivated land as a part of the calling of their castes. Otherwise also the holding structure continued to be fairly iniquitous though the proportion of smaller and medium-size landowners has been expanding (see Table 1).

Provision of Institutional Credit

While land reforms were supposed to deal with the problem of landlordism, the hold of moneylenders over the peasantry was to be weakened by providing credit through institutional sources, initially by credit societies and later by the nationalized commercial banks.

According to the findings of an official survey carried out immediately after Independence from colonial rule, up to approximately 91 per cent of the credit needs of cultivators were being met by informal sources of credit (RBI 1969: 15). Much of this came from usurious moneylenders (69.7 per cent). It was in recognition of this fact that the Indian state planned to expand the network of cooperative credit societies. With the imposition of 'social control' and later their nationalization, commercial banks were also asked to lend to the agricultural sector on priority basis. Over the years, the dependence of rural households on informal sources has come down significantly. While in 1961, an average of only 18.4 per cent of the total credit needs were being fulfilled by institutional sources of credit, in 1981 the corresponding figure had risen to 62.6 per cent (Gadgil 1986: 296).

However, this is not the entire story. The assessment studies on the cooperative credit societies showed that much of their credit went to the relatively better off sections of rural society, and the poor continued to depend on the more expensive informal sources (Thorner 1964; Oommen 1984). This was explained as a consequence of the prevailing structure of land tenures (Herring 1977). The state response was to bureaucratize the cooperative societies. Though in some regions this helped in releasing credit societies from the hold of big landowners, bureaucratization also led to rampant corruption and increasing apathy among those whom they were supposed to serve (Jodhka 1995a). Although banks were never controlled directly by the rural rich, the benefit of their credit has largely gone to those who had substantial holdings (Jodhka 1995b). Yet, despite this inherent bias of institutional credit against the rural poor, its availability played an important role in making the green revolution a success, and it definitely helped to marginalize the professional moneylender in the rural power structure.

Community Development Programme (CDP)

As a strategy of development, the CDP was conceptually very different from both land reforms and the idea of making cheap institutional credit available to cultivators. While the earlier programmes reflected an 'institutionalist' perspective, the CDP had emanated from the 'productionist' approach to rural development. It had been inspired by the agricultural extension service in the United States (Dube 1958: 8) and was based on a notion of the harmonious village community without any significant internal differences and conflict of interests (Dhanagare 1984). There was hardly any mention of the unequal power relations in the village. Its objective was to provide a substantial increase in agricultural production and improvement in basic services, which would ultimately lead to a transformation in the social and economic life of the village (Dube 1958). Its basic assumption was that 'the Indian peasant would of his own free will, and because of his "felt needs", immediately adopt technical improvements the moment he was shown them' (Moore 1966: 401).

The Programme was launched on 2 October 1952 in a few selected 'blocks' and it was soon extended to the entire country. However, the enthusiasm with which the Programme was started could not be sustained. A non-political approach to agrarian transformation resulted in helping only those who were already powerful in the village. Most of the benefits were cornered by a small section of the rural elite.

THE GREEN REVOLUTION AND AFTER

Of all the developmental programmes introduced during the post-Independence period, the green revolution is considered to have been the most successful. It was celebrated the world over and has been studied and debated quite extensively in academia. The green revolution led to a substantial increase in agricultural output, to the extent that it almost solved India's food problem. It also produced significant social and political changes in the Indian village and, in a sense, did bring about an 'agricultural revolution'. In purely economic terms, the agricultural sector experienced growth at the rate of 3 to 5 per cent per annum (Byres 1972), which was many times more than what the rate of growth had been during the colonial period (less than 1 per cent).

The green revolution conceptualized agrarian change in purely technological terms and was based on the 'trickle down' theory of economic growth. The expression 'green revolution' was deliberately coined to contrast it with the phrase 'red revolution'. It carried the conviction that 'agriculture was being peacefully transformed through the quiet working of science and technology, reaping the economic gains of modernization while avoiding the social costs of mass upheaval and disorder usually associated with rapid change' (Frankel 1971: V). The United States played an active role in its conception and implementation. Many have argued that this was because of the strategic, geopolitical interests that the US had at the time in the changing social and economic conditions in the countries of the Third World (Harriss 1987).

The term 'green revolution' had been first used during the late 1960s to refer to the effects of the introduction of higher yielding variety (HYV) seeds of wheat and rice in developing countries. However, the green revolution was not just about the use of HYV seed. It was a package. The new varieties of seeds required fertility-enhancing inputs, i.e. chemical fertilizers, controlled irrigation conditions, and plant-protecting chemicals (pesticides). The other components of the package consisted of providing cheap institutional credit, price incentives, and marketing facilities. In order to back up the application of new technology on local farms, a large number of agricultural universities were also opened in the regions selected for the new programme. It was under the direct supervision of the Ford Foundation that the Intensive Agricultural Development Programme (IADP) was started in 1961. Initially the IADP operated in 14 districts on an experimental basis; it was later extended to 114 districts (out of a total of 325) under the name of the Intensive Agriculture Areas Programme (IAAP) in 1965.

Its advocates argued that the new technology was 'scale neutral' and could be used with as much benefit by small as well as big landowners. However, in the actual implementation, small holdings were not found to be viable units for technological change. Joan Mencher observed that the concerned agriculture officers were far from neutral. 'What they thought was needed to further the green revolution was to forget about small farmers ... because they could not really contribute to increased production. To these officials, progressive farmers are those who have viable farms and who are fairly well-off' (Mencher 1978: 239–40). Interestingly, though, a study from Punjab showed that not only were the smaller landowners as eager to adopt the new technology but that their per acre income from land was slightly higher than that of the bigger farmers (Bhalla and Chadha 1983: 78).

But, participating in the green revolution did not mean the same thing to smaller farmers as it did to bigger farmers. While bigger farmers had enough surplus of their own to invest in the new capital-intensive farming, for smaller landowners it meant additional dependence on borrowing, generally from informal sources. My study of three villages in a green revolution district of Haryana showed that their average outstanding debt from informal sources was the highest even in absolute terms when compared with other categories of farmers (Jodhka 1995c: A124). Although theoretically the new technology was 'scale neutral', it was certainly not 'resource neutral' (Harriss 1987: 231). The new technology also compelled widespread involvement with the market. Unlike traditional agriculture, cultivators in post-green revolution agriculture had to buy all farm inputs from the market for which they often had to take credit from traders or institutional sources. In order to clear the debts, they had no choice but to sell the farm yield in the market even when they needed to keep it for their own consumption. They sold their farm yield immediately after harvesting when prices were relatively low, and bought later in the year for consumption when prices were higher. Thus although the small farmers took to the new technologies, the fact that their resources were limited meant that these technologies ushered in a new set of dependencies. On the other hand, it has definitely strengthened the economic and political position of rich farmers.

One of the manifestations of the growing market orientation of agrarian production was the emergence of a totally new kind of mobilization of surplus-producing farmers who demanded a better deal for the agricultural sector. Interestingly, these 'new' farmers' movements emerged almost simultaneously in virtually all the green revolution regions. Though initiated in the late 1970s, these movements gained momentum during the decade of the 1980s. Using the language of neo-populism (Dhanagare 1991; Brass 1994) and in some cases also invoking traditional social networks and identities of the landowning dominant castes (Gupta 1997), its leaders argued that India was experiencing a growing division between the city and the village. And the village, i.e. the agrarian sector, was being exploited by the city or the industrial sector through the mechanism of 'unequal exchange'.

Those who led these movements were mostly substantial landowners who had benefited most from the developmental programmes and belonged to the numerically large middle-level caste groups, whom Srinivas had called the 'dominant castes' (Srinivas 1994). The members of this new 'social class' not only emerged as a dominant group at village level but they also came to dominate regional/state-level politics in most parts of India. They had an accumulated surplus that they sought to invest in ever more profitable enterprises. Some of them diversified into other economic activities (Rutten 1991) or migrated to urban areas (Upadhya 1988) or entered agricultural trade (Harriss-White 1996). Culturally also, this new class differed significantly from both the classical peasants and the old landlords. As an observer comments:

A typical family of this class has a landholding in its native village, cultivated by hired labour, *bataidar*, tenant or farm servants and supervised by the father or one son; business of various descriptions in town managed by other sons; and perhaps a young and bright child who is a doctor or engineer or a professor. It is this class that is most vocal about injustice done to the village (Balagopal 1987: 1545).

The changes produced by the green revolution also generated an interesting debate among Marxist scholars on the question of defining the prevailing 'mode of production' in Indian agriculture. Though the debate raised a large number of questions, the most contentious revolved around whether capitalism had become dominant in Indian agriculture or was still characterized by the semi-feudal mode of production. A good number of scholars, with some variation in their formulations, argued that the capitalist tendency had started in India with the disintegration of the old system during colonial rule, and that after Independence the process of accumulation had gathered momentum (Patnaik 1990; Thorner 1982). Another set of scholars, on the basis of their own empirical studies mostly from eastern India, asserted that Indian agriculture was still dominated by a semi-feudal mode of production. This position was best articulated by Bhaduri (1984). He argued that landlords-cum-moneylenders continued to dominate the process of agricultural production. Peasants and labourers were tied to them through the mechanism of debt that led to 'forced commercialization' of labour and agricultural yield. This produced a self-perpetuating stagnant and exploitative agrarian structure that could be at best described as 'semi-feudal'. The internal logic of this system worked against any possibility of agricultural growth or the development of capitalism in Indian agriculture (Bhaduri 1984).

However, towards the end of the debate there seems to have emerged a consensus that though it may have its local specificities and considerable regional variations, the capitalist mode of production indeed was on its way to dominating the agrarian economy of India and most certainly that of the regions which had experienced the green revolution (Thorner 1982).

Agrarian Changes and Agricultural Labour

Did the benefits of the green revolution 'trickle down' to agricultural labourers? How did it affect them relationally? These have been among the most debated questions in the literature on agrarian change in India.

In a study comparing wage rates of a pre-green revolution year with those of a year after the new technology had been adopted, Bardhan (1970) showed that while cash wages of agricultural labourers had gone up after the introduction of the new technology, their purchasing power had in fact come down due to overall increase in prices. Though not everyone would agree with Bardhan, few would dispute that though the green revolution brought an overall prosperity to the countryside, it also multiplied income inequalities both within the village and among different regions of the country (Bagchi 1982; Dhanagare 1988). In a way, it was in recognition of the failures of the 'trickle-down' thesis that 'target-group' oriented programmes for poverty alleviation were started during the second half of the 1970s.

During the decade of the 1970s, the proportion of agricultural labour to total population dependent on land also experienced a significant increase. According to one estimate it went up from 16.7 per cent in 1961 to 26.3 per cent in 1971 (Prasad 1994: 15). However, micro-level studies have shown that the increase was not an effect of land sales by marginal landholders. A substantial proportion of the new labourers were tenants evicted from land after the land reforms or they were those who did not own land but were previously self-employed in traditional occupations (Bhalla 1976). The green revolution made many of the traditional occupations redundant and the 'jajmani relations' disintegrated rapidly (Aggarwal 1971; Karanth 1987).

It is generally believed that the process of agricultural modernization is accompanied by a change in the social relations of production, leading to freeing of agricultural labour from relations of patronage and institutionalized dependencies. Some scholars did report in their studies that such a process was under way in the Indian countryside, particularly in the regions where the green revolution had been a success. Breman (1974), for example, observed a process of 'depatronization' being experienced in the farmer–labourer relationship in the villages of south Gujarat. In a later study, he again argued that the inter-generational bondage characterized by extra-economic coercion no longer existed in south Gujarat and that the existing system of attached labour was no longer an unfree relation (Breman 1985). In his study of a Tanjore village in Tamil Nadu, Béteille (1971) had also observed a process of formalization in the relation of landowning castes with village artisans and landless labourers. They had 'acquired a more or less contractual character' (Béteille 1971). On the basis of her study in the same region, Gough too reported that the old type of attached labour that was mainly paid in kind was being replaced by casual day labour, paid largely in cash (Gough 1989:142). Similarly, despite the elements of continuity that she observed, Bhalla reported that in the Haryana countryside relations between farmers and attached labourers were also changing into formalized contractual arrangements (Bhalla 1976).

Highlighting the elements of continuity reported by Bhalla in her study, Bhaduri (1984) argued that the presence of attached labourers and their high indebtedness meant that the relations of production even in the green revolution belt of Haryana were 'semi-feudal'. However, Bardhan (1984) and Rudra (1990) strongly contested the argument that the prevalence of attached labour necessarily meant 'semi-feudal' relations. Bardhan argued that the post-green revolution voluntaristic attached labour was very different from the feudal institution of bonded labour marked by hereditary and long-term indebtedness, entailing continuous and exclusive work for the creditor-employer. On the basis of his own work, he contended that the modernization of agricultural technology had in fact increased the demand for attached labourers, as they were seen to be useful in overseeing the work of casual labourers. Similarly, Rudra argued that the attached labour in the post-green revolution agrarian setting was more like permanent employment in the organized sector than an unfree relationship.

Arguing in a very different mode, Brass (1990) questioned the claims that offered a positive conceptualization of attached labour. Contesting the assumption that the voluntarity of attached labour meant freedom, Brass argued that 'while the recruitment may itself be voluntary, in the sense that labourer willingly offers himself for work, it does not follow that the production relation will be correspondingly free in terms of the worker's capacity to re-enter the labour market' (Brass 1990: 55). Brass argued that in post-green revolution Haryana, where he did a field study, farmers used the mechanism of debt and attachment to 'discipline' labour and 'decompose/recompose' the labour market, which led to 'deproletarianization' of labour. He asserted that the indebted labourers of the Haryana countryside were in fact 'bonded slaves'.

On the basis of my study (Jodhka 1994) in the same region, I have argued that while the attached labourers in Haryana were certainly not like permanent employees in the organized sector, as suggested by Rudra, and that elements of lack of freedom were obvious in their relationship with farmers, they could not be viewed as bonded slaves because of the overall change in the social framework of agricultural production in contemporary Haryana. I have suggested that attached labour in the post-green revolution agriculture should be seen more as 'a system of labour mortgage' where labourers, despite an acute dislike for the relationship, were compelled to accept attachment for interest-free credit. However, their loss of freedom being temporary in nature, they could not be characterized as bonded slaves. There were many cases where the labourers after having worked as attached labourers for some time, could leave the relationship. The growing integration of the village in the broader market and the increasing availability of alternative sources of employment outside agriculture, along with the changing political and ideological environment, had been leading to a process that weakened the hold of landowners over labourers. In some cases developmental schemes such as the Integrated Rural Development Programme (IRDP) being run by the central government also helped.

More recently, scholars have been exploring new questions relating to the process of development and agrarian transition. Some of these could have far-reaching implications for the classical theories of agrarian change. Such studies allow us to inquire into the specific effects of new agrarian technology on the changing position of women in the household and on the farm. Apart from pointing to the 'gender blindness' of much of the development theory and the empirical surveys on issues such as poverty and land rights of women in the region (Dube 1986; Agarwal 1988; 1994), students of gender and agrarian change have also shown how the new technology had a clear bias against women. It marginalized female agricultural wage labour both in terms of work as well as earnings (Chowdhry 1994). Similarly, the questions of ecology and displacement (Guha 1989; Das 1996; Kothari 1996) and the new social movements (Baviskar 1995) against the construction of big dams, once considered 'the temples of modern India', have raised serious critiques of the present models of development.

CONCLUSION

After his extensive tours of the Indian countryside during the early 1950s, Daniel Thorner (1956) suggested that one can conceptualize the Indian agrarian structure on the basis of the form of income derived from the soil, the type of right in the soil, and the form of actual field work that is done. Conceptualized in this way, the Indian agrarian structure can be thought to constitute three main social categories: *maliks* (the landlords or proprietors), kisan (the working peasants), and mazdoors (the labourers). Although speaking from a different perspective, around this time Srinivas (1955) conceptualized the structure of social relations in the Mysore village in a framework of patron–client relationships and vertical ties between landlord and tenant, between master and servant, and between creditor and debtor. He also mentioned that these relations did not always correspond with the structure of caste hierarchies.

Another set of formulations of the prevailing agrarian structure in India before it embarked upon the path of 'development' came from different groups of Marxist scholars. As mentioned earlier, Bhaduri (1984) saw agrarian relations in eastern India as a classical case of a 'semi-feudal' mode of production where the landlord virtually controlled everything through his monopoly over land and credit. Similarly, Bhardwaj (1974) argued that agrarian relations in the Indian countryside were structured around a network of unequal exchange relations between those who possessed land, labour, and credit. However, these exchange relations were not among individuals with free will but were 'interlocked' with each other in such a manner that the prevailing structure worked in favour of the 'strong' and against the 'weak'.

Common to all these formulations was a stress on the fact that a small section of big landowners dominated a large section of agricultural producers through control over resources and ideologies. They were the people who rarely did any physical labour themselves. As Béteille (1980) points out, there was, in fact, an inverse relationship between the extent of manual work performed and the degree of control over land.

Despite a considerable degree of continuity and significant regional variations, these relations have definitely experienced many changes over approximately the last fifty years. Independence from colonial rule and the launching of development programmes started a new phase in the history of Indian agriculture. At a purely quantitative level, the limited institutional changes—i.e. partial implementations of land reforms, adoption of new technology, and state support to the cultivators—have led to considerable expansion in the area under cultivation and the total volume of production.

A substantial volume of the literature shows that the agrarian structure has transformed the direction of a capitalist mode of organization at least in areas that experienced the green revolution, which have extended from traditional crops such as wheat and paddy to new crops such as oil seeds and soya bean. The Indian farmer has increasingly become outward looking, orienting his needs to demands of the market rather than local conventions and earlier traditions, yet the impact of the change on the different categories defined by caste and gender has been a differential one. This is why the changes in agriculture have not secured a better quality of life for all social categories in the agrarian structure of village communities.

REFERENCES

Agarwal, B. 1988. *Structures of Patriarchy: State, Community and Household in Modernising Asia.* New Delhi: Kali for Women.
_____. 1994. *A Field of One's Own: Gender and Land Rights in South Asia.* New Delhi: Foundation Books.
Aggarwal, P.C. 1971. 'Impact of Green Revolution on Landless Labourers: A Note'. *Economic and Political Weekly.* 6(47):2363–5.
Alavi, H. 1990. 'Structure of Colonial Formations'. In Utsa Patnaik, ed., *Agrarian Relations and Accumulation: The 'Mode of Production Debate in India',* 165–82. Delhi: Oxford University Press.
Baden-Powell, B.H. 1892. *Land Systems of British India.* 3 vols. London: Oxford University Press.
Bagchi, A.K. 1982. *The Political Economy of Underdevelopment.* Cambridge: Cambridge University Press.
Bailey, F.G. 1958. *Caste and the Economic Frontier: A Village in Highland Orissa.* Bombay: Oxford University Press.
Balagopal, K. 1987. 'An Ideology of the Provincial Propertied Class'. *Economic and Political Weekly.* 21(36–7):2177–8.
Banaji, J. 1976. 'A Summary of Kautsky's *The Agrarian Question'. Economy and Society.* 5(1):2–49.
_____. 1990. 'For a Theory of Colonial Modes of Production'. In Utsa Patnaik, ed., *Agrarian Relations and Accumulation: The 'Mode of Production Debate in India',* 119–31. Delhi: Oxford University Press.
Bardhan, P. 1970. 'Green Revolution and Agricultural Labour'. *Economic and Political Weekly.* 5(29–31):1239–46.
_____. 1984. *Land, Labour and Rural Poverty: Essays in Development Economics.* Delhi: Oxford University Press.
Bauer, P.T. and B.S. Yamey. 1957. *The Economy of Underdeveloped Countries.* Cambridge: Cambridge University Press.
Baviskar, A. 1995. *In the Belly of the River: Tribal Conflict over Development in the Narmada Valley.* Delhi: Oxford University Press.
Bell, C. 1974. 'Ideology and Economic Interests in Indian Land Reform'. In D. Lehmann, ed., *Agrarian Reform and Agrarian Reformism: Studies of Peru, Chile, China, and India,* 190–220. London: Faber and Faber.
Beidelman, T.O. 1959. *A Comparative Analysis of the Jajmani System.* New York: Association for Asian Studies.
Béteille, A. 1971. *Caste, Class and Power: Changing Patterns of Stratification in a Tanjore Village.* Berkeley: University of California Press.
_____. 1974a. *Studies in Agrarian Social Structure.* Delhi: Oxford University Press.
_____. 1974b. *Six Essays in Comparative Sociology.* Delhi: Oxford University Press.
_____. 1980. 'The Indian Village: Past and Present'. In E.J. Hobsbaum et al., eds, *Peasants in History: Essays in Honour of Daniel Thorner,* 107–20. Delhi: Oxford University Press.
Bhaduri, A. 1984. *The Economic Structure of Backward Agriculture.* Delhi: Macmillan.

Bhalla, G.S. and G.K. Chadha. 1983. *Green Revolution and Small Peasants: A Study of Income Distribution among Punjab Cultivators*. New Delhi: Concept Publishing House.

Bhalla, S. 1976. 'New Relations of Production in Haryana Agriculture'. *Economic and Political Weekly*. 11(13):A23–30.

Bhattacharya, N. 1985. 'Agricultural Labour and Production: Central and South-East Punjab'. In K.N. Raj, ed., *Essays on the Commercialization of Indian Agriculture*, 105–62. Delhi: Oxford University Press.

Blyn, G. 1966. *Agricultural Trends in India 1891–1947*. Philadelphia: University of Philadelphia Press.

Bonnano, A. 1989. *Sociology of Agriculture*. New Delhi: Concept Publishing House.

Brass, T. 1990. 'Class Struggle and Deproletarianization of Agricultural Labour in Haryana (India)'. *The Journal of Peasant Studies*. 18(1):36–67.

——. 1994. 'Introduction: The New Farmers' Movements in India'. *The Journal of Peasant Studies*. 21(3–4):50–77.

Breman, J. 1974. *Patronage and Exploitation: Changing Agrarian Relations in South Gujarat India*. Berkley: University of California Press.

——. 1985. *Of Peasants, Migrants and Paupers: Rural Labour Circulation and Capitalist Production in West India*. Delhi: Oxford University Press.

Byres, T.J. 1972. 'The Dialectics of India's Green Revolution'. *South Asian Review*. 5(2):99–106.

——. 1974. 'Land Reforms, Industrialization and Marketed Surplus in India: An Essay on the Power of Rural Bais'. In D. Lehmann, ed., *Agrarian Reform and Agrarian Reformism: Studies of Peru, Chile, China, and India*, 221–61. London: Faber and Faber.

Chakravarti, A. 1975. *Contradiction and Change: Emerging Patterns of Authority in a Rajasthan Village*. Delhi: Oxford University Press.

Chayanov, A.V. 1987. *The Theory of Peasant Economy*. Ed. Daniel Thorner. Delhi: Oxford University Press.

Chowdhry, P. 1994. *The Veiled Women: Shifting Gender Equations in Rural Haryana 1880–1990*. Delhi: Oxford University Press.

Cohn, B.S. 1987. *An Anthropologist among the Historians and Other Essays*. Delhi: Oxford University Press.

Darling, M. 1947. *Punjab Peasantry in Prosperity and Debt*. Bombay: Oxford University Press.

Das, V. 1996: 'Dislocation and Rehabilitation: Defining a Field'. *Economic and Political Weekly*. 31(24): 1509–14.

Desai, A.R. 1976. *Social Background to Indian Nationalism*. Bombay: Popular Prakashan.

——, ed. 1979. *Peasant Struggles in India*. Bombay: Oxford University Press.

Dhanagare, D.N. 1983. *Peasant Movements in India: 1920–1950*. Delhi: Oxford University Press.

——. 1984. 'Agrarian Reforms and Rural Development in India: Some Observations'. *Research in Social Movements, Conflict and Change*. 7(1):178–93.

——. 1988. 'The Green Revolution and Social Inequalities in Rural India'. *Bulletin of Concerned Asian Scholars*. 20(2):2–13.

——. 1991. 'An Apoliticist Populism: A Case Study of BKU'. In K.L. Sharma and Dipankar Gupta, eds, *Country–Town Nexus: Study in Social Transformation in Contemporary India*, 104–22. Jaipur: Rawat Publications.

Djurfeldt, G. and S. Lindberg. 1976. *Behind Poverty: The Social Formation of a Tamil Village*. New Delhi: Oxford and IBH.

Dube, L. 1986. *Visibility and Power: Essays on Women in Society and Development*. Delhi: Oxford University Press.

Dube S.C. 1958. *India's Changing Villages: Human Factors in Community Development*. New Delhi: Allied Publishers.

Fox, R. 1987. *Lions of the Punjab: Culture in the Making*. New Delhi: Archives Publishers.

Friedland, W.H. 1982. 'The End of Rural Society and the Future of Rural Sociology'. *Rural Sociology*. 47(4):589–608.

———. 1984. 'Commodity Systems Analysis: An Approach to the Sociology of Agriculture'. In H.K. Schwarzweller, ed., *Research in Rural Sociology and Development*, vol. 1:221–35. Greenwich: Jai Press.

Frankel, F.R. 1971. *India's Green Revolution: Economic Gains and Political Costs*. Bombay: Oxford University Press.

Gadgil, D.R. 1933. *Industrial Evolution of India in Recent Times*. London: Oxford University Press.

Gadgil, M.V. 1986. 'Agricultural Credit in India: A Review of Performances and Policies'. *Indian Journal of Agricultural Economics*. 14(3):282–309.

Geertz, C., ed. 1963. *Old Societies and New States: The Quest for Modernity in Asia and Africa*. New York: The Free Press.

Ghose A.K., ed. 1984. *Agrarian Reforms in Contemporary Developing Countries*. New Delhi: Select Books.

Gough, K. 1955. 'The Social Structure of a Tanjore Village'. In M.N. Srinivas, ed., *India's Village*, 90–102. Bombay: Asia Publishers.

———. 1979. 'Peasant Resistance and Revolt in South India'. In A.R. Desai, ed., *Peasant Struggles in India*, 719–42. Bombay: Oxford University Press.

Gouldner, A.W. 1973. *For Sociology: Renewal and Critique in Sociology Today*. Harmondsworth: Penguin.

Greenough P.R. 1982. *Prosperity and Misery in Modern Bengal: The Famine of 1943–1944*. Oxford: Oxford University Press.

Guha, R. 1982. *Subaltern Studies-I: Writings on South Asian History and Society*. Delhi: Oxford University Press.

———. 1983. *Elementary Aspects of Peasant Insurgency in Colonial India*. Delhi: Oxford University Press.

Guha, Ramchandra. 1989. *The Unquiet Woods: Ecological Change and Peasant Resistance in the Himalaya*. Delhi: Oxford University Press.

Gupta, D. 1997. *Rivalry and Brotherhood: Politics in the Life of Farmers in Northern India*. Delhi: Oxford University Press.

Habib, I. 1963. *Agrarian Systems of Mughal India*. Bombay: Asia Publishers.

———. 1982. 'Agrarian Relations and Land Revenue: North India'. In, T. Raychaudhury and Irfan Habib, eds, *The Cambridge Economic History of India*, vol.1:235–48. Delhi: Orient Longman.

Harriss, J. 1987. 'Capitalism and Peasant Production: The Green Revolution in India'. In T. Shanin, ed., *Peasants and Peasant Societies*, 227–45. London: Blackwell.

Harriss-White, B. 1996. *A Political Economy of Agriculture Markets in South India: Masters of the Countryside*. New Delhi: Sage.

Herring, R.J. 1977. 'Land Tenure and Credit-Capital Tenure in Contemporary India'. In R.E. Frynkenberg, ed., *Land Tenure and Peasants in South Asia*, 120–58. New Delhi: Manohar.

———. 1983. *Land to the Tiller: The Political Economy of Agrarian Reforms in South Asia*. Delhi: Oxford University Press.

Inden, R. 1990. *Imagining India*. Oxford: Basil Blackwell.

Jodhka, S.S. 1994. 'Agrarian Changes and Attached Labour: Emerging Patterns in Haryana Agriculture'. *Economic and Political Weekly*. 29(39):A102–6.

———. 1995a. 'Bureacratisation, Corruption and Depoliticisation: Changing Profile of Credit Co-operatives in Rural Haryana'. *Economic and Political Weekly*. 30(1):53–6.

———. 1995b. *Debt, Dependence and Agrarian Change*. Jaipur: Rawat Publications.

———. 1995c. 'Who Borrows? Who Lends?: Changing Structure of Informal Credit in Rural Haryana'. *Economic and Political Weekly*. 30(39):A123–31.

———. 1998. 'From "Book View" to "Field View": Social Anthropological Constructions of the Indian Village'. *Oxford Development Studies*. 26(3):311–31.

Joshi, P.C. 1976. *Land Reforms in India: Trends and Perspectives*. New Delhi: Allied Publishers.

_____. 1987. *Institutional Aspects of Agricultural Development: India from Asian Perspective*. New Delhi: Allied Publishers.

Karanth, G.K. 1987. 'New Technology and Traditional Rural Institutions: The Case of Jajmani Relations'. *Economic and Political Weekly*. 22(51):2217–24.

Kothari, S. 1996. 'Whose Nation? Displaced as Victims of Development'. *Economic and Political Weekly*. 31(24):1476–85.

Krober, A.L. 1948. *Anthropology*. New York: Harcourt, Brace and Co.

Kumar, D. 1982. 'South India'. In Dharma Kumar and Meghnad Desai, eds, *The Cambridge Economic History of India*, vol. II:207–41. Delhi: Orient Longman.

_____. 1992. *Land and Caste in South India*. New Delhi: Manohar.

Lenin, V.I. [1899] 1960. *The Development of Capitalism in Russia*. In *Collected Works*, vol. 3. Moscow: Foreign Languages Publishing House.

_____. [1908] 1962. *The Agrarian Programme of Social-Democracy in the First Russian Revolution 1905–1907*. In *Collected Works*, vol.13. Moscow: Foreign Languages Publishing House.

Lewis, W.A. 1963. *The Theory of Economic Growth*. London: George Allen and Unwin.

Marx, K. 1959. *The First Indian War Of Independence: 1857–1859*. Moscow: Progress Publishers.

Marriot, M., ed. 1955. *Village India: Studies in Little Community*. Chicago: Chicago University Press.

Mayer, P. 1993. 'Inventing Village Tradition: The Late 19th Century Origins of the North Indian Jajmani System'. *Modern Asian Studies*. 27(2):357–95.

Mencher, J.P. 1978. *Agriculture and Social Structure in Tamil Nadu: Past Origins, Present Transformations and Future Prospects*. New Delhi: Allied Publishers.

Moore, B.Jr. 1966. *Social Origins of Dictatorship and Democracy*. Middlesex: Penguin.

Mukherjee, M. 1985. 'Commercialization and Agrarian Change in Pre-Independence Punjab, 1870–1940'. In K.N. Raj, ed., *Essays on the Commercialization of Indian Agriculture*, 51–104. Delhi: Oxford University Press.

Mukherjee, R. 1971. *Six Villages of Bengal*. Bombay: Popular Prakashan.

Neale, W. 1962. *Economic Change in Rural India: Land Tenure and Reform in Uttar Pradesh, 1800–1955*. New Haven: Yale University Press.

Newby, H. 1980: 'Trend Report: Rural Sociology'. *Current Sociology*. 28 (Spring): 1–41.

Oommen, T.K. 1984. *Social Transformation in Rural India*. New Delhi: Vikas Publishing House.

Patnaik, U. 1972. 'Economics of Farm Size and Farm Scale'. *Economic and Political Weekly*. 7(31–3):1613–24.

_____. 1996. 'Export Oriented Agriculture and Food Security in Developing Countries and India'. *Economic and Political Weekly*. 31(35–7):2429–50.

_____, ed. 1990. *Agrarian Relations and Accumulation: The 'Mode of Production Debate in India'*. Delhi: Oxford University Press.

Prasad, K.N. 1994. *Four Decades of Indian Agriculture*. Delhi: Manas.

Radhakrishanan, P. 1989. *Peasant Struggles, Land Reforms and Social Change: Malabar 1836–1982*. New Delhi: Sage Publications.

Redfield, R. 1965. *Peasant Society and Culture*. Chicago: University of Chicago Press.

Reserve Bank of India. 1969. *Report of the All India Rural Credit Review Committee*. Bombay:RBI.

Rudra, A. 1990. 'Class Relations in Indian Agriculture'. In Utsa Patnaik, ed., *Agrarian Relations and Accumulation: The 'Mode of Production Debate in India'*, 251–67. Delhi: Oxford University Press.

Rutten, M. 1991. *Capitalist Entrepreneurs and Economic Diversification: Social Profile of Large Farmers and Rural Industrialist in Central Gujarat, India*. Rotterdam: Academisch Proefschrift.

Satyanarayana, A. 1991. 'Commercialization, Money Capital and the Peasantry in Colonial Andhra, 1900–1940'. In S. Bhattacharya et al., eds, *The South Indian Economy: Agrarian Change, Industrial Structure and State Policy 1914–1947*, 51–77. Delhi: Oxford University Press.

Schwarzweller, H.K., ed. 1984. *Research in Rural Sociology and Development*, vol. 1. Greenwich: Jai Press.

Scott, J. 1976. *The Moral Economy of the Peasantry: Rebellion and Subsistence in Southeast Asia.* New Haven: Yale University Press.

Sen A. 1976. 'Famines as Failures of Exchange Entitlements'. *Economic and Political Weekly.* 11(31–3):1273–80.

———. 1977. 'Starvation and Exchange Entitlements: A General Approach and its Application to the Great Bengal Famine'. *Cambridge Journal of Economics.* 1(1):33-59.

Shanin, T., ed. 1987. *Peasants and Peasant Societies.* London: Blackwell.

Silverman, S. 1987. 'The Concept of Peasant and the Concept of Culture'. In J. Mencher, ed., *Social Anthropology of Peasantry,* 7–31. Bombay: Somaiya Publications.

Srinivas, M.N. 1955. 'The Social Structure of a Mysore Village'. In M. Marriot, ed., *Village India,* 1–35. Chicago: University of Chicago Press.

———. 1994. *The Dominant Caste and Other Essays.* Delhi: Oxford University Press.

Stokes, E. 1978. *The Peasant and the Raj.* New Delhi: Vikas Publishing House.

Thorburn, S.S. 1983. *Musalmans and Moneylenders in Punjab,* Delhi: Mittal Publications.

Thorner, A. 1982. 'Semi-Feudalism or Capitalism? Contemporary Debate on Classes and Modes of Production in India'. *Economic and Political Weekly.* 17(49–51):993–99; 2061–86.

Thorner, D. 1956. *The Agrarian Prospects of India.* Delhi: Oxford University Press.

———. 1964. *Agricultural Co-operatives in India.* Bombay: Asia Publishers.

Upadhya, C.B. 1988. 'The Farmer-Capitalists of Coastal Andhra Pradesh'. *Economic and Political Weekly.* 23(27–8):1376–82.

Weber, M. 1978. *Economy and Society: An Outline of Interpretative Sociology,* vol.1. Eds, G. Roth and C. Wittich. Berkeley: University of California Press.

Wiser, W.H. 1969. *The Hindu Jajmani System.* Lucknow: Lucknow Publishing House.

Wolf, E. 1966. *Peasants.* New Jersey: Prentice-Hall, Inc.

TABLE

Table 1: Changing Structures of Landholdings during the Post-Independence Period

Size	1960–1		1976–7		1990–1	
	Number of holdings (%)	Area operated (%)	Number of holdings (%)	Area operated (%)	Number of holdings (%)	Area operated (%)
Marginal	40.70	6.70	54.60	10.70	59.00	14.90
Small	22.30	12.20	18.00	12.80	19.00	17.30
Semi-medium	18.90	20.00	14.30	19.90	13.20	23.20
Medium	13.40	30.40	10.10	30.40	7.20	27.20
Large	4.70	30.70	3.00	26.20	1.60	17.40
Total	100.00	100.00	100.00	100.00	100.00	100.00

Source : *Indian Agriculture Sector-A, Compendium of Statistics.* September 1995.

Markets

Denis Vidal

Markets and trade have always played an important role in Indian history. Whilst there is evidence of the significance of markets and monetary transactions in medieval India (Subrahmanyam 1994), it is concerning the eighteenth century that we find an abundance of information about the intricate networks of markets which characterized the Indian economy of that period. Such networks linked the periodical market (*hat*) of the countryside with the local urban markets (*mandi, ganj, qasbah*) of small towns, the great bazaars of important commercial cities, and the outposts for long-distance trade outside India (Chaudhuri 1994; Habib and Raychaudury 1982; Bayly 1983). Historians have also demonstrated that monetary transactions were not only limited to the domains of trade or to the collection of state revenue but also entered into other aspects of social life in pre-colonial India. For example, Dirk Kolff has shown the importance of a military labour market both for state formation and for the maintenance of the village economy (Kolff 1990). This richness of historical material makes it surprising that the study of markets and monetary transactions has played such a minor role in the development of the social and cultural anthropology of India. Ironically the main reason for this neglect is that the market has often been perceived as a relatively recent phenomenon and an alien imposition on Indian society and culture.

This neglect does not only concern India. It begs more general questions about the way markets have been studied within the framework of the social sciences and of economic anthropology in particular. It is probably true to say that the progressive hegemony of neoclassic theory in economic literature does not blend well with sociological approaches to the market in spite of recent efforts at reconciliation made by the so-called 'new institutional economics' school.[1] But it is not enough for anthropologists and sociologists to blame economists for monopolizing the field with their limited model of the market; the former are also partially responsible for the development of the situation.

On the one hand, sociologists criticize the neoclassic approach for its failure to consider the social and cultural factors which influence economic behaviour. On the other hand, the same critics will insist that social relationships and cultural values are obliterated by the market. In the first instance, they question the relevance and interpretative value of economic theory from a sociological point of view; but in the second, they find themselves implicitly validating the economist's model of the market, even if they intend to do the opposite. If anthropologists and sociologists are to escape from this double bind, they need not only to question the applicability of the economist's model, but to go one stage further to develop an alternative approach.

Paradoxically, it is amongst anthropologists working in non-western cultures, often perceived as not having market economies, that the tendency to endorse the standard economic interpretation of the market has been most apparent. Placing the emphasis on the social and the cultural specificities of the societies they study, these scholars inevitably recognize the discrepancy between the economic practices they observe and the economic model thought to characterize western societies. However, rather than using their observations to contest the model developed in the West, they tend to assume its relevance only for the West and that its limitation is simply that it cannot be applied cross-culturally.

The intensification of this debate in the anthropological literature of the 1960s and 1970s can be traced back to the influential role played by the work of Karl Polanyi (1886–1964). Polanyi attempted to show that the market economy characterized a specific and very particular moment of western society. It was therefore inappropriate to apply a model which had been built out of these specific circumstances to other societies. He also questioned the notion that the market economy was more 'rational' or more efficient than other forms of economic organization based on different principles. Like many other intellectuals of his time, Polanyi believed that the period of western history which had been marked by economic liberalism was coming to an end.

The ambition of Polanyi and his followers, who became known as the 'substantivists', was to draw up a typology of different kinds of economic organization found throughout the world at different periods in history. In effect, he identified three main economic principles: reciprocity, redistribution, and exchange: 'Reciprocity denotes movements between correlative points of symmetrical groupings; redistribution designates appropriational movements toward a centre and out of it again; exchange refers here to vice-versa movements taking place as between "hands" under a market movement' (Polanyi 1992: 35). He was also anxious to avoid any form of evolutionism and did not want to give undue privilege to the sort of economic organization which characterized modern western societies. The social scientists who opposed this view, and who were collectively known as the 'formalists,' argued to the contrary that, in spite of the obvious differences in the economic organization of societies, the main task at hand was to delineate a few fundamental principles which could be applied to all.

According to the substantivists, the main characteristic of the domination of economic liberalism in the West lay in the separation of the economic domain from social and cultural values and constraints. By contrast, in more 'traditional' societies, economic relationships were 'embedded' within the social fabric and were subordinate to non-economic considerations. Such a conception corresponds well to that developed by Louis Dumont in the Indian context, and it is no coincidence that it was this author who wrote the preface of the French translation of Polanyi's major work, *The Great Transformation* (1957). Basing his argument both on ancient Hindu texts and contemporary ethnography, Dumont argued that one of the fundamental characteristics of Hindu society was that the economic and political domain (*artha*) was subordinate to the moral exigencies of a higher order (*dharma*). This hierarchy of principles was thought to inform the ideology of Indian society as a whole (Dumont 1970).

Most sociologists and anthropologists working in India have, at some level, proved 'substantivist' in their approach. They have tended to place emphasis on the logic of redistribution rather than monetary transactions, as if the latter could be dismissed as an alien imposition on Indian culture and society. Once market exchanges were perceived purely as a modern development, it became possible by contrast to define the ideological features which were supposed to characterize the 'traditional' economic system in India.

However, from the 1980s onwards this simplistic divide between so-called 'traditional' and 'modern' economic systems has been more and more contested. On the one hand, the use of the notion of 'tradition' has been questioned in the works of historians, cultural theorists, and anthropologists (Hobsbawm and Ranger 1983; Breckenridge and Van der Veer 1994). On the other hand, new approaches to economic sociology have emerged. As a result of these developments we find two new tendencies in Indian economic sociology. The first is to recognize and take a fresh look at the importance of markets in Indian culture, the second is to begin to question the dominant model of the market from an Indian perspective. It is on these two tendencies that I wish to focus.

Rediscovering the Importance of the Market in Indian Sociology

Sociologists and anthropologists have tended to draw a clear distinction between monetary transactions and other forms of exchange such as gift giving. The latter has generally been perceived as positive in value as opposed to the former which is thought to dehumanize social relationships. According to this view, it was usually taken for granted that exchanges of gifts not only expressed the values of a society but also reinforced social relationships within it; whilst money transactions implied the erosion of social solidarity and cultural values (Bloch and Parry 1989).

There is no doubt that gifts have positive connotations in western culture; and it is equally true that market transactions are often looked at with suspicion, particularly in certain spheres of life where commercialization may seem sacrilegious from a moral point of view. A good illustration of this is Viviana Zelizer's interesting discussion of the history of life-insurance companies in the United States (Zelizer 1992). She analyses the development of this specific market in terms of a complicated negotiation between mercantile values and particularly sacred human values which seem to contradict each other. She goes on to show that Americans were not only resistant to the idea that life could be evaluated in monetary terms but also to the idea that payment was appropriate as compensation for someone's death. The question raised by such an example is whether monetary transactions and market relationships are always evaluated in the same way in different societies. If economists have tended to universalize western economic logic, anthropologists have tended to universalize anti-market rhetoric. Joel Kahn put it neatly in his critique of Taussig's well-known monograph, *The Devil and Commodity Fetishism in South America* (1980), when he argues that Taussig's approach 'places a Young Hegelian critique of commodities and markets into the mouth of Latin American peasants' (Kahn 1997: 75).

It is precisely this question which has been addressed by Jonathan Parry in his analysis of different types of economic transaction in Varanasi (Parry 1989). Parry argues that one cannot make a clear-cut distinction between gifts and commercial transactions in terms of the morality attached to them. Moreover, in India, it is gift relations, not monetary ones, which are perceived as a potential threat to social relations. Parry also demonstrates that commercial and monetary transactions are treated in a much more neutral perspective in India than in the West and in many other societies.

It is possible to question the generality of Parry's study, located as it was amongst the priests of Varanasi. There are, of course, many varied traditions and streams of thought in Indian culture, some of which do not fit his argument. Sanjay Subrahmanyam, for example, has shown that many currents of medieval poetry and literature in India express a range of ambivalent attitudes to money and trade (Subrahmanyam 1994) However, one should not undermine the importance of Parry's findings. There is, in fact, a large body of evidence in anthropological and historical literature to support his thesis. For example, we find often in India a more lenient and morally neutral attitude to debt and credit than that found generally in the West. In spite of the exploitation of debtors by creditors and of sporadic resistance, there is not as much moral condemnation of the former as one might expect (Vidal 1997; Hardiman 1987, 1996).

Parry's argument is not limited to India. In fact, he goes on to suggest that the condemnation of market relationships seems everywhere to be linked to the valorization of self-sufficiency in the economic domain—whether in the West or in Melanesia. So, reverting to the conventional perspective on Indian society, Parry argues that it may be precisely because economic autarky has never been considered an ideal in Indian society that monetary transactions have not posed a serious threat to cultural values or social relationships. Such insights echo the mounting criticism of the idea that local economic relations can be understood purely in terms of what is known as the *jajmani* system.

The Jajmani System

The jajmani system is a term commonly used by sociologists and anthropologists to summarize economic relationships between members of different castes in the Indian village context. Jajmani relationships were thought to be based on a system of redistribution in kind where the monetarization and commercialization of goods and services hardly existed. This made economic interactions largely independent of market forces. Rather, they were deeply embedded in the social and ritual structures of the caste system.

W.H. Wiser is generally acknowledged to be the first author to have emphasized the importance of the jajmani system in village relations (Wiser 1958). But most village studies from the 1950s onwards make use of the concept even if some of them offer a much more nuanced picture of the rural economy than others, thereby pointing out some of the limitations of the jajmani model (Harper 1959; Pocock 1969). But in spite of these criticisms, the jajmani system came to be identified as some sort of normative principle at the very root of economic relations in village India, making it easy to contrast it with the logic of the market as defined by the West. The jajmani system was a good example of what Polanyi termed a 'redistributive' system, and its study allied Indian sociologists with the substantivist school.

It is for this reason that when C.J. Fuller (1989) and Peter Mayer (1993) systematically exposed the methodological weakness of the arguments which overstressed the importance of the jajmani system in the rural economy a turning point in the economic anthropology of India was reached. In particular, Fuller demonstrated the huge discrepancy which had always existed between the theorization of jajmani relations and the empirical evidence about them. In fact, he showed, beyond any possible doubt, that there was no general economic principle which corresponded to the variety of economic formations found in different parts of India. Neither could it be said that highly localized economic structures could be understood purely in terms of jajmani relations. Monetary transactions often existed alongside transactions in kind and were often an accompaniment to jajmani relations.

Once it is recognized that monetary exchanges are not incompatible with Indian social and cultural values, it becomes possible to re-evaluate the place of the market and trade within the sociological study of India.

Actors in the Market

In Indian markets, the social identity of local traders is often highly specific. Even in major cities like Delhi with a complex history of migration and rapid economic change, the vast majority of traders belong to specific socio-religious groups. Often a particular market is dominated by a particular community. For example, in the principal grain market of Delhi we find that most of the traders belong to the business communities of Haryana. Though the economic context of this market has changed considerably since Independence, there is evidence to suggest that it was these same communities which dominated it back in the first half of the nineteenth century (Bayly 1983: 332). Similarly, in local towns throughout south India grain markets tend to be dominated by traders belonging to specific communities (Harris-White 1996). While such a pattern is no doubt common in many places throughout India, and constitutes an important element of the sociology of the market, it is important to avoid the types of misinterpretations which are often made about its significance.

The first misinterpretation is about how such clusters reproduce themselves. If a trader's son becomes a trader, it is not because he is compelled to continue the tradition of his caste in any simplistic way. Rather, he is likely to explain his choice in terms of the fact that by following the family profession, he will have the best opportunity in terms of immediate access to business know-how, social and trading networks, and material facilities. However, one finds members of the same caste in a variety of different professions.

More generally, gender, caste, regional origin, and economic power are all significant factors of the identity of traders but their particular relevance varies according to specific markets, localities, and professions. It is possible to find a group of traders all of the same caste, even when this caste is not conventionally associated with trading activities. For example, in the street market for Gujarati embroidery in Ahmedabad, all the traders are from the same caste and most are linked by close kinship ties, yet their ancestors had no links with this trade (Tarlo 1997). What matters is not caste identity as such, but the types of networks that a person's identity enables him or her to tap into, both in terms of business opportunities and social connections. This is true not only for traders but for all types of participants in the market. For example, in the grain market of Delhi, it is not only the traders who have a specific identity, but also accountants, peons, and coolies. In each case it is different criterion that is emphasized. In the case of coolies in the grain market of Delhi, for example, it is regional origin, rather than caste identity, which forms the most important basis on which networks are established.

The example of the coolies in Old Delhi also highlights another common stumbling block in the sociological interpretation of markets. It is often assumed that markets can be distinguished according to whether they are organized along corporate or individual lines. However, in old Delhi we find that some coolies are operating purely on an individual basis whilst others, by contrast, pool all their earnings and work together in teams.

Finally, it is a mistake to consider that networks based on different aspects of social identity (caste, religion, locality, kinship, etc.) are necessarily obstacles to the smooth functioning of the market, as economists from Adam Smith onwards have tended to assume. Not only can one demonstrate that it is often by the mobilization of such networks that Indian markets are constituted (Tarlo 1997) and maintained (Lachaier 1997), but also that social networks play an equally crucial role in markets in the West which are generally supposed to be the purest incarnation of neoclassic economics (Carrier 1997).

Once we recognize that the perspective of the conventional economist is undersocialized whilst that of the conventional social anthropologist is generally oversocialized, it becomes clear that the study of socio-economic networks is essential to any empirical understanding of the market. And once such networks are placed at the centre of the analysis, the distinction usually drawn between economic transactions in western and non-western societies rapidly dissolves. Not only do economic transactions in non-western countries appear much less embedded than previously assumed, but also economic transactions in western societies appear much more embedded than economists have supposed (Granovetter 1992).

By rediscovering the importance of markets in India, anthropologists can now make use of the advances made in other social sciences. On the one hand, they can take advantage of research on markets in other parts of the world for studying markets in India, without either sacrificing or exaggerating Indian specificities. On the other hand, they can take advantage of the studies done in India which may have a real sociological content but were conducted under the umbrella of other disciplines such as economic geography, economic history, and political economy. The question which then emerges is how can one make use of these different works, not only in order to get a more satisfying picture of the history, geography, and sociology of markets in India, but also to reconsider the concept of the market itself in a broader context.

Redefining Markets

Analysing the economic writings of Indian nationalist thinkers (from Justice Ranade and his classic address on the Indian Political Economy, delivered at Pune in 1892 to the works of K.T. Telang, Dadhabhai, Bipen Chandra Pal, or G. Subramanya Iyer and others), Bipan Chandra has shown their awareness of the Eurocentric bias of economic theory. This, they felt, limited both its significance and its applicability to India (Chandra 1966). This tradition of defiance helps explain why economists who have worked either in or about India have kept a distance from neoclassic theory, many pointing out its limitations and recognizing the legitimacy of historical and sociological approaches. But although many have criticized the neoclassic theory of the market from the perspective of the political economy, this exercise has often proved little more than an intellectual routine (Basu 1994: 111–18).

Goods, Money, or Commodities?

Markets have been criticized both for dissolving social bonds and for reducing goods to commodities. This point of view has been perpetuated as much by economists as anthropologists. The latter have generally maintained a clear-cut distinction between the status of things which circulate as gifts and those which circulate as commodities (Mauss 1970). In the former case objects are thought to retain something of the quality of the giver whereas in the latter case they become neutralized through the market. However, as Appadurai and others have shown, such a distinction only makes sense if one ignores the trajectories which objects follow before and after they enter the market context (Appadurai 1986).

In his anthropological study of the Muria Gonds, Alfred Gell points out that consumption is generally identified with the destruction of goods and that this may well be because our notion of consumption is conceptualized on the basis of eatables. He goes on to argue that 'consumption as a general phenomenon really has nothing to do with the destruction of goods and wealth, but with their reincorporation into the social system that produced them in some other guise' (Gell 1986: 112). One only has to consider the land market to recognize the inappropriateness of the metaphor of destruction. Such observations highlight the deficiencies of the economic categories so often accepted as uncontested truths.

To take another example, let us consider the market for jewellery which plays a very important role in Indian social and economic life. Much of a woman's jewellery is given to her at the time of marriage. This means that shortly after being purchased in the market place, jewellery will apparently lose its status as 'commodity' and acquire the new status of 'gift.' In fact, jewellery serves several functions at once. Not only is it both a beautifier and symbol of status and wealth but also it is considered a form of quasi-money which can be exchanged for other commodities or used in pawnbroking as a guarantee for loans. Viewed in this context, jewellery plays a very significant role in the monetization of the Indian economy.

What is true for jewellery is also true for other things. In a fascinating historical study, Christopher Bayly has demonstrated the diverse range of roles played by cloth in socio-economic life in India during the eighteenth and nineteenth centuries. He demonstrates how the Moghuls used textiles in a complex circuit of tribute and redistribution in such a way that 'at no point did cloth become "merely" a commodity whose production and distribution was solely determined by market forces'. Bayly also argues that even when cloth is acquired through the market place, it nevertheless retains the qualities associated with the conditions of its production and sale. So, even from this point of view, the distinction usually made between gift relationships and market relationships loses much of its relevance. As with the jewellery example it is not only the distinction between 'gifts' and 'commodities' that is called into question but also that between 'money' and 'commodities'.

The Market and the State

In India, as elsewhere, most of the public debates surrounding the market in the last two decades have focused on the issues of economic liberalization and deregulation. In its crudest and most ideological version, which is also its most common form, the whole debate is reduced to a simplistic dichotomy between the influence of the state, thought to impede the optimal functioning of the economy, and the influence of market institutions, thought to encourage it.

A more refined version of the same argument—largely developed nowadays in economic literature—consists in arguing that non-markert institutions cannot simply be regarded as negative and arbitrary influences on economic life which can be removed at will. State intervention can in fact be motivated by the 'failure' of markets. In such cases 'non-market' institutions are considered a 'rational' answer to the functioning of the economy. This is the line of argument first used by economists like R.H. Coase then Oliver E. Williamson in their explanations of the existence of firms, and on which the theoretical advances put forward by the 'new institutional economics' school are built (Williamson and Winter 1993).

A more socially sensitive form of the same argument is found in the work of Amartya Sen and Jean Drèze, though they would not necessarily identify with this school (Drèze and Sen 1995). In order to widen the debate from its narrow concentration on issues of liberalization, they insist on the importance of distinguishing between different domains: those where state intervention may be considered an impediment to the efficiency of the market and those where state intervention should be considered not only necessary but also desirable. For example, in areas like primary education or public health, they argue that it does not make sense to consider that there is (or could be) any real competition between the market and the state in a country like India. As a matter of fact, state intervention needs to be increased. So whilst it makes sense to debate the relative efficiency of the state and the market in domains where they are 'excluding' each other, one must also recognize that there are many domains where they should rather be complementary (Drèze and Sen 1995: 9–27).

From a sociological and anthropological point of view, the dichotomy between market and state is more than just a question of economic policy. First, in these disciplines, it is generally taken for granted that state and market are largely interdependent institutions. But the interaction between market and state is also much more complicated than is generally assumed. For example, every time individuals are confronted with one or another form of corruption, they are obliged to settle the debate about the 'deregulation' of government activities on their own terms and for their own use. So, an immediate consequence of corruption in ordinary life is to 'privatize' a debate which is more often analysed as a public one. More fundamentally, the accumulative result of this is to blur precisely the sort of distinctions that Drèze and Sen attempt to establish between 'market-complementary' governmental activities and 'market-excluding' ones. For example, access to public social amenities and services in the fields of health and education are often more 'privatized' than they appear. Moreover, while simple acts of corruption displace rather than abolish the distinction between monetary transactions and public services, such a distinction rapidly becomes irrelevant in the case of more insidious forms of corruption based on social networks and patronage. Such considerations are interestingly taken into account by an economist like Kaushik Basu, when he argues that 'the problem with the Indian economy is not that its market is less or more free but that its freedom is in the wrong domains' (Basu 1994: 154).

Buying and Selling

It is not only corruption but also a certain laxity in the enforcement of social and legal norms which must be taken into account for analysing the functioning of the market in India. Such, for example, is the case with the real-estate market. In all Indian cities, but particularly in major ones, a large amount of land is bought, built on, or sold without legal authorization. As a consequence of this, property rights cannot be taken for granted. And even when property rights are not questioned as such, broken contracts are very common and the legal apparatus for dealing with them is slow and inefficient. More generally, in the context of Indian markets, transactions are often made without formal contracts to fall back on. Such occurences are well known and scholars as different as Kaushik Basu and Amiya Kumar Bagchi have noted the importance of taking them into consideration when studying markets in India (Basu 1989: 51–5). This is also why both insist on the importance of trust in market transactions where there is always 'a time lag, however brief, between each agent performing his side of the exchange' (Basu 1989: 53). But even if it is worth noticing that 'where contract-adherence norms are weak, markets function poorly and may not even exist' (Basu 1989: 53), one should also point out the possibility of the opposite phenomenon. In some contexts it is precisely because the level of trust that exists between all sorts of actors that the time lag between transactions may, in fact, be extended as different categories of intermediaries become involved, and the market thereby expands.

The Key Role of Intermediaries

At first sight markets in large Indian cities look as if they might conform to the neoclassic paradigm: the choice of goods is plentiful, as is the competition; customers are free to purchase goods where they wish, to enquire about their quality and to negotiate prices to their advantage. And as long as they are willing to pay cash, the anonymity of buyers and sellers does not impede negotiations. However, only a very small proportion of commercial transactions actually conform to such a description. More usually, customers know exactly where they want to buy. This may be because they are regular clients of a particular shop or because a particular shop has been recommended to them. This is not to say that price and quality do not enter the equation, but rather that commercial transactions are usally enmeshed in a series of other factors where the identities of sellers and buyers are taken into account. These interactions are not dissimilar from what Clifford Geertz describes in his study of Moroccan bazaars (Geertz 1992). The merit of Geertz's analysis is his avoidance of the trap of assuming that one should give a central role to social and cultural factors in explaining bazaar transactions on the one hand, and discarding them automatically while describing market principles on the other. He bases his distinction between markets and bazaars on the way in which knowledge and information are acquired in each. In bazaars, the search for information is primarily intensive because knowledge has to be acquired by asking a large number of diagnostic questions to a few people, rather than a handful of index questions to a large number of people. The former approach, exploring nuances rather than canvassing populations, is what characterizes the bazaar economy in Geertz's view.

However, when one tries to apply Geertz's model of the bazaar to the Indian context, one finds that his analysis applies only to retail transactions. Only here can one draw an effective contrast between 'extensive' and 'intensive' forms of search for economic information; or that one can oppose anonymous styles of market interactions with more personalized ones between buyers and sellers. But when one analyses the sort of commercial transactions which take place between buyers and sellers at the wholesale level, not only the style but also the whole process and inner logic of the transactions totally changes. Not only can one no longer contrast different sorts of economic transactions on the basis of the knowledge that buyers and sellers individually possess, but, more fundamentally, one can no longer consider the confrontation between buyers and sellers as a the central element of the market institution. Rather, it is the presence of intermediaries and the different functions they assume that defines the characteristics of the market.[2]

At first sight, the activity of brokerage might seem a simple act of mediation between supply and demand, and the percentage taken on negotiations made via a broker might simply be considered as one of the many 'transaction costs' known to characterize any market. However, it needs to be recognized that the very existence of brokerage does, in fact, radically change the characteristics of the market. What it does is allow buyers to know what is available in a market well beyond their individual capacities for acquiring information. It also allows traders to know about the demand in the market place well beyond their capacities to accumulate information directly through their networks of clients; third, the mediation of brokers introduces a degree of trust between market partners who would not otherwise know each other sufficiently for entering into commercial relations. This is a particularly crucial point because all significant transactions involve financial credit which presupposes both trust and knowledge about the credibility of the partners involved.

In other words, brokerage cannot be dismissed as marginal to the functioning of the market; on the contrary, it is the most decisive element in the constitution of the market itself. It is through the broker that supply and demand are defined and that the evaluation of customer and trader is made. The same trader may be presnted as a simple shopkeeper to some and as a commercial intermediary or potential business partner to others. Similarly, a customer who might not be taken seriously if unknown to a trader might be considered an important client if introduced in the right manner by the right broker. In other words, both the market actors and the supply and demand undergo a constant process of redefinition with the result that the same market will appear in a very different light according to the identity of different actors.

The role of brokerage in Indian markets is one example which shows why it is necessary to reconsider most of the hypothesis which lies at the foundation of the standard interpretation of markets. What characterizes the institution of brokerage is precisely the fact that it blurs the sorts of distinctions which are usually made between markets and bazaars but, more generally, between 'neoclassic markets' and supposedly less 'rational' economic institutions. Basically, in any market where brokerage prevails, all transactions are concretely made on a very personalized basis between people and intermediaries. And yet, at the same time, the buyers and sellers often remain anonymous to each other.

All over the world, markets are intricate institutional or quasi-institutional spaces in which different sorts of actors, often with different sets of values, interact, and which cannot be understood purely in terms of a confrontation between buyers and sellers. This is certainly the case with India. Barbara Harriss-White's work on the grain market (1996) confirms the impossibility of reducing the function of trade to a simple intermediary stage between production and consumption. In the entire sample of merchant firms that she studied, none limited its activities to buying and selling. All of them were involved to varying degrees in other activities which ran all along the economic chain from agricultural production until the delivery of products to the final selling point. The pattern of their involvement was so diverse that she considered it impossible to classify according to function and had to devise new ways of analysing them in a pluri-functional perspective. Her example demonstrates the impossibility of reducing the market to a simple encounter between buyers and sellers or, at a more abstract level, between demand and supply.

Demand and Supply

Until quite recently, two sorts of theoretical perspectives have dominated the debate in economic literature. On the one hand there are those who insisted on the crucial importance of production in the economic process; on the other are those who focused on exchange. It was also taken for granted by many sociologists that to analyse society from an economic perspective, it was necessary to focus on the domain of production which was considered the driving force behind social and cultural identities. In most of these approaches, the role of consumption was largely ignored. The works of scholars like Werner Sombart or Thorstein Veblen were unusual in according a significant role to the consumption process. However, from the 1970s onwards, an increasing number of social scientists began to insist on the declining importance of the sphere of production in post-industrial societies. Follwoing thinkers like Jean Baudrillard and Roland Barthes, renewed importance was given to the symbolism of consumption and, more particularly, its importance for defining identities (Douglas and Isherwood 1978).

It is no coincidence that this new trend should find an echo in social and cultural anthropology. Most anthropologists, with the exception of Marxists, have always privileged the process of exchange above the process of production. Nevertheless, as I have already suggested, the one form of exchange which anthropologists rarely considered worthy of study was monetary transactions in 'ordinary' markets. So, in spite of the obvious importance of market culture in India, there were very few studies by sociologists and anthropologists which delineated the sorts of cultural practices displayed in Indian markets. Until recently, Ostor's study of bazaars in Bengal could be considered an exception (Ostor 1984). Nevertheless, new research has now been undertaken in this domain (cf., for example, Carrithers and Humphreys 1991; Cadene and Vidal 1997). The other dominant tendency in economic anthropology was to consider consumption and the use of objects largely in terms of their symbolic meaning rather than their utilitarian use. It is only recently that the importance of consumption in the making of social identities has been highlighted in different case studies (Appadurai 1986; Breckenridge 1993). For example, Emma Tarlo's study of the clothing choices made by different groups in India highlights the symbolic importance of consumption practices (Tarlo 1996).

Such works undoubtedly give new insights into a previously neglected domain; but it is also interesting to reflect on the reasons for this sudden interest in consumption in the social sciences.[3] A historical comparison may be helpful here. William Reddy has shown, for example, that until the second half of the eighteenth century, market people in France possessed considerable expertise concerning the goods in which they dealt but had very little interest in how these goods were produced (Reddy 1986). Nevertheless, in the few decades which preceded the French Revolution, new attitudes developed and market people started taking a strong interest in the details of production they had happily ignored until then. Reddy argues that this apparently small change was part of a larger cultural shift which was to completely transform the existing perceptions of the economic process; and this cultural shift took place before any technological transformation had occurred. The question is, might the sort of demonstration that Reddy makes for eighteenth-century France be helpful for understanding contemporary trends? Is it not the case that another cultural shift of similar importance is taking place today in the economic field? But while, in eighteenth-century Europe, the consequence was to affirm the link between the market and production, today it is to reinforce the link between the market and consumption.

Conclusion: Towards an Anthropological Study of Markets

To summarize, the study of markets in the social sciences has long been dominated by two perspectives: the dominant tendency, especially among economists, to analyse the functioning of the market in a formalist manner, leaving little space for sociological or historical consider-ations, and a counter-tendency, especially among sociologists and anthropologists, to dismiss the abstract model of the market because of its ideological content and to focus on the destructive characteristic of the market economy. However, in the case of India, what was fundamentally lacking was the attempt to reformulate the analysis of markets on the basis of Indian material. As far as economists and economic historians were concerned, the question was rather to know which of the existing frames of analysis Indian markets could better illustrate. Whilst attempts to impose a neoclassic frame were few,[4] there was much discussion concerning the exact nature of the Indian economy at different stages of its history, especially from a Marxist point of view.[5] Whilst most sociologists shared the same debates and some-times the same perspective as economists (Breman 1985) the majority of anthropologists sim-ply ignored the existence of the market altogether because it did not fit their idea of India.

There has, nevertheless, been an important renewal of interest in the anthropology of markets in the last two decades. This interest has taken two directions. On the one hand, the study of networks came to play a central role in the study of markets both in non-western and in western contexts. On the other hand, diverse notions and interpretations of the market—including academic ones—have ceased to be perceived either as pure ideologies in the Marxist sense or as more or less adequate representations of the 'real world'. Finally, a few sociologists and anthropologists attempted to contextualize interpretations of 'the market' and to study how people were using such interpretations (Carrier 1997). It was, in a way, only to be expected. This is, after all, what they have done for most institutions they have studied in different cultures.

One of the main strengths of the new sociological perspective on markets is that it should help definitively to dissolve the false dichotomy which has survived for so long between the study of markets in the West and non-West. On the one hand, it enables us to recognize the discontinuities in the progress of market culture in the West. On the other hand, it helps us also to recognize the exaggerated nature of the civilization gap assumed by the distinction between market economy and all other forms of economic organization. As a result, recent advances in economic sociology of the market are no more confined to western economies as the two collective volumes edited by Stuart Plattner and by Roy Dilley show (Dilley 1992). The study of Indian markets is playing an increasing role in this wider process. Kaushik Basu points out:

A developing country provides a fascinating range of institutions. A lot of these remains unexplored because these phenomena are not of primary interest to economists in developed countries and economists in developing nations have a tendency to choose their research agenda from ongoing themes published in the major journals of developed countries [Basu 1994: 115].

In economic sociology and economic anthropology, this trend is slowly being reverted.

ENDNOTES

1. For an anthropological evaluation of this school, cf. Harris et al. 1995.
2. For another interpretation of bazaar transactions in India, cf. Panselow 1990.
3. For one critical interpretation of this trend, see Carrier and Heyman 1997.
4. For an exception, see M.D. Morris 1967.
5. For a critical assessment of these debates, see Subrahmanyam 1994 and 1996.

REFERENCES

Aggarwal, B.L., ed. 1989. *Alternative Economic Structures*. Delhi: Allied Publishers.
Appadurai, A., ed. 1986. *The Social Life of Things: Commodities in Cultural Perspective*. Cambridge: Cambridge University Press.
Basu, K. 1989. 'Limitations of the Free Market: Conjectures, Customs and Norms'. In B.L. Agarwal, ed., *Alternative Economic Structures*, 51–5. Delhi: IAS and Allied Publishers.
———. 1994. *Of People, of Places: Sketches from an Economist's Notebook*. Delhi: Oxford University Press.
Bates, R.H. 1995. 'Social Dilemmas and Rational Individuals: An Assessment of the New Institutionalism'. In J. Harris, J. Hunter and M. Lewis, eds, *The New Institutional Economics and Third World Development*, 27–48. London: Routledge.
Bayly, C.A. 1983. *Rulers, Townsmen and Bazaars: North Indian Society in the Age of British Expansion, 1770–1870*. Cambridge: Cambridge University Press.
Bloch M. and Parry, J. ed. 1989. *Money and the Morality of Exchange*. Cambridge: Cambridge University Press.
Breckenridge, C.A. ed. 1993. *Consuming Modernity: Public culture in contemporary India*. Delhi: Oxford University Press.
Breckenridge, C.A. P. and Van der Veer, eds 1994. *Orientalism and the Postcolonial Predicament*. Delhi: Oxford University Press.
Breman, J. 1985. *Of Peasants, Migrants and Paupers: Rural Labour Circulation and Capitalist Production in West India*. Delhi: Oxford University Press.
Cadène, P. and D. Vidal, eds. 1997. *Webs of Trade*. Delhi: Manohar Publishers.
Carrier, J.G. ed., 1997. *Meanings of the Market: The Free Market in Western Culture*. Oxford: Berg

Carrier, J.G. and J.M.C. Heyman. 1997. 'Consumption and Political Economy'. *Journal of the Royal Anthropological Institute* (n.s.). 3:355–73.

Carrithers, M. and C. Humphreys, eds. 1991. *The Assembly of Listeners: Jains in Society*. Cambridge: Cambridge University Press.

Chakravarty, S. 1993. 'Prologue: Economics as Seen by a Dissenting Economist'. In *Selected Economic Writings*. Delhi: Oxford University Press.

Chandra, B. 1966. *The Rise and Growth of Economic Nationalism in India*. Delhi: People's Publishing House.

Chaudhuri, K.N. 1994. 'Markets and Traders in India during the Seventeenth and Eighteenth Century'. In S. Subrahmanyam, ed., *Money and the Market in India 1100–1700,* Delhi: Oxford University Press.

Dilley, R., ed. 1992. *Contesting Markets; Analyses of Ideology, Discourse and Practice*. Edinburg; Edinburg University Press.

Douglas, M.and B. Isherwood. 1978. *The World of Goods*. Harmondsworth: Penguin.

Drèze, J. and Amartya Sen. 1995. *India: Economic Development and Social Opportunity*. Delhi: Oxford University Press.

Dumont, L. 1970. *Homo Hierarchicus: The Caste System and Its Implications*. London: Weidenfeld and Nicholson.

Fuller, C.J. 1989. 'Misconceiving the Grain Heap: A Critique of the Concept of the Indian Jajmani System'. In M. Bloch, and J. Parry, eds, *Money and the Morality of Exchange,* 33–63. Cambridge: Cambridge University Press.

Geertz, C. 1992. 'The Bazaar Economy: Information and Search in Peasant Marketing'. In M. Granovetter and R. Swedberg, eds, *The Sociology of Economic Life,* 225–32. Boulder: Westview Press

Gell, A. 1986. 'Newcomers to the World of Goods: Consumption among the Muria Gonds'. In A. Appadurai, ed., *The Social Life of Things: Commodities in Cultural Perspective,* 110–38. Cambridge: Cambridge University Press.

Granovetter, M. 1992. 'Economic Action and Social Structure: The Problem of Embeddedness'. In M. Granovetter and R. Swedberg, eds, *The Sociology of Economic Life,* 53–81. Boulder: Westview Press.

Granovetter, M. and R. Swedberg, ed. 1992. *The Sociology of Economic Life*. Boulder: Westview Press.

Habib, I. and T. Raychaudhury, eds. 1982. *The Cambridge Economic History of India,* vol. 1 (c.1200–c1750). Delhi: Orient Longman.

Hardiman, D. 1987. *The Coming of the Devi: Adivasi Assertion in Western India*. Delhi: Oxford University Press.

———. 1996. *Feeding the Baniya: Peasants and Usurers in Western India*. Delhi: Oxford University Press.

Harper, E.B. 1959. 'Two Systems of Economic Exchange in Village India'. *American Anthropologist*. 61:760–78.

Harris, J., J. Hunter and M. Lewis, eds. 1995. *The New Institutional Economics and Third World Development*. London: Routledge.

Harriss-White, B. 1995. 'Maps and Landscapes of Grain Markets in South Asia'. In J. Harris, J. Hunter and M. Lewis, eds, *The New Institutional Economics and Third World Development,* 87–108. London: Routledge.

———. 1996. *A Political Economy of Agricultural Markets in South India*. New Delhi: Sage Publications.

Hobsbawm, E. and T. Ranger, eds. 1983. *The Invention of Traditions*. Cambridge: Cambridge University Press.

Kahn, J.S. 1997. 'Demons, Commodities and the History of Anthropology'. In J.G. Carrier, ed., *Meanings of the Market,* 69–99. Oxford: Berg.

Kolff, D.H.A. 1990. *Naukar, Rajput & Sepoy: The Ethnohistory of the Military Labour Market in Hindustan, 1450–1850*. Cambridge: Cambridge University Press.

Lachaier, P. 1977. 'The Merchant Lineage Firm and the Non-Invisible Hand: Pune, Maharashtra'. In P. Cadène and D. Vidal, eds, *Webs of Trade*, 23–52. Delhi: Manohar Publishers.

Mauss, M. 1970. *The Gift*. London: Cohen and West.

Morris, M.D. 1967. 'Values as an Obstacle to Economic Growth in South Asia: An Historical Survey'. *Journal of Economic History*. 27(4).

Ostor, A. 1984. *Culture and Power: Legend, Ritual, Bazaar and Rebellion in a Bengali Society*. New Delhi: Sage Publications.

Parry, J. 1989. 'On the Moral Perils of Exchange'. In M. Bloch and J. Parry, eds, *Money and the Morality of Exchange*, 64–93. Cambridge: Cambridge University Press.

Pocock, D.F. 1969. 'Notes on *jajmani* relationships'. *Contributions to Indian Sociology*, 6:78–95.

Polanyi, K.1957. *The Great Transformation: The Political and Economic Origins of Our Time*. Boston: Beacon Press.

Polanyi, K. 1992. 'The Economy as Instituted Process'. In M. Granovetter and R. Swedberg, eds, *The Sociology of Economic Life*, 29–52. Boulder: Westview Press.

Polanyi, K., C.M. Arensberg, and H.W. Pearson, eds. 1957. *Trade and Market in the Early Empires*. Glencoe: The Free Press.

Reddy, W.M. 1986. 'The Structure of a Cultural Crisis: Thinking about Cloth in France before and after the Revolution'. In A. Appadurai, ed., *The Social Life of Things: Commodities in Cultural Perspective*, 261–84. Cambridge: Cambridge University Press.

Stein, B. and S. Subrahmanyam, eds. 1996. *Institutions and Economic Change in South Asia*. Delhi: Oxford University Press.

Sombart, W. 1967. *Luxury and Capitalism:* Ann Arbor: University of Michigan Press.

Subrahmanyam S. ed. 1994. *Money and the Market in India 1100–1700*. Delhi: Oxford University Press.

Subrahmanyam S. 1996. 'Institutions, Agency and Economic Change in South Asia: A Survey and Some Suggestions'. In B. Stein and S. Subrahmanyam, eds, *Institutions and Economic Change in South Asia*, 14–47. Delhi: Oxford University Press.

Tarlo, E. 1996. *Clothing Matters: Dress and Identity in India*. Delhi: Viking.

———. 1997. 'The Genesis and Growth of a Business community: A Case Study of Vaghri Street Traders in Ahmedabad'. In P. Cadène & D. Vidal, eds, *Webs of Trade*, 53–84. Delhi: Manohar Publishers.

Taussig, M. 1980. *The Devil and Commodity Fetishism in South America*. Chapel Hill: The University of North Carolina Press.

Veblen, T. 1967. *The Theory of the Leisure Class*. New York: Penguin.

Vidal, D. 1997. 'Rural Credit and the Fabric of Society in Colonial India: Sirohi District, Rajasthan'. In P. Cadène and D. Vidal, eds, *Webs of Trade*, 85–107. Delhi: Manohar Publishers.

Williamson, O.E. and S.G. Winter, eds. 1993. *The Nature of the Firm; Origins, Evolution and Development*. New York: Oxford University Press.

Wiser, W.H. 1958. *The Hindu Jajamani System*. Lucknow: Lucknow Publishing House.

Zelizer, V.A. 1992. 'Human Values and the Market: The Case of Life Insurance and Death in 19th-Century America'. In M. Grandovetter, and R. Swedberg, eds, *The Sociology of Economic Life*, 285–304. Boulder: Westview Press.

The Informal Sector

JAN BREMAN

INTRODUCTION

The term, 'informal sector' dates from the early 1970s when it was coined by Hart in a study on Ghana to describe urban employment outside the organized labour market. This category includes a great diversity of occupations characterized by self-employment (Hart 1971). His chapter, which was based on anthropological fieldwork, brought attention to the enormous variety of economic activities carried out by a large part of the population of Accra in order to survive. These activities were not registered anywhere and were often clandestine in nature or at any rate outside the framework of official regulations. The improvised and inadequate manner whereby this took place demonstrated that the people engaging in them lived mostly in poverty and were to be found at the bottom of the urban landscape.

The concept quickly became popular when the International Labour Organization (ILO), as part of its World Employment Programme, sent out missions to examine the employment situation outside the modern, organized, large-scale, and capital-intensive sectors of the economy. The first of these country reports investigated Kenya and the Philippines (ILO 1972 and 1974). These studies were followed by reports that examined the particular features of the 'informal sector' in a number of Third World cities such as Calcutta, Jakarta, Dakar, Abidjan, and Sao Paulo.[1] To supplement these case studies, the ILO commissioned a number of more analytical essays such as those authored by Sethuraman (1976) and Kanappan (1977), and the World Bank published a paper by Mazumdar (1975).

As a result of the way the concept had been framed and the attention it subsequently drew from development economists and policy makers in particular, the informal sector became, to a significant extent, associated with the economy of the large cities of Africa, Asia, and Latin America. Most of these cases concern societies with a predominantly rural-cum-agrarian identity in which the process of urbanization began relatively recently. The dynamics of this spatial shift in settlement patterns include the declining importance of agriculture as the principal source of economic production and the expulsion from village habitats particularly the growing proportion of the land-poor peasantry. However, this transition has not been marked by a concomitant expansion in the metropoles of 'technologically advanced' and 'modernly organized' industries, aimed at enabling the accommodation of this newly mobile section of the population from the rural hinterland. Only a small part of the labour that reaches the urban areas manages to penetrate the 'secure' zones of regular, more-skilled and hence better-paid work. The majority of migrants must be satisfied with casual labour which is unskilled or pseudo-skilled, has no fixed working hours, provides a low income which, moreover, fluctuates significantly and, finally, is only available seasonally.

The description of the informal sector is characterized by analytical vagueness. In order to indicate the wide repertoire of occupations, commentators often confine themselves to an arbitrary enumeration of activities which one comes across walking through the streets of the Third World metropoles. Included in this parade are market-stall holders, lottery-ticket sellers, parking attendants, vendors of food and drink, housemaids and market women, messengers and porters, ambulant artisans and repairmen, construction and road-building workers, trans-porters of people and cargo, and shoe polishers and newspaper boys. Numerous occupations on the seamy side of society such as pimps and prostitutes, rag pickers and scavengers, quacks, conjurers and confidence tricksters, bootleggers and drug pedlars, beggars, pickpockets, and other petty thieves are not omitted. It is a colourful arrangement of irregularly working people that scratches around for a living close to or at the bottom of urban society and which, in the overwhelming majority of cases, both lives and works in extremely precarious circumstances.

Origins

The division of the urban economy into two sectors can be seen as a variant of the dualism theories that had gained currency at an earlier time. Basing himself on colonial Indonesia, the Dutch economist Boeke voiced the idea at the beginning of this century that native producers had not internalized in their behaviour the basic principles of the homo economicus. Unlimited needs and their deferred gratification in accordance with a rational assessment of costs and benefits did not stand at the forefront of the peasant way of life in the Orient. What marked the orient was the immediate and impulsive indulgence of limited wants. This colonial doctrine of what Boeke referred to as homo socialis would return in later development studies as the image of the working masses in underdeveloped countries obstinately refusing to respond to the primacy of economic stimuli.[2]

The rejection of the axiom that there is a real difference in rationality and optimalization behaviour between western and eastern civilizations ended in the construction of a new con-tradistinction in post-colonial development economics, namely that between the countryside and the city. This spatial contrast corresponded more or less with a sectoral division between agriculture and industry. Western mankind was superseded by the city-industrial complex as the dynamic factor, against which village and agriculture were seen as static and diametrically opposed. The new dualism theory, like its precursor, was associated with the rise of capitalism as the organizing principle of economic life. While the bulk of the peasants in the villages were attributed an outlook restricted to subsistence, modern industry was expected to concentrate outside the agrarian sector and in the urban milieu. According to this line of thinking, the contradiction between both sectors was indeed not of a fundamental nature but merely reflected different stages of social development which corresponded with the traditional–modern di-chotomy. The dualism concept in this sense was used first by Lewis (1954) and subsequently by Fei and Ranis (1964) with the aim of examining the outflow of superfluous labour from the rural subsistence economy and to trace the arrival of this labour in urban growth poles as part of the gradual expansion of non-agrarian production. The evolution of social transformation in developing countries is, in this scheme of interpretation, similar to the capitalist process of change that took place in the Atlantic part of the world in an earlier phase.

It is against this background that the latest version of the dualism model, now under discussion, should be understood. Urban agglomerations are not growing exclusively or even predominantly as centres of technologically advanced industrial production along capitalist lines. In addition to the presence of an economic circuit that does fit this description, there is also a sector consisting of a plethora of activities of a completely different nature. Key terms such as 'modern management' and 'capitalist organization' appear to be scarcely relevant for this sector. The combination of a slow pace of factorized industrialization, the presence of excess labour due to increased demographic growth and the expulsion from the agricultural economy, are given as the principal causes leading to a dualist system in cities of the Third World. The lower echelons in this bipolar order consist of the mass of the working poor who have a much lower rate of productivity than those in the technologically advanced section of the economy. To the latter, this rapidly increasing segment of urban population, as yet and perhaps forever, cannot obtain access.

Can the wide range of activities which informal-sector workers have to depend on for their survival be seen as 'traditional'? This is the stereotypical notion of those modes of production in which emphasis is laid on their old-fashioned and outmoded character. They depend on fairly simple occupational skills and employ very meagre as well as inadequate tools. The sparse availability of means of production based on superior technology results in a return on labour that is almost always quite low. A consequence is that, in order to scrape together a minimum income, the working day is extremely long while the work is also so physically demanding that poor health is a common occurrence. An argument against the tendency to portray the informal sector as traditional and 'pre-capitalist' is the fact that among the enormous variety of activities that fall under this category, very many in fact were created by the capitalist transformation of the urban milieu. It would be misleading to suggest that the observed urban dualism is shaped, on the one hand, by a dynamic growth pole marked by advanced technology and innovative organizational management and, on the other, by a more or less static circuit of long-established, miscellaneous, and stubbornly surviving but outdated pre-capitalist activities. Instead of speaking of a gradually disappearing contradiction between 'modern' and 'traditional', or capitalist versus non-capitalist, in my opinion what should be emphasized is the drastic restructuring of the entire economic system whereby the interdependence between different sectors needs to be identified as the most important element. This conclusion is in part derived from an appraisal of the transformation which took place in the western world over a period of more than a century and for which the dual processes of urbanization and industrialization were of major importance. Without wanting to suggest that societies that until recently were rural/agrarian are currently experiencing a similar process of change, I would nevertheless like to draw attention to the fact that what is now referred to as the informal sector, characterized by many different forms of self-employment and petty commodity production, has for a long time remained a marked feature in the urban economies of the northern hemisphere as well (see Stedman Jones 1971). Research on the various forms of the informal sector in developing countries, as it has been conducted since the 1970s, is handicapped by the virtual lack of comparison with the very profound changes in the organization of work and labour which went together with the emergence of metropolitan economies elsewhere in the world in the last two centuries. This lack of historical perspective coincides with the disciplinary background of the majority of researchers, mainly development economists and policy makers, who have little affinity with the need to understand the problem stated in a time span; they see little need for highlighting instead of obfuscating the continuing effects of the past on the present.

Clarification and Definition of Concepts

One of the first ILO reports on this subject discussed the informal sector by focusing on a set of characteristics: 'easy entry for the new enterprises, reliance on indigenous resources, family ownership, small scale operations, unregulated and competitive markets, labour intensive technology, and informally acquired skills of workers' (ILO 1972). The assumption behind this description is that the opposite of all these features applies to the formal sector of the economy. In this definition, which is built on an implicit contrast, it is not the type of economic activity but the way it is practised that is used as the differentiating criterion. In slightly different formulations, and supplemented with new suggestions, the above list of characteristics is found in a myriad of later studies. It is certainly possible to question the inclusion of some of these traits. For example, highly trained formal-sector professionals such as lawyers or accountants often run their businesses in a manner which does not satisfy the criterion of large-scale operation. And again, it is just as misleading to presume that at the bottom echelons of the urban economy newcomers can establish themselves without any trouble as vendors, shoe polishers, or beggars. Furthermore, features that were initially accorded great importance— such as the foreign origin of capital or technology, the use of mainly waged labour, the large and impersonal distance between the supply of and demand for commodities and services— appear, on closer examination, not to constitute the watershed between formal and informal. The easy answer to this criticism is that urban dualism must be understood not by assuming the validity of each and every separate characteristic but rather by looking at the total fabric in an ideal-type construction. Informal would then be the whole gamut of economic activities characterized by small scale, low capital-intensity, inferior technology, low productivity, predominantly family labour and property, no training or only that obtained 'on the job', easy entry, and finally a small and usually poor clientele. In this formulation, the emphasis lies on the subdivision of the urban economy into two independent circuits, each with its own logic, structural consistency, and dynamics.

Another form of the concept of economic dualism derives from the contrast made between an activity which is officially registered and sanctioned by official legislation and that which is not. The term informal, in this case, refers to operations which are kept out of the sight and control of the government and in this sense are also denoted as the 'parallel', 'underground', or 'shadow' economy. The legal recognition on which the formal sector can rely is not only expressed in the levying of taxes but also in the promulgation of various protective regulations. The much easier access to the state apparatus enjoyed by the owners or managers of formal-sector enterprises leads to disproportionate advantages in the granting of various facilities, such as credit and licences, as well as the selective use of government ordinances as to what is permitted and what is not. The privileged treatment claimed by formal-sector interests creates disadvantages or even renders criminal informal-sector activities when, for instance, these are seen as a hindrance to traffic on the street or as threatening 'public order'. Unregulated activities may also clash with the prevailing state ideology. In the former socialist regimes of central and eastern Europe, producers supplemented their income with transactions on the black market both outside and during official working hours. The conversion of the party leaders in post-Maoist China to free-market thinking went together with the legalization of various economic activities of an informal nature which, until then, had not been allowed or to which a blind eye had been turned.

When first using the concept, Hart did not omit to draw attention to the criminally inclined nature of some of the activities he enumerated. The association of informal with subversiveness or illegality is partly a result of an unwillingness to recognize the economic value of these goods and services. It should also be realized that excluding this great army of the deprived from access to space, water, and electricity, only encourages them to make clandestine use of these services and to contravene public health instructions. Yet the authorities are not slow to conduct large-scale campaigns against such violations of the law. In any case, it is clear that the government is not absent in this milieu but, on the contrary, actively concerns itself with disciplining the sector.

Furthermore, the dividing line in the two-sector model has to be drawn very differently when it comes to the observance of legislation and official regulations. There is a tendency to conceive of the informal economy as an unregistered, unregulated, and hence untaxed circuit. This, however, ignores the ease with which power holders, particularly the personnel in government agencies responsible for implementing formal regulations and laws, see this industry as their private hunting ground once it has been made invisible. Moreover, it would be a great distortion of reality to dissociate phenomena such as fraud, corruption, demands for the payment of speed, protection money, and bribes and, more generally, the conversion of public resources into private profits, from operations in the formal-sector economy where they primarily occur. This goes a long way in explaining why not only the legal incomes of politicians and policy makers, who are part of the elite, but also the basic salaries of many low-ranking health-care workers, police constables, and teachers lag far behind their incomes of an 'informal' nature.

The third and last variant of the formal- informal-sector dichotomy is related to the existence of bifurcated labour markets. A first feature to be discussed is the degree of division of labour. Formal-sector labour is usually performed in a complex work organization that consists of a set of specific tasks which are interrelated but are hierarchically and differently valued and which, to differing degrees, require previous training. The small scale, in combination with the low capital intensity, of informal- sector employment implies very little or no task differentiation and requires skills and knowledge which are picked up in daily practise.

Due to a lack of accurate and ongoing or periodical data collection, there is little known about the size, origin, and composition of the working population in the informal sector. The labour statistics which are maintained are mainly restricted to the supply and demand of permanent workers, who are recruited and dismissed on the basis of objectified criteria in the higher echelons of the urban economy. This registration is a result of, as well as condition for, greater control of the economy by official regulations. It is, therefore, not very surprising that studies of employment and labour relations have primarily focused on the upper segment of the urban order.

Given the above-mentioned characteristics, the alternative name for the informal sector as the zone of unorganized or unregistered labour is understandable, and just as clear as a third synonym, the unprotected sector. There are simply no legal rules concerning either entry into this sector or the conditions and circumstances under which informal-sector labour is put to work. If some elementary standards have been introduced—such as the fixing of a minimum wage, the ban on labour which is deleterious for health and the environment, and the prohibition of child labour or practices of bondage—a machinery for their enforcement is lacking. The organized, registered, and protected character of formal-sector labour is in diametrical opposition to this situation. In terms of organization, there is another advantage enjoyed by formal-sector workers, namely the possibility of setting up their own organizations in order to defend their common interests when dealing with employers or the government. This form of collective action increases the efficacy of the existing protection and is, at the same time, a means of extending this protection. In the informal-sector landscape, trade unions are only rarely encountered. This absence contributes further to the maintenance of low wages and to the social vulnerability and miserable conditions of employment in this sector.

The introduction of the concept 'informal sector' has irrefutably drawn attention to the jumbled mass of activities—unregulated, fragmented, and infinitely diverse—whereby a large part of the working population manages to survive, usually with a great deal of difficulty. Research on urban employment in the past was almost always restricted to labour in factories and other modern enterprises. Its recurring themes were the rural origin of the new working population, its adjustment to an industrial lifestyle, and the labour relations in these large-scale enterprises. With the shift in focus from the formal to the informal sector, the long-fostered idea that the large mass of workers who have not been incorporated in the labour process in a regular and standardized manner should, in fact, be seen as unemployed has been done away with.

On the other hand, the discussion on the informal sector has begged more questions than it has answered. This is the result of a lack of precision in the definition, where everything that is not regarded as belonging to the formal sector is categorized as 'informal'. This assumption, made very early on, gives a distinctly tautological slant to the difference made between the two sectors.[3] The dualism that has been discussed above relates sometimes to the labour market, sometimes to the economic circuits with different modes of production, and, in other cases, to permissible versus clandestine or plainly criminal economic activities. There is often a combination of all these variants with the implicit or explicit suggestion that the different criteria of the dual division run parallel to each other.[4] I fundamentally disagree with this idea. One of the definitional problems arises precisely from the discord between the different dimensions of the dualism concept. For example, it is simply not true that informal-sector workers produce goods and perform services only or even principally for clients in their own milieu, just as it is true that innumerable formal-sector commodities find their way to informal-sector consumers. Furthermore, formal-sector regulations are often avoided by transferring some or even all business activities and industrial production to the informal sector. These are only some arbitrarily chosen examples, amongst many, of the interdependence of the two sectors.

It is significant that authors who base their work on empirical research are often the most critical of this dual conceptualization. From my own long experience of studying rural and urban labour relations in western India, I conclude that the concept is useful in an 'ideal' sense only.[5] I believe that the informal sector cannot be demarcated as a separate economic circuit and/or a segment of the labour force. Attempts to persist with this strict demarcation create innumerable inconsistencies and problems which are discussed later. Instead of a two-sector model, there is a much more complex differentiation of the urban economy which should be the point of departure for structural analysis. The reduction to two sectors, the one capitalist and the other non- or early capitalist, does not reflect the reality of the much greater complexity of work and production. A final objection of perhaps greater importance is that, in assuming such a dualist system, the interrelationships between the various components of the economy threaten to be lost from sight. Instead of splitting up the urban system into two sectors, I want to emphasize the fragmented character of the total labour market and the need to see these fragments not as mutually exclusive, but as connected. This argument is central to my analysis (Breman 1994; 1996).

Size and Dynamics

Estimates of the size of the informal sector are not very precise and the figures which have been reported for various countries or cities differ greatly. This is a variation which does not, however, necessarily signal real differences in economic structure or developments over time. The most frequently cited estimates fluctuate between 30 and 70 per cent of the urban workforce. This very broad range is indicative of the serious lack of terminological clarity. Since the first use of the concept, a trend of upward correction has become apparent—both of the total number of workers and the proportion accounted for by the informal sector. Virtually all recent studies on this subject assume that at least half of the population in large Third World metropoles can be categorized as belonging to the informal sector, while this proportion is even higher for the smaller-sized cities and towns. The changing criteria used—including the nature of the work (industry, trade, transport, or services); the scale of operation (more or fewer than ten workers for each enterprise); use of other production factors than labour (energy and technology)—virtually exclude a systematic comparison of the estimates for different places and years. Based on official statistics, derived from the requirement to register the formal-sector labour, Visaria and Jacob estimated that, in 1972–3, 18.8 million of the total of 236.7 million working people in India belonged to the formal sector. In 1991 their number had increased to 26.7 million out of a total of 343.5 million. Hence, in both the first and last year, formal-sector employment came to less than 8 per cent of the total workforce (1995: 14). I may add here that I have little confidence in the completeness and reliability of the figures on which these estimates are based. Moreover, it should be realized that the data banks on employment and labour relations collected by international organizations such as the ILO and the World Bank are not much better.[6]

A serious methodological problem is that on both sides of the dividing line the working population is constituted very differently. Even the use of the term 'economically active' is of problematic significance for the informal sector. Women, the elderly, minors, and even the less able often participate in the work process, although their labour power is neither always nor fully used. This also applies to the labour power of able-bodied male adults at the peak of their physical strength. The ratio of earners to non-earners in homogeneous, informal-sector households is higher than that in pure formal-sector households. On the other hand, the working members of formal-sector households are more permanently employed. But to estimate that, of the working members of informal-sector households only one in eight is a woman—as Papola calculated on the basis of research in Ahmedabad—indicates significant under-registration in terms of gender (1981: 122). Similarly, until recently there has been systematic underestimation of the extent of child labour. The information to be found in the same source, that children constitute only 8 per cent of the workers in non-registered hotels and restaurants, is highly unlikely. The actual proportion of these young 'helpers' between 5 and 14 years must be at least double this figure.

The length of the working day in the informal sector is considerably greater than that in the formal sector and work often continues into the night. There are also no weekly off days, while annual festivals are celebrated much less or not at all. On the other hand, there are far greater seasonal fluctuations in the annual work cycle. The net effect of all these factors for the size and intensity of the labour power in the formal and informal sectors is difficult to ascertain. In order to obtain an insight into the living conditions of the poor masses, empirical research at the level of the household deserves priority. It is possible to understand the relative elasticity with which unemployment, greatly fluctuating incomes and other adversity are countered only by assuming that many, if not all members of households at the bottom of the urban heap—regardless of age, sex, or degree of physical ability—are, or want to be, partially or completely incorporated in the labour process.[7]

The specific nature of work arrangements in the informal sector seems to suggest a gradual continuum from employment to non-employment rather than a sharp break. The consequence of this peculiarity is that permanence and security are not marked features of informal work performance and that irregularity and vulnerability dominate instead. This particular trait of the informal sector makes an analysis of the labour market an extremely arbitrary and even disputable matter. The attempts to subject non-standardized and irregular work to quantitative analysis in terms of exact measures and clear counts might stem from a research methodology which is based on formal-sector notions. The recurrent complaints from researchers about the chaotic appearance and lack of transparency of the informal sector should be seen in this light. This explains why sociological and economic analyses of the labour market are so strongly distorted in favour of data collection on formal-sector enterprises. Of course, the small size of this sector does not at all justify this bias.

The contrast between the top and bottom of the urban economy is easy to describe. In the broad social spectrum between these polar ends, however, where informal and formal labour merge into each other, there is no clear dividing line. Consequently, I conclude that the image of a dichotomy is much too simple and can better be replaced by the idea of a continuum.

The first studies of the informal-sector concept created the impression that this segment of the urban economy functioned as a waiting room for a rapidly increasing stream of migrants pushed out from the rural economy. It was merely meant to be their first 'stay' in the new environment. The work that they performed provided them with craftsmanship and stimulated them to develop their talents as micro-entrepreneurs. Those who completed this apprenticeship successfully would in the end cross the gap which separated them from the formal sector. The promise of social mobility expressed by this optimistic scenario, however, appears in practice to be fulfilled for only a tiny minority. Time and again the results of numerous investigations show that a very considerable proportion of informal-sector workers are born and raised in the city and, at the end of their working lives, have not come much further than where they started.

A completely different dynamic, in an institutional and not an individual sense, arises from the idea that the informal sector is nothing more than a transitory phenomenon caused by the massive expulsion from the agrarian-rural economy. Given that the growth of formal-sector employment is slower than would be necessary to accommodate fully and immediately the size of this exodus, there is a temporary excess of people in the lower layers of the urban system. As economic growth accelerates, the need for and significance of employment in the informal sector declines and eventually little or nothing of this 'buffer zone' will remain. In my conclusion, I shall show that this representation is nothing more than hopeful expectation.

An Urban Phenomenon?

One of the shortcomings in the debate on the informal sector is the unflagging preoccupation with the urban economy. It is difficult to maintain that there is dualism in the urban order and that the countryside is in contrast characterized by homogeneity. To be sure, the peasant economy *in toto* demonstrates a number of features which are very similar to informal-sector activity. This is true for the way production takes place and it is also reflected in the pattern of employment. On the other hand, it is not so far-fetched to classify plantations, mines, or agro-industries in the rural areas as formal-sector enterprises, as they possess most of the dominant characteristics of this category. Why is attention in the majority of studies on this subject then focused on the urban economy? This preoccupation appears to originate in two misplaced suppositions: first, that the countryside is almost exclusively the domain of agriculture and, second, that agricultural labour is performed by a virtually homogenous peasant population. We are concerned here with a monolithic image which does not allow a sectoral division in terms of formal and informal. Moreover, this three-compartment (one rural and two urban) model seems to indicate the direction of social dynamics: peasants migrate to the city where they find work and an income in the informal sector before making the jump to the formal sector of the economy. Against this line of reasoning inspired by wishful thinking, I maintain that regardless of the reservations that one may have about the validity of the informal-sector concept, it is both theoretically and in practice impossible to declare that this concept is exclusively applicable to the urban domain. There are some other researchers who share this view and focus attention on dualist features manifest in the organization of agrarian production (Jaganathan 1987).

Analyses based on the comprehensive totality of economic activities, irrespective of whether they are located in urban or rural areas, emphasize the small volume of formal-sector employment in India. As mentioned earlier, for example, Visaria and Jacob (1995) arrived at a figure of not more than 8 per cent. According to them this extremely skewed division is primarily caused by the dominant position of the agrarian working population, consisting almost exclusively of informal-sector workers. The ratio of 92:8 is so highly uneven that it cannot be considered as a sound basis for sectoral analysis. This leads me to exclude agriculture, both in terms of production and labour, and to employ the formal–informal dichotomy as a framework of analysis for all other branches of the economy together (in other words, without dividing them according to city or countryside). It is a point of departure which takes care of my objection that there is a tendency to see the informal sector only as an urban phenomenon and helps to highlight the magnitude of informal non-agrarian employment in the rural economy. Skilled crafts of all sorts, trade and transport, as well as services in differing degrees of specialization have always been important occupations in the past as well as at present. The size and importance of this non-agrarian work, performed either as the worker's main or subsidiary activity, has increased significantly in many parts of India in recent decades. Table 1 illustrates the shift in the composition of the workforce in the last twenty years—the declining importance of employment in agriculture in the face of the growth, particularly in informal-sector activity in other economic sectors.

Even if all possible criticism of the accuracy of the figures, in Table 1, which are derived from government statistics, is taken into account, the data are still sufficiently robust to provide an insight into the trend of economic transformation in the long term. First, agricultural employment declined from 74 per cent in 1972–3 to 65 per cent fifteen years later. During the same period, non-agricultural labour rose from 26 to 35 per cent. The number of people employed in agriculture increased from 61.8 million in the first year to 113.6 million in 1987–8. According to another study, non-agricultural work was the main source of income for one out of four men and one out of six women in all rural households in India at the end of the 1980s (Chadha 1993). The growth indicated by these figures is principally propelled by activities which fall under the informal sector. The annual rate of increase in this sector is 4.9 per cent, more than double that of the formal sector.

It is important to observe that an acceleration in the diversification of the rural economy does not correspond to an increasing formalization of employment. One example concerns the emergence of a major agro-industry in the south of the state of Gujarat: every year huge armies of migrant labourers are mobilized from nearby Maharashtra and other catchment areas for the large-scale harvesting and processing of sugarcane; at the end of the campaign, they return (Breman 1994:133–287). I will discuss in the conclusion, this stagnation of formal-sector employment is a more general phenomenon which goes far beyond the city–country contrast; hence, it must be understood in a broader context.

Employment Modality

Self-employment is described in a large part of the literature as the backbone of the informal sector (see Sanyal 1991; Portes et al. 1989). When introducing the concept, Hart mentioned this as the most significant feature. 'The distinction between formal and informal income opportunities is based essentially on that between wage earning and self-employment' (1973: 86). Subsequently, many authors expressed themselves in a similar vein. A quite arbitrary example is Sanyal who, in an analysis of informal-sector policy states, without any reservation or empirical evidence, that the majority of the urban informal-sector population lives from the income gained from self-employment (Sanyal 1991: 41). This is, of course, the well-known image of the army of odd-jobbers and jacks-of-all-trades that travel around in the open air or survive from put-out work performed at home, but always do this on their own account and at their own risk. In such descriptions, emphasis is laid firmly on the ingenuity, the stamina, and the alert reaction to new opportunities demonstrated by these small-scale self-employed workers and last, but certainly not least, on the pride they show in being their own bosses. Some authors speak of these workers as mini-entrepreneurs and tend to describe the informal sector as a breeding ground for more sophisticated entrepreneurship which, as it is larger-scale and capitalist, can only be developed in the formal sector. Under this unrestrained apology for the free market, not only are informal workers trained and hardened in the struggle for daily existence—one can recognize here the profile of self-made men who started small—but once mature, they are able to develop into true captains of industry.

Another and more critical school of thought is represented by authors who describe and analyse the informal sector in terms of petty commodity production (see Smith 1985). In these writings the emphasis lies on the limited room for manoeuvre in which the self-employed have to operate. These works also discuss the dependence of the self-employed upon suppliers who overburden them with poor quality or overpriced products, moneylenders who charge extortionate rates of interest for short-term loans, street vendors who are easy prey for the police, sex workers who are in the hands of their pimps, slumlords who demand protection money, home-workers who can offer no resistance in the face of the practices of contractors or agents who commission their work, etc.

What is portrayed as own-account work carried out at the risk of the producer is in fact a more or less camouflaged form of wage labour. There is a wide diversity of arrangements which actually show great similarity with tenancy or sharecropping relationships in agriculture, where the principle of self-employment is so undermined in practice that the dependency on the landowner is scarcely different from that of a contract labourer. This is true for many actors operating in the informal sector such as the 'hirers' of a bicycle or motor taxi who must hand over a considerable proportion of their daily earnings to the owner of the vehicle, or for the street vendors who are provided their wares early in the morning on credit or commission from a supplier and then in the evening, after returning the unsold remainder, learn if and what they have retained from their transactions.

The façade of self-employment is further reinforced by modes of payment which are often associated with informal sector practices. For example the sub-contracting of production to home-workers is a common occurrence. Piece-rate and job work suggest a degree of independence which differs from the relationship between regular wage workers and employers. In the latter case, the time worked is the unit of calculation of the wage, while the wage is also paid regularly—per day, week, or month. The actual payment of this regular wage confirms the status of the worker as a permanent employee. Putting-out and one-off jobs, on the other hand, are in this aspect much closer to self-employment. And last but not least, there is no valid reason to describe wage labour as a phenomenon that is inextricably bound with the formal sector. The informal sector landscape is covered with small-scale enterprises that not only make use of unpaid labour, requisitioned from the household or family circle, but even more of personnel hired for a special purpose. This does not, however, always take the shape of an unequivocal and direct employer–employee relationship. There are different intermediaries— those who provide raw materials and then collect semi-finished or finished products from home workers, or jobbers who recruit and supervise gangs of unregistered workers—who function as agents for the ultimate patron. In all these cases, it would be incorrect to construct a sharp contrast between self-employment and wage labour corresponding to the informal–formal divide.

Such a division would also conflict with the occupational multiplicity that is characteristic of casualized labour. The bulk of these workers are continually in search of sources of income and perform a wide range of odd jobs within a relatively short time period—a week, a day, or even a few hours. These activities sometimes appear to be characterized by self-employment, sometimes by wage labour, and sometimes by a combination of both. For those involved, the nature of and the manner in which they perform these jobs is not of importance, but what they will pay is. The necessity not to specialize in one occupation but to show interest in a multitude of diverse activities arises from the seasonal fluctuations which are inherent to informal-sector economy. The alteration between the dry and the wet season, or between summer and winter, corresponds with the uneven annual rhythm of a great deal of these open-air occupations. During unsuitable seasons much less use, and sometimes no use at all, is made of the services of building and road-construction workers, quarrymen, brick makers, street vendors, itinerant artisans, and other street workers. But significant fluctuations throughout the year also occur in the demand for labour for numerous activities which take place in roof-covered and enclosed spaces. In their case, it is not the climatic conditions but the changing demand in the annual cycle of certain commodities and services that is the main factor. The months preceding the wedding season are a period of peak production for the manufacture of embroidered *saris,* while religious festivals also give a large but temporary incentive to associated industries. The same applies for the great variety of workers in the tourist industry. Cessation of production, or perhaps a sudden spurt, can be determined by stagnation in the supply of raw materials, cuts in the electricity supply or availability of transport, and price rises or falls. It is a characteristic of informal-sector employment that the use of labour, in size and intensity, is seen as derived from all these market imperfections of a structural or conjunctural nature. In other words, the business risk is passed on to the workers. They must remain available for as long as there is need of their labour, not only in the daytime but also in the evening and at night. Periods of overemployment are then followed by shorter or longer periods of enforced idleness. However, they can derive no rights from this pattern of irregular or suddenly changing working hours in the form of wage supplements or continued payment of wages for hours, days, or seasons during which work was stopped or declined in intensity. The excessive subjection of labour to the highly variable demands made by the production process arises from the presence of an almost inexhaustible labour supply, if not actually then at least potentially. This reserve army consists of men and women, both young and old, who differ from each other more in the degree of previous experience and suitability than in the preparedness to make the required effort for the lowest possible price. To speak of superexploitation of wage workers by employers in the informal sector, but then to regard the self-employed as responsible for their own degree of exploitation, gives, in my opinion, an exaggerated picture of the differences between both categories and ignores their similarities.

The standardization of the conditions of employment in the formal sector of the economy—in terms of wage scales, length of the working day, security, and social benefits—equally applies to obtaining access to the sector. This observation implies that recruitment and promotion are subject to fixed rules related to training, seniority, and other objectively determined qualities of the workforce concerned. Conversely, access to industry in the informal sector is characterized by much greater coincidence and arbitrariness. This difference is, of course, consistent with the more permanent employment in the formal sector and the much more casual and shorter-lasting jobs which dominate in the lower zones of the labour hierarchy. Without wanting to contest that access to employment in both sectors can be differentiated on the basis of these criteria, I would like to add that these differences become blurred when increasing pressure is put on the formal-sector labour market. When supply also exceeds demand in this sector, the standardized rules make way for more subjective considerations in the selection policy. Formalized labour arrangements then appear to be anything but free of arbitrary personal preferences and prejudices which are more often used to describe practices of recruitment and dismissal in the informal sector.

The conclusion that I draw from the above is that the diverse modalities of employment do not confirm the image of a dualist but rather of a fragmented labour market. The distinction made between the two sectors is further complicated by the manner whereby the occupants of formal and informal labour positions try to build fences or barriers in order to guarantee access to the conquered niche of employment for candidates hailing from their own circle, with maximal exclusion of 'outsiders'. The latter are those who do not belong to the category of close family members, neighbours and friends, nor are they members of the same caste, religious group, tribe, linguistic group, regional or ethnic group. Of vital importance for the organization of the labour market is a pronounced state of fragmentation, that is expressed in the innumerable compartments of employment, of which some assume a fluid form while others are demarcated by fairly hard partitions in both the higher and lower levels of the economy.

Social Identity

The very broad spectrum of activities grouped together under the concept of the informal sector are performed by heterogeneously composed categories of working people. Despite the diversity, there are still a number of common features in the social profile of these masses. In the first place, these workers have little or no formal training and the majority are often totally illiterate.

Second, they have no source of income besides the earnings from their own labour. Even the acquisition of the most simple tools—a shovel and basket or bowl for carrying earth in the case of road workers; a barrow, oil lamp, and scales for a street vendor; a little wooden box with polish and brushes for shoe polishers—represents an investment which beginners cannot afford out of their own savings and for which they have to take a loan. The moneylenders operating in this sector charge a high interest rate even for the small amounts and short-term repayments which they grant.

The acute lack of creditworthiness of informal-sector workers is closely connected to a third feature: the extremely low wages which they receive for their strenuous efforts. It is precisely these paltry returns that force informal-sector workers to make use of all hands, big ones as well as nimble fingers, which are available in their household. In the case of migrants, this leads them to leave behind 'dependent' family members who are no longer (or not yet) able to work to an extent that would at least compensate for the extra costs needed for their maintenance. In this weighing up of pros and cons, a role is also played by how much of the income should be spent on housing. In order to keep this expenditure as minimal as possible, seasonal migrants in particular make do with a very primitive roof over their heads, improvised from waste material that happens to be available, or they even set up a bivouac under the open sky. Migrants who establish themselves for longer periods far from home may sometimes hire living space together, in the case of single men, or attempt, if accompanied by wife and children, to find their own accommodation preferably with water and sanitary facilities, however primitive, in the immediate vicinity.

A fourth feature is the much higher participation of both women and children in the informal sector of the economy. The vulnerability of this labour force has also to be understood in gender and age tems. Even more exploited and subordinated than men are children and women. A wide variety of studies has documented the magnitude, identity, and conditions of work of both these categories (see Mies 1982; Karlekar 1982; Banerjee 1985; Tom 1989; Banerjee 1991; Kapadia 1995; Banerjee 1979; Rodgers and Standing 1981; Jugal et al. 1985; Punalekar 1993 and Sahoo 1995).

Finally, informal work has a low status. This is partly the sum of the features mentioned in the preceding paragraphs in combination with the substitutability and irregularity of the work, and partly the result of the socially inferior origin of this workforce: in India the large majority of them are members of backward or Untouchable castes. Although the word 'coolie' is no longer fashionable, the derogatory connotation implied by its use in the past covers quite well the lack of respect that is associated with this sort of work. The strenuous physical effort that is often demanded, goes with sweat, filth, and other such bodily features which bear the odium of inferiority and subordination. Besides being tainted with the stigma of pollution, these characteristics also undermine the health of the workers in a way which leads to their being prematurely worn out. In addition to all these hazards, the women and children are often exposed to sexual harassment. Female and child domestic servants are at risk from their employers, and such members of workgangs from the foremen. Lack of dignity results from their inability to cope with misfortune, such as illness, or to save for the considerable expense involved in important life-cycle rituals which have to be observed. By taking an advance on these occasions they try to meet their social obligations even though it leads to a form of labour attachment to their employer or an intermediary, which restricts even further their already limited room for manoeuvre.

Does it follow from the above that informal-sector workers have a style of living and working in common with each other which could categorize them as belonging to one homogeneous social class? In comparison with the labour aristocracy employed at the top of the formal-sector economy—permanently employed, well educated, with a daily rhythm in which work and free time are sharply marked, reasonably well paid and hence creditworthy, living in reasonable comfort and consequently aware of their social dignity and respect—the many-times-greater army of workers without all these prerogatives form one uniform mass. But closer examination reveals that there is no simple division into only two classes. At the very broad bottom of the economic order there are striking differences between, for example, migrants forced to wander around various sites of employment in the open air and labourers who operate power looms or other simple machines in small workshops. It is true that the textile workers go every day to work for the same boss, at least for the time being, but they cannot derive from their regular employment at the same site any claim to decent treatment or even the right to a minimum form of security.

In an earlier work (Breman 1994) I classified informal-sector workers into three classes:

First, a petty bourgeoisie who, besides the owners of mini-workshops, self-employed artisans, small traders, and shopkeepers, also include those who earn their keep as economic brokers or agents, such as moneylenders, labour contractors, intermediaries who collect and deliver piece-work and home work, and rent collectors. Compared with the lower ranks of formal-sector labour, the income of this category is not infrequently on a much higher level. In reports which tend to value the informal sector as a breeding ground for entrepreneurs, the emphasis lies on the right type of behaviour. Those who belong to this social category set great store by their relative autonomy—they exhibit a need to avoid subordination to others in general and an aversion to wage dependence in particular—and show, by good bourgeois attributes such as thrift and hard work, that they are striving to improve their individual positions within the social hierarchy.

Second, the subproletariat, who subsume the largest segment of informal-sector workers, consists of a colourful collection of casual and unskilled workers who circulate relatively quickly from one location of temporary employment to another. It includes both labourers in the service of small workshops and the reserve army of labour who are recruited and dismissed by large-scale enterprises according to the need of the moment. The subproletariat also include, itinerant semi-artisans who offer their services and (paltry) tools for hire at morning markets, day labourers, home workers, vendors, and the long parade of occupations practised in the open air, including the shoe polisher and messenger. They differ from the residual category by having, if not a permanent, at least a demonstrable form of accommodation, and by keeping a regular household even if all the members are not always able to live together as a family. This is achieved by a labour strategy that is based on a rational choice of options which are time and place bound and by attempts to invest in education, health, and social security, even though the irregularity of their existence and the inability to accumulate consistently, excludes any firm plans for the future. Although their misery (from which many often escape into drunkenness) is great, these workers are still distinguished from the category of the last resort, which I am inclined to describe as 'paupers'. These are the lumpen, the dregs of society with criminal features, whose presence nobody values. They are the 'declassed' who have often broken contact with their family or village of origin, who have no fixed accommodation, and who maintain no regular contacts with other people in their immediate environment. These people not only lack all means of production but also do not have the labour power and stamina needed to be able to meet their daily minimal requirements in full. Thus alienated even from the means of consumption, they easily fall into a state of pauperization and form a ragbag of crushed, broken-spirited rejects—single men, widows or divorced women with children, children without parents, the mentally or physically handicapped, and the superfluous elderly.

It is important to note that this classification does not mean that an unambiguous, clearly hierarchical formation of three discrete social strata has crystallized. A household can consist of members who have been absorbed in the labour process in various ways; it is not always the case that all members of one household work in either the formal or informal sector. A consequent lack of consistency in terms of class position and associated lifestyle is, however, rectified by part of the household sometimes breaking away or being pushed off to form a new household.

The fluidity in the transition between the different social classes, as well as shifts in the proportional distribution among them that occur over time, under influence of contraction or expansion of the economy, mitigate against a division which is either unduly rigid or too static. It is hence empirically not easy to delimit the largest segment of the working population, the subproletariat, from the other collectivities. Upward and downward mobility are both possible, in theory, and occur in practice at all levels to some degree, although it is very exceptional for this mobility to apply for one individual all the way from the bottom to the top or vice versa. In most cases, mobility is limited to much shorter movements.

Organization and Protection

One of the most common criteria for the operationalization of the formal–informal-sector dichotomy is whether or not labour has managed to get organized. The protection enjoyed by workers in large-scale and capital-intensive enterprises is the result of action taken by them for the collective promotion of their interests, including wage levels, rules for recruitment, promotion, and dismissal, hours of work, and secondary terms of employment. Not all those who have found a niche in the formal sector are in fact members of such trade unions. On the other hand, it is even less common for workers in the informal sector to join together in an effort to improve their position. Still, this has actually occurred in a limited number of cases and it is interesting to observe that these initiatives arise from or focus on very vulnerable groups. This applies, for example, to the Self-Employed Women's Association (SEWA) which is based in Ahmedabad. In Kerala, both within and outside agriculture, different trade-union-like organizations have been established with the explicit objective of reinforcing the rights of informal-sector workers (Kannan 1988; Pillai 1996). Becoming acquainted with the occasional successful experience is relevant for answering the question of how the emergence of trade unions can be facilitated in the lower echelons of the economy. There is hardly any difference of opinion concerning the urgent need for such a course of action. Why then, with a few exceptions, are they absent in the informal-sector landscape?

The explanation must be sought firstly in the subaltern identity of these working masses and the manner in which they are absorbed in the labour process. The workers concerned are mostly young men and women who belong to the lowest levels of the social hierarchy, who can often neither read nor write, and who have arrived in an alien environment as migrants. They manage to survive with casual and irregular work which often gives them the appearance of being self-employed. The work performed is not connected with a fixed location but is subject to constant change. Besides having to move from place to place looking for employment they also need to engage themselves in a variety of different activities at intervals of a year, season, week, or even day.

This profile of occupational multiplicity demonstrates how difficult it is to bring together in an organization these casual, unskilled, itinerant, fragmented, and poverty-stricken masses on the basis of their common interests. Furthermore, any attempts at unionization made in the separate branches of informal-sector industry, come up against barriers erected by employers and their agents, such as intermediaries and labour contractors. This resistance is sometimes expressed in the form of intimidation or instant dismissal of workers who not only try to press for their own interests but also for those of others. Even worse, it can come to actual violence or the terrorizing of labour activists by gangs of thugs or hired killers whom the employers don't hesitate to use.

Are the existing trade unions established by and for formal-sector labour who have permanent jobs, are better trained, and usually higher paid, aware of the miserable state of the masses who populate the lower zones of the economy? And more important still, can they be persuaded to see these irregular workers, with low social visibility and fragmented into unconnected, fluid segments, as potential members of their organization? The answer seems to be 'no', or at least 'hardly at all'. This disinclination arises partly from all sorts of practical problems such as, for instance, the difficulty involved in mobilizing an amorphous and floating multitude on the basis of shared interests. The task set is further complicated by the necessity encouraging these differing and diverse interests to have bargaining dialogue with a very great number of micro-employers. This effort requires large overhead costs which would be impossible for members who belong to the economically most-vulnerable categories to finance. Furthermore, experience shows that the needs and problems of informal-sector workers are quite different from labour arrangements in the formal sector of the economy. These differences in needs demand a type of organization and promotion of interests of which conventional trade unions have little experience, many of them not at all. Even more important, the union leadership is not prepared, in the light of these much wider aims, to reformulate its mission and to operationalize the new agenda into a concrete plan of action. In the final analysis, the trade unions close ranks to restrict access. The miserable lot of informal-sector workers is not seen as a challenge but as a threat to the much better deal—the outcome of a long-lasting struggle for a reasonable degree of security, prosperity, and dignity—enjoyed by labour in the formal sector. The strategy of fending off the mass of excluded workers explains why, conversely, the latter feel little affinity with the recognized trade-union movement. Both the union leadership and members do not appear to unduly worry themselves over the question of how they could contribute to improving the lot of the informal workers and instead tend to see them as scabs. They regard the reserve labour army with scorn, as it supplies the strike-breakers who unscrupulously accept the jobs, temporarily made available by formal-sector workers who have gone on strike, in the hope of being able to occupy them permanently. Only in recent years, and under the pressure of stagnating or even declining levels of employment in the formal sector, have the established labour organizations dropped their indifferent or even hostile attitude. At the initiative of the International Congress of Free Trade Unions (ICFTU), a conference was held in 1988 on the transformation of the international economic order and the concomitant trend of informalization of employment modalities. It had become clear to insiders as well as outsiders that the trade-union movement was threatened with marginalization by its exclusive concentration upon a relatively small elite engaged under formal terms of employment. The leadership finally realized that a large part of the working masses did not recognize the trade-union movement as an ally in the struggle against deteriorating working conditions. The unions that were members of this international federation were urged to make the informal-sector issue a high priority one. A report that appeared only a year later described as a first aim the formalization of the gigantic army of unprotected and unorganized workers (ICFTU 1989). They should enjoy the same legal protection as employees in the formal sector. It will be clear that this demand was characterized by a woefully inadequate sense of reality. Moreover, it demonstrated a very poor understanding of the dynamics of the informal sector. The formula to achieve this new goal was confined to the suggestion about accelerating what, according to conventional wisdom, would be the predictable result of the process of economic development. It was a naive supposition, and after this recommendation very little has happened in the routine practice of trade-union activities.

The lack of support from the established trade-union movement does not mean that informal-sector workers passively accept the labour regime forced upon them. Many make efforts, often repeatedly so, to combat the insecurity and miserable conditions of employment by trying to negotiate a somewhat better deal with their particular employers. They do this by emphasizing their subordination and loyalty to their patrons in exchange for which they appeal to the patrons' discretionary power to grant favours. Given the abundant supply and limited demand for labour, employers are bent upon reducing even further the already small space in which the massive army in search of work must operate. Thus they use all sorts of arrangements which lead to a curtailment of their employees' room for manoeuvre. Mechanisms to tie the worker further to the employer, such as providing an advance on salary or paying in arrears show similarities with forms of unfree labour which occurred in the past (Breman 1993), but differ from them by a more articulated contractual and capitalist slant. Against this background, it is understandable why much labour resistance assumes the shape of sabotage, obstruction, avoidance, and other deeds of covert protest, summarized by the term, 'weapons of the weak' (Scott 1985, 1990).

Despite the severe sanctions which are brought to bear on attempts to form a common front and openly express latent feelings of solidarity, collective signals of resistance are the order of the day in the informal sector. Reasons discussed in the preceding paragraphs explain why, for example, strikes 'suddenly' break out, rarely spread to the whole branch of the industry, and also die out relatively quickly. The weak capacity to resist makes it understandable why these actions are usually spontaneous, local, and short in duration. But there is also in part an under-reporting of some forms of resistance, as they occur infrequently, or not at all, in employment under formal conditions. The registration of labour resistance has been unduly focused on the nature and course of the social struggle in the formal sector. Proto-trade unions, such as those that existed in Europe's pre-industrial past, could be an interesting point of departure for comparison with the manifestation of labour unrest and industrial action in the informal sector of the economy of today.[8]

The protection enjoyed by formal-sector workers arises from a gradual shift in the balance of power between capital and labour over a period of roughly one hundred years. The introduction and implementation of separate legislation for protecting labour (in the same way, although not to the same extent, that the rights of capital were safeguarded) would be inconceivable without the intermediary role of the state. What has been the role of national and local government in regulating the informal sector of the economy? For one thing, the impression often created that there is absolutely no official interference is incorrect. Where there is universal suffrage, which is actually exercised with reasonable freedom in India since Independence, the political system cannot afford to ignore completely the working masses which make up the majority of the electorate. This consideration is of relevance for explaining why minimum wages have been fixed for landless labourers, why the practices of illegal labour contractors are restricted, why various ordinances regulate the movement of migrants, and why violations of the prohibition of bonded labour are punishable by law, to mention just a few examples. In many states of India, there are detailed rules regulating employment for many occupations, even for casual labour that is limited to particular seasons of the year (Breman 1996). What is lacking, however, is an effective machinery to implement these regulations, as well as the appointment of an adequate number of officials responsible for their enforcement. Moreover, civil servants who are allocated inspection responsibilities in practice make use of their mandate to obtain extra income; it is an example of the abuse of public authority for private advantage that occurs at all levels of bureaucracy.

Policy and Globalization of the Labour System

After the 'discovery' of the informal sector, amazement was expressed in many publications that such a large part of the population survived or even thrived on it. The reaction of the authorities was evidence of the need felt for regulation. At the same time, the way in which regulation took place made it clear that this involvement was not motivated so much by the desire to improve the lives of these workers but arose largely from irritation over their escape from government control. In this negatively coloured assessment, the informal sector was seen as a conglomerate of activities which were inconvenient and caused trouble. The parasitic or openly criminal features attributed to these workers reinforced the tendency of the government to protect the public and the economy from these 'useless, unhealthy, or downright dangerous' elements. Bicycle taxis and peripatetic vendors were driven from the streets, while 'unfavourably' located slums, if they were not razed to the ground, were removed from public view by enclosures. City beautification was the slogan which in many countries was used to justify this persecution and banishment (Breman 1983).

The plea for a more positive attitude, first made by the ILO in particular, was the beginning of a new direction that at least promised to end the open hunt on informal-sector workers and their trades. The argument in support of this policy was that the returns from these activities not only provided a living for those involved but also that they were of genuine use from a more general economic perspective. In order to increase the efficiency and effectiveness of this sector, an extensive package of supportive measures was recommended, varying from better training, more (and more accessible) credit, expansion of the markets for informal commodities as well as services, to, finally, greater tolerance in issuing government permits. Whether these proposals should be understood as reflecting a policy of formalization remains unanswered, as most of them were never implemented. A scenario with which policy makers felt more at ease was to not involve themselves with the informal sector at all, in either a positive or negative sense. The persecution and unbridled mania for regulation by bureaucrats at all levels was discontinued but without switching over to active protection. A well-known and influential advocate of this formula, with a very strong neo-liberal leaning, is De Soto, who has created great enthusiasm for it among leading politicians and international agencies (De Soto 1986). This is understandable, as the policy of non-state intervention he advocated tends to leave the existing relations of deep-seated inequalities in the distribution of property and power untouched and goes on to legitimize a situation which guarantees the domination of formal-sector interests, both capital and labour.

I have already indicated in the preceding discussion that in populist-inspired interpretations of the informal-sector phenomenon, attention has been focused, to a significant extent, on self-employment as an important element in the definition of the sector. To suggest that these workers operate on their own account and at their own risk leads to an analysis focusing on micro-entrepreneurship with all its positive features: ingenuity, versatility, boldness, industriousness, and flexibility. This is also an image that pleases these neo-liberal politicians and policy makers because, in their perception, success or failure is purely an affair of the actors themselves as individuals. They feel no need to look for the causes of this success or failure in the structure of society, of which informal-sector workers form such a major segment, nor in the unequal opportunities which are inherent to it.

The continuous formalization of employment in the urban and rural economy did not eventually materialize. In most cases, including India, there has even been a reversal of the trend: a chipping away of the formal conditions of employment which are being replaced by casual and short-term labour arrangements as part of an overall change in the organization of industrial production. An example is the closure of textile factories in Bombay and Ahmedabad. In these locations, power looms for the manufacture of rayon were transferred to thousands of small-scale workshops in new urban growth poles such as Surat (Breman 1996). The new international economic order demands the addition of more capital to the industrial process, but this takes place in a manner that guarantees the availability of abundant labour and the payment of very low wages, and provides employment only when needed. The pattern of employment still runs along informal-sector lines, to the extent of becoming, in recent decades, an ideological maxim, a credo. What is heralded as the 'flexibilization of production' is actually contracting-out of work, replacing time-wage with piece-rate and permanent with casual workers. This trend implies not only a deterioration in the working conditions of formal-sector workers, but also undermines the role of the trade unions which have promoted the interests of this privileged section.

The further implementation of the recent policy calls for the dismantling of the existing labour legislation. In addition to a considerable drop in wages, the inevitable result is a cutting back of the social-security benefits that have been built up over many years and, in the end, a reappraisal of perceptions of dignity and self-esteem. The decline in the quality of workers' lives has been exacerbated in many developing countries by the simultaneous introduction of structural adjustment programmes. These schemes, imposed by the World Bank and the International Monetary Fund (IMF), have included a drastic reduction in subsidies which kept food and transport prices low, and of expenditure meant to facilitate public access to education, health, and housing.

Labour in an Integrating World is the title of the 1995 World Bank Annual Report. According to this document, the dualism that determines the organization of the labour market arises from the unjustified preferential treatment of formal-sector workers. In this view, the labour arrangements in the informal sector are not perceived as a problem, or as modalities of employment which contribute to the perpetuation of poverty. Rather, they are recommended as a solution to the situation of immense deprivation suffered by such a large part of humanity. The argument made for the withdrawal of state involvement in the labour system, for the repeal of existing protective legislation, and for the abolition of more effective enforcement of minimum-wage regulations, is part of a political-economic doctrine founded upon the unfettered freedom of the market as the guiding principle. The organization of economic production, in a period of growth characterized not by a lack of labour but of capital, benefits the latter at the cost of the former. The providers of work, under these conditions, pay the lowest possible price after the rejection of social-security rights which, directly or indirectly, require wage supplements.

The crumbling away of the welfare state where it had previously existed, as well as its halting development where it had only just begun to come into sight, can be seen as confirmation of a trend in which the slowly advancing emancipation of labour in recent decades appears as if it were being reversed into subordination and insecurity. The progressive polarization of social classes accompanying these dynamics has given rise in Europe to a debate which concentrates on the inclusion-exclusion contrast, which seems to mark the return of the old dualism concept in yet another form.

ENDNOTES

1. For Calcutta, see Lubell (1974) and Bose (1974); for Dakar, see Gerry (1974); for Jakarta, see Sethuraman (1976); for Abidjan, see Joshi et al. (1976); and for Sao Paulo, see Schaefer (1976).
2. Examples are 'the law of inverse wage elasticity' formulated by Boeke (1953) and the idea of the 'target worker' which enjoyed such great popularity in the early literature on the essence of the development process (Nurkse 1953).
3. 'The informal sector, as its name suggests, is not formal in its character', according to Sethuraman (1977: 196); see also Gerry (1974: 1).
4. One author who subscribed to this idea was Oteiza, who predicted that 'the end of the century will see, to an even more pronounced degree, the existence of two labour markets with two different occupational structures and levels of income, corresponding to two clearly distinctive sectors of the economy—the modern and the traditional sector' (1971: 196). Without using the terms 'modern' and 'traditional', Sethuraman (1976: 10–12) suggests the same distinction.
5. In the sense understood by Weber, namely the almost exaggerated emphasis on the principal characteristics in a way which seldom occurs in social reality.
6. For critical comments raised on the lack of adequate quantitative evidence in the documents published by both organizations, see Mazumdar (1995: 19).
7. See also Bienefeld (1975: 20). A complicating factor is that not all members of a household are necessarily employed in the same sector. This fact argues in favour of a choice to be made between income levels and type of economic activity when elaborating the formal/informal opposition. A combination of both leads to contradictions or discrepancies in the operationalization of the dichotomy.
8. See various contributions in the volume edited by Lis et al. (1994).

REFERENCES

Aziz, A. 1984. *Urban Poor and Urban Informal Sector.* New Delhi: Ashish Publishing House.

Banerjee, B. 1985. *Women in the Unorganised Sector.* Delhi: Sangam Books.

———. 1986. *Rural and Urban Migration and the Labour Market.* Bombay: Himalaya Publishing House.

———. 1991. *Indian Women in a Changing Scenario.* Indo-Dutch Studies on Development Alternatives. 5. New Delhi: Sage Publications.

Banerjee, N. 1978. *Unorganised Women Workers: The Calcutta Experience.* CSSSC Occasional Paper. Calcutta: Centre for Studies in Social Sciences.

Banerjee, S. 1979. *Child Labour in India: A General Review with Case Studies of the Brick making and Zari-embroidery Industries.* London: Antislavery Society.

Bhalla, A. and F. Lapeyre. 1997. 'Social Exclusion: Towards an Analytical and Operational Framework'. *Development and Change.* 28(3):413–34.

Bienefeld, M. 1975. 'The Informal Sector and Peripheral Capitalism: The Case of Tanzania'. *Institute of Development Studies Bulletin.* 6:53–73.

Bose, A.N. 1974. *The Informal Sector in the Calcutta Metropolitan Economy.* Geneva: ILO.

Boeke, J.H. 1953. *Economics and Economic Policy of Dual Societies as Exemplified by Indonesia.* Haarlem: H.D. Tjeenk and Zoon.

Breman, Jan. 1983. 'The Bottom of the Urban Order in Asia; Impressions of Calcutta'. *Development and Change.* 14:153–83.

_____. 1985. *Of Peasants, Migrants and Paupers: Rural Labour Circulation and Capitalist Production in West India*. Oxford: Clarendon Press.

_____. 1993. *Beyond Patronage and Exploitation: Changing Agrarian Relations in South Gujarat*. Delhi: Oxford University Press.

_____. 1994. *Wage Hunters and Gatherers: Search for Work in the Urban and Rural Economy of South Gujarat*. Delhi: Oxford University Press.

_____. 1995. 'Labour, Get Lost; A Late-Capitalist Manifesto'. *Economic and Political Weekly*. 30:2294–300.

_____. 1996. *Footloose Labour: Working in India's Informal Economy*. Cambridge: Cambridge University Press.

Bromley, R. and G. Gerry, eds. 1979. *Casual Work and Poverty in Third World Cities*. New York: John Wiley & Sons.

Brown, P. and R. Crompton, eds. 1994. *Economic Restructuring and Social Exclusion*. London: UCL Press.

Chadha, G.K. 1993. 'Non-farm Employment for Rural Households in India: Evidence and Prognosis'. *The Indian Journal of Labour Economics*. 36:296–327.

De Soto, H. 1986 [1997]. *El Otro Sendero*. Lima: Editorial E L Barranco. In English translation: *The Other Path; The Invisible Revolution in the Third World*. New York: Harper & Row.

Fei, J.C. and G. Ranis. 1964. *Development of the Labour Surplus Economy; Theory and Policy*. Illinois: Homewood.

Gerry, C. 1974. *Petty Producers and the Urban Economy: A Case Study of Dakar*. World Employment Programme, Working Paper 8. Geneva: ILO.

Gerry, C. and C Birkbeck. 1981. 'The Petty Commodity Producer in Third World Cities: Petit Bourgeois or "Disguised" or Proletarians'. In Beckhoffer and Euiot, ed., *The Petite Bourgeoisie: Comparative Studies of the Uneasy Stratum*, 121–53. London: Macmillan.

Gore, C., G. Rodgers, and J. Figueiredo. 1995. *Social Exclusion: Rhetoric, Reality, Response*. Geneva: International Institute for Labour Studies.

Government of India. Report of the Committee on Child Labour. 1979. Ministry of Labour.

Gulati, L. 1982. *Profiles in Female Poverty: A Study of Five Poor Working Women in Kerala*. Delhi: Hindustan Publishing Corporation.

Hart, K. 1973. 'Informal Income Opportunities and Urban Employment in Ghana'. In R. Jolly, ed., *Third World Employment* 66–70. Harmondsworth: Penguin.

Holmstrom, M. 1984. *Industry and Equality: The Social Anthropology of Indian Labour*. Cambridge: Cambridge University Press.

ICFTU. 1989. *On Organising Workers in the Informal Sector*.

ILO. 1972. *Employment, Incomes and Equality: A Strategy for Increasing Productive Employment in Kenya*. Geneva: ILO.

_____. 1974. *Sharing in Development: A Programme of Employment, Equity and Growth for the Philippines*. Geneva: ILO.

_____. 1976. *World Employment Programme: Research in Retrospect and Prospect*. Geneva: ILO.

Jaganathan, N.V. 1987. *Informal Markets in Developing Countries*. Delhi: Oxford University Press.

Jolly, R., E. de kadt, H. Singer, and F. Wilson, eds. 1973. *Third World Employment* Harmondsworth: Penguin.

Joshi, H. and V. Joshi. 1976. *Surplus Labour and the City: A Study of Bombay*. Delhi: Oxford University Press.

Joshi, H., H. Lubell, and J. Mouly. 1976. *Abidjan: Urban Development and Employment in Ivory Coast*. World Employment Programme. Geneva: ILO.

Jones, Stedman G. 1971. *Outcast London*. London/Oxford: Clarendon Press.

Jugal, B.N. et al. 1985. *Child Labour: The Twice Exploited*. Varanasi: Gandhian Institute of Studies.

Kanappan, A., ed. 1977. *Studies of Urban Labour Market Behaviour in Developing Countries*. Geneva: ILO.

Kannan, K.P. 1988. *Of Rural Proletarian Struggles: Mobilization and Organization of Rural Workers in South-West India*. Delhi: Oxford University Press.

———. 1992. 'Labour Institutions and the Development Process in India'. In T.S. Papola and G. Rodgers, eds, *Labour Institutions and Economic Development in India*, 49–85. IILS, Research Series no. 97, Geneva.

Karlekar, M. 1982. *Poverty and Womens' Work: A Study of Sweeper Women in Delhi*. Delhi: Shakti Books.

Kapadia, K. 1995. *Siva and Her Sister: Gender, Caste and Class in Rural South India*. Boulder/Oxford: Westview Press.

Lewis, W.A. 1954. 'Economic Development with Unlimited Supplies of Labour'. *The Manchester School of Economic and Social Studies*. 22:139–91.

Lis, C., J. Lucassen, and H. Soly, eds. 1994. *Before the Unions: Wage Earners and Collective Action in Europe, 1300–1850*. International Review of Social History, Supplement 2. Cambridge: Cambridge University Press.

Lubell, H. 1974. *Calcutta: Its Urban Development and Employment Prospects*. Geneva: ILO.

Mathew, P.M. ed. 1995. *Informal Sector in India; Critical Perspectives*. New Delhi: Khama Publishers.

Mazumdar, D. 1975. *The Urban Informal Sector*. World Bank Staff Working Paper. Washington: World Bank.

———. 1995. 'Labor Issues in the World Development Report: A Critical Assessment'. Unpublished paper, Centre for International Studies, University of Toronto.

Mies, M. 1982. *The Lace Makers of Narsapur*. London: Zed Books.

Nieuwenhuys, O. 1994. *Children's Life Worlds: Gender, Welfare and Labour in the Developing World. An Anthropological Study of Children and Their Work in a Kerala (Indian) Village*. London: Routledge.

Noronha, E. 1996. 'Liberalisation and Industrial Relations'. *Economic and Political Weekly* (Review of Labour). 31:L14–L20.

Nurkse, R. 1953. *Problems of Capitals Formation in Underdeveloped Countries*. New York: Oxford University Press.

Oteiza, E. 1971. 'The Allocation Function of the Labour Market in Latin America'. *International Institute for Labour Studies Bulletin*. 8:190–205.

Papola, T.S. 1981. *Urban Informal Sector in a Developing Economy*. New Delhi: Vikas Publishing House.

Papola, T.S. and G. Rodgers, eds. 1992. *Labour Institutions and Economic Development in India*. International Institute for Labour Studies, Research Series no. 97. Geneva: IILS.

Pillai, S.M. 1996. 'Social Security for Workers in Unorganised Sector. Experience of Kerala'. *Economic and Political Weekly*. 31:2098–107.

Punalekar, S.P. 1993. *Seeds of Marginalization and Instability: A Study of Children in Gujarat Cities*. Surat: Centre for Social Studies.

Portes, A. M. Castells, and L.A. Benton. 1989. *The Informal Economy: Studies in Advanced and Lesser Advanced Countries*. Baltimore: Johns Hopkins University Press.

Rodgers, G. and G. Standing, eds. 1981. *Child Work, Poverty and Underdevelopment*. Geneva: ILO.

Safa, Helen, ed. 1982. *Towards a Political Economy of Urbanization in Third World Countries*. Delhi: Oxford University Press.

Sahoo, U.C. 1995. *Child Labour in Agrarian Society*. Jaipur/Delhi: Rawat Publications.

Sanyal, B. 1991. 'Organizing the Self-Employed'. *International Labour Review*. 130:39–56.

Schaefer, K.1976. *Sao Paulo: Urban Development and Employment*. World Employment Programme. Research Working Papers. Geneva: ILO.

Scott, J.C. 1985. *Weapons of the Weak: Everyday Forms of Peasant Resistance*. New Haven: Yale University Press.

———. 1990. *Domination and the Arts of Resistance: Hidden Transcripts.* New Haven: Yale University Press.

Sethuraman, S.V. 1975. 'Urbanisation and Employment: A Case Study of Djakarta'. *International Labour Review.* 112:191–205.

———. 1976. *The Urban Informal Sector: Concept, Measurement and Policy.* World Employment Programme Research (Working Papers). Geneva: ILO.

———. 1977. 'The Informal Sector in Developing Countries: Some Policy Implications'. *Social Action.* July–September.

Singh, M. 1990. *The Political Economy of Unorganised Labour: A Study of the Labour Process.* New Delhi: Sage Publications.

Smith, G. 1985. 'Reflections on the Social Relations of Simple Commodity Production'. *The Journal of Peasant Studies.* 13(1):99–108.

Tom, I. 1989. *Women in Unorganised Sector: Technology, Work Organisation and Change in the Silk Industry, South India.* Delhi: Usha Publication.

Van Der Loop, Th. 1992. *Industrial Dynamics and Fragmented Labour Markets: Construction Firms and Labourers in India.* Netherlands Geographical Studies, 139. Utrecht/Amsterdam: Netherlands Geographical Studies.

Visaria, Pravin and P. Jacob. 1995. *The Informal Sector in India: Estimates of its Size, and Needs, and Problems of Data Collection.* Gujarat Institute of Development Studies, Working Paper Series no. 70. Ahmedabad: Gujarat Institute of Development Studies.

Wertheim, W.F. and G.H. van der Kolff, eds. 1966. *Indonesian Economics; The Concept of Dualism in Theory and Policy.* The Hague: W. van Hoeve Publishers.

World Bank. 1995. *Workers in an Integrating World. World Development Report 1995.* New York: Oxford University Press.

TABLE

Table 1: Agricultural and Non-agricultural Workers (in millions) Classified According to Formal/Informal Sector 1972–3 to 1987–8

Branch of Industry	1972–3			1977–8			1983			1987–8		
	Formal	Informal	Total	Formal	Informal	Total	Formal	Informal	Total	Formal	Informal	Total
Agriculture	1.1	173.8	174.9	1.2	189.7	190.9	1.3	206.3	207.6	1.4	209.7	211.1
Non-agriculture*	17.7	44.1	61.8	20.0	57.9	77.9	22.7	72.5	95.2	24.3	89.3	113.6
Total	18.8	217.9	236.7	21.2	247.6	268.8	24.0	278.8	302.8	25.7	299.0	324.7

* : This category includes mining and quarrying, manufacturing, construction, electricity, gas and water, trade, hotels and restaurants, transport, storage and communication services.

Source : National Sample Survey (NSS) as cited in Visaria and Jacob (1995: 17–18),

The Indian Nation-State

The Indian nation-state, imagined and struggled for during the anti-colonial movement, was formally inaugurated in 1947 and given constitutional sanction in 1950. Of its two components, viz. state and nation,[1] the former was largely an adapted continuation of the modern apparatus of the colonial state, whereas the latter was the anti-colonial creation of the Indian national movement, especially of its Gandhi-Nehru phase. In the processes leading to, and culminating in, the transfer of power from the British rulers to the leadership of the Indian nationalist movement and the attendant process of constitution making, the state apparatus of colonial modernity became transformed by, and anchored in, the moral-political concerns of Indian nationalism. Appropriately stressing the newness of the independent nation-state, Jawaharlal Nehru, India's first Prime Minister, announced its birth, at midnight of 14–15 August 1947, as 'a moment, which comes but rarely in history, when we step out of the old to the new, when an age ends, and when the soul of a nation, long suppressed, finds utterance' (Nehru 1949: 3).

How was this 'nation' suppressed by colonialism and how has it found its new expression in the post-colonial state? What has been its post-Independence career?

In their different ways, the British colonial state in India and the anti-colonial nationalist movement which it gave rise to, marked major departures from the structure of political authority and the culture of political identities as they had existed in pre-colonial/pre-modern Indian society. Those departures or discontinuities constitute the birthmarks of the distinctive identity of the contemporary Indian nation-state. This state, however, even while resolutely pursuing modernity, does claim a certain moral-cultural or cultural-political continuity with tradition or, to repeat Nehru's words, with the long-suppressed 'soul' of the Indian nation. This continuity is formally expressed, often for symbolic purposes, in several different places and ways, some of which include: (i) Article 1 of the Constitution, which identifies India as 'Bharat', reminiscent of Bharatvarsha (the land of the progeny of Bharat, celebrated in the great epic, Mahabharata); (ii) the use of an adaptation from the Sarnath lion capital of Mauryan emperor, Ashoka, as the state emblem of India; (iii) the incorporation, into that emblem, of the inscription, satyameva jayate (Truth Alone Triumphs), which is taken from the Mundaka Upanishad; (iv) the incorporation of Ashoka's dharmachakra (Wheel of Law) on the national flag of India; and (v) the constitutionally directed (Article 40) efforts of the state to promote panchayati raj, the form of village republics in ancient India.

What then were the characteristics of state formations and their patterns of legitimization in India in pre-colonial times?

The Subcontinental State Under the Mauryan and Gupta Dynasties

In India's long pre-colonial history, a centralized pan-Indian state was the exception rather than the rule. The prevailing pattern was one of resilient power structures at the level of the village community and several regional kingdoms of varying power with changing interrelationships with one another. True, many of these regional states did often pursue ambitions for subcontinental hegemony, but only on very few occasions were they successful. In fact, prior to British colonial rule, there have been only three brief periods 'when the parochial loyalties of family, caste, and region have been transcended by a larger pan-Indian vision of what a united India might be' (Larson 1997: 140–1). These three 'pan-Indian visions' were those of the Mauryan empire under Ashoka (third century BC), whose legitimacy rested partly on Kautilya's *Arthashastra* (science of wealth) and partly on the Buddhist *dhamma*; the Gupta empire under Chandra Gupta II (fourth and early fifth centuries AD), with its legitimation by a composite Hindu religious culture which absorbed several ideas from Buddhism and Jainism; and the Mughal empire under Akbar (sixteenth century) with its largely Indo-Islamic legitimation.

The infrequency of the formation of centralized or strong subcontinental states and their early mortality in India's long history are generally interpreted as having to do partly with the frequency of foreign invasions and partly with the fact that structures of political authority remained rooted 'in lineage and kinship networks and primordial loyalties rather than in associational structures and impersonal norms' (Kumar 1997: 398). The power of the dominant clans, lineages, and castes of a given local society was legitimized by the Brahmanical religion (Frankel 1989: 2). In ancient India, the transition from nomadic and semi-nomadic tribal communities to agricultural settlements took the form of caste society, which has proved to be a change-inhibiting system of social stratification (Kulke and Rothermund [1986] 1998: 39–41). In caste society, the political agency of the people was either circumscribed (in the case of the Brahmins and the Kshatriyas) or altogether precluded (in the case of the other, lower castes, namely the Vaishyas and Shudras, as well as the untouchables, the Aspriyas). Moreover, there was a peculiar embedding or reinforcing relationship between the ritual hierarchy based on religious notions of purity and pollution and the hierarchies of wealth and power—peculiar in the sense that the lowest levels of all these hierarchies tended to coincide, whereas their highest levels were differentiated from each other. In this ingenious system of social stratification, it was extremely difficult for the ordinary people to pinpoint any locus of compounded privileges or the social/human causation of, or political responsibility for, the compounded deprivations of those who found themselves at the bottom of the hierarchies of status, wealth, and power. This had a change-inhibiting impact, especially at the level of the local village community. Its social order, which was indeed one of inequality, was interpreted by the Brahmins as 'natural' or 'pre-given' (in/by the immutable, sacred *shruti* [revealed] texts), and not politically constructed by historically situated human agents. In a society which is thought to be made up of such 'pre-ordered' or 'pre-governed' village communities, the state or the political sphere had only a very limited or marginal role to play. It had no sovereignty in any political sense; it did not have to engage in any legislative or judicial activities for creating or transforming the social order, be it the order of gender relations or of production relations. Thus, as Francine Frankel writes, 'the failure of centralized states to emerge in the subcontinent was directly linked to the strength of Brahmanical ideology in providing sacral legitimation for localized dominance relations.

These religious beliefs made the state unnecessary for the preservation of social harmony [1989: 1–2]'.

This is not to deny the limited space which the Brahmanically legitimized social order assigned to the state or the political-administrative sphere (of the Kshatriyas). Under Brahmanical edict, the state had to uphold or maintain, without any change, the pre-given social order of *varnashramdharma* and punish those who infringed it. The state of course also had to perform the basic function of providing protection to the community from its external enemies. Accordingly, the caste system provided for a very limited functional autonomy to its 'political' segment, the Kshatriyas, to raise and administer the required revenues and to manage its bureaucracy, police, and army. A part of the state's revenues had to be used to construct and maintain temples, whose priests crowned the kings and advised them on their *rajadharm* (king's duty) of upholding the varnashramdharma.

Given the limited or constrained nature of their differentiation or autonomy from the Brahmanically legitimized 'pre-given' or 'natural' social order, the institutions of the state could not develop as political institutions. Hence the formation of the first centralized pan-Indian state, namely the Mauryan empire, could come about only through radical departures from the old religiously legitimized social order—departures which established a clear differentiation or autonomy of the political sphere from the socio-religious sphere.[2] Such departures were made since the sixth century BC, first, by heretical movements within religion, namely, Buddhism and Jainism,[3] and, second, by the radically new, secular-pragmatic theory of the state and government contained in the *Arthashastra,* attributed to Kautilya, the mentor and minister of Chandragupta Maurya (c. 321–298 BC), the founder of the Mauryan empire.

As noted by Romila Thapar, some of the ways in which the 'reforms' or 'heresies' of Buddhism and Jainism contributed to changing the socio-economic system, were: the support of the investment of economic surplus in commercial activities rather than its consumption in ritual functions,[4] the formation of the Buddhist *sangha,* with the monastery, which was supported by the lay followers; as its main institution; and the participation of the emperors, qua *chakravartins* (universal rulers with not only administrative functions but also legislative and judicial sovereignty), in the Buddhist Councils held at Rajagrha and Pataliputra. The most important departure of Buddhism and Jainism from Brahmanism was their advocacy of a universalistic ethics for 'the entire range of castes in an effort to equate people not socially but at least at the level of ethical action' (Thapar 1984: 109–11; Prasad 1974: 209–11).

Buddhism and Jainism, however, were primarily heretical movements within the religious sphere and, with the exception of the later phase of Ashoka's rule, did not exert much direct influence on the state.[5] According to Louis Dumont, the Jain and Buddhist reaction against Brahminic supremacy 'has been effected through renunciation, and not within the social order itself; in other words it occurred on a level transcending society' (Dumont 1970: 74). I would, however, maintain that the affirmation of human agency by the individual in her/his religious life did have a revolutionary impact on political life in the sense that the political agency of the individual could no longer be de-legitimized by Brahmanical ideology. In fact, since its beginning, Buddhism has been associated with a republican view of political life and a contractarian view of the state. Moreover, during the time of Ashoka, Buddhism 'was not merely a religious belief; it was in addition a social and intellectual movement at many levels, influencing many aspects of society' (Thapar [1966] 1997: 85).

Yet it cannot be denied that the earlier strand of Buddhism, with its emphasis on renunciation and monastic life, could not have been the answer to the need for political unity and centralization in the wake of the incursions into India by Alexander of Macedon. That need was met by the theory of state which was provided by Kautilya's *Arthashastra*. According to it, the answer to the dangers of anarchy was to be found neither in renunciation nor in excessive individualism, but in a strong, centralized state under a sovereign king. What was required, in other words, was a clear or secular differentiation or autonomy of the political from the socio-religious. The *Arthashastra* provided for such a clear autonomy. As V.R. Mehta writes: 'While the earlier literature [e.g. the *Dharmasutras*] had subordinated the king to brahmanical authority, and the *Shantiparva* gave the king some discretion, when we come to Kautilya, we find that the king is given the last say in all matters' (Mehta 1992: 86). The autonomy of the political sphere from the socio-religious sphere was stretched to the extent of giving to the former its own moral standard, namely the principle of the end justifying the means. With the acquisition of such a sovereignty by the state, religion became a private affair of the citizens. Moreover, according to Kautilya, the king is no more a mere protector or upholder of a pre-given socio-religious order; he has sovereign legislative, judicial, and executive powers. 'In the Arthashastra,' writes Dumont, 'the king exerts a complete hold on everything, and in the first place on the soil' (1970: 83).

It was this radically new theory of state that guided and informed the formation and consolidation of the first centralized imperial Indian state under the Mauryan dynasty of Chandragupta, Bindusara, and Ashoka. Its formation through conquests and consolidation through a centralized bureaucracy rested on the fiscal security provided by an economy of expanding agriculture, craft guilds, and trade. The intervention of the state for such expansion, however, was by and large confined to the metropolitan or core region of the empire, whereas in the peripheral regions the presence of the imperial state, through its centralized administration, was usually confined to the collection of taxes, tributes and, during campaigns or conquests, plunder. The taxes and tributes thus collected were used to pay the large army and bureaucracy and the spies, who worked in the guise of ascetics, mendicant women, prostitutes, merchants, and students.

Romila Thapar has used the symbolism of the wheel and the *mandala* theory of state to describe the relationship between the core region of the Mauryan empire, which served as a firm and secure 'hub of power', and its peripheral areas. Just as a wheel is marked by a differential distribution of power, so in the Mauryan empire there was 'a differentiation between power at the centre of the circle and at the rim' (Thapar 1984: 161). Or, as the mandala theory stipulates, the core region and its peripheral areas stood in a kaleidoscopic; relationship marked by a constant vacillation between friendship-and-hostility, between the central king and his circle (mandala) of friendly, hostile, and neutral kings (cf. Ghoshal 1959: 93–4).

Towards the close of Ashoka's rule, the Mauryan state experienced some severe socio-economic and religious conflicts, namely conflicts between the Brahmins and the heterodox sects (Buddhists and Jains) and the disaffection of the rising mercantile communities whose interests clashed with the revenue requirements of the bureaucratic-militaristic state. Taxes were in fact collected 'from every conceivable human activity with which the state could be associated' (Thapar 1984: 160). Heavy taxation and bureaucratic controls did not contribute to the expansion of economic activity. The harassment of traders blocked economic progress and led to a fiscal crisis of the state (Kosambi 1970: 165 and 1975: 216).

Confronted by these problems, Ashoka felt that the *Arthashastra* framework of double or separate standards for the state and for the people had to be replaced by, or at least brought under the purview of, a new common or universal ethics that would not only unite the state and its citizens but also bring about toleration among the religious sects. Accordingly, he expounded and propagated a new, universal dhamma (the Prakrit word used in Buddhist literature for the Sanskrit word, dharma). Dhamma, for Ashoka, meant neither piety nor the rules of caste society, but a spirit of righteous conduct and social responsibility. Its main principles were non-violence, public works or people's welfare, and, most importantly, toleration, especially of opposing religious sects. In one of his rock edicts, he propagated the principle of toleration in the following way:

> The Beloved of the Gods [i.e. Ashoka] does not consider gifts of honour to be as important as the essential advancement of all sects. Its basis is the control of one's speech, so as not to extol one's own sect or disparage that of another on unsuitable occasions. ... On each occasion one should honour another man's sect, for by doing so one increases the influence of one's own sect and benefits that of the other man, while, by doing otherwise, one diminishes the influence of one's own sect and harms the other man's ... therefore concord is to be commended so that men may hear one another's principles [(Thapar (1966) 1977: 87)].

Although Ashoka's actual policy of dhamma made only a very small contribution to bringing about social unity and political stability, his role in emphasizing the need for moral legitimacy of the actions of the state has remained a lasting legacy in India. 'It can even be said,' to quote Kosambi, 'that the Indian national character received the stamp of *dhamma* from the time of Asoka. The word soon came to mean something else than "equity", namely religion—and by no means the sort of religion Asoka himself professed' (1970: 165).

The Brahmanic reaction to the Buddhist dhamma was one of the factors contributing to the decline of the Mauryan empire. The former led eventually to a great religious-cultural resurgence and creativity, culminating in what is referred to as the 'classical Hindu' period of Indian history under the imperial rule of the Gupta dynasty (AD 320–500). However, the Hindu religion from which the legitimacy of the imperial rule of the Gupta emperors was derived was a remarkably pluralist religion, containing within it three major sects/cults (of Shiva, Vishnu/ Krishna, and Durga/Kali). The Gupta rulers were also tolerant towards and supportive of other religions, notably Buddhism and Jainism. There was also a Christian community in South India. According to many historians, the Gupta emperors pursued a composite pan-Indian moral-cultural vision that accommodated religious and regional differences. The *Lawbook of Yajnavalkya*, which served as a guide to the Gupta rulers, not only drew a clear distinction between secular and religious law but also removed some of the legal discriminations against the Shudras and some of the legal privileges which the Brahmins had earlier enjoyed. Yet it must be remembered that the primary interest of the Gupta rulers was to rule and not to bring about social revolution. Their rule sustained and was sustained by the 'Aryan patriarchal society', which, among other things, practised pre-puberty marriages and *sati* (Thapar [1966] 1977: 152 and 166; Dandekar [1958] 1988: 236–40). Under the rule of the Gupta dynasty, there was a revival of some aspects of the old Brahmanical ideology (for example caste hierarchy, Vedic rituals, and the horse sacrifice). The Gupta period was also associated with some new additions to, or redactions of, the *smriti* literature, especially the *Dharmashastra* and the *Bhagwad Gita*, which, among other things, presented the moral philosophy of *nishkama karma* (the duty of disinterested action).

The religious pluralism and toleration of the imperial state of the Guptas was associated with the flourishing of trade and commerce both across the regions within the empire and across the oceans, especially with Southeast Asia, where both Buddhists and Hindus visited and settled. There was also an association between the religious pluralism of the imperial state and the considerable degree of political and administrative autonomy which the provinces or regions had.

The degree of centralization of rule which was achieved under the Mauryan or the Gupta dynasties was not continued or repeated until the coming of the Mughals in the sixteenth century. In the intervening period, the Indian polity was loosely integrated under a succession of what has come to be alternatively designated as 'pyramidally segmented states' (Stein 1980) or 'imperial formations' (Inden 1990). In their separate ways, theoretical constructs such as these are meant to differentiate the medieval Indian polity from the unitary, centralized, territorial state of European modernity.

Pyramidally Segmented States or Imperial Formations?

According to Burton Stein (1980), a pyramidally segmented type of state was formed in medieval south India, especially during the Pallava, Chola, and Vijayanagara periods, by the interlinking of 'relatively self-sufficient, enduring, and often quite ancient localized societies'.

Such a state is not an amalgamation or absorption of localised units into an organic greater unit such as implied in the unitary state, but is an arrangement in which the local units—segments—retain their essential being as segmental parts of a whole. One reason why each of the segmental units remains autonomous is that each is pyramidal, that is, each consists of balanced and opposed internal groupings which zealously cling to their independent identities, privileges, and internal governance, and demand that these units be protected by their local rulers [Stein 1980: 275].

In this polity, sovereignty was dual in the sense that while the king exercised an essentially ritual sovereignty in all the zones (*nadus*) of the state, he wielded actual political sovereignty or control only in the core or central zone of the state system, leaving the intermediate and peripheral zones to the political sovereignty or control of the 'little kings' and chiefs. However, because all the segmentary units recognized the king as the single, incorporative, ritual authority, they together constituted a state system of the segmentary type. It was segmentary rather than unitary or centralized in the sense that it had a vertical discontinuity of actual power relations, with the 'little kings' and chiefs of the peripheral zones retaining their own armies and administrators. Inter-segmentary cooperation was brought about in acts of defence or aggression against others and was cemented by their common recognition of the ritually incorporative sovereignty of the king of kings. This came about in Tamil Nadu during the Pallava period, when the Aryan/Brahmanical conception of 'ritually incorporative kingship' or sovereignty was introduced. To quote Stein again: 'The pre-Pallavan, or Classical, period was one in which three kingships and a great number of chieftainships existed among Tamils; from the Pallava period, the Tamils could have but one great king, one who, by means of ritual, incorporated all lesser rulers' (1980: 276).

Because its political unity was based only or essentially on the sacral or ritual rulership of the king over the segmentary units, which were in complementary opposition to one another, the pre-modern, pyramidally segmented state, in contrast to the modern, unitary, centralized state, constituted a fluid and indeterminate political structure with vague boundaries and shifting capitals. The fixed or stable elements of the state existed only at local levels, which were under the control of dominant cultivating or merchant groups and of the 'little kings'. As protectors of the locality, these 'little kings' could obtain resources by force. But since their rulership had a ritual or sacral character as well, they had to redistribute some of their amassed resources through the '*dharmic* activities' of giving *dana*s (gifts) to temples and Brahmins. The hundreds of nadus which comprised south Indian society under the Pallavas or the Cholas were unified not through any technical or bureaucratic mechanisms but through the 'idiom of a *dharmic* universe realized through the sacral kingship' of the ruling dynasty (Stein 1980: 365).[6]

The segmentary model of the state in 'medieval' south India has been criticized for its overemphasis on the segmentariness of the polity and the essentially ritual nature of the sovereignty of its king. Alam and Subrahmanyam (1998: 34) feel that the regular fiscal flows which were maintained between the localities and the core region of the Vijayanagar kingdom made it more than a mere segmentary state based essentially on ritual sovereignty. According to Ronald Inden (1990), the Indian polity during the so-called medieval period had a greater and, indeed, different type of unity than what is granted to it by Stein's notions of pyramidal segmentation and ritual sovereignty. Rejecting Stein's dichotomy between the higher ritual sovereignty of the Great King and the lower political sovereignties of the 'little kings', Inden seems to suggest that the so-called ritual or dharmic activities were also political activities and vice versa.

Instead of Stein's dichotomy between the ritual/sacral sovereignty of the Great King and the political sovereignty of the 'little kings', Inden speaks of the chakravartin's 'compound activity' whereby he seeks both *dig-vijaya* (conquest of the quarters, whereby other kings are brought into 'the circle of kings' or the imperial formation) and dharma-vijaya (cosmomoral victory). Inden writes

All of the major [Indian] religious orders incorporated into their soteriologies the idea of a universal monarch or paramount king of India, a 'great man' (*mahapurusha*) who, endowed with special powers, was able to complete a 'conquest of quarters' of India in the name of a still greater agent, the one taken as overlord of the cosmos. The names given to this compound activity, the 'conquest of quarters' (*dig-vijaya*) and 'conquest in accord with cosmomoral order' (*dharma-vijaya*), referred to a royal progress that was supposed to display the performer of it as the overlord of each of the four directional regions, together with a middle region, taken to comprise the whole of the earth [Inden 1990: 229–30].

Inden does concur with Stein in denying to the medieval-Indian state the centralized political control and administration that characterize the modern nation-state. He also sees in medieval India a succession, not of mere ritually integrated kingdoms, but of real 'imperial formations' which approximate the *Arthashastra* model of the 'circle of kings' (mandala, *rajamandala*) under the paramount control or domination of a chakravartin (universal monarch).[7] Each one of these imperial formations consisted of 'one (or more) empires and a number of other kingdoms'. Through 'dialectical and eristical relations with one another', they together formed 'a scale of polities, or rulerships that overlapped one another'. Among them, there was frequent competition for the position of the 'highest polity in the scale' (Inden 1990: 267).

According to Inden, the Indian polity functioned as an imperial formation under the Chalukyas, the Rashtrakutas, the Cholas, and the Vijayanagara rulers. Under their rule, the core or middle region of Indian polity was displaced from the Ganga-Yamuna region on to their own imperial domains. He also claims that Indian polity under the rule of the Rashtrakuta dynasty (AD 753–975) was one of a total of only four imperial formations which made up the whole of Eurasia and North Africa in that period, the others being the Arab, Chinese, and Greek imperial formations.

Patrimonial-Bureaucratic States

The Mughal empire, especially under Akbar's rule (1556–1605), has been viewed as 'the culmination of pre-modern state administration in India' (Kulke 1995: 32). It had a centralized administrative machinery, called the *mansabdari* system, in which there was a fusion of military and civil services into a single, hierarchic bureaucracy under the emperor. Each administrative-military officer had a definite number rank (*mansab*), generally determined by the number of cavalry (*sawars*, horsemen), he had to raise and maintain out of his emoluments and which, when needed, were available to the emperor. The payments were either in cash or by an assignment of the land-revenue of a specified area (*jagir*), under the control of the mansabdar and his subordinate revenue collectors, including the *zamindars*.

The empire was divided into *subahs* (provinces), *sarkars* (subdivisions), and *mohallas* (revenue circles). More or less the same administrative structure was developed in each subah. Yet, as pointed out by Alam and Subrahmanyam, there was noticeable variation in land-revenue administration from region to region, rather than an 'unremitting centralization based on an elaborate and uniform bureaucracy which has "penetrated" the countryside (1998: 15). The zamindars in the countryside as well as bankers and traders retained a certain degree of autonomy. Moreover, as many new regions were conquered and incorporated into the empire, regional and local variations had to be recognized so that the state eventually resembled a "patchwork quilt" rather than a "wall-to-wall carpet"' (Alam and Subrahmanyam: 33). Notwithstanding the absence of any 'unremitting centralization' in the administrative set-up of the Mughal empire, it needs to be noted that the Mughal state was seen 'in all of the subcontinent as the only true source of sovereignty' (Alam and Subrahmanyam 1998: 57).

The rise and consolidation of this great patrimonial-bureaucratic state in India coincided with, and was, in its later phase, helped by, the dawn of modern technology in Europe. Especially significant was the role of artillery, 'the most brilliant and dreadful representative of modern technology' in those times, when there also arose absolute monarchies in Europe (Ali 1995: 264). As pointed out by M. Athar Ali (1995: 274–5), even though the Mughal army was mainly a cavalry force, artillery did play a significant role in it. Its infantrymen included 'match-lock men, gunners, cannoneers[,] and rocketeers' and thus they had a decisive advantage against the traditional chiefs, including the Rajputs.

Another product of early European modernity was the influx of silver into the international market, resulting from the Spanish 'discovery' of South America. This made it possible for the Mughal emperors, especially Akbar, to replace the existing debased coinage (largely of copper content) that had a new currency system, with the highly valued silver-based rupee as the basic unit. This contributed to the expansion of commerce and credit, and also to the centralization of the state.

Some of the subjects of the Mughal state became aware of early modern European scientific knowledge and questioned the finality of traditional knowledge. For instance, Abul Fazl, Akbar's ideologue, propagandist, and adviser, questioned those who were opposing sciences that were not based upon the Quran (Ali 1995: 275). There were also 'revisionist' movements, like the Mahdavi movement, which challenged earlier interpretations of Islamic doctrines. 'All these,' writes M. Athar Ali, 'were symptoms of a cleft in the hitherto solid structure of faith in the traditional cultural heritage of Islam' (1995: 276). Partly in response to this new situation and partly for other reasons (like the majority status of the Hindus in the population and Akbar's marriage to a Hindu princess), Akbar pursued a policy of religious tolerance and promoted regular, inter-religious discussions. More importantly, he devised a new, eclectic set of beliefs called Divine Faith (*Din-el-Ilahi*), which contained elements from Islam, Hinduism, and Zoroastrianism. Din-e-Ilahi, however, was not made a state religion. Moreover, in the administration of justice, Akbar assumed the role of an interpreter of the Islamic law, which he occasionally supplemented by imperial edicts (*qanun-e-shahi*).

Despite these advances in military-fiscal organization and moral-political legitimation, the Mughal state basically remained a patrimonial-bureaucratic state, in which the empire was identified with the person of the emperor and personal loyalty to the emperor was equated with loyalty to the state. This is well expressed by J.F. Richards:

From an external perspective, the bureaucratic structure of the empire[,] with its specialized offices, systematic procedures, and hierarchies of technically proficient officials, was the most impressive aspect of the empire. However, the core of the imperial system embedded within the outer structure was formed by the complex matrix of ties of loyalty and interest between the *amirs* and the emperor [1998: 129].

Some of the patrimonial-bureaucratic features of the Mughal state are brought out by Stephen Blake in his reading of Abul Fazl's *Ain-i Akbari* (Institutes of Akbar), as follows:

In its depiction of the emperor as a divinely aided patriarch, the household[,] as the central element in government, members of the army as dependent on the emperor, the administration as a loosely structured group of men controlled by the Imperial household and travel as a significant part of the emperor's activities, the Ain-i Akbari supports the suggestion that Akbar's state was a patrimonial-bureaucratic empire [1995: 302].

A variant of the Mughal patrimonial-bureaucratic state was the patrimonial-*sultanist* state of Tipu Sultan (1783–99), which functioned as a semi-independent state under the carapace of the sovereignty of the Mughal state. Under this sultanism, the army was the first institution of the state and its ruler was above all a war commander, demanding the personal loyalty of the subordinates. Sultanism essentially meant the elimination of the tribute-paying intermediaries and the instantiation of a centralized machinery of fiscal control.[8]

Given its essential character as an extended patrimonial-bureaucratic system, the Mughal state cannot be said to have been constituted according to the distinctly modern values and principles of the formation and legitimation of the state. In effect, the subcontinent of India, to quote M. Athar Ali once more, 'had a centralized quasi-modern state without any developing sense of nationhood' (1995: 277) among the mass of the imperial subjects. In fact, one of the contributing factors to the decline of the Mughal imperial authority was the resistance movements not only of the peasants and other regional and local groups but also of the zamindars, who capitalized on the peasants' grievances against the state and mobilized them for their own political ends (Alam 1998: 472; Bhadra 1998).

The patrimonial-bureaucratic structures of the Mughal state were initially relied upon by the colonial regime, which, as we shall see below, eventually replaced it by the fully bureaucratized, modern, unitary state based on European principles (Stein 1985: 412–13). Another point of continuity and change between the Mughal and colonial states pertained to the use of what Foucault calls the modern technologies of power (Foucault 1979: part 3, ch. 3). The Mughal state did use some rudimentary, early modern versions of modern technologies of power and surplus extraction such as surveys, measurements, accounts, and audits. Also, panopticons-style prisons (designed to enable the warder to directly observe prisoners without being seen by them) were built at Poona and Ratnagiri. Through these new technologies of power exercise, the Mughal state eliminated some of the intermediary structures and acquired direct control over its subjects. These early modern technologies of power/knowledge, however, were more fully developed and used by the colonial state and used for substantively new purposes (Perlin 1985: 263, 475, 477).

The Colonial State

The British colonial state in India marked a substantial break with the previous state forms. This had to do with its European origins and orientations or purposes, which were inextricably linked with the career of capitalist modernity on a world scale.

The English East India Company, founded in London in 1600 under the Charter rights given by the British government, began its trading activities in India by securing privileges from Mughal emperor Jahangir, in 1619 for setting up and fortifying 'factories' or trading centres. Operating from those trading centres, the functionaries of the Company eventually resorted to political conspiracies, military conquests, and the instantiation of Company raj. These actions constituted the proto-state of colonial modernity, to be replaced, after the 1857 Great Revolt, by the fully designed and formally proclaimed colonial modern state.

The Company's securing of *Diwani* (the high office entitling its incumbent to collect all revenues) in Bengal in 1765 from the Mughal emperor constituted the 'inaugural moment of the *raj*' (Guha 1997: 156). Diwani enabled the Company to legitimize its military conquest of Bengal (in the battles of Plassey and Buxar) and to launch its new career as the incipient proto-state of British colonialism in India. As *Diwan,* the Company claimed legality for its new function of administering civil justice and collecting and administering land revenues, which were used to finance further trade and military conquests, and to pay an annuity of 400,000 pounds sterling as tribute to the British exchequer. By the Pitt's India Act of 1784, the British government brought the Company raj under its indirect rule. After the suppression of the Great Indian Revolt of 1857, the indirect rule of Great Britain over India was converted into direct imperial rule. This was effected through an Act passed by British parliament and proclaimed in India by Queen Victoria in November 1858. By this Act and Proclamation, the British Indian colonial state was formally created, with its sovereignty appropriated by the British Crown. This colonial state came to exercise direct rule over two-thirds of the territory and four-fifths of the population of the country, while the rest of the territory and population were left to the rule of the native princes, subject to the 'paramount' overseeing of resident agents of the Viceroy.

The Company raj received initial support from Indian financial and merchant capitalists, who saw themselves as standing to benefit more from the larger trade networks of the East India Company than from the military fiscalism of the Mughal *nawabs* or from the sultanist or warrior states of Mysore, the Marathas, or the Sikhs. For instance, Robert Clive's victory in the Battle of Plassey was crucially dependent on the support he received from the merchant bankers Jagat Seth and Omichand. As the Company raj became consolidated, Indian commercial and trading groups were reduced to very inferior status, although some of them found avenues for business in some of the British colonies in Africa, West Asia, and Southeast Asia.

Being both colonial and modern at the same time, the state of the British Indian empire marked a substantial departure from India's pre-modern/pre-colonial state structures as well as from its modern mother state in England. The most obvious way in which the colonial state differed from the pre-colonial states lay in the greatness and pervasiveness of its activities. Commenting on some of those 'great' activities of the new state on the eve of its reorganization according to the Government of India Act of 1935, Edward Thompson and G.T. Garratt wrote:

On the merely material side the new Federal Government will take over the largest irrigation system in the world ... some 60,000 miles of metalled roads; over 42,000 miles of railway ...; 230,000 scholastic institutions ...; a great number of buildings. The vast area of India has been completely surveyed, most of its lands assessed, and a regular census taken of its population and its productivity. ... The postal department handles nearly 1500 million articles yearly, the Forestry Department not only prevents the denudation of immense areas, but makes a net profit of between two and three crores. These great State activities are managed by a trained bureaucracy, which is today almost entirely Indian [Thompson and Garratt (1934) 1962: 654].

These 'great State activities', which, as noted by Thompson and Garratt ([1934] 1962) were to leave a 'permanent mark upon Indian life', had to do with the colonial state's superiority in military technology, financial resources, administrative or bureaucratic rationality, and, above all, its colonizing purpose, namely the incorporation of India, as a colony, into the imperialist capitalist system. The central task of the colonial state was the internal disarticulation of the colonial economy and the external articulation of its segments with the requirements of the metropolitan or core country of the then emerging imperialist system of capitalist production and exchange. Some of the requirements of that core country, namely Britain, were the import of raw materials, especially agricultural and mineral products, and the export of its own manufactured goods. Accordingly, the colonial state, departing from the military fiscalism of the Mughal state and its subordinate/successor sultanist kingdoms in the region, developed modern, centralized, sovereign state institutions for transforming and restructuring the economy, culture, laws, etc. of the colony. Thus, besides promoting or supporting colonial plantations, forced cultivation of indigo or opium, irrigation, mining, trade, transport, communications, and selected industries, the new state introduced institutions of modern western education and bourgeois legal and judicial systems (Kaviraj 1994: 36 and 38).

For carrying out these unprecedented, mammoth tasks, the colonial state replaced the erstwhile, patrimonial-sultanist, civil-cum-military bureaucracy with a modern, specialized military and civil bureaucracy, based on a colonial version of the rational, impersonal, non-arbitrary, competitive principles of merit, efficiency, neutrality, etc. The colonial state constituted a curious mixture of modernity and tradition. It tried to accommodate its own modern, unitary sovereignty with the sovereignties of the traditional rulers, the *rajas* and *maharajas*. Even its own modern, paramount, unitary sovereignty was initially presented, for the purpose of legitimation, as a continuation and improvement of the institutional and symbolic order of the pre-colonial state, for example the institution of the Mughal *durbar* (Cohn 1983; Kaviraj 1994). By doing so, the colonial state secured legitimacy for its rule from the forces of tradition, which, in turn, received a fresh lease of life under the paramountcy of the modern-colonial state. For the sake of social stability and state legitimacy, the colonial state also followed the personal laws of the Islamic *sharia* and an order of precedence according to caste hierarchy.

As mentioned in earlier paragraphs, the colonial state marked a radical departure not only from its pre-colonial predecessor states but also from its mother state in Britain, to which it was in fact held responsible. Colonialism was based on the justificatory assumption that the colony and its people were different from, inferior to, and therefore colonizable by the 'enlightened' or 'rational' masters of the modern, industrialized metropolis. The colonial state therefore sought to 'prove' the truth of that assumption in two interrelated ways. First, it subjected the land and people of India to the specifically modern regime of power and knowledge, which, following Michael Foucault (1979), we may refer to as the power of cognitive regimes or disciplining categories of knowledge and rules of logic. Thus, under colonial rule, not only was the law codified and the bureaucracy rationalized, but a whole apparatus of specialized technical services was instituted in order to scientifically survey, classify, and enumerate the geographical, geological, botanical, and meteorological properties of the natural environment and the archaeological, historical, anthropological, linguistic, economic, demographic, epidemiological characteristics of the people [Chatterjee 1993: 19–20].

These new or modern technologies of disciplining knowledge/power/rule, namely surveys, enumerations, classifications, accounting and auditing, and the associated conceptual baggage and binary logic of rational exclusion or marginalization, were put into operation by the colonial state in order to bring about an unprecedented centralization of rule, especially of the monetary system. As noted earlier, the revenues extracted from the traditional society by the modern, specialist cadres went into supporting the military operations or the international trading activities of the Company raj. This led to 'money famines', demonetization of the countryside, and the decline both of indigenous banking and manufacturing industries (Perlin 1985: 477–8). After the replacement of the Company raj by direct Crown rule through the Secretary of State and the Viceroy, the Indian economy had to pay what were called 'home charges', which included the cost of the Secretary of State's office (in London), costs of wars fought to expand or defend the empire, pensions for the military and civilian personnel, and a guaranteed annual interest on the investment in Indian railways. There was also a substantial de-valuation of the silver-based Indian rupee when it was plugged onto the gold-based exchange standard (Bose and Jalal 1998: 99–100).

The second way in which the colonial state attempted to 'prove' the justificatory assumption of colonialism (namely that the colonial subjects were a racially inferior people) was by 'demonstrating' that the legitimizing principles of the modern, liberal-democratic state, for example the principles of liberal equality, rule of law, and responsiveness to public opinion, were not universalizable until after the fulfilment of the so-called 'civilizing mission' of colonial rule. Even though the colonial state did set up institutions of modern western education in India and even though some of the constitutional reforms of the colonial rulers did provide for restricted Indian representation in provincial and central legislative assemblies as well as in municipal and other local boards, the colonial government did not give Indian judicial officers the same rights as their British counterparts to try cases in which European British subjects were involved.[9] Similarly, the principle of the freedom of opinion and expression was denied to the colonized subjects by the colonial government, whenever that opinion and expression clashed with those of the European community.[10]

The colonial state was formed by, and for, an alien bourgeois class. While the rule of that class was hegemonic in its home country as there was, in its civil society, widespread acceptance of the bourgeois-liberal conceptions of the individual, society, state, and democracy, its state in the colony lacked any such hegemony.[11] No doubt, the colonial state was responsible to the parliamentary-democratic government and public opinion of Britain. Those, however, were, for the historical period in question, avowedly imperialistic. The colonial state maintained its rule or power partly through coercion, partly through the continuation of some of the old discourses and practices of legitimation, and partly by forming a new middle class of English-educated Indians, who, it was hoped, would appreciate and advocate the benefits of the modern state that was imported from Britain. As it turned out, it was this middle class, whose acquisition of modern education made them see the utter illegitimacy or 'untruthful' nature of the colonial state and who provided the moral-intellectual and organizational leadership of the successful anti-imperialist nationalist movement.

In the course of the Indian nationalist movement, many of its leaders emphasized the fact that while in the entire tradition of Indian political thought and practice, the state had to seek its legitimacy in terms of moral-political principles, such as the principles of dhamma, dharma, or Din-e-Ilahi, the colonial state made itself the source of the law which created and sustained the colonial mode of the drain of wealth from India to the imperialist circuit of modern capitalism. This colonial-modern conception of the role of the state and of the rule of law was in fact inscribed over the seat of imperial power at the Central Secretariat in New Delhi. It read: 'Honour the State, the Root of Law and Wealth' (Sudarshan 1995: 59).

The Indian Nation-State—Democratic, Secular, and Developmental

It was in resistance to that state and its laws that the anti-colonial nationalist movement took shape in India and eventually succeeded in securing the transfer of power from the colonial rulers to its own leadership. The nationalist movement was spearheaded by the western-educated middle-class intelligentsia and the emergent indigenous bourgeoisie. Under the leadership of Mahatma Gandhi, the movement acquired a mass base among the peasantry, who had been the worst sufferers of the colonial system and who had previously risen in uncoordinated, violent rebellions (Chatterjee 1986 and 1993). The Gandhian era also saw a major reorganization of the Indian National Congress, whereby its provincial units were made to correspond to the linguistic regions rather than to the administrative provinces of the colonial state. The structure and functioning of the party were also made democratic. These democratic and linguistic-federal practices of the Indian National Congress, which were in clear opposition to the arbitrary and despotic practices of the colonial state, were thought to prefigure the future, independent nation-state. In fact, the central objective of the nationalist movement, in its mature phase, was the replacement of the colonial state by a democratic, sovereign nation-state, which, unlike the colonial and pre-colonial states, was to play a central, directing role in economic development and social justice.

The future, independent state was 'imagined' by the nationalist movement, especially in its final, Gandhi-Nehru phase, to be one which would sustain, and be sustained by, a complex conception of pluralist, civic-communitarian nationalism, rather than by any simple ethnic, religious, or linguistic nationalism. The former, unlike the latter, entailed a state-centred (rather than, say, caste- or religion-oriented) 'imagining' or 'construction' of a composite or pluralist national political community marked by the equal citizenship of all the peoples of India, irrespective of their religious, caste, linguistic, regional, or gender differences. 'In effect,' writes Rajni Kothari (1995a), 'it was stateness that gave to the new entity, at once, an encompassing, representative, and transcendent quality.' The state, moreover, was to respect the principle of the equality of all religions. The relationship of the new nation-state to the diverse pre-existing social, regional, linguistic, religious, or cultural identities was imagined 'in part to be one of transcendence, though it was far more to be one of encompassing them and in some ways even representing them in a composite manner' (Kothari 1995b). In the Indian nation-state, as imagined by the nationalist movement,

there was no way ... for any person to be *only* Indian and nothing else; indeed, one could not be an Indian without being some other things at the same time. Being a Bengali or Tamil or Punjabi, or Hindu, or Muslim or agnostic, was not contradictory to being an Indian. Indianness was a complex and multilayered identity which encompassed other such identities without cancelling them [Kaviraj 1995c: 119].

The Indian nation-state, as pointed out by Bhikhu Parekh is both an association of individuals and a community of communities, recognizing both individuals and communities as bearers of rights. The criminal law recognizes only individuals whereas the civil law recognizes most minority communities as distinct legal subjects (1992: 171).

Only a democratic, federal, 'secular' state could sustain and be sustained by such a rich or great 'composite' nation.

Actually, however, the end of the career of the British colonial state in India in 1947 came about through the formation of *two* sovereign nation-states, India and Pakistan.[12] Why the country was partitioned and how the colonial state [or, how the end of the colonial state] contributed to defining the state–religion relationship within, and interstate relations between, them are some of the most important questions to be addressed in any study of the post-colonial states of the Indian subcontinent. Such an exercise falls outside the purview of the present work. I will, however, briefly consider the implications of partition for the 'secular' and centralized nature of the Indian nation-state.

The demand of the Muslim League for a separate state for Indian Muslims was based on the claim that they constituted a distinct 'nation', and not just a 'minority'. Those, like the leaders of the Indian National Congress, who opposed that demand did so on the counter-assertion that the Muslims and the other religious communities together constituted the 'composite' or 'pluralist' Indian nation. Eventually, the creation of Pakistan as a separate nation-state was not done through any homologous translation of the religious identity of the Indian Muslims into a national-political identity. Actually, partition was the result of a modern, political-ideological use of religion, which Jinnah and the Muslim League pursued and which was agreed to, quite readily, by the colonial rulers (who had earlier introduced the system of separate electorates for minorities) and, more reluctantly, by the Indian National Congress. Pakistan was created not as an Islamic state of all the Indian Muslims, but as a separate state made up of the territory of only the Muslim-majority provinces and Muslim-majority districts of Punjab and Bengal.[13] After Partition, Pakistan had a Muslim population of about 60 million, while about 40 million Muslims continued to live in various parts of India. Hence the idea of India as a 'composite', 'pluralist', or 'secular' nation-state did not become less salient after Partition.

In fact, the Indian Constitution contains explicit provisions that guarantee to all persons equal freedom of conscience and religion and that prohibit the state from discrimination against any citizen on grounds of religion (Smith 1963; Pantham 1997; Bhargava 1998). In 1973, a full bench of the Supreme Court ruled that secularism is a constitutive feature of the basic structure of the Constitution. In 1976, the Constitution was amended to add the word 'secular' to the Preamble and to make the preservation of 'the rich heritage of our composite culture' a fundamental duty of all citizens.

Since the 1980s, however, there has been a shift in the legitimizing ideology of the Indian nation-state from secular nationalism to a religious-majoritarian nationalism. Associated with this, there has also been a shift in the state's developmental ideology from socialism or 'growth with justice' to the idea of the liberalizing state. These shifting trends are briefly sketched below.

It is pertinent to recall here that the partition of the country had a centralizing effect on state building in India (as well as in Pakistan). This is well brought out by Partha Chatterjee who writes that partition provided the state-builders in India with the opportunity to consolidate the powers of the state under a centralized political leadership which had a reasonably clear consensus on the objectives of state policy and which faced relatively little organized political opposition. The presence of a strong Muslim League opposition with potential support from large landed interests and the princes would have definitely made the task far more difficult [1998: 7].

Chatterjee goes on to maintain that Partition facilitated the formation of a new, relatively more cohesive ruling-class coalition, which was led by the industrial bourgeoisie and the urban middle-class intelligentsia and which also included, for reasons of electoral mobilization of the masses, locally dominant rural propertied classes.

A strong, centralized state, rather than a Gandhi-inspired decentralized system of government, was chosen by the state builders of independent India, led by Nehru and Sardar Vallabhbhai Patel, for coping with certain immediate problems of governance, such as Partition-related riots between Hindus and Muslims, the incursion of tribesmen from Pakistan's North West Frontier Province into Kashmir, a peasant uprising in Telengana, and problems connected with the integration of the hundreds of princely states, in one of which (Hyderabad) the Indian army had to intervene.[14] A strong, centralized state was also seen to be necessary for pursuing one of the major goals of the nationalist movement, namely-planned economic development, especially industrialization.[15] Hence it seemed sensible to the leadership of the independent nation-state to continue with the centralized structure of the colonial state apparatus. Not only the structure but also the Indian personnel of the civil bureaucracy, the police, and the army were retained and expanded in a big way. Also retained was the judicial system along with the system of civil and criminal laws. In fact, about two-thirds of the Constitution of independent India was drawn from the (colonial) Government of India Act of 1935.

The major institutional departures from the colonial state were: (i) the institutions of sovereign statehood (the indirectly elected President as Head of State) and parliamentary democracy based on universal adult franchise; (ii) a set of constitutionally guaranteed fundamental rights to all citizens, a set of principles to guide state policies; (iii) a centrally tilted federal system with a constitutional distribution of powers between the States; and the Union of India, and an independent judiciary vested with certain powers of judicial review.

The overriding objectives of the new independent nation-state were the preservation of its national sovereignty and unity and the fostering of economic development and social justice. These objectives had been the guiding motives of the Indian nationalist movement. Its opposition to the colonial state was based on the grounds that it was an alien institution serving to exploit and underdevelop India for the benefit of the people of the imperialist country. The independent Indian nation-state was imagined to be the historically necessary and legitimate means to end imperialist exploitation and to usher in a process of national economic development *with* social justice.[16]

Concerning the state's role in economic development, Partha Chatterjee writes: A developmental ideology ... was a constituent part of the self-definition of the postcolonial state. The state was connected to the people-nation not simply through the procedural forms of representative government, it also acquired its representativeness by directing a programme of economic development on behalf of the nation. The former connected, as in any liberal form of government, the legal-political sovereignty of the state with the sovereignty of the people. The latter connected the sovereign powers of the state directly with the economic well-being of the people (1997: 86–7).

Whatever strategy of economic development was to be chosen by the state, it had to be in conformity with the newly acquired national Independence and the newly established democratic framework. No doubt, state power was controlled by a ruling-class coalition of the indigenous bourgeoisie, the rich farmers, and the professional-bureaucratic class. The interests of these classes had to be accommodated in the developmental strategy.

The actual strategy of economic development chosen by the state under Nehru's leadership was a state-planned or 'mixed' path of capitalist industrialization. According to it, the state or 'public' sector undertook the responsibility for the development of heavy industries and social overheads, with the medium and consumer industries as well as the agriculture being left to the private sector. The state sector of heavy industries was intended to bring about a pattern of import-substituting industrialization leading to a self-reliant economy.

Obviously, this state-planned and state-dependent capitalist industrialization required both capital accumulation and democratic legitimation; this was a historically unprecedented pair of requirements. In the pioneer capitalist countries (England and France), the democratization of the franchise took place only after the primary or 'primitive' accumulation required for the launch of capitalist industrialization had been obtained through a variety of non-democratic, coercive methods of appropriating the means of production from the peasants. And when it did eventually take place, those capitalist countries were able to secure the democratic legitimation of the state not merely through the institutions of liberal-representative democracy but also through social-democratic or welfare-state measures.

In India, the capital required for setting up the state-controlled heavy industries was obtained through taxation, loans, and foreign assistance, especially from the USSR. The requirement of democratic legitimation of the state and its 'mixed' capitalist strategy of economic development was attended to in two ways. First, the planning of economic development was entrusted to a body of technical experts and bureaucrats who were not directly tied to the requirement of electoral legitimation. Second, the state leadership gave up the claims to socialism proprie dicta or to welfare-state democracy, which some of them had been propagating earlier. Instead, a vaguely defined ideology of a 'socialistic pattern of society' was used to secure electoral legitimation for the state, with the 'public-sector' heavy industries being presented as the necessary means to take India along an independent or self-reliant 'middle' path between free-enterprise capitalism and state-dominated communism.

Nehru genuinely believed that he was leading the construction of a post-colonial, secular-democratic nation-state and launching a 'socialistic', 'third way' of self-reliant development.[17] There can be no denying that the Nehruvian phase of the Indian nation-state does have a very impressive record of achievements in many areas. The preservation of the unity and sovereignty of the Indian nation-state and its democratic and secular character is indeed a most significant achievement. Thanks to it reconstruction under the Gandhi–Nehru leadership, the Indian nation-state has been able to produce 'the most noteworthy spell of democratic governance for about a fifth of mankind for close to a half century' (Kaviraj 1995a: 128). Another praiseworthy achievement of the Nehruvian state is its preservation of India's political sovereignty through an ingenious and impressive foreign policy of non-alignment. Also notable is a certain degree of self-reliance achieved in the heavy industries sector as well as a fairly good infrastructure for further industrialization. 'Almost alone among non-Communist states,' writes Sunil Khilnani, 'it [India's developmental state] managed to prolong until the 1980s a quite exceptional insulation from the vagaries of the global economy' (1992: 204). Other accomplishments include the

442 HANDBOOK OF INDIAN SOCIOLOGY

elimination, through land reforms, of some of the most glaring anomalies of feudal landlordism and the establishment of free primary schools and health centres.

Along with these praiseworthy achievements, there have also been some glaring distortions and decelerations in the process of economic change. The five-year plans, the series of periodically revised industrial policies, and the system of tax reliefs and state financial aid to the private sector, combined with a system of licensing and controls, resulted in the formation of 'a centralized powerful state, combining its monopoly of the means of repression with a substantial ownership of the means of production, propelling as well as regulating the economy' (Bardhan 1984: 36). The actual course of economic change, despite the aforementioned achievements, led to a retarded pattern of industrial development and an associated fiscal crisis of the state. This had to do with the growth-inhibiting 'rationalities' which were pursued by each of the three major partners of the dominant/ruling-class coalition.

Of them, industrial capitalists pursued their interest in securing inputs from the public sector at below-market prices, export subsidies, etc., while rich farmers managed to obtain subsidized fertilizers and seeds, higher procurement prices, etc. The latter also stalled land reforms[18] and derived benefits from the state in the name of the Green Revolution (Kaviraj 1995b: 120, 123; Frankel 1978). The third partner of the coalition, the political-bureaucratic class, reaped 'ruler's rents' and other benefits through state controls and regulations. The newly set-up public sector undertakings also served to increase their power and patronage enormously. By exercising its licensing, regulative, and controlling role in a selective manner, this class has been able to prevent any class-based challenge from industrialists and traders. In this way, as pointed out by Bardhan, the autonomy of the Indian state is reflected more often in its regulatory (and hence patronage-dispensing) than developmental role (Bardhan 1984: 39).

It must nevertheless be acknowledged that the Nehruvian state did set up a regime of curbs on monopoly houses and of some transfers 'not only to the landed rich, but also to broad sections of the peasantry, the working class, and to a minuscule extent, even to the rural poor' (Patnaik 1995: 204). Even though the monopoly houses did *actually* gain from the operations of the Nehruvian state, the latter did not officially identify the 'national interests' with the interests of any particular social class. Specifically, the relative autonomy of the Indian economy from metropolitan capital was maintained. This was obviously beneficial to Indian economy in general and to the domestic bourgeois and proto-bourgeois groups in particular in the 1950s and 1960s. However, in the 1970s, when the world economy went through a pronounced transnationalization of production, the opportunities it provided were not seized by India's state-bureaucratically managed strategy of import-substituting industrialization (Kaviraj 1995a: 123).

Re-imagining the Nation-State: Majoritarian Democracy and Economic Liberalization

Since the late 1980 and early 1990s, both domestic regulation of private capital and the protection of the Indian economy from penetration by foreign capital have been supplanted by a regime of economic liberalization, which provides for, among other things, domestic deregulation of private-sector enterprises, import liberalization, export facilitation, privatization or 'disinvestment' of profitable public-sector units, and the opening up of the domestic economy to foreign private capital.

Underlying this change is a shift in the legitimizing ideology of the state from one of a 'socialistic pattern of society' to that of a market-friendly, liberalized, open-door economy. Associated with this, there is also a shift in the ideology of the electoral legitimation of the state. The state has moved from the secular/pluralist notions of nationalism and democracy to religious-majoritarian redefinitions of these terms. These post-1980 shifts were the political responses of state leaders to a series of crises affecting the legitimacy, governability, and fiscal viability of the nation-state—crises in the making of which some of their own earlier actions and some of the actions of their predecessors had played a role.

In the latter part of the 1960s, there was an intense power struggle within the Congress party between Indira Gandhi and a powerful group of (regional) state-level bosses who had initially backed her rise to leadership. The former proved victorious through some clever left-leaning, populist moves, which undercut the power of the state-level bosses of the party and undermined the norms and procedures of inner-party democracy. In the name of a left-leaning populism, Gandhi's government nationalized the large banks and abolished the privy purses of the former rulers of the princely states. These steps were put to good use by Indira Gandhi in the 1971 parliamentary elections, when, bypassing the regular party organization and its regional 'vote-banks', she made direct appeals to the electorate in the name of a populist-socialist programme of *garibi hatao* (poverty removal). The huge electoral success of this strategy contributed to overcentralization of power in her hands. This had adverse effects on both the democratic functioning of the Congress party and on the federal framework of the relationship between centre and states. At the same time, the masses, who had given electoral support to garibi hatao, started popular movements (especially in Bihar and Gujarat) demanding radical reforms from the government. Those protest movements had the backing of the urban middle class as well as the rural 'vote banks', whom Indira Gandhi had defeated in the elections. Neither the ruling Congress party nor the governmental bureaucracy was prepared to translate populist radicalism into any programme for the structural transformation of society in favour of the poor. In the wake of the ensuing 'steep decline in the legitimacy of the government in an unusually short time', the government under Indira Gandhi imposed Emergency (1975–7) and exhorted people to suspend their political rights to enable the government to bring about socio-economic change (Kaviraj 1995c: 113). Freed from democratic pressures, the government undertook or supported, among other things, such measures as the eviction of beggars from the big cities and forced sterilization of the poor in some urban locales. Some ideas were also floated in favour of a Brazilian-type liberalization of the economy (Kaviraj 1995a and 1995b).

Indira Gandhi's party was voted out of power in the 1977 elections. The victorious but heterogeneous Janata coalition fell apart after just three years of running the government. In 1980, Indira Gandhi and her party were returned to power. This time, the challenge to the power of the central government headed by her came from regionalist movements in the Punjab, Telugu Desham, Assam, and, indeed, Kashmir. These were vertically, and *not* horizontally mobilized movements, which combined the numerical strength of the poor and the financial resources of the well-to-do. The conflicts between these vertically mobilized united regions/states and the centre led Indira Gandhi to make a shift in her own mobilizational strategy from a horizontal to a vertical approach, which included a religious-majoritarian approach. This was obviously a shift away from secularism. There was also a simultaneous shift away from the socialistic, 'poverty removal' role (or promises) of the state towards a new role, namely the liberalization of the economy. The government successfully negotiated 'for the largest loan ever granted by the IMF' and took steps to liberalize imports, 'automatically' license some twenty important industries, and decontrol the pricing of certain industrial products (Kohli 1989: 308).

In the final phase of Indira Gandhi's rule, then, there was a certain shift in the ideology of the Indian nation-state away from secular-socialist democracy and nationalism towards a religious-majoritarian conception of nationalism and democracy and a vaguely conceived idea of a liberalized economy. An insight into the nature of the association between economic liberalization and the religious-majoritarian redefinition of the democratic nation-state may be gained from the following observation by Atul Kohli:

Those who wanted to argue for business interests faced a dilemma: in a poor democracy like India, how do you mobilize the support of the majority, who are after all very poor? One solution to this puzzle was to cut the majority-minority pie at a different angle. If the poor were majority by the criterion of wealth, Hindus were the religious majority. Appeals to the majority religious community against minority communities, then, can be an alternative strategy for seeking electoral majorities by downplaying class issues [1989: 309].

The religious-majoritarian approach to electoral democracy and nation building is professed and practised in an unambiguous way by the Bharatiya Janata Party, which is leading the ruling coalition of parties at the present. That approach is a distortion of secular, pluralist democracy in the sense that it upholds one of the basic principles of the latter, namely that of majority rule, by dissociating it from what in fact is its twin, inseparable principle, namely that of the inviolability of the fundamental rights of the minority, be it a present minority or some future minority—of conscience, opinion, belief, religion, or even disbelief in any religion.[19]

The policy of economic liberalization has also been continued and progressively stepped up under all the succeeding governments since the late 1980s. The proximate reason for the change of track by the post-colonial, developmental nation-state on to a path of economic liberalization, entailing a closer integration into the global market economy, was the escalation of the government's fiscal deficit, which culminated in a very severe balance-of-payments crisis in 1991. In that year, India did not have enough foreign-exchange reserves to pay for its imports for even two weeks. The loans which the Indian government successfully negotiated with the International Monetary Fund and the World Bank to meet the crisis were tied to the conditionalities requiring India to follow a programme of short-term macro-economic stabilization measures and long-term 'structural adjustment and reform', whereby the state is rolled back from the arena of production and regulation and the economy is left to be shaped by private initiative and the private sector rather than by state intervention or the public sector. This programme includes, besides the devaluation of the rupee, steps to curb inflation and to reduce the government's fiscal deficit (by reducing its subsidies and capital expenditures and by disinvestment of the shares of profitable public-sector units) and liberalize or free private capital from the regime of regulations, quotas, licences, controls, import-restrictions, etc. Another important feature of the new policy is the opening up of the Indian economy to foreign private capital, be it productive capital or finance capital.

An assessment of the pros and cons of this liberalizing 'structural adjustment programme', which the Indian nation-state has been pursuing since its fiscal and foreign-debt crisis of the late 1980s and early 1990s, is beyond the scope of the present chapter.[20] It is, however, pertinent to mention some of the ways in which these liberalizing reforms may be seen to be intimating a fundamental change in the nature and role of the nation-state. First, the state is withdrawing from long-term developmental activity and is now yielding space to the private sector. For instance, the capital expenditure of the central government showed a steady decline from 5.9 per cent of the GDP in 1990–1 to 3.6 per cent in 1994–5. Second, the state is changing from a market-controlling to a market-friendly institution.[21] Liberalization, to state the obvious, frees market forces from the erstwhile regime of state controls. Finally and most importantly, the nation-state is losing, to a considerable extent, the 'post-colonial' relative autonomy which it has hitherto had vis-à-vis metropolitan capital. For instance, as acknowledged by the World Bank in its 1995 Economic Memorandum on India, the '[c]onditions on portfolio investment by foreign institutional investors ... are much more liberal in India than in Korea ... Taiwan and China' (Kurien 1996: 90).[22] Yet it needs to be asserted that a not-too-insignificant measure of effective political autonomy is still available to the nation-state of India as it is to developing countries—a measure of autonomy that, alas, does not find appropriate reflection in the current liberalizing regime of structural adjustments and reforms!

Acknowledgements

The research for this paper was undertaken while I was a C.R. Parekh Visiting Fellow in the Department of Politics, University of Hull. The helpful discussions I have had with Bhikhu Parekh are gratefully acknowledged.

ENDNOTES

1. The modern 'nation-state' is the product of a process of 'state building', which, according to Charles Tilly (1975: 27), entails 'territorial consolidation, centralization, differentiation of instruments of government from other sorts of organization, and monopolization (plus concentration) of the means of coercion'. In Europe, this process of state building passed through three stages of political unification and consolidation: (i) the formation of composite states under the leadership of a single dynasty, without any administrative unification; (ii) the institutionalization of absolute sovereign monarchies or military-fiscal states; and (iii) the transformation of the former into absolute, popular, 'national' sovereignty or, in other words, the modern representative republic (cf. Hont 1994: 179). As Hont points out,

   The difference between a modern 'absolutist' state, striving to unite the country and homogenize its institutions, and a 'nation-state' is thus no more than a higher stage of the very same 'state-building' process, a 'nation-state' is merely an 'absolutist' state whose subjects or citizens identify themselves with it, and regard it as a collective expression of themselves as a 'nation'. The pairing of the notions of 'nation' and 'state' makes sense when in people's imagination their nationality and their territorial political unit, which has emerged from a history of 'conquest and coalescence', becomes [sic.] fused [1994: 182].

   On the meaning of the modern concept of the 'state', see Skinner (1989) and Parekh (1996). A stimulating discussion of 'the changing idea and/or mythology of the Indian state' may be found in Nandy (1989, 1992).
2. An impetus for political consolidation was provided by the invasion of north India by Alexander of Macedonia in 327–25 BC.
3. Interestingly, the founders of Jainism and Buddhism came from the Kshatriya castes of tribal republics.
4. According to A.L. Basham (1988 [1958]: 116), some of the Buddhist texts encouraged 'a solid bourgeois morality'. Similarly, Jainism, with its stress on frugality, facilitated commercial activity. Its emphasis on non-violence made it favour trade and urban life over agriculture which involved the killing of insects and pests (Thapar [1966] 1977: 65).
5. Towards the close of his reign, Chandragupta Maurya is believed to have patronized Jainism and eventually become a Jain monk, while the most illustrious of Mauryan emperors, Ashoka, embraced and promoted Buddhism after his victory in the Kalinga war.
6. Stein's 'segmentary state' has some similarity with Stanley Tambiah's 'galactic polity' (1976), in which, to use S.H. Rudolph's words, the leading king, the *rajadhiraj*, and the lesser rulers are 'unified by a field of force characterized by both repulsion and attraction' (1987: 739).

7. Inden (1990: 238, n. 22) too feels that Tambiah's 'galactic polity' (1976) comes close to his own conception of the 'imperial formation'.

8. It is interesting to note that sultanism attracted Max Weber's attention, as he saw in it a stage fairly close to the rationalized bureaucracy of the modern state. See Weber (1978: vol. I, 231–2).

9. In this connection, see the analysis of the so-called Ilbert Bill Affair in Partha Chatterjee (1993: 20–1).

10. In this context too Partha Chatterjee (1993: 22–4) makes a relevant examination of what has come to be known as the Nil Durpan Affair.

11. For a very insightful study of colonial rule as 'dominance without hegemony', see Guha (1997). See also Kaviraj (1994).

12. Pakistan went through a subsequent split in 1971, when Bangladesh seceded and became a new sovereign state. These two states, together with the Indian state, have been interpreted by L.I. Rudolph and S.H. Rudolph as representing 'two latter-day representatives of the regional kingdom and one of the subcontinental imperial state' (1987: 66).

13. As invented by Chaudhri Rahmat Ali, a Cambridge University student, in 1933, the name 'PAKISTAN' stands for Punjab ('P'), the Afghan Province ('A'), Kashmir ('K'), Sind ('S'), and Baluchistan ('tan').

14. The army also intervened to liberate Goa from Portuguese control in 1960.

15. L.I. Rudolph and S.H. Rudolph refer to this as 'high stateness' and associate it with India's 'imperial legacies and the contemporary requirements of an interventionist, managerial state pursuing welfare and socialist objectives' (1987: 73).

16. Articles 38 and 39 of the Indian Constitution direct the state 'to promote the welfare of the people by securing and protecting as effectively as it may a social order in which justice—social, economic, and political—shall inform all the institutions of the national life' and to ensure that 'the operation of the economic system does not result in the concentration of wealth to the common detriment'.

17. Partha Chatterjee and Sudipta Kaviraj have shown that the Nehruvian strategy of economic development was actually a strategy of 'passive' capitalist revolution, in which the bourgeoisie, because of its underdevelopment by imperialism, is required to make compromises with the old or pre-capitalist dominant classes (Chatterjee 1997; Kaviraj 1988. See also Pantham 1980, 1995: Ch. 3).

18. The reasons for, and consequences of, the absence of thoroughgoing land reforms in India's strategy of capitalist development are analysed in Patnaik (1998: 39–48).

19. As pointed out by Sudipta Kaviraj, the main problem with the religious-majoritarian conception of democracy is that by demanding 'unequal rights of permanent dominance on grounds of a purported majority', it imposes 'permanent disabilities on other groups' (1995c: 118).

20. Several aspects of the policy of economic liberalization in India are critically examined in Byres (1997); Bhaduri and Nayyar (1996); and Nayar (1992); Sridharan (1993); Kohli (1989); Kurien (1996); and Patnaik (1995 and 1996).

21. It must indeed be admitted that economic liberalization makes a belated recognition of the market as a positive institution of the economy. The market, however, cannot be a substitute for the state just as the state cannot be a substitute for the market. Hence the role of the state under economic liberalization has to be examined not so much in terms of the extent of state intervention as in terms of the nature and purpose of such intervention. In fact, the liberalizing programme of 'structural adjustment and reform' represents a transformed, rather than a reduced, form of state intervention. That transformation tends to go in the direction of a more centralized and authoritarian state. This, to a great extent, has to do with the 'conditionalities' of the international financiers and the so-called 'discipline' of the 'market forces'. see Ghosh (1997); Patnaik (1995 and 1996); and Bhaduri and Nayyar (1996).

22. Kurien (1996: 89) shows that the international capital that has come to India since liberalization has been more of finance capital than productive capital. He maintains that under liberalization, India has opened up its economy to foreign capital 'way beyond what was necessary and prudent'.

REFERENCES

Alam, M. 1998. 'Aspects of Agrarian Uprisings in North India in the Early Eighteenth Century' in M. Alam and S. Subrahmanyam, eds, *The Mughal State. 1526–1750*. Delhi: Oxford University Press.

Alam, M. and S. Subrahmanyam, eds. 1998. *The Mughal State, 1526–1750*. Delhi: Oxford University Press.

Alavi, H. 1973. 'The State in Postcolonial Societies: Pakistan and Bangladesh'. In K. Gough and H.P. Sharma, eds, *Imperialism and Revolution in South Asia*. 145–73. London: Monthly Review Press.

Ali, M.A. 1995. 'Towards an Interpretation of the Mughal Empire'. In H. Kulke. ed. *The State in India*, 1000–1700, 267–77. Delhi: Oxford University Press.

Austin, G. 1996. *The Indian Constitution: Cornerstone of a Nation*. Oxford: Clarendon Press.

Bayly, C. 1990. *Indian Society and the Making of the British Empire*. Cambridge: Cambridge University Press.

Bardhan, P. 1984. *Political Economy of Development in India*. Delhi: Oxford University Press.

———. 1997. 'The State against Society: The Great Divide in Indian Social Science Discourse'. In S. Bose and A. Jalal, eds, *Nationalism, Democracy and Development: State and Politics in India*, 184–95. Delhi: Oxford University Press.

Basham, A.L. [1958] 1988. 'Jainism and Buddhism'. In Wm. T.de Bary et al., comps, *Sources of Indian Tradition*. Reprint. Delhi: Motilal Banarsidass.

Bhadra, G. 1998. 'Two Frontier Uprisings in Mughal India'. In M. Alam and Subrahmanyam, eds, *The Mughal State. 1526–1750*. Delhi: Oxford University Press.

Bhaduri, A. and D. Nayyar. 1996. *The Intelligent Person's Guide to Liberalization*. New Delhi: Penguin Books.

Bhargava R. ed. 1998. *Secularism and Its Critics*. Delhi: Oxford University Press.

Blake, S.P. 1995. 'The Patrimonial-Bureaucratic Empire of the Mughals'. In H. Kulke, ed., The State in India 1000–1700. Delhi: Oxford University Press.

Bose, S., and A. Jalal, eds. 1997. *Nationalism, Democracy and Development: State and Politics in India*. Delhi: Oxford University Press.

———. 1998. *Modern South Asia: History, Culture, Political Economy*. Delhi: Oxford University Press.

Bose, Sumantra. 1997. '"Hindu Nationalism" and the Crisis of the Indian State'. In S. Bose and A. Jalal, eds, *Nationalism, Democracy and Development: State and Politics in India*. 104–64. Delhi: Oxford University Press.

Byres, T.J. 1988. 'A Chicago View of the Indian State'. *Journal of Commonwealth and Comparative Politics*. November: 246–69.

———. ed. 1997. *The State, Development Planning and Liberalization in India*. Delhi: Oxford University Press.

Chandra, B. 1980. 'Colonialism, Stages of Colonialism and the Colonial State'. *Journal of Contemporary Asia*. 10(3):272–85.

Chatterjee, P. 1986. *Nationalist Thought and the Colonial World*. Delhi: Oxford University Press.

———. 1993. *The Nation and Its Fragments: Colonial and Postcolonial Histories*. Delhi: Oxford University Press.

———. 1997. 'Development Planning and the Indian State'. In P. Chatterjee, ed., *State and Politics in India*. 271–97. Delhi: Oxford University Press.

———. ed. 1998. *The Wages of Freedom: Fifty Years of the Indian Nation-State*. Delhi: Oxford University Press.

Cohn, B.S. 1983. 'Representing Authority in Victorian India'. In E. Hobsbawm and T. Ranger., eds, *The Invention of Tradition*, 165–209. Cambridge: Cambridge University Press.

Dandekar, R.N. [1958] 1988. '*Artha*, the Second End of Man'. In Wm.T.de Bary et al., comps, *Sources of Indian Tradition*, 236–57. Reprint. Delhi: Motilal Banarsidass.

Dirks, N. 1987. *The Hollow Crown: Ethnohistory of an Indian Kingdom*. Cambridge: Cambridge University Press.

Doornbos, M. and S. Kaviraj. eds. 1997. *Dynamics of State Formation: India and Europe Compared.* New Delhi: Sage Publications.

Dumont, L. 1970. *Religion, Politics and History in India.* Paris: Mouton Publishers.

Dunn, J. ed. 1992. *Democracy, the Unfinished Journey.* Delhi: Oxford University Press.

_____, ed. 1995. *Contemporary Crisis of the Nation-State.* Oxford: Basil Blackwell.

Eisenstadt, S.N. and H. Hartman, eds. 1997. 'Historical Experience, Cultural Traditions, State Formation and Political Dynamics in India and Europe'. In M. Doornbos and S. Kaviraj, eds, *Dynamics of State Formation: India and Europe Compared.* 35–53. New Delhi: Sage Publications.

Embree, A.T. 1977. 'Frontiers into Boundaries: From the Traditional to the Modern State'. In R.G. Fox, ed., *Realm and Region in Traditional India,* 255–80. New Delhi: Vikas.

Foucault, M. 1979. *Discipline and Punish: The Birth of the Prison.* Harmondsworth: Penguin.

Frankel, F.R. 1978. *India's Political Economy 1947–1977.* Princeton: Princeton University Press.

_____. 1989. 'Introduction'. In F.R. Frankel and M.S.A. Rao, eds, *Democracy and State Power in Modern India,* vol. I. Delhi: Oxford University Press.

_____. 1990. 'Conclusion: Decline of a Social Order'. F.R. Frankel and M.S.A. Rao, eds, *Democracy and State Power in Modern India.* 482–517. Delhi: Oxford University Press.

Ghosh, J. 1997. 'Development Strategy in India: A Political Economy Perspective'. In S. Bose and A. Jalal, eds, *Nationalism, Democracy and Development*; State and Politics in India. 165–83. Delhi: Oxford University Press.

Ghoshal. 1959. UN. *A History of Indian Political Ideas.* Bombay: Oxford University Press.

Guha, R. 1997. *Dominance without Hegemony: History and Power in Colonial India.* Cambridge, Mass: Harvard University Press.

Hont, I. 1994. 'The Permanent Crisis of a Divided Mankind: "Contemporary Crisis of the Nation-State" in Historical Perspective'. *Political Studies.* 42:166–231.

Inden, R. 1990. *Imagining India.* Oxford: Basil Blackwell.

Kaviraj, S. 1988. 'A Critique of the Passive Revolution'. *Economic and Political Weekly.* November (Special Number):2429–44.

_____. 1991. 'On State, Society and Discourse in India'. In J. Manor, ed., *Rethinking Third World Politics.* 72–99. London: Longman.

_____. 1994. 'On the Construction of Colonial Power: Structure, Discourse, Hegemony'. In S. Engels and S. Marks, eds, *Contesting Colonial Hegemony: State and Society in Africa and India.* 19–54. London: British Academic Press.

_____. 1995a. 'Crisis of the Nation-State in India'. In J. Dunn, ed., 115–129. *Contemporary Crisis of the Nation-State.* Oxford: Basil Blakwell.

_____. 1995b. 'Dilemmas of Democratic Development in India'. In A. Leftwich, ed., *Democracy and Development,* 114–138. Cambridge: Polity Press.

_____. 1995c. 'Democracy and Development in India'. In A.K. Bagchi, ed., *Democracy and Development.* 92–130. Delhi: Macmillan.

_____. 1997. 'The Modern State in India'. In M. Doornbos and S. Kaviraj, eds, *Dynamics of State Formation: India and Europe Compared.* New Delhi: Sage Publications.

Khilnani, S. 1992. 'India's Democratic Career'. In J. Dunn, ed., *Democracy, the Unfinished Journey.* Delhi: Oxford University Press.

_____. 1997. *The Idea of India.* London: Hamish Hamilton.

Kohli, A. ed. 1988. *India's Democracy: An Analysis of Changing State-Society Relations.* Princeton: Princeton University Press.

_____. 1989. 'Politics of Economic Liberalization in India'. *World Development.* 17(3):305–28.

_____. 1990. *Democracy and Discontent: India's Growing Crisis of Governability.* Cambridge: Cambridge University Press.

Kosambi, D.D. 1970. *The Culture and Civilization of Ancient India in Historical Outline.* Delhi: Vikas.

_____. 1975. *An Introduction to the Study of Indian History.* Bombay: Popular Prakashan.

Kothari, R. 1988. *The State against Democracy: In Search of Humane Governance*. New Delhi: Ajanta Publications.

———. 1995a. 'Globalisation and Revival of Tradition: Dual Attack on Model of Democratic Nation-Building'. *Economic and Political Weekly*. 25 March.

———. 1995b. 'Under Globalisation: Will Nation-State Hold?' *Economic and Political Weekly*. 1 July.

Kulke, H., ed. 1995. *The State in India, 1000–1700*. Delhi: Oxford University Press.

Kulke, H. and D. Rothermund. [1986] 1998. *A History of India*. London: Routledge.

Kumar R. 1997. 'State Formation in India: Retrospect and Prospect'. In M. Doornbos and S. Kaviraj, eds, *Dynamics of State Formation: India and Europe Compared*. New Delhi: Sage Publications.

Kurien, C.T. 1996. 'Economic Reforms–7: What Next?' *Frontline*. 23 February: 88–91. This seven-part series of articles have appeared in book-form, *Economic Reforms and the People*. Delhi: Madhyam Books.

Larson, G.J. 1997. *India's Agony over Religion*. Delhi: Oxford University Press.

Mehta, V.R. 1992. *Foundations of Indian Political Thought*. Delhi: Manohar Publishers.

Mitra, S. 1990. 'Between Transaction and Transcendence: The State and the Institutionalization of Power in India'. In S. Mitra, ed., *The Postcolonial State in Asia*. 73–99. Hermel Hempstead: Wheatsheaf.

———. 1991. 'Desecularising the State: Religion and Politics in India after Independence'. *Comparative Studies in Society and History*. 755–77.

Moore, B. 1966. *Social Origins of Dictatorship and Democracy*. Boston: Beacon Press.

Nandy A. 1989. 'The Political Culture of the Indian State'. *Daedalus*. 118:1–26.

———. 1992. 'State'. In W. Sachs, ed., *The Development Dictionary*, 264–74. London: Zed Books.

Nayar, B.R. 1989. *India's Mixed Economy*. Bombay: Popular Prakashan. 264–74.

———. 1992. 'The Politics of Economic Restructuring in India: The Paradox of State Strength and Policy Weakness'. *Journal of Commonwealth and Comparative Politics*. 30(2):145–71.

Nehru, J. 1949. 'A Tryst with Destiny' (speech in the Constituent Assembly of India at the midnight of 14–15 August 1947). In J.L. Nehru. *Independence and After*, New Delhi: Government of India, Publications Division.

Pantham, T. 1980. 'Elites, Classes and The Distortions of Economic Transition in India'. In Sachchidananda and A.K. Lal, eds, *Elite and Development*. 71–96. New Delhi: Concept Publishing House.

———. 1995. *Political Theories and Social Reconstruction: A Critical Survey of the Literature on India*. New Delhi: Sage Publications.

———. 1997. 'Indian Secularism and its Critics'. *Review of Politics*. 59(3):523–40.

Parekh, B.C. 1992. 'The Cultural Particularity of Liberal Democracy'. *Political Studies*. (Special Issue). 40:160–75.

———. 1995. 'Jawaharlal Nehru and the Crisis of Modernization'. In U. Baxi and B.C. Parekh, eds, *Crisis and Change in Contemporary India*. 21–56. New Delhi: Sage Publications.

———. 1996. 'The Nature of the Modern State'. In D.L. Sheth and A. Nandy, eds, *The Multiverse of Democracy*. 27–49. New Delhi: Sage Publications.

Patnaik, P. 1995. 'Nation-State in the Era of Globalization'. *Economic and Political Weekly*. 19 August: 2049–54.

———. 1996. 'A Note on the Political Economy of the Retreat of the State'. In P. Patnaik, *Whatever Happened to Imperialism and Other Essays*. 194–210. New Delhi: Tulika.

———. 1998. 'Political Strategies of Economic Development'. In P. Chatterjee, ed., *The Wages of Freedom: Fifty Years of the Indian Nation-State*. 37–60. Delhi: Oxford University Press.

Perlin, F. 1985. 'State Formation Reconsidered'. *Modern Asian Studies*. 19(3):415–80.

Prasad, B. 1974. *Theory of Government in Ancient India*. Allahabad: Central Book Depot.

Richards, J.F. 1998. 'The Formation of Imperial Authority under Akbar and Jahangir'. In M. Alam and S. Subrahmanyam, eds, *The Mughal State. 1526–1750*. Delhi: Oxford University Press.

Rudolph, L.I. and S.H. Rudolph. 1985. 'The Subcontinental Empire and the Regional Kingdom in

Indian State Formation'. In P. Wallace, ed., *Region and Nation in India*. 40–59. New Delhi: Oxford and IBH.

———. 1987. *In Pursuit of Lakshmi: The Political Economy of the Indian State*. 731–46. Hyderabad: Orient Longman.

Rudolph, S.H. 1987. 'Presidential Address: State Formation in Asia—Prolegomenon to a Comparative Study'. *Journal of Asian Studies*. 46(4).

Sathyamurthy, T.V. 1996. 'State and Society in a Changing Political Perspective'. In T.V. Sathyamurthy, ed., *Social Change and Political Discourse in India,* vol. 4. *Class Formation and Political Transformation in Post-Colonial India*. 437–75. Delhi: Oxford University Press.

Sen, A. 1982. *The State, Industrialization, and Class Formations in India*. London: Routledge and Kegan Paul.

Skinner, Q. 1989. 'The State'. In T. Ball et al. eds, *Political Innovation and Conceptual Change*. 90–131. Cambridge: Cambridge University Press.

Smith, A. 1991. 'The Nation: Invented, Imagined, Reconstructed?' *Millennium: Journal of International Studies*. 20(2):353–68.

Smith, D.E. 1963. *India as a Secular State*. New Delhi: Oxford University Press.

Sridharan, E. 1993. 'Economic Liberalization and India's Political Economy: Towards a Paradigm Synthesis'. *Journal of Commonwealth and Comparative Politics*. 31(3):1–29.

Stein, B. 1980. *Peasant State and Society in Medieval South India*. Delhi: Oxford University Press.

———. 1985: 'State Formation and Economy Reconsidered'. *Modern Asian Studies*. 19(3):387–413.

Stokes, E. 1959. *The English Utilitarians and India*. Delhi: Oxford University Press.

Sudarshan, R. 1995. 'The Political Consequences of Constitutional Discourse'. In T.V. Sathyamurthy, ed., *Social Change and Political Discourse in India*, vol. I: *State and Nation in the Context of Social Change*. Delhi: Oxford University Press.

Tambiah, S.J. 1976. *World Conqueror and World Renouncer: A Study of Buddhism and Polity in Thailand against a Historical Background*. Cambridge: Cambridge University Press.

Thapar, R. [1966] 1977. *A History of India*. vol. 1. Reprint. Harmondsworth: Penguin Books.

———. 1980. 'State Formation in Early India'. *International Social Science Journal*. 4:655–60.

———. 1984. *From Lineage to State: Social Formations in the Mid-First Millennium* BC *in the Ganga Valley*. Delhi: Oxford University Press.

Thompson, E. and G.T. Garrat. [1934] 1962. *Rise and Fulfilment of British Rule in India, 1600–1935*. Reprint. Allahabad: Central Book Depot.

Tilly, C. 1975. 'Reflections on the History of European State-Making'. In C. Tilly, ed., *The Formation of National States in Western Europe*. Princeton: Princeton University Press.

Wallerstein, I. 1986. 'Incorporation of the Indian Subcontinent into Capitalist World Economy'. *Economic and Political Weekly*. 21(4).

Washbrook, D. 1981. 'Law, State and Agrarian Society in Colonial India'. *Modern Asian Studies.* 15:649–721.

———. 1990. 'South Asia, the World System and World Capitalism'. *Journal of Asian Studies*. 49(3):479–508.

Weber, M. 1978. *Economy and Society*. Ed G. Roth and C. Wittich, vol. I. Los Angeles: University of California Press.

Yadav, Y. 1990. 'Theories of the Indian State'. *Seminar*. 367. (March): 1–5.

The Nature of Indian Democracy

SUDIPTA KAVIRAJ

THE PROBLEM OF INDIAN DEMOCRACY

It is often assumed, without enough clarification, that the continued success of democracy in India is in some senses a surprise, that the continuance of democracy itself is some kind of a problem to be explained. There are several possible grounds for such scepticism. The most common view sees the obstacle to democracy as economic. Without some economic development, it is argued, political democracy is not possible. The reason for this is that sharing in a general atmosphere of economic prosperity reduces the desperation and sharpness of social conflicts. The second argument is based on social structure or, alternatively, culture. The most familiar form that this argument takes is as follows. Indian society has traditionally been based on caste and other strong community identities. Caste is explicitly based on principles of hierarchy, and goes against political equality. Attachment to traditional communities or sects is resistant to the principles of abstract equal citizenship under a common state. The successful operation of democracy requires that individual electors should vote on the basis of their considered individual judgement, and on the basis of their perception of their self-interest. Caste and community attachments, it is argued, would defeat a succesful operation of democracy. The historical record of Indian democracy, however, shows that such objections are indecisive. Despite continued poverty, and the undeniable influence of caste and communities on political choice, the democratic system in India has functioned with vitality.[1] However, the social and cultural conditions in which democratic institutions have functioned have made Indian democracy operate in ways which are quite locally specific.

The Nature of Indian Democracy

John Stuart Mill began his treatise on representative government by noting two different ways of thinking about governments. The first theory treated governmental institutions like machinery that is deliberately conceived and constructed by human contrivance, without much regard for the form or kind of society in which this machinery is supposed to work. The second, Mill thought, regarded governmental forms as institutions which grow out of the fundamental tendencies of the social structure. Interestingly, in the literature on Indian democracy we can find traces of these two unreconstructed views of either extreme constructivism or sociological determinism. Broadly, the early academic works on Indian democracy accepted an uncritical legal constructivism, and spent its intellectual resources in perfecting legal institutions when faced with political challenges.[2] Since the 1970s, the academic study of Indian democracy has tended to move away from institutional formalism towards political sociology. Now the central questions about the 'nature' of Indian democracy involve an analysis of what has happened to the recognizable forms of institutional democracy adopted by the Indian state after Independence, what the structure of society has done to these state forms, and what the state form, in its turn, has done to the structures of social life. Democracy can be viewed in two rather different ways and is said to contain two contradictory types of possibilities. The idea of democratic government was evidently regarded as historically transformative by the political elite which established the state after Independence. It believed that operating under the principles of democratic government ordinary people would learn new rules of political and social equality. But historical comparisons of democratic experience show that democratic government also has a tendency to bring social cleavages into overt, public expression through the openness of its political process. And evidently, in certain circumstances there can be a tension between these two sides of the historical consequences of democratic government.

The Origins of Indian Democracy

Although the political elite after Independence behaved as if the choice of democracy as a form of government was a foregone conclusion, that belief itself is an interesting fact to explain. Neither traditional Indian social rules, nor the rules according to which British authorities governed India for about two hundred years, could be called democratic: that is based on a recognition of political or social equality.[3] Why did the successful national movement think of democracy as the only appropriate form of government? The historical sources of Indian democratic thought were several, and it was also a history of considerable complexity. First, the intellectual following of democratic ideas was historically uneven. Indian writers and political groups were quick to discern the internal differentiations and complexities of the democratic idea in the West. They noticed the difference particularly between a liberal, individualist, legalistic strand which embraced both individualism and emphasis on legal procedures and a radical, populist strand intolerant of procedural obstacles to social justice. Internal discussions on democracy would usually form a conversation between three different positions, to simplify the considerable variations of emphasis and inflexion. Some writers opposed the idea of any implantation of institutions from the West on the grounds that these were inappropriate for Indian culture. But, increasingly, two other strands were to emerge to make powerful arguments for adoption of western practices. One was a strand of liberal, individualistic thought which used rationalistic arguments to undermine justifications of the caste system and reject religious superstitions.[4] And a second, community-oriented, political strand interpreted democracy in a more radical, and at the same time less individualistic, fashion. The weight of political opinion and actual political support fluctuated between these three types of thinking. After the early influence of liberal and individualistic ideas, in the second half of the nineteenth century in Bengal one sees a clear emergence of a critique of western forms of ideology and a distinct preference for what was regarded, sometime quite erroneously, as more indigenist social forms and principles.[5] However, there was a second kind of complexity always accompanying this explicit debate. Even the strands which supported western ideological trends had to introduce startling translations and improvisations, especially when [or, 'mainly because'] they wrote in the vernacular—translations which would be difficult to characterize in terms of standard western categories.[6]

Administrative and cultural practices of colonialism contributed to the growth of democratic ideas in some ways. Colonial rule had immense impact on the systems of property holding in Indian society; much of colonial law insisted on private property. The meticulous institutionalization of private property in various spheres, like landholdings, introduced crucial ideas about individual ownership and assisted individuation with regard to economic practices in elite Indian culture. Perhaps more significantly, the colonial government in the nineteenth century introduced ideas of procedural as opposed to arbitrary government. Conceptions of fair procedure and just government existed in traditional society, but these were different from the modern ideas about impersonality of power and associated notions of legal impartiality. This familiarized Indians with ideas of a rule of law, though it was common practice to suspend it in case of European offenders. But the fact that some of the most powerful individuals associated with early colonialism, individuals who often acted like medieval despots, when away from the restrictions of the British Parliament, were formally tried and indicted, reinforced the idea that modern governance was a rule of law. Under the new dispensation, political activity did not consist in turning the arbitrary will of the rulers in one's favour, but to act in a public sphere to pressurize them into enacting more equitable laws. The introduction of western education was driven by a complex combination of motivations on the part of colonial rulers, and showed the extreme diversity of opinion among them. In part, it was driven by the condescending altruism of giving to Indians the knowledge on which modern civilization was based; in part, it was meant to produce a class of reliable bureaucratic under-labourers. But the most strikingly paradoxical effects of modern education were political. The more British education sought to convince Indians about the wonderful narrative of western enlightenment and freedom, the more it undermined the ideological grounds of colonial rule.[7] Familiarity with the history and the institutions of the West enabled Indians to desire more perfect forms of such institutions and helped them criticize British authority on the basis of principles which the British could not morally reject. But, obviously, the processes by which Indians could acquire a strong preference for democratic government in the strict sense were severely restricted in colonial India. Such preferences were found mainly in elite groups which have access to English education or among those who have serious contacts with the institutions of colonial legality; it was only in those groups that could either understand, value, feel attracted towards, or reflect critically on the western democratic ideals.

Democratic ideas emerged more powerfully and circulated more widely after the rise of the nationalist movement, particularly after it assumed mass character with the coming of Gandhi in the 1920s. Gandhi's tactics bridged the crucial gap between two broad strands of anti-colonial politics that had existed before him but never managed to converge. Middle class dissatisfaction with British rule assumed the form of constitutionalist-liberal agitation against the colonial government, which constantly emphasized the procedural and legalistic elements of modern politics and tried to embarrass the British authorities by quoting their own principles, thereby proving the 'un-British' character of governance in India. The colonial administrative discourse operated inside the British political ideology of the times, which generally advocated democracy as the best form of government, but argued that Indians were unprepared for self-government on cultural grounds. Liberal-constitutional agitation, however, sought to prove the Indian middle class was capable of governing. But since this agitation was confined primarily to the new colonial middle classes, it had little support outside the colonial cities. By contrast, peasant uprisings represented the most radical form of protest against colonial rule, but these were usually restricted to particular regions, and often showed utter incomprehension of the system of legal rules that the colonial administration had put in place (see Guha 1981).

Understandably, peasant militants showed less regard for the intricacies of colonial legality as compared to the lawyers who mostly formed the leadership of the Indian National Congress in its early stages.

As long as the two strands of opposition to colonialism remained separate, British authorities in India could retain their power without much difficulty. The constitutionalist agitation of the middle classes rarely broke out of the strict limits of political mendicancy, and the anger of the peasantry, though much more troublesome and destructive, could always be surrounded and eventually crushed by the use of military power. Gandhi's emergence as the prime leader of Indian nationalism brought these two social forces into a powerful combination for the first time, immediately posing far more difficult problems for British colonial power.

The legacy of the Congress for Indian constitutional democracy was far more direct and positive, although not entirely free of paradoxes. Nehru claimed in the *Discovery of India* that Congress was the most democratic organization he knew, defending it against the British colonial charge that it was an organization dominated by a small elite and manipulated by its major leaders. But the practice of political procedure inside the Congress is interesting because it shows some trends which would persist in post-Independence Indian politics. The formal organizational structure of the Congress was certainly democratic, with members choosing Pradesh Congress Committees which sent their delegates through a democratic representative process to the annual sessions of the AICC, the major forum for the declaration of policies, if not their actual formulation. The Congress maintained an astonishing adherence to formal rules of procedure. Even large-scale agitations, which were to convulse India for long periods, were ceremonially launched at Congress sessions by the procedurally fastidious passing of resolutions, like the famous Quit India resolution of August 1942.

Political practice in the Congress thus showed a shrewd awareness that democracy required a balance between the participatory and procedural sides of the democratic idea: unlike many other popular movements, the Congress never claimed that large mobilizations of people were their own justifications.[8] Under the conditions of stress and enthusiasm in which successful national movements function, this was an amazing characteristic and not a mean achievement. However, Gandhi was always particular about his rather idiosyncratic notion of discipline, which he contrasted with the anarchy and disorder associated in his mind with violence. His construal of what discipline meant in particular circumstances could be extremely odd. But his ability to impose a certain kind of political discipline and orderliness on the potentially anarchic forces of Indian nationalism was quite evident from the success with which he could bring to instant suspension huge mass movements in the middle of their disorderly career. The manner in which the civil disobedience movements of the 1920s and 1930s were brought to a sudden but orderly end were miracles of control, though it is quite natural that his critics interpreted these acts very differently.

Communists and socialists like Nehru evidently associated more value with the participatory, mobilizational, activist side of the idea of democratic movements, and deplored Gandhi's sudden withdrawals as arbitrary and authoritarian, in the sense that what appeared the right course of action to Gandhi was allowed to trump what the thousands of activists in the movement actually thought. So while these were enormous acts of will, for Gandhi mythicized his political role, it implied a totally illegitimate assumption of their capacity of decision by him, and evidently had a strongly negative impact on democratic politics. They correctly detected the small seed of authoritarianism at the heart of even the most benign form of charismatic politics. At other times, when the Congress was not engaged in leading mass movements but occupied in more mundane politics of the everyday, Gandhi's attitude towards procedural forms could be deeply puzzling. When Subhas Chandra Bose defeated Pattabhi Sitaramayya, the candidate he had favoured, Gandhi declared this as his own defeat, forcing a reluctant Bose to step down, eventually splitting the Congress. From another angle, however, Gandhi was usually willing to compromise with political opponents—his critics inside the Congress, Jinnah and the Muslim League, and, most significantly, the British. His actions, however, often had an air of moral generosity which was suited to his ethical style but they were really somewhat removed from the rejection of extremism required by political liberalism.

Despite these complexities, the Congress legacy was mainly positive in its contribution to a democratic form of government in independent India in two ways: first, its internal functioning was often startlingly attentive to procedures and legal niceties; and second, from the early part of the century, and especially after 1937, it took part in representative government at the provincial level. Until the very end, the institutions were based on only limited representation, never involving more than about 16 per cent of the entire population. The eve of constitution making was marked by several interesting contradictions. The Congress, which had campaigned for the introduction of adult suffrage which it considered essential for a possible Constituent Assembly, eventually accepted the unrepresentative assembly that the departing British administration offered. At the same time, it is remarkable that most sections of political opinion about the form of government to be adopted after Independence chose some form of parliamentary democracy. The constitution, which introduced universal suffrage, was adopted by an Assembly which was not, to crown the irony, itself based on adult franchise. But this shows several peculiar features of the institutional form of Indian democracy. It was not a form of government that emerged out of irresistible popular demand, but rather a paternalistic elite construction driven by two rather different impulses. The educational and political culture of the Indian elite made it likely that they would regard parliamentary democratic government as the most appropriate to India after Independence. But it was also somewhat tragic luck which gave it its actual form.

The historical circumstances of Partition fatally weakened those forces which might have been less than enthusiastic about liberal democratic procedural forms—both the Muslim League with its fear of Hindu majoritarian rule and the assorted opposition to liberal-democratic ideas found from Hindu chauvinists to communists. There was a window of opportunity for the more democratic section of the Indian elite to construct the constitution relatively unhindered. The property restrictions in voting which chose members of the Constituent Assembly also appear to have favoured this institutional construction. Communists, for instance, had only one member in the Assembly, while in the first general elections, they formed the largest opposition group. The moment of constitution making therefore marked a strange and tragic elite consensus.[9] The politics of colonial India, despite the largely democratic ideals of the Congress, failed to produce any consensual or even compromise result, and failed to tackle the most serious conflict about religious nationalism. But after that serious opposition hived off from India, the business of finding relatively consensual settlements among the Indian elite became much easier.

The Constitutional Structure of Democracy

The preamble to the constitution declared with suitable solemnity that the people of India had resolved 'to give to themselves' the classical principles of freedom, equality, fraternity, and justice. A minor irony of this gesture was that it was made in English, a language understood by a small segment of the population, and some of its more indigenist members regretted weakly at the end of its deliberations that it would have been more appropriate if these principles had been given to the people in a language of their own.[10] Yet, given the complexity of the situation, even that was not an uncontested or simple issue. In the Constituent Assembly, there was little contestation about the adoption of democratic government. Because of the elite consensus in India's politics at that moment, no one doubted that parliamentary democracy was the most appropriate form of government for India. Most of the discussions in the Assembly concerned more detailed matters of institutional architecture: of combining elements from the American with the basic structure of the Westminster model. The eventual constitutional arrangement adopted a Westminster-style parliamentary government with a cabinet and the principle of collective responsibility to the central legislature.

It adopted a constitutional president as head of state, but sought to demarcate the difference in executive authority by making his election indirect. However, a troublesome flaw in the constitution was leaving the jurisdiction of the President, in times of confusion or absence of a clear-cut majority in parliament, strangely, to be governed by the conventions of British parliament. This assumed that future generations of legislators would be as conversant with the technicalities of British law and Erskine May as the one who wrote the constitution. It is hardly surprising that as legal training of legislators has declined in later years, such matters, in the absence of clear constitutional directives, have become increasingly contentious.

Independent India also slowly developed a very different culture of legality, with much less emphasis on legal technicality and the pertinacious accumulation of precedents. Consequently, after the decline of the comfortable majorities of the Congress in the 1980s, governmental changes have become increasingly uneasy; they are heavily dependent on the judicious use of discretionary powers by the President. If his decisions are politically awkward, morally questionable, and contested by major parties, this could become a source of serious problems for the smooth procedural functioning of Indian democratic institutions. In ordinary times, however, there has been little controversy about the powers of the cabinet and the President. The major institutional innovations of Indian democracy lay in the manner in which its draftsmen combined elements of more consensual forms with the majority rule of the Westminster model. The second chamber, the Rajya Sabha, was based on democratic but not numerically equal representation of the states, and several important types of legislation were made dependent on special majorities.[11] The Constitution accepted the principle of representation of constiuent states along with that of popular representation, which was expressed in a federal structure. In accordance with federal principles, the constitution distributed powers between the central and state governments, but the experience of the Partition changed legal thinking on federalism fundamentally.

Before Partition became a certainty, it was generally acknowledged that after Independence India would have a very loose federal structure; after Partition, the understandable anxiety about territorial integrity favoured a far more centralized federalism. The central government not merely received a much larger number of subjects, but also the most insignificant ones, including the undefined residual powers.[12] Besides, the Constitution gave the central government power to dislodge state administrations in circumstances in which the former thought constitutional government had become impossible. In the aftermath of Partition, this highly centralized federal design drew little protest from regionally based political groups. But after 1967, in situations where the centre and the states were controlled by different parties, this emergency power has been used with alarming frequency and often with questionable justification. Political evolution after the 1960s saw increasingly strident demands for greater regional autonomy from parties which recognized that their influence was unlikely to expand beyond specific regions.

However, in several areas the constitutional structure improvised to produce legal rules to suit Indian conditions, and came out with remarkably interesting features. Because of the specific historical conjuncture, and the unrestricted influence of reformist leaders in the Constituent Assembly, the institutional structure paid serious attention to the eradication of caste discrimination, which it expected, along with affiliation to religious communities, to be the primary obstacle to the working of formal democracy. The first innovation was in the definition of the underlying form of nationalism which supported the institutions of the constitution. Historically, Indian nationalism had been an internally variegated ideology, with often strongly contradictory trends coexisting within its capacious spread. Apart from the question of how to deal with the two-nation theory which asserted that the two main religious communities constituted natural nations, there was the further problem of how the two levels of nationalist-patriotic sentiments could be reconciled. Historically, nationalism, rode on the back of intense cultural self-assertions of regional language cultures and the rise of modern vernacular literatures. The constitutional system had to find a way in which the nationalism of the linguistic regions and of the entire country could properly be reconciled.

The institutional solution to the problem of regional and administrative diversity was of course federalism. But underlying the entire idea of Indian federalism was the question of how far the ideal of the cultural unity of the new nation should be taken, and what its form should be. In the Constituent Assembly, there was an opinion which followed the precedent of western nation-states and demanded a single indigenous language to form the basis of a single national culture. In the aftermath of the Partition, it was particularly plausible to argue that without the unifying structure of a single culture based on a single language the new state would fall apart, or simply lack cultural substance as a nation.[13] It was also likely that this line of argument would increasingly slide towards a Hindu self-definition of the Indian nation. Despite strong representations of this strand within the Constituent Assembly, the drafting committee defended its idea of a pluralistic, two-tier nationalism. It recognized the legitimate demands of linguistic cultures and did not consider them hindrances to a feeling of an all-India nationalism. Federalism therefore was not just an administrative- territorial arrangement, it reflected the pluralistic and layered form of the nationalism that was officially accepted by the state.

Adoption of this idea was necessarily incomplete in the first stage of institution making. The Constitution initially established a Byzantine and complicated system of different types of states, but the reorganization of the states in linguistic terms after 1956 brought legal structures in line with this pluralistic conception of Indian nationalism.[14] The Nehruvian state remained concerned about the long-term effects of this concession to linguistic nationalism of the regions.[15] In its early stage, Nehru's government energetically, pursued a policy of propagation of Hindi which brought hostile reaction and political discontent in south India and West Bengal, leading to Nehru's retreat in the face of dissatisfaction. This, however, had rather contradictory consequences over the longer term. The imposition of Hindi on reluctant regions immediately after Independence, may have created difficult political problems similar to ones that the neighbouring state of Pakistan faced because of an unwisely homogenizing linguistic policy. But leaving things without reform meant unrestrained continuance of the cultural and professional privilege of English and the classes who controlled it—a policy unlikely to ever contribute to a democratic eradication of cultural access to social privilege. Fortunately, however, the Indian state has not faced direct trouble over the question of language and its distribution of life chances.

Another important innovation of the constitutional structure of democracy was the set of provisions for reverse discrimination in favour of groups which were considered historically backward. The Constitution not only formally abolished untouchability, but enacted provisions against discrimination on the basis of caste, the most common principle of conventional Hindu social life. The adoption of measures directed against caste practices was not a direct inheritance of a nationalist consensus. At least two strands of Indian nationalism were seriously opposed to the abolition of caste-based conduct. Hindu nationalists were, for obvious reasons, opposed to the abolition of castes, so central to the practice of common Hinduism, though it must be noted that modern Hindu nationalism always contained a serious reformist tradition as well, which, while using Hinduism as the basis of the Indian nation, wished internal hierarchies on the basis of caste to be abolished.[16] Yet the caste question could produce paradoxically complex issues. Gandhi, for instance, was intensely opposed to the practice of untouchability, but not to everyday conduct based on caste.[17] The radical approach to everyday conduct on caste therefore received its support mainly from the reformist, socialist elements in Congress around Nehru and the crusading zeal of B.R. Ambedkar who came to play a crucial role in the drafting of the Constitution. Thus the Constitution established a number of crucial provisions for reverse discrimination in favour of the former untouchable castes. About a fourth of government jobs and educational places were to be reserved for these Scheduled Castes and Tribes. This expressed a foundational belief in the connection between constitutional democracy and social change in the direction of greater equality. Government moves towards extending the scope of reservations for the lower castes(with the Mandal Commission recommendations, for instance) have often been bitterly disputed by parties drawing their support from the higher caste groups, but interestingly, no organized section in Indian politics has asked for an abolition of the existing reservations.

THE HISTORICAL TRAJECTORY OF INDIAN DEMOCRACY

Democratic politics in India during the Nehru years (1946–64) seemed to follow the rules and conventions associated with western democracy. First of all, the procedural rules of democratic government were in general punctiliously observed, though sections of political opinion were at times unhappy about individual cases. Elections were held punctually, and generally there were no strident complaints about vote rigging or violent exclusion of particular groups. Former untouchable groups, however, have later claimed that they simply did not vote in the early general elections in certain parts of the country.[18] Formal rules of cabinet government were also carefully observed. Some important incidents showed, however, that in case of disputes of an extremely serious nature, such procedural observances could be fragile. The most celebrated case of this kind was when the Communist government in Kerala, elected by a thin but eventually firm majority, was dismissed by the Nehru government on the wholly unconvincing excuse that constitutional government was becoming impossible. In fact, the government had undertaken radical measures which affected the Catholic church's control over the state's educational structure. This showed that if radical attacks were planned through perfectly constitutional means by a duly elected government, even a normally procedurally correct government under Nehru could construe these as constitutional anarchy and dismiss it. Similarly unsavoury incidents took place with far greater frequency after the Congress experienced its first major loss in elections in 1967.

Indira Gandhi and Institutional Decline

The fourth general elections of 1967 marked a watershed in the history of Indian democracy in several ways. At the level of party politics, they obviously marked the end of a period in which the Congress could simply assume electoral victory and concentrate on developmental policies entirely free of immediate electoral pressures. This introduced a new kind of politics in which government policies were to have a much more direct and visible connection with electoral commitments. Sometimes, such commitments were so general and radical as to be entirely unrealizable, and certainly the making of such commitments eventually harmed the parties that made them, although Congress under Indira Gandhi (1966–84)[19] initially gained an immense advantage through the slogan of *garibi hatao* (remove poverty). The 1967 elections also showed a more interesting sociological trend. Congress policies for heavy industrialization placed obvious emphasis on industrial groups and looked after their interests through protectionism, low pricing of raw materials, etc. Although the agricultural sector also gained by the absence of an agricultural income tax, powerful farmers' lobbies, formed by the mid-1960s complained against an urban-industrial bias and clamoured for greater attention to agricultural interests. There was a slow but steadyalienation of farmers' groups from the Congress in the northern states from the late 1950s. By the fourth general elections, these disgruntled elements left the Congress and formed their own political parties, usually siding with the opposition. Thus for the first time in the history of elections, the opposition votes were unified, to the great disadvantage of the Congress. Apart from asserting the new power of the farmers' interests in national politics, this also started the process of the splintering of the Congress party. Eventually, the absence of a single ruling party and the unending squabbles among opposition groups introduced an utterly chaotic period of constant defections. This showed how the institutional structure, essentially drawn from some major western models, could face serious crisis with a change in the social composition of the party elites. If party leaders, unlike the Nehru period, were ignorant or defiant of known legal conventions, the institutional system might prove extremely fragile. In fact, the following decade of Indira Gandhi's regime offered a misleading picture of apparent orderliness that was actually created by the irresistibility of Mrs Gandhi's power rather than by a restoration of institutional discipline.

Historically, Indira Gandhi's rule reversed some of the fundamental principles by which Nehru's regime had ruled India and conducted the business of Indian democracy. First, she re-established the control of the Congress over the Indian political system by entirely abrogating the internal democratic functioning of her party. As the Congress in the 1970s still occupied so much of India's political space, this raised the question of how the democratic functioning of parties related to the democratic operation of the formal system. It was hardly surprising that as Indira Gandhi got away with disregard of procedural rules inside her party, she would try to extend this behaviour to state institutions as well. She began to ignore institutional conventions in appointment of Supreme Court judges and conduct of cabinet affairs, but as opposition to her government intensified and slowly turned into an unprecedented nationwide movement which she was unable to control, she eventually took resort to a quasi-legal authoritarianism. The Emergency (May 1975–December 1979) had a very thin legality. It was adopted by a legislature elected by a large but clearly outdated, over which Indira Gandhi exercised undisputed control; it put to mendacious use provisions put into the Constitution to avert threats to the entire institutional system or the territorial integrity of the country. Emergency provisions were meant to avert threats to the state, not to individual politicians. Although it was technically within its formal provisions, the Emergency violated the spirit of the Constitution, and mainly sought to deflect the effect of a ruling by Allahabad High Court questioning the method of Indira Gandhi's election in the previous general elections. The politics of populism leading to the Emergency, again, showed some interesting features of democratic evolution in India. It was dramatic evidence of a dissonance between participation and procedure. The fact that Indira Gandhi faced a rebellion in much of the country only three years after she had won an unprecedented majority showed a disconnection between the elective procedure and popular opinion. By her populist rhetoric and partly because of the success in the war with Pakistan, Indira Gandhi won an immensely impressive mandate. But this actually deflected attention from the record of her previous government, so popular discontent spilled onto the streets soon after her resounding victory. The declaration of the Emergency passed off without much popular protest, with major political groups watching with caution a situation which was entirely without precedent. But when they were allowed some minimal freedom to organize, the other political groups reasserted themselves and set up a single party to oppose the Congress in 1977.

The episode of the Emergency showed, paradoxically, both the fragility of democratic institutions and their underlying legitimacy, if not strength. Their fragility was demonstrated by the weary and unenthusiastic manner in which advent of the first authoritarian regime in India was treated, and by the fact that for about two years it faced little resistance except of unorganized local people driven to desperation. Yet its end showed in some ways the opposite: a failure of nerves on Indira Gandhi's part to rule indefinitely without electoral sanction, though she was so immensely misinformed by a sycophantic bureaucracy that she probably expected to get a reduced mandate. This was in any case a reluctant acknowledgement of the principle that the exercise of political power required elective sanction. When the electorate was given a chance, they showed their determination for the continuance of democratic government by voting her out comprehensively. Indira Gandhi's period in uncontested authority also marked a departure from the liberal rules of democracy that Nehru followed. One of the major features of Nehru's government, as of the structure of the Congress party itself, was a commitment to compromise—between various ideological positions, regional interests, and social classes. Majority rule, therefore, never polarized opinions or interests to an extent where some political groups would become irretrievably alienated from the political process and the state itself.[20]

Indira Gandhi's tendency to use her electoral majority to destroy and alienate opposition, and to deny her adversaries even the general protection democratic procedures provide, led to a kind of political hostility that although initially expressed through democratic processes was nevertheless new. Parties began to dredge more deeply for slogans and often began to mobilize along caste and religious community based ties. Indira Gandhi's years in Indian politics worked an astonishing transformation in the language and issues of politics. During the Nehru years, the main lines of party demarcation and political conflict were broadly ideological. The Communists and the Swatantra Party represented ideologically leftist and right-wing opposition to the Congress's resolute centrism. From the point of view of understanding democracy, this contrast can be seen not only as a conflict between ideological positions, but also as a conflict between political extremism and a politics of compromise. One of the major departures of Indira Gandhi from Nehru's political style was a conversion of Congress politics into one of perpetual confrontation. Excessive centralization ironically resulted in major outbreaks of regional discontent, sliding, because of her abrasive handling, into immediate militancy and, eventually, insurgency. By the time Indira Gandhi was assassinated, she had left behind seriously impaired institutions and a string of regional insurgencies which have proved intransigent to all subsequent governments.

Non-dominant Coalitions

After Indira Gandhi's death, Indian democracy clearly entered a new historical phase. The aspects of this phase were the decline of the Congress, which had previously occupied centre stage in Indian politics, and the rise of Hindu nationalism in various forms, primarily the growing influence of the Bharatiya Janata Party (BJP). After Independence, the nationalism of the state was represented by the Congress, and despite its many internal complexities and undoubted untidiness, the party held its ideology and political practice within some generally recognized parameters. It rarely succeeded in realizing the shining ideals of complete secularism, an unequivocal commitment to egalitarianism, or the perfect observance of procedures. Judged against such high standards, the Congress always came out seriously tarnished and sordid. Despite that, in retrospect, it achieved success of a kind. This success was to be measured, paradoxically, in negative terms: despite furtive use of religious feelings, it did not use overt communalism; its members did not always observe rules but could be shamed into retreating when serious procedural flaws could be revealed; it did little directly for social equality but admitted a general commitment of the state in that direction—at least had a bad conscience.

The historic achievement of the Congress lay not in what it achieved but in what it averted. Consequently, the Congress's slow fragmentation and apparently irreversible decline inevitably left a huge ideological vacuum in Indian politics. Two very different forces have tried to fill it in recent years. There is still considerable support in India for a strong, territorially integrated, powerful nation-state. The groups who promulgate such a position are naturally disappointed by the collapse of the Congress version of nationalist ideology which animated this nation-state. The strongest alternative to this nationalist vision is now the one offered by the BJP with a Hindu nationalist conception of India. This ideology shares with the Congress ideal the territorial integrity of the nation-state. What it does not share with the Congress ideal is the principle of secularism and pluralism as fundamental, inalienable aspects of the definition of nationalism (Jaffrelot 1996: Ch. 11)—it is not merely a Hindu majoritarian vision, but also necessarily hostile to the implicit pluralism of Indian culture. Thus it is opposed to two central principles of Indian society, one traditional, the other modern. It is opposed to the pluralist and politically egalitarian conceptions of modern secular democracy,[21] but, ironically, it is equally opposed to the traditional pluralism of Hindu religion. The success of the Hindu nationalists would preserve the territorial integrity of India, but turn its internal political culture into something utterly different. If experience with BJP regional governments is any guide, it might not offer a remarkably superior administration, but would certainly destroy the confidence of India's large religious minorities in the neutrality of the nation-state.

The second type of political force which might offer an alternative to the Congress is a congeries of regional groups which have no national perspective or vision and simply bargain with other regions and whichever party is at the centre for maximum regional advantage. Although it is customary for nationalists to deride these groups for their parochialism, in the long run this null nationalism might be an excellent foil to the BJP's tendency towards homogenization. The fact that these groups do not have a strong, determinate idea of what the nation should be like, or what should be its cultural form, ideological content, etc. tends to indicate that they would accept a pluralistic nationalism and, collaterally, a procedural conception of democracy. These parties are likely to be satisfied by a decision arrived at by a particular procedure (consultation, compromise, some form of weighted voting, etc.) rather than a strong association with a particular content of nationalism. For similar reasons, they are also less likely to impose a particular cultural, linguistic, ideological, or religious character on the whole nation, simply because they implicitly recognize their inability to speak for the nation as a whole. Given the strength of their respective support and social bases, it is unlikely that in the short term any of the main contenders in democratic politics in India would completely overwhelm the other. The BJP's support is unlikely to fade away or collapse suddenly. Although the Congress might fragment and decline even further, the counterweight to the BJP in the form of a coalition of groups which oppose it on secular or caste grounds is not likely to have an imminent collapse. Indian politics looks bound in the foreseeable future to muddle through on the basis of perishable coalitions. This might strengthen the procedural aspects of democracy by bringing into relief how important institutional forms are in case of indecisive electoral results. Since all parties suffer from insecurity in electoral terms, they might all equally value the impartiality of titular and supervisory agencies like the Election Commission or the President and state Governors. In a strange fashion, this might also gladden the hearts of economic liberalizers by shifting effective powers from the state to the market and by immobilizing the state agencies for long periods. But this consequence would go against the long-term tendency of Indian democracy to allow the state to extend its control over steadily larger areas of economic life, and marginal groups have tried to acquire some control over state resources by means of electoral power. Reduction of the effective control of the state's realm of decisions would mean a restriction of the scope of social life which was amenable to democratic power.

Major Features of Indian Democracy

The Problem of Representation

Indian democracy in its early years was marked by a paradox: its formal principles were democratic, based on formal equality of citizens, but the actual social structure through which it functioned was still highly aristocratic. Thus the political elite, who represented different social and political groups in the highly verbal arena of democratic politics were usually members of the educated middle class, predominantly urban elite. Democratic politics gives greater importance to certain types of assets: by nature, it values cultural capital. It is thus not surprising that in the first two decades of the operation of democratic government the legislators and politicians, irrespective of their political opinions, came from a narrow, recognizably homogenous urban upper-class elite. Political activities of all kinds in the narrower sense—in state institutions, the file-maintaining work of the bureaucracy, the verbal disputations inside the legislatures, and the legally technical proceedings of judicial process—were all carried out in impeccable English. This, of course, restricted access to the relevant democratic forms for ordinary people who did not have the right education or cultural capital. Political representatives of untouchable castes were figures like Ambedkar or Jagjivan Ram who shared the culture of the elite and could speak their 'language'. Similarly, Communist legislators were mostly from educated cultural and social backgrounds, despite their political sympathies. Representation, one of the most fundamental processes, was thus of a specific kind— representatives who could represent interests of marginal or less dominant groups like the former untouchables or the workers and peasants through the trade-union movements and Communist parties, were socially and culturally unlike the groups they spoke for.

Slowly, over the late 1950s and early 1960s, some inevitable consequences of democratic politics were discernible. Land reforms in the countryside, particularly in areas where formerly the *zamindari* system was in place, created a space for the emergence of a new class of richer farmers who acquired wealth and political influence locally, but did not immediately aspire to the culture of the urban elites. Their representatives slowly broke into the state legislatures initially altering their internal patterns of functioning, use of language and styles, and, finally, the entire internal culture of legislative and electoral politics. Democratic politics also slowly mobilized underprivileged groups like the lower castes and the poorer peasantry. Gradually, this led to a fundamental restructuring of the representational system of the parties. In the 1950s most parties were ideological, and claimed to represent mixed constituencies, mobilized on the basis of distributive principles of various sorts. Congress, Swatantra, the Communists, and the Socialists were all 'national' parties in a certain sense, and felt unwilling to be associated with the interests of any particular primordial group. The Communists claimed particular title to represent the working class. This was not based on primordial identity, but rather on an economic interest defined in terms of class.

By the 1970s, the early signs of a fundamental redefinition of this format of representation were clearly observable. Two processes occurred simultaneously to alter the meaning of representation in the party system. First, there was a subtle but undeniable change in the nature of some parties. The Socialists from the 1960s slowly lost all other support and became a northern regional party except in name. The Communists, after their splits in 1964 and 1968,[22] slowly lost influence in other regions and became entrenched in West Bengal, Kerala, and Tripura and started behaving much like a regional party. The Congress did the same, only in a way that was less discernible because it continued to retain some influence in most regions. Under Indira Gandhi, the Congress began using appeals to religious identities, especially clearly in Punjab and Jammu and Kashmir, wooing the Hindu minorities in these states and alienating the Sikh and Muslim majorities. But what was more permanently damaging to democratic institutions was the enticement to religious groups to think of themselves as political communities. This undermined the randomness of outcomes and the indeterminacy of the constitution of majorities, slowly forcing the politics of these states in the direction of irresoluble conflict between religious communities.

But the more obvious shift in the field of political parties has been the development of straightforward identity-based parties which have equated the idea of identity with that of interest. Since the 1980s, two types of parties have emerged as the most powerful players in the political field. First, there are parties based on religious identities like the Akali Dal in Punjab, the BJP in most of north and western India and some of the political groups in Kashmir which drifted from an initially regionalist to a clearly religious self-indentification, and caste-based parties of various types, galvanized by the suggestions and opposition to the recommendations made by the Mandal Commission.[23] Between these two types of new political parties, political parties based on other types of affiliations, especially associational ones, have constantly been on the retreat. One accompanying feature of such homogeneous identity-based parties, unsurprisingly, has been a different form of representation. To represent a backward-caste group, it is now seen as necessary to have the outward manifestations of behaviour that both its members and others associate with these groups. The idea that any other individual who

464 HANDBOOK OF INDIAN SOCIOLOGY

does not have the necessary identity features can represent them or their interest politically has been fatally undermined.

Politics of this kind acknowledges only representation by likeness. Often this logic of representation has been carried even further by implicating the bureaucracy into this politics. For instance leaders of successive governments in Uttar Pradesh have openly declared that only Scheduled-caste officers can advance the interests of Scheduled-caste groups, and therefore have promoted officers from these groups quite openly. This brings the logic of segmentation on which the caste order is based into the operation of democratic government with potentially unpredictable results. Although a departure from the previous idea of representation, which was at the bottom was aristocratic, democratizes politics in a certain sense. There are certainly precedents of this type from the history of western democracy, particularly from the history of labour parties, which often based the idea of representation on this kind of social resemblance. At the same time, it complicates the question of trust which must underlie modern institutions, including democratic political forms. It might introduce something like a non-territorial social partition between different identity groups. The effect of this has been that the discourse of rights has assumed increasingly complex form. While most groups speak in terms of a language of rights, the bearers of these rights are increasingly seen to be communities and primordial groups rather than individuals and their associational interests. The obvious consequence of this will be, if this trend is taken to its logical end, that democratic decisions will become frozen into segmented groups aligned in relations of unalterable, permanent majorities and minorities—a condition under which democratic decisions would become increasingly misleading and meaningless.

The politics of representation has another aspect as well. Democracy is often justified as a government based on the choice of the people. Obviously, this is an idea that has to be further refined. If choice means taking actual decisions about policies or outcomes, it is misleading to say that the electorate chooses. It seems necessary to think of the process of choice as stretching from a wide and general end where the electorate participates through elections to a narrow, specific end at which the government or its relevant bodies take actual decisions about individual policies. This does not deny the reality of an exercise of choice by the electorate, it locates choice in the relations between political parties and their personnel, with some very broad, occasionally ambiguous declarations of policies. This should properly be seen as a mandate, to be distinguished, in a strict sense, from a choice. Further down the line, there can be other forms of choice like assent or acquiescence to general directions or policy objectives, which are eventually further focused by the real act of policy decisions. One of the major questions in a democracy is how the electorate can use the necessarily blunt instrument of a mandate to get policy decisions of its liking. The change in the nature of political formations in India is closely associated with a change in the nature of the mandates that parties have put forward to the electorates. There is a broad trend of parties which is far away from large ideological postures like socialism or laissez faire, which were too broad to affect people's livelihoods or incomes, to far more specific expectations of redistribution of government resources for particular groups. The lack of interest in large public investments like infrastructure, observed by economists, might be linked to this political fact. The fragmentation of the party system has made the adoption of economic policies benefiting sectional interests more likely than government investment in general welfare or common interests.

It has been widely noted that the success of democracy has led to results that appear paradoxical in terms of conventional modernization theories. Those theories assumed that with the rise of industries and the entrenchment of modern democratic politics, social individuation would be greatly advanced and ordinary people would feel less attached to their primordial communities. But the actual consequence of democratic processes has confounded such expectations. As democracy applied pressure on groups to combine and use the pressure of large numbers, voters have been mobilized often on the basis of their community self-understandings. Through this caste identities have been politically reinforced. Instead of caste affiliations slowly fading and disappearing from political life, these identities have become incresingly assertive and important in the making of party political moves, baffling observers.[24] At the same time, it is difficult to regard these parties as manifestations of traditional caste identities. Conventional caste practices were concerned with social activities like marriage, commensality, and enjoyment of property. New caste forces are concerned primarily with the acquisition and maintenance of political power. Since political power in a democratic regime depends on large numerical groups, the trend in caste politics has gone in the direction of forming new kinds of alliances across the traditional segmentation of caste groups. This has led to the formation of entirely new kinds of caste affiliations like Scheduled Castes(created by Constitutional contrivance) or 'intermediate castes' created by the drive for large coalitions for electoral purposes. The consequence of this has been equally puzzling: instead of the principle of equality reducing caste identification, there is increasingly a tendency to assert caste identities while claiming equality *among* them. The imbrication of particularist, identity-based-claims and universalist, equality-based-claims was entirely unforeseen by the earlier theory or by constitutional designs or indeed by the traditional principles of the caste order. Thus democracy has certainly affected the structure of social inequality in India in terms of caste. It has surely reduced the practice of caste inequality both by the first wave of constitutional reforms in the 1950s and the second wave of electoral politics of the 1980s and 1990s. While the first set of moves intended to work towards greater individual equality, the second set have mobilized opinion against hierarchical caste practice by mobilizing and reinforcing caste identities themselves, not by trying to abolish them.

Democracy and Regional Interests

Sceptical views about Indian democracy often regard regional pluralism as a threat to democratic government. In the institutional arrangements of politics, regional diversity is supposed to be addressed by devices of federalism rather than of democratic government. But if democracy is interpreted as government by consent, where political solutions would not be imposed on people who do not like them, a strong connection between principles of federalism and democracy can be seen: federalism is a representative arrangement for India's various regions. Representation for regions has worked in two different ways. Initially, it functioned through the internal federalism of the Congress party itself, not through regional parties. In the Nehru period, the Congress maintained its earlier consensual principles of functioning by making sure representatives of various regions enjoyed office, which was also reflected in cabinet making. Although from a formal point of view, the first three decades of Indian politics might appear to have been totally dominated by a single 'national' party, with very little power to regional groups, regional representation has in fact worked quite well through the Congress. However, centralizing tendencies in the Congress during Indira Gandhi's time led to more intense regional resentment against her regime, with regional parties successfully capturing state governments. Irresponsible and partisan use of the Constitutional clause for dismissing state governments exacerbated this relation, and the 1970s and 1980s were marked by increasingly insistent demands for redistribution of financial powers between the states and the centre. Regional parties have been primarily of two types, representing quite different types of opposition to the centre. Some groups were simply confined to regions in terms of support, such as the Socialists in the Hindi areas in the 1960s, or the Communists in West Bengal and Kerala since the mid-1960s. Since the 1960s, however, regional parties appeared which had merely regional political demands, and therefore could not aspire to any national influence. The Akali Dal, the DMK, the AGP, etc., owed their political existence to regional issues. In some cases, when outplayed by the Congress or a nationalist coalition, some of these regional groups have tended to move in the direction of secessionism. The relation between democracy and regional dis-affection presents a complex and mixed picture in Indian politics. In at least three cases—Punjab, Kashmir, and Assam—attempts to resolve conflict through democratic elections have not succeeded, because, some claim, democratic procedures were not punctiliously observed for a long time in earlier phases. If regional demands are not reconciled early, they have tended to move uncontrollably towards confrontation and have eventually led to the disruption of the state itself. The movements for regional autonomy in these regions claimed not a better deal within the Indian Union but the right to break away from the Indian state itself. There have been other cases, by contrast, where serious concessions by the central government successfully defused conflict and brought intense regional secessionism back into the folds of electoral politics. The DMK in Tamil Nadu, the nativist agitation in Andhra, the Mizo separatist move-ment, and even the National Conference in Kashmir under Farukh Abdullah were enticed back into parliamentary politics after serious conflict. In the 1990s, with the decline of 'national' parties the relation between regional politics and Indian democracy is falling into a different pattern. Since neither the Congress nor the BJP appears likely to command a stable and unassisted majority in parliamentary elections, national governments would have to depend on coalitional support of regional parties. Suddenly, the relation between regional and national parties might become strangely altered. Since major parties would depend on their support for forming governments, they would have to concede substantial governmental power and in-fluence to regional groups. Instead of thinking of themselves as players confined to regional politics, and having a predominantly negative relation with dominant national groups, regional parties would now have to play an increasingly significant role at central level. Ironically, this might induce them to look at the central government in a different light, and alter the rules by which the centre–states game has been played for the last fifty years.

Democracy and Economic Policy/Development Policy

Theorists of democracy with a predominant interest in political economy were wont to argue once that democracy is probably detrimental to economic growth. The primary reasons given for this were two: first, democratic politics led to instability of government policies regarding economic matters. Business groups found it difficult to adjust to potentially conflicting economic strategies followed by ideologically divergent political parties who might succeed each other in office. Authoritarian governments, by contrast, were able to follow stable economic strategies over long periods, making it easier for business to make long-term calculations. Second, democratic politics, it was often suggested, made for too close a connection between electoral politics and government distribution of economic resources. Since winning elections depends quite often on making short-term economic promises to particular sectional interests, democratic regimes are chronically incapable of making detached, long-term policies about deveopment of the whole economy, because such policies does not manage the requisite 'insulation' of economic policy making from electoral pressures. Democracy in India shows a rather paradoxical picture in this respect. First, on long-term continuity of economic or development strategy, government change rarely affected fundamental strategy. On the contrary, at times, the continuity was quite startling. For example, in 1977 when the Janata Party succeeded Indira Gandhi's Congress, it was logical to expect serious change, since it was a combination of political groups which had opposed Congress policies of state-led development on various grounds. Yet the government did little to alter the basic package of policy orientations on economic matters. Curiously, the most significant shifts in economic strategy marked by liberalization since the early 1990s were introduced by a minority Congress government, but no party seriously opposed them at the time. After a coalition of leftist and regional parties replaced the Congress government, they deliberately continued with the policies of liberalization instead of scrapping them. Short-term concessions of economic policy before elections have also been rare at central level, though in state elections such quick distribution of state resources has been fairly common. However, since the state governments' resources are generally quite meagre, the effect of such behaviour has not been significant.

Indian democratic politics, however, shows the impact of democracy on economic policies in a different way. Democratic politics was surely responsible for the continuous increase of the sphere of the state's interference in the economy. Though originally introduced by standard Fabian Socialist arguments, taken from Britain, about capturing the 'commanding heights' of the economy, it slowly degenerated into a different kind of politico-economic practice. The state's control over enormous economic resources meant that these could be used for political purposes by political elites. The only means of acquiring control over these resources was through winning elections. Despite important differences about economic policy, nearly all groups of politicians benefited from this access. This meant, by implication, that electoral politics determined, to some extent, how this reservoir of resources was to be spent.

Paradoxically, the tendency towards economic liberalization, though justified by liberal arguments about the harmony between democracy and markets as systems of choice, is likely to reduce this indirect popular control over state resources. If the state is slimmed down, and this fund of resources wrenched away from its grasp, the impact of political democracy in the structural operations of the Indian economy is bound to be significantly reduced. This tends to show that not under all circumstances are the logics of democracy and capitalism fully congruent; in the Indian case, at least, liberalization would tend to make them diverge dramatically.

Democracy and Social Inequality

At the time of the adoption of the Constitution, one of the major arguments in favour of adult suffrage was that it would eventually reduce social inequality. But social inequality in India existed in two forms. The first is status inequality based on caste, which is still, despite socio-economic changes during the colonial period, deeply entrenched in Indian society. The Constitution abolished status inequality on the basis of caste, at least in public matters, by the radically simple device of the legal declaration of the right to equality. But legal declarations, while powerful statements about a society's principles, do not always necessarily change social behaviour. Advantage based on caste could not be simply abolished by legal delcaration because social inequality also meant unequal economic conditions and life chances. Curiously, the rights in the Constitution bestowed status equality on its citizens and helped maintain economic inequality at the same time, since some essential aspects of social inequality—especially in property and incomes—were part of the liberal regime of rights. It was believed at the time of Constitution making that democracy would support social equality in two different but complementary ways. First, the Constitution gave the state the right to use reverse discrimination in favour of backward castes, reserving academic places for them and, more directly, reserving government jobs. To the extent, lower-caste individuals got these jobs or places, they acquired either equality of condition or a chance to secure it. State employment, however, offered opportunities for a relatively small number of people, and the importance of reservations of posts in government service was often of symbolic rather than of great statistical significance. Reservations in education and other measures were expected to work as a larger process of bringing in social equality, and the Constitution envisaged a phasing out of these reservation rules after opportunities had become more generally equal. It is in the second kind of measures that the effect of democracy has been disappointing. Democratic pressure on legislatures has constantly extended the reservation rules of the state, both in terms of time and in terms of their coverage, most notably through the recommendations of the Mandal Commission. But democratic politics has failed to bring pressure on the state to provide greater equality in the provision of education, health, and skills through which economic inequality can be addressed in the long term. In recent decades, the shift in political conflict to questions of identity, like caste and religion, has tended to overshadow this apsect of social equality. It must be noted, however, that the demands for advance of the lowest castes, although made on the grounds of identity, do have an effect on economic equality in an indirect fashion.

In India, historical experience appears to show that democratic politics tends to bring social conflicts out into the open. It makes them more public, occasionally magnifies them and, only at times makes them easier to settle because of this publicity. If the outer parameters of the state are accepted, it does tend eventually to assist in the resolution of conflicts. In democratic contexts, due to immediate expression of popular or sectional grievances, both the government and the ruling elites as well as other parties with opposed interests get to know about these disaffections quite quickly. Democratic openness thus works as a kind of early warning system, and allows other groups to adjust to such demands. But once demands gained currency, democratic government encouraged two rather contradictory tendencies: it allows radical groups to exacerbate differences of opinion and conflicts of interests. But at the same time, since demands of either social groups like castes or classes or regional forces have to argue their case against other views, it tends to create a climate in which accommodation is eventually possible. This can lead to the trend towards the composition of differences and de-radicalization that liberal theorists have usually found in democratic politics. After fifty years of Independence, the historical strength of Indian democracy is undeniable, and this is shown in the fact that no major party ever offers arguments against democracy. But the subtler threat to democracy might come from forces which wish to use the power of democracy in a way which keeps some sections of society permanently excluded, which would mean a violation of the spirit of democracy through the use of its electoral forms.

ENDNOTES

1. Rajni Kothari argued ingeniously that traditional Indian culture was based on religious pluralism, and could thus form a cultural base for the functioning of democracy. (Kothari 1970).
2. For an example of the constitutionalist approach to the problems of Indian democracy, see Pylee.

Besides these, however, there was an immensely detailed and erudite literature on technical constitutional law, of which one of the best known works.

3. For an account of the evolution of colonial government in India.

4. This strand was represented in Bengal, where some of these early intellectual moves were played out by the movement called Young Bengal.

5. For a detailed analysis of three writers who represent this tendency—Bankimchandra Chattopadhyay, Bhudev Mukhopadhyay and Vivekananda—see Raychaudhuri 1999?

6. To take a well known example—again from late-nineteenth-century Bengal, there was a great deal of discussion about the exact semantic connotations of *Dharma* and religion, and Haraprasad Shastri the famous socio-linguist wrote about these translation problems.

7. The best example of this kind of argument is to be found in Dadabhai Naoroji's *Poverty and the Un-British Rule in India*, first published in Britain in 1899.

8. Thus the arguments, taken from Hannah Arendt's analysis of totalitarian politics, widely used in the conventional political science literature of the 1950s and 1960s against popular nationalist mobilizations could not be used against the Congress.

9. For detailed analyses of the workings of the Constituent Assembly, see Austin (1964); Chaube and; Dattagupta (1978).

10. Rajendra Prasad, the president of the Constituent Assembly expressed his regret in the valedictory session, speaking in Hindi.

11. The most important of these provisions is, of course, the amendment of the Constitution itself.

12. The division of powers between the central and state governments is set down in the ninth schedule of the Indian Constitution, with the centre awarded 97 separate heads, the states 64, treated as concurrent subjects on which the centre's laws would override the states', with the residuary powers given to the centre.

13. For discussions on the Constituent Assembly, see Austin (1964: Ch. 12).

14. For an account of the evolution of Indian federal institutions in this period, see Chandra (1965: Ch. 2).

15. Nehru's reservations about conceding linguistic states are recorded in Gopal (1989: vol. II, Ch.).

16. Christophe Jaffrelot (1996) provides a detailed historical analysis of the various trends in Hindu nationalist thinking. See esp. Ch. 1.

17. Because of his odd belief that caste practices could be non-discriminatory, that is a registration of difference rather than inequality.

18. These complaints have been made mainly to academic researchers or journalists covering elections in rural constituencies.

19. But this phase of renewed Congress dominance could be stretched to 1990, the death of Rajiv Gandhi and the coming of the first Congress minority regime under P.V. Narasimha Rao.

20. Some critics of the argument that asserts the difference in political styles between Nehru and Indira Gandhi point to Nehru's attitude towards Naga rebels and the general troubles in India's north-eastern region. But those were cases of areas which were never properly integrated into the Indian state, rather than of areas pushed into militant opposition by government policy.

21. The BJP claims that its politics represents true secularism, and those of other parties 'pesudo-secularism' that concedes illegitimate concessions to the minorities. But the claim that religious minorities must conform to certain ideas, laid down eventually by the Hindu majority, goes against the fundamental principle of equal treatment of religious groups.

22. The Communist Party of India first split in 1964. Subsequently, the larger fragment, the CPI(M), split again in 1968, with the radical wing, popularly known as the Naxalites, forming a militant anti-electoral movement committed to winning power by violent revolution. While the CPI(M) has thrived electorally in specific regions, while slowly becoming de-radicalized, the Naxalite movement was crushed by the state's use of force, and later splintered into a number of warring groups.

23. The Mandal commission was appointed by the central government to look into the operation of reverse discrimination policies over the long term, and to make further suggestions. The Commission suggested a substantial increase in the scope of reservations, at times increasing it well beyond 50 per cent. This has polarized Indian political opinion as nothing else had for the last several decades. Its views have drawn primarily three types of response. First, some groups have enthusiastically supported them as a means of realizing social justice. Second, other parties, based understandably on upper caste support, have condemned them as denial of rights to equality of opportunity and treatment. Some other groups, while not openly contesting the recommendations, have supported drastic reduction of state control over employment and resources, since these principles are more difficult to apply to the private sector.

24. The earliest, and in some ways the best, analysis of this trend remains Kothari's (1970) analysis.

REFERENCES

Austin, Granville. 1964. *The Indian Constitution: Constitution of a Nation*. Oxford: Clarendon Press.

Brown, Judith. *Modern India: The Origins of an Asian Democracy*. Oxford University Press.

Chandra, Asok. 1965. *Federalism in India*. London: George Allen and Unwin.

Dattagupta, S. 1978. *Justice and Political Order in India*. Calcutta: K.P. Bagchi.

Gopal, S., ed. 1989. *Jawaharlal Nehru*, vol. II. London: Frank Cass.

Guha, Ranajit. 1981. *Elementary Aspects of Peasant Insurgency in Colonial India*. Delhi: Oxford University Press.

Jaffrelot, Christophe. 1996. *The Hindu Nationalist Movement and Indian Politics*. London: Hurst.

Kothari, Rajani. 1970. *Politics in India*. Delhi: Orient Longman.

———. 1970. *Caste in Indian Politics*. Delhi: Orient Longman.

Naoroji, Dadabhai. [1889]. *Poverty and the Un-British Rule in India*.

Raychaudhuri, Tapan. 199. *Europe Reconsidered*. Oxford University Press.

Collective Violence

JONATHAN SPENCER

C ollective violence is an expression used to describe certain specific kinds of violence: the violence of the urban crowd (rather than the violence of the state), and the violence of the public arena (rather than the violence of domestic relations). Although the term appears self-evident and satisfactorily value-free, the boundaries between collective violence and the rule of law, between acts of the crowd and acts of warfare, between the aberrant moment of riot and the 'normal' violence of political life, are by no means as clear-cut as is usually implied. In South Asia, 'collective violence' is now often used interchangeably with the more contentious term 'communal violence'. In both Europe and South Asia, the study of collective violence has until recently been dominated by the work of social and economic historians, and it is only relatively recently that it has returned to the empirical agenda of anthropologists and sociologists. In Europe and North America, the urban disturbances of the 1960s provoked a brief flurry of studies on crowd violence, but interest waned until the collapse of the Soviet empire and the break-up of Yugoslavia reminded Europeans of the continued power of the call to community, ethos, or nation. In South Asia, anthropologists and sociologists have responded to the disturbing rise in collective violence since the late 1970s with a number of important studies emerging in the 1990s.

This chapter will start with a review of the curious position of violence in classic western social theory, as well as the special place it occupies, with its Gandhian alternative, non-violence, in South Asian political theory. It will then briefly review the comparative evidence on violence and non-violence from social and cultural anthropology, before turning to recent empirical and theoretical work from South Asia in the 1980s and 1990s. In keeping with the so-called crisis of representation in the social sciences, since the 1980s the analysis of violence has been preoccupied in part with the political and moral problems of writing about violence.

Violence and Theory

Collective violence could be said to be the evil twin of the Enlightenment march of Reason. The French Revolution can be remembered for both the apparent triumph of the politics of universal reason and the recognition of the radical political potential of the Parisian crowd. For Marx, violence was famously the 'midwife' involved in the birth of any new social order. For Weber (1948), addressing German students in the revolutionary aftermath of the First World War, violence was the 'decisive means' of modern politics, and the fact that the politician's power was in the last analysis based on the command of force presented one of the key ethical dilemmas of modern politics. For Durkheim, somewhat more abstractly, violence was one of those natural human propensities which required the disciplining of the conscience collective if human community was to function. In all these cases, though, violence was in a curious way treated as a given, a necessary part of the theoretical background, rather than an object itself requiring sustained theoretical attention. The writings of leading theorists of violence, such as the syndicalist Georges Sorel (1950), have been ignored for most of the century. If it is true that Hannah Arendt (1969) and Frantz Fanon (1965), probably the two most important mid-century theorists of violence, have returned to intellectual fashion in the 1990s, their specific suggestions on violence and power are still relatively neglected.

Three moments stand out in what Keane (1996) calls this 'long century of violence' in Europe and North America: the experience of the slaughter in the trenches of the First World War; the Nazi project for a Final Solution; and the dropping of atomic bombs on the Japanese cities of Hiroshima and Nagasaki. All involved complex processes of collective agency and enormous suffering, yet, in an odd way, all have been treated as aberrant or atypical, as temporary departures from the smooth road of normal politics in modern societies. The problems they posed for intellectuals were often transposed into the register of morality and aesthetics and not, again until surprisingly recently, into problems of social and political theory. The analogue in India is obviously the experience of Partition, which, as Gyanendra Pandey has recently argued, has become a site of 'collective amnesia', another aberration or departure from the teleological narratives of the Indian nation (Pandey 1992). If it has taken the rather different theoretical efforts of Michel Foucault (1984) and Zygmunt Baumann (1993) to remind western intellectuals of the complicitous relationship between these moments of extreme violence and the institutional forms of political modernity, it has been the mounting tide of so-called communal violence since the early 1980s that has forced South Asian intellectuals to re-examine the relationship between violence and their own local forms of political modernity.

In this century, the great South Asian contribution to the political theory of violence is, of course, the recognition in Gandhian theory and practice of the political potency of collective non-violent action. This is explicitly invoked as an example in Hannah Arendt's radical argument for a distinction between 'power', which is an effect of collective non-violent action, and its obverse, force, which in its reliance on violence betrays an absence of what she sees as real power (Arendt 1969). Yet the very success of Gandhian political practice in the anti-colonial struggle has generated further complicating distortions. Just as India can be stereotypically represented as the land of non-violence, so too is the story of the nationalist movement told as a teleology of non-violence with no intelligible space left for the moments of collective violence which also formed part of it. Recently, though, it has become apparent that historical and sociological investigations in South Asia require the recognition of the coevality and interdependence of both violence and non-violence (Vidal et al. 1993).

Violence and Anthropology

Just as violence has long been taken to be a sign of the primitive, the savage, or the uncivilized, or alternatively, of the deviant, the individual, and the unsocialized, so anthropology has long been concerned to show that violence obeys rules, is part of culture, and even fulfils certain social functions. Classic functionalist accounts of institutions such as the feud stress that these bind people together, through the shared norms and expectations that participants invoke, even as they appear to divide them. But, despite this well-worn interpretative path, violence retains its capacity to unsettle and disturb.

Theoretically, violence lurks behind many important anthropological conceptions of the human and the social. Violence represents 'natural' drives which society must tame and repress if it is to survive: this broad idea can be found in western political philosophy (classically in Hobbes), as well as in Freudian psychoanalysis, Durkheim's notion of humans as 'homo duplex', and Mauss's implicit argument in his essay on 'The Gift' that gifts are society's means of overcoming the inevitability of war. From these perspectives emerges the linked notion of society, or most often the state, as the monopolist of 'legitimate' violence. The place of violence as a sign of the natural and unsocialized is even more marked in socio-biological arguments about human nature and genetics, such as those employed by Napoleon Chagnon (1983) in the complex controversy about Yanomamo violence in lowland South America. Not surprisingly, such emphases have generated a counter-literature in which ethnographic examples are employed to suggest that peaceful sociability is the 'natural' condition (Howell and Willis 1989).

As a comparative discipline, anthropology's most useful contribution has probably been its documentation of the fact that violence is pre-eminently collective rather than individual, social rather than asocial or anti-social, usually culturally structured, and always culturally interpreted. This was already implicit in functionalist interpretations of violence, but in recent years it has been greatly extended as anthropologists have reported the experience and interpretation of violence from the point of view of (among many others) paramilitaries in Northern Ireland, Indian riot victims, and torture survivors in Sri Lanka. Here the anthropology of violence becomes part of a new anthropology of the body in which the body becomes a privileged site for the inscription of signs of power.

What is more difficult is to escape the assumption that questions about violence are inevitably questions about human nature. Simon Harrison (1989), writing about the Avatips of the Sepik river area of New Guinea, argues that the Avatips distinguish between two types of sociality linked to two different concepts of the person. The unmarked type, so to speak, is one in which everyday social relations are lived in an idiom of peaceful equality; the other type of sociality, encountered in the world of men's politics and men's warfare, is marked by assertion, aggression, and potentially uncontrollable violence. This second type is not, however, treated as a natural property of men, but rather as something which has to be created and sutained in ritual action. In order to perform those acts of violence which warfare requires (and warfare itself is politically necessary if Avatip society is not to descend into entropy), Avatip men have to acquire the capacity to be violent.

Harrison's argument is an excellent example of the way in which cultural accounts of other people's ideas about violence, gender, and personhood can serve to undermine powerful western assumptions about human nature. Such cultural accounts do not, though, clarify any of the definitional confusions in the analysis of violence. Even in societies with an explicit concept which we could translate as 'violence', not all acts involving the deliberate inflicting of physical pain, or marking or damage to another's body are defined as 'violent'. Are sacrifice, circumcision, tattooing, fighting, and biomedical procedures ranging from appendectomy to electro-convulsive therapy, all usefully classifiable as acts of 'violence'? How should we classify acts of witchcraft and sorcery, actions which are clearly *intended* to cause bodily harm, even if we doubt their efficacy? What of attempts to break down such literal assessments of violence, like Bourdieu's (1977) use of the term 'symbolic violence' to refer to acts of coercion which are usually unaccompanied by overt physical violence? One way to imagine an anthropology of violence is to see it as a kind of mapping of the different moral and aesthetic evaluations people in different contexts make of their actions on the bodies of others. Instead of constituting a discrete and self-evident object of study, the broad category of 'violence' seems to contain particularly valuable evidence which can help us explore the links between two connected aspects of human life: what Mauss called the 'techniques of the body'; and the inter-subjective world of signs and communications (1950).

Collective Violence in South Asia

When confronted with events like the anti-Tamil riots in Colombo in July 1983, or the killings of Sikhs in Delhi in the wake of Indira Gandhi's assassination the following year, the immediate reaction is usually to ask, how are these things 'still' possible? But in asking this question we are already treating the events as historically 'normal', however bad, wrong, or anachronistic we may think them to be. The view of history implicit in this reaction is brought out in Pandey's reconstruction of colonial interpretations of 'communal violence':

The violence of the 'native' has other, specifically Oriental, characteristics. It is a helpless, instinctive violence, it takes the form of 'convulsions' and, in India, these are more often than not related to the centuries' old smouldering fire of sectarian strife. That is all there is to the politics of the indigenous community. That is the Indian past [Pandey 1990: 65].

There are, in fact, two components of this view of communal violence. One is the idea that violence happens in 'convulsions' and is 'helpless' and 'instinctive'; the other attaches these convulsions to certain identities—'communities'—and treats this attachment as 'ancient', 'primordial', or (in a peculiarly inappropriate term favoured by political scientists) 'parochial'.

There is, of course, an alternative tradition in the human sciences. This is the idea, which runs in a line from Marx to Fanon and thence to myriad left-wing commentators, that some violence is a necessary accompaniment of social transformation. In the actions of the 'mob' we may, with a little historical digging, recover the structural necessity of class struggle. The best of this work has greatly enriched our understanding of the moral structure of collective action in Europe and America in the eighteenth and nineteenth centuries. It has, however, tended to concentrate on those kinds of violence—grain riots rather than religious riots, machine breaking rather than lynchings—which fit most readily into the template of putative social revolution. The insights of this strand of Marxist social history have been most successfully applied to South Asian examples by the historian Ranajit Guha (1983) and his colleagues involved in the early volumes of *Subaltern Studies*.

Yet what is usually called communal violence seems particularly ill-suited to this explanatory framework, because its distinguishing feature is rarely the powerless attacking the powerful, or the poor taking on the powers that be. Communal violence, especially in the colonial and immediately post-colonial period, most often involves sections of the urban poor attacking each other. Colonial rulers may have seen the resulting 'disorder' as a challenge to their authority, but only the naive would assume that this meant that those involved actually intended to attack their rulers but somehow got sidetracked into attacking each other. More generally, there is a widespread tendency to confuse economic explanations with rational explanations. The sometimes tortuous search for the material 'reality' behind the appearance of religiously, ethnically, or linguistically based violence too often confuses rationality and rationalization, explanation and explaining away, as if the murder of a family is somehow more intellectually and morally acceptable if it can be shown to be connected to the pursuit of land or business, and is morally more problematic if it is connected to religious or cultural symbols. This is not to deny that economic factors play a part in what are characterized as communal riots, even as religious idioms can be detected in what might be thought to be more straightforwardly economic or political actions. What is most discomfiting, though, is the necessary recognition that similar patterns of order and meaning can be found in collective violence of apparently different provenance, that participants in religious riots are as likely to see their actions as being informed by considerations of morality and justice as participants in grain riots or peasant insurgencies.

One great gain of Marxist approaches to collective action and collective violence has been a successful break from the unthinking condemnation and scapegoating which characterize most immediate reactions to crowd violence. The moral intensity of the search for scapegoats has the effect of separating these events off from the processes of 'normal' politics. In 1983, the Sri Lankan government took refuge in a version of events which blamed the anti-Tamil riots on a coterie of left-wing conspirators who were allegedly exploiting the people's sensitivity to the threat of separatism in order to destabilize the regime. Many of the affected Tamils, and not a few left-liberal Sinhala, took comfort in an alternative explanation which heaped all the blame at the door of elements of the ruling United National Party (UNP), who were widely believed to have been prominent in the more overtly 'organized' episodes of the violence. The UNP may well have been involved in the July violence (as sections of the Congress Party were alleged to have been prominent in Delhi the following year), but this in itself 'explains' nothing; it merely indicates that any adequate explanation has to treat the violence of the riots as one moment in a longer political process. This requires us to look more broadly at violence and power in South Asian political systems, especially the 'normal' use of violence by agents of the state, and at the fuzzy borderline between state and civil society, private violence and official violence (Brass 1997).

Morality is, however, important in analysing these events. As was long ago pointed out in two classic studies of European riots (Davis [1973] 1975; Thompson 1971), crowds seem to obey moral imperatives of their own and their violence is often structured in terms of 'legitimate' targets and appropriate punishments. In the case of riots studied by Davis and Thompson these targets and punishments were structured according to values which are widely accepted within the community. In early modern France, Protestants excelled in the destruction of religious objects and religious property, while Catholics were more prone to attack the persons of their religious opponents; Protestants were interested in exhuming the bones of those venerated by Catholics, but Catholics were more concerned with the desecration of Protestant corpses. Ideas of justice were prominent in French religious riots as in English grain riots. But the morality which the crowd sought to impose seems not to have been based on the new heaven of a transformed society. Rather, it invoked a retrospective vision of a world restored to its proper order, where the sinner has been punished and the righteous are left free to go about their business.

Recent violence in South Asia seems also to have been motivated by similar ideas of justice and morality, 'legitimate' targets and appropriate punishments. In Delhi in 1984 these targets were Sikh men and their punishment was not merely death, but death administered in a particular, stylized way: Sikhs caught by the crowds had their skulls cracked and were then burnt. In Colombo, and elsewhere in Sri Lanka in 1983, the appropriate punishment seems to have been the destruction of Tamil property; killing seems to have been mostly reserved for those Tamils (mis)identified as members of the separatist Tigers. Again the killings employed a distinctive repertoire of violence: stabbing and burning were the favoured modes of destruction for those the crowd identified as Tigers. However uncomfortable it may make us feel, we need to confront the possibility that some of these actions may, for those taking part, be interpretable as extensions of 'everyday forms of resistance', even though the source of injustice in this case is defined in religious or ethnic, rather than class, terms.

As Charles Tilly points out, 'at any point in time, the repertoire of collective actions available to a population is surprisingly limited' (Tilly 1978: 151). The evidence suggests that riots are—perhaps not so surprisingly—informed by many of the same values that inform everyday life. This is not to say that Delhi Hindus or Colombo Buddhists go about their daily business wracked with the idea of death and mutilation. But those—generally quite small—sections of the population which actively participate in riots seem to do so in the belief that they are acting morally, imposing a justice which the official organs of the state cannot or will not impose. In doing this, they seem able to invert the most obvious interpretation of their actions: Sinhala rioters seem to have believed they were acting in their own defence when they killed innocent Tamils in 1983, and the few police cases that followed the Delhi riots mention self-defence as the motive for the killings. What the crowd was doing to Sikhs and Tamils was what the crowd believed Sikhs and Tamils were doing, or going to do, to them.

Crowds and Perception

We are, in this context, severely constrained by the shortage of evidence on the ideas and explanations of the rioters, the social composition of the crowds, and the central organizing symbols for their actions. But we do have some evidence concerning what we could call the collective context of collective violence. Violence and disorder have the capacity to create their own characteristic forms of inter-subjectivity. We know this form of inter-subjectivity as it reaches us in the shape of 'rumours'. The crowd usually knows these 'rumours' as 'facts' and acts upon them. In Colombo in 1983 people believed a Tiger attack on the city was imminent. The Tigers, it was said, had travelled from Jaffna, hanging on the undersides of trains, or moving by road wearing military uniforms under the robes of Catholic priests. Tamils who made any display of resistance to the actions of the crowds found themselves identified as 'Tigers' and liable to be murdered. As in earlier riots, there were constant rumours of an attack on the Temple of the Tooth in Kandy. (In 1915 rumours of an army of Muslims making its way up to Kandy from the coast were sufficiently convincing to persuade the colonial authorities to turn out the militia to meet them in several towns.) The rumours inverted what was actually happening. The Tamils were treated as the 'real' aggressors; the response of the crowd was merely self-defence. In some cases the security forces also attacked Tamil civilians, apparently convinced that by doing so they were attacking Tigers.

Similarly in Delhi in 1984, the roles were inverted in the crowd's perception of the situation: the Sikhs who were being attacked were the 'real' aggressors, and recurring rumours supported this view of the situation. What is striking about these rumours to an observer is the tenacity with which people hold them to be true; the collective interpretation, propagated and developed within the crowd, has the power to override the evidence of the witness's own eyes and ears. Again, this evidence from South Asian violence in the 1980s connects to historical reconstructions of the place of rumour in violent disturbance, both in South Asia (Guha 1983) and elsewhere. In the case of communal violence in the 1980s, though, one can no longer simply celebrate rumour as the idiom of the subaltern of marginal.

Confronted with evidence like this, what we seem to need is an adequate theory of the crowd. The theory we need has to be a theory of collective psychology. 'Collective' because this experience of the crowd is the same experience that is at the heart of Durkheim's description of collective effervescence. 'Psychology' because what needs explaining is what it is about these circumstances that predisposes people to accept certain representations as real and true, either in the absence of immediate empirical evidence or, in many cases, in direct contradiction to what they see around them. Nor is it simply a matter of perception; the actions of people in crowds can include inversions of 'normal' behaviour, inversions which range from grown men crying on football terraces to small groups of killers acting out collective fantasies of hell and punishment (which is one way in which we can interpret the killings in Sri Lanka in 1983).

The psychoanalyst Sudhir Kakar has described some of the psychological processes which may underlie the actions of crowds. The ethnic 'other', he suggests, acts as a container for 'one's disavowed aspects' (Kakar 1990: 137). Muslims, for example, become the medium through which Hindus can represent aspects of themselves—particularly in the area of aggression and physical violence—which they cannot openly acknowledge. Crowds—whether gathered for religious purposes or assembled for attack on some other rival group—share the capacity for what he calls 'self-transcendence' and this 'self-transcendence' may then manifest itself either in acts of demonic violence or displays of loving self-sacrifice, depending on the structure of the situation itself. Kakar's conclusion is apparently pessimistic: the possibility of acts of violence and destruction is rooted in our unconscious sense of self and is always liable to erupt in the particular conditions of mass action. It is, therefore, foolish to imagine that we can ever rid ourselves of the threat of ethnic violence; instead, we should concentrate on ways of managing the processes which underlie it.

The main problem with this analysis is Kakar's use of an extremely broad brush. Veena Das stresses that we should not treat all crowds as the same—in particular, we need to investigate the difference between violent and non-violent crowds; non-violent crowds 'who, following Gandhian techniques, are willing to allow their own bodies to be violated, and, conversely, violent crowds who must inflict pain and injury upon surrogate victims in order to be avenged' (1990: 28). We could expand this further. There are the crowds who participate in secular, ludic celebrations of identity—mass sporting events—as well as those who participate in religious festivals; these crowds, as we all know, contain the potential for violence and destruction, but it is nevertheless striking how little this potential is realized. Ritual displays of aggression are more often than not quite sufficient; what Kakar characterizes as 'actual physical violence and destruction' is the exception rather than the rule. When exceptions do occur, they require a more nuanced explanation of their precise causes, although such explanation will have to touch on the psychological processes which Kakar describes.

It is significant that the Sri Lankan anthropologist, Stanley Tambiah, ends his survey of collective violence in South Asia (1996) with a reconsideration of both the turn-of-the-century crowd psychology of Gustave Le Bon, and of Durkheim's ideas about the birth of the sacred in the heightened experience of collective action. But as a consideration of the political context of Le Bon's work should remind us, 'the crowd' itself is a complex representation which serves to personalize, demonize, and homogenize the agents and practices of violence. In fact, local research shows that the spatial distribution of collective violence is anything but homogeneous, as neighbouring areas within the same city suffer quite different levels of violence at the same time. To understand this statistical irregularity, we need specifically to reconstruct the work of political agents and often extremely local, social and political contexts. To the extent that the notion of 'the crowd' glosses over these particularities, it is a hindrance to understanding collective violence (Das 1996).

Violence, the State, and Normal Politics

In the discussion so far, it has been convenient to isolate some kind of collective meta-agent—called 'the crowd'—as our object of concern. In fact, though, we know that rumours and misapprehensions are not confined to participants in collective action, rumours circulate all the time. It is just that they reach a special intensity in particular circumstances. The presence on the street of crowds is not necessarily the causal factor in the dissemination of collective misinterpretations, but is perhaps better viewed as a symptom of some more pervasive cause. The rumours which circulated in Colombo in 1983 and Delhi in 1984 drew on pre-existing stereotypes about Tamils and Sikhs and provided a plausible interpretation of what must otherwise have been a threateningly disorienting time. They can only be interpreted and understood if we treat these 'organizing images', as Das (1990) describes them, as the products of everyday concerns, heightened and distorted by extraordinary circumstances. We need, then, to attempt a more precise delineation of the circumstances which predispose people to accept apparently absurd misrepresentations of what is actually happening. In the past, collective violence was often associated with festivities thought to be periods of ordered licence. Now as often as not they are tied to the events of national political history; the violence following Indira Gandhi's death can be treated as a feature 'of the more general inversion of order which prevails to mark the passing away of a great leader'. Local arguments become transmuted as they are reinterpreted in the terms of national political differences; national political events become the occasion for local disturbances. Sometimes there is a coincidence of both markers of disorder: in Sri Lanka in 1983 (and earlier in 1981) violence broke out in response to news of killings by the Tigers in the north, news which coincided with the time of the Buddhist full-moon holiday.

The evidence reviewed so far throws into question a number of customary responses to collective violence: far from being an irruption of unreasoning pre-social passions, it seems to display not merely a logic, but a logic which is both moral and collective. So the interpretation of the actions of crowds and the symbols and rumours around which they organize can tell us something about how collective violence takes its particular form in South Asia. But it seems unlikely that it can tell us why it occurs at some times rather than others. For that we need to reinsert our category of 'collective disorder' back into the flow of 'normal' political time. Moments of violence are not discontinuous, isolated from the processes of 'normal' politics, and there is much recent evidence from which to question the complacent political distinction between the 'legitimate' violence of the state and the brutality of the crowd. In general, the pattern is the same as we find in Europe: 'repressive forces are themselves the most consistent initiators and performers of collective violence' (Tilly 1978: 177). Again this needs to be interpreted in the context of 'normal' politics in post-colonial South Asia. In Sri Lanka, for example, the police have long been known to be a source of brutality, and from the inception of universal suffrage in 1931 electoral politics has been marked by the selective use of violence and intimidation. But there has, nevertheless, been an escalation in the level of political violence since the 1960s, much as there appears to have been in India. In the months before the 1983 riots in Sri Lanka, groups of government supporters publicly beat up prominent opponents and even tried to intimidate high-court judges. For many observers who were in the country at the time, the riots themselves seemed a logical continuation of the steady growth of 'semi-official' violence over the preceding decade. In Sri Lanka, political use of 'official' and 'semi-official' violence over the decade that followed the UNP's accession to power in 1977 created a situation in which a generation of young people came to believe that the only valid idiom of protest was the same idiom used by the powers that be. The result was the spiral of terror and counter-terror that followed the arrival of the Indian Peace Keeping Force in 1987 and the violent opposition to its arrival led by the Janata Vimukti Peramuna (JVP). There is no sensible way in which we can tell the story of the 1983 riots without referring to the broader use of violence by both the state and its political opponents, both before and after the riots.

The most impressive attempt to construct a full political context for acts of collective violence is Paul Brass's *Theft of an Idol* (1997). This book, based on very rich, long-term field data from UP, analyses the politics of violence in terms of circulating discourses of violence. Why do some acts of violence become politically significant, and other, equally shocking, ones go unnoticed? How is it that some violent clashes become known more widely as 'communal', even when there is little or no 'communal' component at the original moment of conflict? Brass deals with these issues through an uneasy mixture of Foucaultian, and more conventional political scientific, theorizing. Perhaps the most compelling feature of Brass's study, though, is his description of the place of violence in 'normal' political and social relations in rural north India:

[T]here is no law and order in the countryside. Rather there are sets of forces operating in pursuit of their own interests, which include *dacoits*, police, villagers who belong to distinct castes and communities, and politicians. These forces do not operate on opposite sides of a dichotomous boundary separating the mechanisms of law and order from those of criminals, but are integrated in relationships in which criminal actions bring some or all of them into play with unpredictable results. In this context, a criminal act does not necessarily or even likely lead to a police investigation, a report, the filing of a case, pursuit of the criminals, and their being hauled up before a court. Rather, it provides an occasion for the testing of relationships and alliances or for the forming of new ones. In the ensuing encounters, force and violence are always a possibility [Brass 1997: 75].

Just as a concern with 'the crowd' may occlude our grasp of the local politics of violence, so a concern with the intense moment of collective, or communal, violence can distract our analytic gaze from the high incidence of violence in everyday encounters with the state in much of rural South Asia.

In an important study of Hindu–Muslim violence in Hyderabad in 1990, Sudhir Kakar (1996) has presented some remarkable evidence on the world of the perpetrators of collective violence. In particular, he describes his meetings with two well-known leaders of urban violence—one Hindu, one Muslim. Although Kakar is concerned with analysing the personality type of the men of violence, his description allows us to glimpse important factors in the socio-political context of contemporary violence. Both men are known to the police for their alleged involvement in acts of violence and intimidation; both have roots in the world of traditional wrestling, and their public personas as men of violence and influence combine old and new concerns about leadership, community, and the cultivation of the male body; and both talk openly about their role in previous Hindu–Muslim disturbances. What is most striking, though, are the telling glimpses of the political milieu in which Kakar's 'warriors' emerge and flourish—a world of dubious property deals and rough politics, in which the roles of police and criminal can be combined or reversed, and in which citizens in pursuit of 'justice' rarely have much confidence in the official procedures of the state and turn instead to local political bosses and their violent enforcers.

In other words, understanding collective violence in South Asia requires an understanding of the political circumstances which make such violence possible. This includes the exploitation of symbols of identity and fears of the other by local and national politicians, as well as the place of violence in the pattern of 'normal' politics and the tolerance of high levels of violence by official agencies. But it also requires a complementary understanding of the symbols, organization, and culture of the crowd, or of the participants, that I pointed to in the earlier discussion.

Language, Narrative, and Reflexivity

Some of the most original and impressive recent analysis of collective violence is contained in the final section of Veena Das's *Mirrors of Violence* (1990) in which Amrit Srinivasan, Valli Kanapathipillai, and Veena Das record and interpret the voices of the survivors of the Colombo and Delhi riots. The strengths of these analyses are the strengths of classic ethnography: clear documentation allied to theoretical sophistication and sensitive interpretation, voices recorded and situated in their social, cultural, and political contexts. But this work differs in one crucial respect from the usual work of the ethnographer—it is explicitly therapeutic. The people whose voices are recorded demanded that their testimony be transcribed and preserved. The title of Das's chapter is taken from one survivor's remark to a visiting academic: 'It is our work to cry and your work to listen.'

Reading the survivors' stories is often harrowing and often moving. Kanapathipillai reproduces the terrifying first-hand account of a middle-aged schoolteacher, locked into a room in her own house with her children while Sinhala men try to break down the door. Das starts her chapter with the impossibly sad case of a woman called Shanti who lost her husband and three sons in the Delhi violence; racked with guilt at her failure to protect her children, Shanti eventually commits suicide; she was the only survivor from her colony to do this. Yet the authors do not merely record the testimony of the witnesses, they also describe the processes by which those affected tried to piece together a world which had been turned upside down and transformed into a scene of terror. There are differences in the reactions of men and women, adults and children, the middle class Tamil whose voices are heard in Kanapathipillai's article. The family emerges as a crucial mediating institution—a source of strength for the Tamils, but also a source of friction for the widowed Sikh women. The experience of violence was also gendered—in Delhi the killers singled out Sikh males and the surviving women found themselves dealing with new, unfamiliar areas of life, lawyers, bureaucrats, and civil rights' activists.

These analyses bring out what has become a major theme of the work of the 1990s—the problems of narrative, representation, and reflexivity involved in writing about violence. In her chapter, Srinivasan talks of the 'epistemic space' of the survivor, a space which mediates between 'life and death, chaos and order, speech and silence' (Srinivasan 1990: 307). In recording the testimony of survivors it seemed best to 'keep lay perceptions and understandings of the collective crisis free of exogenous theory' (Srinivasan 1990: 310). Das also writes about the need to avoid a titillating or voyeuristic style in writing about the experience of survivors. For her, the survivor's record is particularly important because it can show us how suffering 'may be transformed into redemption'; the survivor carries 'the responsibility of creating a reflexive understanding of our situation and our times' (Das 1990: 33–4).

One common experience, of course, is the survivors' demand that their sufferings and injustice are recorded and publicized by the observer. Given the potency of memories of past violence in the motivation of present and future violence, there is an understandable pressure to suppress or play down the testimony of those who have suffered more recently. Moreover, as the discussion of rumour should have made clear, the issue of memory is not at all straightforward.

Kakar starts his account of riots (1996) with his memories of the violence of Partition, memories dominated by the horrific eye-witness accounts told by members of his immediate family. Then, disarmingly, he confesses to the reader that he is now unable to sort out what he 'really' saw as a child from the morass of stories, second-hand accounts, rumours, and fantasies that circulated at the time of the violence. He, like other recent writers confesses to being forced to adopt a more personal, less 'objective' tone than might be considered normal or desirable for a social scientist. Valentine Daniel introduces further complexities in his study of the impact of violence on Tamils from the hill country of Sri Lanka (Daniel 1996). He starts his book with the issue of how to write about violence without prurience, to write an 'ethnography' rather than a 'pornography' of violence. Later he describes how during an interview the same woman, describing her father's brutal death at the hands of the security forces, pleaded with him to 'tell the world' exactly what had happened, then later beseeched him not to let anyone know the indignities and shame he had suffered. Daniel uses this moment of powerful ambivalence as the key to meditation on both the necessity and the impossibility of documentation, on the need to challenge the prevailing 'master narrative' of violence, and, perhaps even more radically on the need to realize that even the 'master narrative' was plural and evanescent.

Daniel is not alone in his predicament. Brass (1997) swings between a Foucaultian concern with discourses of violence and a much more conventional urge to establish 'what really happened'. This urge to document, to construct an authoritative version of what happened, is by no means confined to modern social scientists. Colonial officials often conducted enquiries and published reports, seeking to impose narrative coherence on the world of rumour and real or imagined atrocity. The practice has been continued, some of the time at least, by the post-colonial state, although the reports have been read with increased cynicism as the involvement of politicians and police gets quietly swept under the official carpet. Since the early 1980s, there has been a growing trend for groups of academics and activists to visit areas affected by violence in order to compose their own, more independent and trustworthy, reports. In an important article reflecting on his experience as a member of one such team, Gyanendra Pandey acknowledges the impossibility of this task:

Violence produces the necessity of evidence gathering, of uncovering hidden processes and contradictions that we might normally prefer to ignore, but violence also wipes out 'evidence' and even, to a large extent, the possibility of collecting it in a manner and form that is deemed acceptable by today's social sciences [1992: 35].

In Pandey's expereince volunteers became aware of a sense of rehearsal, or the recitation of 'official versions' of the experience of violence, from the victims they interviewed. There were pressures to create a questionable balance by including stories of violence on 'both sides', although all the evidence suggested that the violence was overwhelmingly directed against one community, and so on.

Pandey reaches two main conclusions. The first is the need to identify and challenge the unspoken assumptions about the nation-state and the teleology of the nation which can be shown to structure much writing about collective violence in post-colonial South Asia. The second is a plea to recognize the necessary limits, the provisionality, of social scientific analyses of collective violence. Both points are explored in telling detail in Shahid Amin's *Event, Metaphor, Memory* (1995). This work focuses on a moment of collective violence—the attack on the north Indian police station of Chauri Chaura by a group of Gandhian volunteers in 1922 in which twenty-three policemen were killed—and combines oral history with archival reconstruction to remarkable effect. Amin demonstrates how the procedures of the colonial legal system produced one, highly tendentious, offical version of the event, even as the shocked reactions of Gandhi and other Congress officials produced another. But Amin discovered that even local memory could not be relied upon to produce a more authoritative account of what had actually happened: sometimes details that were 'remembered' could be shown to be factually 'wrong', at other times the broad shape of memory had been clearly influenced by the later importance of the event as nationalist metaphor.

Given the seriousness of the problem of collective violence in post-colonial South Asia, it would be quite understandable for the reader to express some impatience and dissatisfaction at articles such as mine. Is it not typical of the times, it could be asked, for academics to indulge in fashionably post-modern exercises in deconstruction when what is required is some robust combination of fact and explanation? This criticism would, though, be misplaced. If the important work of the 1980s and 1990s on collective violence has demonstrated one thing, it is the representational potency of violence, or stories about violence, as signs or tokens in the everyday politics of community and exclusion. Tales of who-did-what-to-whom do not merely circulate within communities, to a very great extent they are instrumental in creating those communities. Striking examples of this process can be found in the symbolism of martyrdom among both Sikh and Tamil militants: the suicide bomber who dies in pursuit of a separate state for Sri Lankan Tamils thereby binds the survivors more closely to that ideal with a combination of grief and guilt. Sociologists and anthropologists know far more about all aspects of collective violence than they did in the 1960s or 1970s. Not least, some are now acknowledging that the best critical response to the place of violence in the certainties of communal rhetoric is a careful and sober reminder of our uncertainty, of the necessary limits of our knowledge of complex social and political phenomena.

REFERENCES

Amin, S. 1995. *Event, Metaphor, Memory: Chauri Chaura 1922–1992*. Delhi: Oxford University Press
Arendt, H. 1969. *On Violence*. New York: Harcourt, Brace and World.
Baumann, Zygmunt. 1993. *Modernity and the Holocaust*. Oxford: Polity.
Bourdieu, P. 1977. *Outline of a Theory of Practice*. Cambridge: Cambridge University Press.
Brass, P. 1997. *Theft of an Idol: Text and Context in the Representation of Collective Violence*. Princeton: Princeton University Press.
Chagnon, N. 1983. *Yanomamo: The Fierce People*. New York: Holt Rinehart and Winston.
Daniel, E.V. 1996. *Charred Lullabies: Chapters in an Anthropography of Violence*. Princeton: Princeton University Press
Das, V., ed. 1990. *Mirrors of Violence: Communities, Riots and Survivors in South Asia*. Delhi: Oxford University Press.
———. 1996. 'The Spatialization of Violence: Case Study of a "Communal Riot"'. In K. Basu and S. Subrahmanyam, eds, *Unravelling the Nation: Sectarian Conflict and India's Secular Identity*, 157–203. Delhi: Penguin.
Davis, N.Z. [1973] 1975. 'The Rites of Violence'. In N. Z. Davis, ed., *Society and Culture in Early Modern France*, 152–87. Stanford: Stanford University Press [originally published *Past and Present*. 59].
Fanon, Frantz. 1965. *The Wretched of the Earth*. London: Macgibbon and Kee.
Foucault, M. 1984. 'Space, Knowledge and Power'. In P. Rainbow, ed., *The Focault Reader*, 239–56. London: Penguin.

Guha, R. 1983. *Elementary Aspects of Peasant Insurgency in Colonial North India*. Delhi: Oxford University Press.

Harrison, S. 1989. 'The Symbolic Construction of Aggression and War in a Sepik River Society'. *Man* (n.s.). 24(4):583–99

Howell, S. and R. Willis, eds. 1989. *Societies at Peace: Anthropological Perspectives*. London: Routledge.

Kakar, S. 1990. 'Some Unconscious Aspects of Ethnic Violence in India'. In V. Das, ed., *Mirrors of Violence*, Delhi: Oxford University Press.

_____. 1996. *The Colors of Violence: Cultural Identities, Religion, and Conflict*. Chicago: University of Chicago Press.

Keane, J. 1996. *Reflections on Violence*. London: Verso.

Mauss, M. 1950. 'Les Techniques du Corps'. In M. Mauss, ed. *Sociologie et Anthropologie*, 363–86. Paris: Presses Universitaires de France.

Pandey G. 1990. *The Construction of Communalism in Colonial North India*. Delhi: Oxford University Press

_____. 1992. 'In Defense of the Fragment: Writing about Hindu-Muslim Riots in India Today'. *Representations*. 37:27–55

Riches, D. ed. 1986. *The Anthropology of Violence*. Oxford: Blackwell.

Sorel, G. 1950. *Reflections on Violence*. Illinois, Glencoe: Free Press.

Srinivasan, A. 1990. 'The Survivor in the Study of Violence'. In V. Das, ed., *Mirrors of Violence*, 305–20. Delhi: Oxford University Press.

Tambiah, S.J. 1996. *Leveling Crowds: Ethnonationalist Conflicts and Collective Violence in South Asia*. Berkeley: University of California Press.

Thompson, E.P. 1971. 'The Moral Economy of the English Crowd in the Eighteenth Century'. *Past and Present*. 50:76–136

Tilly, C. 1978. *From Mobilization to Revolution*. Reading, MA: Addison-Wesley.

Vidal, D., G. Tarabout, and E. Meyer, eds. 1994. *'Violences et Non-Violences en Inde'* (*Purusartha* 16) Paris: EHESS.

Weber, M. 1948. 'Politics as a Vocation'. In H. Gerth and C.W. Mills, eds, *From Max Weber: Essays in Sociology*, 72–128. London: Routledge.

Index